Short Stories
Stories
for Students

National Advisory Board

Short Stories
for Students

Presenting Analysis, Context, and Criticism on
Commonly Studied Short Stories

Volume 10

Michael L. LaBlanc and Ira Mark Milne, Editors

GALE GROUP

Detroit
New York
San Francisco
London
Boston
Woodbridge, CT

Short Stories for Students

Staff

Series Editors: Michael L. LaBlanc and Ira Mark Milne.

Contributing Editors: Elizabeth Bellalouna, Elizabeth Bodenmiller, Anne Marie Hacht, Polly Rapp, Jennifer Smith.

Managing Editor: Dwayne Hayes.

Research: Victoria B. Cariappa, *Research Team Manager.* Maureen Eremic, Barb McNeil, Cheryl Warnock, *Research Specialists.* Andy Malonis, *Technical Training Specialist.* Barbara Leevy, Tamara Nott, Tracie A. Richardson, Robert Whaley, *Research Associates.* Scott Floyd, Nicodemus Ford, Sarah Genik, Timothy Lehnerer, *Research Assistants.*

Permissions: Maria Franklin, *Permissions Manager.* Margaret A. Chamberlain, Edna Hedblad, *Permissions Specialists.* Erin Bealmear, Shalice Shah-Caldwell, Sarah Tomasek, *Permissions Associates.* Debra Freitas, Julie Juengling, Mark Plaza, *Permissions Assistants.*

Manufacturing: Mary Beth Trimper, *Manager, Composition and Electronic Prepress.* Evi Seoud, *Assistant Manager, Composition Purchasing and Electronic Prepress.* Stacy Melson, *Buyer.*

Imaging and Multimedia Content Team: Randy Bassett, *Image Database Supervisor.* Robert Duncan, Dan Newell, *Imaging Specialists.* Pamela A. Reed, *Imaging Coordinator.* Dean Dauphinais, Robyn V. Young, *Senior Image Editors.* Kelly A. Quin, *Image Editor.*

Product Design Team: Kenn Zorn, *Product Design Manager.* Pamela A. E. Galbreath, *Senior Art Director.* Michael Logusz, *Graphic Artist.*

Copyright Notice

Table of Contents

Why Study Literature At All?

Short Stories for Students is designed to provide readers with information and discussion about a wide range of important contemporary and historical works of short fiction, and it does that job very well. However, I want to use this guest foreword to address a question that it does *not* take up. It is a fundamental question that is often ignored in high school and college English classes as well as research texts, and one that causes frustration among students at all levels, namely—why study literature at all? Isn't it enough to read a story, enjoy it, and go about one's business? My answer (to be expected from a literary professional, I suppose) is no. It is not enough. It is a start; but it is not enough. Here's why.

First, literature is the only part of the educational curriculum that deals directly with the actual world of lived experience. The philosopher Edmund Husserl used the apt German term *die Lebenswelt*, "the living world," to denote this realm. All the other content areas of the modern American educational system avoid the subjective, present reality of everyday life. Science (both the natural and the social varieties) objectifies, the fine arts create and/or perform, history reconstructs. Only literary study persists in posing those questions we all asked before our schooling taught us to give up on them. Only literature gives credibility to personal perceptions, feelings, dreams, and the "stream of consciousness" that is our inner voice. Literature wonders about infinity, wonders why God permits evil, wonders what will happen to us after we die. Literature admits that we get our hearts broken, that people sometimes cheat and get away with it, that the world is a strange and probably incomprehensible place. Literature, in other words, takes on all the big and small issues of what it means to be human. So my first answer is that of the humanist—we should read literature and study it and take it seriously because it enriches us as human beings. We develop our moral imagination, our capacity to sympathize with other people, and our ability to understand our existence through the experience of fiction.

My second answer is more practical. By studying literature we can learn how to explore and analyze texts. Fiction may be about *die Lebenswelt*, but it is a construct of words put together in a certain order by an artist using the medium of language. By examining and studying those constructions, we can learn about language as a medium. We can become more sophisticated about word associations and connotations, about the manipulation of symbols, and about style and atmosphere. We can grasp how ambiguous language is and how important context and texture is to meaning. In our first encounter with a work of literature, of course, we are not supposed to catch all of these things. We are spellbound, just as the writer wanted us to be. It is as serious students of the writer's art that we begin to see how the tricks are done.

Seeing the tricks, which is another way of saying "developing analytical and close reading skills," is important above and beyond its intrinsic literary educational value. These skills transfer to other fields and enhance critical thinking of any kind. Understanding how language is used to construct texts is powerful knowledge. It makes engineers better problem solvers, lawyers better advocates and courtroom practitioners, politicians better rhetoricians, marketing and advertising agents better sellers, and citizens more aware consumers as well as better participants in democracy. This last point is especially important, because rhetorical skill works both ways—when we learn how language is manipulated in the making of texts the result is that we become less susceptible when language is used to manipulate us.

My third reason is related to the second. When we begin to see literature as created artifacts of language, we become more sensitive to good writing in general. We get a stronger sense of the importance of individual words, even the sounds of words and word combinations. We begin to understand Mark Twain's delicious proverb—"The difference between the right word and the almost right word is the difference between lightning and a lightning bug." Getting beyond the "enjoyment only" stage of literature gets us closer to becoming makers of word art ourselves. I am not saying that studying fiction will turn every student into a Faulkner or a Shakespeare. But it will make us more adaptable and effective writers, even if our art form ends up being the office memo or the corporate annual report.

Studying short stories, then, can help students become better readers, better writers, and even better human beings. But I want to close with a warning. If your study and exploration of the craft, history, context, symbolism, or anything else about a story starts to rob it of the magic you felt when you first read it, it is time to stop. Take a break, study another subject, shoot some hoops, or go for a run. Love of reading is too important to be ruined by school. The early twentieth century writer Willa Cather, in her novel *My Antonia*, has her narrator Jack Burden tell a story that he and Antonia heard from two old Russian immigrants when they were teenagers. These immigrants, Pavel and Peter, told about an incident from their youth back in Russia that the narrator could recall in vivid detail thirty years later. It was a harrowing story of a wedding party starting home in sleds and being chased by starving wolves. Hundreds of wolves attacked the group's sleds one by one as they sped across the snow trying to reach their village. In a horrible revelation, the old Russians revealed that the groom eventually threw his own bride to the wolves to save himself. There was even a hint that one of the old immigrants might have been the groom mentioned in the story. Cather has her narrator conclude with his feelings about the story. "We did not tell Pavel's secret to anyone, but guarded it jealously—as if the wolves of the Ukraine had gathered that night long ago, and the wedding party had been sacrificed, just to give us a painful and peculiar pleasure." That feeling, that painful and peculiar pleasure, is the most important thing about literature. Study and research should enhance that feeling and never be allowed to overwhelm it.

Thomas E. Barden
Professor of English and
Director of Graduate English Studies
The University of Toledo

Introduction

Purpose of the Book

The purpose of *Short Stories for Students* (*SSfS*) is to provide readers with a guide to understanding, enjoying, and studying short stories by giving them easy access to information about the work. Part of Gale's "For Students" Literature line, *SSfS* is specifically designed to meet the curricular needs of high school and undergraduate college students and their teachers, as well as the interests of general readers and researchers considering specific short fiction. While each volume contains entries on "classic" stories frequently studied in classrooms, there are also entries containing hard-to-find information on contemporary stories, including works by multicultural, international, and women writers.

The information covered in each entry includes an introduction to the story and the story's author; a plot summary, to help readers unravel and understand the events in the work; descriptions of important characters, including explanation of a given character's role in the narrative as well as discussion about that character's relationship to other characters in the story; analysis of important themes in the story; and an explanation of important literary techniques and movements as they are demonstrated in the work.

In addition to this material, which helps the readers analyze the story itself, students are also provided with important information on the literary and historical background informing each work.

This includes a historical context essay, a box comparing the time or place the story was written to modern Western culture, a critical overview essay, and excerpts from critical essays on the story or author (if available). A unique feature of *SSfS* is a specially commissioned overview essay on each story, targeted toward the student reader.

To further aid the student in studying and enjoying each story, information on media adaptations is provided, as well as reading suggestions for works of fiction and nonfiction on similar themes and topics. Classroom aids include ideas for research papers and lists of critical sources that provide additional material on the work.

Selection Criteria

The titles for each volume of *SSfS* were selected by surveying numerous sources on teaching literature and analyzing course curricula for various school districts. Some of the sources surveyed include: literature anthologies, *Reading Lists for College-Bound Students: The Books Most Recommended by America's Top Colleges*; *Teaching the Short Story: A Guide to Using Stories from Around the World,* by the National Council of Teachers of English (NCTE); and "A Study of High School Literature Anthologies," conducted by Arthur Applebee at the Center for the Learning and Teaching of Literature and sponsored by the National Endowment for the Arts and the Office of Educational Research and Improvement.

Input was also solicited from our advisory board, as well as educators from various areas. From these discussions, it was determined that each volume should have a mix of "classic" stories (those works commonly taught in literature classes) and contemporary stories for which information is often hard to find. Because of the interest in expanding the canon of literature, an emphasis was also placed on including works by international, multicultural, and women authors. Our advisory board members—educational professionals—helped pare down the list for each volume. Works not selected for the present volume were noted as possibilities for future volumes. As always, the editor welcomes suggestions for titles to be included in future volumes.

How Each Entry Is Organized

Each entry, or chapter, in *SSfS* focuses on one story. Each entry heading lists the title of the story, the author's name, and the date of the story's publication. The following elements are contained in each entry:

- **Introduction:** a brief overview of the story which provides information about its first appearance, its literary standing, any controversies surrounding the work, and major conflicts or themes within the work.

- **Author Biography:** this section includes basic facts about the author's life, and focuses on events and times in the author's life that may have inspired the story in question.

- **Plot Summary:** a description of the events in the story.

- **Characters:** an alphabetical listing of the characters who appear in the story. Each character name is followed by a brief to an extensive description of the character's role in the story, as well as discussion of the character's actions, relationships, and possible motivation.

  Characters are listed alphabetically by last name. If a character is unnamed—for instance, the narrator in "The Eatonville Anthology"—the character is listed as "The Narrator" and alphabetized as "Narrator." If a character's first name is the only one given, the name will appear alphabetically by that name.

- **Themes:** a thorough overview of how the topics, themes, and issues are addressed within the story. Each theme discussed appears in a sepa-

rate subhead, and is easily accessed through the boldface entries in the Subject/Theme Index.

- **Style:** this section addresses important style elements of the story, such as setting, point of view, and narration; important literary devices used, such as imagery, foreshadowing, symbolism; and, if applicable, genres to which the work might have belonged, such as Gothicism or Romanticism. Literary terms are explained within the entry, but can also be found in the Glossary.

- **Historical Context:** this section outlines the social, political, and cultural climate *in which the author lived and the work was created.* This section may include descriptions of related historical events, pertinent aspects of daily life in the culture, and the artistic and literary sensibilities of the time in which the work was written. If the story is historical in nature, information regarding the time in which the story is set is also included. Long sections are broken down with helpful subheads.

- **Critical Overview:** this section provides background on the critical reputation of the author and the story, including bannings or any other public controversies surrounding the work. For older works, this section may include a history of how the story was first received and how perceptions of it may have changed over the years; for more recent works, direct quotes from early reviews may also be included.

- **Criticism:** an essay commissioned by *SSfS* which specifically deals with the story and is written specifically for the student audience, as well as excerpts from previously published criticism on the work (if available).

- **Sources:** an alphabetical list of critical material quoted in the entry, with bibliographical information.

- **Further Reading:** an alphabetical list of other critical sources which may prove useful for the student. Includes full bibliographical information and a brief annotation.

In addition, each entry contains the following highlighted sections, set separate from the main text:

- **Media Adaptations:** where applicable, a list of film and television adaptations of the story, including source information. The list also includes stage adaptations, audio recordings, musical adaptations, etc.

- **Topics for Further Study:** a list of potential study questions or research topics dealing with the story. This section includes questions related to other disciplines the student may be studying, such as American history, world history, science, math, government, business, geography, economics, psychology, etc.

- **Compare and Contrast Box:** an "at-a-glance" comparison of the cultural and historical differences between the author's time and culture and late twentieth-century Western culture. This box includes pertinent parallels between the major scientific, political, and cultural movements of the time or place the story was written, the time or place the story was set (if a historical work), and modern Western culture. Works written after the mid-1970s may not have this box.

- **What Do I Read Next?:** a list of works that might complement the featured story or serve as a contrast to it. This includes works by the same author and others, works of fiction and nonfiction, and works from various genres, cultures, and eras.

Other Features

SSfS includes "Why Study Literature At All?," a guest foreword by Thomas E. Barden, Professor of English and Director of Graduate English Studies at the University of Toledo. This essay provides a number of very fundamental reasons for studying literature and, therefore, reasons why a book such as *SSfS*, designed to facilitate the study of litererture, is useful.

A Cumulative Author/Title Index lists the authors and titles covered in each volume of the *SSfS* series.

A Cumulative Nationality/Ethnicity Index breaks down the authors and titles covered in each volume of the *SSfS* series by nationality and ethnicity.

A Subject/Theme Index, specific to each volume, provides easy reference for users who may be studying a particular subject or theme rather than a single work. Significant subjects from events to broad themes are included, and the entries pointing to the specific theme discussions in each entry are indicated in **boldface.**

Entries may include illustrations, including an author portrait, stills from film adaptations (if available), maps, and/or photos of key historical events.

Citing Short Stories for Students

When writing papers, students who quote directly from any volume of *SSfS* may use the following general forms to document their source. These examples are based on MLA style; teachers may request that students adhere to a different style, thus, the following examples may be adapted as needed.

When citing text from *SSfS* that is not attributed to a particular author (for example, the Themes, Style, Historical Context sections, etc.), the following format may be used:

> "The Celebrated Jumping Frog of Calavaras County." *Short Stories for Students.* Ed. Kathleen Wilson. Vol. 1. Detroit: Gale, 1997, pp. 19-20.

When quoting the specially commissioned essay from *SSfS* (usually the first essay under the Criticism subhead), the following format may be used:

> Korb, Rena. Essay on "Children of the Sea." *Short Stories for Students.* Ed. Kathleen Wilson. Vol. 1. Detroit: Gale, 1997, p. 42.

When quoting a journal essay that is reprinted in a volume of *Short Stories for Students,* the following form may be used:

> Schmidt, Paul. "The Deadpan on Simon Wheeler." *The Southwest Review* Vol. XLI, No. 3 (Summer, 1956), pp. 270-77; excerpted and reprinted in *Short Stories for Students,* Vol. 1, ed. Kathleen Wilson. (Detroit: Gale, 1997), pp. 29-31.

When quoting material from a book that is reprinted in a volume of *SSfS,* the following form may be used:

> Bell-Villada, Gene H. "The Master of Short Forms," in *Garcia Marquez: The Man and His Work* (University of North Carolina Press, 1990); excerpted and reprinted in *Short Stories for Students,* Vol. 1, ed. Kathleen Wilson. (Detroit: Gale, 1997), pp. 90- 91.

We Welcome Your Suggestions

The editor of *Short Stories for Students* welcomes your comments and ideas. Readers who wish to suggest short stories to appear in future volumes, or who have other suggestions, are cordially invited to contact the editor. You may write to the editor at:

Editor, *Short Stories for Students*
Gale Group
27500 Drake Road
Farmington Hills, MI 48331-3535

Literary Chronology

1771: (Sir) Walter Scott is born in Edinburgh in 1771.

1799: Honore de Balzac is born in southwestern France.

1824: Sir Walter Scott's "Wandering Willie's Tale" first appears in Scott's novel entitled *Redgauntlet*. The tale is not directly part of the action of the novel; it is simply a story told by one of the characters to another, and in fact is merely the most developed of such stories contained in the novel.

1832: Sir Walter Scott dies.

1842: Honore de Balzac's "La Grande Breteche" is published in France. The story is set in 1830 and describes events that happened in the year 1815 to 1816—a turbulent time in France. After the Revolution in 1789, the bourgeoisie, or middle class, struggled to consolidate its power and to retain the political and economic victories it had won over the nobility and the church. By the time of the events of the story, the reign of Napoleon Bonaparte had come and gone, but the old class divisions remained beneath the surface of a new, freer, France.

1850: Balzac dies a newlywed in his Paris apartment in August.

1876: Sherwood Anderson is born on September 13 in Camden, Ohio.

1881: P. G. Wodehouse is born on October 15 in Hong Kong, where his father is stationed as a member of the British civil service.

1888: Katherine Mansfield Beauchamp is born to a wealthy family in Wellington, New Zealand, on October 14.

1894: James Thurber is born in Columbus, Ohio, on December 8, the middle of three sons.

1894: Isaac Babel is born on July 13 in Russia to Jewish parents, and is given the full name Isaac Emmanuilovich Babel.

1903: Kay Boyle is born to a wealthy family in St Paul, Minnesota.

1909: Eudora Welty is born on April 13 in Jackson, Mississippi. Her father is an insurance executive, and her mother is a teacher.

1919: P.G. Wodehouse's "Jeeves Takes Charge" is first published in England in his collection of stories entitled *My Man Jeeves*. "Jeeves Takes Charge" is one of the earliest of dozens of stories and several novels detailing the comical misadventures of Bertie Wooster, a befuddled young Englishman, and his resourceful butler, Jeeves.

1920: Mansfield's *Bliss, and Other Stories* is published, and secures the author's literary reputation.

1923: Katherine Mansfield dies of a massive pulmonary hemorrhage in January at the age of thirty-four.

1925: Flannery O'Connor (birthname Mary Flannery O'Connor) is born on March 25 in Savannah, Georgia, as the only child of Edwin Francis and Regina Cline O'Connor.

1926: Isaac Babel's "My First Goose" appears in his work entitled *Red Cavalry*, Babel's first collection of vignettes and stories—none longer than four pages. This interconnected cycle of stories, considered by many critics to be Isaac Babel's best work, is also considered one of the most important contributions to twentieth-century Russian literature. The stories showcase Babel's gift for disturbing imagery and complex philosophy. *Red Cavalry* initially gained popularity in serialized newspaper form and commanded international critical attention.

1928: William Trevor is born in County Cork, Ireland, to Protestant parents.

1929: Milan Kundera is born in Brno, Czechoslovakia, on April 1.

1933: Sherwood Anderson's "Death in the Woods" is published in final form as the title story in his 1933 collection entitled *Death in the Woods and Other Stories*. Anderson had worked on "Death in the Woods" periodically for nine years, and had published earlier versions as a sketch in *A Story-Teller's Story* (1924) and as a chapter in his autobiographical *Tar: A Midwest Childhood*. (1926).

1933: Susan Sontag is born on January 16 in New York City.

1935: Kay Boyle wins widespread critical acclaim for the first time as her "The White Horses of Vienna" wins the O. Henry Award for best short story of the year. Despite this honor, reviewers hold mixed opinions of the story, which examines the rise of Nazism in Austria. Many reviewers, however, do appreciate Boyle's obvious talent. The following year, the story is included in her Boyle's fourth volume of short fiction.

1936: Andre Dubus is born into a middle-class Southern family on August 11 in Lake Charles, Louisiana.

1940: Isaac Babel, after being arrested in 1939 by the Soviet regime for reasons that are unclear and after being beaten in prison until he confessed to spying against the Soviet regime, is sentenced to death and shot.

1941: Sherwood Anderson dies during a trip to South America.

1941: Eudora Welty's "Why I Live at the P.O." appears in *Atlantic* magazine. The story was inspired by a lady ironing in the back room of a small rural post office, whom Welty glimpsed while working as publicity photographer in the mid-1930s. Wetly has just started her writing career, and the story is among the first that she has published. The story is also included in her first collection of short stories entitled *A Curtain of Green*, which appears this same year.

1942: James Thurber's "The Catbird Seat" is first published in the November 14 issue of *The New Yorker*. "The Catbird Seat" also appeared in Thurber's 1945 collection, entitled *The Thurber Carnival*.

1948: Leslie Marmon Silko is born on March 5 in Albuquerque, New Mexico.

1961: James Thurber dies on November 2 of pneumonia following a stroke.

1963: Flannery O'Connor wins her second O. Henry Award, this time for "Everything That Rises Must Converge," a powerful depiction of a troubled mother-son relationship. In 1965 the story is published in her well-regarded short fiction collection *Everything That Rises Must Converge*.

1963: Milan Kundera's "The Hitchhiking Game" is first published as part of his collection of stories entitled *Laughable Loves*.

1964: Flannery O'Connor dies of kidney failure as a result of complications caused by lupus.

1975: P. G. Wodehouse dies, shortly after being knighted.

1978: Andre Dubus's "The Fat Girl" is published in his collection entitled *Adultery and Other Choices*. "The Fat Girl" is deemed one of his best short stories.

1981: Leslie Marmon Silko's short story "Lullaby" first appears in her *Storyteller* (1981), a book in which Silko interweaves autobiographical reminiscences, short stories, poetry, photographs of her family (taken by her father) and traditional songs. The book as a whole is concerned with the oral tradition of storytelling in Native American culture.

1986: William Trevor's ''The News from Ireland'' is published, a work that hearkens back almost 150 years to the Great Famine, a cataclysmic event in Ireland's history that left over a million Irish dead from hunger and drove as many as two million to leave their country of birth.

1986: Susan Sontag's ''The Way We Live Now'' first appears in the *New Yorker* magazine.

1999: Andre Dubus dies of a heart attack.

Acknowledgments

The editors wish to thank the copyright holders of the excerpted criticism included in this volume and the permissions managers of many book and magazine publishing companies for assisting us in securing reproduction rights. We are also grateful to the staffs of the Detroit Public Library,the Library of Congress, the University of Detroit Mercy Library, Wayne State University Purdy/Kresge Library Complex, and the University of Michigan Libraries for making their resources available to us. Following is a list of the copyright holders who have granted us permission to reproduce material in this volume of **Short Stories for Students (SSfS)**. Every effort has been made to trace copyright, but if omissions have been made, please let us know.

COPYRIGHTED MATERIAL IN *SSfS*, VOLUME 10, WERE REPRODUCED FROM THE FOLLOWING PERIODICALS:

Connecticut Review, v. XVIII, Spring, 1996 for ''Not Noticing History: Two Tales by William Trevor'' by Richard Bonaccorso. Reproduced by permission.—*Critique,* v. XIII, 1971. Copyright (c) 1971 Helen Dwight Reid Educational Foundation. Reproduced with permission of the Helen Dwight Reid Educational Foundation, published by Heldref Publications, 1319 18th Street, NW, Washington, DC 20036-1802.—*The Explicator,* v. 40, Summer, 1982; v. 45, Spring, 1987. Copyright 1982, 1987 by Helen Dwight Reid Educational Foundation. Both reproduced with permission of the Helen Dwight Reid Educational Foundation, published by Heldref Publications, 1319 18th Street, NW, Washington, DC 20036-1802.—*Michigan Academician,* v. XXVIII, January, 1996. Copyright (c) The Michigan Academy of Science, Arts, and Letters, 1996. Reproduced by permission of the publisher.—*MLN,* v. 97, May, 1982. (c) 1982. Reproduced by permission of The Johns Hopkins University Press.—*Modern Fiction Studies,* v. 24, Autumn, 1978. Copyright (c) 1978 by Purdue Research Foundation, West Lafayette, IN 47907. All rights reserved. Reproduced by permission of The Johns Hopkins University.—*Modern Fiction Studies,* v. 32, Summer, 1986. Copyright (c) 1986 Helen Dwight Reid Educational Foundation. Reproduced with permission of the Helen Dwight Reid Educational Foundation, published by Heldref Publications, 119 18th Street, N. W., Washington, DC 20036-1802.—*Narrative,* v. 2, 1994. Reproduced by permission.—*The Southern Quarterly,* v. XXVII, Summer, 1989. Copyright (c) 1989 by the University of Southern Mississippi. Reproduced by permission.—*Studies in Short Fiction,* v. IV, Spring, 1967; v. VII, Fall, 1970; v. XI, Spring, 1974; v. 17, Spring, 1980; v. 23, Winter, 1986. Copyright 1967, 1970, 1974, 1980, 1986 by Newberry College. All reproduced by permission.—*Twentieth Century Literature,* v. 28, Winter, 1982; v. 32, Summer, 1986. Copyright 1982, 1986, Hofstra University Press. Both reproduced by permission.—*The University of Windsor*

Review, v. XVI, Fall-Winter, 1981. (c) The University of Windsor Review. Reproduced by permission.

COPYRIGHTED MATERIALS IN *SSfS*, VOLUME 10, WERE REPRODUCED FROM THE FOLLOWING BOOKS:

Love, William F. From *Dorothy L. Sayers: The Centenary Celebration.* Edited by Alzina Stone Dale. Walker and Company, 1993. Copyright (c) 1993 by Alzina Stone Dale. Reproduced by permission.—Spath, Eberhard. From *Functions in Literature: Essays Presented to Erwin Wolff on His Sixtieth Birthday.* Edited by Ulrich Broich, Theo Stemmler, and Gerd Stratmann. Max Niemeyer Verlag. (c) Max Niemeyer Tubingen 1984. Reprinted by permission of the publisher.

PHOTOGRAPHS AND ILLUSTRATIONS APPEARING IN *SSFS*, VOLUME 10, WERE RECEIVED FROM THE FOLLOWING SOURCES:

—Anderson, Sherwood, 1984, photograph by Alfred Stieglitz. The Library of Congress.—Babel, Isaac, photograph. AP/Wide World Photos, Inc. Reproduced by permission.—Boyle, Kay, photograph. New York World-Telegram, Sun Collection, Prints and Photographs Division, The Library of Congress.—de Balzac, Honore, photograph. Archive Photos. Reproduced by permission.—Dubus, Andre, photograph. AP/Wide World Photos. Re-produced by permission.—Edward VII, print.—Kundera, Milan, photograph. Archive Photos. Reproduced by permission.—Mansfield, Katherine, photograph. Corbis-Bettmann. Reproduced by permission.—O'Connor, Flannery, photograph. AP/Wide World Photos. Reproduced by permission.—Scott, Sir Walter, illustration. AP/Wide World Photos. Reproduced by permission.—Silko, Leslie Marmon, photograph by Robyn McDaniels. (c) Robyn McDaniels. Reproduced by permission.—Sontag, Susan, photograph. AP/Wide World Photos. Reproduced by permission.—Thurber, James, 1954, photograph by Fred Palumbo. NYWTS/The Library of Congress.—Trevor, William, photograph by Jerry Bauer. (c) by Jerry Bauer. Reproduced by permission.—Welty, Eudora, 1962, photograph. NYWTS/The Library of Congress.—Wodehouse, P.G., 1940, photograph. AP/Wide World Photos. Reproduced by permission.

Cliff Palace dwellings, Mesa Verde, Colorado, photogrph by Lisa Dawson. Corel Corporation. Reproduced by permission.—Harlem, 125th Street near the Apollo Theater, 1930's, New York City, photograph. National Archives and Record Administration.—Hippies (crowd walking down city streets), San Francisco, California, 1967, photograph. AP/Wide World Photos. Reproduced by permission.—Irish famine victims (receiving help from Mrs. Kennedy), Kilrush, Ireland, 1849, photograph. Corbis-Bettmann. Reproduced by permission.

Contributors

Don Akers: Don Akers is a free-lance writer whose work has appeared in college journals and educational publications. Entry on "Jeeves Takes Charge." Original essay on "Jeeves Takes Charge."

Kate Bernheimer: Kate Bernheimer has a master's degree in creative writing and has edited *Mirror, Mirror on the Wall: Women Writers Explore Their Favorite Fairy Tales* (Anchor/Doubleday 1998). Entry on "My First Goose." Original essay on "My First Goose."

Cynthia Bily: Cynthia Bily teaches writing and literature at Adrian College in Adrian, Michigan, and writes for various educational publishers. Entry on "The Catbird Seat." Original essay on "The Catbird Seat."

Liz Brent: Liz Brent has a Ph.D. in American Culture, specializing in cinema studies, from the University of Michigan. She is a freelance writer and teaches courses in American cinema. Entries on "The Hitchhiking Game" and "Lullaby." Original essays on "The Fat Girl," "La Grande Breteche," "The Hitchhiking Game," "Lullaby," "The Way We Live Now," and "The White Horses of Vienna."

Sheldon Goldfarb: Sheldon Goldfarb has a Ph.D. in English and has published two books on the Victorian author William Makepeace Thackeray. Entry on "Wandering Willie's Tale." Original essay on "Wandering Willie's Tale."

Rena Korb: Rena Korb has a master's degree in English literature and creative writing and has written for a wide variety of educational publishers. Entries on "Bliss," "The Fat Girl," "The News from Ireland," and "The White Horses of Vienna." Original essays on "Bliss," "The Fat Girl," "The News from Ireland," and "The White Horses of Vienna."

Sarah Madsen Hardy: Sarah Madsen Hardy has a doctorate in English literature and is a freelance writer and editor. Entries on "Death in the Woods," Everything That Rises Must Converge," "The Way We Live Now," and "Why I Live at the P.O." Original essays on "Death in the Woods," Everything That Rises Must Converge," "The Way We Live Now," and "Why I Live at the P.O."

Elisabeth Piedmont-Marton: Elisabeth Piedmont-Marton teaches American literature and directs the writing center at Southwestern University in Texas. She writes frequently about the modern short story. Entry on "La Grande Breteche." Original essay on "La Grande Breteche."

Bliss

Katherine Mansfield
1920

By the time of her death, Katherine Mansfield had established herself as an important and influential contemporary short story writer. Her appeal can be traced to her focus on psychological conflicts, her oblique narration, and her complex characters that seem to be on the brink of a major epiphany.

One of her finest short stories, ''Bliss,'' serves as prime examples of these defining qualities. The protagonist of the story, Bertha, experiences a sense of rapture as she reflects on her life, which later turns to disappointment and resignation as she discovers that her husband is having a love affair with her friend.

Mansfield's *Bliss, and Other Stories*, published in 1920, secured the author's literary reputation. While readers and critics at the time generally lauded the short fiction collection, a few reviewers objected to its controversial subject matter—infidelities, discussions of sexuality, cruel and superficial characters. Today ''Bliss'' is one of Mansfield's most frequently anthologized stories and still resonates with modern readers.

Author Biography

Katherine Mansfield Beauchamp was born to a wealthy family in Wellington, New Zealand, on October 14, 1888. She was educated in London and

decided early on that she wanted to be a writer. She studied music, wrote for the school newspaper, and read the works of Oscar Wilde and other English writers of the early twentieth century.

After three years in London she returned to New Zealand, where her parents expected her to find a suitable husband and lead the life of a well-bred woman. However, Mansfield was rebellious, adventurous, and more enamored of the artistic community than of polite society.

She began publishing stories in Australian magazines in 1907, and shortly thereafter returned to London. A brief affair left her pregnant and she consented to marry a man, George Bowden, whom she had known a mere three weeks and who was not the father of her child. She dressed in black for the wedding and left him right after the ceremony.

Upon receiving word of the scandal and spurred on by rumors that her daughter had also been involved with several women, Mansfield's mother immediately sailed to London and placed her daughter in a spa in Germany. During her time in Germany, Mansfield suffered a miscarriage and was disinherited. After returning to London, Mansfield continued to write and was involved in various love affairs.

In 1911, Mansfield published her first volume of stories, *In a German Pension*, most of which had been written during her stay at the German spa. That same year she fell in love with John Middleton Murry, the editor of a literary magazine. Although they lived together on and off for many years, her other affairs continued.

Together Mansfield and Murry published a small journal, the *Blue Review*, which folded after only three issues. However, the experience led to friendships with members of the literary community of the day, including D. H. Lawrence and Virginia Woolf. In 1918, Mansfield was granted a divorce from Bowden, and she and Murry married.

Stricken with tuberculosis in 1917, Mansfield became very ill. She continued to write, publishing her collections *Bliss, and Other Stories* and *The Garden Party, and Other Stories* in 1920 and 1922 respectively. The title story of the former collection, ''Bliss'' garnered much critical success, both in England and the United States. Its success established Mansfield as a major talent.

Her short fiction received favorable critical attention, and she continued to write even after her health forced her to move to Fontainebleau in France. Though she was separated from Murry for long periods towards the end of her life, it was he who saw that her literary reputation was established by publishing her last stories and her collections of letters after she died of a massive pulmonary hemorrhage in January, 1923, at the age of thirty-four.

Plot Summary

''Bliss'' opens with Bertha Young reflecting on how wonderful her life is. As she walks home, she is overwhelmed by a feeling of bliss; she feels tremendously content with her home, her husband, her baby, and her friends.

At home, she begins to prepare for a dinner party she is having that evening. She reflects on the guests that will be arriving soon: Mr. and Mrs. Knight, an artistic couple; Eddie Warren, a playwright; and Pearl Fulton, Bertha's newest friend. Bertha wishes that her husband, Harry, would like Pearl; he has expressed some misgivings over the women's burgeoning friendship and Bertha hopes they will eventually become friends too.

As Bertha waits for her guests, she looks out on her garden. Her enjoyment of a pear tree with wide open blossoms, which she sees as representing herself, is ruined by two cats creeping across the lawn. Bertha meditates on how happy she is and how perfect her life is. She goes upstairs to dress, and soon thereafter her guests and husband arrive for dinner.

The group moves into the dining room, where they eat with relish and discuss the contemporary theater and literary scene. Bertha thinks about the pear tree again. She also senses that Pearl shares her feelings of bliss, and she is simply waiting for a sign from the other woman to show her recognition of the empathy between them.

After dinner, as Bertha is about to make the coffee, Pearl gives her the sign by asking if Bertha has a garden. Bertha pulls apart the curtains to display the garden and the pear tree. Bertha imagines that Pearl responds positively to the tree, but she is not sure if it really happened.

Over coffee, the group talks about a variety of topics. Bertha perceives Harry's dislike for Pearl and wants to tell him how much she has shared with her friend. She is suddenly overcome by a feeling of sexual desire for her husband. This is the first time she has felt this way, and she is eager for the guests to leave so she can be alone with Harry.

After the Knights leave, Pearl and Eddie are set to share a taxi. As Pearl goes to the hall to get her coat, Harry accompanies her. Eddie asks Bertha if she has a certain book of poems. Bertha goes to retrieve the book from a nearby table. As she looks out into the hallway, she sees her husband and Pearl embrace and make arrangements to meet the next day. Pearl reenters the room to thank Bertha for the party. The two guests leave and Harry, still cool and collected, says he will shut up the house. Bertha runs to the window to look at the pear tree. She cries "''Oh, what is going to happen now?'''" but outside the pear tree is just the same as ever.

Katherine Mansfield

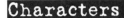

Characters

Pearl Fulton

Pearl Fulton is Bertha's enigmatic new friend in the story. With her indirect way of looking at people and her half-smile, she appears distant and mysterious. Although Bertha acknowledges that she and Pearl have not had a really intimate conversation, on the night of the dinner party Bertha senses an intimate attachment between them. This feeling of attachment is confirmed when Bertha discovers that Pearl is having an affair with her husband, Harry.

Mrs. Knight

Mrs. Knight and her husband are guests at Bertha's dinner party. Though she is "awfully keen on interior decoration," Mrs. Knight dresses herself in wild clothing and resembles a giant banana peel.

Norman Knight

Norman Knight is about to open a theater that will show thoroughly modern plays.

Mug

See Norman Knight

Eddie Warren

Eddie Warren is an effeminate playwright. He is described as always being "in a state of acute distress" and over the course of the evening complains about his taxi ride to the party.

Bertha Young

Bertha, a young housewife, is the main character in the story. Despite the fact that the story is told from her perspective, readers learn few concrete details about her. She appears to enjoy a fairly leisurely life, as she and her husband are financially comfortable. However, though she claims she and her husband are "pals," her home life would seem not as ideal as she views it; her marriage lacks passion, and the nanny clearly keeps her at a distance from her young daughter.

Bertha's most notable characteristic is her inexplicable state of happiness. As the story opens, she is pleased with all life offers her. During her dinner party, she seems to find joy in almost everything she sees: the lovely pear tree in the garden, which seems to represent both herself and Pearl Fulton; her smart and cosmopolitan friends; the bond she is forging with Pearl. She even sexually desires her husband for the first time in her life and looks forward to spending the rest of the evening alone with him. By the end of the story, however, this world in which Bertha finds such pleasure is shattered when she discovers that her husband is having an affair with Pearl.

Harry Young

Harry is Bertha's husband. He provides a good income for his family, enjoys good food, and has a zest for life. However, his most notable characteristic is his duplicitous nature: while he declares to Bertha that he finds Pearl Fulton dull, he is secretly engaged in a love affair with her. In fact, during the dinner party, he pretends to dislike Pearl. Yet he risks exposure of the affair when he embraces Pearl in the hallway while his wife is in the next room.

Themes

Marriage and Adultery

The themes of marriage and adultery are central to ''Bliss.'' Bertha believes (or makes herself believe) she has a fulfilling, complete marriage. Although she characterizes her husband as a good pal, she still contends they are as much in love as they ever were.

The climactic event of the story—Bertha's realization of Harry's affair with Pearl—proves that her husband does not share his wife's contentment. As Harry's affair demonstrates, he is not happy with the lack of passion in their marriage. Harry's actions reveal his duplicitous nature: not only has Harry been hiding the affair from his wife, he also pretends to dislike Pearl in order to cover it up. The risk that Harry takes in kissing Pearl in his own home, as well as his method of hiding his true feelings, indicate the likelihood that he and Pearl share a very strong connection.

Change and Transformation

Change and transformation are subtle themes in the story. Bertha's extreme sense of bliss, along with her new feelings of desire for her husband, show that she is undergoing a profound change in her life. She wonders if the feeling of bliss that she had all day was actually leading up to her increased attraction to her husband. At the end of the story, she wants nothing more than for the guests to leave so she can be alone with Harry.

Bertha's transformation into a sexual being is abruptly halted when she sees her husband kissing Pearl Fulton. She realizes that she can no longer look at her world as perfect, nor can she move forward to a new relationship with Harry. When she runs to the window to look at the pear tree she finds that it is ''as lovely as ever and as full of flower and as still.'' This is a clear sign that the change Bertha has undergone will be brought to an abrupt halt, for the pear tree—which is seen to represent Bertha—remains exactly the same.

Modernity

The concept of modernity is an important aspect of the story. Bertha constantly characterizes the elements of her life—her relationship with her husband and her friends, for instance—as being thoroughly modern. However, Bertha's view of modernity would seem to be a liking for things that are shallow, superficial, and duplicitous. She has rationalized her poor sexual relationship with her husband as ''being modern'' because they are such good pals. Thus, in Bertha's mind, a modern marriage needn't be based on love or attraction but simply on the bonds that would make two people friends.

Her view of the modern marriage hurts her relationship with Harry as he experiences dissatisfaction at the state of their relationship. Even Bertha and Harry's philosophy of raising children is perceived as modern. Bertha seems to spend little time with her daughter, instead entrusting her to a jealous nanny; moreover, Harry claims to have no interest in his daughter.

Bertha's friends are also considered thoroughly modern—but they appear utterly ridiculous. Mrs. Knight is described as a cross between a giant monkey and a banana peel. Her modern ideas for decorating—including french fries embroidered on the curtains and chairbacks shaped like frying pans—seem distasteful and ugly. Plays and poems mentioned by the guests seem dismal and pseudo-intellectual, and the satire reaches a high point in Eddie Warren's lauding of a poem that begins, ''Why Must it Always be Tomato Soup?'' The guests and their interests, rather than seeming ''modern'' and ''thrilling,'' seem merely excessive and absurd.

Style

Point of View and Narration

The story is told from a third person, limited point of view. This means that readers are privy to only Bertha's perspective. In "Bliss," all events are filtered through Bertha, and her overexcited way of viewing the world forms the story's narrative technique. That the narration is studded with questions, interjections, and exclamations only emphasizes Bertha's perspective.

Bertha's emphatic and constant reassurances of how happy she is also serves to emphasize the fact that she may be hiding something from herself. Clearly, she is not truly as content with her life as she claims to be. The facts presented by the narrative reinforce this idea. For instance, Bertha spends very little time with her child. Her lack of meaningful activity also demonstrates the hollowness of her life. When she draws up a list of all the things she has—money, a nice house, modern friends—she ends with the pathetic inclusion of a "wonderful little dressmaker" and "their new cook [who] made the superb omelettes." Bertha's narration demonstrates the incompleteness of her life, though she cannot acknowledge it.

Satire

Satire is the use of humor, wit, or ridicule to criticize human nature and societal institutions. Indirect satire, as found in "Bliss," relies upon the ridiculous behavior of characters to make its point. Bertha describes her friends as "modern" and "thrilling" people, yet they are presented as ridiculous figures. Mrs. Knight resembles some kind of monkey, wearing a dress reminiscent of banana peels. The most notable characteristic of Eddie Warren, who appears to be a writer, is his white socks and his affected way of speaking.

Although these people aspire to be sophisticated and artistic, their conversation reveals how little regard they truly have for an aesthetic sense of beauty. Mrs. Knight, an interior decorator, wants to design the room of a client's home around a fish-and-chip motif. The poems and pieces of literature enjoyed by Eddie Warren border on the grotesque. Truly, Bertha's friends seem to have no idea of true artistry; instead, they wrap themselves up in what they believe to be fashionable talk about artistic ideas.

It is also clear that the group is more about talk and less about creating art. She thinks "what a decorative group they made, how they seemed to set one another off." In Bertha's mind, as in the group itself, the image of oneself as an artistic person is more important than actually being one.

Topics for Further Study

- Read another of Katherine's Mansfield's London stories, such as "Marriage à la Mode." Then compare Mansfield's use of satire and imagery in the stories, as well as her presentation of characters and relationships. Which story do you think is more successful? Why?

- In "Bliss," Mansfield mentions several poems and plays. Locate and read one of these "modern" poems and plays of the early 1920s. How does this poem or play relate to the themes of Mansfield's story? Does it add to your understanding of that era? In what way?

- J. F. Kobler wrote, "A first-time reader of a Mansfield story may have similar feelings of bliss while experiencing the story and may well not understand their source." Write a paragraph describing your initial reactions after reading "Bliss" for the first time.

- Mansfield drew on her intimate knowledge of the bohemian London art scene to write "Bliss." Based on this story, what are your perceptions of the scene and the people who populated this segment of society?

Symbolism

The most important and complicated symbol in "Bliss" is the pear tree: it represents different people at different times throughout the story. First and foremost, it represents Bertha because she believes that "its wide open blossoms [are] as symbol of her own life." When Bertha first notices the tree, she is intent on pursuing the belief that her life is full and rich, open to wondrous possibilities.

Later on in the story the pear represents Pearl Fulton. Like the pear tree, Pearl, dressed in silver, emits a shimmery, ethereal glow. Thus both Pearl and Bertha—who are actually rivals—are connected to each other by association with the pear tree.

However, the pear tree also takes on a masculine identity in its phallic description: "it seemed, like the flame of a candle, to stretch up, to point, to quiver in the bright air, to grow taller and taller'' under the gaze of the women. In this manifestation, the pear tree can be seen as representing Harry, who further unites the two women.

In addition, the pear tree seems to be reaching toward the moon, which previously had been identified with Pearl. Thus Harry's sexual desire, which Bertha now wants for herself, is clarified as reaching toward Pearl, not Bertha.

Historical Context

Post-World War I Art

In the aftermath of the devastation of World War I, artists expressed their shock at the horrors of war and their disillusionment with modern society. Art that emerged in the post-war period showed a marked departure from past forms as artists rejected traditional ways of expressing their ideas. For instance, James Joyce's novel *Ulysses* (1922) experimented with a stream-of-consciousness narrative. Poets often abandoned traditional rhyme and meter. Playwrights such as Bertolt Brecht saw the theater more as a classroom than as a place of performance. In his plays, characters would step out of their roles and directly address the audience.

The Bloomsbury Group

In the 1910s, and 1920s, London was a hubbub of literary and artistic activity. At the center of this activity was the Bloomsbury group, one of London's foremost intellectual and artistic circles. Members of this group rejected conventional ideas on religious, artistic, social, and sexual matters. Bloomsbury members included writer Virginia Woolf, painter Vanessa Bell, novelist and essayist E. M. Forster, art critic Roger Fry, and economist John Maynard Keynes. Attendees at the regular Thursday night meetings included such British literary luminaries as George Bernard Shaw and William Yeats.

In 1917, Leonard Woolf established the Hogarth Press, which went on to publish Sigmund Freud's works in English, T. S. Eliot's poetry, and Mansfield's short stories, among other pieces. The Bloomsbury group also set up the Omega Workshop, which lasted from 1913 to 1919. At the workshop, painters applied their ideas of abstraction and decorated ordinary objects, such as screens and chairs, in what today would be called modern design. Through their artistic work and ideas, the members of the Bloomsbury group were influential practitioners of twentieth-century modernism.

The British Economy

In 1920, Britain headed into a cycle of economic depressions, which were to last until World War II. Unemployment quickly reached 1.5 million, where it remained for most of the decade. A government committee was appointed to find remedies for this depressed economic situation; unfortunately, some of the remedies the committee recommended were ignored in light of pressure from other economic interests. As a result, the situation did not significantly improve throughout the decade.

The Modern British Woman

World War I had forced many women to join the ranks of male workers. At the outset of the war, the British government actively set out to recruit women as men went to war. Millions of British women entered government departments, factories, and private offices. They worked in many capacities, from clerical jobs to manufacturing.

Such increased employment and economic opportunities were important factors in women's emancipation. By 1918 the Franchise Act gave all women over the age of twenty-eight the right to vote (all men over the age of twenty-one were given this right by the same law). Soon the first British female sat in the House of Commons. However, women did not have equal voting rights as men until 1928, when the Representation of the People Act, known as the ''flapper act,'' was passed.

As in the United States, young British women used fashion to reflect their changing status in society: shorter skirts and bobbed hair became the rage amongst young women in both countries. Despite these advances, most married women remained dependent on their husbands, and working women were paid less than men for equal labor. Women were not promoted to positions of power, such as judges, corporate CEOs, or managers.

Some women publicly decried this inequality. Beatrice Hastings wrote feminist articles published in the *New Age* in which she frankly discussed such topics as the sexual subjection of women to their husbands or the refusal of British universities to grant degrees to women. Laws passed in 1919 and 1923 also gave women rights equal to those of men in cases of divorce.

Compare & Contrast

- **1920s:** Between 1910 and 1920, the number of divorces in Britain tripled, from about 600 to 1,700. The Matrimonial Causes Act of 1923 made it easier for a wife to obtain a divorce. This legislation allowed a woman to divorce her husband without having to prove cruelty or desertion in addition to adultery.

  Today: With the advent of the Divorce Reform Act, which passed in 1971, divorce could be obtained by either party without grounds. Like in the United States, divorce is common in modern-day Great Britain.

- **1920s:** By 1918, as part of the Franchise Act, British women over the age of twenty-eight had the right to vote. Yet it was not until 1928, with the passage of the Representation of the People Act, that women were given equal rights in terms of voting.

  Today: For a few decades, several women have held important political positions in Great Britain. The most powerful of these women was Margaret Thatcher, who served as the country's prime minister from 1979 to 1990.

- **1920s:** About ten percent of British people own their own homes.

  Today: Approximately two-thirds of British people own their own homes. Owner-occupied homes are the most prevalent form of housing.

- **1920s:** At the beginning of the decade, women make up about thirty percent of the British workforce. This number drops as Britain undergoes an economic crisis later in the decade.

  Today: Women make up more than 44 percent of the British workforce.

Modern British Society

British society underwent significant changes in the 1910s and 1920s. By 1914 the discrepancies between the lifestyles of the rich and poor were far less evident. Fewer people had servants, poorer people had access to the same goods as the wealthy, and middle-class society came to hold greater political power. More people owned homes that had the comforts of electricity and modern plumbing. The workweek was reduced in 1918 from 56 hours to 48 hours. Working-class people also saw improvements as new forms of recreation—particularly dance halls and talking films—enhanced their leisure hours.

Critical Overview

The story "Bliss" was first published in *The English Review* in 1920. Later that year, it became the title story for Mansfield's second collection, *Bliss, and Other Stories.* The story (and the volume) helped solidify Mansfield's reputation as an important contemporary writer.

Many early reviewers lauded the collection and Mansfield's unique narrative voice. Conrad Aiken, in a review for *Freeman*, called Mansfield "brilliant" and remarked upon her "infinitely inquisitive sensibility." Several reviewers drew a parallel between Mansfield's work and that of the Russian writer Anton Chekhov. Aiken noted this similarity but also countered any claims that Mansfield "borrowed" from Chekhov: "One has not read a page of Miss Mansfield's book before one has said 'Chekhov'; but one has not read two pages before Chekhov is forgotten."

Malcolm Cowley also commented on the resemblance to Chekhov. He deemed the collection to be a "voyage of adventure" filled with Mansfield's "own experiments and successful experiments."

Many reviewers paid particular attention to "Bliss." The anonymous reviewer for the *Times*

Literary Supplement maintained, "it is all beauty till the end; beauty so deeply known and so discerningly expressed that that special condition of springtime exaltation seems here finally and fully held." The review ended with this positive judgment: "Miss Mansfield, with the air of dispassionately reporting, is making all the while her own world. In other words, she is an artist in fiction."

A reviewer for *The Athenaeum* contended that despite the "shock and disillusionment, . . . [and] seemingly wanton destruction of faith, vision, or happiness," in stories such as "Bliss," readers "are left believing . . . in human virtue and integrity."

Yet some critics focused on the story's cruel or disagreeable aspects. A reviewer for the *Spectator* countered these accusations early on: "That is not to say that they ["Bliss" and "Je ne parle pas francais"] are cheerful stories; they are anything but that; they have not, however, that element of trivial discomfort so dominant in modern fiction." This reviewer also acknowledged, however, that both stories would likely "shock some people by their outspokenness on some subjects usually left alone." The reviewer continued, "but surely the only real test for 'book ethics' is whether they will . . . be likely to do good or harm. Judged by this standard, we cannot imagine anyone objecting to Miss Mansfield's book."

Succeeding generations of critics and readers also singled out "Bliss" as one of Mansfield's finer stories. In 1934, the poet T. S. Eliot, in his *After Strange Gods*, put forth the story as an example of the modern mood. While early reviewers and critics tended to focus on literary and stylistic aspects of the story—as well as how it reflected contemporary society—as the years have passed, critics have broadened their scope of inquiry.

For instance, recent criticism of the story has explored Bertha's sexual desire (both for Harry and Pearl Fulton), which earlier critics disregarded. In addition to Bertha's sexuality, commentators hold differing views of many key facets of the story, such as their analysis of Bertha's personality, why Bertha experiences feelings of bliss, and what these feelings actually mean to her.

It is also interesting to note the way specific criticism has changed since the publication of "Bliss." The review in *Athaeneum* referred to one of Mansfield's "finest pieces of characterization" of "'ordinary' people" such as "the vigorous Harry." Most contemporary critics, however, find Harry to be crass, aggressive, and crude.

When a number of Mansfield's books, journals, and letters were reprinted in the 1980s, reviewers again discussed the story. Katherine Dieckmann, in the *Village Voice Literary Supplement,* responded to Murry's assertion that Mansfield's stories were "read and loved by innumerable simple people," and not the academics or critics. She contended: "Bosh. Read Mansfield's story "Bliss" and it's immediately apparent how deeply connected she was to this cultured world—both critical of it and quite willingly a part of it. . . . The upshot of "Bliss" is that these social animals eat away at your soul."

Recent critics, however, contend there is much more to the story than simply Mansfield's effective use of satire. In fact, commentators laud the effective and unusual use of symbolism and imagery on multiple levels, the deft psychological portrait of Bertha, and Mansfield's evocation of mood in the story.

Criticism

Rena Korb

Korb has a master's degree in English literature and creative writing and has written for a wide variety of educational publishers. In the following essay, she focuses on Bertha's feelings of bliss as a way of understanding the story.

In 1919, Katherine Mansfield wrote in a letter to a friend:

> O this Spring—It makes me long for happiness. That is so vague. Each year I think—this year I shall not feel it so keenly—but I feel it more. Why are human beings the only ones who do not put forth fresh buds—exquisite flowers and leaves? . . . Really, on some of these days one is tired with *bliss*. I long to tell someone—to feel it immediately shared—felt without my asking 'do you feel it?'—Do you know what I mean?

Within the year, Mansfield had channeled her own feelings of exultation into "Bliss"—a story that helped solidify her literary reputation. The story demonstrates Mansfield's skill as writer while evoking a milieu of social superficiality and stagnation. At the same time, the story operates on a more emotional level, one to which countless readers have responded positively without precisely knowing why.

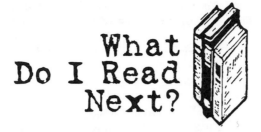

What Do I Read Next?

- Like "Bliss," Ellen Glasgow's 1923 story "The Difference" explores the consequences of adultery when a Victorian woman learns of her husband's affair.

- Virginia Woolf's *Mrs. Dalloway* (1925) chronicles one day in the life of Clarissa Dalloway, an upper-class Londoner.

- Evelyn Waugh's satirical novel, *A Handful of Dust* (1934), examines the complex nature of contemporary morality.

- "Weekend" (1978), a short story by Ann Beattie, explores the relationship between a husband and wife after the husband's numerous affairs.

- Edith Wharton's short story "Roman Fever" (1934) challenges Victorian morality while exploring a pivotal moment in a woman's life.

- F. Scott Fitzgerald's *This Side of Paradise* (1920) explores the Jazz Age generation that emerged in the United States 1920s. This novel reveals the new morals and cynical attitude of younger Americans.

"Bliss" relates a fateful day in the life of Bertha Young. Bertha, a thirty-year-old housewife, tenaciously clings to the belief that she has all that is good in the world: a fine, dependable husband; "an adorable baby"; "modern, thrilling friends"; and the material comforts that money can buy.

Yet as day merges into evening, it becomes clear that Bertha's declarations of happiness serve as a mere cover-up for all that her life lacks. This feeling reaches its culmination when she finds out that her husband Harry is having an affair with her friend, Pearl Fulton—the very friend she had believed was the only person to share her overflowing emotions.

The richness of "Bliss" allows for much discussion; critics have focused on different aspects of the story—those they deem most essential to its understanding—such as character analysis, sexual desire, and Mansfield's use of symbolism, imagery, and satire. Just as critics do not always agree on what is the most important facet of "Bliss"—what makes the story "work" and indeed survive the decades—neither do they always agree in their analysis of what remains at the core of the story: Bertha's feelings of bliss.

Critics remain divided over the genesis of these feelings that grip Bertha so strongly. J. F. Kobler, author of *Katherine Mansfield, A Study of the Short Fiction*, maintains that her feelings derive from a natural source; much as, it would seem, did Mansfield's own feelings as described in the letter of 1919. "Bertha definitely feels what is happening to her," he writes, "but she cannot discover [its] source."

In contrast, Saralyn R. Daly has asserted in *Katherine Mansfield* that Bertha's overwhelming protestations of happiness stem from her denied awareness of Harry's affair.

Most critics, however, attribute Bertha's neurotic behavior to her growing dissatisfaction with her life. Her feelings of bliss are thus artificially manufactured as a means to hold on to her facade of happiness. Indeed, Bertha, laughing at how beautiful she finds the fruit she has arranged, even declares, "'I'm getting hysterical.'"

In addition to the hints inherent in Bertha's words, the story's narrative style indicates all that she is trying to keep from herself. The opening paragraphs demonstrate her inability to perceive her life through her own eyes. Instead, she speaks as if she is in the process of observing herself. Though she speaks glowingly of moments when she wants to "laugh at—nothing, at nothing, simply" and of the feeling of "absolute bliss!" that comes over her

> It is not surprising that before discovering Pearl's and Harry's affair, Bertha reaches out to Pearl. The narrative states that 'Bertha had fallen in love with her, as she always did fall in love with beautiful women who had something strange about them.'"

as she walks home, it is subtly revealed that her words are not her own. She questions, "Why be given a body if you have to keep it shut up in a case like a rare, rare fiddle?" but then immediately edits her own thoughts: "No, that about the fiddle is not quite what I mean."

Later, while visiting her daughter in the nursery, Bertha returns to this turn of phrase: "Why have a baby if it has to be kept—not in a case like a rare, rare fiddle—but in another woman's arms?" Bertha's repetition of the phrase shows her experimentation with finding a way to express her feelings, but she is only able to rework an expression she was not happy with in the first place.

Mansfield wrote of the former scene to her husband John Middleton Murry. "What I *meant*. . . was Bertha, not being an artist, was yet artist manqué enough to realise that these words and expressions were not and couldn't be hers. They were, as it were, *quoted* by her, borrowed with . . . an eyebrow . . . yet she'd none of her own." Thus, early in the narrative, Bertha reveals her engagement in an act of self-deception and self-creation.

As Bertha continues to congratulate herself on her privileged life, her very words indicate the rationalization taking place in her mind. "Really—really—she had everything," she thinks, as if trying to convince herself. The list that she manufactures moves swiftly from family and home to praises for her dressmaker and her cook. Harry and she "were as much in love as ever," but then she qualifies this statement with the revelation that they were "really

good pals." Indeed, Bertha later reveals that she has never felt any sexual passion for her husband.

Her friends are "keen on social issues" but as their conversation at the dinner party shows, her friends are more concerned with inflating their own egos. Their lack of social conscious is revealed through Eddie Warren's description of "'A *dreadful* poem about a *girl* who was *violated* by a beggar *without* a nose in a little wood. . .'"

Bertha's claims of a good life ring hollow. She cannot even find solace in her daughter—though the moment in the nursery seems to be when Bertha really lets down her defenses. She readily acknowledges that she "did not dare to" question the nanny's authority; later, the baby is snatched back by the nanny "in triumph" when Bertha takes a phone call. Bertha's lack of a close relationship with her daughter is not surprising given that the child, Little B, serves more as a reflection of her mother than her own person.

Part of Bertha's problems stem from her inherent immaturity, as underscored by her last name, "Young." Bertha's immaturity (as well as that of her friends) prevents her from achieving any meaningful connections with those who surround her. She is not able to adequately mother her child despite the fact that while feeding Little B "all of her feelings of bliss came back again." She does not experience sexual satisfaction with her husband nor is she able to truly communicate with him, as evidenced by her inability to keep him on the telephone when she "only wanted to get in touch with him for a moment."

Of Bertha's circle, only Pearl Fulton seems to possess a modicum of maturity (and it is significant that she is not really a member of Bertha's crowd but rather Bertha's latest "find"). Yet Bertha finds it difficult to truly connect with her new friend. Though she and Bertha had "met a number of times and really talked" her true essence eludes Bertha, who cannot break past Pearl's wall of reserve. Of course, as the story demonstrates, Pearl's maturity can be crudely construed as a sexual one—and her reserve could come from the knowledge that she is betraying Bertha.

It is not surprising that before discovering Pearl's and Harry's affair, Bertha reaches out to Pearl. The narrative states that "Bertha had fallen in love with her, as she always did fall in love with beautiful women who had something strange about them." Bertha's affection for Pearl seems to stem from her search for something or someone meaningful and different—which, compared to those she surrounds herself with, implies a person of some substance. Pearl Fulton, as the newest comer, still has that potential, while her friends and family have failed to inspire Bertha to experience *true* feelings of bliss.

Harry's coarseness is revealed in his "talk about food and glory in his 'shameless passions for the white flesh of the lobster'"; his inclinations show his predatory and aggressive nature. Eddie Warren's inherent foolishness and pretentiousness is revealed when he talks about a poem that begins with an "*incredibly* beautiful line: 'Why Must it Always be Tomato Soup?'"; he finds the poem so "'*deeply* true . . . Tomato soup is so *dreadfully* eternal.'"

Clearly, such people are no match for Bertha, who finds artistic pleasure in something as simple as the arrangement of fruit. Pearl, on the other hand, is the only person who seems to relate to Bertha's emotion. While the other guests are "dabbing their lips with napkins, crumbling bread, fiddling with forks and glasses and talking," Bertha remains silent. After dinner, when Pearl asks Bertha whether she has a garden, Bertha takes this as a sign.

Unfortunately, Bertha is simply reading into Pearl's actions. This is subtly acknowledged when, as the two women are regarding the pear tree, the narration reads, "And did Miss Fulton murmur: 'Yes. Just *that*.' Or did Bertha dream it?" For Bertha, this feeling of shared communication opens her own life up to numerous possibilities, foremost that of feeling passion for her husband.

Instead of fulfilling her desires, however, Bertha discovers Harry and Pearl in a silent embrace. Thus does Bertha's burgeoning transformation come to an end. While she had hopes of evoking a change in her life, based on a feeling of shared emotion—which her life so sorely lacks—she resigns herself to a profound loneliness. The pear tree, which symbolizes Bertha (note that the pear tree is bathed in the white of the moon and rises against a jade-green sky, and Bertha dresses in a white dress, jade beads, and green shoes and stockings), remains unchanged, "as lovely as ever," as Bertha's life seems destined to go forward, unchanged.

Because "Bliss" is so full of multiple meanings and symbolism, a thorough understanding of it on a textual level is difficult to achieve. Yet the story also succeeds on a more undefinable level. As Kobler maintains: "A first-time reader of a Mansfield story may have similar feelings of bliss while experiencing the story and may well not understand their source. Why does this story on this reading create such pleasure for this particular reader?"

Kobler's question may prove impossible to answer, but countless readers over the generations would agree with his assessment.

Source: Rena Korb, for *Short Stories for Students*, Gale, 2000.

Armine Kotin Mortimer

In the following essay, Kotin Mortimer argues that a second story exists within "Bliss," one that is critical to the understanding of the story as a whole.

When the heroine of Mansfield's well-known, extraordinary short story discovers her husband's infidelity less than a page before the end, a *second story* untold in the first but necessary to its meaning erupts into the narrative, to devastating effect. The devious second story construction leads, and often misleads, the reader, who interprets clues and applies general cultural competence to "retell" the once-submerged second story. Appealing to the reader's cooperation in its complex processes, the story subverts the reading subject, placing her in the position of the unknowing heroine.

"The truth is," Katherine Mansfield wrote in her journal, "one can get only *so much* into a story; there is always a sacrifice. One has to leave out what one knows and longs to use. Why? I haven't any idea, but there it is. It's always a kind of race to get in as much as one can before it *disappears*." Suggesting Hemingway's principle of the iceberg, this double-edged observation, both naive and devious, insinuates an interpretive strategy: it challenges the reader to find the disappeared text. If we assume that the sacrificed material of the second story in "Bliss" contained what Mansfield knew and longed to use, still we may not agree on what she knew. Some readers soft-pedal the homosexualities of Mansfield's relations, or eliminate them altogether, while others make them a necessary ingredient in any interpretation of her fictions. I favor neither extreme. Let us recognize, as many have, that Bertha Young and her text are lacking knowledge; they are in the position of the analysand. As the analyst, however, I prefer not to claim to discover a particular referential knowledge behind the text (taken to be the "language" spoken by the analysand), but rather to be *knowledgeable about the functioning of language*. This wording borrowed from Shoshana Felman aptly describes the stance

"
'The truth is,' Katherine Mansfield wrote in her journal, 'one can get only <u>so much</u> into a story; there is always a sacrifice. One has to leave out what one knows and longs to use. Why? I haven't any idea, but there it is. It's always a kind of race to get in as much as one can before it <u>disappears.</u>"

I take in reading "Bliss." I am interested in showing how the text reveals its own strategies for manipulating the reader, while it convinces us to apprehend a character as if she were a real person. In other words, I wish to be attentive not just to what Susan Stanford Friedman calls the horizontal axis, the "movement of characters within their fictional world," but especially the vertical space-time, referring to the "writer and reader in relation to each other," in particular the "interplay of the semiotic and the symbolic." "Bliss" is a good example of how the represented events of the story mirror the way language drives the narrative. Furthermore, although the story has an undoubted lesbian meaning that compels us to read out homosexual desire, it is rich enough to enjoy wider interpretations. The second-story construction, whose effects "work" only once, throws up a fortification protecting what Mansfield knew, and this is what guides our interpretive strategy. In question is not so much what hidden knowledge we may reveal about Bertha as what we may know about how the story moves us.

The dazzling feeling of bliss that Bertha Young shares with her "find," Miss Pearl Fulton, lies mysteriously hidden. At dinner, she thinks she has seen the enigma behind Miss Fulton's smile: "But Bertha knew, suddenly, as if the longest, most intimate look had passed between them—as if they had said to each other: 'You, too?'—that Pearl Fulton, stirring the beautiful red soup in the grey plate, was feeling just what she was feeling''; Miss Fulton too has swallowed a bit of the sun. The reader will find out, with Bertha, that she is not wrong, but that this should not be cause for joy. Bertha ponders what could make her so certain of this knowledge: "What she simply couldn't make out—what was miraculous—was how she should have guessed Miss Fulton's mood so exactly and so instantly. For she never doubted for a moment that she was right, and yet what had she to go on? Less than nothing." Together, they look at the beautiful pear tree in the garden, "understanding each other perfectly." Setting this "perfect" understanding against a backdrop of grotesques taints the shared feeling with both comic and tragic irony. Bertha can hardly wait for her idiotic guests to leave so she can tell her husband in bed about her wonderful feeling. And it is then that she realizes with a shock that the name she must give to her feeling, instead of the euphemistic "bliss," is desire: "For the first time in her life Bertha Young desired her husband."

Husband Harry, however, professes to dislike striking blonds like Miss Fulton, and the reader has little choice but to interpret his rude behavior as Bertha does. In the last page and a half the narrative takes pains to describe the characters' movements: Pearl Fulton goes toward the hall to get her coat; Bertha is following her to help, but her husband brushes past, repenting his coldness; as a good hostess, she must then remain in the drawing room to listen to Eddie Warren's italicized praise of Bilks's *new* poem, "Why Must it Always be Tomato Soup?" and to fetch the anthology containing it from a table near the hall door—"And she moved noiselessly to a table opposite the drawing-room door and Eddie glided noiselessly after her. She picked up the little book and gave it to him; they had not made a sound." This elaborate staging, insisting implausibly on the silence of both characters, announces to the reader at the very least *that* something is going to happen, if not exactly *what*. As Bertha looks up to see Harry helping Miss Fulton with her coat, the second story bursts upon her like a tornado:

> And she saw. . .Harry with Miss Fulton's coat in his arms and Miss Fulton with her back turned to him and her head bent. He tossed the coat away, put his hands on her shoulders and turned her violently to him. His lips said "I adore you," and Miss Fulton laid her moonbeam fingers on his cheeks and smiled her sleepy smile. Harry's nostrils quivered; his lips curled back in a hideous grin while he whispered: "Tomorrow," and with her eyelids Miss Fulton said "Yes."

With Bertha, we embrace the entire second story in an instant. We feel certain that Harry Young and Pearl Fulton have already become lovers, for he is a proficient reader of her eyelids, and it seems likely that "To-morrow" follows a "To-day." At the same moment, we realize that Bertha, through whose eyes the entire story is told, has been a particularly bad guide for us (leading us down the garden path?). Her understanding of Miss Fulton is far from "perfect," and her reading of her husband's behavior is always wrong. For the first-time reader, who does not know the second story until it surfaces, the second story sweeps away mistaken interpretations and irreparably changes the first. As Mansfield wrote, "[w]ithout [the sense of crisis] how are we to appreciate the importance of one 'spiritual event' rather than another? What is to prevent each being unrelated—complete in itself—if the gradual unfolding in growing, gaining light is not to be followed by one blazing moment?" The blazing moment, the eruption of the second story into the first, links the spiritual events of Bertha's bliss in a sudden new light, which casts into shadows the "gradual unfolding in growing, gaining light." Until these moments, our reading is necessarily naive; it becomes devious when the second story bursts into the first.

The exclusive focus on Bertha and the scintillating expressiveness of her discovery of desire also take our attention away from any clues to the threatening tornado. Our second reading finds them. The first story is highly indexical (rather than functional), particularly in its treatment of the sublime bliss. Preeminent among symbols indexing the mysterious and enchanting feeling is the pear tree in perfect full bloom at the end of the garden, which Bertha takes as an icon of her own life. She dresses for dinner in a flowing white dress with a jade necklace, and green shoes and stockings, thus uncannily presaging the white-blossomed pear tree against the jade-green sky at dusk. Yet this index also serves as an early clue to the reader, if not to Bertha, that the bloom is not her own, for later in the moonlight the tree turns silver, "silver as Miss Fulton" in her elegant dress. When Miss Fulton asks to see the garden, Bertha takes this request as an enigmatic "sign," and when she sees the pear tree, Bertha fancies she says "Yes. Just *that*." As Miss Fulton and Bertha together gaze at the slender tree, it indexes their "perfect" understanding: "Although it was so still it seemed, like the flame of a candle, to stretch up, to point, to quiver in the bright air, to grow taller and taller as they gazed—almost

to touch the rim of the round, silver moon." Symbolic of the fullness of desire, no doubt suggestively phallic, the fantastical tree finally stands as an index not of Bertha's bliss but of Miss Fulton's, which remains undisturbed at the end of the story. With Miss Fulton's farewell words echoing in Bertha's mind ("Your lovely pear tree—pear tree—pear tree!"), she runs to the window and cries, "Oh, what is going to happen now?" The story thus closes on a question that calls explicitly for a further narrative, and the only answer, in the final one-sentence paragraph, is again indexical and not functional: "But the pear tree was as lovely as ever and as full of flower and as still." Bliss remains—not Bertha's but Miss Fulton's.

A second index, which the reader probably ignores on a first reading, is also found in the garden when Bertha first looks out, before the guests arrive: "A grey cat, dragging its belly, crept across the lawn, and a black one, its shadow, trailed after. The sight of them, so intent and so quick, gave Bertha a curious shiver. 'What creepy things cats are!' she stammered, and she turned away from the window." The cat is the vulgar counterpart to the sublime pear tree, the defect that dooms the "perfect" symbol. Yet if it passes unnoticed in the first story, it reappears after the second story has erupted. When Miss Fulton leaves after murmuring "Your lovely pear tree!," Eddie follows her "like the black cat following the grey cat." For Bertha now that the tornado has burst upon her, the silvery, blond Miss Fulton, with her moonbeam fingers, has become the creepy gray cat that slithered snake-like below the beauty of the miraculous tree. Against a pervasive array of vibrant and compelling colors, in this narrative, black and gray are merely two intensities of non-color. Not only has Miss Fulton become a sinister, treacherous cat, the devious introduction of evil into paradise, but she has lost her shining silver mystery and taken on a dullish gray—no enigma but a trite, brutal platitude. The gray cat is a distant clue to the second story, but the reader is not allowed to give it a precise interpretation until the second story has shattered the first. Everything was not perfect, after all, in the garden.

There are many other clues, but the most intriguing lie in the very feeling of bliss and the muted mystery of its origin in Miss Fulton. After the shared fantasy of the phallic pear tree, the following paragraph offers, on second reading, an insertion point for a clue addressed to the reader: "How long did they stand there? Both, as it were, caught in that circle of unearthly light, understanding each other perfectly, creatures of another world, and wondering what they were to do in this one with all this blissful treasure that burned in their bosoms and dropped, in silver flowers, from their hair and hands?'' The third person plural, the stressed word ''both,'' the plural noun ''creatures'' all tell us that Miss Fulton's case is exactly like Bertha's. As Judith Neaman believes, ''Bertha's 'crushes' on women are nothing new in her life, but her desire for her husband is both new and startling to her.'' Yet this crush on Pearl Fulton also remains in the second-story mode, leaving us to supply the details: without knowing it, Bertha ''found'' Miss Fulton because Harry had already become her lover.

This untold story lies buried in such a well-fortified location that the reader's access to its ramifications leads through many deviations. Let us first see how the story misleads the reader by proposing meanings that turn into red herrings. Given the ironic context, the reader may, during a first reading, assume that the developing point of the story lies in the contrast between the sublime sensation of bliss and the grotesque social mores the story satirizes—between the sensually poetic internal feeling and the ridiculously ugly external portrayal. Mr. Norman Knight, putative producer of plays, who evolves in a milieu in which writers named Oat write plays called ''Love in False Teeth,'' screws and rescrews a large tortoise-shell-rimmed monocle into an eye and is called ''Mug.'' Mrs. Norman Knight, whose orange coat sports processions of black monkeys and who seems to be wearing a dress made of scraped banana skins, is nicknamed ''Face'' and is going to decorate a room with a ''fried-fish scheme, with the backs of chairs shaped like frying pans and lovely chip potatoes embroidered all over the curtains.'' Effete Eddie Warren, poet and admirer of poems with ''*incredibly* beautiful'' first lines about food (''It's so *deeply* true, don't you feel? Tomato soup is so *dreadfully eternal*''), is terrorized by taxi-drivers and always speaks in italics. A very large portion of the story is devoted to the pretentious and inane conversation among these remarkable specimens of the superficial, self-satisfied bourgeoisie, providing a comic backdrop to the seemingly sublime drama within Bertha. The narrative induces the reader to pursue this contrast even into the relation between husband and wife; although Bertha's tenderness toward Harry does not readily allow us to see him as an utter grotesque, like his guests, we doubt that this blunt, superficial, ''extravagantly cool and collected'' pasteboard confection will rise to Bertha's

sublime heights. His first manifestation in the story already reveals that he is not on Bertha's poetic level. So brusque is he on the phone that she cannot tell him about her new feeling, and she concludes that civilization is idiotic. Everything that goes on around Bertha is external and ridiculous except Miss Fulton; when the Norman Knights leave, Bertha feels that ''this self of hers'' has taken leave of them forever; she has moved to a different plane, in the sole present company of Miss Fulton, and in the naively anticipated company of her husband. We predict an outcome that would include a rude awakening, an abrupt fall from the heights of bliss to the new discovery of her husband's mundane reality, and, possibly, Pearl Fulton's.

In this way, or in another, the reader formulates erroneous hypotheses on a first reading which must be rejected or at least significantly revised on a second reading. If, like John Middleton Murry, we see mainly that caricature contradicts pathos, then we will only describe the story as a ''sophisticated failure.'' Any failure on our part would consist in not seeing how the story masks and thus reveals its messages by forcing mistaken interpretations. Although it appears that authorial irony is directed only toward the grotesques, and not toward Bertha, it is the story's intentions that are ironic. Little prepares us for the supremely ironic discovery that what Miss Fulton shares with Bertha is also her husband, not just the wonderful feeling of bliss, and that the day when sexual desire finally flares up in her, after several years of marriage, is the very day she will see it destroyed. The knowledge Bertha acquires only shows her that her vision was defective. Thus our reading neurosis takes the form of an interpretive construction or delirium that is simply wrong. While erroneous hypotheses protect the reader from the second story, the second reading forces one back to read and recognize the ironic treatment of the heroine. It is then that the reader becomes as devious as the second story.

Bertha founders in a ''snare'' in the narrative, and the reader with her, when she thinks her husband is ''simple'' and really dislikes Miss Fulton, and when she interprets the way Miss Fulton refuses a cigarette as an expression of her hurt (''she felt it, too, and was hurt''). For much of the story, Bertha's desire to explain the mysterious attraction of Miss Fulton, the elusive feeling of bliss, the miraculous unspoken knowledge, only leads to blockage of the enigma. No detective she, the solution explodes upon her unbidden and unwanted. What I now want to show is that shared sexual desire, the essence of the enigma, is the very thing that makes it difficult for Bertha to understand the mystery.

What Bertha catches sight of in the hallway is the tip of the iceberg—the only part of the second story that is visible, momentarily and by accident. Readers' competence, including Bertha's, leaves no doubt whatsoever that the rest of the second story has happened just as surely as we know an iceberg lies, as Hemingway said, seven-eighths under water. Bertha is forced to let the entire second story into her consciousness. In this structure there is a kind of internal intertextuality: the text refers not to an intertext outside the story, but to one that lies within—under water, as it were—the familiar story of the unfaithful husband. When Bertha sees her husband embrace Miss Fulton, she learns not only the nature of the secret Miss Fulton contains, but also that there is a *real* secret about mundane events, what one might call a degraded version of the mysterious enigma she had perceived. Until that point the wall surrounding the second story construction can fairly be called a fortification, a product of her own nascent sexual desire.

Chicane and *redan*, both describing deviations in fortified walls, are Lacanian terms for the fortifications characteristic of obsessive neurosis. In "L'agresivité en psychanalyse" Lacan describes the obsessive neurosis as "une décomposition défensive, si comparable en ses principes à celles qu'illustrent le redan et la chicane, que nous avons entendu plusieurs de nos patients user à leur propre sujet d'une référence métaphorique à des 'fortifications à la Vauban'" ["a defensive decomposition, so comparable in its principles to those that illustrate the *redan* and the *chicane*, that we have heard several of our patients employ with regard to their own selves a metaphorical reference to 'Vauban-like fortifications.'"] The structure of these bastions is "particulièrement destinée à camoufler, à déplacer, à nier, à diviser et à amortir l'intention agressive" ["particularly aimed at camouflaging, displacing, denying, dividing and deadening the aggressive intention"]. When Bertha interprets Harry's behavior toward Miss Fulton as rude, unkind, or sarcastic, when she concludes that Harry really dislikes Miss Fulton, Bertha is producing a neurotic interpretation that functions, unconsciously, to defend her from a fact that her conscious mind has no purchase on, namely that if the feeling she shares with Miss Fulton is sexual desire, then Miss Fulton too must be feeling desire.

Instead, the entire narrative about Bertha's shared feelings with Pearl Fulton presents a neurotic, unconscious camouflage, displacement, disavowal, division, and deadening of Miss Fulton's aggressive intentions, to use Lacan's terms. Like another bit of the iceberg, the text supplies openings to its own devious structures. At the revelation of Bertha's indescribable feeling, the text stops just short of realizing the source of Miss Fulton's feeling too. She has been mentally telling Harry: "I shall try to tell you when we are in bed to-night what has been happening. What she and I have shared." A break in the page follows, after which the narrative continues: "At those last words something strange and almost terrifying darted into Bertha's mind. And this something blind and smiling whispered to her: '. . .you and he will be alone together in the dark room—the warm bed . . . .'" She and her husband had been "such good pals" and she had not loved him "in that way," but now she desires him "ardently! ardently! . . . Was this what that feeling of bliss had been leading up to? But then—" and here the text of her thoughts is interrupted by the pedestrian needs of the grotesque Mug and Face. The attentive reader will come to see that the dash stands for and eliminates (camouflages, displaces, etc.) the repressed thought: *Miss Fulton* desires Harry Young "ardently! ardently!" and loves him "in that way." The story might have erupted at that dash, had there not been the defensive decomposition of Bertha's "perfect" understanding of Miss Fulton. The rhetorical indices of her perfect understanding—for instance, the terms "miraculous," "exactly," "instantly," "never doubted for a moment"—bolster the fortification. Instead, the break in her thoughts is only a clue to the alert reader, who must, I believe, wait for a second reading to fill in the dash with the story of Miss Fulton's bliss—the internal intertext. Although this dash does not represent an ellipsis during which the entire second story takes place (like a famous dash in Kleist's "Die Marquise von O . . ."), by the second reading one probably wonders if Bertha is as naive as she seems. The bulk of the first story, then, can be read as an example of Lacan's *chicane*, the zigzag structures in the wall designed to prevent the passage of enemy forces, or the devious, circuitous, surreptitious formulations of the narrative which lead the reader astray—the erroneous hypotheses about the first story, the false clues or snares, the inadequate, defective, or devious vision of our reader's guide—in all, the failure of narrative reliability hidden behind the walls thrown up by Bertha's apparent self-knowledge, her "growing, gaining light."

We might profitably compare this second story structure to the repetition of a primal scene. In Freud's original formulation, the primal scene portrays the child witnessing the mother and father in sexual embrace. As is well known, however, Freud revised this bald account by claiming the scene could just as well be only a fantasy. Carrying the metaphor into the textual domain, Ned Lukacher writes that primal scenes are *interpretive constructions*. Thus it suffices to see the mute scene in the hall; from it Bertha and the reader construct the entire second story. The love affair Harry Young is having with Pearl Fulton could well be described as the forgotten primal scene of Bertha Young's new bliss. Miss Fulton has already had the experience that Bertha's story refers to, and Bertha's sublime feeling is only an ironic repetition, a degraded version of the original, a mere copy. The second story here is thus a kind of primal scene which the first story conveniently "forgot" to tell the reader (or Bertha), thus protecting her new-found bliss, until the fortification is breached.

That moment we may well call a Lacanian instant, the event by which Bertha learns that her desire is the desire of the other. Lacan's well-known statement that desire is the desire of the other occurs in "La subversion du sujet et la dialectique du désir." Until this moment, Bertha thinks—and the reader with her—that she has reached a new knowledge of her feeling, when she identifies it as sexual desire. Here the narrative is unflinchingly direct: "For the first time in her life Bertha Young desired her husband." But it is also deceptive in its directness; to say that Bertha desired her husband is to mask, by exploiting the simplicity of this phrase, the complexity of the relations of desire that lead to the final moment. Discovering Miss Fulton's desire for Harry, Bertha learns that her new desire for her husband is not simple but complex, for the second story soon demonstrates that her knowledge is rather what Lacan calls "nescience," misrecognition or misprision, found in the structure of the fantasy: "Car là se voit que la nescience où reste l'homme de son désir est moins nescience de ce qu'il demande, qui peut après tout se cerner, que nescience d'où il désire" ["For there is it seen that the misprision in which man remains of his desire is less misprision of what he is asking for, which can after all be discerned, than misprision of where he desires from."] That is, misrecognition of desire does not come from not knowing its object, which can be and is discovered, but from the fact that the self does not know where desire comes from. "Unknowing" is a misrecognition of the fact that desire is the desire of the other.

In psychoanalysis, unknowing occurs in the family trinity; the girl's desire for the father is the mother's desire. Among others, a reading in this vein emerges from the symbolic structures of the story. Throughout, while Bertha is called by her first name, like a child, and her last name, Young, only underscores her youth, Miss Fulton is never called simply Pearl. The opening segment of the story explicitly opposes maturity ("thirty" and "sensible") to youth as Bertha Young arrives home ("she wanted to run instead of walk, to take dancing steps on and off the pavement, to bowl a hoop"). The next narrative segment concerns an episode I have not mentioned so far, because it seems to have very little to do with the events in the dining room, drawing room, and hall after the guests arrive, events that seem to constitute the entire story. After arranging the many-colored fruit in the blue bowl and the glass dish, Bertha runs upstairs to the nursery where Nanny has just finished bathing and feeding her daughter. Here Nanny is the authority, disapproving of this unwanted interruption, and Bertha is just the "poor little girl in front of the rich little girl with the doll." Even her desire for her daughter is breached in this way. In this scene too Bertha completes a reflection she had begun as she waited on the stoop to be let in, having childishly forgotten her key, a reflection interrupted (as many of Bertha's thoughts are) when the maid opened the door. There she had thought: "Why be given a body if you have to keep it shut up in a case like a rare, rare fiddle?," but had then corrected herself: "No, that about the fiddle is not quite what I mean. . . . It's not what I mean, because—Thank you, Mary," she stops, as the door is opened. The dash is later filled in when Bertha begs Nanny to let her finish feeding her daughter: "How absurd it was. Why have a baby if it has to be kept—not in a case like a rare, rare fiddle—but in another woman's arms?"—a woman who, in this scene, stands in for a mother, and has a visibly but paradoxically greater authority and power. "In another woman's arms" is precisely where Bertha will at last see the reality of her husband. In the triangle relating Harry, Bertha, and Miss Fulton, Bertha stands in the position of the child who discovers her desire for her father, and immediately thereupon discovers that she is merely repeating her mother's desire.

This rather simplified triangle stands for all possible permutations of the relations of desire, which never become fixed. The second story subverts the first story just as the unconscious subverts the subject, splitting it; the story subverts the discourses of the self that produce knowledge and understanding. With its second-story structure, ''Bliss'' says that a discourse of desire is not sayable; it is among the things that the narrative has to sacrifice (as Katherine Mansfield wrote in her journal), the better to command understanding. For the ''*so much*'' one can get into a story reveals the traces of what disappears. We demand to know quite little of the second story, and most of what we do know is based on our general competence; the story is ''in'' the first story in the form of a perverse secret that ceases to be secret for the first story. Rather, it is the very process and structure of hiding (the forgetting of the primal scene, the fortification, the sighting of the tip of the iceberg) that give the story its chilling efficacy; it exists for these structures of hiding, structures that mostly censure saying but allow it to erupt in minimal form (''Tomorrow,'' says Harry Young) to confirm what they have shown by hiding. The narrative with its second-story structure forces us to produce in our reading, as Shoshana Felman writes, an ''analysis of the unconscious (the repressed) not as hidden but on the contrary as *exposed* —in language—through a significant (rhetorical) displacement.'' Connoting both dissertation form and voyeuristic pleasures, the word ''exposed'' well expresses the ambiguous effectiveness of the second-story structure. In these rhetorical and unavowed (camouflaged, etc.) structures, what Katherine Mansfield knew, and suppressed, lies revealed. She knew how fragile desire is; she did not let on that she knew the misadventure awaiting her heroine. She knew why Bertha was blissful, but kept it in the second-story mode. She knew desire throws up fortifications, and she lent her reader an ample supply of obstacles.

The dynamic of this narrative process is an instance of what Lacan calls *fading*. Originally meaning the weakening of the signal in radio transmissions, allowing intermittent reception of other wavelengths, the term is used in typically metaphoric fashion to describe the situation in psychoanalysis in which the unconscious speaks intermittently of things the subject has no knowledge of, because of its subordination to the signifier. The subject is thus subverted and split, and the fading is the point at which the speaker's desire can never be recognized. Rather than force a purely psychoanalytic reading in which the text would be compared to a patient undergoing analysis, I would prefer to take ''fading'' as a metaphor for a literary structure of

significant complexity. That is what Barthes does when he borrows Lacan's concept to explain the plurality of a text, in a section called ''Le fading des voix'' the fading of voices. Most utterances, in a classical text, speak from a known voice. It happens, writes Barthes, that

the voice is lost, as if it were disappearing into a hole of the discourse. The best way to imagine the classical plural is then to listen to the text as a shimmering exchange of multiple voices, posed on different wavelengths and seized at times by an abrupt fading, whose gaps permit the enunciation to migrate from one point of view to the other, without warning.

Fading subsumes all the double, devious, and ironic mechanisms of the narrative; ''Bliss'' is plural in intermittently and partially allowing the second story to be heard. In the breaches Bertha's thoughts make in the story of the grotesques, the second story throbs behind the wall of her fortification, until, with the fading of these inane and ironic voices, one hears the point at which Bertha's desire can never be recognized. In the lapses of the ''shimmering exchange of multiple voices'' the ones in Bertha's head, another voice is heard, intermittently, as if from a different wavelength—a voice posing questions for the reader. When the story stops, the reader continues, telling herself the story of the adulterous love affair, from its still obscured beginning in female desire to its vulgar exposure among the grotesques. It is a measure of the power of ''Bliss'' that readers want to go well beyond its ending to say ''what happens'' next; but does the reader have an answer to Bertha's question? Harry's love affair will obviously bring changes to Bertha's desire for her husband, but how much can the reader say about Bertha's comprehension of Pearl Fulton? How vast and deep is Bertha's forced insight?

It is my contention that each reader will answer differently, and the gist of my answer ties in the dynamic of fading. Bertha can never recognize her relation to her self, no more than anyone can. Fortifications remain necessarily in place. Her homosexual desire is revealed only in the structures that hide it and keep it hidden even beyond the end of the story. Bertha is not allowed to recognize the censor that guards the door of insight; that role is strictly the reader's. We think we have at last understood the mystery, found out the secret, solved the enigma, but we do so only if we think of Bertha as a real person. Are we not deceived when the narrative explains: ''Bertha had fallen in love with [Pearl Fulton], as she always did fall in love with beautiful women who had something strange about them''? Is this an excessive, rhetorical expression of Bertha's enthusiasms, or is the text forcing us to argue that the direct, overt meaning is the disguised one? As long as we affirm that we are knowledgeable about how language—the language of narrative—functions, then reading turns our knowledge to misprision about where our desire to know comes from. No more than Bertha do we know what is going to happen now.

Source: Armine Kotin Mortimer, ''Fortifications of Desire: Reading the Second Story in Katherine Mansfield's 'Bliss''' in *Narrative*, Vol. 2, No. 1, 1994, pp. 41–52.

Judith S. Neaman

In the following essay, Neaman argues that allusions to the Bible and Shakespeare's Twelfth Night *offer answers to questions that have troubled critics.*

''Bliss'' Katherine Mansfield's most ambiguous story of initiation, poses many problems, some of which have plagued critics for years. What is Bertha's ''bliss''? What does Pearl Fulton represent and to what does her name allude? Why a pear tree instead of an apple? Was Bertha really cold? Is she hysterical? Would *would* ''happen now''? Why, at the end of such a crisis of disillusionment, is the pear tree ''as lovely as ever''? Yet, Mansfield has answered these questions in the story by interweaving allusions to two sources—the Bible and Shakespeare's *Twelfth Night*—whose major role in ''Bliss'' has been largely ignored. These allusions not only answer the crucial questions but they also illuminate the meaning of the tale, while simultaneously charting the anatomy of its creation.

Perhaps because critics have seen all too clearly the obvious tree of knowledge blooming in Bertha's garden, none seems to have detected the first overt clue to the thematic importance of the Bible. It appears as a familiar echo in the words, ''for the first time in her life, she desired her husband.'' In Genesis 3.16, among the punishments God metes out to the disobedient Eve is: ''thy desire *shall* be to thy husband and he shall rule over thee.'' In visiting this affliction on Bertha at the very moment that she first experiences marital lust, Mansfield appears to indicate an easy familiarity with the long tradition of biblical commentary. According to both Augustinian and Talmudic interpretation, lust entered the world as a result of the Fall. ''Bliss'' pursues the theme by chapter and verse.

In the same chapter of Genesis, directly before and after Eve is first sentenced to a life of connubial

desire, there are numerous phrases so similar in image and content to those Mansfield uses in ''Bliss'' that the story seems to be almost a gloss upon the Bible. The evidence that the words of Genesis were deeply embedded in her mind appears in a diary entry of February 1916 in which she remarks that, since she came to Bandol where she wrote ''Bliss'' in 1918, she has ''read the Bible for hours on end.'' She wrote here of wanting to know ''if Lot followed close on Noah or something like that. But I feel so bitterly that they ought to be part of my breathing.'' Furthermore, during the same brief period of feverish work in which she produced ''Bliss,'' Mansfield wrote the story ''Psychology'' in which a character playfully remarks, ''And God said; 'Let there be cake. And there was cake. And God saw that it was Good.'''

In both stories, words or phrases from Genesis appear in brief but they set up reverberations which guide the reader's responses to all subsequent events. In ''Bliss,'' Mansfield's more indirect use of the words of Genesis is overbalanced by a closer attention to the intent and material of it. In fact, the parallels between the biblical work and Mansfield's story are so close that the words of Genesis may inform the reader not only of what Bertha's life was before the day of her maturation but also of what her future will be. In this way, Genesis answers Bertha's last question: ''What is going to happen now?'' If, like a modern Eve, Bertha has lived in a fool's paradise which is destroyed by knowledge, then she and Harry are destined to repeat, in a modern form, the fate of their first models. This is so much the case that God himself answers Bertha's question about her future. What ''will happen now'' is that Bertha will desire only her husband and he will dominate her life. ''In sorrow [she] will bring forth children'' while Harry, who has tasted another form of the forbidden fruit of knowledge, will now eat ''the herb of the field'' ''in sorrow . . . all the days of [his] life'' (Gen. 3.17). Bertha's future children will be begotten in sorrow and bitterness born of the knowledge she has gained. She will know that Harry sees her as Adam saw Eve after the Fall—as the ''mother of all living'' (Gen. 3.20), which, in Mansfield's punning paraphrase, is Berth A' Young.

Because Mansfield's metamorphosis of this chapter of Genesis remains so close to its source, readers will not be surprised to find still further relations between the words and events of ''Bliss'' and those of Genesis 3. The garden in which this young pair learns the consequences of sin is populated not only by a wondrous tree about which all knowledge revolves but also by animals. Following her own associative thought patterns, Mansfield has linked the denizens of the first garden and the Youngs' garden with the behavior of Adam and Eve and also with Darwinian evolutionary theory. The Norman Knights are also compared to first forebears by their name but they are now the forebears of English society. Mansfield compares them to monkeys, for "Face" Knight, so perfectly matched with her mate, "Mug," is wearing a funny little coat with monkeys all over it and looks "like a very intelligent monkey."

Here the reader must wonder if Mansfield is using her Bible to deliver a post-Darwinian stab at English society. The rest of Face's outfit echoes Adam's and Eve's first attempt at clothing, which they made in Genesis 3 to hide their shame at their newly discovered nakedness. As God created for Adam and his helpmeet "coats of skins" (3.21) to help them "hide their shame," so Face wears a yellow silk dress that looks like "scraped banana skins" and she is later described as "crouched before the fire in her banana skin." No sooner has Bertha noticed the simian clothing and physiognomy of her guest than Mr. Norman Knight remarks on parenthood and paradise, "This is a sad, sad fall!... When the perambulator comes into the hall—...."The final link of this particular chain which seems to stretch through Mansfield's mind from Bible to "Bliss" is forged when Norman Knight remarks in parting, "You know our shame."

Gradually, it becomes apparent that the innocent Bertha and her hairy mate, an emotional primate if there ever was one, have opened their house and garden to beasts from a number of literary fields. Eddie Warren, his last name removing all doubt of his nature and habitat, is a stuttering rabbit. Terrified by his taxi ride, dressed in white socks and an enchanting white scarf to match, Eddie speaks in conversational tones and patterns that often echo those of Alice in Wonderland's white rabbit.

Pearl has been called a moon to Bertha's sun and a parallel to the pear tree, which has also been identified with Bertha and Harry. However, Mansfield's descriptions of Pearl emphasize not only Pearl's lunar qualities (she is dressed "all in silver with a silver fillet binding her head" and her fingers, "like moonbeams, are so slender that a pale light seemed to come from them") but also focus the reader's attention on her "cool arm," "heavy eyelids," and "[mysterious] half smile." Pearl is such an adept at enigma that everyone who encoun-

> "The parallels between the biblical work and Mansfield's story are so close that the words of Genesis may inform the reader not only of what Bertha's life was before the day of her maturation but also of what her future will be."

ters her assigns her another identity. Her conversation merely amplifies the mystery, for it is barely audible; she whispers and intimates. Bertha is not even certain what Pearl murmured about the pear tree or if she had guessed that Pearl said, "just that" when she looked out at the tree in the garden. Yet, it is Pearl who ask if there is a garden, Pearl whose "cool arm could fan—fan—start blazing—blazing the fire of bliss that Bertha did not know what to do with."

Enigmatic, dressed in scaly silver, full of whispers and murmurs, Pearl is infinitely tempting. Her lidded eyes conceal her passion for Harry. But she is secretive, intimating, cool-skinned and cool-souled, in other words, "the subtlest beast of the field" (Gen. 3.3). Thus, Bertha cannot see the truth until she glimpses the kiss. With that kiss, Bertha's innocence falls and her blissful illusions are destroyed. Only then does Bertha begin to see her mysterious friend in a new light. No longer the distant and enchanting moon of Bertha's hopes, Pearl now appears to her hostess to resemble the seductive gray cat who had provoked a shiver of sexual revulsion in Bertha earlier in the evening. One critic believes that Bertha's new vision of Pearl is evoked by a horror of the bestiality she perceives in her former love, since she considers that Pearl's purity has been sullied by the heterosexual behavior Bertha abhors. But, if we see Pearl as a serpent, the common Talmudic and patristic interpretation of the serpent's role in tempting Eve seems far more appropriate a view.

According to this traditional understanding of the Bible, it was the serpent's seduction of Eve that first induced her to lust for Adam. Pearl's seduction of Bertha awakens Bertha's lust for her own husband. In fact, Bertha's image of Pearl followed by Eddie, as the seductive gray cat followed the black cat, is so distorted a view of Eddie that it makes little sense if Pearl is not seen as the serpent. Mansfield has, after all, painted Eddie as effeminate at least and homosexual at most, hence hardly a likely candidate for seduction by a woman. Clearly the "grey cat, dragging its belly . . . [as it] crept across the lawn, and a black one, its shadow trail[ing] after," reminds Bertha, and is intended to remind readers of "Bliss," of the serpent of Genesis which God punished by decreeing that it should crawl on its belly.

In every possible way, Pearl fulfills the role of the serpent in the garden. She is one of those beautiful women with "something strange about them" with whom Bertha is always falling in love. Like the rest of these temptresses, she is strangely secretive while seeming to be *so* open and Bertha is certain that they "share" something. Until Bertha gains the carnal knowledge which will be revealed to her, she is incapable of understanding that what they share is a lust for Harry. By the time Bertha realizes that the "bliss" with which she has burned is sexual desire and then sees that desire mocked (all within moments), she has tasted the fruit of the tree and found it a bitter dessert to the banquet of sight and taste she has laid for herself and her guests. That the discoveries which cause her so much pain should take place at a dinner party celebrated in a house with a flowering fruit tree is no coincidence.

Critics who have noted the importance of the imagery of food and eating in this tale have ignored standard biblical associations among lust, fruit, and knowledge so clearly introduced in Mansfield's references to the food and eating which led to the Fall and lead to this fall. Bertha's first important act in the story is associated with these elements. The reader can see this link in her conflict between the enjoyment of temptation and her fear of succumbing to it. First she luxuriates in the beauty of the fruits she has bought for the party. Then, as she begins to fear the intensity she tries to repress it, crying, "No, no. I'm getting hysterical." As the tale and Bertha's growth simultaneously progress, the images of fruit and eating become less abstract and aesthetic and more active and hostile, for their connection with sex, flesh, and desire is clarified. Pearl rolls a tangerine between her luminous fingers. Harry loves the "white flesh" of lobster and "pistachio ices—green and cold like the eyelids of Egyptian dancers." The most emotinally evocative dish is made of eggs, reminding us of the embryonic Youngs and their new infant. In the forms of the new cook's omelettes and the "admirable soufflé," eggs become the crucial bonds in the marriage, inspiring Harry's praise which makes Bertha almost weep "with childlike pleasure."

After Bertha sees Harry and Pearl embracing, the nature of the imagery shifts from its focus on the food to be eaten to a new emphasis on the act of eating it. With this shift, the cannibalism which has been vaguely implied now becomes glaring. When Harry kisses Pearl "with his lips curled back in a hideous grin," the reader, like Bertha, sees him devouring this delectable woman whose serenity he had earlier attributed to a "good stomach." Hence, fruit becomes the visible apple of temptation (at one point in the story it is a tangerine turning in Pearl's fingers), and eating becomes the act of lust born of knowledge.

If fruits and flesh and the devouring of these represent desire and consummation as well as knowledge, then instruments and the music *not* played on them represent human bodies and sexual frustration and/or repression. Marilyn Zorn quotes Mansfield's letter of May 24, 1918, to Ottoline Morrell in which Mansfield cries, "What might be so divine is out of tune—or the instruments are all silent and nobody is going to play again." For her purposes, Mansfield's succeeding words are irrelevant, for ours, they are central. "There *is* no concert for us. Isn't there? Is it all over? Is our desire and longing and eagerness, quite all that's left? Shall we sit here forever in this immense wretched hall—waiting for the lights to go up—which will never go up." That is precisely what Bertha does at the end of course, and it is Harry who "shut[s] up shop" or turns out the lights. The musical refrains, though they occur only three times in the story, are central and the association between the fruits, the passion, and the music becomes increasingly specific. Music is "the food of love." Like the eating of the fruit, the playing of music, in this tale at least, is forbidden.

At the very outset of the tale, Bertha longs to dance, bowl a hoop, or "simply laugh at nothing" in the streets to express her bliss. "Oh, is there no way you can express it without being 'drunk and disorderly'? How idiotic civilization is! Why be given a body if you have to keep it shut up in a case like a rare rare fiddle?" Bertha's protest against the social requirement that she quash her ebullience becomes a louder aria when Nanny removes the baby from her embrace: "How absurd it was. Why have a baby if it has to be kept—not in a case like a rare string fiddle—but in another woman's arms?"

Finally, the fiddle—shaped like a pear and analogue, like the pear, to a woman's body—grows into a piano. Now fully aware and unsuccessfully trying to repress her thoughts and fears about that moment at which she will share the bed with a husband she suddenly desires, Bertha runs to the piano. "What a pity someone does not play! What a pity someone does not play!" Indeed, Bertha's body has not been played, nor has she played. But now the fruit of carnal knowledge is about to be transmuted into the music of desire and the passion arising from both is about to suffer "a dying fall," a hidden pun on both the original fall from grace and the musical form of a "dying fall."

Associating the tree of knowledge with the food of love, Mansfield has subtly alluded to Shakespeare's *Twelfth Night*, a play she knew almost by heart, which celebrates the Feast of Twelfth Night or Epiphany. This reference creates a musical tie which binds all the images and references of "Bliss." Like the primary biblical allusion, this secondary Shakespearean allusion from the opening lines of the play not only recapitulates the theme of the Fall but, in so doing, explains in part why Bertha's beloved tree is a pear tree. The lines alone explain the musical references in "Bliss" and show the relations between love, food, and the shattering of Bertha's innocence:

> If music be the food of love, play on; Give me excess of it that surfeiting, The appetite may sicken and so die. — That strain again!—it had a dying fall! (*Twelfth Night* I.1.4)

To observe Mansfield's whole train of thought, the reader must consider the entire play. *Twelfth Night* is a play of pairing and couples, of confused and confusing sexuality, of female love which leads to male-female unions. The pear tree of "Bliss" may be Mansfield's conscious or unconscious pun on pair, as Magalaner suggests, for the story is itself full of pairs and even possibly alter egos. More important, Mansfield was interested throughout her life in "shadow selves," as she called them in a letter to Murry of 1920. But the connections among the pairing and the pear tree and the structure and imagery of *Twelfth Night* run deeper still.

Large portions of the play take place in a garden which belongs to Olivia; there, to oblige Orsino,

Viola courts Olivia. Viola is dressed as a man and Olivia does, indeed, conceive a passion for her, only to discover that she is not eligible. It is only after meeting Viola's twin, Sebastian, whom Viola had feared was dead, that Olivia transfers her affection to him and gives him a pearl as a love token. Viola, one cannot help noting, is closely related to the viol or fiddle to which Bertha compares her caged body, and Bertha is, at first, Pearl's wooer, sadly winning her for Harry. Thus, the theme of sexual confusion, of pairing of opposites, of "shadow selves" which Mansfield had cherished so long and embodied in her story "Sun and Moon," is everywhere in "Bliss" Bertha and Harry, Bertha and Pearl (Bertha's gift to Harry), the black and gray cats, Pearl and Eddie, and the spiritual twins, Mug and Face, recapitulate this favorite theme, one which Magalaner has noted. In *Twelfth Night*, as in "Bliss," heterosexual love is the goal toward which the play strives and pairing is, after all, just another name for copulation, suggesting the lust which the fruit of the tree evoked.

But Mansfield's personal and aesthetic interests might have been far more effective than her reading in directing her choice of associations which formed "Bliss." Since girlhood, Mansfield had been both a cellist and a passionate lover of gardens and pear trees. Magalaner notes that, a year before she wrote "Bliss" Mansfield mentioned, in a letter to Ottoline Morrell, the importance of writing about a flower garden with people in it:

> walking in the garden—several pairs of people—their conversation—their slow pacing their glances as they pass one another.

A kind of, musically speaking, conversation set to flowers. In Murry's volume the letter immediately succeeding the letter to Ottoline Morrell was a note to Virginia Woolf about the sketch "Kew Gardens":

> Yes, your Flower Bed is very good. There's a still, quivering changing light over it all and a sense of those couples dissolving in the bright air which fascinates me—

Of all the plants and trees in a garden, a pear tree was one of the most important to Mansfield and, at the time of the writing of "Bliss," she must have been thinking of it. Convinced that she was dying after the major hemorrhage which preceded the writing of this story by a few days, she thought constantly of her beloved brother, Chummie, who had recently been killed in the war. How often the two of them had sat on the bench beneath the pear tree in Tinakori Road in New Zealand and exchanged confidences. The new home which she and Murry first rented in England had a garden with a pear tree.

If these two types of sources, the biographical and the literary, consistently clarify Mansfield's use of images and symbols in the story, it would be illogical to ignore their potential influence upon the meaning of the story. Might they not also, central as they seem to be to Mansfield's consciousness at the time she wrote "Bliss," shed light on the relationship between Bertha and Pearl, for example? Upon this love, some critics of the story have dwelled far too emphatically. Mansfield's friend Virginia Woolf, for example, hated "Bliss," which she considered a shallow, maudlin tale of lesbianism. Later critics, like Nebeker, have argued that Bertha's real goal is Pearl and that the sorrow she experiences is a result of Pearl's rejection of her for Harry. But nothing in the story suggests this. In fact, Bertha considers a bedtime discussion with Harry about what she and Pearl share. She imagines that this conversation will promote the spiritual understanding that will culminate in their first passionate physical union. In both *Twelfth Night* and "Bliss" youthful and innocent love is homosexual, as if both authors were chronicling the normal English schoolgirl stage of maturation. Heterosexual love is the source of the excitement, the growth, the real passion. Bertha's "crushes" on women are nothing new in her life, but her desire for her husband is both new and startling to her. Ultimately, Bertha's disillusionment over the impossibility of fulfilling her terrifying but exciting new desire matures her, for, through this loss of hope, she learns the sorrow of knowledge. Finally, it is Harry's "cool" voice which sets the seal on Bertha's fear and suffering.

Critics have cited Bertha's frigidity as the most incontrovertible proof of her lesbianism. After all, Bertha seems to have admitted to frigidity when she reflected that "it had worried her dreadfully at first to find that she was so cold." Despite the fact that readers conventionally accept a narrator's statements about him or herself, Bertha's self-evaluation, in this instance, cannot be taken at face value, no matter how afraid she is of her first real sexual encounter. Too much of her behavior argues against frigidity. She experiences bliss, she resents the restrictions of a society that demands she "cage" her body, she enjoys her child's flesh and resents the woman who withdraws it from her, she aches to communicate her bliss to Harry though it is hopeless to do so. Bertha is highly sensual, glorying in the

colors of fruit, in smells and sights, in feelings she can hardly contain. Surely these are not the responses of a frigid woman. The source of her conviction that she is frigid lies elsewhere—at the site of her "discovery" that she is so cold. It is the same source from which she learns that her desire to dance and sing, to hold her child are symptoms of "hysteria." That source is the society she identifies as the one which will call her "drunk and disorderly" if she gives vent to her passions; it is the "idiotic civilization" which demands that she imprison her feelings and her body. Harry, and she have "discussed" her problem and he has explained that he is "different."

That Bertha's testimony about her own proclivities is not necessarily reliable is attested to by the sardonic tone, the desperate contradiction of her "Really, really—she had everything. . . ." She is missing something—something that throws a pall over her marriage, and surely part of what she is missing is the understanding husband who would not hasten her off the phone, truncate her expression of feeling. Is the rest the passion she lacks or is it, as Mansfield's portrayal of Harry's callousness suggests, the passion he tells her she lacks? Throughout the story, Bertha acts the good wife and mother, observing the conventions of social respectability which pinion her whims and moods. The purveyors of these conventions appear in the forms of Nanny and Harry, yet she still emerges as a passionate woman. When she finally experiences the marital lust so "improper" in a good English matron, Bertha learns that the fruit of desire is death, for there is always a snake in the garden and the music of passion always suffers a "dying fall."

In marrying these sources to produce so carefully unified a story, Mansfield has disclosed the cast of her mind. Critics who have often pointed out how autobiographical the tale is, have neglected one major aspect of Mansfield's autobiography to which both her letters as well as her journals draw attention. Mansfield was devoted to Shakespeare and the Bible and was especially absorbed in Genesis at the time she wrote "Bliss." She spoke of her desire to know the Bible as well as she knew Shakespeare, whose words she recited constantly. In a letter to Murry, dated March 4, 1918 written only a week after completing "Bliss," Mansfield remarked to Murry: "My Shakespeare is full of notes for my children to light on." Magalaner noted a letter to Murry written just days before the completion of "Bliss" in which Mansfield speaks of her love for

Murry in terms of food and eating. She concludes, "'Hang there like fruit, my soul, till the tree die!' The tree *would* die."

Twelfth Night is much on her mind. She notes often at this time that she is thinking of death (because of her own severe hemorrhage and Chummie's death), and these morbid thoughts intermingle with visions of gardens and food. She is filled with what she calls either "a rage of bliss" or bliss she longs to "share unexplained." Coincidentally perhaps, both the story and the title of "Sun and Moon" are conceived at this same time. The intellectual and emotional recipe for "Bliss" is revealed in these threads of thought recorded in Mansfield's journals and letters. How she regarded the conclusion of the story is not. Yet, the mystery of the concluding lines is solved by finishing the speech from *Twelfth Night* which both opens the play and sets the musical key of the story.

The work ends on an elegiac note: innocence dies quickly, but those who see their paradise fade survive. They live out long lives in a twilight sorrow, illuminated only by a memory of an irretrievable bliss.

> O, spirit of love, how quick and fresh art thou! That, notwithstanding thy capacity Receiveth as the sea, naught enters there, Of what validity or pitch soe'er, But falls into abatement and low price Even in a minute! (*Twelfth Night* I.1.9–15)

Twelfth Night tells us what has happened; Genesis tells us that what happened once will happen—again and again. The pear tree remains "as lovely as ever and as still" because, like the tree of knowledge, it remains firmly rooted in perfect Eden. Only Bertha is expelled. The lasting beauty and seductiveness of the tree sound an ironic note of contrast with the imperfection of the love they provoke and disclose. In the mythic world in which the pear tree, now forever out of Bertha's reach, blooms eternally without blemish, Eddie Warren's last words about the eternal quality of the lines: "Why must it always be tomato soup?" bear the wisdom of the Shakespearean clowns; they are set against an archetypal quest for knowledge which will always end in the "too dreadfully eternal" discovery that sweet fruit turns bitter when bliss fades. Accompanied by the unplayed music of *Twelfth Night* Bertha Young relives the epiphany of Genesis in a London garden.

Source: Judith S. Neaman, "Allusion, Image, and Associative Pattern: The Answers in Mansfield's 'Bliss,'" in *Twenti-*

eth Century Literature, Vol. 32, No. 2, Summer, 1986 pp. 242–54.

Walter E. Anderson

In the following essay, Anderson explores the psychological aspects of mood and feeling within the conventional love-triangle plot of "Bliss."

In her study of Katherine Mansfield's art, Anne Friis draws special attention to the style, which "hints and suggests rather than asserts. It is indirect, it is elliptic." Mansfield abbreviates crucial thoughts or statements with dots and dashes, and "by the use of those punctuation marks she waives a mass of description and psychology." In her short story "Bliss" this technique is most apparent, perhaps, in a significant passage occurring just after Bertha Young has her first experience of sexual desire for her husband: "But now—ardently! ardently! The word ached in her ardent body! Was this what that feeling of bliss had been leading up to? But then then—." Only a proper understanding of the psychological meaning of the story's action enables us to complete correctly that final sentence. Previous critics generally seem to agree that "Bliss" embodies a provocative study in mood and feeling within a conventional love-triangle plot. The climax has been seen as Bertha's discovery that her husband Harry and her friend Pearl Fulton are lovers, a revelation which shatters her growing sense of marital bliss. In accordance with this interpretation, Robert Heilman identifies two main ironies: "Bertha's realization that her admired Miss Fulton shares her own unique bliss, and then her discovery that the shared mood has the same origin for each—love for Harry." Edward Shanks faults Mansfield for making this central subject so obvious. All her art, he argues, goes into establishing the precarious external dependency of Bertha's bliss, "and it is a disastrous descent to a lower plane when, at the end, she appears to say, 'Disillusionment, you see, might have come in some such way as this. . . .'" Actually the story is more subtle than Shanks imagines and more complexly ironic than Heilman has proposed, because the point of Bertha's disillusionment is not that both she and her friend love Harry and Harry loves Pearl instead of his wife, but that Bertha also loves Miss Fulton.

It is safe to say that Pearl Fulton does not, contra Heilman, share Bertha's "unique bliss," as Bertha, in the course of the party, imagines she must. In guessing Miss Fulton's mood, Bertha ad-

> "'But now--ardently!
ardently! The word ached in
her ardent body! Was this
what that feeling of bliss
had been leading up to? But
then then--."

mits that she actually has "less than nothing" to justify her suspicion that their inclinations coincide. The entire bearing of the action suggests that Bertha's and Pearl's desires have neither the same origin nor the same object, yet Bertha, in her dreamy self-delusion, gives free rein to her coursing desire. Almost completely unaware of the homosexual nature of her attraction to Pearl, Bertha quite logically supposes that her passion—though fanned throughout the evening by imaginary communications with Miss Fulton—is for her husband Harry. If she desires Harry, "then then—" (the sentence Bertha is unable to complete) what has Miss Fulton had to do with it all? Being together in a "warm bed" with Harry, she asks in apparent disbelief, "was this what that feeling of bliss had been leading up to?" The answer is no. But she cannot fill in the sexual gaps—hence the all-significant dash and her wondering perplexity, both in this scene and at the close, when she recalls the "lovely pear tree—pear tree—pear tree." Earlier in the evening she had ecstatically contemplated this tree in company with Miss Fulton, the touch of whose arm kindled Bertha's passion into a blaze. After dinner, over coffee and cigarettes, Bertha imagines that Miss Fulton at last "'gave the sign'" for which she had long been waiting. The indefiniteness of the sign forces the reader to mark the disparity between Miss Fulton's words and what Bertha makes of them: "'Have you a garden?' said the cool sleepy voice." In answer, all Bertha can do is "obey," ecstatically:

> And the two women stood side by side looking at the slender, flowering tree. Although it was so still seemed, like the flame of a candle, to stretch up, to point, to quiver in the bright air, to grow taller and taller as they gazed—almost to touch the rim of the round, silver moon.

> How long did they stand there? Both, as it were, caught in that circle of unearthly light, understanding each other perfectly, creatures of another world, and wondering what they were to do in this one with all this blissful treasure that burned in their bosoms and dropped, in silver flowers, from their hair and hands?

> For ever—for a moment? And did Miss Fulton murmur: "Yes. Just *that*." Or did Bertha dream it?

The thoughts and feelings here belong to Bertha's dream, so different from what Pearl—the silver moon, the silver flower to Bertha's yearning desire—must be thinking as she stands next to her lover's wife. Both the "as it were" and the final question undercut Bertha's hopes for a silent communion with her "new find." Before understanding the significance of this moment for Bertha, we must consider those earlier passages of thought and feeling which resonate both with it and with the startling scene of disillusionment immediately following.

Early in the story we receive an insight into Bertha's stifled sexual feelings. "How idiotic civilization is," she thinks: "Why be given a body if you have to keep it shut up in a case like a rare, rare fiddle?" The thought of her body's not being used bears implications causing her to resist her analogy: "'No, that about the fiddle is not quite what I mean,' she thought, running up the steps and feeling in her bag for the key . . . 'It's not what I mean, because—'" (*ibid.*). Beyond a certain point, Bertha would not go, and she nervously allows herself to be distracted from pursuing her thoughts. The idea would bring Harry to mind, simultaneously forcing her to acknowledge that Harry cannot be blamed for her sexual indifference. The real issue that Bertha will not pursue is the origin of this indifference. Just before the close of the story, Mansfield reveals the crucial fact that Bertha and her husband are simply good pals:

> Oh, she'd loved him—she'd been in love with him, of course, in every other way, but just not in that way. And, equally, of course, she'd understood that he was different. They'd discussed it so often. It had worried her dreadfully at first to find that she was so cold, but after a time it had not seemed to matter. They were so frank with each other—such good pals. That was the best of being modern.

Although modernity had its advantages, civilization was idiotic if one's body was shut up in a case. When Bertha compares her lack of desire with Harry's sexual appetite (his difference), she thinks of herself as "cold." Yet she obviously is, as we have seen, a woman of ardent, though repressed, passions. Although she tries to pretend that she is happy ("She had everything": baby, money, house, cook, friends, and a husband) she still feels unsatisfied. This evening gives her a sense of other possibilities, vague perhaps, yet overwhelmingly powerful.

Hours before the dinner party, Bertha's excited anticipation of Pearl's imminent visit causes her bosom to glow unbearably as if a "shower of little sparks" were exploding, though the reader only learns later that Pearl has caused this excitement. Bertha "hardly dared to breathe for fear of fanning it higher." She observes in the mirror her "trembling lips" and feels that she is "waiting for something . . . divine to happen . . . that she knew must happen . . . infallibly" (Mansfield's ellipses). To appease her excitement, she rushes up to the nursery to hold her baby girl. But when the nanny deprives her of this outlet, "all the feeling of bliss came back again, and again she didn't know how to express it—what to do with it." She flies to the phone to answer Harry's call and "to get in touch for a moment" with him, but finds "nothing to say." Her thoughts return to her expected guests and the arrangement of the living room: "As she was about to throw the last [sofa cushion] she surprised herself by suddenly hugging it to her, passionately, passionately. But it did not put out the fire in her bosom. Oh, on the contrary!" Releasing the cushion, Bertha beholds the "tall, slender pear tree in fullest, richest bloom" standing "as though becalmed" at the end of the garden. Anne Friis and Chester Eisinger interpret the tree as a symbol of nature's indifference to human suffering. A few other critics, however, perceive a phallic symbolism in the tree, and connect it with Harry. The tree does not stand either for Harry's sexuality or for a pure, spiritual relationship with a woman, which Helen Nebeck claims is what Bertha seeks. The flowering pear tree is a composite symbol representing in its tallness Bertha's homosexual aspirations and in its full, rich blossoms, her desire to be sexually used. As Bertha flings herself down on the couch in ecstasy, "she seemed to see on her eyelids the lovely pear tree with its wide open blossoms as a symbol of her own life": the open flowers image her female sexual self, but the meaning and object of the tree's tall assertiveness, the "masculine" part of her sexual feelings, eludes her conscious recognition. To the end of the story it remains a strongly felt urge only vaguely defined.

Mansfield initially presents Bertha in a state of unfocused, semihysterical bliss heightened by thoughts of Miss Fulton, her most recent "find," whom she had met at the club: "And Bertha had fallen in love with her, as she always did fall in love with beautiful women who had something strange about them." Mention of her falling in love elicits at first only casual attention, since the phrase characterizes Bertha's hypersensibility and exaggerated manner of expression. We note, however, that Bertha habitually finds and picks up beautiful women, afterward trying to draw them out. Toward what end, she does not specify: "Up to a certain point Miss Fulton was rarely, wonderfully frank, but the certain point was there, and beyond that she would not go." Bertha does not consciously know herself the tendency of her own solicitations.

When her guests begin to arrive, she forgets until Harry enters the house that "Pearl Fulton had not turned up." Her thoughts shuttle back and forth from Harry to Miss Fulton in a pattern of association which gains significance as the crisis builds. When Pearl does arrive, Bertha smiles, "with that little air of proprietorship that she always assumed while her women finds were new and mysterious." Upon seizing Pearl's arm, Bertha feels much as she did earlier in the afternoon when sparks seemed to light up in her bosom: "What was there in the touch of that cool arm that could fan—fan—start blazing—blazing—the fire of bliss that Bertha did not know what to do with?" Although Pearl does not look directly at her hostess, Bertha is sure, "as if the longest, most intimate look had passed between them—as if they had said to each other: 'You, too?'—that Miss Fulton . . . was feeling just what she was feeling." Mansfield repeats the "as if" to heighten the contrast between the apparent facts and what Bertha would most like to believe. For her part, Pearl is simply casual, blasé; she may be thinking about Harry, but Bertha clearly does not. In believing that she and Pearl are intimately in touch, Bertha is doomed to disappointment at the close of the evening.

For the moment everything that happens seems to fill her brimming cup of bliss: "Everything was good—was right." And always, "in the back of her mind, there was the pear tree. It would be silver now, in the light of poor dear Eddie's moon, silver as Miss Fulton." After connecting the silver moon and the silvery blond Pearl, Mansfield expands her primary symbolism in an event which climaxes Bertha's mood. Bertha feels that she has read Miss Fulton's mind exactly, yet she is not absolutely certain: "she never doubted for a moment that she was right, and yet what had she to go on? Less than nothing." Consequently she hopes that her friend will "'give a sign'," though "what she meant by that she did not know, and what would happen after that she could not imagine.'' While she waits for the sign to come, as she feels it infallibly must, she simply has to "laugh or die." She diverts herself by observing Mrs. Norman ["Face"] Knight, who, "like a very intelligent monkey," is habitually "tucking something down the front of her bodice— as if she kept a tiny, secret hoard of nuts there." The thought causes Bertha to dig her nails into her hands. Then comes the sign, so Bertha imagines, and the visit to the garden to contemplate the pear tree, as described above.

The adjectives—"tall," "slender," and "still"—for the tree specifically recall Bertha's earlier perception of it while squeezing the sofa cushion with passion. The phrase "wondering what they were to do . . . with all this blissful treasure" parallels Bertha's previous feelings, which she "didn't know how to express" or "what to do with." The latter phrase also occurred in the description of Bertha's thoughts upon taking hold of Pearl's arm after her arrival. "Treasure that burned in their bosoms" echoes the earlier phrase, "in her bosom there was still that bright glowing place— that shower of little sparks coming from it." Some urge inside Bertha grows taller and taller as she stretches, quiveringly, toward the silvery blond Miss Fulton, much as the pear tree seems to her to stretch up and touch the "rim" of the round, silver, feminine moon. The color silver now draws to itself, along with previous associations, the sexually symbolic silver flowers. Bertha has no more knowledge of what her own feelings mean than she would know what to do were Miss Fulton actually to go beyond a certain point, in frankness, and give the sign she secretly longs for. She is left wondering what she is to do with her unknown and unfulfilled desires.

When the lights in her house are turned on, Bertha returns to the world in which her marriage to Harry is a simple fact. Ironies multiply as Bertha imagines that she can share with him the feelings Pearl Fulton has inspired. The conflicting tendencies within her psyche emerge in thoughts at cross-purposes: "Oh, Harry, don't dislike her. You are quite wrong about her. She's wonderful, wonderful. And, besides, how can you feel so differently about someone who means so much to me. I shall try to tell you when we are in bed tonight what has been happening. What she and I have shared." Here Bertha attempts to transfer her unconscious feelings for the woman onto her relationship with the man, according to what she knows her feeling for him conventionally ought to be. For the *first* time in her life, we are told, she feels sexual desire for her husband, and it is a "strange and almost terrifying" thought. Somehow she feels perplexed that her bliss has been leading up to Harry; it was Pearl, after all, who seemed to fan the flames of her ardor. "But then then—'' why Harry? or, if Harry, what has Miss Fulton had to do with her excitement? Bertha breaks off, not pursuing the implications even this far.

As the guests take their leave, a stunned Bertha beholds Harry embrace and kiss Pearl. Her eyes focus on Miss Fulton, who laid her "moonbeam fingers" on his cheeks and smiled "her sleepy smile." The sign she had so much desired has been reserved for Harry, and her pearl slips from her grasp like quicksilver. Bertha touches those slender fingers only in parting, as Miss Fulton holds her "hand a moment longer" to praise her "lovely pear tree." The unwitting irony of her praise is devastating. In another moment she is gone, leaving Bertha feeling empty and hopeless. Bertha, confused and in pain, rushes to the window to view the pear tree: "Oh, what is going to happen now?" she wonders. Her pent-up desires are still in full flower, as are the tree and its flowers that symbolize them.

Throughout "Bliss" Mansfield ironically plays off a conventional love triangle against an unconventional one, forcing the reader to make the necessary adjustment. She subtly controls her symbolism and other modes of suggestion and indirection to convey both the tendency of Bertha's peculiar feelings and her lack of self-knowledge, the degree of ignorance in her bliss. In her essay examining Katherine Mansfield's theory of fiction, Eileen Baldeshwiler reveals the degree to which this author cared about her craft, how much she delighted in achieving the perfect detail and the sufficient balance between form and subject. "Bliss" adequately illustrates both the care and the craft. But even more perfectly, it exemplifies, perhaps, the kind of joy which every practitioner of the art of fiction must feel when he successfully detaches the object from himself. Mansfield carefully articulates this feeling in her letters, parts of which Baldeshwiler summarizes: "'But when I am writing of "another" I want so to lose myself in the soul of the other that I am not.' The act of faith, of surrender, requires 'pure risk,' the absolute belief in 'one's own essential freedom.' It is hard to let go, 'yet one's creative life depends on it and one desires to do nothing else.'" Certainly we may suppose that Mansfield felt her own essential freedom when lost in the soul of Bertha Young and her short-lived bliss.

Source: Walter E. Anderson, ''The Hidden Love Triangle in Mansfield's 'Bliss''' in *Twentieth Century Literature*, Volume 28, No. 4, winter, 1982, pp. 397–403.

Marilyn Zorn

In the following essay, Zorn argues that cultural bias is responsible for the misunderstanding and misrepresentation of ''Bliss'' by critics.

It is perhaps inevitable, given our cultural bias, that Bertha Young, who yearned to share her feelings of ''bliss'' with her husband and friends and failed to find the language that would communicate it, has been misunderstood and misrepresented by the critics of this most popular of Katherine Mansfield's stories. Even a largely sympathetic critic like Sylvia Berkman has had difficulty with Bertha, seeing her as representative of the brittle set among which she moves, an example of a ''modern metropolitan woman'' who is ''callous, tempermental, selfish and unreasonable,'' demanding ''servile, undeviating attention'' from her men. Miss Berkman is uneasy with this mold for Bertha, for she goes on to admit: ''Bertha Young in 'Bliss' to my mind exemplifies a misapplication of this tone, she seems not so much detestable as immature and stupid, an impression I do not believe Miss Mansfield meant to convey.'' Marvin Melanger also identifies Bertha with her social set and stresses the satirical element of the story. Bertha's ''hysteria,'' her frigidity, her mind's apparent ''confused internal chaos'' make her ''a highly unreliable grade for the reader.'' Eisinger goes so far as to say that the pear tree and Bertha's identification with it is ''nothing short of myopic sentimentalization.''

Poor Bertha! According to these critics, she is quintessentially a female stereotype: timid, sentimental, childish, frigid, naive, self-deluding. Such a figure (no matter how self-contradictory some of those qualities might be) of course deserves the disillusionment which comes to her at the end of the story when she discovers her husband's and friend's affair. Perhaps her worst fault, as Melanger insists, is that she has thought herself happy. Even her bliss is suspect: ''. . . in the very words which the author frames her insistence, she demonstrates the emptiness of the claims.'' Katherine Mansfield is thus brought forward as a witness against her character. And what seems to be primarily a critic's reaction against the character is attributed to the author.

But to strip Bertha of her human dignity and to make the story into an unpleasant little exposé of a social group and of a child-woman is to fail to

> "Bertha Young in 'Bliss' to my mind exemplifies a misapplication of this tone, she seems not so much detestable as immature and stupid, an impression I do not believe Miss Mansfield meant to convey."

recognize the author's state of mind during the writing of the story and her hopes and intentions for her art. For Katherine Mansfield was not thinking small or smart at the time ''Bliss'' was composed. The story was written a week after the hemorrhage which signalled the seriousness of her lung condition. Like Keats in a similar situation she was henceforward convinced that she did not have enough time left to seal the accomplishment her work had promised. She turned her back on her earlier, for her less satisfactory, work on the *New Age* and her stories in the collection. *In a German Pension.* Indeed, she forbade republication of that work at a time when she needed money, and it would have been undoubtedly profitable for her to republish it because she no longer wanted to be identified as a clever, satirical voice.

And she no longer needed to be. With signs of her mortality before her eyes, ''Bliss'' nevertheless occurs during a strongly productive time in her career. Highly excited by ''Je ne parle pas francais'' and by J. Middleton Murry's reaction in praise of the story, she writes, ''But what I felt so seriously as I wrote it was—oh! I am in a way *grown up* as a writer—a sort of an authority.'' In another letter of this time she borrows an image from ''Bliss'': ''Oh dear, oh dear! you have lighted such a candle! Great beams will come out of my eyes at lunch and play like search-lights over the pommes de terre.'' Clearly, for all the playfulness of her language, she is exhilarated by the sense her art has matured. Clearly also there is in her letter to Murry at the conclusion of the first draft of ''Bliss'' the conviction that the stories are crowding up on her, that the writing is a matter of necessity and that her powers are sufficient to her inspiration: ''One extraordinary thing has happened to me since I came out here. Once I start them they haunt me and plague me until they are finished and as good as I can do.'' In accord with that sense of power comes also a heightened sensitivity to nature which Katherine Mansfield ascribes to her illness. On February 20, 1918, the day after she hemorrhaged, she wrote to Murry: ''Since this little attack I've had, a queer thing has happened. I feel that my love and longing for the external world—I mean the world of *nature*—has suddenly increased a million times.'' It is this awareness of the signatory aspect of nature which links Katherine Mansfield to the Romantic poets. Like Keats and Shelley, she sees nature as a veil for the ideal world, offering intimations of a beauty and state of being which are transcendent, never possible except in hints and brief glimpses offered in the natural beauty of the world. It is the poet's task to testify to the visionary world's possibility, but he or she is continually aware that such insight also includes its transcendence. Hence to be a messenger of such a world also means that one must speak of its corruption in the real world. When Katherine Mansfield tells Murry that she has two starting points for writing—the sense of joy and the ''cry against corruption,'' —she is being as true to Shelley's vision that life ''Stains the white radiance of Eternity'' as any twentieth-century writer can be. Moreover, ''Bliss's'' theme encompasses exactly the visionary joy and the cry against corruption which we associate with the Romantics. One of the unacknowledged sources for the story is Shelley's poem ''The Question,'' which she cared enough about to memorize and which she mentions both to Murry and to Lady Ottoline Morrell in letters at this time.

The poem is a sensuous description of a flowering countryside on a spring morning. There are animistic images which show the earth and the stream embracing, followed in the next stanza by the birth of flowers. The moon's presence on this morning scene is also invoked through the flower imagery, increasing the sense of the strange in the poem and suggesting both the poet's vision and the unifying presence of love. Pearl Fulton perhaps acquired her coolness and her connection with the moon from stanzas two and three:

> Daisies, those pearled arcturi of the earth / The constellated flower that never sets . . . / And in the warm hedge grew lush eglantine / Green cowbine and the moonlight-colored may

The silver blossoms offered by Pearl and Bertha in the moment with the pear tree are an echo of the poem's speaker offering ''visionary flowers'' to his lover in the fifth stanza. Finally, the poem's last line asks the question which troubles Bertha throughout the story: ''Oh, to Whom'' can the vision be communicated? A year later, the season, the emotion, and Shelley's poem are still linked together in the author's mind. In another letter to Ottoline Morrell she speaks of her sensitivity to the spring and her desire to share her feelings with someone: ''Why are human beings the only ones who do not put forth fresh buds—exquisite flowers and leaves? . . . We have all been wintry far too long—Really, on some of these days one is tired with *bliss*. I long to tell someone—to feel it immediately shared—.''

A major assumption about the story must be, then, that Bertha's state of mind and her need to share it with her friends and husband are seen as perfectly valid by the author. The lack of awareness on the part of those close to her is seen as their incapacity, not Bertha's. Her intuition of the new life which might grow out of her awareness, her brief glimpse of ideal womanhood, and her awakened sexual desire are genuine in the story—not fraudulent and not sentimental. The failure of the vision is the result of those elements in the society and in the individual which Katherine Mansfield identified as corrupting.

Since it would be difficult to speak of Bertha, the most childlike of the story's characters, as corrupt, it is better to ask what has caused Bertha's vision to falter. There is no denying the irony with which the author views her character. She chips away at the illusory nature of Bertha's happiness until at the end nothing seems to be left of it. Still, there she is throughout the story with her ''bliss,'' the only character who is so graced. Moreover, Katherine Mansfield gives her the two central metaphors of the story: the vision of the pear tree and the analogy for art, ''playing.'' In speaking of Bertha to Murry, Katherine Mansfield calls her an ''artist manquée'' and indicates that Bertha has the discrimination to separate language which is her own from language she has borrowed from someone else. She is able therefore to know what is genuine in herself, if not yet in others. Bertha shows the same aesthetic sense in her remark about the piano: ''What a pity someone does not play; what a pity someone does not play.'' The remark must be taken symbolically. Bertha's intuitions about love and her child have used the same analogy: what good is the rare violin if it is shut up in a case and never played? Indeed, Katherine Mansfield uses the same analogy to Ottoline Morrel: ''What might be so divine is out of tune—or the instruments are all silent and nobody is going to play again.'' It is obviously not enough for the artist to have the vision; there must be a language to communicate it and a community of listeners who speak the language to understand it when it is spoken. It is Shelley's question again: ''Oh to Whom?''

Yet supposing Bertha had the tongues of angels to aid her, it has traditionally been her language which has drawn most criticism from her readers. One might suggest that that is so, not because Bertha's speech is so empty and vacuous, but because she sounds like a woman, or our concept of how a particular kind of middle-class woman sounds. Indeed, if one compares her speech to the characteristics of female speech identified by Robin Lakoff in *Language and Woman's Place*, the resemblance is striking. The thesis of Lakoff's book is that because women have accepted secondary roles in public and private life, they are accustomed to think of themselves as powerless. Their status is reflected by their women's speech. When they use women's speech, they reinforce all over again the conviction that they are powerless. Thus, in women's speech, Bertha's feeling of joy will seem insignificant, not only to her husband, but to her critics as well. When Melanger criticizes Bertha's language he is reacting against it in Harry's stead: ''The breathless ecstasy of the passage quoted (the passage beginning 'Really—really—she has everything') gives the lie to the words themselves. The twice repeated 'really' and overenthusiastic 'everything' reveal the emptiness of the lines.'' Of the nine characteristics which denote female language for Lakoff, six are Bertha's. She uses ''so'' and ''such'' as intensifiers. She has a range of adjectives which only women use, like ''divine'' and ''little precious'' and ''incredibly beautiful.'' She uses the tag question to avoid self-assertion; she hedges; she speaks in italics. Further, the author has for her a variety of sentence forms to imply elevated emotion and sensitivity: the rhetorical question, the exclamation, repetition, the abrupt shift in syntax signalled by the dash, the unfinished sentence. When Bertha's breathless, exclamatory perceptions are contrasted with Harry's talk about digestion or the small talk of the dinner guests, the distance between their sensibilities is emphasized. Also emphasized is the difference in female and male speech.

Thus, a major effect of Bertha's speech is to reinforce her sad awareness that she will not be able to communicate her vision, unless a sympathetic woman friend will share it. Because her language for experience must stress its affective and subjective qualities, there will be few reference points in such a language beyond the self unless there is congruence of emotion. Yet Harry's response to Bertha's emotion is to deny it and to hood his own. Bertha, in trying to tell her husband about her ''bliss'' during the phone conversation, recognizes that it will seem absurd to him and breaks off their exchange. Her very sensitivity to her husband's insensitivity, her secret admiration for his deflating jokes about her enthusiasms, insures that she will not ask for intimate communication with him. Thus she will remain the impersonal ''good pal'' she perceives he wishes her to be in their marriage.

Bertha's set generally seems to discount the language of emotion and enthusiasm or to parody it by exaggerating the banal until genuine emotion seems suspect. Bertha feels her estrangement from them throughout the dinner party with the result that she grows more and more tense. The woman who felt ''bliss'' earlier now feels a kind of hysteria at her inability to communicate with them. Because Pearl has seemed sympathetic, she desperately waits for a ''sign'' that she has shared her emotion. But she is unable to distinguish true intimacy from false, and so the moment at the window before the pear tree turns out to be one more imposture. ''Your lovely pear tree'' thus becomes a symbol of the desirability of human intimacy and the betrayal of it.

It is important that the reader not undervalue Bertha's vision, although in terms of the story it is unrealized. For it is one of the poles of feeling in the story. Without it, Bertha's disillusionment is empty of significance, as empty as one of her guest's stories. Since it is the pear tree that draws together the characters and their emotions in the story, it is well to look more closely at the images the author associates with the tree. By the time Bertha and Pearl stand before the pear tree in their moment of intimacy, both of the women have been identified with it. Moreover, Bertha's bliss, supposedly enveloping both the women at this moment, has also been identified with it. The earlier imagery for the bliss has been a series of sun images, which Bertha internalizes. Now the sun image is linked with the moon through the candle metaphor, which seems to project an ideal order of relationship in nature: ''Although it was so still it seemed, like the flame of a candle, to stretch up, to point, to quiver in the bright air, to grow taller and taller as they gazed . . . almost to the rim of the moon.'' Images which link the sun and the moon are for Katherine Mansfield holistic. They suggest the earthly paradise, the condition of pre-lapsarian innocence. A dream story of a childhood experience shared by her brother and herself is called ''Sun and Moon.'' The children are allowed to wait up for a party their parents are giving. They see the feast in all its splendor before the guests arrive. Afterwards, they are allowed to approach the banquet table after the party is over. Their parents are drunk, and the food and ices are spoiled. The result is that the children will have nothing to do with the adult party world and demand to be taken away. In their moment before the pear tree, detached from the real world and its relationships, Bertha and Pearl have the same kind of perfection that the children, Sun and Moon, possess. They are described as ''creatures of another world, and wondering what they are to do in this one with all this blissful treasure that burned in their bosoms and dropped, in silver flowers, from their hair and hands?'' In their ideal selves there is no distinction between the two women. They equally bear treasures of bliss and offer visionary flowers. What Bertha has discovered is the potential life all women possess. What the vision suggests is that there are possibilities of relationships which are gracious and free.

Finally the story shows that these potential relationships are corrupted and thwarted by the character of human interaction in the world. For against Bertha's momentary glimpse of Pearl's and her own ideal self is projected another demonic vision of the world and its way with women.

Beginning with Face, the women in the real world of the story are threatened with actual and imagined acts of violence. In counterpoint to Bertha's vision, the talk at the party is a continuous barrage of horror stories. In her ''monkey'' attire, Face feels that the train she has journeyed upon, ''rose to a man and simply ate me with its eyes.'' The actress at the Alpha is the ''weirdest little person. She'd not only cut her hair, but she seemed to have taken a dreadfully good snip off her legs and arms and her poor little nose.'' Art itself gives expression to the violence: they talk about the poem about a ''girl who was violated by a beggar without a nose.'' Indeed, Harry's passion for the white flesh of lobster and green pistachio ices makes erotic love exactly like eating, and together with Face's experiences, vaguely cannibalistic. His vulgarity is given a sinister turn by the double entendre in the joke about his daughter: ''My dear Mrs. Knight, I shan't feel the slightest interest in her until she has a lover.'' At that point in the story, both of the male guests show by their actions that they know, if Bertha doesn't, about the affair with Pearl. Even

Pearl, who might seem to have come off the winner in the real world of the story, is shown as vulnerable to the questionable ethics of relationships between men and women. For it seems she will be eaten, after all, in Harry's terms. Her blindness is subtly expressed. Along with the Giaconda smile, she is described as one who ''lived by listening rather than seeing.'' It is clear she is caught up in the force which Bertha imagines as ''blind and smiling'' when she imagines desire. In these circumstances, the image is ambiguous and even terrible. The only person who seems to have responded to the ideal Pearl is Bertha, and in their world, they must be rivals.

Katherine Mansfield, then, has not written a satire of a foolish woman who overvalues her life's happiness; nor has she written a satire of the pretensions to art of a group of Philistines. What she has done is to write a somber story about the potential for love and beauty in human relationships, which can be glimpsed but not realized. Certainly, a woman like Bertha, condemned to inarticulateness by her female language, cannot realize it. Yet her openness to ''bliss'' and the potential in life, and her desire to share the vision, do make her the heroine of the story. The question with which Bertha ends the story is not unhopeful. She has been questioning all day. Her ''Oh what is going to happen now?'' is certainly resigned, certainly an admittal of powerlessness at this final moment. But it does look forward to the future. It acknowledges her losses. It propels her forward into the life she must lead.

Source: Marilyn Zorn, ''Visionary Flowers: Another Study of Katherine Mansfield's 'Bliss''' in *Studies in Short Fiction,* Vol.17, No. 2, spring 1980, pp. 141–47.

Marvin Magalaner

In the following essay, Magalaner examines the autobiographical elements in Katherine Mansfield's ''Bliss.''

Since the death of Katherine Mansfield more than fifty years ago, the kind of attention her short stories have received has followed an understandably meandering path. Shocked by the romantic aura of her early demise—in France, no less, of a sudden consumptive attack, almost in the presence of her husband, and hardly out of her twenties—critics could scarcely be blamed for accentuating the sorrow and the pity of her end and for seeking in her stories clues to the real Mansfield not available in the scattered biographical writings of friends and relatives. In the United States, Sylvia Berkman's serious examination of Mansfield's writings marked the beginning of a new and scholarly approach to Mansfield's fiction. The short stories lent themselves admirably to sensitive interpretation according to the rules of the New Criticism and became, indeed, one of the staples of almost all anthologies of the 1950s and afterward.

If only as a corrective, perhaps the time has come to put Katherine Mansfield back into her stories. Though her own attitude toward autobiography in art is ostensibly ambivalent—as I shall try to demonstrate later—there is no doubt that she joins D. H. Lawrence and Aldous Huxley among others in parading those she knew in real life through the pages of her fiction—and no one more consistently than herself. One need look no further than her letters and her *Journal* for evidence that her acquaintances and her relatives furnished materials out of which her fictional people developed. Her despair at the death of her brother "Chummie" during the First World War gave way to her expressed determination to re-create his and her New Zealand existence, complete with sheep, grandmother, mists, parents, and siblings as a memorial to her beloved. The Burnell family, the Sheridan family, Laurie, Laura, the coachman, all are firmly based in autobiography, even when they take on the independent life of fictional characters. And the essential John Middleton Murry, Mansfield's husband, is more thoroughly encapsulated in the few pages of Mansfield's "The Man without a Temperament" than in the hundreds of pages of his own autobiography.

It may be instructive to look once again at a frequently discussed short story of Katherine Mansfield called "Bliss" to demonstrate, if possible, the significant ways in which the author as human being, as wife, as woman, and as emotional and intellectual entity plays a role in the story. Numerous additional parallels might have been traced, but I want merely to indicate the extent of the practice by offering and following up one or two examples.

This short story, completed by Mansfield in 1918, offers the reader one day in the life of Bertha Young, a fashionable thirty-year-old wife and mother. From afternoon to late evening, the graph of her emotions moves from the heights of joyous exhilaration (bliss) to the depths of despair, as she discovers her husband's infidelity in the suddenly grasped relationship between Harry and Bertha's special friend, Pearl Fulton. It is a day for other discoveries,

> "The idea for the artist . . . is to arrange the details of the autobiographical past that the precious kernel of selfhood is separated from the chaff of vital statistics of a life. . ."

too: that Bertha's mystical relationship cannot be regained; that Bertha's relationship to her own child is less firm than the child's ties to her nurse; that Bertha's position as hostess to a bizarre group of bohemian pseudo-intellectuals does not qualify her to enter into communion with them, or them with her; in short, that Bertha's plunge from innocence to awareness will affect her future existence in every regard.

On the first page of "Bliss," Katherine Mansfield defines the feeling of "absolute bliss" that has taken possession of Bertha momentarily in these terms: "as though you'd suddenly swallowed a bright piece of that late afternoon sun." From this point on, the story depends heavily upon the imagery of food, of eating and drinking, and on other suggestions of oral satisfaction like smoking cigarettes. Bertha's first duty upon entering her home is to arrange the fruit tastefully, a simple task engendering an emotional reaction in her that verges on the "hysterical." Her next encounter is a muted struggle with Nanny over the right to feed her own child the evening meal. The remainder of the story centers on the dinner party, the guests, the conversation at table, coffee and cigarettes in the drawing room, the episode of the pear tree and the moon in the garden, and Bertha's culminating epiphany of her betrayal by Pearl and her own husband.

Even when the plot does not require allusions to digestion, chewing, biting, swallowing, drinking, the alimentary canal, indigestion, and the like, "Bliss" intrudes such allusions at every turn. Pearl's aloof smile is jokingly attributed by Harry to a frozen liver, or "pure flatulence," or perhaps to "kidney disease." The reader is told gratuitously that the Youngs' new cook makes "the most superb omelettes." Mrs. Norman Knight complains that the bourgeois passengers on the train "ate" her with their eyes and then goes on to characterize the episode as "too absolutely creamy." This same guest is imagined by Bertha as having "made that yellow silk dress out of scraped banana skins," and she sees Mrs. Knight's earrings as "little dangling nuts." Harry's infatuation with Pearl Fulton is disguised through his ability to "talk about food and to glory in" a "shameless passion for the white flesh of the lobster" and "the green of pistachio ices—green and cold like the eyelids of Egyptian dancers," a predilection that recalls to the reader a reference on the same page to the "heavy eyelids" of Pearl Fulton.

Most obviously, during the dinner itself, all the arty chit-chat centers on the imagery of eating. A play by Michael *Oat* is entitled *Love in False Teeth.* The playwright's newest effort is given as "Stomach Trouble." And as they dine, "their spoons rising and falling—dabbing their lips with their napkins, crumbling bread, fiddling with the forks and glasses and talking," Pearl fingers a tangerine, Mrs. Knight tucks something "down the front of her bodice—as if she kept a tiny, secret hoard of nuts there, too," and the group hears of a "fried-fish scheme" of interior decoration, chairs "shaped like frying pans and lovely chip potatoes embroidered all over the curtains." A call for new writers to desert the romantic for the realistic is put in terms of the necessity to vomit in contemporary literature: "The trouble with our young writing men is that they are still too romantic. You can't put out to sea without being seasick and wanting a basin. Well, why won't they have the courage of those basins?" Literary allusions steeped in the imagery of food end with mention of two poems: *"Table d'Hôte"* and "Why Must it Always be Tomato Soup" (sic).

I have discussed elsewhere the internal aesthetic relevance and artistic appropriateness of such imagery to this short story. My intention here is quite different. It is to demonstrate that the abundance of such imagery in "Bliss" is entirely consistent with Katherine Mansfield's own patterns of thought and feeling, not at all merely a device for literary exploitation.

Mansfield sums it up in a particularly meaningful letter to her husband, John Middleton Murry:

> Darling, this is just a note, sent with the letters. Eat all that extra ration of meat—eat *all* [italics Mansfield's] you can—as I do. God! this darling boat—swinging lazy with the tide. Give Fergusson my love. . . . Tell me as soon as you know about your holiday and try and eat fruit while the warm weather lasts—and

remember what you are to me. It's no joke. *My love seems all to be expressed in terms of food* [italics mine].

This letter, dated May 22, 1918, was written just three months after Mansfield completed the short story "Bliss." Murry, in his autobiography, quotes another letter from Katherine Mansfield in which she first expresses her overwhelming love for him and her happy anticipation of his arrival: "What drowsy bliss slept in my breast!" She continues, "I thought of what I would have ready for you," but she substitutes for amorous embraces a more explicit and less emotionally charged menu—"soup and perhaps fish, coffee, toast (because *charbon de bois,* which is *much* cheaper than coal, makes lovely toast, I hear), a pot of confitures, a vase of roses . . ." [ellipses Murry's].

While it is perhaps natural for one in love to wish to offer food and drink to the beloved, a rather more specialized perversity allows the loved one to *become* the food itself, as Bertha is transformed into a fruit and Pearl into lobster and ices. Thus, in a letter to Murry written only a few days before "Bliss" was completed, Mansfield makes the imaginative leap:

> 1:15. Well. I wish you had eaten my *tournedos*; it was such a good 'un. The great thing here is the meat, which is superb. Oh, but now I am turned toward *home* everything is good. I eat you. I see you. . . . I'd die without you. "Hang there like fruit, my soul, till the tree die!" The tree *would* die.

Though I shall resist developing it at this point, the emerging scenario and its relevance to "Bliss," certainly seems clear enough: the loving wife's desire to share her food with her absent husband, the transformation of the husband into the meat which the wife will enjoy, and the invocation by the wife of her own soul, seen as the fruit of a fruit tree which would die if the husband deserted the wife. During the ten days that followed the posting of this letter, Mansfield would be composing her short story. She would also be writing Murry to complain of the all-devouring solicitude of her long-time friend and companion, Ida Baker, whose tangled relationship to Mansfield and Murry recalls distortedly the triangle in "Bliss": "'It's no good looking cross because I love you [she imagines Ida Baker saying to her], my angel, from the little tip of that cross eyebrow to the *all* of you. When am I going to brush your hair again?' I shut my teeth and say 'Never!' but I really do feel that if she could she'd EAT me."

I shall resist also turning this article into a catalogue of Mansfield's allusions to food in so many of her private writings. In fantasy, she visualizes her reunion with her husband as a communion at table: ''Ah, Love, Love, when I come back—we shall be so happy. The very cups and saucers will have wings, and you will cut me the only piece of bread and jam in the world, and I will pour you out a cup of *my* tea.'' In the same letter, she sees Ida Baker as a ''ghoul'' demanding desperately to overpower with attentions a weaker person ''more or less delivered up to her.'' ''As long as I am to be massaged she's an angel, for then *c'est elle qui manage.*'' When rebuffed in her charity, however, Ida Baker is ''all hungry fury.'' Mansfield recalls how Ida ''ate me before my eyes, and I really *revolted.*'' Summing it up, she decides, in appropriate imagery, that ''Her passion for me feeds on my hate'' and that is what ''I can't stomach.''

Significantly, the two persons to whom Katherine Mansfield felt closest in her adult life, Ida Baker and John Middleton Murry, she imagines as eating her or being eaten by her—and sometimes as involved in a combination of both processes. Consuming and being consumed—in human interaction, in love, in sex, in hate—blurs the distinction between the consumer and the consumed. We are what we eat, nutrition editors tell us, but Mansfield invested the idea with symbolic overtones that go far beyond the scientific.

Eventually, Mansfield discovers that her role of dependence upon Ida Baker and Murry has been instrumental in forging an unacceptable bond among the three. They have become an unhealthy trinity, impossible as a threesome, difficult to separate into viable couples: Katherine and Ida, on the one hand; on the other, Katherine and Murry. Her complaint to Murry about their marriage is first of a lack of ardor: ''You never once held me in your arms and called me your wife.'' But this grievance is coupled with distress that she and Murry have no marital privacy while Ida shares their married life. ''I am jealous—jealous of our privacy—just like an eagle. If I felt that you and she discussed me even for my own good—I'd . . . dash myself on the rocks below.'' Many years later, Murry found it ''difficult'' to ''reconcile affection for and dependence upon'' Ida with Mansfield's ''passionate hatred of her.'' So tangled does the thread of the multiple relationship become that Mansfield actually imagines herself married to Ida. ''How I should beat her if I were married to her! It's an awful thought.'' To Murry, Mansfield confides:

> . . . our hate had got to such a pitch that I couldn't take
> a plate from her hand without shuddering. This *awful*

relationship living on in its secret corrupt way beside my relationship with you is very extraordinary; no one would believe it. I am two selves—one my true self—the other that she creates in me to destroy my true self.

Years later, weeks before her own death, she was still trying to sort out her many selves, revealing to Murry that he matters ''more and more'' to her now that ''I am not so 'identified' with you'' and recording in the same letter Ida's past identification with her also: ''She had got to the pitch of looking after me when she gave me a handkerchief without my asking for it. She *was* me [italics Mansfield's].''

Katherine Mansfield's *Journal* neatly sums up her view that the self is manifold:

> Of course, it followed as the night the day that if one was true to oneself . . . True to oneself! which self? Which of my many—well really, that's what it looks like coming to-hundreds of selves? For what with complexes and repressions and reactions and vibrations and reflections, there are moments when I feel I am nothing but the small clerk of some hotel without a proprietor, who has all his work cut out to enter the names and hand the keys to the wilful guests.

These reflections lead us back to ''Bliss,'' and to the strange relationship among the principals, Bertha, Harry, and Pearl. Married for some years, Bertha and Harry typify the conventional pair, male and female, in monogymous society. Yet their association as ''pals'' rather than true lovers reveals either a flaw in their marriage or a larger imperfection in contemporary society. Perhaps it reveals both. But what concerns the reader of the story is the specific relationship among the three characters.

I would suggest that the Bertha-Harry, Bertha-Pearl, Pearl-Harry combinations comprise one ever-shifting personality unit and that sanction for this view may be found not only in the story but in Mansfield's autobiographical references. That Mansfield considered herself to be almost mystically part of Murry is evident from numerous allusions in her private writings. ''Mysterious fitness of our relationship! . . . he and I, different beyond the dream of difference, are yet an *organic whole.* We are . . . the two sides of the medal, separate, distinct and yet making one.'' Indeed, later on in her *Journal,* Mansfield elevates to a principle her idea of the ''relationship between 'lovers.''' ''We are,'' she says, ''neither male nor female. We are a compound of both. I choose the male who will develop and expand the male in me; he chooses me to expand the female in him. Being made 'whole.' Yes, but that's a process. By love serve ye one another . . . .'' (And this love, incidentally, is expressed in the concern of the lover regarding the food taken by the beloved: ''. . . We had bouillabaisse. I wondered what you had. Yes, I am not one but *two*. I am *you* as well as myself. You are another part of me, just as I am a part of you.'' But, as I have quoted above, Mansfield feels herself invaded and violated by Ida Baker—''I am two selves—one my true self—the other that she creates in me to destroy my true self.''

In ''Bliss,'' Pearl Fulton is Bertha's acknowledged ''find.'' She is the only one with whom Bertha can communicate completely—and without the need of speaking. Both women are associated with the colors green and white, Pearl with the green of pistachio ices and the white meat of the lobster, Bertha with a white dress, jade beads, and green shoes and stockings—the colors of the pear tree in bloom. Harry is formally married to one of these green and white women. His ''find,'' ironically, is not his wife at the moment but Pearl. And when Bertha imagines how she and Harry will communicate in bed that night, how she will tell him what she and he have shared, she does not yet realize that the shared object is Pearl who, at parting, will also exchange messages with Harry silently, with no need to speak aloud.

''*Everything has its shadow,*'' Katherine Mansfield tells Murry in a letter of 1920. I propose that in the Betha-Pearl combination Harry is really dealing with two aspects of one personality—with two faces of Eve, the innocent and virginal type represented by Bertha, and the moon-like Pearl whose charms belong to everyone. In a story which boasts a gray cat and a black cat, ''its shadow,'' so that the reader finds it difficult to decide whether he is dealing with one or two cats, the implications of Harry's situation are not obscure. And further, if the man and woman, according to Mansfield, are really an organic whole, if she and Murry are not two but one, it is quite possible that Bertha-Harry-Pearl, sharing each other, consuming and being consumed by each other, alternately warm and cold, attracting and repelling, neither fully male nor fully female, form a unitary trio indissoluble in nature rather than a human triangle subject to marriage, divorce, legal separation, and other civilized mechanical arrangements.

For Mansfield does reject in her life the constraints of ''reality'' by which most human beings live. She *can* be part of Murry voluntarily,

part of Ida Baker by violation of personality. She can feel deep affection for her female companion at one moment, loathing the next. She can have total confidence in the fidelity of Murry in one letter and be sure that he is unfaithful in the next.

She can even be a tree, as Bertha is in ''Bliss'':

I wonder if you [Murry] would feed on this visible world as I do. I was looking at some leaves only yesterday . . . and suddenly I became conscious of them—of the amazing ''freedom'' with which they were ''drawn''—of the life in each curve—but not as something *outside oneself,* but as part of one—as though like a magician I could put forth my hand and shake a green branch into my fingers from . . . ? And I felt as though one receive— accepted—absorbed the beauty of the leaves even into one's physical being. Do you feel like that about things?

It is clear that Murry *did* feel like that (though Harry, his fictional shadow, would not have had the sensitivity to be aware of such rarefied matters). Murry expresses their oneness even more clearly and with real certainty. In a letter to Mansfield quoted in his autobiography, he says:

It's no use talking about these identities of ours. I have not the slightest doubt (seriously) that we are manifestations of the same being. . . . Don't think I'm mystical if I explain it like this. The night *when we discovered the Heron together* [their dream house], we became one being. . . . The Heron is more than the symbol of our love, it is the creation of our one being. From that night on we have been fused in soul, so that our correspondences now seem to me the most natural and inevitable thing in the world.

Murry adds thoughtfully, ''Now, I am perfectly aware that if I were to say this to anybody else but you, they would think me raving. But to me it is simple truth in exactly the same way as 2 + 2 = 4.''

Thus in the world inhabited by Mansfield and Murry (and the ever immanent Ida Baker) human identities can and do merge, people can absorb the characteristics of plants and trees, and even the moon can acquire human attributes, as in the poem by Mansfield in which the question is asked:

''Is the moon a virgin or is she a harlot?'' Asked somebody. Nobody would tell.

In ''Bliss,'' where virginal matron and harlot meet as Bertha-Pearl, there is no need to pursue the question.

The relation of Bertha and Pearl, a mystically hybrid fruit of the single pear tree (pair tree?), is matched by the creation and literary accentuation of pairs throughout the story: of masculine Harry and effeminate Eddie as stalkers of Pearl Fulton, of Face and Mug as indistinguishable halves of a married couple, and even of the gray cat and the black cat, its shadow, out in the garden.

To Lady Ottoline Morrell, Katherine Mansfield had confided a year before the writing of ''Bliss'':

> . . . *who* is going to write about that flower garden. It might be so wonderful, do you know *how* I mean? There would be people walking in the garden— several *pairs* of people—their conversation—their slow pacing—their glances as they pass one another. . . . The ''pairs'' of people must be very different and there must be a slight touch of enchantment—some of them seeming so extraordinarily ''odd'' and separate from the flowers, but others quite related and at ease. A kind of, musically speaking, conversation *set* to flowers . . . And I see B—, who hasn't the remotest idea of getting them into harmony. Perhaps that's not fair. But it's full of possibilities. I must have a fling at it as soon as I have time.

There seems little doubt that these outlines eventually were fleshed out to accommodate the governing principle of ''Bliss'' and maybe to give form to ''The Garden Party'' and one or two other stories.

I have deliberately avoided a detailed, fact-by-fact biographical approach to Mansfield's ''Bliss'' for I believe that conclusions drawn from such a study would not be particularly meaningful here. I have refrained from drawing parallels that are there to be drawn between Mansfield's autobiographical writings and the associations suggested in her short story: her flirtation from time to time with lesbianism; her great fear of abandonment; her realization, whether justified or not, that Murry was interested in other women because his own wife was unable to satisfy his emotional and other needs. These details are already public and accessible; moreover, demonstrating their applicability to ''Bliss'' would have little more than a statistical corroborative effect.

For Mansfield, though she knew the immense value of autobiographical materials in fiction, quickly perceived that the faithful rendering of such details fell far short of basic artistic necessity. At the same time, she recognized that the cathartic value of such verisimilitude to the writer was essentially limited. Like Joyce and Gide—perhaps like all artists of distinction—she saw early that autobiography in fiction was merely the jumping-off place for the creation of meaningful art. During the last few years of her short life, she engaged in an intensely personal attempt to eradicate the personal element in life and art so that what transcended the personal and individual would shine forth as continuing and permanent.

To Hugh Walpole, Mansfield had written:

> I sympathise more than I can say with your desire to escape from autobiography. Don't you feel that what English writers lack today is experience of Life. I don't mean that superficially. But they are self-imprisoned. I think there is a very profound distinction between any kind of *confession* and creative work— not that that rules out the first by any means.

Three days later, she writes to Murry that ''we only live by somehow absorbing the past—changing it. I mean really examining it and dividing what is important from what is not (for there IS waste) and transforming it so that it becomes part of the life of the spirit and we are *free of it.* It's no longer our personal past, it's just in the highest possible sense, our servant. . . .'' Then, in an aside, she adds, ''I used to think this process was fairly *unconscious.* Now I feel just the contrary. . . . ''

During the same year, Mansfield wrote:

> . . . there are signs that we are intent as never before on trying to puzzle out, to live by, our own particular self. *Der Mensch muss frei sein*—free, disentangled, single. Is it not possible that the rage for confession, autobiography, especially for memories of earliest childhood, is explained by our persistent yet mysterious belief in a self which is continuous and permanent; which, untouched by all we acquire and all we shed, pushes a green spear through the dead leaves and through the mould, thrusts a scaled bud through years of darkness until, one day, the light discovers it and shakes the flower free and—we are alive—we are flowering for our moment upon the earth? This is the moment which, after all, we live for,—the moment of direct feeling when we are most ourselves and least personal.

The idea for the artist, then, is so to arrange the details of the autobiographical past that the precious kernel of selfhood is separated from the chaff of vital statistics of a life—that, in short, the true Self emerges from the welter of information regarding the past life of the self. In the particular, Joyce had said, lies the universal.

Perhaps Bertha Young grows older in ''Bliss'' because she is at the end able to separate the details of her household tragedy, to absorb her past, and to be ''alive— . . . flowering for our moment upon the earth,'' like the pear tree which, as the story ends, is ''as lovely as ever and as still.''

Source: Marvin Magalaner, ''Traces of Her 'Self' in Katherine Mansfield's 'Bliss''' in *Modern Fiction Studies*, Vol. 24, No. 3, autumn, 1978, pp. 413–22.

Sources

Aiken, Conrad, Review of *Bliss, and Other Stories*, *Freeman*, May 11, 1921, p. 210.

Cowly, Malcolm, Review of *The Garden Party, and Other Stories*, *Dial*, August, 1922, pp. 230–32.

Dieckmann, Katherine, ''Body English: The Short, Sexy Life of Katherine Mansfield,'' *The Village Voice Literary Supplement*, May, 1988, p. 27.

Hanson, Claire, and Andrew Gurr, *Katherine Mansfield*, New York: St. Martin's Press, 1981.

Kobler, J. F., *Katherine Mansfield: A Study of the Short Fiction*, Boston: G. K. Hall & Co., 1990.

Magalaner, Marvin, *The Fiction of Katherine Mansfield*, Carbondale and Edwardsville, IL: Southern Illinois University Press, 1971.

Review of *Bliss, and Other Stories*, *Athenaeum*, January 21, 1921, p. 67.

Review of *Bliss, and Other Stories*, *Spectator*, January 15, 1921, p. 83.

Review of *Bliss, and Other Stories*, *Times Literary Supplement*, December 16, 1920, p. 855.

Further Reading

Berkman, Sylvia, *Katherine Mansfield, A Critical Study*, New Haven, CT: Yale University Press, 1951.
   A thematic and stylistic analysis of Mansfield's stories.

Boddy, Gillian, *Katherine Mansfield: The Woman and the Writer*, Victoria, Australia: Penguin Books, 1988.
   An overview of Mansfield's life, including numerous photographs and the major short stories.

Daly, Saralyn R., *Katherine Mansfield*, Revised Edition, New York: Twayne Publishers, 1994.
   An overview of Mansfield's writings.

Mansfield, Katherine, *The Journal of Katherine Mansfield*, edited by John Middleton Murry, Hopewell, NJ: Ecco Press, 1983.
   Selections from Mansfield's journals edited by her husband.

———, *Selected Letters of Katherine Mansfield*, edited by Vincent O'Sullivan, Oxford: Clarendon Press, 1989.
   Selected letters written by Mansfield.

———, *Selections, Critical Writings of Katherine Mansfield*, edited by Clare Hanson, New York: St. Martin's Press, 1987.
   Mansfield's non-fiction writing, including essays and book reviews.

Tomalin, Claire, *Katherine Mansfield, A Secret Life*, New York: Alfred A. Knopf, 1988.
   A biography of Mansfield.

The Catbird Seat

James Thurber

1942

First published in the November 14, 1942, issue of the *New Yorker,* "The Catbird Seat" also appeared in Thurber's 1945 collection, *The Thurber Carnival.* Since that time, the story has been published in dozens of anthologies for high school and college students, and Thurber has been called America's most important twentieth-century humorist.

The story chronicles a battle of wills between the fussy Erwin Martin, head of a filing department, and Ulgine Barrows, the firm's efficiency expert who threatens to bring change into Martin's well-ordered existence. With comic irony, Martin uses his reputation as a meek and pleasant man against the flashy Mrs. Barrows. The character of Martin is typical of what critics have called Thurber's "Little Man," a common working man who is baffled and beaten down by life in United States in the twentieth century.

The title "The Catbird Seat" derives from the speech patterns of Red Barber, the radio announcer for the Brooklyn Dodgers baseball team in the 1940s. Thurber, a devoted baseball fan, was among those who enjoyed the colorful expressions Barber sprinkled throughout his commentary. As Joey Hart, Martin's assistant explains, sitting "in the catbird seat" means being in an advantageous position. Although it is Mrs. Barrows who seems strong and bold and powerful, it is Martin who wins in the end.

Author Biography

Thurber was born in Columbus, Ohio, on December 8, 1894, the middle of three sons. When he was six, his brother accidentally shot him in the eye with an arrow, leaving him blind in that eye.

Thurber attended public school in Columbus, and then Ohio State University, where he was a bright but careless student who earned low grades and was rather unpopular. He wrote humorous pieces for the campus newspaper and literary magazine, but left college in 1918 without a degree. He worked as a code clerk, and then as a reporter, columnist, and correspondent for various newspapers before settling in New York in 1926.

After dozens of rejections, he finally had an article accepted by the *New Yorker,* and soon was hired as staff writer. He had the good fortune to share an office with E. B. White, who was the first to appreciate Thurber's drawings; Thurber later credited White with helping him develop a cleaner, stronger writing style. Over the next decade the two writers became the strongest influences on what is still known as "The *New Yorker* style."

During the 1930s Thurber published short pieces in the *New Yorker* and other magazines, and several books, including an autobiography, *My Life and Hard Times* (1933), and a spoof of psychology, *Let Your Mind Alone!* (1937). He also earned acclaim for his drawings.

As his friends often commented, Thurber was not much like the shy, nervous protagonist of many of his stories. He was wealthy and successful, and was frequently compared with Mark Twain. By 1940 the sight in his good eye was failing, but he continued writing and drawing, with the aid of large paper and a good secretary. In 1942, nearly blind, he wrote one of his most enduring stories, "The Catbird Seat."

Three years later the story was included in *The Thurber Carnival* (1945), which stayed on the bestseller lists for almost a year. For the first time, Thurber's work drew serious critical attention—no longer was he regarded as "just a humorist." Over the next fifteen years he tried out new forms including children's fantasy stories, and television and film adaptations of his earlier work.

On November 2, 1961, Thurber died of pneumonia following a stroke. Widely regarded as the most important American humorist of the twentieth century, he had published more than twenty books and hundreds of stories and drawings.

Plot Summary

"The Catbird Seat" opens in a crowded cigar store in New York City, where Mr. Erwin Martin is buying a pack of Camel cigarettes. As the narrator points out, this is an unusual act for Martin, who is generally known as a nonsmoker. But the reason for his purchase is soon made clear: he is planning to murder Mrs. Ulgine Barrows.

Martin is the head of a filing department in a large corporate firm; he is characterized as a neat and precise man who is known for his "cautious, painstaking hand." Back in his apartment, drinking a glass of milk, he contemplates the horrible Mrs. Barrows. He resents her for her "quacking voice and braying laugh," her constant chattering, and her use of colorful phrases she picks up from the radio.

Quoting Red Barber, the announcer for the Brooklyn Dodgers, she asks him seemingly nonsensical questions like "Are you lifting the oxcart out of the ditch?" and "Are you sitting in the catbird seat?" The expressions are Southern colloquialisms picked up by Barber during his years in Tallahassee, Florida. "Sitting in the catbird seat," for example, means holding an advantage. Even though the source and the meaning of the lines has been explained to him, Martin finds her way of speaking "annoying" and "childish."

Yet the most serious offense she has committed is her "willful, blatant, and persistent attempts to destroy the efficiency and system of F&S." Nearly two years ago, she met the elderly company president, Mr. Fitweiler, at a party, and charmed her way into a new job as his special adviser. Since then she has fired several loyal employees and driven others to quit.

Now she has turned her attention to the filing department, even hinting that perhaps some of the file cabinets are no longer needed. For Martin, who has worked with the F&S files for twenty-two years, this threat to his well-ordered system is reason enough to kill her.

Martin plans to go to Mrs. Barrows's apartment and kill her. He buys the Camel cigarettes—not her brand—so he can leave one in her ashtray and throw the police off his trail.

On the night of November 9, 1942, he eats his dinner as usual and sets off for his evening stroll, which this time takes him to her apartment. He finds her alone and accepts her invitation to come in. While she is in the kitchen fixing drinks, he looks around her apartment for a murder weapon, but finds nothing suitable. Then a new idea comes to him.

When Mrs. Barrows returns with his drink, he takes out one of his cigarettes, and lights it. She is surprised by his unusual behavior. He raises his glass, and makes a toast that insults ''that old windbag,'' the company president. He tells Mrs. Barrows that he intends to make a bomb and blow up Mr. Fitweiler, and that he will be ''coked to the gills'' on heroin when he does it. Shocked and indignant, Mrs. Barrows throws him out, but not before he sticks out his tongue at her and announces, ''I'm sitting in the catbird seat.''

The next morning, Martin arrives at work at his usual time, and behaves in his normal ''neat, quiet, attentive'' manner. Mrs. Barrows arrives soon after, storming in and promising to report Martin to the boss. Martin pretends he does not know what she means, and she charges into the president's office, where she is heard yelling.

More than an hour later, Mr. Fitweiler sends for Martin. Apologetically, he explains that Mrs. Barrows has come in with a crazy story about Martin drinking, smoking, and threatening the boss. Martin calmly denies having been to Mrs. Barrows's apartment, and Fitweiler believes him, knowing that Martin is his best employee and that he does not drink or smoke. Mrs. Barrows, he explains, has been under a lot of strain, and this must account for her wild accusations.

Naturally, Mrs. Barrows is furious that Martin denies their encounter, but her rage only makes it clear to Mr. Fitweiler that she has suffered a nervous breakdown. Mrs. Barrows is taken away. Mr. Fitweiler apologizes again to Martin, and Martin returns to his files.

Characters

Ulgine Barrows

As the ''newly appointed special adviser to the president of the firm'' of F&S, Mrs. Barrows has

James Thurber

been hired to ''bring out the best'' in the company. In eighteen months on the job (which she obtained by cuddling up to the president, Mr. Fitweiler, at a party) she has fired three loyal employees, driven another to resign, and made changes in nearly every department. Now she plans to reorganize Mr. Martin's area, the filing department.

Mr. Martin despises her large and commanding presence, her loud ''quacking voice and braying laugh,'' and her habit of repeating the colorful phrases of her favorite baseball announcer, Red Barber. When she reports Mr. Martin's shocking threats, Fitweiler does not believe her. Instead, he summons a psychiatrist. In a rage she screams accusations at Martin, confirming Fitweiler's belief that she has gone mad.

Mr. Fitweiler

Mr. Fitweiler is the aging president of the firm of F&S. Almost two years before the story begins, he met Ulgine Barrows at a party, where she ''worked upon him a monstrous magic.'' Shortly afterwards, he hired her and began to follow her suggestions for reorganizing the company. Fitweiler is formal and autocratic; after twenty-two years of working together he still calls Mr. Martin by his last name, and Martin calls him ''sir.''

Media Adaptations

- Read by Wolfram Kandinsky, "The Catbird Seat" was recorded on audiocassette in 1984. It is available as part of an unabridged reading of *The Thurber Carnival,* produced and distributed by Books on Tape, Incorporated.

- "The Catbird Seat" was adapted in 1960 as a British feature film, *The Battle of the Sexes,* starring Peter Sellers as Mr. Martin. The film is not available on videocassette.

Joey Hart

One of Mr. Martin's assistants in the filing department, Joey Hart explains to Martin that Mrs. Barrows' colorful expressions are taken from the baseball announcer Red Barber.

Erwin Martin

Mr. Martin is the protagonist of the story. He is described as a small, neat, quiet man. He has never taken a drink of alcohol or smoked a cigarette, and he has no family or friends. For twenty-two years he has worked for the firm of F&S, eventually rising to the position of head of the filing department. He takes great pleasure in keeping the files as orderly as the rest of his life.

When the loud and aggressive Mrs. Barrows joins the firm and threatens to make changes in his filing system, he goes to her apartment planning to kill her. Suddenly he realizes that he could have her removed from the firm by discrediting her instead. Because Martin is such a "drab, ordinary little man," not even Mrs. Barrows believes that he has planned her demise.

Miss Paird

One of Mr. Martin's two assistants in the filing department, Miss Paird is "always able to find things out." She spreads the story of how Fitweiler and Barrows met, and tries to eavesdrop when Barrows storms into Fitweiler's office.

Themes

Men and Women

One of the more important themes of "The Catbird Seat" is the struggle for men and women to understand each other and live together. In Thurber's work, the battle is always between a weak, nervous man and a strong, domineering woman. It was a recurring theme in his work, most notably in fictional works like *The Owl in the Attic* (1931) and the "The Secret Life of Walter Mitty" (1939). When "The Catbird Seat" was adapted as a movie in 1960, the film was called *The Battle of the Sexes.*

Many of Thurber's stories and drawings explore the struggles between men and women in marriage. In "The Catbird Seat" the arena is the workplace. In Thurber's world, men and women can never understand each other. Like Mr. Martin and Mrs. Barrows, they speak different languages; moreover, women always want to change things.

In this story, many of the traditional male and female characteristics are reversed. It is Mrs. Barrows who drinks alcohol, smokes cigarettes, and follows baseball. Mr. Martin drinks milk, has never smoked, and does not know who Red Barber is. Mrs. Barrows is loud, with a commanding presence. Mr. Martin "maintain[s] always an outward appearance of polite tolerance."

So if conventional behaviors are considered, Mrs. Barrows is the more "masculine" of the two, and Mr. Martin the more "feminine." Martin himself finds her masculinity offensive. Though he tries to "keep his mind on her crimes as a special adviser," he cannot help dwelling on "the faults of the woman as a woman."

The stereotype of the feminist who emasculates men is common in twentieth-century fiction. Yet Mrs. Barrows does not strip Mr. Martin of his manhood, but actually forces him to solve his own problem—to "act like a man," for the first time. The moral of the story seems to be that strong women should be eliminated in order to maintain the status quo.

For Jesse Bier, author of the critical history *The Rise and Fall of American Humor* (1968), "The Catbird Seat"

represents the ultimate victory of put-upon man over matriarchism. Thurber's work is a joyfully vengeful and tireless attack on womanhood. . . . Thurber's stories . . . are the very acme in our literature of controlled wish fulfillment and triumphant, sustained

Topics for Further Study

- If "The Catbird Seat" were set today instead of in 1942, who might play the Red Barber role? Name a few famous entertainment or sports figures that use unusual language or unique ways of expressing themselves. Give an imitation of these distinctive qualities.

- Interview someone who works in a business office. How has the office environment changed since Mr. Martin worked for F&S? How has it remained the same? You might consider relationships between bosses and employees, relationships between employees, and hiring and firing procedures.

- Mr. Martin is an oddity because he does not smoke or drink. Does the story ultimately present Martin's abstinence as a weakness or a strength?

- Investigate the psychological phenomenon of the "persecution complex." Does Mr. Fitweiler's explanation for Mrs. Barrows's behavior seem plausible?

- Search for the phrase "catbird seat" using two or three Internet search engines. How many different publication titles and product names include the phrase? Which of these uses seem to be based on an understanding of the phrase's origin?

---

opposition to everything that Woman, especially the aggressive American woman, stands for."

Many critics sense this anger in Thurber; but others find him cheerfully resigned to the battle of the sexes. Catherine McGehee Kenney's *Thurber's Anatomy of Confusion* describes his handling of the theme as "both bright and melancholy, enlightening and saddening, amusing and frightening."

Alienation and Loneliness

Underlying the inability of men and women to communicate is a deeper truth: all people are essentially alone. Men cannot communicate with women, but they cannot communicate with each other, either. The "battle" between men and women is simply the most visible demonstration of how isolated people are from one another.

In eliminating Mrs. Barrows, what is Martin protecting? The same job he has held for twenty-two years, working for a boss who barely knows him and still calls him by his last name. When he steps out of his routine to buy cigarettes, the clerk does not even glance at him.

In fact, Martin relies on this isolation and anonymity to carry out his plan unnoticed. Only the reader will note that once Martin has achieved the greatest victory of his life, he has no one to share it with.

Style

Irony

The term "irony" refers to a difference between appearance and reality, between what might be expected and what actually happens. Often, as in Thurber's work, irony comes out of a grim sense of humor and to make a serious point.

It is ironic that Martin's well-established reputation as a timid, quiet man makes it possible for his outrageous plan to succeed. To his boss and co-workers, the thought of Martin drinking, smoking, and saying "I'll be coked to the gills when I bump that old buzzard off" seems ridiculous.

The central irony of the story is found in the title. It would appear to be Mrs. Barrows who sits "in the catbird seat." She has the ear of the president, she has mysterious feminine charms, and she has a strange language that Martin cannot understand. Yet as the story plays out, her strength is what brings her down.

In the end, Martin is able to use the title phrase as a weapon against the woman who taught it to him. Mrs. Barrows charges him with "sticking your tongue out, saying you were sitting in the catbird seat, because you thought no one would believe me when I told it!" She recognizes Martin's plan, but she cannot stop it; Mr. Fitweiler knows that Martin would never use such a phrase. Ironically, in the end it is Martin, not Mrs. Barrows, who sits in the catbird seat.

Imagery

The term "imagery" refers to the representation in words of something that is experienced through the senses—but it can be much more than that. Images are not only a way of giving readers a sudden and vivid picture of what something looks like, but also a sense of what it is like.

For example, Thurber uses vivid animal imagery to describe Mrs. Barrows. To Martin's ears, she has a "quacking voice and braying laugh." She romps through the halls of F&S "like a circus horse." In her fury after she confronts Mr. Fitweiler with her accusations, she brays and snorts and bawls.

Thurber does not expect the reader to consciously absorb and add up the animal imagery, and to analyze which animal Mrs. Barrows is most like. Instead, the intention and the effect are subtle. Each animal image quietly follows another, building up in the reader's mind, as Mrs. Barrows's many offenses build up in Martin's. Subconsciously, the reader forms an impression of Mrs. Barrows as animal-like. By creating that distance between the reader and Mrs. Barrows, Thurber makes it seem less shocking—and more fitting—that she should be "rubbed out."

In the *Explicator* in 1982, Marilyn Underwood examines the bird imagery in the story, and finds that Thurber chose his birds carefully to enhance his characterization. The catbird, she points out, is a quiet bird that can be riled; the sparrow (Mrs. Barrows) is known for invading territory of other birds; the martin is a type of swallow, associated with the formal and precise swallowtail coat men used to wear.

Again, the imagery serves to reinforce structures and meanings that are presented more overtly through plot and dialogue. By using layers of imagery, Thurber strives to make his story a richer experience.

The story also features a cluster of football images, used in scenes where Thurber wishes to underscore conflict. Mrs. Barrows first meets the company president at a party, where she helps him escape from a drunken man who thinks Fitweiler is "a famous retired Middle Western football coach." By the end of the scene, she has become special advisor to the president. At the end of the story, when an enraged Mrs. Barrows lunges for Martin, Thurber turns to football again: "Stockton, who had played a little football in high school, blocked Mrs. Barrows as she made for Mr. Martin." This time, the scene ends with Mrs. Barrows's dismissal.

Martin, too, has his brief moment of strength, when he summons his courage and goes to Mrs. Barrows's apartment. Hearing her braying welcome, "He rushed past her like a football tackle, bumping her." His plan is to kill her, to use physical force to have his victory. He realizes after only a few minutes in her apartment not only that she seems "larger than he had thought," but that he can use his cunning instead of his body.

Linking these three scenes by utilizing football imagery, Thurber emphasizes the difference between Mrs. Barrows and Mr. Martin. Of course, Mrs. Barrows's colorful expressions come from baseball, a sport Thurber followed closely. Mrs. Barrows appreciates baseball, while Martin does not; this difference emphasizes the contrast between her "masculinity" and his "femininity."

Historical Context

Humor in the Modern Period

Although Thurber has often been compared with the nineteenth-century humorist Mark Twain, this has more to do with their importance than with their subjects or styles. American humor in the nineteenth century and earlier featured rural or western heroes like Huck Finn, Davy Crockett, and Uncle Remus, slow-talking but clever country folk who made up in "horse sense" what they lacked in education. A staple of this kind of humor was the

Compare & Contrast

- **December 8, 1941:** After a Japanese surprise attack on Pearl Harbor, the United States declares war on Japan and enters World War II. The war will continue until August 14, 1945.

  Today: The United States is involved in several international conflicts, but has not officially declared war since 1941.

- **1941:** The Brooklyn Dodgers baseball team wins the National League pennant, but loses the World Series to the New York Yankees. Red Barber is the baseball announcer for the Brooklyn Dodgers.

  Today: The Dodgers now play in Los Angeles, where they moved in 1958. Most fans follow the games on television, which became popular in the 1950s.

- **1940s:** In metropolitan areas like New York City, outerwear for businessmen includes gloves and formal hats, usually of felt, with creased crowns and narrow brims that go all the way around.

  Today: Businessmen usually are seen without hats of any kind, except in severe weather.

- **1942:** Although women work at manufacturing jobs formerly held by men, relatively few women work in offices. Most of these businesswomen are unmarried, like Miss Paird and the apparently unattached Mrs. Barrows. Women in influential positions are rare.

  Today: Although sociologists have described a "glass ceiling" that prevents many women from being promoted to the top ranks of large corporations, women do appear at every level of business.

---

humiliation of the conniving "city slicker" who thought he could use his education and sophistication to win the fight or the contest or the girl.

When the *New Yorker* was founded in 1925, it strived to present a new type of humor, focusing on life in the modern city. The central characters of the new humor were formally educated, spoke "proper" English, and worked in offices instead of on the land. This humor was different for another reason: where earlier humor had celebrated the triumph of the pioneer spirit with its energy and cleverness, the new humor offered its heroes only hollow victory and loneliness.

Thurber and his colleagues at *The New Yorker* did not invent the school of urban humor, but became its most important contributors. Charles S. Holmes, in his introduction to *Thurber: A Collection of Critical Essays*, describes Thurber's heroes as lost in a modern world that lacks the stability of the past:

> Trapped in a world of machines and gadgets which challenge his competence and threaten his sanity, a world of large organizations and mass-mindedness which threatens his individuality, and—most painfully—a world of aggressive women who threaten his masculine identity, he is forced to go underground, so to speak, and to fight back in small, secret ways.

Erwin Martin is more like the protagonists of the novels of Henry James than he is like the wise folk heroes of Mark Twain.

Psychology and Modern Man

During the early part of the twentieth century, Sigmund Freud revolutionized the understanding of human psychology and originated the practice of psychoanalysis. His many books, including *The Interpretation of Dreams* (1900) and *Three Contributions to the Sexual Theory* (1905), were widely read and discussed by both professionals and general readers; moreover, such terms as "the unconscious" and "the Oedipus complex" became part of the American vocabulary. From the beginning, Thurber rejected many of Freud's ideas, including his theories in *Wit and Its Relation to the Unconscious* (1905) that humor arises from impulses beyond the humorist's control.

Throughout his career, Thurber used psychology and its misapplications as a target for his humor. His first book, *Is Sex Necessary?* (1929) makes fun of Freud's theory—as interpreted in popular culture—that an obsession with sex underlies all human activity. He also spoofs the many "pop psychology" books that appeared in the 1920s. In *Let Your Mind Alone!* (1937) Thurber parodies the self-help book genre. The problem with modern popular psychology, he implies, is that it assumes that motivation and behavior are consistent from one person to another.

"The Catbird Seat" demonstrates the failures of popular Freudian psychology. Martin succeeds because he is different, because his mind does not work like it is "supposed" to, and because he knows he can count on everyone else to accept modern psychology as truth. When Mr. Fitweiler confronts Martin, his talk is laced with the vocabulary of pop psychology: "Mrs. Barrows . . . has suffered a severe breakdown. It has taken the form of a persecution complex. . . . It is the nature of these psychological diseases . . . to fix upon the least likely and most innocent party as the—uh—source of persecution."

Fitweiler has not come to this conclusion on his own, but rather with the help of his psychiatrist. After all, "these matters are not for the lay mind to grasp." The newness of psychology, and the quickness with which it was adopted by a public who only barely understood it, gave Thurber much material for his work.

Critical Overview

Thurber published hundreds of short stories and essays during his career, and while he was one of the few writers to be widely admired both by the critics and by the general public, there is little serious criticism of his work.

"The Catbird Seat" was one of four stories Thurber published in 1942, and it was included in the volume *Best American Short Stories of 1943*. Thurber liked the story, and chose it for the 1945 retrospective collection of his best work, *The Thurber Carnival*.

The *Thurber Carnival* was widely reviewed. Critic and editor William Rose Benét, writing in

The Saturday Review of Literature, praised the book's humor and handling of psychology, and called it "one of the absolutely essential books of our time."

A reviewer for the London *Times Literary Supplement* ranked Thurber as America's most important humorist. Poet and critic Malcolm Cowley's review in *The New Republic* found traces of French expressionism and surrealism in Thurber's work, but hoped that the humorist would turn his considerable talents to creating longer, more worthy, pieces.

Yet several reviewers lauded Thurber's mastery of the short form, and predicted that this volume would finally bring his work serious critical attention. *Chicago Tribune* reviewer Fanny Butcher wrote that she expected Thurber's reputation to move from "cult into a literary culture."

In the intervening years, a handful of book-length critical studies on Thurber have been published. Each points to "The Catbird Seat" as an example of Thurber's finest work, but spends only two or three pages discussing it, usually in contrast to "The Secret Life of Walter Mitty."

For Catherine McGehee Kenney, the two stories must be considered together: "Martin is really Mitty's second cousin, acting out the fantasies of Hollywood films that Mitty had only dreamed about. Taken together, these two stories represent the height of Thurber's powers as a short-story writer."

Robert Elias also compares Martin to Mitty, finding that they both "win not too dissimilar victories over the commonplace, the dead level of practicality, the enemies of the imagination." He includes both stories among a short list of Thurber's "important and challenging masterpieces."

Only a few scholarly articles have been written specifically about "The Catbird Seat." These critical studies have pointed out that Mr. Martin is unlike Thurber's typical male protagonist in actually achieving victory over his female tormentor. Moreover, Earl Dias claimed in 1968 that the victory is undercut by Martin's own femininity.

Thomas Kane proves that Martin's victory occurs on Armistice Day. Fourteen years later, another article appeared, in which Marylyn Underwood examined the implications of Martin and Mrs. Barrows ("Mrs. Sparrows") both having bird names.

A street scene of 1940s New York City, which serves as the setting for 'Catbird Seat.'

In the preface to his *James Thurber* (1964), the first book-length study of the author's work, Robert Morsberger comments on the state of Thurber scholarship:

> Perhaps no other distinguished contemporary has been so neglected critically: for, in spite of his immense popularity at home and abroad, he has received little serious critical attention and that only in book reviews or brief articles. One difficulty for reader and critic is that most of Thurber's pieces are short and are scattered over thirty years of periodicals and more than two dozen books. Most of his pubic read him intermittently, relishing the individual selections but failing to survey the whole of his achievement.

The Thurber Carnival has never gone out of print. "The Catbird Seat" has been included in many of the major high school and college short story anthologies of the last third of the twentieth century. Thurber has not reached the heights of "literary culture" that Fanny Butcher envisioned, however. Like Mark Twain, with whom he is frequently compared, he is studied primarily as a "humorist," not as a "serious" or "major" figure.

Still, generation after generation of new students study the story, using it as a model of irony and characterization and as a prime example of how a writer can use language for comic effect.

Criticism

Cynthia Bily

Bily teaches writing and literature at Adrian College in Adrian, Michigan, and writes for various educational publishers. In the following essay, she discusses isolation and invisibility in "The Catbird Seat."

When James Thurber published "The Catbird Seat" in the *New Yorker,* he was already famous. He had published dozens of stories in the magazine, and ten books of humorous writings and cartoons. Each new book was heralded with reviews in all the major publications in the United States and in Europe.

Yet individual short stories, while they were welcomed by regular readers of the *New Yorker,* were scarcely noticed by critics; "The Catbird Seat" was no exception. Not until it was included in the best-selling collection *The Thurber Carnival* did it earn its place among the most popular and most widely anthologized American short stories of the twentieth century.

The "The Catbird Seat" was recognized as a prime example of a Thurber story: the weak but imaginative little man oppressed by a large and strong woman; the spoof of amateur psychologists; the suffocating climate of the modern business office; and the understated humor in ridiculous situations.

These elements can be found in many of Thurber's short fiction, most notably in stories featuring the character of Mr. Monroe in *The Owl in the Attic* (1931) and Walter Mitty in "The Secret Life of Walter Mitty," published in the *New Yorker* in 1939.

Like Mr. Monroe and Mr. Mitty, Mr. Martin of "The Catbird Seat" copes with a haranguing woman—or tries to—by dreaming of himself as strong and capable enough to overcome his foe. While Mr. Martin is merely unpleasant and Walter Mitty is charming, Erwin Martin, the hero of "The Catbird Seat" is ultimately sad and pitiful.

One important difference between Martin and the others is his living arrangements: he is a bachelor living in an apartment in New York City. He has no family, no friends, and no a pet. The New York of "The Catbird Seat" is not the writhing, exciting city, but an empty and lonely place where a person can go all day without a friendly word.

Thurber states and restates this idea throughout the story. When Martin buys his cigarettes in "the most crowded store on Broadway," no one speaks to him and the clerk does not even look at him. If any of his coworkers had seen him buying cigarettes they would have been surprised, but "No one saw him." Every evening he eats alone, reading the paper, and apparently chats with no one before he leaves for a solitary stroll.

Martin counts on his invisibility to carry out his plan to rid himself of the presence of Mrs. Barrow; he knows that "no one would see his hand" because no one ever sees him. He is so trained in hiding behind a mask, in maintaining "always an outward appearance of polite tolerance," that even Miss Paird, one of the two people with whom he works closely every day, is completely fooled by it.

Miss Paird believes that Martin actually likes Mrs. Barrows. Martin has never shown his dislike, but gives Mrs. Barrows his "look of studious concentration." In the excitement of waiting to carry out his plan, he behaves strangely—he polishes his glasses a few extra times and sharpens "an already sharp pencil"—but again, no one notices.

On the night of the intended murder, Martin takes an unusually long walk to pass the time. He is worried about being noticed, but in fact this New York City is deserted and no one is watching. Mrs. Barrows's apartment house has "no doorman or other attendants," and at 9:18 p.m. her street is empty except for Martin, a man passing, and a man and woman talking. "There was no one within fifty paces when he came to the house"—convenient when one is planning a murder, but unusual for Manhattan. Inside, there is "nobody" in the hallway.

Mrs. Barrows is not a "nobody." She is a person other people notice, whether they wish to or not. She romps and hollers and shouts silly phrases. Men notice her at parties. Bosses are taken with her and hire her as "special advisers." Where Martin has his "look of studious concentration," hers is an "amused look." What does she see? Even a man as studious as Martin is driven "near to distraction" by her. It is more than he can stand.

The problem with Mrs. Barrows is that she seems to see right through his cloak of anonymity. As soon as he sees her (from under his eye shade) looking around the filing department, "taking it in with her great, popping eyes," he worries that she will see him for the person he really is.

What Do I Read Next?

- "The Secret Life of Walter Mitty" (1939) is Thurber's best-known short story. Mitty is a mild-mannered man who shuts out his nagging wife and other troubles by daydreaming about himself as hero.

- Thurber's *The Thurber Carnival* (1945) is collection of over one hundred stories and drawings by Thurber and represents the best of his humorous work written during the 1930s and 1940s.

- *Remember Laughter: A Life of James Thurber*

(1994), by Neil A. Grauer, is the most accessible of the Thurber biographies. It includes photographs and a selection of Thurber's most famous drawings.

- Robert Benchley's *My Ten Years in a Quandary* (1936) portrays common American men struggling with the frustrations of twentieth-century life.

- *America's Humor: From Poor Richard to Doonesbury* (1978), by Walter Blair and Hamlin Hill, is a history of American humor.

Ironically, Mrs. Barrows, the person whom Martin dislikes most in the world and the last person he would allow himself to be honest with, is in some ways the only one who truly sees him. As soon as Martin enters her apartment, Mrs. Barrows sees what his two assistants have missed all day: "What's after you? . . . You're as jumpy as a goat."

Of course, Mrs. Barrows is not as perceptive as she thinks she is—or as Martin fears. As an efficiency expert she has a good eye for fine details, but not for broad strokes, and she is taken in by Martin's outrageous performance.

Just as Martin is undone by Mrs. Barrows's largeness and loudness, Martin's large gestures fool Mrs. Barrows. He gives the performance of his life, a startling imitation of Mrs. Barrows herself. He leaves her building. "No one saw him go." He walks home alone. "No one saw him go in."

The next morning at the office, everyone is suddenly seeing everyone else; in one paragraph Thurber emphasizes seeing and not seeing. When Mrs. Barrows announces she is going to report Martin to Mr. Fitweiler, he gives her "a look of shocked surprise." When she storms out of the office, she leaves Martin's two assistants "staring after her."

Martin returns to work, and the assistants look "at him and then at each other." Martin's look is a

disguise, a lie. He is not surprised, but only playing a part. The assistants look at Mrs. Barrows, and then at Martin, and then at each other, but they do not see anything. They have no idea of what is going on.

For a brief instant, Mrs. Barrows almost understands what Martin has done. A "new glint" comes into "her popping eyes" and she says, "If you weren't such a drab, ordinary little man . . . I'd think you'd planned it all." Yet as Martin has known all along, the idea of him drinking and smoking and making bomb threats is too impossible to be believed. "Can't you see how he has tricked us, you old fool?" shouts Mrs. Barrows. "Can't you see his little game?"

Mr. Fitweiler cannot see it. The only Erwin Martin that Mr. Fitweiler has ever seen—and will ever see—is "the head of the filing department, neat, quiet, attentive." His perception will never change because he will never really look.

When Martin leaves Mr. Fitweiler's office after Mrs. Barrows has been sent home, he has a moment of pleasure that makes his step "light and quick." Of course, no one sees it. By the time he reenters the filing department offices, he has resumed his usual step, and "a look of studious concentration." He will not share his triumph with anyone, and no one will notice that he is relieved. Martin's plan was to "rub out" Mrs. Barrows.

> " The next morning at the office, everyone is suddenly seeing everyone else; in one paragraph Thurber emphasizes seeing and not seeing."

In fact, Martin himself has already been rubbed out, erased and written over with the legend of Mrs. Barrows. No one really looks at him, or tries to learn about him, because they think they already know all there is to know. Martin was right: his plan will succeed because no one ever pays attention to anyone else.

Yet he should take no comfort in this. The sad thing about Erwin Martin is that he is invisible and alone every day—not just when he is hiding a murder plot—and he can't imagine any other way to live.

When Thurber wrote "The Catbird Seat" he had just undergone the last of five unsuccessful eye operations. He had lost one eye in an accident when he was a young boy, and now the other was stricken with cataracts and other ailments. Only in his forties, Thurber was practically blind, and he was forced to find new ways to write and to draw.

Not surprisingly, he responded to his condition by becoming withdrawn and depressed. If the story of Erwin Martin seems more bleak than Thurber's other tales of henpecked men, perhaps it is because the writer was struggling in his own life with questions of seeing and being seen.

Source: Cynthia Bily, for *Short Stories for Students*, Gale, 2000.

Burton Kendle

In the following essay, Kendle discusses the difficulties of translating literature into popular film, with specific attention to Thurber's "The Catbird Seat."

My pleasurable recognition of the Aged P, Dickens's lovable and thematically crucial character who doddered briefly across the screen in David Lean's *Great Expectations* (1946), generated a perplexing question. I wondered whether the movie image would have been meaningful to someone who had not spent the previous two weeks rereading and teaching the novel. This concern, added to others I felt about Lean's version, led me to a number of more general questions about the process of translating a work of fiction to film. Is a film adaptation an independent entity accessible to even an unlettered viewer, or does the adaptation exist primarily as an homage to, or even a series of illustrations from, the original? Such speculations inevitably involve assessments of the intrinsic worth of the literary work: are we perhaps relatively complacent about films that translate undistinguished novels like *The Godfather* or *Gone With the Wind,* and do we make unfair demands of films that adapt masterpieces like *The Brothers Karamazov?*

Soon after my disappointing experience with *Great Expectations*, I saw Charles Crichton's *The Battle of the Sexes* (1961), a screen version of James Thurber's story ''The Catbird Seat,'' for the first time in thirty years. My delighted response stimulated an assessment of my different reactions to the two films. Had I been less awed by Thurber's work than by Dickens's and therefore more accepting of Crichton's major changes in setting, plot, and tone? Why did Lean's highly regarded film with its brilliant visual effects and fine performances frustrate me? Perhaps a clue lay in the films' treatment of the grotesque comic elements of the originals, a treatment that raises key questions about the strengths and possibilities of the two forms, and the different problems of adapting novels and short stories to the screen. Thurber's small masterpiece of misogyny, an impressive example of the short story genre, brilliantly encapsulates his obsessive theme of male-female relationships and shrewdly creates a sense of the power dynamics of New York's business and social worlds (Dickens obviously has a broader canvas and room for fuller detailing in his picture of London). Just as Dickens challenges filmmakers to find a means of condensing the material without destroying the novel's richness, Thurber's brief story offers perhaps greater difficulties because of the small number of episodes from which it creates its world and because its cartoon-like characters might seem untranslatable to a full-length film. Crichton's adaptation raises the serious question of how to invent additional episodes while remaining true to the spirit of Thurber's original and how to seduce a sophisticated audience into spending time with outrageous comic stereotypes. . . .

Charles Crichton's version of Thurber's "The Catbird Seat" disarms criticism immediately. Though the film title, *The Battle of the Sexes*, sounds lurid, Thurber's story *does* focus on the planning of a perfect murder and culminates with the brutal heroine, an "industrial consultant," being pushed over the edge of sanity and apparently relegated to an institutional future by the milquetoastish protagonist, a clerk in the firm she plans to reorganize. (In Thurber's unpublished first version of the story, the clerk does successfully carry out the crime.) The material and characterizations are so exaggerated that they might seem more suited to a cartoon than to a film with human performers. In fact, Thurber's thematically similar "fable," "The Unicorn in the Garden," in which the hulking despotic wife of the mild-mannered protagonist is hauled off to the "booby-hatch," apparently as the result of his sly manipulation of her mental state (the seemingly strongest females are the most vulnerable in Thurber's cosmos), did become a brilliant UPA cartoon in the fifties. But Crichton and witty screenwriter-producer Monja Danischewsky have skillfully muted Thurber's grotesqueness without destroying the comedy. The film smoothly shifts Thurber's original Manhattan setting to Edinburgh after the significantly bow-tied American efficiency expert so offends even her American colleagues that they send her on a fact-finding mission to Scotland. Thurber's heroine, the uneuphoniously named Mrs. Ulgine Barrows (Mr. Barrows' fate is never mentioned) is more humanely rechristened Angela Barrows for the film. Though a reader might envision the American Hope Emerson or the British Peggy Mount in the role, the film wisely casts the Canadian-born Constance Cummings, who appeared in many undistinguished American movies of the thirties before settling in England and turning up every few years in with impressive performances in films like *Blithe Spirit* or plays like *Long Day's Journey Into Night* with Olivier. The stylish Cummings, whose couturier is listed in the credits, skillfully humanized Thurber's harridan and is sufficiently attractive to make plausible the budding gallantry of protagonist Peter Sellers at the end. The film thus successfully dramatizes the sexual tension in Thurber's power struggle and wittily implies the force of such tension in all male-female relations. Sellers's performance suggests the sly Alec Guinness persona of the Ealing comedies (Crichton had directed Guinness in *The Lavender Hill Mob*). But Sellers's fussy Scotsman is, in fact, overshadowed by Robert Morley, who upstages everyone by appearing a few times in kilts as Cummings's would-be suitor, a

> "... a clue lay in the films' treatment of the grotesque comic elements of the originals..."

character invented for the film. Morley's casting as a romantic rival suggests that the film's version of the gender wars will be, to put it mildly, idiosyncratic. From the film's opening shots of kilted bagpipers, as a voiccover calls Edinburgh "one of the last bastions of male supremacy, in which the shortest skirts are worn by men," the audience pleasurably senses that it is being controlled by master manipulators of stereotypes, both sexual and national.

Thurber's monstrous Mrs. Barrows, who "bawls," "snorts," metaphorically "swings at the firm's foundation stones with a pickax," "catapults through doorways," and governs many other violent verbs, becomes in the film an explicitly American phenomenon, Europe's punishment for Columbus's voyage. The brief appearance of a brash female American tourist with a timid husband in the showroom of the venerable weaving firm that is the Morley family business both supports the negative generalizations about domineering American women that structure the film and also makes Cummings less grotesquely cartoonish by contrast. Thus, she does not have to embody all the frightening American womanhood that terrorizes Thurber's hero and that Sellers and his co-workers feel as a perpetual threat. This altered image of Mrs. Barrows allows her a more humanized appearance and behavior. Like Thurber's original, she still does her share of braying: "If there is any night life in this dump, I haven't found it yet" is her ugly American assessment of Edinburgh. But she is really too attractive to make the audience comfortable laughing at her final breakdown and defeat, as can readers of the story. Some time after Sellers has successfully driven her from the firm and apparently from Morley's life, Sellers sees her as she walks tearfully, still unaccountably in Edinburgh (has the atmosphere of the city gotten to her despite its lack of night life?), and still elegantly dressed and carrying impressive shopping bags. He shyly offers her flowers, as the voiceover mentions man's greatest hazard, "a woman's tears."

Danischewsky and Crichton, having assessed what is workable in print as opposed to what is possible on film, obviously respect Thurber's material without necessarily venerating it and give it an individual, often hilarious spin. Surprisingly, most of the film's sexual comedy derives not from Cummings's potentially lethal relationship with Sellers, who rather overdoes his subdued slyness, but from her abortive courtship by Morley. After a stage success as Oscar Wilde, a role he repeated in a 1960 film, Morley established his essential screen persona in his first film, *Marie Antoinette* (1938), as Louis XVI, a physical and erotic disappointment to Norma Shearer's character. A successful paterfamilias in real life, Morley created a fussy, purse-lipped character who is perhaps less sexually ambiguous than infantilely pre-sexual, or at times, as *The Battle of the Sexes* wittily demonstrates, is too fastidious or hypochondriacal to let himself go in any way. The film begins its teasing of Morley's sexuality early on when, looking for the company chauffeur, he accosts the wrong man, ''Are you my chap?'' and receives a rude but amused response, ''No, I'm promised to another.''

Though the film derives a great deal of its humor from the spectacle of Morley as a suitor, it is equally fair (or unfair) to both sexes. The story's Mrs. Barrows seems the familiar hulking female of Thurber's cartoons. He never gives a detailed description of her, but Mrs. Barrows's barely-controlled violence of speech and behavior as she explodes into rooms and bellows baseball jargon (''Are you tearing up the pea patch? . . . Are you sitting in the catbird seat?'') suggests a threatening physical presence. In one bizarre episode she ''bounced'' in the protagonist's office and yelled ''Boo,'' a sign that she is aware both of her power to terrorize and of her cartoon origins. In softening but not eliminating this aggressive aspect of Mrs. Barrows, the film acknowledges that literary grotesques are difficult to make credible on film, which must deal with images of real people. Instead of deleting such comic exaggeration, as did Lean, Crichton balances the grotesque and the believably human. (The recent British television version of Muriel Spark's comic novel *Memento Mori* failed primarily because director/co-screenwriter Jack Clayton could not find appropriate visual equivalents for Spark's material. Clayton shied too far from confronting the physical and psychological breakdowns of a group of upper-class Londoners, a phenomenon that seems grimly amusing in the privacy of the reader's imagination but would be painful to watch on screen, especially when the actors are approximately the same age as the characters they portray. Clayton, who had directed *The Innocents* (1961), a fine adaptation of James's ''The Turn of the Screw,'' muted the humiliation of Spark's characters and imposed a comparatively happy ending on Spark's no-nonsense religious finale in an unsuccessful attempt to make her vision palatable to a mass audience. He was thus unable to sustain the balanced treatment of grotesques evident in Crichton's film.)

The Battle of the Sexes goes flaccid at times and fails to find a rhythm for the climactic farce sequence when Sellers tries to escape from Cummings's flat after his presumably serious attempts to kill her, and she tries to convince Morley that the teetotaling, non-smoking Sellers has really been there lighting cigarettes, drinking, talking of being coked to the gills (a phrase he learned from a film thriller), and making insulting comments about Morley. Sellers actually tried harder (and more farcically) to kill Cummings than does the story character, but the film's kinder, gentler atmosphere absorbs this material without turning Sellers into a monster. The wonderful dialogue, some transcribed from Thurber, some invented by screenwriter Danischewsky, redeems this episode, as it does the entire film. Cummings complains of Morley, ''Oh, but you're so helpless; if only there were a man here,'' a comment that both establishes her femininity and raises questions about both men. She had earlier, however, told Morley, to rebuff his unconvincing attempt at an embrace, ''I wish you wouldn't think of me as a woman—I'm your business partner.'' Sex, which motivates all three characters consciously and unconsciously, must thus compete, often unsuccessfully, with a variety of commercial and health concerns. Morley, who hypochondriacally keeps a thermometer on his office desk, is disturbed by a nude pre-Columbian statue which Cummings has purchased for his office, and which Sellers destroys, presumably because if offends *his* puritanism.

In the film's world of reversed and undercut sexual stereotypes, it is possible simultaneously to savor the cruelty of the comedy and to feel grudging compassion for the plight of the flustered characters, an effect that improves upon Thurber's more single-minded misogyny. Crichton and Danischewsky thus demonstrate appropriately humanized equivalents for Thurber's cartoonish exaggeration. Lean and his collaborators, on the other hand, in their laudable effort to convey the seriousness of Dickens's material, fail to recognize the crucial role of the comic grotesque in defining and enriching Dickens's world. By essentially eliminating such grotesqueness (Miss Havisham is the film's only example of the grotesque, but she is hardly comic), Lean both dilutes the richness of Dickens's world and ironically undercuts the seriousness of his themes.

Source: Burton Kendle, "Lean Dickens and Admirable Crichton: Film Adaptations of Literature" in *Michigan Academician*, Vol. XXVIII, No. 1, January 1996, pp. 19–27.

Marylyn Underwood

In the following essay, Underwood examines some of the deeper devices Thurber employs in the story.

Critics of James Thurber's "The Catbird Seat" invariably refer to his humorous tone, his control of language, and his effective characterization in this tight-plotting short story. But this is not all, one needs to dig deeper to unearth what devices Thurber uses to make this story the success it is. One device in particular has been overlooked by critics. A biologist would not have been so negligent: he would have looked at the catbird's *seat* and would have seen an instant correlation to the events and characters in Thurber's story.

Anyone who picks up a copy of Peterson's *A Field Guide to the Birds of Texas* (Boston: Houghton Mifflin, 1963) will find on page 182 a description of the catbird. This bird is unobtuse, "skulks in undergrowth," and is hard to rile. However, upon being disturbed, it will come out from the underbrush, where it meshes with its environment because of its drab coloring, and will flare its tail feathers, showing a rusty tuft of seat (or "under tail-coverts") to the cause of its disturbance.

This description is significant to understanding Thurber's short story. Consider who is first "sitting in the catbird's seat" or "sitting pretty"—Mrs. Ulgine Barrows, an upstart, a new-comer, a defiler, an intruder in the territory of Erwin Martin. That her name sounds much like *sparrows* is equally significant. Note the imported sparrow's characteristics: a little gray bird that takes territory away from the domestic bird by "settling in" noisily, eating the seeds of the domestic, and making, literally, a mess of the former domestic bird's habitat. The sparrow, with its conical-shaped short bill, is quick and effective in pecking away the foundations of the former owner's home. Soon only sparrows inhabit the territory, the take-over complete.

> "Mr Martin, astute as he is austere, comprehends this eventuality, but, like the catbird, remains quiet and unobtuse--until she invades his territory."

Mrs. Ulgine Barrows is "sitting in the catbird's seat," flaunting her tail (if you will) in the face of everyone in the office of F&S. She is an import, having been brought in by Mr. Fitweiler. She "eats the seeds" of the employees at F&S, taking from them the sustenance, the employment that has been theirs for years. Aggressive as an efficiency expert, she has several fired, others just quit. If she is not stopped, the very foundations of F&S will crumble. Mr. Martin, astute as he is austere, comprehends this eventuality, but, like the catbird, remains quiet and unobtuse—until she invades his territory.

Consider now Mr. Martin and the connotations inherent in his name. The martin is a member of the swallow family, a small gray bird with long wings, a forked tail, swift and graceful flight. *Swallowtail* is a term for *cutaway,* a man's formal coat with tails. Indeed, it is easy to imagine Mr. Martin clad in a cutaway, as he is precise in nature, impeccable in character, and haughty in his regard for his occupation and position.

Mr. Fitweiler innocently brings Mrs. Barrow to his firm—as if in a *fit* (defined as "a sudden, acute attack" and "a highly emotional reaction") to the F&S *weiler* or *hamlet.* Also innocently, he allows her to quack and bray commands, yell and bawl obscenities, and chip and pick "at the foundation stones" of F&S. Thurber's descriptive terms of Ulgine Barrows are similar to the terms used to describe the calls of yet another bird—the cuckoo-burro—which is distinguished by a raucous, braying, laughing call that approximates the ass for which it is appropriately named (as is apparently Mrs. Barrows).

Barrows' asininity does not concern Mr. Martin, though it bothers him; but her invasion of his territory does, to the extent that he plans his strategy which he changes at the last minute. Instead of "rubbing her out," he flaunts his tail jauntily by being obnoxious, by exhibition of characteristics not his own. In short, he shows a color heretofore covert. When the deed's done, he very unobtrusively returns to his underbrush, the W20 file, "wearing a look of studious concentration," while his antagonist is removed from the coveted "catbird's seat."

Source: Marylyn Underwood, "Thurber's 'The Catbird Seat'" in *The Explicator,* Vol. 40, No. 4, summer 1982, pp. 49–50.

Sources

Benét, William Rose, "Carnival with Spectres," in the *Saturday Review of Literature*, February 3, 1945, p. 9.

Bier, Jesse, *The Rise and Fall of American Humor*, New York: Holt, Rinehart and Winston, 1968, p. 224.

Butcher, Fanny, "His Unique Art Reaches Wider Public," in *Chicago Tribune Books*, February 4, 1945, n.p.

Cowley, Malcolm, "James Thurber's Dream Book," in the *New Republic*, March 12, 1945, pp. 362–363.

Dias, Earl J., "The Upside-Down World of Thurber's 'The Catbird Seat,'" in *CEA Critic*, February, 1968, pp. 6–7.

Elias, Robert H., "James Thurber: The Primitive, the Innocent, and the Individual," in *Thurber: A Collection of Critical Essays*, edited by Charles S. Holmes, Englewood Cliffs, NJ: Prentice-Hall, 1974, p. 97.

Holmes, Charles S., Introduction to *Thurber: A Collection of Critical Essays*, Englewood Cliffs, NJ: Prentice-Hall, 1974, p. 4.

Kane, Thomas S., "A Note on the Chronology of 'The Catbird Seat,'" in *CEA Critic*, April 1968, pp. 8–9.

Kenney, Catherine McGehee, *Thurber's Anatomy of Confusion*, Hamden, CT: Archon Books, 1984, p. 62, 148.

Morsberger, Robert E., *James Thurber*, New York: Twayne, 1964, n.p.

"On the Thurber Trail," in *Times Literary Supplement*, November 3, 1945, p. 520.

Underwood, Marylyn, "Thurber's 'The Catbird Seat'", in *Explicator*, Summer, 1982, pp. 49–50.

Further Reading

Bowden, Edwin T., *James Thurber: A Bibliography*, Columbus: Ohio State University Press, 1968.
    This valuable resource lists and describes every known writing and drawing published by Thurber in books and magazines, including those in translation.

Kinney, Harrison, *James Thurber: His Life and Times*, New York: Henry Holt and Company, 1995.
    Considered the definitive biography of Thurber.

Long, Robert Emmet, *James Thurber*, New York: Continuum Publishing, 1988.
    An overview of Thurber's life and works, more useful for its observances of common themes and contexts than for its discussion of any individual work.

Morsberger, Robert E., *James Thurber*, New York: Twayne, 1964.
    Published three years after Thurber's death, this overview was the first book-length study of his work. It was also the first serious attempt place Thurber among America's great writers.

Thurber, James, *The Years with Ross*, Boston: Atlantic Monthly Press, 1959.
    A memoir of Thurber's years writing for *The New Yorker* under the guidance of Harold Ross, who edited the magazine from 1925 until his death in 1951.

Toombs, Sarah Eleanora, *James Thurber: An Annotated Bibliography of Criticism*, New York: Garland, 1987.
    A well-organized and thorough listing of over one thousand books, articles, and reviews discussing Thurber's writings, drawings, plays and productions.

Death in the Woods

Sherwood Anderson
1933

Sherwood Anderson published early versions of "Death in the Woods" as a sketch in *A Story-Teller's Story* (1924) and as a chapter in his autobiographical *Tar: A Midwest Childhood* (1926). He worked on "Death in the Woods" periodically for nine years before publishing it in final form as the title story in his 1933 collection *Death in the Woods and Other Stories.*

According to many critics, Anderson's artistic powers were waning at this point in his career; yet "Death in the Woods" stands out as a masterpiece, paralleling the brilliance of the stories collected in his best known work, *Winesburg, Ohio.*

"Death in the Woods" chronicles the deceptively simple story of the life and death of a poor and downtrodden farm woman. The narrator, an adolescent boy at the time of these events, observes her dead body—a formative moment in his development as a man and an artist. He puts together the pieces of her story, which takes on mystery and mythic meaning as he reflects back on it years later.

"Death in the Woods" exemplifies Anderson's pared-down writing style and brooding, bittersweet tone. The story is most notable for the stark simplicity of its subject matter and the contrasting intricacy of its self-conscious narration.

Author Biography

Anderson was born on September 13, 1876, in Camden, Ohio. In his early years, his large family moved frequently and struggled with poverty. When Anderson was eight, the family settled in Clyde, Ohio, the small town that became the model for his famous book *Winesburg, Ohio* and the setting for many of his other writings. From a young age, Anderson was an ambitious, responsible, and enterprising fellow.

At the age of nineteen, Anderson left Clyde for Chicago, where he worked as a laborer and fell in love with the city. For the rest of his life, he would always be torn between the excitement of life in the big city and the charms of small-town life.

Anderson served in the Army during the Spanish-American War and then studied at Wittenberg Academy for a year before returning to Chicago to work as an advertising copywriter. After twelve years and much success in the advertising field, he married and started his own business in the town of Elyria, Ohio.

It was during these years in Elyria that Anderson first began to write. With his business and marriage failing, he had a nervous breakdown in 1912. Two years later, he got divorced and moved back to Chicago to begin his career as a fiction writer.

In Chicago he fell in with an influential circle of writers, such as Floyd Dell, Carl Sandburg, Burton Rascoe, and Robert Morss Lovett. He wrote his first novel and began the stories that were to be published as *Winesburg, Ohio* in 1919.

With *Winesburg, Ohio* Anderson was recognized as one of the most important American writers of his generation. He soon made his first trip to Europe and met literary luminaries such as Gertrude Stein and James Joyce. Anderson also became an instrumental mentor for younger modernist writers William Faulkner and Ernest Hemingway, who were soon to eclipse him in stature.

Anderson never matched the triumph of *Winesburg, Ohio*. He continued to publish prolifically, but seldom with great success. In the 1920s Anderson bought two newspapers and became involved in labor politics, championing the proletarian cause. He died in 1941 during a trip to South America.

Plot Summary

The narrator of "Death in the Woods" introduces the central character of the story: an anonymous old woman who periodically comes to town to sell a few eggs and buy a few supplies. The woman is known only by her last name, Grimes.

The story is the narrator's fictionalized account of her life and death, focusing on one fateful trip into town.

The narrator recounts what he knows of Mrs. Grimes's background, things that "must have stuck in my mind from small-town tales when I was a boy." The old woman's husband, Jake Grimes, was a known horse thief. He came from a family that had once been prosperous, but Jake and his father had squandered their money.

Jake met his wife when she was a young "bound girl," an orphan working for a German farmer in exchange for her room and board. There were rumors that the farmer sexually harassed and perhaps even raped the girl. Jake came to work for the farmer and began to take the girl out. The farmer caught them, and he and Jake fought. The girl confided in Jake about the farmer's abuse.

Jake married the girl out of defiance toward the farmer. They had a son and a daughter, but only the son survived. She settled into a life of caring for the animals on their impoverished farmstead and making sure there was food for her husband and son.

Jake's threshing business failed because of his dishonest reputation, so he resorted to cutting firewood at a small profit. Jake and his son went on trips and got drunk together while the woman tried to manage the small farm. She no longer was intimate with her husband or even spoke to him. Not yet forty years of age, she had begun to look old.

One winter day, Mrs. Grimes went into town with a few eggs to trade in exchange for some supplies. She went to the butcher to beg for some meat scraps for the family dogs that accompanied her. The butcher was kind to her and expressed anger at her husband and son for letting her go out on such a cold and snowy day. It was the first time anyone had spoken to her warmly in a long time.

The woman set out for home with the heavy grain bag of food on her back. She decided to take a shortcut through some woods in the hope of getting home before dark. Part of the way through, she stopped to rest in a small clearing and fell asleep under a tree. She would never wake up from that sleep.

The four dogs that accompanied the old woman were used to foraging for food, so they killed a few rabbits while she slept. Excited, they began to play and circle the woman, beating a track in the snow around her in a "kind of death ceremony." One at a time they came up to the woman and stuck their noses into her face, waiting for her to die.

When she eventually died there in her sleep, the dogs dragged the woman out of the clearing by the grain bag tied to her back—tearing her dress but leaving her body intact—and took the food out of the bag.

The narrator recounts hearing that a local hunter had found a dead body in the woods. The narrator and his brother accompany the town marshal and a party of men as they go out and investigate. They know that they will be late for supper but choose to go because "we would have something to tell." The hunter reports that the body belonged to a beautiful young girl.

When they get there they view the body—the first naked woman the narrator has ever seen. Frozen in the snow, the old woman looks young and lovely. The boys return home, and the narrator's brother tells the dramatic story of the body in the woods. The narrator isn't satisfied with his brother's account, but says nothing.

Mrs. Grimes's body is not identified until the next day. The narrator hears fragments of her life story around town. He says that the story was something he had to pick up slowly over time, "like music heard from far off." Years later he remembers and recounts the story of her death.

Sherwood Anderson

Characters

The Butcher

The butcher is the last person to talk to Mrs. Grimes before she dies. Taking pity on her, he gives her a generous portion of meat that makes her pack too heavy and causes her to stop and rest in the cold.

The German Farmer

The German farmer once hired Mrs. Grimes as a "bound girl," which meant that she lived on his farm, cooked for him, and fed his animals. She suffered from his unwanted sexual advances until she married Jack Grimes.

Jake Grimes

Jake Grimes is married to Mrs. Grimes. He is a profligate, a drunk, and a known horse thief. Jake counts on his wife to make ends meet at their small farm, and does not contribute to the family economy. He expects her to provide for him and treats her with indifference or cruelty; the marriage is a loveless one. After Mrs. Grimes dies, the townspeople suspect Jake and his son of wrongdoing. Though they have alibis, they are banished from the town.

Mrs. Grimes

"Death in the Woods" chronicles the story of a woman, known as Mrs. Grimes, who lives on the outskirts of town. The narrator recounts her sad history as a "bound girl" and an abused wife as a background to the story's central drama—the events surrounding her freezing to death in the woods and the ensuing discovery of her body.

The old woman is the story's central character, but she remains an enigma because her life experiences are filtered through the narrator's consciousness; therefore we know that the narrator has filled in the gaps with experiences from his own life.

Anderson is known for creating characters based on the concept of the "grotesque." While the word *grotesque*—meaning something that is outlandishly or incongruously distorted—normally has a negative connotation, Anderson viewed such distortion or imbalance sympathetically, as part of the human condition.

In some ways, the old woman is a grotesque. Her life—as the narrator views it—revolves around the feeding of animal life. With other people, she is uncommunicative and isolated. However, in her death she becomes a mythic figure that represents womanhood.

The Hunter

The hunter discovers the old woman's dead body in the woods. He reports that the body belonged to a "beautiful young girl."

The Marshal

The marshal leads a party of men to the site in the woods where the hunter found the body. He questions the hunter and initially suspects murder.

The Narrator

The narrator is a boy growing up in the town near where Mrs. Grimes lived. He did not know her personally but reports the facts of her life and death. He passes along information that he has heard, as well as recounting a few experiences as a direct observer—most notably, the discovery of the woman's body in the woods.

Viewing the body has a strong impact on him: it is the first naked woman's body that he has ever seen and he, like the others, perceives her as beautiful and young. When he and his brother return home that night, it is his brother who reports what happened.

The narrator is dissatisfied with his brother's rendering of the story, and this is his motivation for retelling the story in its current form years later, when he is an adult. The narrator admits that he added details from his own experience until Mrs. Grimes's story becomes something "complete" and thus beautiful.

The Narrator's Brother

The narrator's brother is delivering papers when word reaches town about a woman's body found in the woods. He joins the party rather than finishing his task and knows that this will make him late for supper. When the narrator and his brother return home, it is the brother who recounts the remarkable events.

Old Woman

See Mrs. Grimes

Old Woman's Son

The old woman's son is nameless throughout the story. Like his father, he gets drunk and treats the old woman like a servant. The son has a sexual relationship with a "rough" woman that he conducts under his mother's nose. She is not particularly offended, having "got past being shocked early in life."

Themes

Human vs. Animal

The main theme of the story, as described by the narrator, concerns Mrs. Grimes's aim to "feed animal life"—including both humans and animals. She spends her life trying to sustain other life forms.

In other words, she feeds the German farmer and his wife, her husband and son, and the animals on their farm, making no particular distinction between them. The men in her life are crude, self-absorbed, abusive, not significantly different from animals.

Mrs. Grimes is an outsider in the town; therefore it seems natural that she dies in the woods, surrounded by dogs. In turn, the dogs are endowed with civilized, almost human qualities. Anderson even assigns dialogue to them: "Now we are no longer wolves. We are dogs, the servants of men. Keep alive, man! When man dies we become wolves again." Moreover, the dogs do not eat the woman's body when she dies, which preserves the human/animal distinction.

In life, the woman goes unnoticed by the townspeople. In death, she becomes an object of fascination for the narrator as he grows up and remembers and reconstructs her story. The events of her simple life take on mystery and beauty as the narrator crafts them into art, a high expression of humanity.

Sex Roles

The old woman's role as a provider of food is closely tied to her gender role. Feeding is conventionally seen as woman's work. There is no emotional, nurturing quality to her constant feeding of others; in fact, she views this role as a duty and a burden.

Nevertheless, the fact that she provides sustenance is closely associated with femininity and women's biological role in gestating and nursing babies. Some critics have interpreted the woman as an "earth mother," representing the sustenance offered by a feminized nature. However, this is a dark portrait of Mother Nature as a powerless, passive woman forced to endure the abuse of men.

The theme of woman's role as a provider of food is echoed by her role as an object of sexual desire. Feeding even becomes a metaphor for sex: "Thank heaven, she did not have to feed her husband—in a certain way. That hadn't lasted long after their marriage and after the babies came." Sex is another form of providing for the physical needs of the men around her. The woman's sexuality is prematurely depleted, as her hard life and loveless marriage render her old before her time.

In death it is restored. Her slight, frozen body looks young again, and both the hunter and the narrator see her as a beautiful object of desire. In this sense, she can be understood as representing an idea or prototype of Woman in all of the phases of her life cycle.

Since this was the first naked woman's body that the narrator had ever seen, her representation of womanhood is crucial to the development of his own adolescent sexuality. As Jon S. Lawry writes in *PMLA,* viewing her body in the snow is, for the narrator, "no mere event, but rather definition for him of the mystery and beauty of woman."

Topics for Further Study

- Do you find Mrs. Grimes a sympathetic character? Why or why not? Cite specific passages from the text to support your point of view.

- The narrator states that it was the woman's destiny to "feed animal life." Do you feel that this adequately explains the significance of the story? What are some of the other ideas and themes present in "Death in the Woods"?

- Critics have suggested that Anderson's writing style was influenced by post-impressionist artists Paul Cezanne, Vincent van Gogh, and Paul Gaugin. Do some research into these artists' ideas about perception. How do they relate to the style of "Death in the Woods"—particularly, the narrator's changing perceptions of the old woman?

- In his preface to *Winesburg, Ohio* Anderson describes his characters as "grotesques." Research some critical responses to Anderson's idea of "the grotesque" and relate your findings to "Death in the Woods." How does this concept help you to understand Anderson's portrayal of the old woman?

Truth and Fiction

"Death in the Woods" is a story within a story that comments upon the creative process. The narrator recounts Mrs. Grimes's life; yet he also reflects on his status and qualifications as a narrator, telling, in effect, the story of how he came to understand and relate the story in its present form.

The narrator is both a witness and participant in some of the events of the story—most notably, the discovery of the body—but he makes it clear that the old woman's tale is closer to fiction than truth. Most of the story he has either heard secondhand or extrapolated from his own experiences. Interrupting his narration of the old woman's past, he interjects, "I wonder how I know all of this. It must have stuck in my mind from small-town tales when I was a boy."

He initially claims that he has little knowledge of the woman, and he admits that details of the story were "picked up slowly, long afterwards," from his own experiences. Yet as he relates the story years later, he deems it "the real story"—more complete and satisfying than the version his brother told on the night the body was discovered. His story—crafted and fictionalized—transcends anecdote and becomes a thing of beauty, mystery, and meaning.

Style

Point of View

Point of view is probably the most striking and significant stylistic feature of "Death in the Woods."

The story is narrated in the first person by a man looking back on an event that happened in his hometown when he was a youth.

At first his qualifications for telling the old woman's story seem somewhat dubious. The narrator is limited in his view of events—a fact that he frequently calls to his readers' attention. To him, the old woman was "nothing special. She was one of the nameless ones that hardly anyone knows, but she got into my thoughts. I have just suddenly now, after all these years, remembered her and what happened." He initially describes the old woman only as a type, not an individual, and admits that his sources of information are not particularly reliable.

Much of the old woman's past he recounts based on anecdotes and gossip and experiences of his own that he later merges with her story. For example, he recalls seeing Jake Grimes at the local livery barn and quotes his speech, only to admit, "He did not say anything, actually. 'I'd like to bust one of you on the jaw,' was about what his eyes said. I remember how the look in his eyes made me shiver."

The narrator feels a need to understand the woman's life and death. Eventually, he finds beauty in the "completion" he is finally able to bring to the story *as* a story, without regard to its factual accuracy. Just as important as this thematic "completion" is the mystery and resonance the story gains through the narrator's own personal investment in its symbolic significance.

The narration of "Death in the Woods" shows how a formative moment in the narrator's personal experience acquires meaning over time. Anderson's subtle manipulation of point of view highlights the fiction-making process and illustrates how an active imagination can create mystery and beauty.

Structure

"Death in the Woods" does not just tell the old woman's tale, but *re*-tells it. Thus its structure is based on repetition, which may begin to explain why several critics have described the story as being similar in form to a poem.

At the first telling of the story, the narrator's brother gives an unsatisfactory version of the story while the narrator remained silent. Thus the whole text can be understood as the narrator's retelling of that initial, formative, unprocessed experience that he could not articulate. "The whole thing, the story of the old woman's death, was to me as I grew older

like music heard from far off. The notes had to be picked up slowly one at a time. Something had to be understood," reads the narrator's famous reflection on the his impulse to retell.

Lawry suggests that "Death in the Woods" is structured by "the narrator's progress from recorder to creator." It opens with the narrator's account of a certain type of old woman, describing trips into town and characterizing her as "nothing special." This is the first and most brief telling of the old woman's tale, from which little meaning is derived.

His authority to tell the story grows as he describes climactic scene of her death. "I knew about it all afterward, when I grew to be a man, because once in the woods in Illinois, on another winter night, I saw a pack of dogs act just like that." As he adds scenes and parallels from his own life to Mrs. Grimes's story he becomes a creator of her story.

Historical Context

Anderson's Midwest

When Anderson wrote "Death in the Woods," the modernist literary movement was raging; many American writers took up explicitly modern themes—such as the disenfranchisement of the middle-class during the Industrial Revolution and effect of technological change on human existence—to explore the distinctive experiences, mores, and sensibilities of the early twentieth century.

Anderson is unique because his writing style is decidedly modern—his pared-down style is often compared to that of modernist giants Gertrude Stein and Ernest Hemingway—but his subject matter is not. To the contrary, Anderson's stories appear to take place in something of a historical vacuum. While many modernists gathered in and wrote about the world's cosmopolitan cities—Paris, London, New York—Anderson wrote about life in the American Midwest.

"Death in the Woods" takes place in a Midwestern town, likely based on Anderson's childhood home of Clyde, Ohio. In the 1890s, Clyde was a town of a few thousand people on the brink of expansion and modernization. It had its own respectable institutions and cultural events, but its streets weren't paved and had no electric streetlights. It was, in the words of biographer Kim Townsend, "still a frontier town."

Compare & Contrast

- **1930s:** American women have a life expectancy of sixty-five years, five years longer than their male counterparts.

  Today: Women in the United States still outlive men by approximately five years, though life expectancies have changed (female life expectancy is seventy-nine years, male life expectancy is seventy-four years of age).

- **1930s:** For generations the United States has been become an increasingly industrial and urban society. However, as a result of the Great Depression, for the first time in decades there is a reverse in the rural-urban migration pattern, with slightly more people leaving cities and returning to their towns of origin.

  Today: A movement called "new urbanism" or "neo-traditionalism" seeks to restore the small-town American way of life. Disney designs and builds an entire town, Celebration, Florida, based on old-fashioned city planning and social values.

- **1930s:** The United States ceases to be a primarily agricultural nation, but 25% of the population still lives on farms. There are 6,300 farms in the United States. Most farms are 50–99 acres, but more farmers live on small farms of less than ten acres than live large farms of more than a thousand.

  Today: There are approximately 2,000 farms in the United States. The farm population has dropped to approximately two percent of the total population of the country. Most food is grown on huge "factory farms" owned by corporations.

- **1930s:** Working women have little protection against sexual harassment. In fact, the courts do not name sexual harassment as an illegal form of discrimination until 1976.

  Today: Sexual harassment is a public issue in workplaces across the country, where strict new anti-harassment policies are introduced and implemented.

Anderson recalled it as a warm and intimate community where people knew and looked after each other. These qualities were becoming scarce by the time Anderson began to write about his Midwestern childhood, and his representations are always tinged with nostalgia for a way of life on the verge of extinction.

Autobiographical Connections

A different version of "Death in the Woods" appeared as part of Anderson's autobiography, *Tar: A Midwest Childhood.* Beside the story's small-town setting, there are other significant autobiographical elements to the story.

In many of Anderson's writings he expresses hostility toward his good-for-nothing father and sympathy for his long-suffering mother. In "Death in the Woods," the Grimes marriage can be seen as an exaggeration of the dynamics between Anderson's parents: Anderson's father, Irwin, was unable to hold a steady job; he drank too much; cheated on his wife; and would disappear for days on end. During these times, his mother Emma kept the impoverished family warm and fed. "Emma was continually providing," Townsend writes. She died of tuberculosis when Anderson was eighteen.

Another parallel between the woman in "Death in the Woods" and Emma Anderson is Anderson's description of his mother as having been a "bound girl," rejected by her own mother and sent to work to support herself until adulthood. His account of his mother's youth (which may not be factually accurate) has striking similarities to the history of the woman in the story.

"Our mother had been so bound out, to some farming family somewhere in the southern part of the state of Ohio, and my father, no doubt then a young dandy, had found her there and married her,'' Anderson writes in his *Memoirs.*

He describes his mother's life:

> She must have worked, all her life, even from child-hood, for others, a childhood and young girlhood of washing dishes, swilling cows, of waiting at table, a kind of half-servant in a house of strangers to her own blood, only after marriage and children to become a wash woman.

Townsend considers Anderson's lifelong interest in working women and his attitude toward women in general as a direct result of his unresolved feelings toward his mother. "He would always think of her as Woman, a figure who inspired him to do good, to write," Townsend writes. "If he could not approach her when she was alive, he would approach her through his works."

Critical Overview

A prolific writer, Anderson published eight novels, four collections of short stories, autobiographical works, poems, plays, and essays. Critics agree that his reputation rests on his influential short fiction, although his stories seem to range greatly in quality.

Anderson published his most important and influential work, *Winesburg, Ohio,* when he was forty-three years of age. By 1926, after two novels were panned by the critics, his critical reputation suffered. Although Anderson's style is modernist, his themes and subject matter are not, which led him to be considered as old-fashioned or irrelevant before his time.

Soon after Anderson's death, there was a renewed critical interest in his work. In the 1940s several anthologies of his fiction appeared and the first two biographies of Anderson were published. In his critical study *Sherwood Anderson,* Rex Burbank asserted, "No other writer has portrayed so movingly the emerging consciousness of the culturally underprivileged Midwesterner with neither condescension nor satiric caricature."

The fact that Anderson's reputation was in decline may have influenced the early reviews of 1933's *Death in the Woods and Other Stories.* Reviewers of the book were tepid in their praise.

"This collection of short stories neither augment nor diminish the affection with which America regards Sherwood Anderson," maintained T. S. Matthews of the *New Republic.*

Matthews continued: "The almost childish unevenness of his performance, shown in most of his earlier books, is echoed in *Death in the Woods;* but as almost always there are compensating high spots."

Many critics singled out the title story as one such "high spot." As Louis Kronenberger contended: "In a few of the short stories here there are a simplicity and tenderness, there are evocations of phrases and moments in American life which, as things go, are the real thing."

In the opinion of Ray Lewis White, editor of *The Achievement of Sherwood Anderson:*

> In only one case were critics of Anderson's later work seriously wrong in their judgment. *Death in the Woods* (1933), Anderson's last collection of short stories, contains works that are among our finest short fiction. . . . Perhaps because these were stories and not extended writing, Anderson recaptured the tender charm of *Winesburg, Ohio, The Triumph of the Egg,* and *Horses and Men.*

Other critics also consider this volume as one of Anderson's best, and singled out "Death in the Woods" for special praise. Writing in the introduction to the *Portable Sherwood Anderson,* Horace Gregory described the story as a "masterpiece":

> Beyond any other story that Anderson wrote," Gregory opines, ["Death in the Woods"] "was the summing up of a lifetime's experience, and in its final version it became Anderson's last look backward into the Middle West of his childhood."

Recent Anderson criticism has explored the themes and mechanics of the story, with special attention to the narrator's point of view. Writing in *PMLA,* Jon S. Lawry offered an extended interpretation of the narrator's complex relation to his subject:

> The creative narrator is not, as is usually the case with narrators in Anderson's stories, involved with his subject through personal concerns, familial relation, or friendship. The distance between them, however, serves to enhance their sympathetic contact; they have only disinterested humanity in common.

David R. Mesher also focused on the underlying importance of the "narrator-turned-creator," who openly admits that he has "fabricated the most important elements of the story he is telling" and "projects the reality of his own psychology onto the history of his subject."

Criticism

Sarah Madsen Hardy,

Madsen Hardy has a doctorate in English literature and is a freelance writer and editor. In the following essay, she discusses Anderson's ideas about what is commonplace and what is beautiful as expressed in "Death in the Woods."

"Death in the Woods" opens with a description of its central character, the old woman, as a familiar type that anyone from a small town would recognize. She is a common and simple woman who lives on the outskirts of town, coming there only occasionally to beg and barter for a few supplies.

The narrator initially characterizes Mrs. Grimes as "nothing special." She is not known personally to anyone in the community, and, being such a familiar figure, she is easy to ignore. "People drive right down a road and never notice a woman like that."

Having emphasized her anonymity, the narrator then goes on to tell and retell her tale, which, by the end of the story, has taken on mythic proportion. The imagined scene of her death is full of solemn mystery, and the meaning of her life is revealed as transcendent.

In his introduction to *The Portable Sherwood Anderson,* Horace Gregory calls the story "universal," praising Anderson's skill in "giving the so-called common experiences of familiar, everyday life an aura of internal meaning." Through reconstructing her tale over time, the narrator transforms an old woman's life and death into a piece of art.

In his work Anderson focused on the lives of simple and downtrodden people as his subjects, often representing them as the embodiment of a kind of purity and integrity that he saw as becoming increasingly rare in modern American life. He is praised by critics for a deceptively simple, declarative writing style that had a great influence on Ernest Hemingway, the modernist writer most famous for simple, spare prose.

As opposed to his worldly contemporaries, who also wrote in this modern style, Anderson considered himself provincial and unsophisticated. In his most famous book, *Winesburg, Ohio,* Anderson uses a youthful, autobiographical narrator who denies his own artistry in statements such as, "It needs the poet here," implying that his own descriptions are nothing special.

"Death in the Woods" shares with *Winesburg* a plain-speaking narrative voice and descriptions that are short, direct, and free of figurative language. However, in this story the narrator has become confident in his storytelling capabilities—someone who knows what a powerful story is and how to tell it beautifully.

Like his narrator, Anderson came back to the story again and again over a period of many years. He first drafted a version of "Death in the Woods" on the back of the manuscript to *Winesburg, Ohio,* which was published in 1919. He published significantly different versions of the story in *A Story-Teller's Story* and *Tar: A Midwest Childhood,* where it was presented as a sketch and an autobiographical anecdote respectively.

Neither of these versions is equal the artistry of the final version. In the final version, which was published as a short story in a volume of the same name, the mature narrator reflects on the artist's role in giving form and meaning to his commonplace subject matter.

So how does such a modest character as the old woman acquire such mythic stature? And how does a mere anecdote come to be retold as something "complete," with meaning that transcends its specific place and time? One can fruitfully explore these questions by focusing on Anderson's description of the recovery of the old woman's body from the woods clearing where she died. "The scene in the forest had become for me, without my knowing it, the foundation for the real story I am now trying to tell," the narrator says.

This scene is transformational to the narrator as a man, in terms of the development of his idea of womanhood. It is also transformational to him as an artist, in terms of the development of his ideas of what makes a powerful story. Both of these issues involve questions of aesthetics—that is, questions about what is defined as beautiful. Thus there is an implicit parallel between the narrator's struggle to understand female and literary beauty.

Important to Anderson's complex idea of womanhood is the issue of sexuality. Though it may be hard for contemporary readers to believe, in his time Anderson was known for his shockingly direct discussions of sex.

In "Death in the Woods," Anderson demystifies sexuality through his narrator's descriptions of the woman's difficult life. He frankly describes how the woman, as a young "bound girl," was nearly raped

What Do I Read Next?

- *Winesburg, Ohio* (1919), Anderson's collection of interlocking short stories set in a fictionalized Midwestern town, is considered his finest work.

- *The Triumph of the Egg* (1921) is another classic short story collection written by Anderson. The fable-like title story is narrated by a child who openly fictionalizes an account of his father's failures.

- Written by Theodore Dreiser, *An American Tragedy* (1925) traces the downfall of Clyde Griffiths. The story is a scathing indictment of American materialist values.

- *Main Street* (1920), a novel by Sinclair Lewis, chronicles the story of a big-city girl who marries a small-town doctor. Lewis gently satirizes the provincial Minnesota setting, which is based on his own hometown.

- *The Nick Adams Stories* (1972) are Ernest Hemingway's famous semi-autobiographical stories about his boyhood set mainly in rural Michigan. The Nick Adam stories were influenced by Anderson, sharing with his works autobiographical themes and simple language.

---

by her employer. "He tore her dress down the front. The German, she said, might have got her that time if he hadn't heard his old woman drive in at the gate." He is matter of fact about her son's disrespectfully flagrant affair with a "rough enough woman, a tough one." Also he describes her relief at no longer having to be intimate with her husband.

Here, sexuality is base and ugly. It is represented as nothing more than an inevitable part of the cycle of "animal life" in which the woman is trapped. Beauty, it would seem, has nothing to do with it.

Furthermore, the woman herself is characterized as so negligible that it is not even necessary to describe her appearance or to say that she isn't beautiful. From the start, she is described as *old* and, implicitly, sexually irrelevant, despite the fact that she is barely middle-aged.

However, later in the story the woman undergoes a strange transformation that renders her young, beautiful, and eerily alluring—she dies. The narrator and his brother join a party of men who go out into the woods clearing where a hunter has discovered the body of an unidentified woman, which he describes as that of a "beautiful young girl." When they arrive, they see her naked body and he, along with the others in the party, also perceives her as beautiful. This is the first time he has ever seen a woman's naked body.

In death, which usually corrupts the body, the woman is instead restored to youthful perfection—at least in the collective imagination of the town's men. "It may have been the snow, clinging to the frozen flesh, that made it look so white and lovely, so like marble."

Whiteness is associated with purity, and marble suggests the idealized nudes of ancient sculpture. She has become an aesthetic object, transformed by the projected ideas and desires of the community of men as much as by the cold and snow.

The old woman is unknown when she trudges into town on her thankless chore, and she is equally unknown when her youthful-looking body is reverentially carried back to town. Yet she has been completely transformed from a base and sexless beast of burden into a tragic and mysterious beauty. These are two crucial and opposing ways that men see women that the narrator must try hard to piece together as he grows into a man.

The woman's transformation in turn transforms the young narrator. "She did not look old, lying there in that light, frozen and still. One of the men turned her over in the snow and I saw everything."

In viewing her, the narrator glimpses two of life's darkest and most essential secrets—that of sexuality and that of death.

This startling vision has the quality of a revelation. He sees ''everything''—which makes sense both as a boy's embarrassed way of describing her nudity and as a statement about how the scene marked the end of his childish innocence, forever altering his outlook on the world.

He goes on, ''My body trembled with some strange mystical feeling and so did my brother's. It might have been the cold,'' which has a similar effect of mixing literal-minded and transcendental interpretations of the experience. Throughout the story, Anderson offers such a dual perspective—romanticizing his plain subject matter and de-romanticizing it at once.

Like the woman, the narrator's rendition of her story is transformed from something simple and crude into something transcendent and beautiful. He recognizes right off that the experience has the makings of a good story—''something to tell. A boy did not get such a chance very often.''

However, he also cannot tell it completely—in a way he considers authentic and therefore beautiful—until he has matured. And this, like the woman's transformation, is not a matter of uncovering objective truth, but of seeing in the crude and commonplace glimpses of beauty.

The narrator needed to wait to tell her story in order to reconstruct it, ''like music hear from far off,'' from a combination of observation, hearsay, and empathetic conjecture. In his viewing of her dead body and his retelling of her story, the ''real'' beauty that is found is not objective, but created in the eye and imagination of the beholder.

While Anderson has sometimes been denigrated as a ''primitive'' artist—vivid but naive in his representations of simple subject matter—''Death in the Woods'' reveals his degree of self-consciousness and artistic control. In this story, one of the strongest works of his later career, he can be seen as reflecting on his artistic process.

Through his narrator—a mature man fictionalizing a formative experience from his youth—Anderson reveals something about his own relationship to the simple people who populate his fiction. Amidst the crude and commonplace Anderson perceives mystery, and uses his art to transform the life

> **"** This startling vision has the quality of a revelation. He sees 'everything'--which makes sense both as a boy's embarrassed way of describing her nudity and as a statement about how the scene marked the end of his childish innocence, forever altering his outlook on the world.**"**

stories of those who are ''nothing special'' into things of beauty.

Source: Sarah Madsen Hardy, *Short Stories for Students*, Gale, 2000.

Clare Colquitt

In the following essay, Colquitt examines Anderson's belief that art is a means for a man to find personal salvation whereas women find their destiny through childbirth.

Like most writers, Sherwood Anderson was vitally concerned with the workings of the imagination and the creation of art. For Anderson, these concerns were also inextricably linked to questions of personal salvation. In letters to his son John, himself a painter, Anderson asserted that ''The object of art . . . is to save yourself'': ''Self is the grand disease. It is what we are all trying to lose'' (*Letters*). Given Anderson's faith in the redemptive possibilities of art, it is not surprising that the writer frequently compared ''literary [and nonliterary] composition to the experience of pregnancy and deliverance, and also to the poles of maleness and femaleness in life'' (*Letters*). One letter composed three years before the author's death well illustrates Anderson's understanding of the problematic nature of such ''deliverance'':

> The trouble with the creative impulse . . . is that it tends to lift you up too high into a sort of drunkenness and then drop you down too low. There is an artist

> 'There is a woman hidden away in every artist. Like the woman he becomes pregnant. He gives birth. When the children of his world are spoken of rudely or, through stupidity, not understood, there is a hurt that anyone who has not been pregnant, who has not given birth, will never understand'"

lurking in every man. The high spots for the creative man come too seldom. He is like a woman who has been put on her back and made pregnant, but even after he gets the seed in him, he has to carry it a long time before anything comes out. (*Letters*)

If, as Anderson claims, "There is an artist lurking in every man," so, also, did the writer believe that there is a woman "lurking" in every artist. Indeed, the image of the male artist whose "lurking" burden is the female within is depicted repeatedly in the correspondence, perhaps nowhere more explicitly than in a letter Anderson sent late in life to his mother-in-law, Laura Lou Copenhaver: "There is a woman hidden away in every artist. Like the woman he becomes pregnant. He gives birth. When the children of his world are spoken of rudely or, through stupidity, not understood, there is a hurt that anyone who has not been pregnant, who has not given birth, will never understand" (*Letters*).

The assumptions "hidden away" within such assertions are easily gleaned from letters in which Anderson frankly acknowledges his "old-fashioned" views about men and women. In another letter to his son John, Anderson admitted, "I do not believe that, at bottom, they [women] have the least interest in art. What their lover gives to work they cannot get" (*Letters*). As a result, the writer held that the sole "high spot" available for women to experience in life is childbirth. To be sure, Anderson understood that the biological impulse also moves man,

but, as he makes clear in letters to his male friends, the love of woman "isn't enough for an eager man": "No woman could ever be in herself what we want or think we want" (*Letters*). Thus, whereas woman's destiny is circumscribed by biology, man's destiny transcends the purely physical and finds consummate expression only in the creation of art. As Anderson explained to Dwight MacDonald in 1929:

> There is no purpose other than the artist's purpose and the purpose of the woman. The artist purposes to bring to life, out of the . . . hidden form in lives, nature, things, the living form as women purpose doing that out of their lovely bodies.
>
> The artist there[fore] is your only true male. . . . (*Letters*)

The "tru[ly] male" quality of Anderson's artistic imagination and of his polarized worldview is forcefully represented in his short stories and novels, as well as in his letters and memoirs. Indeed, to speak of woman's destiny in the context of Anderson's fiction is to call to mind what is undoubtedly one of the master storyteller's most disturbing tales, "Death in the Woods." Written at the "peak of his [creative] powers" (Howe), "Death in the Woods" has provoked a varied critical response, ranging from interpretations that see the tale much as Anderson claims he did, as a biological allegory depicting woman as feeder, to more recent interpretations that focus less upon the plight of the old farm woman and more upon the narrative consciousness that constructs her story. This shift of focus has led several critics to conclude that "Death in the Woods" is "a story about the creation of a story" (Joselyn; see also Robinson), hence Anderson's many attempts to unveil the mechanics of the creative process through the workings of the tale's narrative center, an older man who looks back to one scene from his childhood out of which he will spin his yarn. To borrow from the title Anderson gave to his first published memoir, "Death in the Woods" has been increasingly viewed as "a story teller's story." As Wilfred Guerin argues, "It is a story about how fragments become a whole and have meaning, partly through the workings of the unconscious, partly through the conscious memory."

That there exists an intricate bond connecting the "real story" ("Death") of an old woman's life and death and the "creating" consciousness who narrates her tale has long been acknowledged. Critics have also observed that the relationship between narrator and reader is similarly complex. As early as 1959, Jon Lawry astutely perceived that the narrator's tortuous labors to give meaning to the death he describes are offered as both an interpretative and experiential model for the reader of "Death in the Woods" to follow: "The audience is invited to enter as individuals into a process almost identical with that of the narrator. . . . to share directly not only the narrator's responses but his act of discovering and creating those responses." What few critics have since examined, although both Lawry and William Scheick point toward the issue, are the implicatory bonds that result when the reader blindly accepts this enticing invitation; for if the reader succumbs to the narrator's interpretative wiles, he becomes enmeshed in a web of guilt that connects him not only with the "I"/eye of the tale but also with the other men and boys in the woods who pruriently feed upon the body of a dead woman. By further exploring the peculiar design of this web, I hope to illuminate the obsessive concern evidenced in this short story with the process of reading and making meaning. This is of course the very experience that Anderson's reader must also enact if the story is to be grasped, as the narrator himself claims to have done, as an aesthetic whole: "A thing so complete has its own beauty."

Several critics have noted the somewhat unorthodox alternation of tenses that operates throughout "Death in the Woods," as in the first paragraph of the story: "She was an old woman and lived on a farm near the town in which I lived. All country and small-town people have seen such old women, but no one knows much about them. Such an old woman comes into town driving an old worn-out horse or she comes afoot carrying a basket." Although critics differ as to the effects of such shifts, many would agree with Guerin's explanation that "In this and in the second paragraph of the story the historical present tense of the verbs makes clear the timeless quality of the regularity of such old women and their doings." Diverting the reader's attention from the particular to the general, from the life of one old woman to the experience of "such old women," the narrator strives to "universalize" his story in a timeless setting by removing the "she" of his opening description from history and by granting himself the authority to speak of "all country and small-town people" in categorical terms. Such ahistorical maneuvering complements another effect of this passage that no critic has yet observed: "Death in the Woods" begins much like a fairy tale. Further, any reader who reflects upon the tales passed on in childhood may note a slight echo here with one of our culture's most famous allegories of female feeding, the Mother Goose story of the old

woman who lived in a shoe. In addition, the reader may come to see Anderson's narrative as cautionary, particularly if other tales of wolves, women, and dark woods come to mind. From this initial description then the reader comes to two important realizations. First, the frame in which the "Death in the Woods" occurs is both fanciful and remote, a timeless realm that suggestively resonates with the surreal landscape of children's stories. Second, the reader learns that the tale is not to be interpreted simply as the narrative of an isolated farm woman but rather as a fiction that has universal implications. After all, one of the first statements the narrator makes about the old woman is that she is "nothing special."

Having been thus directed toward the ostensible subject of the story, the reader soon finds that the interpretative process is effectively impeded by obtrusive references the narrator makes concerning his own past. Indeed, in the opening section of "Death in the Woods," the reader learns almost as much about the narrator's childhood as about the plight of old country women. Interestingly, the narrator's allusions to his past closely resemble the boyhood recollections set forth in Anderson's memoirs; yet, despite the similarities that seem to link the storyteller with his tale, Anderson himself "persistent[ly]" interpreted the narrative of Mrs. Jake Grimes in thematic, not autobiographical, terms:

> In a note for an anthology Anderson wrote that "the theme of the story is the persistent animal hunger of man. There are these women who spend their whole lives, rather dumbly, feeding this hunger. . . . [The story's aim] is to retain the sense of mystery in life while showing at the same time, at what cost our ordinary animal hungers are sometimes fed." (Howe)

Anderson's reading is a superb illustration of what John Berger calls critical mystification—"the process of explaining away what might otherwise be evident"—for as Irving Howe noted more than thirty years ago, this interpretation is "apt, though limited. . . . Anderson could hardly have failed to notice that the story may be read as an oblique rendering of what he believed to be the central facts about his mother's life: a silent drudgery in the service of men, an obliteration of self to feed their 'persistent animal hunger,' and then death." Regardless of the limits of Anderson's analysis, one fact is clear: Anderson, like his narrator, is trying to steer critics of "Death in the Woods" away from the realm of history—from the varying records of a writer's conflicted relationship with his mother—to the hallowed domain of myth. Having fastened upon a presumably "safe" and unalterable interpretation of his story, Anderson thereby avoids public confrontation with painful memories of his childhood.

How painful those memories were is suggested in several of Anderson's more revealing letters. Of these, perhaps none more poignantly illustrates the writer's anguished ties to his past than one addressed but never mailed to Paul Rosenfeld. Given the highly personal nature of its contents, it is easy to see why Anderson chose not to post it; for far more than a simple communication to a friend, this lengthy letter represents an aging artist's "effort to justify" his politics and clarify his "obligation" as a writer (*Letters*). Of primary importance to Anderson in 1936 was his relationship with the proletariat, a relationship that led the writer to remember the tedious "hopelessness" of his mother's struggles to support her family:

> You must remember that I saw my own mother sicken and die from overwork. I have myself been through the mill. I have worked month after month in factories, for long hours daily, have known the hopelessness of trying to escape. I have seen my own mother stand all day over a washtub, washing the dirty linen of pretentious middle-class women not fit to tie her shoelaces, this just to get her sons enough food to keep them alive, and I presume I shall never in my life see a working woman without identifying her with my mother. (*Letters*)

Several points immediately emerge from this passage. First, Anderson sees a significant portion of his own adult experience as closely resembling his mother's. As members of the working class, they have both "been through the mill." Second, this excerpt obliquely suggests how much their lives diverged, for, unlike his mother, Anderson "escaped" and rose out of his class to enjoy a successful career as a writer. That he did so, he implies, is in some part a testament to his mother's decision to sacrifice herself "just to get her sons enough food to keep them alive." Not surprisingly, a legacy of unresolved guilt still haunts the writer. Anderson avoided his mother's fate, it seems, precisely because he chose another course; for Anderson, self came first. Indeed, the proliferation of I's in this passage points toward the egocentric nature of his interests. In short, Anderson as artist is evidently more enthralled by his own vision of martyred motherhood than by the grim particulars of his mother's impoverished existence, hence the heavy reliance upon varying forms of the verb "to see" in the passage above: "I saw," "I have seen," "I shall never . . . see."

This shift of focus away from the mother and toward the artist parallels the narrative stratagems employed in the opening section of "Death in the Woods." Here the narrator also moves quickly to guide the reader's attention away from his apparent subject, an old farm woman, to what is ultimately his larger concern—himself. Particularly jarring is the narrator's first substantial digression concerning the liver he was forced to eat as a child, a digression that interrupts his account of what old women do when they come to town:

> Such an old woman . . . takes [eggs] to a grocer. There she trades them in. . . .

> Afterwards she goes to the butcher's and asks for some dog-meat. Formerly the butchers gave liver to anyone who wanted to carry it away. In our family we were always having it. Once one of my brothers got a whole cow's liver at the slaughterhouse near the fair grounds in our town. We had it until we were sick of it. It never cost a cent. I have hated the thought of it ever since.

Clearly, this is a narrator who needs close watch, for as such digressions multiply, the reader becomes increasingly fascinated not with the "real story" of an old woman's death but rather with the peculiar manner in which her story is told. This first digression is peculiar enough, suggesting as it does a puerile hostility on the narrator's part toward his past as well as the bonds of poverty and sickness that bridge the narrator's memories of his childhood with the experience of "nameless" country women. At this juncture, the narrator also reveals that when he first noticed the woman he soon identifies as Mrs. Jake Grimes, he himself was literally sick in bed with "inflammatory rheumatism," a statement that takes on added significance when he subsequently remarks that Mrs. Grimes had journeyed to town even though "she hadn't been feeling very well for several days . . . ." Given the vehemence of these boyhood reflections, the reader might justifiably wonder at this point if the "inflammatory" child has ever fully recovered, for as the unpredictable narrator continues to weave his tale, the reader begins to sense that this man is still none too well.

Following this unsettling digression, the narrator sketches the rough outlines of Mrs. Grimes's life. Through him we learn that in her youth she worked as a "bound girl" for a German farming couple: "At the German's place she . . . cooked the food for the German and his wife. . . . She fed them and fed the cows in the barn, fed the pigs, the horses and the chickens. Every moment of everyday, as a young girl, was spent feeding something." That her life was neither one of ease nor happiness becomes plain when the narrator discloses that the "young thing" was sexually abused, perhaps raped, by her employer. Interestingly, however, the reader's knowledge of the bound girl's life is unstable, for the narrator evidences uncertainty concerning the particulars of her story. Thus, in the opening section of "Death in the Woods," the narrator first hesitantly supposes that the young girl was "bound"—"You see, the farmer was up to something with the girl—she was, I think, a bound girl . . ."—whereas only shortly afterwards he claims that he knows the woman was so: "I remember now that she was a bound girl and did not know where her father and mother were." Such wavering causes the reader to question the narrator's confidence in the truth of the tale he says he has only "suddenly" remembered: "I have just suddenly now, after all these years, remembered her and what happened. It is a story." By calling attention in this way to the manipulative possibilities of narration, Anderson directs his audience to larger questions concerning the nature of "story" telling. As Mary Joselyn observes, "the fact that [Anderson] goes out of his way several times to tell us that the story might have been told . . . differently is important, for these statements emphasize that the process of creation is essentially one of choice and of selection."

The role that choice plays in the shaping of fiction is stressed on several occasions in "Death in the Woods" when the narrator returns to scenes or conversations that he has previously described. In the opening section of the story, the narrator records two conversations that take place between the bound girl and Jake Grimes, another employee on the German couple's farm. Although the conversations are not identical, the subject of these talks is: both focus upon the sexual abuse that the young girl allegedly suffered on the farm. The narrator first recounts that before Jake became the bound girl's lover, she confided in him that "when the wife had to go off to town for supplies, the farmer got after her. She told young Jake that nothing really ever happened, but he didn't know whether to believe it or not." Between this and a later dialogue occurs a fight involving the German and his hired hand, which the narrator delightfully describes: "They had it out all right! The German was a tough one. Maybe he didn't care whether his wife knew or not." In the midst of this passage, the reader gradually realizes that the narrator could not possibly know all the details he provides of the scene, for there were no witnesses to the brawl. Indeed, the narrator himself seems aware of this problem when he parenthetically inserts: "(I wonder how I know all this. It must have stuck in my mind from small-

town tales when I was a boy)." Following this admission, the reader learns of the conversation that takes place after the fight when Jake finds his lover "huddled up . . . crying, [and] scared to death." Now, however, the narrator's phrasing suggests that the bound girl's "stories" are not to be believed: "She told Jake a lot of stuff, how the German had tried to get her, how he chased her once into the barn, how another time . . . he tore her dress open clear down the front." The narrator's unwillingness to grant the woman any degree of credibility in either of these confessions is further emphasized when he reveals that Jake Grimes "got her pretty easy himself, the first time he was out with her," an assertion that may once again lead the reader to wonder how the narrator can possibly "know all this."

What Anderson himself knows of course is how to construct a story, a story that, as its narrative voice becomes increasingly assured, causes the reader to question any interpretation offered concerning the meaning of the life and death of Mrs. Jake Grimes. Indeed, as the description of the fight scene suggests, the narrator identifies himself less with the plight of the "young thing" who is "scared to death" than with the men who are able to bind such women to their will. This is, moreover, not the only occasion in which the narrator reveals his sympathy with brutal forms of masculine expression, as is evident in the second section of the story when Mrs. Grimes makes her last trip to the butcher's:

> she went to the butcher and he gave her some liver and dog-meat.

> It was the first time anyone had spoken to her in a friendly way for a long time. The butcher was alone in his shop when she came in and was annoyed by the thought of such a sick-looking old woman out on such a day. . . . [He] said something about her husband and her son, swore at them, and the old woman stared at him, a look of mild surprise in her eyes as he talked. He said that if either the husband or the son were going to get any of the liver or the heavy bones with scraps of meat hanging to them that he had put into the grain bag, he'd seen him [*sic*] starve first.

In spite of the narrator's tacit assumption that his audience will see this interchange as positive, many readers imagining this encounter might question how "friendly" such a conversation would appear to a woman grown accustomed to "the habit of silence" who suddenly finds her family being sworn at and threatened by a man she hardly knows.

Immediately following this passage, the narrator depicts the death that has been anticipated since the opening lines of the story. In this middle section of the narrative, the old woman starts her journey home. Laden with a sack of provisions too heavy for her, Mrs. Grimes decides to take "a short cut over a hill and through the woods. . . . She was afraid she couldn't make it" otherwise. In the midst of her "struggle" home, the old woman "foolish[ly]" allows herself to rest against a tree and "quietly" falls into a sleep from which she never completely awakes. The interest in the "strange picture" her death presents lies with the several dogs that are "running in circles. . . . round and round" her sleeping form: "In the clearing, under the snow-laden tree and under the wintry moon they made a strange picture, running thus silently in a circle their running had beaten in the soft snow." At this point, the narrator shocks the reader by disclosing that he also has been part of a similarly "strange picture": "I knew all about it afterward, when I grew to be a man, because once in the woods in Illinois, on another winter night, I saw a pack of dogs act just like that. The dogs were waiting for me to die as they had waited for the old woman that night when I was a child . . . ." Like most critics, Jon Lawry dismisses this revelation as fictive, suggesting that Anderson is striving to unveil the "negative capability" necessary to the artist. According to Lawry, even the narrator knows that at this moment he is telling tales. Evidence in the memoirs, however, suggests that the adventure in the Illinois forests may be interpreted less figuratively; for the experience the narrator records seems modeled on a "strange performance" Anderson himself claims to have witnessed when, as a young man, he awoke to find himself encircled by a pack of dogs:

> In the forest on the winter night dogs kept leaving the mysterious circle in which they ran and coming to me. Other dogs ran up the log to put their forelegs on my chest and stare into my face. It seemed to me, that night, that they were caught by something. They had become a wolf pack. . . .
>
> That there was such a thing as man, that they were the servants of man, that they were really dogs not wolves in a primitive world. That night I stood the strange performance as long as I could and then I arose and ran. . . . I shouted. I . . . picked up a stick and ran among the dogs, hitting out at them. (*Memoirs*)

"It was on that night," Anderson avers, that he "got the impulse for one of [his] best stories" (*Memoirs*)— "Death in the Woods."

In many respects these three "moonlit" pictures are strikingly similar, as if Anderson is attempting to suggest that the shared experience of the "primitive world" unites all human beings. To be sure, within the story itself, this is the moment at which the narrator most identifies with the plight of the dying woman; yet as soon becomes clear, his identification with her is remarkably short-lived. Indeed, the narrator survives the nightmarish "performance" precisely because he, like the combative writer depicted in the memoirs, is "young" and male and "ha[s] no intention whatever of dying" ("Death"). By contrasting the two male-centered portraits with the "strange picture" of Mrs. Grimes's death, I hope to show how fundamentally separate these varying wintry images are. A brief look at the history of the composition of "Death in the Woods" will aid this contrast.

If, as Anderson claims, "the telling of the tale is the cutting of the natal cord" (*Story*), then the creation of "Death in the Woods" was an exceptionally laborious birth. In his memoirs Anderson reveals that he "did not succeed in writing it at once. It was one of the stories I wrote, threw away and rewrote many times." One fragmentary reference to an "old woman . . . who died alone in a wood on a winter day" appeared in 1924 in a passage from *A Story Teller's Story* where Anderson describes at some length the "strange life" that peopled his boyhood imagination:

> As a boy lying buried in the hay I presume I had some such notion as that and later as a man standing by a lathe in some factory some such notion must have still been in my mind. I wanted then to be something heroic in the eyes of my own mother, now dead, and at the same time wanted to be something heroic in my own eyes too.
>
> One could not do the thing in actual life so one did it in a new world created within one's fancy.
>
> And what a world that fanciful one—how grotesque, how strange, how teeming with strange life!. . .
>
> There are so many people in that land of whom I should like to tell you. . . . There is the old woman accompanied by the gigantic dogs who died alone in a wood on a winter day, the stout man with the grey eyes and with the pack on his back who stands talking to the beautiful woman as she sits in her carriage, the little dark woman with the boyish husband who lives in a small frame house by a dusty road far out in the country.

Somehow this "grotesque" image of an old woman's death became fused in the artist's imagination with that "strange performance" depicted in the posthumously published memoirs. There as well the experience in the woods looms larger than life as if the dogs roaming within and without Anderson's "fancy" world were all "gigantic[ally]" "large German police dogs." Although Anderson never admitted to being "frightened" by this "primitive" encounter, certainly most people would see this experience as threatening:

> How long I lay there that night I'll never know. I was warmly clad. It is possible that I slept and dreamed although I do not think so.
>
> The dogs had become silent and then suddenly there was one of them, a large German police dog with his bare leg on my chest. He was standing, his hind legs on my legs, his forelegs on my chest and his face close to my face. In the moonlight I could look directly into his eyes.
>
> I thought there was a strange light in his eyes. Was I frightened? Well, I can't remember. (*Memoirs*)

Importantly, neither passage from these autobiographical writings is dominated by sexual overtones; nor does an undated precursor of "Death in the Woods" entitled "The Death in the Forest" depict as sexually menacing the "big ugly dogs" that accompany Ma Marvin (Mrs. Grimes in the final version) on her journey to town. Rather, the narrator simply mentions as a matter of fact that "of course [the] pack . . . one always saw lying about Ike Marvin's ruined saw mill . . . had come with her." This early version of the story differs from "Death in the Woods" in other ways as well. Notably, in "The Death in the Forest," the "Marvin dogs . . . gro[w] bold" only after the old woman is dead, at which time they tear through the bag on her back in order to get "the hunk of salt pork within." Between this and the final version of the story we know as "Death in the Woods," Anderson drastically reenvisioned the particulars of this scene. Whereas the "Marvin dogs" were merely "big" and "ugly," the "Grimes dogs" are "all tall gaunt fellows," and when one of them "left the running circle and came to stand before" the half-conscious woman, the "dog thrust his face close to her face. IIis red tongue . . . hanging out." Clearly, this image represents a significant departure from those winter landscapes depicted in the memoirs and in the undated manuscript of "The Death in the Forest." Bluntly put, in "Death in the Woods" the narrative thrust is directed elsewhere, for the threat Mrs. Grimes faces from these "tall gaunt fellows" is the threat of rape, as becomes plain when the narrator records what happens after the sleeping woman dies.

The seven dogs, which had run round Mrs. Grimes as if operating by "some old instinct, come down from the time when they were wolves" now drag her thinly clad corpse into the open. As they rip the food sack from her back, they tear through her clothing "clear to the hip," conveniently leaving her body unharmed. This last image echoes the earlier "rape" scene in which the German farmer tore the bound girl's "dress open clear down the front," even as it also nicely complements the second section of "Death in the Woods" in which the narrator reasserts woman's role as feeder. According to his report, Mrs. Grimes's married life was merely an extension of the monotony she knew on the German couple's farm: "Horses, cows, pigs, dogs, men . . . [all] had to be fed." Even her sexual relations with her husband are imaged by the fixated narrator as a form of feeding when he envisages Mrs. Grimes's relief at no longer being sexually desirable: "Thank heaven, she did not have to feed her husband—in a certain way. That hadn't lasted long after their marriage."

In the final sections of "Death in the Woods" the process of reading and interpretation is brought to the fore, for the first person to discover the partially exposed body is a hunter who seemingly "misreads" the scene. "Something, the beaten round path in the little snow-covered clearing, the silence of the place, the place where the dogs had worried the body trying to pull the grain bag away or tear it open—something startled the man and he hurried off to town" to tell "his story": "'She was a beautiful young girl. Her face was buried in the snow.'" Once again, the reader notes the narrator's identification not with the woman herself but rather with the man who had been so "frightened" by his discovery that he "had not looked closely at the body": "If something strange or uncanny has happened in the neighborhood all you think about is getting away from there as fast as you can." This rationalization sets the stage for the "mystical" transformations that result when a "crowd of men and boys," including the narrator and his brother, accompany the hunter back into the forest. Following this journey, the young boy knows that he and his brother, like the hunter before them, will "have something to tell."

The "fragments" with which narrator pieces together his story are modeled upon the hunter's wish-fulfilling vision of the "beautiful young girl":

> She did not look old, lying there in that light, frozen and still. One of the men turned her over in the snow and I saw everything. My body trembled with some strange mystical feeling and so did my brother's. It might have been the cold.
>
> Neither of us had ever seen a woman's body before. It may have been the snow, clinging to the frozen flesh, that made it look so white and lovely, so like marble.

What the narrator remembers from this epiphanic moment is "only the picture there in the forest, the men standing about, the naked girlishlooking figure, face down in the snow. . . ." He further acknowledges that "the scene in the forest had become for me, without my knowing it, the foundation for the real story I am trying to tell. The fragments, you see, had to be picked up slowly, long afterwards." As several critics have observed, this "real story" can be interpreted on one level as the boy's sexual awakening, or as William Scheick has argued, his failure to do so. On another level, however, this experience represents an aesthetic metamorphosis: the "slight thing," who previously moved through town unnoticed, becomes in death a symbol for the feminine ideal, an objet d'art worthy to serve as the "foundation" for a "real story."

This final metamorphosis—woman into art—can prove disturbing, particularly if the reader has accepted Anderson's invitation "to enter . . . into a process almost identical with that of the narrator" (Lawry). Yet no matter how appealing this invitation is, our experience of this "mystical" transformation differs considerably from what the male posse "saw" in the woods, for even as Anderson's trembling narrator reenvisions this scene, we know, as the crowd in the forest does not, exactly who this woman is. Indeed, it is only when her body is carried back to town and protected from men's eyes by the blacksmith's coat that the beautiful marbled nude is discovered to be the naked corpse of the old Mrs. Grimes. In distinguishing between Mrs. Grimes's shifting status as "naked" and "nude," I follow John Berger's analysis of these terms set forth in his insightful study *Ways of Seeing*. There Berger asserts that "To be naked is to be oneself," as Mrs. Grimes is when there are no men or boys about pruriently relishing the "lovely" vision of her "frozen flesh." Mrs. Grimes becomes "nude," however, when she is put "on display." As Berger maintains, "To be nude is to be seen naked by others and yet not recognized for oneself. A naked body has to be seen as an object in order to become a nude. (The sight of it as an object stimulates the use of it as an object.) Nakedness reveals itself. Nudity is placed on display." Had the crowd encircling the "faceless" torso not been exclusively male, Mrs. Grimes might have been identified more quickly. That Anderson himself sensed this is suggested by a significant revision he made in the course of composing his story. In the early version of the tale I have already discussed, "The Death in the Forest," the crowd that "went out to Grimes' woods" includes both men and women: "Even women who had no babies to look after went." Largely because

of this, the townspeople's discovery of Ma Marvin's clothed body seems quite prosaic when compared with that "mystically" male moment in "Death in the Woods" when the men and boys "see" only a projection of their collective imagination.

Importantly, the narrator returns in the final section of "Death in the Woods" to the episode in which he also "had a half-uncanny, mystical adventure with dogs in an Illinois forest." What startles the reader in this passage is not the narrator's repeating himself—he has done that before—but rather the vague confession that prefaces this second reference to the "mystical adventure": "Things happened. When I was a young man I worked on the farm of a German. The hired-girl was afraid of her employer. The farmer's wife hated her. I saw things at that place." If nothing else has previously alerted the reader to the narrator's disturbing identification with the community of males that, within the bounds of this short story, routinely victimizes women, this hesitant admission should; for here the narrator firmly locates himself in a position of power identical to that of Jake Grimes, a position that grants him the ability to "get" frightened "young things" to satisfy his various hungers. Contrary to what William Scheick has argued, the young boy's sexual development clearly has progressed according to the definition of masculinity accepted by "all country and small-town people."

Several critics have discerned the shattering effect with which Anderson's male narrators depict their initial sexual encounters with women. Judith Fetterley's analysis of "I Want to Know Why" pertains well to "Death in the Woods": "What Anderson's boy resists is not just growing up, it is specifically growing up *male*." Yet as Fetterley demonstrates in her criticism of the earlier story, and as I hope to have shown in my own study of "Death in the Woods," any resistance felt by Anderson's narrators on this score is eventually overcome. Indeed, one might argue of "Death in the Woods," as Fetterley does of "I Want to Know Why," that the story is "infused with the perspective it abhors, because finally to disavow that perspective would be to relinquish power." Or in the terms offered within Anderson's own interpretation of "Death in the Woods," to abandon power is to become like one of those "women who spend their whole lives, rather dumbly, feeding" the "persistent animal hunger of man." Thus, despite the narrator's attempts to sympathize with the "simple story" of Mrs. Jake Grimes, his allegiances are ultimately with the powerful and most definitely closed male community—with the "crowd of men and boys" who go to the woods, with the "frightened" hunter and the "friendly" butcher, and most especially with the two men who strive to "get" the bound girl. Admittedly, the narrator does seem to regard Mrs. Grimes more compassionately than any other man who is fed by her; yet the story he tells deals less with the miserable reality of an old woman's life than with the transforming power of artistic genius. Indeed, it is only *as* an artist that the narrator can justify this woman's life by envisioning her in death as a "slight" but nonetheless "beautiful" "thing." The "foundation" of this "real story" of the artist-as-a-young-man may rest upon the bones of a dead woman, but certainly little concerns her. In short, the narrator/artist can effectively ignore the political realities facing "such old women" by making of one woman's life a poetical whole, a lyric that suggests that Mrs. Grimes's destiny—and by implication, the destiny of her sex—is biologically determined: "The woman who died was one destined to feed animal life. Anyway, that is all she ever did. She was feeding animal life before she was born, as a child, as a young woman working on the farm of the German, after she married, when she grew old and when she died." The many cyclical images within the story, as well as the narrator's passing references to his own mother and sister, reinforce such a constricted view of woman's fate.

The essential hopelessness that pervades Anderson's fiction has long been recognized. As Robert Morss Lovett observed in 1922,

> This hopelessness is not an interpretation playfully or desperately imposed on the phenomena of life from without by thought or reason; it springs from within; it is of the essence of being. . . . It is as if, to use Cardinal Newman's words, man were implicated from birth in some "vast aboriginal calamity"; only instead of placing the fall of man historically in the Garden of Eden Mr. Anderson traces it biologically to the egg.

To recall that Mrs. Jake Grimes herself takes eggs to market in order to buy food for her family; to recall that this woman dies only when she "foolish[ly]" deviates from her customary route home; to recall that the narrator interprets her existence solely in terms of feeding—to recall these is to realize that Anderson's own aesthetics are most narrowly "bound." Naturally the story proves unsettling to many readers today; for if we are taken in by the interpretative web Anderson's narrator seductively dangles before us, if we also become trembling voyeurs in the woods, then we also implicate ourselves in that "vast . . . calamity" of

masculinist convention that proceeds to dehistoricize woman by objectifying her into art. We may of course recognize the alluring contours of this web without becoming ensnared in the trap, which led one of America's most distinguished storytellers, Edgar Allan Poe, to maintain that the "most poetical" of melancholy subjects is not the story of a real woman's life but rather the "death of a beautiful woman" as imagined by the artist who loves her.

Source: Clare Colquitt, "The Reader as Voyeur: Complicitous Transformations in 'Death in the Woods'" in *Modern Fiction Studies*, Vol. 32, No. 2, Summer 1986, pp. 175–90.

William J. Scheick

In this essay, Scheick looks at the role of the narrator in Anderson's "Death in the Woods," specifically the attempt to gain mastery over an unpleasant situation through a compulsion toward repetition in describing the situation, in this case the old woman's death.

In spite of its generally recognized excellence, "Death in the Woods" has frequently escaped careful study. It has been read as a story presenting death as inevitable though not terrible, concerning the pathos of a woman's life and the narrator's response to her death, and focusing on the narrator's enlarged consciousness of the human condition. More perceptive is a recent emphasis on the old woman's representation of the Demeter-Proserpine-Hecate trilogy and on four transformations that occur in the account. Most valuable are two essays concentrating on Sherwood Anderson's notions about art as revealed in the story. None of these studies focuses on the narrator in depth. To do so, however, not only indicates that an alleged narrative problem in the story—"a clumsiness in perspective that forces the narrator to offer a weak explanation of how he could have known the precise circumstances of the old woman's death"—is in fact a crucial feature but also reveals hitherto unacknowledged aesthetic features.

On the surface the story seems a simple allegory on feeding. What has not been sufficiently stressed concerning this theme is the narrator's preoccupation with male (and by implication his own) involvement in the recurrent feeding cycle: "things had to be fed. Men had to be fed, and the horses that weren't any good . . . . Horses, cows, pigs, dogs, men." This view pertains not merely to man's animal hunger for food but, in a disturbing way for the narrator, includes the adult male's hunger for the sexual victimization of women. At one point the

"He cannot pass beyond that frozen mystical moment when he unconsciously identified with the dead woman."

narrator revealingly remarks of the old woman: "Thank heaven, she did not have to feed her husband—in a certain way. That hadn't lasted long after their marriage and after the babies came." Throughout the story the narrator symptomatically discloses a fascination with and a repulsion to this aspect of male feeding. He intends, for instance, his description of the scene in which the dogs tear the dead woman's dress "clear to the hips" to parallel directly an earlier episode in her youth when a German farmer "tore her dress open clear down the front," with the ironic difference that "the dogs had not touched her body."

His perception of man's relation to animal feeding, in this double sense, becomes an important factor in assessing the reason why and the manner in which the narrator tells his story, as we shall see. Equally significant is his awareness of a connection between sex and death. Twice in his report of the battle between the German farmer and Grimes for sexual possession of the woman, then "a young thing," the narrator remarks that she was "scared to death." That this phrase is more than a cliché for him becomes clearer when he relates his first encounter with sex, which occurs in the woods when he sees the dead woman, stripped to the hips: "One of the men turned her over in the snow and I saw everything. My body trembled with some strange mystical feeling." What he experiences and begins to comprehend is more than he can express; *mystical* is the only word he has for it. But as his relation obliquely indicates, he has received a most disturbing impression of the relation between feeding, sex, and death.

In attributing this strange feeling to the weather—"It might have been the cold"—the narrator unconsciously provides a clue to what has happened to him. In one sense during that mystical moment he identifies with the cold dead body, which no longer looks old but as young as his own. Significantly just

as the woman had learned "the habit of silence," so, too, he now "kept silent and went to bed early." Furthermore, throughout the story, the product of his long silence, it becomes increasingly clear that the narrator is incorporating the facts (insofar as he has ascertained and imagined them) of the old woman's life into his own experience, with the consequence that he completely identifies with several events in her life. He, too, he tells us, had been circled by dogs one winter night.

Whether or not this incident really occurred is less important than that it underscores the narrator's identification with the old woman. However, the reader's suspicion as to its authenticity is aroused by the revelation of another incident paralleling one during the woman's youth: "Things happened. When I was a young man I worked on the farm of a German. The hired-girl was afraid of her employer. The farmer's wife hated her." What he says may be true, however unlikely the coincidence seems; but what is important is the level at which he identifies with the woman, resulting in a story that finally recounts *their* experience rather than merely *hers*. The narrator's capacity for imaginative interpretation is evident in a scene in which Grimes confronts the men of the town: "When he was leaving he turned around and stared at the men. There was a look of defiance in his eyes. 'Well, I have tried to be friendly. You don't want to talk to me . . . .' He did not say anything actually. 'I'd like to bust one of you on the jaw,' was about what his eyes said." Similar interpretation occurs throughout the story whenever the narrator elliptically moves from objective observation of the woman's dilemma to imaginative identification with her thoughts.

As a result of this intense identification, the narrator readily mixes past and present tense in his account. His confusion of tenses represents a suspension of time identical to what occurs during a mystical experience. He cannot pass beyond that frozen mystical moment when he unconsciously identified with the dead woman. His incomprehensible and therefore inarticulate impression of the underlying bond between feeding, sex, and death has proved traumatic for him; and now he remains suspended between the past of the woman's experience and the future of his own destiny as a mature male.

He cannot escape nor does he really seek release from this frozen moment. To advance would mean that he must embrace maturity, become an adult male, and like grown men partake of sexual feeding. His arrested state of psychological development, the consequence of his trauma, simulates death, the ideal state: ''A thing so complete has its own beauty.'' Such a suspended condition permits him to preserve childhood innocence, to reject the threatening reality of what he has perceived in the woods—''I saw everything''—concerning man and himself as a future adult male. Significantly the narrator stresses that the ''frozen and still'' body of the old woman took on, in death, the appearance of regained youthfulness, that it ''looked like the body of some charming young girl.'' Through death the old woman has regained innocence and beauty; and through his identification with this woman, though a simulation of her death with regard to the frozen suspended state of his psychological development, the narrator hopes to reinstate his earlier condition of unconscious innocence.

From another but germane perspective, the narrator has participated in a traditional rite held in the woods and intended to initiate him into the world of adult sexuality. Clearly only men and boys go to see the body, and even the dogs circling the body are male. This ritual provides for the narrator's first encounter with sex, but he fails to emerge from the initiation with a mature outlook. Ironically his development is arrested, and death rather than participation in life becomes for him the ideal condition, a state of suspension whereby he can maintain youth and innocence. Thus, not only does his story chiefly take place between summer and fall, but his psychological condition is likewise symbolically suspended between the summer of his youthful, pre-initiation innocence (past-present) and the autumn of his conscious, adult awareness (present-future). To progress to the autumn stage would necessitate his development as a mature male who, with regard to feeding, will victimize women. Indeed contributing to his trauma is the realization, appropriately arising after his experience in the woods, that he is already guilty of victimizing women in terms of feeding (and by implication its symbolic connection to sex and death): ''When he [my brother] got back to town he would have to go on distributing his papers before he went home to supper. . . . we would both be late. Either mother or our older sister would have to warm our supper.''

The narrator's paralysis between the summer and autumn of his psychic development is reflected not only in his mingling of past and present tense but also in his simple, rather terse sentences, very unsophisticated in vocabulary and style, which time

and again sound as if a child were speaking: ''In a woods, in the late afternoon, when the trees are all bare and there is white snow on the ground, when all is silent, something creepy steals over the mind and body.'' Such verbal simplicity belies the real complexity of the mystical experience he has undergone; but it is entirely organic to his suspension in an eternal present staving off maturity and reinstating innocence. Especially pertinent in this regard is the narrator's evasiveness when referring to sexual matters. Such remarks as ''the farmer was up to something with the girl'' and ''maybe she did not have any father. You know what I mean'' emphasize the child persona of the narrator, though in fact he is a grown man. Even his comment that ''things happened,'' pertaining to the German farmer's sexual interest in the young girl, and that he ''saw everything,'' referring to the naked body in the snow, suggest the narrator's evasiveness when speaking about sexual matters as well as his perception of some large unexpressible truth beyond the specifics of the immediate incidents. Clearly ''Death in the Woods'' does not present a ''matured narrator,'' nor does it represent a ''mature man's creation,'' as two critics have claimed.

Although the narrator apparently prefers his frozen, deathlike condition, he does experience a counter instinct, the thrust toward maturity. A tension results from the conflict between these two instincts, a neurotic anxiety necessitating the narrator's attempt to restructure his experience in order to fathom what has happened to him: ''The fragments, you see, had to be picked up slowly, long afterwards,'' for ''something had to be understood.'' What he almost consciously recognizes about feeding, sex, and death has remained as elusive as his first mystical encounter with their meaning: ''The whole thing, the story of the old woman's death, was to me as I grew older like music heard from far off. The notes had to be picked up slowly one at a time.'' Painstakingly the reality of what he had perceived had to be retrieved from the unconscious. Never in control of his problem, however, the narrator constantly remains at the receiving end of his experience and its aftermath. Consequently, it is ''just *suddenly* now, after all these years'' (italics added) that he discovers fragments emerging into consciousness. Although one might argue that he seems to understand a little better what these fragments mean, it is even truer that he is unable to piece them together with utter clarity: ''I wonder how I know all this. It must have stuck in my mind from small-town tales when I was a boy.''

Because the fragments are only dimly perceived and essentially beyond his control, the narrator's story is related in a disjointed manner with segments out of chronological order. What strikes the rational mind as murky, disorderly fragments in fact represents a disguised underlying pattern to the unconscious. Struggling for a glimpse of this pattern the narrator's conscious mind must continually circle around the woman's frozen body in a manifestation of what Freud described as a compulsion toward repetition, a tendency to repeat an unpleasant incident in order to gain mastery over it. The circle in fact is the principal image in the narrator's account, for he does not regress to an earlier period but tries to stand still. Paradoxically in striving to restructure his experience, the narrator performs the very activity he seeks to escape; he, too, is fed by the woman, for she remains the substantive, vital core of his story and his experience. Like the dogs running "silently, in a circle," around her body, like the hunter and the other men who later surround it, the narrator compulsively circles and recircles "the oval in the snow." In a sense he is guilty of precisely the act he tries to renounce, a situation he does not consciously realize but seems to sense intuitively at the end of his relation: "even after her death [she] continued feeding animal life."

The narrator's story, then, is not about *a* death or *the* death in the woods but, as the title reads, death in the woods. The old woman has died and so has the narrator, who in identifying with her emerges from his initiation rite psychologically frozen. Even the narrator senses that the scene in the forest represents only "the *foundation* for the real story" which he is "now *trying* to tell." (italics added). In his attempt to resolve the tension between the instinct to remain psychologically suspended in simulation of death (thereby retaining innocence) and the other instinct to mature (thereby consciously facing painful reality), the narrator continually circles the subject and the meaning of his story, compulsively trying, albeit never quite managing, to attain composure. Composure remains as unattainable as the exact meaning of his narrative, the meaning that his brother's version failed to make clear and from which his own account retreats: "I shall not try to emphasize the point." The final sentence of the story summarizes the narrator's plight: "I speak . . . that you may understand why I have been *impelled* to *try* to tell the *simple* story *over again*" (italics added). This recapitulation, reflected in the narrative technique and imagery of "Death in the Woods," evinces the narrator's

compulsion toward repetition as he circles and recircles the elusive, the always incomplete and uncomprehended significance of his initiation experience in the woods. This psychological circular pattern is objectified in the simulated frozen ideal state of death, that timeless present in which the narrator remains suspended between an innocent unconscious past and a conscious future as an adult male who expresses animal hunger with all its symbolic implications with regard to women. Like the old woman in her youth, the narrator was, as a boy, "scared to death."

Source: William J. Scheick, "Compulsion Toward Repetition: Sherwood Anderson's 'Death in the Woods'" in *Studies in Short Fiction*, Vol. XI, No. 2, Spring 1974, pp. 141–46.

Sister Mary Joselyn

In the following essay, Sister Mary Joselyn examines the themes of transformation that are interwoven in the thematic and structural elements of the story.

Although Sherwood Anderson's "Death in the Woods" is widely regarded as the author's masterpiece and has been closely studied by at least two critics, its depths have not yet been plumbed. It is not the claim of this short paper to do so, either, but rather to indicate some dimensions of the story that so far have scarcely been identified but which in fact have both structural and thematic importance. An appreciative reader of the modern short narrative marvels at Anderson's skill in this story—the "circling," resonating effect created by the several retellings of the events, the deft but strong and pointed ironies thrown off as it were in passing, a time scheme intricate in the extreme yet managed in a relaxed and casual-seeming style, above all the unerring movement back and forth between the mode of ordinary realism and a highly-charged, universalized and poetic vein. It is this characteristic of "Death in the Woods," no doubt, that prompted Horace Gregory's observation that though its external form is "plainly that of a story, its internal structure is that of poetry; it has the power of saying more than prose is required to say, and saying it in the fewest words." A sentence that illustrates this quality occurs near the end of the narrative, in the climactic fourth section, where, describing his feeling as a boy gazing on the snowy circle where the woman's body lies, the narrator says, "Darkness comes quickly on such winter nights, but the full moon made everything clear." The first part of the sentence is purely a statement of fact from and about the "real" world, a generalization framed in the present tense as a truism should be, but the second clause leaps out of the level of realistic detail to suggest a more universal realm where deeper issues are raised—the meaning of seeing, the amazing possibility of seeing better in a transforming half-light, of perceiving something not revealed clearly by the physical sight. Thus the second clause not only goes beyond the first but offers a commentary upon it, constituting a critique of the consciousness that originated it and indeed of the context of meaning available to such a consciousness. The concern of this paper, however, rather than defining the perfect amalgamation of modes that the story demonstrates, will be centered upon the "transformations" that occur in the narrative.

One of Jon Lawry's chief findings in "'Death in the Woods' and the Artist's Self in Sherwood Anderson" is that a main theme of the story is the creation of the narrator's consciousness as a man and as an artist. Lawry has correctly identified a transformation theme in the story, as has Mary Rohrberger in relating the woman's life to the metamorphosis of Proserpine, Demeter, and Hecate. Yet both readings are incomplete, for, whether or not one accepts the full mythical interpretation, it can be shown that "Death in the Woods" is built upon at least four transformations, which Anderson has interwoven with unparalleled skill. If, for purposes of analysis, Anderson's intricate time scheme is restructured as straightforward chronology, the outline of the four basic changes of the story immediately becomes clearer. The most obvious of these—and the one that provides the firmest "story line"—concerns the transformation of Mrs. Grimes.

Piece by piece Anderson fills in the picture of the stages of the woman's life. Almost at the end of the story, the narrator refers to Mrs. Grimes's girlhood "at the German's, and before that, when she was a child and before her mother lit out and left her." The girl, the narrator guesses, probably became a "bound girl" of the German farmer because she did not have any father: "You know what I mean." Bound children were often cruelly treated, were "slaves really." At any rate, the farmer's pursuit of the "young, scared" girl, the hatred and suspicion of the farmer's wife, as well as the girl's own inability to resist the rakish Jake Grimes when he appeared led to a situation by which "She got past being shocked early in life." As Mrs. Grimes and the mother of two children—the daughter died and the young son became a drunkard like his father—the woman sees her existence turn into a

> **Thus the whole is implicit in each of the parts, and by these means and others, Anderson succeeds in creating a perfectly integrated work of art."**

sordid round of silent, slavish labor that, before she is forty, has driven her to the edge of madness.

In the second section of the story Anderson develops in his brilliantly incantatory prose the picture of the woman in her symbolic role as feeder and nourisher of life. As a young girl at the German farmer's, she had spent every moment of the day feeding animals and men, and this work continues and increases after her marriage. Anderson's rhythmic cadences move from simple realism to mnemonic thematic statement: ". . . things had to be fed. Men had to be fed, and the horses that weren't any good but maybe could be traded off, and the poor thin cow that hadn't given any milk for three months. Horses, cows, pigs, dogs, men." The "feeder" motif remains in the background of all the remaining sections of the story, shading into irony as the maddened dogs tear the food pack from the woman's shoulders after she freezes to death in the snow. Near the conclusion of the narrative, Anderson returns explicitly to the feeder theme as the narrator attempts, however fumblingly, to probe the deeper meaning of the woman's life:

> The woman who died was destined to feed animal life. Anyway, that is all she ever did. She was feeding animal life before she was born, as a child, as a young woman working on the farm of the German, after she married, when she grew old and when she died. She fed animal life in cows, in chickens, in pigs, in horses, in dogs, in men. . . . On the night when she died she was hurrying homeward, bearing on her body food for animal life.

While the interpretation of the woman's life afforded in the narrator's recapitulation contains truth, it does not exhaust it. For this, another stage in the woman's metamorphosis is necessary.

When a hunter finds the woman's body in the circle of snow around which the dogs have run their ritual chase, it is "frozen stiff . . . the shoulders . . .

so narrow and the body so slight that in death it looked like the body of some charming young girl.'' The man who finds the body is succinct: ''I didn't see any wounds. She was a beautiful young girl. Her face was buried in the snow. No, I didn't know her.'' Finally, the narrator presents his own direct view of the scene when the men and the two boys go to the woods. He remembers that ''She did not look old, lying there in that light, frozen and still. . . . It may have been the snow, clinging to the frozen flesh, that made it look so white and lovely, so like marble.'' Years later, the memory of the picture there in the forest is still vivid to the narrator: ''the men standing about, the naked girlish-looking figure, face down in the snow, the tracks made by the running dogs and the clear cold winter sky above.'' The woman's metamorphosis is complete; she has passed from girl to woman, feeder, and victim, then to the perpetual, ''frozen'' embodiment of the young girl, caught in ''marble.'' Through the stages of her transformation her meaning—''A thing so complete has its own beauty''—has been dramatically revealed. But other transformations, some not so dramatic and complete, take place in ''Death in the Woods,'' one of the most interesting of them being the change in the narrator himself.

The most circuitous of the narrative threads in the story traces the development of the central consciousness, that of the narrator, itself. Lawry has already carefully analyzed the stages in the completion of the man's sense of his self through his telling of the woman's story expressed as a work of art. According to Lawry, ''the discovery of the 'I' necessarily involves the artistic expression of that discovery.'' The ''I'' is revealed in three stages, as the boy before the woman's body, as the young man facing the circle of dogs in Illinois, and as the older man still holding to his ideal picture of woman. One may question Lawry's apparent conviction of the finality of this transformation; rather it would seem that since the narrator is still mulling over the deepest significance of what he has experienced, he is himself still ''in process,'' his own future promising still further transformations.

A minor transformation (minor, that is, in relation to the plot of the story but not to its themes) is the change, also uncompleted, of the seven dogs into wolves. Much is made by the narrator of the large, gaunt-looking animals always hanging around the Grimes's place near the sawmill on the creek. ''Such men, as Jake Grimes,'' the narrator holds, ''always keep just such dogs. They kick and abuse them, but they stay.'' Two or three of the dogs

insistently follow the woman as she goes about her chores, and four of them are with her on her walk into town to sell eggs and beg a packet of dog-meat from the butcher. On the return trip the animals trail behind her sniffing at the bag on her back. The narrator vividly re-creates, in the third section of the story, the actions of these huge, hungry animals:

> The Grimes dogs, in order to keep from starving, had to do a lot of foraging for themselves, and they had been at it while the old woman slept with her back to the tree at the side of the clearing. They had been chasing rabbits in the woods and in adjoining fields and in their ranging had picked up three other farm dogs.

> After a time all the dogs came back to the clearing. They were excited about something. Such nights, cold and clear and with a moon, do things to dogs. It may be that some old instinct, come down from the time when they were wolves and ranged the woods in packs on winter nights, comes back into them.

> The dogs in the clearing, before the old woman, had caught two or three rabbits and their immediate hunger had been satisfied. They began to play, running in circles in the clearing. Round and round they ran, each dog's nose at the tail of the next dog. In the clearing, under the snow-laden trees and under the wintry moon they made a strange picture, running thus silently, in a circle their running had beaten in the soft snow. The dogs made no sound. They ran around and around in the circle.

Perhaps the woman opened her eyes and saw the animals before she died, noticing how the bolder ones came up to her with their red tongues hanging out and their faces thrust at hers. The circling of the dogs, thinks the narrator, may have been a kind of death ceremony, for the primitive instinct of the wolf aroused in the animals by the night and the running may have made them ''somehow afraid.'' Perhaps they said to themselves: ''Now we are no longer wolves. We are dogs, the servants of man. Keep alive, man! When man dies we become wolves again.''

The woman dies but the dogs do not become wolves; their transformation is not completed. The dogs stop running and gather about Mrs. Grimes, toppling her body face downward in the snow to loosen the bag in which the meat is tied, led by the most agile and quick of the animals. The narrator insists, ''Had the dogs really been wolves that one would have been the leader of the pack.'' The dogs drag the woman's body into the clearing and tear her dress from her shoulders but do not touch the corpse itself. Although the animals act like wolves and have ''lost'' man in death, the narrator refuses to acknowledge their regression. This metamorphosis, then, remains incomplete, at least to the narrator.

The fourth transformation takes place at a different level. The first three changes, as the story's *donnée,* its material, are for the most part reported, verifiable incidents that occurred in the natural, "real" world, but the fourth transformation consists of the alteration itself of these facts into a work of art. There is no question that, as all readers will observe and as Lawry has noted in detail, "Death in the Woods" is not only a story but a story about the creation of a story. Lawry, it would appear to this writer, oversimplifies, though, in identifying the process of the creation of the narrator's consciousness with the process of the creation of the story. Certainly the two metamorphoses are related, but they are not identical. Possibly the most profound change in the narrator occurs when he finds the true *subject* of his story, but as a matter of fact the narrator is himself an outcome of the writer's art.

As evidence that Anderson is writing about the process of art, the fact that he goes out of his way several times to tell us that the story might have been told (seen, imagined) differently is important, for these statements emphasize that the process of creation is essentially one of choice and of selection. When, for example, the older brother tells the story of the woman's death the evening after it happened, the narrator remembers, "I kept silent .... It may have been I was not satisfied with the way he told it." Then there is the culminating section of the narrative—

> You see it is likely that, when my brother told the story, that night when we got home and my mother and sister sat listening, I did not think he got the point. He was too young and so was I. A thing so complete has its own beauty.
>
> I shall not try to emphasize the point. I am only explaining why I was dissatisfied then and have been ever since. I speak of that only that you may understand why I have been impelled to try to tell the simple story over again.

As the process of art is a process of choice, it may also be imperfectible, forever unfinished. If, in this view, art is responsible—and responsive—to existence itself, and existence is in continuous state of change, art could not be other than unfinal. The aesthetic undertaking is difficult ("the story *I am trying* to tell") and it is slow ("The notes had to be picked up slowly one at a time").

Anderson's handling of the problems of verisimilitude, too, may emphasize the improvisatory character of the art process. Repeatedly the narrator indulges in explanations of how he "knew" some fact or event, though on the other hand Anderson does not hesitate to write in strict omniscient-author point of view when the material seems to call for it. Throughout Section Three and again in Section Four the account of the dogs' ritual dancing before the dying woman is presented at firsthand from the woman's point of view, yet near the end of Section Four, the narrator goes to the trouble of saying "I knew all about it afterward when I grew to be a man because once in a woods in Illinois, on another winter night, I saw a pack of dogs act just like that." The reader is inclined to feel the explanation—and others like it—is a pointless awkwardness; still these statements may be used to stress the gap between mere fact and what the imagination makes of it in the act of art.

The narrative contains other hints and implications relating to the aesthetic process, for instance on the way subjects are discovered. Over and over in "Death in the Woods," reference is made to the memory as a source of art: the story is sprinkled with the phrase "I remember," and more than once detail, even irrelevant detail, is brought in with no more purpose than to situate an event in the past, as in the generalized account of women's dealings with butchers in former days—

> ... she goes to the butcher's and asks for some dog-meat. She may spend ten or fifteen cents, but when she does she asks for something. Formerly the butchers gave liver to anyone who wanted to carry it away. In our family we were always having it. Once one of my brothers got a whole cow's liver at the slaughterhouse near the fairgrounds in our town. We had it until we were sick of it. It never cost a cent. I have hated the thought of it ever since.

While details like these serve to establish tone and may contribute something to the characterization of the narrator, their chief purpose would seem to be to stress the pastness of events and to reinforce indirectly the idea that memory is the main repository from which the subjects of art are drawn.

Anderson also suggests, however, that certain meaningful, more static scenes or "pictures" also may be the source of art. Thus the narrator, mulling for years over some of the events appearing in the story asserts, "I remember only the picture there in the forest. ... The scene in the forest had become for me, without my knowing it, the foundation for the real story I am now trying to tell." The implication would seem to be that when these "pictures" or quintessential scenes have been forced to reveal their meaning, a work of art will be the result. The end of the process consists, doubtless, in understanding what has been seen. At the highest point of concentration in "Death in the Woods," when the men finally turn over the body of the woman in the snow, the narrator avers "I saw everything" and "My body trembled with some strange mystical feelings . . . ." Again, of the same moment: "I had seen everything, had seen the oval in the snow, like a miniature race track, where the dogs had run, had seen how the men were mystified, had seen the white bare young-looking shoulders, had heard the whispered comments of the men." The materials of art, then, may be events or pictures; the act of art is to determine their meaning, for "The fragments, you see, had to be picked up slowly, long afterwards." The notes of the strange, far-off music must be "picked up slowly one at a time," for "Something had to be understood."

It is through these four interlocking transformations, then, that Anderson creates his story. As Mrs. Grimes undergoes a three-fold metamorphosis, the narrator himself is altered from the young boy who witnessed the original events to the youth facing the circle of dogs in Illinois to the older man with his picture of ideal woman and his artist's view of the events. A minor but not insignificant transformation is that of the seven dogs in the woods into wolves, a change not completed, like that of the other (major) transmutation, that of the welding of the materials of art into the work of art. Two of the changes are presented more or less directly, in their chronological order, that of dogs into wolves and events into story, while the other two transformations, those of boy into youth and man and of girl into frozen ideal or statue, are presented in a much more roundabout, circumstantial, "existential" manner. Casual as the linking of the metamorphoses may seem to be, a perusal of the story will show how intricate their inter-relationship really is, with one change occupying the foreground and the other three the background of each of the sections of the story. Thus the whole is implicit in each of the parts, and by these means and others, Anderson succeeds in creating a perfectly integrated work of art.

Source: Sister Mary Joselyn, "Some Artistic Dimensions of Sherwood Anderson's 'Death in the Woods'" in *Studies in Short Fiction,* Vol. IV, No. 3, Spring 1967, pp. 252–59.

Sources

Anderson, Sherwood, *Sherwood Anderson's Memoirs*, edited by Ray Lewis White. New York: Harcourt, 1942.

Burbank, Rex, *Sherwood Anderson*, New York: Twayne, 1964.

Gregory, Horace, ed., *The Portable Sherwood Anderson*, New York: Viking Press, 1946.

Kronenberger, Louis, *New York Times*, April 23, 1933, p. 6.

Lawry, Jon S., "'Death in the Woods' and the Artist's Self in Sherwood Anderson," in *PMLA,* Vol. 74, No. 3, June, 1959, pp. 306–11.

Matthews, T. S., Review, in the *New Republic*, June 7, 1933, p. 105.

Mesher, David R., "A Triumph of Ego in Anderson's 'The Egg,'" *Studies in Short Fiction*, Vol. 17, No. 2, Spring, 1980, pp. 18–83.

Townsend, Kim, *Sherwood Anderson*, Boston: Houghton Mifflin, 1987.

White, Ray Lewis, ed., *The Achievement of Sherwood Anderson*, Chapel Hill: University of North Carolina Press, 1966.

Further Reading

Burbank, Rex, *Sherwood Anderson*, New York: Twayne, 1964.
Offers a clear and concise overview of Anderson's life, work, and the critical reception of his work.

Small, Judy Jo, *A Reader's Guide to the Short Stories of Sherwood Anderson*, New York: G. K. Hall, 1994.
This guide offers insight into his influences and sources, as well as critical interpretations of selected stories.

Townsend, Kim, *Sherwood Anderson*, Boston: Houghton Mifflin, 1987.
This biography offers detailed information about Anderson as both a writer and a man. Townsend views him sympathetically and argues for his continued relevance.

Everything That Rises Must Converge

Flannery O'Connor

1963

Just one year before her death in 1963, Flannery O'Connor won her second O. Henry Award for "Everything That Rises Must Converge," a powerful depiction of a troubled mother-son relationship. In 1965 the story was published in her well-regarded short fiction collection *Everything That Rises Must Converge.*

Most critics view "Everything That Rises Must Converge" as a prime example of O'Connor's literary and moral genius. The story exemplifies her ability to expose human weakness and explore important moral questions through everyday situations. Considered a classic of the short story form, "Everything That Rises Must Converge" has been anthologized frequently.

The story describes the events surrounding a fateful bus trip that an arrogant young man takes with his bigoted mother. The mother insists on her son's company because she doesn't like to ride the bus alone, especially since the bus system was recently integrated. The tensions in their relationship come to a head when a black mother and son board the same bus.

O'Connor utilizes biting irony to expose the blindness and ignorance of her characters. The story's title refers to an underlying religious message that is central to her work: she aims to expose the sinful nature of humanity that often goes unrecognized in the modern, secular world.

Author Biography

Born on March 25, 1925, in Savannah, Georgia, Mary Flannery O'Connor was the only child of Edwin Francis and Regina Cline O'Connor. She was raised in a devout Roman Catholic family, which was an anomaly in the American South.

When O'Connor was thirteen, her father was diagnosed with disseminated lupus, a hereditary disease. The family moved to Milledgeville, Georgia, her mother's hometown, where they lived in her mother's ancestral home at the center of town. Edwin O'Connor died two years later.

O'Connor attended parochial school in Savannah but graduated from public high school in Milledgeville. She then attended the Georgia State College for Women, where she social sciences and had an avid interesting in cartooning.

After graduation she was determined to write and eventually earned a master's degree at the prestigious University of Iowa Writer's Workshop. While still enrolled there she dropped "Mary" from her name and published her first short story, "The Geranium."

After college, she did a residency at the Yaddo writer's colony in Saratoga Springs, New York. In 1949 she moved to New York City. Later she lived for a time with the literary couple Robert and Sally Fitzgerald and worked on her first novel, *Wise Blood,* in their Connecticut home before falling ill with lupus in 1950.

After her diagnosis, she returned to Milledgville for good. Accompanied by her mother, she moved to a dairy farm called Andalusia on the outskirts of town. Here O'Connor divided her time between convalescing, raising peacock, and writing.

In 1952 *Wise Blood* was published, followed by her short story collection *A Good Man Is Hard to Find* in 1955 and her novel *The Violent Bear It Away* in 1960. She was the recipient of a number of fellowships and was a two-time winner of the prestigious O. Henry Award for short fiction.

O'Connor's devout Catholicism influenced her resilient attitude as she faced a debilitating disease. Her treatments had painful side effects and, in combination with the lupus, softened the bones in her hips so that she required crutches. When her health allowed, she gave readings and lectures and entertained. Despite constant discomfort, she continued to write fiction until her health failed.

In 1964 O'Connor died of kidney failure as a result of complications caused by lupus. Her final work, *Everything That Rises Must Converge,* was published posthumously the following year.

Plot Summary

Set in the South in the early 1960s, "Everything That Rises Must Converge" opens with the protagonist, a young writer named Julian, reflecting on the reasons that he must accompany his mother to her weekly weight-loss meeting. She goes to the meetings because she has high blood pressure, but considers them one of her "few pleasures."

However, Julian's mother has refused to ride the bus alone since the bus system became racially integrated. Julian dreads the trips, but feels obligated to do as she wishes.

On the evening when the story takes place, Julian's mother is indecisive about whether to wear a garish new hat. She eventually decides to wear it, commenting that the hat was worth the extra money because others won't have the same one.

As they walk to the bus stop, Julian's mother reviews her family legacy, which has given her a strong self-identity. She implies that it does not matter that she is poor because she comes from a well-known and once prosperous family of the pre-Civil War South.

Mentioning her family's former plantation, Julian's mother talks about slavery. Julian remembers the mansion, which he regards with secret longing, while his mother continues to reminisce about her nurse, an "old darky" whom she considers "the best person in the world." Julian finds his mother's condescension and racism intolerable.

They get on the bus and his mother tells their fellow white passengers about her son's ambitions as a writer. He deals with his embarrassment by detaching himself from the action; in this state, he considers his mother objectively. He thinks about the sacrifices she has made for him, yet feels superior to her racist and old-fashioned ideas, including her pride in the past.

A black man gets on the bus. Julian moves across the aisle in order to sit next to him, which he knows will bother his mother. Wishing to seem sympathetic, he attempts to strike up a conversation with the disinterested man. Nevertheless, he enjoys his mother's discomfort; he begins to fantasize about bringing black friends home, or even a mixed-race girlfriend.

At the next stop a black woman and her young son board the bus. The woman is wearing the same flamboyant hat as Julian's mother. Taking the only seats available, the woman sits next to Julian and the boy sits next to his mother.

Julian is amused by the identical hats and by the idea that, according to their seating, his mother and the black woman have "swapped sons." Julian's mother recovers her composure and strikes up a conversation with the little boy next to her. The black woman reprimands her son and, when a seat becomes available, moves him next to her. But Julian's mother continues to joke with the boy.

The four of them get off the bus at the same stop. Julian tries to stop his mother from giving the little boy a penny, but she tries to do it anyway. Enraged by her condescension, the boy's mother strikes her to the ground. Julian tells his mother that she got what she deserved. She appears confused and initially declines his offer to help her up.

She looks at him like she doesn't know him and heads in the direction of home. He goads her, calling after her that the hat looked better on the black woman than on her and that "the old world is gone. The old manners and your graciousness is not worth a damn." She is breathing hard but Julian doesn't recognize that she is in physical distress.

She asks for her Grandpa, then for her childhood nurse, Caroline. Julian looks at her face, finally realizing that she is having a stroke. He runs to her crying, calling her "darling," and "sweetheart," and "Mama," as her face distorts and her eyes close. He goes for help but knows that it is too late.

Characters

Caroline

Caroline was Julian's mother's nanny when she was a young child. Julian's mother refers to her as an "old darky" but also claims that "there was no

Flannery O'Connor

better person in the world." Caroline is the last person Julian's mother calls for before she dies, suggesting a return to childhood and also a genuine intimacy with the woman.

Carver

Carver is the little African American boy who boards the bus with his mother. He sits next to Julian's mother, who does not regard black children with the same suspicion that she does adults. She finds him cute and regains her composure by joking with him playfully. She offers him a penny in what she thinks of as a gesture of gentility.

Colored Woman

An African American woman gets on the bus with her young son and is forced to take a seat next to Julian. She wears the same hat as Julian's mother—a hat that Julian's mother had considered too expensive—thus representing the Negro's "rise" in Southern society. Julian finds bitter humor in the fact that the two women wear the same hats and that, according to their seating configuration, they have "swapped sons."

The African American woman is direct and aggressive, lacking the cutting condescension and the gentile manners of Julian's mother. She resents Julian's mother for ingratiating herself with her son and slaps her when she offers him a penny.

Julian

Julian is the protagonist of "Everything That Rises Must Converge." A young white man in his early twenties who has recently graduated from college, he lives with his mother and contributes minimally to the household by selling typewriters.

The story focuses on his conflicted relationship with his mother and his rejection of her old-fashioned, racist ideology. Although grateful for her financial and emotional support, Julian is proud of himself for being able to see her objectively and not allowing himself to be dominated by her.

The issue of race relations triggers a major conflict between mother and son. Julian considers himself as liberal and progressive because he rejects his mother's racist views; yet it becomes clear his views come from an attempt to antagonize his mother, not from a thoughtful worldview. He has "an evil urge to break her spirit" and he succeeds, only to regret it deeply.

Julian's Mother

Julian's mother is an older Southern lady. Descended from a respected, wealthy family, she is now virtually impoverished. Almost every dollar she has goes to her beloved son, Julian; this financial support has allowed him to complete college and attempt a life as a writer.

Julian's mother holds old-fashioned racist views: she strongly favors segregation, believes that blacks were better off as slaves, and blames civil rights legislation as the main cause of her deteriorated social and economic standing. Yet she holds on to her ideas of gentility and graciousness; after all, that is the way a Southern lady would act.

"Everything That Rises Must Converge" focuses on her complex, troubled relationship to Julian as he tries to confront her on these views. On an integrated bus, he forces her to address her prejudices, hoping to teach her a lesson about race relations, justice, and the modern world.

When the stress of bearing his antagonism is exacerbated by a physical attack, she has a stroke. As she dies, she looks at her son as if she doesn't know him and asks for her childhood nurse, who was a black woman.

Negro Man

Julian sits next to a well-dressed, African American man in order to make a point about his own views on racial integration and to antagonize his mother. Julian asks the man for a light, wishing to strike up a conversation. The man has no interest in talking to him.

Themes

Social Class

Julian's mother reminds him that they come from a "good" family—one that was once respected for its wealth and social standing. Her family name is central to her identity, reinforcing her belief in her value as a human being and her superiority to those around her.

Yet Julian and his mother now live in a run-down neighborhood that "had been fashionable forty years ago." She has sacrificed everything for her son and continues to support him even though he has graduated from college. As a consequence, she has to worry about spending $7.50 on a hat and must ride the bus along with African Americans, which she considers degrading.

Julian finds his mother's preoccupation about the family name ridiculous, but he secretly believes that he has the aristocratic qualities that she claims to value. He thinks of the family's lost mansion with longing, asserting that "it was he, not she, who would've appreciated it."

Morals and Morality

Morality is a recurring theme in O'Connor's work, and "Everything That Rises Must Converge" is no exception. The story concerns questions of right and wrong, with the contrasting moral sensibilities of Julian and his mother forming the basis of the plot's conflict.

Julian's mother relies on custom and tradition for her moral sensibility, claiming that "how you do things is because of who you *are*" and "if you know who you are, you can go anywhere." She believes in polite social conduct, and considers herself to be superior to most other people—especially African Americans.

She is fiercely loyal to those whom she identifies as part of her proud tradition, especially her son.

In her eyes, upholding her duty to her family and her family name is the key to goodness.

Julian has great disdain for his mother's moral outlook. He dismisses her notions of proper conduct as part of an old social order that is not only immoral, but also irrelevant. Julian believes that by sitting next to the African American man on the bus, he is teaching his mother a valuable moral lesson.

He considers his views on integration liberal and progressive, but they turn out to be merely an attempt to punish his mother. The events of the story reveal him to be blinded by self-centeredness, arrogance, and resentment. In the end, he is morally responsible for his mother's death; but his cries for help at the story's close suggest "his desperate awareness of the dark state of his own soul," as Robert D. Denham contends in the *The Flannery O'Connor Bulletin*.

Knowledge and Ignorance

Julian considers himself intellectually superior to those around him. He believes that he sees reality with detachment and objectivity, an "inner compartment of his mind" that is "the only place where he felt free of the general idiocy of his fellows."

However, the ironic narration reveals Julian to be the most self-deceiving character in the story. His seething resentment of his mother and "evil urge to break her spirit" are evidence of his lack of objectivity and his deep, emotional involvement with his mother.

His liberal views on race relations have more to do with a desire to lash out at her than they do with being open-minded or tolerant. In fact, he looks down on his mother for living "according to the laws of her own fantasy world, outside of which she never steps foot," but it is he who spends much of the bus trip deep in fantasy about punishing his mother by bringing home a black friend or a mixed-race girlfriend.

In the final scene, Julian is ignorant as to the reality of his mother's medical condition. When he realizes that she is dying he experiences the first moment of true understanding described in the story. At this point, he feels a sense of intimacy with his mother, calling her "darling," "sweetheart," and "Mamma." The closing line suggests that his mother's death—and the confrontation with his own cruelty and selfishness—will open up the possibility for self-knowledge for Julian, one based on "convergence" rather than detachment.

Topics for Further Study

- Do you think that O'Connor is too unsympathetic to her characters? Do they seem to you like grotesque distortions of humanity or more like regular people you've met? Support your opinion with specific passages from the text.

- Many critics view O'Connor's use of irony as integral to her moral outlook. Discuss her use of irony in relation to one of the moral questions raised in the story.

- O'Connor wrote from a Roman Catholic perspective. Do you think that one needs to be Catholic to fully understand "Everything That Rises Must Converge"? How do you think your own religious or spiritual beliefs (or the lack thereof) influence your response to the story?

- Julian's mother derives many of her opinions from her heritage as part of the slave-holding aristocracy of the pre-Civil War South. Do some research about the conventions and belief systems regarding interactions between blacks and whites in the Old South. How does this information help you understand the interactions between the story's various characters?

Style

Ironic Narration

"Everything That Rises Must Converge" is narrated in the third person, meaning that the events in the story are described from the position of an outside observer. The narrator has access to Julian's inner thoughts, private motivations, and fantasies.

While Julian believes himself to be perfectly objective, the events are described in terms of his emotionally charged relationship with his mother. Yet just because the narrator has access to Julian's innermost thoughts does not mean that readers are meant to empathize with him. As the story continues, the narrator's perspective becomes more distinct from Julian's; by the end, readers are in a position to criticize Julian as strongly as he has criticized his mother.

The narrative technique O'Connor uses to create this effect is called irony. Irony refers to the difference or imbalance between the surface meaning of the words and the effects that they create. Irony allows O'Connor to expose Julian's lack of self-knowledge and his distance from a state of grace.

O'Connor employs another form of irony at the story's conclusion: the difference between intentions and effects. Throughout the story Julian wishes evil on his mother and tries to punish her by pushing his liberal views on her. When the stress of the bus trip leads to a stroke, his wish comes true. Ironically, this leads him to recognize his own weakness rather than revealing hers. He wanted to teach her a lesson, but he ends up learning one himself. O'Connor's ideas about redemption rely on this kind of ironic reversal.

Satire

O'Connor is known for her biting satire, which is the use of ridicule, humor, and wit in order to criticize human nature and society. In "Everything That Rises Must Converge," her characters are all satiric extremes. Sometimes called "grotesques," each character expresses some distortion of human nature; these distortions are also emphasized through physical traits.

Julian's mother "holds[s] herself very erect under the preposterous hat, wearing it like a banner of her imaginary dignity." A self-pitying Julian "wait[s] like Saint Sebastian for the arrows to start piercing him." According to O'Connor's belief system, weakness and sin plague human nature. She wrote from an orthodox Catholic perspective about a secular and profane world and, thus, saw it as her calling to portray sin in no uncertain terms.

As Walter Sullivan asserted in the *Hollins Critic,*

It was Flannery O'Connor's contention that the strange characters who populate her world are essentially no different from you and me. They are drawn more extravagantly, she would admit, but she claimed that this was necessary because of our depravity: for the morally blind, the message of redemption must be writ large.

Some critics find O'Connor's satire heavy-handed, but others argue that her harsh portrayals must be understood in relationship to her more subtle use of irony and in contrast to the glimpses of redemption she offers her fallen characters at the violent conclusions of her stories.

Symbolism

O'Connor's first creative outlet was cartooning, and her stories are dominated by strong visual symbols. In "Everything That Rises Must Converge," the key symbol is the green and purple hat, which is described as "hideous" and "atrocious."

Despite her misgivings about its expensive price, she decides to keep the hat because, she says, "at least I won't meet myself coming and going." This means that Julian's mother believes that she will never meet anyone else wearing the same hat. Yet the turn of phrase "meet myself" suggests how strongly the hat reflects the wearer's identity—which compounds the irony when she encounters an African American woman on the bus wearing the same hat.

In this way, she "meets herself" in the figure of an African American woman. Their connection is further emphasized by the fact that "she and the woman had, in a sense, swapped sons." Julian sits next to the black woman and her young son sits next to Julian's mother, thus creating an additional layer of symbolic mirroring.

That the African American woman wears the same hat—a hat that Julian's mother had to scrimp to pay for—is testament to how far Julian's mother has fallen economically and socially. It also illustrates how far African Americans have risen in American society. The African American woman's social "rise" brings a kind of "convergence" between the two women, but not the transcendent sort referred to in the title.

Historical Context

Southern Race Relations

The generation gap between Julian and his mother manifests itself through their disagreement over race relations, an issue that was a pressing part of public discourse in the early 1960s.

At the turn of the twentieth century, a series of "Jim Crow" laws had been instituted throughout the South; these laws enforced segregation of public places. In fact, for the first half of the twentieth century, blacks and whites used separate facilities: parks, restaurants, clubs, restrooms, and transportation.

In 1954 a landmark Supreme Court decision, *Brown vs. Board of Education,* deemed school

Compare & Contrast

- **1960s:** The Civil Rights movement becomes a viable and powerful movement. After the passage of a series of laws ordering the desegregation of schools, interstate transportation, and various other public accommodations, the Civil Rights Act of 1964 desegregates all public places.

- **Today:** Affirmative action, which led to greater integration in schools and workplaces in the 1970s and 1980s, is challenged in a series of court cases as a form of reverse discrimination.

- **1960s:** In 1966 the Supreme Court strikes down a Virginia law prohibiting interracial marriage; Virginia had been one of sixteen states still outlawing such marriages. In 1967 Secretary of State Dean Rusk's daughter, who is white, makes headlines by marrying a black man. Rusk offers to resign from his post, but President Lyndon Johnson refuses to accept his resignation.

- **Today:** Interracial marriage no longer makes headlines. There are a number of prominent interracial couples in public life. The number of interracial marriages has tripled since 1967 and there are over a million biracial families.

- **1960s:** The oldest of the post-war "baby boomers" reach adolescence and young adult-

hood. Many of this generation differ from their parents in their desire to express their individuality and challenge prevailing social mores and assumptions. A generation gap emerges, with parents and children often having very different attitudes toward important issues.

- **Today:** "Baby boomers" reach middle age, having raised their children in a less conflicted and more tolerant society.

- **1960s:** Founded by wealthy philanthropists in 1906, the Young Women's Christian Association (YWCA) has declined from its former status as an important charitable organization and community center. Instead, it is primarily used as an inexpensive gymnasium and hotel. In 1960 its cafeteria becomes the first pubic dining facility in Atlanta to desegregate. By this time it has become a secular institution.

- **Today:** There are still 326 YMCAs, at least one in every American state. The organization's objectives include social justice and services for women, as well as physical fitness. No mention of religion is made in the YWCA mission statement.

---

segregation as inherently unequal. In the aftermath of this decision, African Americans won the right to share public transportation with whites in a number of Southern cities. In 1960 "sit-ins" at segregated lunch counters became a popular method of protesting against segregation. Such actions spurred the burgeoning Civil Rights Movement, which would lead to important social and legislative changes over the next decade.

In "Everything That Rises Must Converge," Julian's mother refuses to ride the bus alone; this implies that sharing the same vehicle with African Americans would compromise either her safety or her dignity.

Catholic Theology

A devout Roman Catholic, O'Connor differed from other writers in her generation in that she wrote from a deeply religious perspective. "I see from the standpoint of Christian orthodoxy," she asserts. "This means that for me the meaning of life is centered on Redemption by Christ and what I see in the world I see in its relationship to that."

While religious issues are not explicit in "Everything That Rises Must Converge," O'Connor's vision of the sinful nature of the human race dominates the story. "The novelist with Christian concerns will find in modern life distortions which are repugnant to him, and his problem will be to make these appear as distortions to an audience which is used to seeing them as natural,'' O'Connor contends.

''Everything That Rises Must Converge'' refers to the ideas of a Jesuit theologian and scientist named Pierre Teilhard de Chardin (1881–1955). In a book called *The Phenomenon of Man* (1955), which attempts to reconcile the science of evolution with a Christian vision, Teilhard theorizes that after the rise of *homo sapiens* evolution continues on a spiritual level toward a level of pure consciousness called Being. While species diversified biologically until humans came to dominate the earth, evolution began to take the form of rising consciousness and led back toward unification or convergence. At the end of time, all Beings will be as one in God.

Some critics maintain that O'Connor's reference to Teilhard must be ironic, since in the story there is so little evidence of convergence; but others suggest that Julian's revelation at the story's close can be seen as a first step toward the higher consciousness that is God. Julian is negatively affected by his pride, arrogance, and anger. Yet when his mother dies, he recognizes the evil he has done.

The stories throughout the collection create situations where a flawed character comes to a ''vision of himself as he really is, and makes possible a true rising toward Being,'' asserts Dorothy Tuck McFarland in *Flannery O'Connor.*

> That this rising is inevitably painful does not discredit its validity; rather, it emphasizes . . . the tension between the evolutionary thrust toward Being and the human warp that resists it—the warp which O'Connor would have called original sin.

Critical Overview

O'Connor is widely considered one of the most significant writers ever produced by the United States. She was the subject of an unusual amount of critical attention as a young writer, and this fascination has continued over the decades since her death.

Less than a decade after O'Connor started writing, scholars began serious critical interpretation of her work. A special issue of the journal *Critique* was devoted entirely to her writing in 1958. Early approaches to her fiction tended to

focus on the grotesque extremes of her characterization and the bleak violence of her plots.

As she responded to early interpretations with explicit explanations of her beliefs about art and faith in various lectures and essays (collected in 1969 under the title *Mystery and Manners: Occasional Prose*), the critical focus shifted toward O'Connor's moral framework and her religious vision.

The posthumous publication of her last collection of stories, *Everything That Rises Must Converge,* further solidified O'Connor's reputation as one of the strongest and most original American voices of her generation.

Granville Hicks described the stories in the collection as ''the best things she ever wrote. They are superb, and they are terrible. She took a cold, hard look at human beings, and set down with marvelous precision what she saw.''

Even Walter Sullivan, writing one of the book's weaker reviews in the *Hollins Critic,* credited these ''last fruits of Flannery O'Connor's particular genius'' for ''work[ing] their own small counter reformation in a faithless world.''

The main criticism of the volume focused on O'Connor's singular purpose and the constant repetition of her main themes. ''She had only a few ideas, but messianic feelings about them,'' contended the *Nation*'s Webster Schott. He praised her for doing what she does superbly:

> Myopic in her vision, Flannery O'Connor was among those few writers who raise questions worth thinking about after the lights are out and the children are safely in bed. What is reality? What are the possibilities for hope? How much can man endure?

Critical attention to her work continues. The way she expressed her Roman Catholic faith remained a subject of fascination and debate for scholars. Her literary influences have been discussed, as well as her place within the Southern Gothic regional tradition.

Dorothy Tuck McFarland maintained:

> While [O'Connor] was an artist of the highest caliber, she thought of herself as a prophet, and her art was the medium for her prophetic message. It was her intention that her stories should shock, that they should bring the reader to encounter a vision he could face with difficulty or outright repugnance. And she wanted her vision not only to be seen for what it was but also to be taken seriously. She was confident enough of her artistic powers to believe this would happen, even if it took fifty or a hundred years.

Civil Rights icon Rosa Parks sits at the front of a Montgomery, Alabama, city bus in the aftermath of the Supreme Court ruling banning segregation on public transit vehicles. O'Connor's story, which tackles the issue of race relations in the 1960s, revolves around a bus ride taken by a Southern mother and son.

She did not need to wait so long.

Criticism

Sarah Madsen Hardy

Madsen Hardy has a doctorate in English literature and is a freelance writer and editor. In the *following essay, she discusses how O'Connor's religious vision shapes the seemingly secular content of "Everything That Rises Must Converge."*

In many essays and public statements, O'Connor identifies herself as a Catholic writer and asserts that her aims as an artist are inextricably tied to her religious faith. She claims that it is her specific goal to offer a glimpse of God's mystery and, thus, to lead readers—whom she sees as, for the most part,

What Do I Read Next?

- *A Good Man Is Hard to Find* (1955) is O'Connor's first collection of short stories. It shares the unique moral outlook of "Everything That Rises Must Converge."

- O'Connor's novel *The Violent Bear It Away* (1960) concerns a young boy's resistance to his calling as a prophet.

- *The Collected Stories of William Faulkner* (1995), edited by Erroll McDonald, gathers Faulkner's short fiction. These stories explore moral dramas against a Southern backdrop. O'Connor is most often compared to Faulkner.

- *A Curtain of Green and Other Stories* (1941), a collection of stories by Eudora Welty, shares O'Connor's flare for local idiom, but takes a gentler approach to its eccentric characters.

- *The Heart Is a Lonely Hunter* (1940), the first novel by Carson McCullers, describes the moral isolation of a deaf-mute girl in a small Southern town.

- *The Second Coming* (1999), by Walker Percy, is a tragicomic novel chronicling a man's search for love and religious meaning.

---

spiritually lost in the modern, secular world—back toward the path of redemption.

This information may be somewhat bewildering for those first approaching O'Connor's writing through her short story "Everything That Rises Must Converge." While some of her other fiction focuses on specifically religious themes, this story, involving the generational and ideological conflict between mother and son, seems to be thoroughly secular in nature.

Set in the South in the early 1960s, "Everything That Rises Must Converge" is firmly grounded in the social history of that time and place. Julian, the arrogant and alienated son, abhors his mother's racism and resents her attachment to outdated ideas of Southern aristocracy. Their differences come to a head during a ride they take together on a recently integrated city bus. The questions the story raises are obviously moral, but how they relate specifically to Christian theology is not immediately apparent.

The story contains a few passing mentions of heaven and sin, but these words are not used in a serious theological sense. (For example, exasperated with his mother's indecisiveness, "Julian raised his eyes to heaven.") There is a single reference comparing Julian to Saint Sebastian, a Christian martyr, but it is used ironically, in order to show Julian's exaggerated self-pity.

In another remote reference to religion, Julian's mother attends a weight reduction class at the 'Y'—the Young Women's Christian Association. But at the time O'Connor wrote, the YWCA, which was founded on Christian values, had become a secular institution. It seems that the few references to Christianity are largely emptied of meaning.

However, the first bit of research into "Everything That Rises Must Converge," reveals that the title of the story refers to the philosophy of an obscure Jesuit theologian, Pierre Teilhard de Chardin. Teilhard offers a Catholic version of the science of evolution, theorizing that lower life forms evolved toward greater diversity and complexity, rising to the level of man, who exists at the midpoint between animal life and God. At this point, evolution continues—yet only on a spiritual level.

Instead of diversifying biologically, humanity takes a path of convergence—that is, a path toward intersection or union—rising toward the unification of spirit in God. Referring to the Christian concept of revelation, Teilhard posits that at the end of time human spirit will have at last risen to the ultimate point of convergence, where all people are as one in Christ.

O'Connor states in her title that everything that rises must converge. This sounds optimistic and affirmative—which faith, by nature, is. What can this theory have to do with the bleak view of human nature that O'Connor presents in the story?

It is helpful to remember that Teilhard conceives of humankind as the *midpoint* between the ultimate unity of offered by God and the chaotic savagery of animal life. O'Connor writes from this midpoint, grounding her fiction in the contemporary secular word, a world she sees as sinful and benighted.

"If the Catholic writer hopes to reveal mysteries, he will have to do it by describing truthfully what he sees from where he is," she writes in "The Church and the Fiction Writer." (This and the other writings by O'Connor cited in this essay are collected in *Mysteries and Manners,* edited by Sally and Robert Fitzgerald.)

What O'Connor sees when she looks at the world from her Catholic perspective is mostly dark, chaotic, and divisive. "An affirmative vision cannot be demanded of [the Catholic writer] without limiting his freedom to observe what man has done with the things of God," she maintains.

Staring into the weaknesses of the human heart, O'Connor finds that what man has done is not good. "[The Catholic writer] may find in the end that instead of reflecting the heart of things, he has only reflected our broken condition and, through it, the face of the devil we are possessed by," she writes in another essay on the topic, "Novelist and Believer."

Returning to the events of the story, it is possible to see them now in a theological light. In "The Catholic Novelist in the Protestant South," O'Connor contends, "The Catholic novel can't be categorized by subject matter, but only by what it assumes about human and divine reality." She considers it her calling to write about her here and now, which is the South in the 1960s, not heaven.

O'Connor portrays the fallen nature of humankind in terms of what she sees from where she is: the arrogance and blindness that divides son from mother, as well as white from black. She portrays the pain and folly that are "our broken condition," the recognition of which is the only means for the human soul to rise toward grace.

The textual references to rising in "Everything That Rises Must Converge" refer literally to problems of race and social class that were reaching a

> " These are some of the ways that O'Connor shows the terribly compromised ways that people 'rise' and 'converge.' Is she so different from Julian, though? For she takes such a dim view of the all-too-human characters she creates. Are they really redeemable?"

boiling point when O'Connor wrote the story. These issues demonstrate clearly enough the failure of humans to achieve spiritual unity.

Julian's mother perceives the rise of African American people as related to her own family's fall from the social and economic heights it enjoyed before the Civil War. She thinks that she knows who she is—meaning she knows where her family belongs in a rigid racial and social hierarchy.

The fact that the family is no longer rich means to her that society is out of order—but this does not cause her to doubt her inherent superiority or the validity of the categories that divide people from one another. "I tell you," she says to Julian, meaning to comfort him about his failure to live up to his ambitions or to make any money, "the bottom rail is on the top."

She attributes their reduced circumstances to the improving rights of African Americans, evidence that "the world is in a mess everywhere." Referring to the social and economic progress of African Americans in the South, the result of the incipient Civil Rights Movement, she says, "They should rise, yes, but on their own side of the fence."

The conflict in the story originates in part because blacks don't rise "on their own side of the fence," but insist on equal rights by means of integration, which can be seen as a kind of social convergence. Like the rising in the story, the convergence that O'Connor portrays reflects the social strife of her times.

Julian's mother is uncomfortable with social convergence between blacks and whites on a most literal level. She won't ride the bus without her son, imagining some abstract danger or indignity in simply sharing space with people of a different race.

Moreover, she reserves a special condescending pity for people of mixed race, who can be understood as the fullest realization of black-white convergence. "The ones I feel sorry for . . . are the ones that are half white. They're tragic."

However, cultural and political changes have made this kind of convergence inevitable. O'Connor demonstrates this through the symbol of the hat, evidence that Julian's mother has "fallen" and the black woman has "risen" to a point where they "meet themselves" as they sit across from each other on a public bus in identical hats. This convergence has embarrassment as its main effect—a far cry from the transcendent convergence Teilhard envisions of the end of time.

Yet this is O'Connor's point: to show, at this point in human history, the unevolved state of the human soul through her characters' weaknesses.

If Julian's mother resists convergence by placing her faith in social separation and hierarchy, Julian takes an even more extreme position, attempting to cut himself off from identification with other people all together, leaving him arguably even further from grace than his mother.

Julian's mother doesn't mind living in an apartment in a declining neighborhood or going to the 'Y' with poor women, while Julian fantasizes about making enough money to move into a house where "the nearest neighbor would be three miles away." This represents not only Julian's longing for status, but also the distance at which he holds himself from fellow humans.

His feelings of superiority are not explicitly tied to race or class, but they take an even more acute form than those of his mother. While she is naive, believing that she treats people well through her misguided gentility, Julian openly wishes ill on others.

"It gave him a certain satisfaction to see injustice in daily operation," the narrator reports as Julian observes a white woman change seats after a black man sits near her on the bus, "It confirmed his view that with a few exceptions there was no one worth knowing within a radius of three hundred miles."

O'Connor again characterizes Julian in terms of his desire to resist any kind of human connection when she describes the "inner compartment of his mind" that is "the only place where he felt free of the general idiocy of his fellows." Julian attributes what he believes is his judgment and insight to his ability to sever bonds—especially that with his mother. "Most miraculous of all, instead of being blinded by love for her as she was for him, he had cut himself emotionally free of her and could see her with complete objectivity." He fiercely resists his mother's hold on him, despite her devoted love.

These are some of the ways that O'Connor shows the terribly compromised ways that people "rise" and "converge." Is she so different from Julian, though? For she takes such a dim view of the all-too-human characters she creates. Are they really redeemable?

O'Connor would answer with a resounding yes. "[The Catholic novelist] cannot see man as determined; it cannot see him as totally depraved. It will see him as incomplete in himself, as prone to evil, but as redeemable when his own efforts are assisted by grace," she asserts in "The Catholic Novelist in the Protestant South."

At the end of the story, both Julian and his mother are offered some opportunity for the kind of true convergence that Teilhard envisions. As she dies, Julian's mother calls out for Caroline, her black nursemaid, showing that this early emotional bond ultimately transcends her self-justifying beliefs about racial superiority. Julian, who until the very end rails against his mother, finally breaks out of his distancing "inner compartment" and calls out for his her in child-like terms of affection, "Darling, sweetheart . . . Mamma, Mamma!"

These are changes not of the head but of the heart. The sky does not open to reveal God. These changes are earthbound and real.

In *The True Country*, his study of the place of Catholic theology in her writing, Carter W. Martin explains that O'Connor's fiction "gives dramatic, concrete form to the humble and often banal insight that enables the individual man to move toward grace by rising only slightly. It is *this* movement that she means when she speaks of our slow participation in redemption." O'Connor writes about the distance of her characters from a state of grace, but with an abiding faith in the humans ability to—someday, *slowly*—cross that distance.

Source: Sarah Madsen Hardy, for *Short Stories for Students,* Gale, 2000.

Alice Hall Petry

Petry's discussion in this essay centers on the echoes of Margaret Mitchell's novel Gone with the Wind *that she perceives in ''Everything That Rises Must Converge'' and the resonance these echoes add to the reader's understanding of the story.*

Flannery O'Connor knew only too well that she could not assume her audience brought a solid background in Christianity to their readings of her fiction. It was part of the price she paid for being an insistently Roman Catholic writer in the increasingly secularized United States of the mid-twentieth century. One element which she could count on being familiar to any American reader from any socioeconomic or educational stratum was, however, Margaret Mitchell's *Gone with the Wind* (1936). That familiarity enabled O'Connor to incorporate into her fiction various echoes of Mitchell's novel, echoes sometimes transparent and sometimes subtle, sometimes parodic and sometimes serious. In ''A Late Encounter with the Enemy,'' for example, the reference to the ''preemy'' of twelve years before indicates that ''General'' George Poker Sash had attended the world premiere of the novel's movie version in Atlanta in 1939. Sadly, Sash's finest hour had come not during the Civil War, but during the premiere of the movie which, seventy-five years later, had romanticized and popularized the conflict. Likewise, in ''A Good Man Is Hard to Find'' the grandmother tells little John Wesley that the plantation is ''Gone with the Wind. Ha. Ha,'' her pallid joke pointing, once again, to the pervasive acceptance of Mitchell's rendering of the most painful era in southern history. One O'Connor story which has a special kinship with Mitchell's classic story is ''Everything That Rises Must Converge.'' Taken together, these echoes of *Gone with the Wind* —some blatant parallels, some ironic reversals— underscore the story's thesis that Julian's and his mother's responses to life in the South of the civil rights movement are unreasonable and, ultimately, self-destructive precisely because those responses are based upon actions and values popularized by Mitchell's book. Even worse, in several instances, actions and values are pathetic distortions of what Mitchell presents in *Gone with the Wind.*

A clear connection between ''Everything That Rises Must Converge'' and *Gone with the Wind* is the mother's hat. As Patricia Dinneen Maida points

> One element which she could count on being familiar to any American reader from any socioeconomic or educational stratum was, however, Margaret Mitchell's <u>Gone with the Wind</u> (1936). That familiarity enabled O'Connor to incorporate into her fiction various echoes of Mitchell's novel, echoes sometimes transparent and sometimes subtle, sometimes parodic and sometimes serious."

out, O'Connor is ''highly selective'' in her choice of details; John Ower confirms this by arguing the importance of the mother offering little Carver a new Lincoln penny in lieu of a Jefferson nickel. Of course, the ugly hat which the mother has purchased for an outrageous $7.50, a hat identical to that of the large black woman, will help confirm that they are ''doubles'' and, thereby, will make a statement about racial equality. But there is more to the hat than this. Note O'Connor's careful description of it, presented twice: ''It was a hideous hat. A purple velvet flap came down on one side of it and stood up on the other; the rest of it was green and looked like a cushion with the stuffing out. [Julian] decided it was less comical than jaunty and pathetic.'' The purple of the hat suggests bruising. Thus it is very appropriate for a woman whose eyes seem bruised and whose face looks purple as her son torments her, and who will literally be struck to the ground by an overstuffed purse. Less obvious is the irony that her black double has no doubt suffered the bruises of psychological and physical abuse during her life in the South, bruises which are less apparent to whites who, for generations, had been conditioned to believe that blacks have less sensitivity to blows than whites. In addition, various commentators have pointed out that the color purple has religious associations, most notably Easter redemption and penance. At the same time, the antipodal orientations conveyed by the purple flap—''down on one side . . . up on the other''—graphically depict the twin socioeconomic movements in the South: the downward movement of aristocratic families like the Godhighs and the Chestnys, and the upward movement of ''upwardly mobile'' blacks who, because of improved economic status, have ''as much freedom to pursue absurdity as the whites.'' In part, then, the hat's purple flap renders semiotically the impact of the civil rights movement on southern society. Less clear, however, is why the rest of the hat is green and looks ''like a cushion with the stuffing out''—less clear, that is, unless one remembers *Gone with the Wind*. Overwhelmed by the familial and regional crises engendered by the Civil War, the widowed Scarlett O'Hara is all the more personally dismayed by the attire of Emmie Slattery, a ''poor white trash'' neighbor who has suddenly stepped up economically by marrying the underhanded Jonas Wilkerson, and who is considering buying Tara: ''And what a cunning hat! Bonnets must be out of style, for this hat was only an absurd flat red velvet affair, perched on top of [Emmie's] head like a stiffened pancake.'' The velvet pancake, however ''absurd,'' does not go unnoticed by Scarlett's creative self, for shortly thereafter the threadbare mistress of Tara, desperate for $300 more for municipal taxes, resolves to construct a new outfit out of household goods and coerce the sum out of Rhett Butler. With the help of Mammy, Scarlett makes a dazzling dress out of the mansion's ''moss-green velvet curtains'' and a petticoat out of the satin linings of the parterres; her pantalets are trimmed with pieces of Tara's lace curtains. Even the plantation's rooster surrenders his ''gorgeous bronze and green-black tail feathers'' to decorate the green velvet hat. Ashley Wilkes is duly moved: ''he had never known such gallantry as the gallantry of Scarlett O'Hara going forth to conquer the world in her mother's velvet curtains and the tail feathers of a rooster.'' As Dorothy Walters points out, the fact that Julian's mother's hat looks like a cushion without its stuffing makes her ''instantaneously ridiculous. . . . Imagery deflates ego. What the character conveys is not what he intends,'' but if one remembers the Scarlett O'Hara connection, it is clear that the hat suggests the mother's desperate bid for dignity, for a Scarlett O'Hara-type ''gallantry,'' as much as it does a deflation of her ego. True, Julian's mother did not actually make her hat out of a cushion, but it is entirely possible that, at some

level, Julian's mother—herself a widow from a good southern family down on her luck—may have been identifying with the plucky Scarlett, using her as a role model of a lady who survives by making do with what she has. Indeed one could say of Scarlett just as readily as of Julian's mother that she ''had struggled fiercely to feed and clothe and put [her child] through school,'' and Scarlett eventually does attain the economic and social prominence that Julian's mother can only dream of through her son, a would-be writer. Perhaps Scarlett's own makeshift outfit looked as ''jaunty and pathetic'' as the hat of Julian's mother; but it surely was unique (Scarlett would never ''meet [her]self coming and going,'' and the encounter with Rhett ultimately led to her successful business career. The redoubtable Scarlett must have been a role model for many women in the same situation as Julian's mother, so the hat—''hideous,'' ''atrocious,'' ''preposterous''— may be seen as her pathetic attempt to emulate not simply a southern belle in dire straits, but the most famous belle of them all. Whether Julian's mother consciously has Scarlett in mind is a moot point. What matters is that she is conducting herself like a romanticized fictional character from a book set a century before. Times, however, have changed.

Nothing illustrates these changing times more readily than the issue of ladyhood, an issue which permeates both ''Everything That Rises Must Converge'' and *Gone with the Wind*. Julian's mother insisted that ''ladies did not tell their age or weight''; she was ''one of the few members of the Y reducing class who arrived in hat and gloves''; and she entered the bus ''with a little smile, as if she were going into a drawing room where everyone had been waiting for her.'' Julian's mother, in short, regards herself as the consummate lady. It is precisely here that she parts company most glaringly with Scarlett, who herself ''found the road to ladyhood hard.'' Scarlett scorns those well-bred women, financially ruined by the Civil War, who cling desperately to the manners and trappings of the antebellum South. ''She knew she should believe devoutly, as they did, that a born lady remained a lady, even if reduced to poverty, but *she could not make herself believe it* now.'' For all her self-imagined kinship with archetypal belles like Scarlett, Julian's mother is actually more akin to these pathetic women who cannot give up the past. True, Scarlett creates for herself a magnificent outfit, one befitting a lady; but she does it only because she needs the $300 from Rhett. If not for this emergency, she would have continued wearing the slippers reinforced with carpeting and the "raggedy," much mended dress which her harsh postwar life on Tara demanded. She is practical and has no illusions about herself or about what she must do to survive. Julian's mother, however, is but a pale copy of Scarlett. She was practical enough to finance Julian's college education, and she realizes that the $7.50 she paid for the hat should be put towards the gas bill; but she only sent him to a third-rate college, and she capitulates with notable ease to her son's suggestion that she forget the bill and keep the hat. Likewise, she lives in a poor neighborhood only because forty years before it was "fashionable," whereas Scarlett would never fool herself into thinking that past glory had any true bearing on one's current situation. She wants to retain Tara, after all, out of principle and as a matter of family pride, not because it is chic.

The situations of Scarlett and Julian's mother are, of course, superficially similar, and one can see why the example of *Gone with the Wind* would appeal to a middle-aged southern woman of "good" family in the early 1960s. Scarlett is trying to survive in a South undergoing social, economic and racial upheavals due to the Civil War, while Julian's mother is trying to survive in a South undergoing similar upheavals caused by the civil rights movement, World War II and the Korean conflict. Julian's mother states repeatedly that "'the world is in such a mess,'" and that "'the bottom rail is on the top.'" This is precisely how Scarlett perceives her own world: "Ellen's [Scarlett's mother's] ordered world was gone and a brutal world had taken its place, a world wherein every standard, every value had changed." Scarlett's immediate response to this realization is chillingly like Julian's: she blames her mother. Scarlett's Julian-like cynicism and rudeness

> helped her to forget her own bitterness that everything her mother had told her about life was wrong. Nothing her mother had taught her was of any value whatsoever now and Scarlett's heart was sore and puzzled. It did not occur to her that Ellen could not have foreseen the collapse of the civilization in which she raised her daughters, could not have anticipated the disappearing of the places in society for which she trained them so well. It did not occur to her that Ellen had looked down a vista of placid future years, all like the uneventful years of her own life, when she had taught her to be gentle and gracious, honorable and kind, modest and truthful. Life treated women well when they learned those lessons, said Ellen.

Scarlett's resentment towards Ellen O'Hara may help explain Julian's own palpable contempt for his mother. She represents a world, a lifestyle that Julian wants but can never attain, and he bullies her like Scarlett bullies her sisters, wishing he could slap his mother and hoping that some black would help him "to teach her a lesson." But where the resilient Scarlett eventually comes to forgive her mother for the loss of her world, Julian cannot forgive his. He literally torments her to death.

For Scarlett, Julian and his mother, the focal point of the world they have lost is the ancestral mansion. Julian's great-grandfather had a plantation and two hundred slaves, and Julian dreams of it "regularly. He would stand on the wide porch, listening to the rustle of oak leaves, then wander through the high-ceilinged hall into the parlor that opened onto it and gaze at the worn rugs and faded draperies." But Julian's memory of it is marred: "The double stairways had rotted and been torn down. Negroes were living in it." The prospect of the family mansion undergoing such a reversal is also what haunts Scarlett. Part of the reason she so fears the purchase of Tara by its former overseer for his wife Emmie (the local "dirty tow-headed slut") is that "these low common creatures [would be] living in this house, bragging to their low common friends how they had turned the proud O'Haras out. Perhaps they'd even bring negroes here to dine and sleep." But, once again, Scarlett differs significantly from Julian and his mother: she is truly adaptable. To save Tara, "she changed swiftly to meet this new world for which she was not prepared," even taking advantage of her status as a "lady"—a status which, as noted, she does not take too seriously—to cheat male customers in her lumber business. Julian and his mother utterly lack Scarlett's imagination and resourcefulness, although they have both deluded themselves into thinking they do possess these qualities. As Sister Kathleen Feeley notes [in *Flannery O'Connor: Voice of the Peacock*], Julian's mother, "secure in her private stronghold . . . can afford to be 'adaptable' to present conditions, such as associating at the YWCA with women who are not in her social class." However, this is hardly "adaptability" as the enterprising and non-sentimental Scarlett would understand it. Nothing illustrates this inability to adapt more graphically than the death of Julian's mother at the end of the story.

The death scene itself echoes *Gone with the Wind*. Ellen, Scarlett's mother, dying of typhoid, had regressed to her childhood: "'she think she a lil gal back in Savannah,'" and called for her long-dead sweetheart, Philippe. Likewise, Julian's mother regresses to her secure childhood and calls for her mammy Caroline, a request which indicates that, ''for all its defects, the older generation had more genuine personal feeling for Negroes than [Julian's] with its heartless liberalism'' [according to John R. May in his book *The Pruning Word: The Parables of Flannery O'Connor*]. The death of Julian's mother results from her ''loss of illusion'' and, concomitantly, her awareness that she can never adapt to the newly-revealed reality: [as Leon V. Driskell and Joan T. Brittain wrote in *The Eternal Crossroads: The Art of Flannery O'Connor*] it is ''more than she can bear, but mercifully her mind *breaks*'' (emphasis added)—a perfect verb to use since, like a brittle stick, Julian's mother responds to the stress of her realization by ''breaking'' physically and psychologically. Her son, albeit physically alive, is psychically shattered, pathetically calling ''Mamma!'' as he enters ''the world of guilt and sorrow.'' In sharp contrast, Scarlett is like a reed. She bends under duress, adjusts, survives.

What Julian's mother could not accept, and what Julian had only deluded himself into believing that he did accept, is not that everything rises, but that everything that rises must *converge*. Hence her insistence that it's fine if blacks rise as long as they stay on their side of the fence, and her dismay over mulattoes, those emblems of the process of racial convergence. The fact that the black woman wore an identical hat (O'Connor takes care to describe it twice) is another blatant emblem of convergence, which Julian's mother had tried to deny ''by reducing the other woman to a subhuman level and seeing the implied relationship between them as a comic impossibility'' [as Dorothy Tuck McFarland wrote in her book *Flannery O'Connor*]—that is, by responding as if the black woman ''were a monkey that had stolen her hat.'' It is reminiscent of Scarlett's shocked reaction to Emmie's dressing like a lady (which she is not). Scarlett's response to the convergence which she sees around her in postwar Georgia is more constructive: she accepts what she must and changes what she can. Scarlett must often swallow her pride, learning the lumber business from scratch and even, in effect, offering herself to Rhett in exchange for negotiable currency. But survive and thrive she does, and ''ladylike'' behavior be damned. And if it turned out that ladylike behavior could be damned so readily in 1865, what could be more pathetic than trying to retain it in 1960?

The superficial similarities in their situations may have led Julian's mother to emulate Scarlett, consciously or otherwise. But as Kathryn Lee Seidel argues [in *The Southern Belle in the American Novel*], Scarlett is ''both conventional and unique,'' as is evident from her green eyes. Writes Seidel: ''Of all the belles I have studied, she is the only one with green eyes. By assigning Scarlett this eye color, Mitchell both acknowledges and overturns this small detail of the belle stereotype. It is a technique Mitchell uses masterfully throughout the novel; with it, *she compliments her audience's knowledge of and affection for the stereotype, but uses it for her own purposes*'' (emphasis added). O'Connor is using an identical technique in her presentation of Julian's blue-eyed mother, who evidently has extracted selectively for emulation only the most conventional, most romantic aspects of southern womanhood that were popularized by *Gone with the Wind*. Without the ''unique'' qualities that are so vital in the characterization of Scarlett (her personal toughness, imagination, adaptability), the emulation of those conventional aspects is pathetic—and especially so in a middle-aged woman living a century after the Civil War. No doubt Julian's mother would be flattered to see the connection between herself and Scarlett O'Hara signified by the cushion-like hat; and no doubt Scarlett herself would find that connection a grim commentary on the self-image of Julian's mother.

There is no copy of *Gone with the Wind* in Flannery O'Connor's personal library; but in view of her considerable knowledge of southern literature, it is difficult to believe that she had never read Mitchell's novel. And one can surmise readily which features of it would be of special interest to O'Connor: the Georgia setting; the lovely description of ante-bellum Tara surrounded by flocks of turkeys and geese, birds being, of course, a life-long love of O'Connor's; the startling scene wherein Scarlett's father—like O'Connor, an Irish Catholic living in Protestant Georgia—is given a Church of England funeral (the ignorant mourners ''thought it the Catholic ceremony and immediately rearranged their first opinion that the Catholic services were cold and Popish''); even the references to Milledgeville, O'Connor's hometown (e.g., Scarlett admits to Mammy, '''I know so few Milledgeville folks'''). It is far more to the point, however, that O'Connor could readily assume that other American readers and movie-goers, of whatever faith or region, would be familiar with Mitchell's story and would respond to echoes of it in her writings. As is illustrated by the case of ''Everything That Rises Must Converge,'' those echoes could be used, comically or otherwise, to help guide our responses to the often enigmatic fiction of Flannery O'Connor.

Source: Alice Hall Petry, ''Miss O'Connor and Mrs. Mitchell: The Example of 'Everything That Rises,''' in *The Southern Quarterly,* Vol. XXVII, No. 4, Summer 1989, pp. 5–15.

Alice Hall Petry

O'Connor's use of the YWCA as the destination of Julian's mother is Petry's focus in this article, in which the critic shows how ''the Y serves as a gauge of the degeneration of the mother's Old South family and, concomitantly, of the breakdown of old, church-related values in the United States of the mid-twentieth century.''

As Patricia Dinneen Maida has pointed out, Flannery O'Connor ''does not flood her work with details; she is highly selective—choosing only those aspects that are most revealing.'' The justice of this observation in regard to ''Everything That Rises Must Converge'' was confirmed recently by John Ower, who argues persuasively that Julian's mother's having to offer a penny to the little Black boy in lieu of a nickel illustrates the ascendancy of Lincolnesque racial tolerance over Jeffersonian segregation in the South of the Civil Rights Movement. O'Connor's capacity to utilize detail symbolically in ''Everything That Rises'' is evident even in the destination of Julian's mother: the local ''Y.'' Mentioned no less than five times in this brief story, the Y serves as a gauge of the degeneration of the mother's Old South family and, concomitantly, of the breakdown of old, church-related values in the United States of the mid-twentieth century.

As Julian's mother is wont to point out, she is related to the Godhighs and the Chestnys, prominent families of the Old South whose former status is conveyed nicely by the high-ceilinged, double-staircased mansion which Julian had seen as a child, and of which he still dreams regularly. But with the end of the plantation system, the mother's glorious ancestry is meaningless: she has had to work to put her son through a third-rate college, she apparently does not own a car (hence the dreaded, fatal ride on the integrated bus), and she lives in a poor neighborhood which had been fashionable forty years earlier. One of the most telling indicators of her loss of socioeconomic status is, however, also one of the most subtle: she participates in a program at the YWCA.

As Maida notes, a reducing class at the Y is a ''bourgeois event''; but more than this, it suggests how much Julian's mother, and the socioeconomic system she represents, has declined by the early

> " Mentioned no less than five times in this brief story, the Y serves as a gauge of the degeneration of the mother's Old South family and, concomitantly, of the breakdown of old, church-related values in the United States of the mid-twentieth century."

1960s. The Young Women's Christian Association has been functioning in some form in the United States since 1866; the national organization of the ''Young Women's Christian Association of the United States of America'' was effected in 1906. From the beginning, it was a group whose local chapters were organized and financed by the very wealthy, including Grace Hoadley Dodge (1856–1914), the daughter and great-granddaughter of prominent American philanthropists. The civic-minded Miss Dodge managed to supplement her own generous personal contributions by soliciting enormous gifts from captains of industry such as George W. Vanderbilt, and YWCA chapters spread throughout the United States, including the rapidly industrializing post-World War I South. In the late nineteenth-and early twentieth-centuries, then, a woman with the family background of Julian's mother would have been an organizer and financial supporter of the YWCA; but to actually participate in the programs would have been unheard-of, since the Association was intended specifically to benefit ''young women of the operative classes''—that is, young women who were either immigrants or poor native-born country girls seeking employment in large cities, and who were ''dependent on their own exertion for support.'' That the reducing class Julian's mother attends is for ''working girls over fifty'' is thus not only a transparent joke on the self-image of a middle-aged woman (i.e., a fifty-plus ''girl'') but also a sad commentary on Julian's mother having become one of the desperate members of ''the operative classes'': with the loss of the

Godhigh/Chestny plantation, she is simply another poor, naive country girl trying to survive in a hostile urban environ ment. And the hat and gloves she pathetically wears to the Y—those emblems of wealth and respectability of women such as Grace Dodge—serve only to underscore her socioeconomic decline.

At the same time that it sought to help working girls on a personal level, the YWCA of the United States was a surprisingly important force in national and international affairs. At the turn of the century the YWCA, under the leadership of its ''industrial secretary'' Florence Simms, was actively involved in exposing the poor working conditions of women and children and campaigning for legislation to improve those conditions. Through the publication of books, pamphlets, and magazines (such as *Association Monthly*, begun in 1907) and a series of well-publicized national conventions and international conferences, the YWCA called for America's participation in the World Court and the League of Nations; sought the modification of divorce laws, improved Sino-American relations, and world-wide disarmament; advocated sex education as early as 1913; and, through the platform known as the ''Social Ideals of the Churches,'' campaigned vigorously for labor unions—a bold move at a time (1920) when anything resembling Bolshevism was anathema. In short, in its early years, the YWCA never shrank from controversial social issues and often was a pioneer in facing and correcting social problems. That stance was perhaps best illustrated by the 1915 convention in Louisville, Kentucky, in which Black and white members of the YWCA met to discuss ways to improve race relations in the United States. In fine, had ''Everything That Rises'' been written in 1915, that YWCA to which she travels throughout the story might well have been the common meeting-ground of Julian's mother and her ''black double''; but only 45 years after the pioneering interracial convention in Louisville, the YWCA had declined to the point where, far from being a center of racial understanding and integration, it was essentially a free health club for poor white women. The Black woman, after all, gets off at the same bus stop as Julian's mother, but there is nothing to suggest that she, too, is headed for the Y. And much as the YWCA had lost its earlier status as a force for racial understanding, it also had lost its status as a source of practical help: although the Y is only four blocks from where his mother collapses, Julian does not go there for help; and, unlike the early days when the YWCA would literally send its members to factories to conduct prayer meetings for the working women, no one from the Y comes to Julian's mother's aid. Where only a few years before the Y would have been the first source of aid for a desperate woman, by the early 1960s, it was as meaningless and impersonal as the gymnasium to which it had been reduced. The startling decline of the once powerful, liberal, and comforting YWCA parallels the decline of the Old South—and the old America—embodied in Julian's mother. As [Leon V.] Driskell and [Joan T.] Brittain observe [in The Eternal Crossroads: The Art of Flannery O'Connor] ''the-world around her has changed drastically and no longer represents the values she endorses.''

The aspect of the YWCA's decline which would most have disturbed a writer such as O'Connor, however, is its secularization, for she knew only too well that the average American of the twentieth century was out of touch with Christianity. From its inception, the YWCA was regarded as the ''handmaid of the Church''; in the early years, ''The Sunday afternoon 'gospel meeting' was the heart of the whole organization; always there were Bible classes, and mission study extended the interest beyond the local community and out into the world,'' while the improved working conditions and wages of the working girls were seen not as ends in themselves, but as means of generating ''true piety in themselves and others.'' But as early as World War I, the religious dimension of the Association was losing ground—a phenomenon noted with dismay by YWCA leaders, who nonetheless recognized that it was part of a nation-wide move towards secularization: ''The period extending from the day when Bible study was taken for granted as being all-important to the day when there might be no Bible study in the program of a local Association shows changes, not only in the Association, but in religion in general.'' Those changes were reflected in the requirements for admission to membership in the YWCA. To join the nineteenth-century ''Ladies' Christian Association,'' a woman had to prove herself a member ''in good standing of an Evangelical church''; by 1926, church membership was no longer a requirement, and the declaration that ''I desire to enter the Christian fellowship of the Association'' was deemed adequate for membership. Small wonder that the gymnasium, a standard feature of even the earliest YWCA chapters since bodily health was seen as conducive to spiritual health, became divorced from its Christian context: for many Americans after mid-century, ''the Y'' is synonymous with ''the gym.'' Indeed, the secularization of the YWCA is conveyed dramatically by its nicknames. To its earliest members, the Young Women's Christian Association was known informally as "the Association." That emphasis on Christian sisterhood is obscured by the popular abbreviation "YWCA," and it is completely lost by the Association's slangy contemporary nickname, "the Y"—a term with an implied emphasis on youth. It is ironically appropriate, then, that a "working girl over fifty" in youth-minded America would go to the Y for a reducing class, apparently oblivious to the Association's tradition of Christian living and racial understanding. For O'Connor, Julian's mother would be painfully typical of most mid-century Americans, who neither understand nor appreciate the meaning and purpose of the original Young Women's Christian Association. As such, Julian's mother's situation—like the degeneration of the YWCA into a gymnasium—is a gauge of the secularization of American life and the loss of the "old" values and standards.

Source: Alice Hall Petry, "O'Connor's 'Everything That Rises Must Converge,'" in *The Explicator,* Vol. 45, No. 3, Spring 1987, pp. 51–54.

John Ower

In the following essay, Ower comments on the significance of the penny that Julian's mother gives the young black boy and the nickel she would ordinarily have given, arguing that "the designs of these pieces suggest a nexus of meanings relating to the social, racial and religious themes" of the story.

In O'Connor's story, the violent climactic "convergence" of black and white races is precipitated by Julian's mother offering a coin to a little Negro boy. Her customary gift to black children is a nickel, but she has been able to find only a cent in her pocketbook. That the fateful coin is a penny, and that it is newly minted, are both emphasized by O'Connor through being twice mentioned. The author thereby hints the significance with regard to "Everything that Rises . . ." of the Lincoln cent and Jefferson nickel (the two coins current in 1961 when O'Connor's story was written). The designs of these pieces suggest a nexus of meanings relating to the social, racial and religious themes of "Everything that Rises . . . ."

The obverse of the Lincoln cent bears the portrait of its namesake, to the left of which is the motto "LIBERTY." The chief feature of the reverse is a representation of the Lincoln Memorial. These three details have an obvious relevance to

> **"** The 'new penny' Julian's mother does discover indicates the time has come for Southern whites to accept social change, abandon their obsolete racial views, and relate to Negroes in a radically different way."

O'Connor's sympathetic concern with the "rise" of Southern blacks from slavery towards true freedom and socio-economic equality. Thus, the features of the Lincoln cent just mentioned suggest (1) the freeing of Negroes by the "Great Emancipator" and (2), by extension, the activity of the Federal Government in O'Connor's own day to ensure the rights of Southern blacks. Regarding the second, the Supreme Court decision of 1954 and its aftereffects (including the sit-ins of 1960) constitute the immediate historical background for the action of "Everything that Rises . . . ." The story suggests how the crumbling of the "Jim Crow" system was making possible a new "liberty" for Negroes in the South. Blacks have gained both a greater physical freedom in their world and increased opportunities for socio-economic mobility. This twofold access of "liberty" is exemplified by the well-dressed Negro man with the briefcase who sits with the whites at the front of the bus. The new possibilities for betterment opening to blacks are intimated not only by the abovementioned details of the Lincoln cent but also by its "bright," shiny freshness.

Julian's mother is unaware of the ways her "new penny" suggests the historical "rise" of Southern blacks, and would be dismayed if she recognized such implications. She represents the reactionary element among white Southerners who want to reverse history with respect to race relations. Julian's mother would like to return to the days of segregation ("They should rise, yes, but on their own side of the fence") and seemingly even to the era of slavery ("[Blacks] were better off when they were [slaves]"). The retrograde desire of Julian's mother to reduce Negroes to their antebellum servitude stands in ironic contrast to her penny as recalling Lincoln's emancipation of blacks. Furthermore, the date on the obverse of the "new" (presumably 1961) cent is exactly a century after the start of the Civil War, and almost a hundred years after the Emancipation Proclamation (1863). The 1961 date thus underlines just how antiquated are the racial views of Julian's mother.

As opposed to the Lincoln cent, the Jefferson nickel in part suggests the conservative and patrician outlook of Julian's mother, the quasi-mythical old South in which she psychologically dwells. In particular, Jefferson's life strikingly parallels that of the aristocratic grandfather whom Julian's mother so reveres. Both men were slaveholding plantation owners, and both were governors of their home states. It is by virtue of such distinguished ancestry that Julian's mother identifies with the antebellum Southern aristocracy, to whom she romantically attributes a lofty preeminence balanced by "graciousness." That combination of qualities is suggested by the palladian architecture of Jefferson's "stately home" Monticello, depicted on the reverse of the nickel. Monticello further ties in with the Godhigh country mansion as a symbol of the aristocratic heritage and accompanying social pretensions of Julian's mother. Just as the somewhat Olympian Monticello suggests the superior position of the white aristocracy in a class and racially stratified order, so does the plan of the Godhigh house (the owners being elevated above the black cooks who work on the ground floor). It is from such an apparently secure social eminence that Julian's mother looks down on Negroes with a blend of snobbish condescension, "graciousness" and paternalistic benevolence. That set of attitudes is expressed by Julian's mother in bestowing small change upon black children. The Jefferson nickel is especially appropriate as the usual coin for such largesse because it implies the identification with the old Southern aristocracy that largely determines the racial views of Julian's mother.

However, the aforementioned connotations of the Jefferson nickel are in contrast with meanings implied by the motto "LIBERTY" on the obverse of the coin. The slogan brings to mind Jefferson's chief fame as a champion of democratic ideals. In relation to "Everything that Rises . . . ," Jefferson's advocacy of "liberty" and equality is (1) basically antithetical to the cherished social assumptions and racial views of Julian's mother and (2) essentially in keeping with the movement towards freedom and equality for blacks implied by the Lincoln cent. Concerning the second point,

Jefferson although a slaveholder himself found the South's "peculiar institution" morally repugnant. He accordingly devoted considerable effort to advocating the gradual emancipation of Negroes, and he likewise freed some of his own blacks at his death. Jefferson's enlightened attitudes towards slavery, which anticipate Lincoln's Emancipation Proclamation, are diametrically opposed to those of Julian's mother. Far from seeing slavery as morally repellant, she believes that blacks were "better off" in servitude, and is proud that an ancestor owned two hundred Negroes. Such sentiments are undercut through the Jefferson nickel by implicit contrast with the views of one of America's foremost political and social thinkers.

Another detail of both the Lincoln cent and Jefferson nickel which is relevant to "Everything that Rises . . ." is the motto "E PLURIBUS UNUM" ("Out of many, one"). While the slogan is intended to refer to the United States as a nation federated out of various states, it also suggests the American ideal of a unified society tolerantly encompassing racial and ethnic diversity. Both possible meanings of "E PLURIBUS UNUM" are germane to the racial situation that existed in the South in 1961. Since the main impetus towards desegregation came from the U.S. Federal Government, the resistance of Southern white reactionaries threatened to create strife not just between the races, but also between Dixie and the rest of the nation. The first of these potential conflicts is suggested in "Everything that Rises . . ." when the black woman assaults Julian's mother. The second is implied by the Lincoln cent as recalling the Civil War. In opposition to both possible evils, the motto "E PLURIBUS UNUM" indicates how the South should accept the will of the Federal authorities and help create a society where the races can coexist in harmony.

The motto "E PLURIBUS UNUM" also ties in with the theology of Teihard de Chardin that influenced O'Connor when writing "Everything that Rises . . . ." Teihard maintains in *The Phenomenon of Man* that an eschatological evolution is moving the human race from "diversity to ultimate unity." Such a "convergence" will be completed at "Omega point" with the oneness of all men in Christ. In order for convergence to occur, individuals must surrender their "personal or racial egotism" and join with one another in love. Teilhard's convergence of mankind from "diversity to ultimate unity" is of course brought to mind by the motto "E PLURIBUS UNUM." The slogan would thus for O'Connor relate both to God's plan for unifying all men and to U.S. history, suggesting the two are connected. More specifically, O'Connor evidently saw the progress of race relations in the South since the Civil War as part of the convergence of all humanity towards Omega point. The segregationist views of Julian's mother and her like accordingly constitute a sinful resistance to God's redemptive plan for mankind. That opposition is caused in the case of Julian's mother by a "personal . . . [and] racial egotism" arising from her pride of ancestry and class status. Such "egotism" is suggested by the name Godhigh borne by Julian's grandmother. The name stands in neat ironic antithesis to the motto "IN GOD WE TRUST" on the Lincoln cent and Jefferson nickel, a slogan which implies a humble self-surrender to the divine plan moving man towards convergence.

In "Everything that Rises . . .," the penny and the nickel thus relate the racial situation in the South of 1961 to a larger cultural, historical and spiritual context. On the one hand, the Lincoln cent suggests a century of political, social and economic progress elevating blacks towards a final Teihardian convergence with whites. On the other hand, the Jefferson nickel most obviously intimates a conservative, aristocratic mentality contributing to Southern white resistance to integration. The ultimate defeat of such reaction is implied when Julian's mother cannot find a nickel to give the little black boy. O'Connor is suggesting that the old South called to mind by the five cent piece is gone forever. The "new penny" Julian's mother does discover indicates the time has come for Southern whites to accept social change, abandon their obsolete racial views, and relate to Negroes in a radically different way. Instead, Julian's mother stubbornly clings to a quasi-mythical past and refuses to accept the realities of the present. This wrongheaded strategy is seen when she tries to use the coin suggesting a new order in a way appropriate to the old. The violent rejection of the "condescending" penny by the black woman is for Julian's mother an appropriate, if ultimately tragic, initiation into verities she so willfully denies.

Source: John Ower, "The Penny and the Nickel in 'Everything That Rises Must Converge,'" in *Studies in Short Fiction,* Vol. 23, No. 1, Winter 1986, pp. 107–10.

Marion Montgomery

[In the following essay, Montgomery examines the character of Julian in detail, finding the "convergence" of the title in Julian's confrontation with himself, when he realizes that he has "destroyed that which he loved through his blindness."]

Flannery O'Connor's "Everything That Rises Must Converge" first appeared in *New World Writing Number 17,* in 1961, from which it was selected for inclusion in both *Best American Short Stories of 1962* and *Prize Stories of 1963: The O. Henry Awards.* It appeared posthumously, as the title story of the final collection of her fiction, in 1965. It has, in consequence, had special attention called to it over a period of years and has received critical, if sometimes puzzled, readings at a number of hands. Predictably, much (though not all) of that attention has centered upon the topical materials it uses, the "racial" problem which seems the focus of the conflict between the story's "Southern mother" and her liberal son. That sort of attention is one of the inevitable by-products of the turmoils that have engaged us since the story's initial publication, turmoils that fulfill Unamuno's prophecy that soon we would be dying in the streets of sentimentality. In the interest of getting beyond the topical materials of the story, to those qualities of it that will make it endure in our literature, I should like to examine it in some detail, starting, as seems most economical, with a particularly superficial evaluation of it which Miss O'Connor called to my attention.

When the story appeared as first prize winner of the 1963 *O. Henry Awards,* it was remarked in one of those primary sources of Miss O'Connor's raw material, the Atlanta *Journal-Constitution:*

> . . . her basic plot line is provocative and witty: an old-guard Southern lady, afraid to ride the buses without her son since integration, parades out for an evening dressed in a new and expensive hat. On the bus she encounters a Negro woman in the same hat. Unfortunately the denouement of the story (the good Southern lady drops dead) is uncomfortable. It is pushed just too far.

An Olympian, anonymous evaluation, by one who has not even noticed that Julian is the protagonist. Almost two years later, when the posthumous collection appeared, there followed a praiseful review of the collection in which its author was called "the most gallant writer, male or female in our contemporary culture," in which review Julian's mother is again specifically identified as the story's "protagonist."

One no longer expects to discover incisive reviews in newspapers, more's the pity, and these notices themselves are of little importance except that they show forth a good bit of the context from which Miss O'Connor drew the materials of her fiction. She had immediate access to her "Christ-

> " The tragedy is Julian's, in which he recognizes that he has destroyed that which he loved through his blindness. He has so carefully set himself off from his mother that, through the pretenses of intellect, he is as far removed from her as Oedipus from Jocasta. But the Christian implications of Julian's tragedy separate him from Oedipus. Guilt and sorrow come of knowing that one has spurned love."

O'Connor's sharpness in reading that particular "Southern" mind:

> Sixteen-year-old Dixie Radcliff, daughter of an Amesville, Ohio, clergyman, is in jail, classified as an adult charged with being an accessory to murder. She is a tenderhearted child who doesn't like to see anyone hurt. Because of this feminine revulsion to seeing people hurt, she remained in the car while her friend and lover, young Donald Boggs, killed four men. Donald, she says, was considerate. He did not ask Dixie to do more than tie the victims' hands behind their backs. He then took them away from the car so that Dixie would not see the killing. . . .

> There is no particular moral to draw from this sordid, pitiful story. That Don is a dangerous criminal, with a compulsion to kill, and that he is uninhibited by any sense of fear or moral conviction is plain. That Dixie Radcliff is a retarded child is plain. . . .

> Dixie will offend most those who say that children become delinquent today because of a lack of religious influence about the home. Dixie Radcliff grew up, apparently, with a religious influence about her like her clothes or skin. . . . She must have heard papa preach, pound the pulpit and flog the devil and his works a thousand times or more. . . .

> . . . The psychiatrists who worked over Dixie found she knew quite well all that was going on and knew it was wrong and wicked.

> Was the motivation of Don Boggs (and Dixie) something in their genes—or in their environment—or both? We never will know. So we will send them both to jail and forget about it.

haunted" figures through local radio programs; one need only canvass the location stations between 11:00 A.M. and 2:00 P.M. during the week and on Sunday mornings to hear the voices of her prophets, though not their substance, and to see what a true ear she had for that speaking voice. But she used as well the Atlanta daily papers (called by rural Georgians as often as not "them lying Atlanta papers"). In them, for instance, she could see every Saturday a fundamentalist column, run as a paid advertisement with the title "Why Do the Heathen Rage," the title she had given the novel she left unfinished. There was also on Saturday the famous Pickrick ads of Lester Maddox, with their outrageous turns of wit in the midst of absurdities. But these were only a part of what interested Miss O'Connor in the newspapers. There were also displays of the mind of her Julians and Sheppards and Raybers, in the editorial columns and on the book review page. As to what was constantly available to her, consider these excerpts from a regular column [by Ralph McGill in the Atlanta *Constitution,* September 23, 1965]. It is a Sheppard's or a Rayber's version of *A Good Man is Hard to Find*, underlining by contrast Miss

That Miss O'Connor's Raburs and Sheppards are with us as decisively as our Misfits is, I think, sufficiently evidenced by these excerpts from a Pulitzer winner's remarks, remarks that are vaguely disturbed by an anticipation of the fundamentalist reaction and by society's lack of primary concern for Don and Dixie over their hapless victims. The statement that Dixie is clearly retarded does not fit with the assertions of the psychiatrists. Nor does it seem to reside in the columnist's awareness that he has in fact drawn a moral from the story: namely, that parents and environment are either or both responsible for the unhappy plight of Don and Dixie. The columnist's position is that of a determinist, and if the grandmother in Miss O'Connor's story faces her Misfit with the same excuses for evil, she is able to do so from what she has absorbed from the Raburs and Sheppards who have inherited from the priest position of authority in moral matters, with the media as effective pulpit. (Still she was reared with a sounder understanding of evil as she finally admits.)

It is easier of course to make gestures of compassion or brotherhood in the daily press than to deal directly with our Dixies or Dons whom Miss O'Connor translates as a Misfit or Rufus Johnson. What she shows in the inescapable confrontations is, first, the stock responses such as the grandmother's or the columnist's or Sheppard's. Then she presses those responses, through the presence of antagonists, to the point where the response proves inadequate. The modern innocent so confronted is forced to acknowledge the existence of evil and of an older innocence, as the first step toward recovery. This we see in the grandmother's development following her encounter with the Misfit, but the same procedure is used in "Everything That Rises Must Converge" with an important exception. Here the central character is not a country grandma moved to Atlanta, but an aspiring candidate for the *intelligentsia*. Also the confrontation and the stock response to the confrontation occur in the same character. That is, Julian is, in effect, two presences in the story, the Julian who assumes himself aloof and detached from the human condition by virtue of his superior intellect and the Julian who destroys his mother before our eyes. The climax of the story occurs at a point where he recognizes his participation in the catastrophe that has occurred. I think we may make the point clear by first looking at the point of view Miss O'Connor has chosen, a point of view which led the newspaper reviewers to mistake the mother as the central character.

From the first sentence of the story we have it established that this is Julian's story, though with a sufficient freedom in the related point of view to allow the author an occasional intrusion. "Her doctor had told Julian's mother that she must lose twenty pounds on account of her blood pressure, so on Wednesday nights Julian had to take her downtown on the bus for a reducing class at the Y." It is always *Julian's mother*; she is given no name. And we see her through Julian's eyes. The rest of the first paragraph, for instance, carries as if in Julian's sardonic mind, indirect reflections of his mother's words. Who else would speak of herself as one of "the working girls over fifty"? And there is a mimicry of his mother by Julian in such an indirect statement as this: ". . . because the reducing class was one of her few pleasures, necessary for her health, and *free*, she said Julian could at least put himself out to take her, considering all she did for him." The first paragraph concludes with a statement which is not quite neutral on the author's part, a statement we are to carry with us into the action: "Julian did not like to consider all she did for him, but every Wednesday night he braced himself and

took her." The *but* indicates that on Wednesdays the consideration is inescapable, but also that Julian is capable of the minor sacrifice of venturing into the world from his generally safe withdrawal into "a kind of mental bubble." With the story so focused that we as readers are aware that we watch Julian watching his mother, the action is ready to proceed, with relatively few intrusions of the author from this point.

Our reading of Julian's mother, then, is made for us by him, so that one might very well see "the basic plot line" as dealing with "an old-guard Southern lady, afraid to ride the buses," as our anonymous reviewer put it. But our author gives a careful control of our reading, particularly in the imagery Julian chooses to describe his mother. Julian's distortions are those that a self-elected superior intellect is capable of making through self-deception; he is an intellect capable of surface distinctions but not those fundamental ones such as that between childish and child-like. In short, Julian takes himself to be liberated, older than his mother since he is more modern. He feels burdened by his retarded mother and so is free to enjoy the pleasure of his chosen martyrdom to her small desires. Still, there is no one available to him capable of appreciating him, and so no one to know, other than himself, the constancy of his sacrifice. While the mother doesn't hesitate to declare her sacrifices for him openly, he only acts out the pain of his own with expressions of pain and boredom. Standing slouched in the doorway, unwilling audience to her self-torture over paying $7.50 for a hideous green and purple hat, he is "waiting like Saint Sebastian for the arrows." He sees himself "sacrificed to her pleasure," and a little later finds himself depressed "as if in the midst of martyrdom he had lost his faith." In the bus, which he hates to ride more than she, since it brings him close to people, he sits by a Negro "in reparation as it were for his mother's sins." The disparity between his reading of his situation and our seeing that situation for what it is, is sufficient to put us on our guard in evaluating the mother.

Nevertheless, she too is full of a language disproportionate to her position, as he points out with pleasure. She repeats the cliches on the general decay of her civilization, recalling the days when her family was substantial. Her arguments are inherited, rather than learned as are Julian's, for Julian has, in his view of the matter, gotten on his own a first-rate education from a third-rate college, with the result that he is free. That is, he is already "as disenchanted with [life] as a man of fifty.'' His mother, in his account of the matter, is living a hundred years in the past, ignoring the immediate circumstances of her existence. It is rather obvious from what has been so far said that Julian is not only the central character of the story, but in many respects a less spectacular version of the Misfit. Disillusioned with life, he wants to be no closer than three miles to his nearest neighbor, as he says. That failing, since his ancestral ''mansion'' is lost to him, the only pleasure he gets from life is meanness, specifically that of torturing his mother by reminding her of the new world she lives in. But unlike the Misfit, his meanness is paralysed force, gesture without motions. He cannot make a decisively destructive move, since that would require his own self-shattering involvement. Actually it is he who lives in the past, though only his own private past, for he can deal only in abstractions fed by reverie and memory. Through reverie he builds a fantasy version of the world as he would have it be, which is of course not the one he actually inhabits.

Thus it is that he sees his mother as childish. Her eyes, ''sky blue, were as innocent and untouched by experience as they must have been when she was ten.'' Again, ''she might have been a little girl that he had to take to town.'' He detaches accidents from essence, and mistakes them for essence. A pseudo-existentialist, he builds a fairyland, that ''magnificent ersatz of the science of Phenomena'' [Jacques] Maritain declares existentialism to be. For, unlike [Jean-Paul] Sartre's Orestes, Julian's destruction of his mother is not deliberate. He mistakes self-justification for self-affirmation. It is a relatively simple matter then to make the mother be what it is comfortable to him to suppose her. From being simply as innocent as when she was ten, she becomes eventually an obnoxious child whom ''he could with pleasure have slapped.'' She becomes so through the exercise of his withdrawal, leading him finally to feel ''completely detached from her.''

But words, even when poorly used or deliberately distorted, have a way of redounding upon the user. It is thus with the terms Julian uses in his careless abstractions. In addition to the metaphors of his mother as child and himself as martyr, there is also the metaphor of evil that slowly worms its way into his language. At the bus stop, he finds in himself ''an evil urge to break her spirit.'' Neither *evil* nor *spirit* here carries full meaning, for he intends only to express his impulse to embarrass her in public. He sets about that petty meanness out of a

vanity which sees as his own most ''miraculous'' triumph that ''instead of being blinded by love for her as she was for him, he had cut himself emotionally free of her and could see her with complete objectivity. He was not dominated by his mother.'' Love is at this point no more than an emotional attachment as seen with the intellectual freedom Julian professes; so too is evil. And so the possibility of catastrophe is remote indeed to his thinking as he sets about harassing his mother. Thus, when he gives the woman with protruding teeth and canvas sandals ''a malevolent'' look, he is practicing his revenge upon the mother at a level very close to June Starr's sticking out her tongue at Red Sammy's wife. He is more nearly naughty than malevolent. His childishness is fed by his satisfaction in seeing ''injustice in daily operation,'' since that observance ''confirmed his view that with few exceptions there was no one worth knowing wihtin a radius of three hundred miles.'' It is this state of withdrawal that we must be aware of in seeing his actions on the bus. When he sits down by the Negro man, he stares across at his mother ''making his eyes the eyes of a stranger.'' His tension lifts ''as if he had openly declared war on her,'' which of course he has, thus making his withdrawal from the world possible. His only reaction to those about him is that of hate, but his expression of that hate is capable only of irritating, except in the case of that one person in his world who loves him, his mother.

It is in respect to that love that the story's title is to be read. For in the first instance *convergence* carries the sense [Thomas] Hardy gives it in ''The Convergence of the Twain.'' It is only after the devastating collision Julian experiences that any rising may be said to occur. The collision is presented initially in the comical exchange of sons, Julian for the small Negro boy, on the bus. One notices, as Julian sees the large Negro woman get on the bus, that she has a hat identical to that his mother wears. But Julian, observing the accident of color, does not notice it. He can connect nothing with nothing. As in the grandmother's first encounter with the Misfit, Julian is aware only that there is something vaguely familiar about her, the huge woman waiting for tokens. When it finally dawns on him that it is the hat that is familiar, he thinks the problem solved. It is only begun. Feeling triumphant, he awaits his mother's recognition of the hat, for it seems the chance he has waited to teach her ''a lesson that would last for awhile.'' But the real shocker is that he discovers his own likeness to the Negress, the ironic exchange of sons becoming ultimately more terrifying that he anticipated. We see this by observing the Negro mother in comparison to what we know of Julian, ours being an advantage scarcely available to Julian. Though he is very much annoyed by her physical presence as she crowds him in his seat, he doesn't look at her, preferring rather to visualize her as she stood waiting for tokens a few minutes earlier. His is a retreat into the memory such as he accuses his mother of, and in that retreat he realizes that it is the hat that is familiar. It is at this point of recognition that he sees his mother's eyes once more and interprets them. ''The blue in them seemed to have turned a bruised purple. For a moment he had an uncomfortable sense of her innocence, but it lasted only a second before principle rescued him.'' Principle, as abstraction imposed upon the concrete circumstances, rather than derived from them, delays for the moment the threat of the abyss to Julian. He sees that his mother ''would feel'' the symbolic significance of the purple hat but not ''realize'' it, as he, Julian, is capable of doing. His mother is to him just like the Negro woman in the world his mother refuses to acknowledge.

But that is merely reverie's abstraction on Julian's part, for the Negro woman is very much unlike his mother. The facts of her size and color are accidental dissimilarities which Julian's sophistication removes, but there is an essential unlikeness to his mother that underlines the strange woman's kinship to Julian. She, like Julian, is unaware of the possibilities of love. The Negro child, Carver, acts toward Julian's mother to the discomfort of the Negro mother, but with an innocence that Julian can't claim for his childishness. When the mother has snatched the child back, he presently escapes back to ''his love,'' Julian's mother. Afterward the Negro woman slaps the ''obnoxious child'' as Julian only imagines doing to his mother. When the game of Peek-a-boo starts between Julian's mother and Carver, Carver's mother threatens to ''knock the living Jesus'' out of the child. And later, we see her carry the child down the bus steps by its arm as if it were a thing and not a child. She then shakes Carver angrily for his conspiracy of love.

At this point we might reconsider Julian's mother as an ''old-guard Southern lady.'' It is perfectly true that her words are such as to make her appear condescending to her ''inferiors'' when they are black. And she sees little difference between herself and such people as the white woman with the protruding teeth, a person with far fewer historical credentials than she, this last failure one which

Julian is very much embarrassed by. But there is a more fundamental rightness about Julian's mother than her inherited manners and social clichés reveal. So long as Julian is allowed to deal with the surfaces—with her stock words and responses to the immediate social situation—he is safe to enjoy his pretended indignation within his mental bubble. He can make a surface response to surface existence. It is when he is forced to go deeper that horror intrudes, as when for a moment he glimpses a childlike innocence in his mother's blue eyes, from which horror ''principle'' rescues him back to his portrait of her as childish. Eventually, though, a ''terrible intuition'' gets the better of him as he realizes that his mother will give Carver a coin. ''The gesture would be as natural to her as breathing.'' He, rather than his mother, can feel now the symbolic significance of her act, though he is not yet ready to ''realize it.'' For the world Julian insists upon as changed from the world he takes his mother to dwell in is the world of time untouched by that transcendent love that begins to threaten him. Julian's and the Negro woman's world is one in which a penny is hardly an acceptable substitute for a nickel, or any gift at all suitable since it represents an intrusion that can only seem condescension of the Haves to the Have-nots. Julian's is that world of history out of the eighteenth century in which Progress and Change have removed the obstacle of ''Original Sin'' through an intellectual exercise. Julian's mother cannot make distinctions of minor significance, as her son is capable of doing with his college-trained mind. But being child-like, she can make major distinctions, even as Carver can. The mother's gesture of love with the penny has removed from it any concern for the worldly value of her gift. It is a bright coin, given with an affection misunderstood by both Julian and Carver's mother. In the world made by a George Washington Carver with synthetics on the one hand and by Sartre with synthetic existence on the other (the worlds pursued by the Negress and Julian respectively) things and actions have a value in respect to their surfaces. *Action* and *thing* precede *essence* and *intrinsic value*. In such a world, where the possibilities of love are ignored, things and actions are ultimately only mechanical. Thus it is to be expected that the Negro woman explodes ''like a piece of machinery,'' striking Julian's mother with the lumpy pocket book. And Julian, a more subtle machine of his own making, is like a clock, capable of telling only the present confused moment. He is trapped by history, his mother's and his own.

His mother lying on the ground before him, the Negro woman retreating with Carver "staring wide-eyed over her shoulder," Julian picks up his old theme. "That was your black double," he says. He reads the significance of the event to her: "The old manners are obsolete and your graciousness is not worth a damn." But for the first time he remembers bitterly "the house that was lost to him." In his earlier remembrance it has been a *mansion* as contrasted to his mother's word *house*. Now when he insists to her "You aren't who you think you are," the words begin immediately to redound upon him. For now his mother's blue and innocent eyes become "shadowed and confused." He does not try "to conceal his irritation," and so there is no sign of love in his face. That is why she looks at him "trying to determine his identity." He begins to abandon his separateness ("Are *we* walking [home].") Still, when she ignores him, he reads her the stock lesson of our moment of time. The Negro woman is "the whole colored race" rising up against such people as his mother. The mistake Julian is incapable of seeing is that the Negro woman is more than the colored race; she is the human race, to which he himself belongs through the burden of man's being a spiritual mulatto. The mother's earlier words, simple-minded in Julian's view, that she feels sorry for "the ones that are half white" since "They're tragic" take on theological symbolism still beyond his ken. In the presence of his mother dying, he sees her eyes, one moving as if "unmoored," the other fixing on him and finding "nothing." It is the final terrible mirror to his being which he has fleetingly seen reflected in the Negro woman on the bus. But now he cannot deny his own condition by any act of abstraction, by "principle," his old means of escaping his emptiness. His mother's return to her childhood at the moment of death, her acting "just like a child" a Julian says, leads her to call for "Grandpa" and then for her old nurse "Caroline." Only at this point does Julian realize her serious condition. But his reaction is in regard to his own safety rather than hers. Stunned, he is aware of "a tide of darkness" that seems to be "sweeping her from him." The word *mother* no longer suffices, and it is the beginning of a new Julian when he calls out his frightened "Mamma, Mamma!"

The story, then, is one in which Julian discovers, though he does not understand it, the necessity of putting aside childishness to become a little child. It recalls those errors of our childhood in which we take pleasure in our superiority over those younger than we. That superiority we take, with pride, to be a measure of our intellectual station. But the shocking revelation comes as we realize that the pinnacle of this moment's superiority on which we rise is tomorrow's dark valley out of which it is difficult to see. Or in another figure also appropriate to our story we play childishly with our supposed inferiors, as Julian does: we hold up before a mirror a message only we can decipher in its backwardness since we were privy to its writing. Or we write the mirror image and hold it up to be reflected aright for others to read with awe and wonder at our cleverness. What is shattering to us is the larger mystery of our own life which includes childishness but which our intellect cannot comprehend. Thus Julian delights in the mirror reflection of his mother in the Negress, only to discover the dark woman a truer image of himself, the denier of love. Thus too those metaphors of love and hate play mirror tricks as they grow larger than their childish use by Julian, so that "true culture" appears no longer simply "in the mind" as he insists early. Perhaps it is "in the heart," as his mother insisted. Setting out with "the evil urge to break her spirit," he has finally succeeded in breaking his own.

The convergence in the story then, at its most fundamental level, is not that of one person with another but of Julian with the world of guilt and sorrow, the world in which *procedures* have replaced *manners*, both of which are surface aspects of that world. For, while the *spectacle* of the convergence of Julian's mother with the Negro mother is indeed a convergence in a "violent form," as one critic of the story [John J. Burke, S. J., in "Convergence of Flannery O'Connor and Chardin" in *Renascence*, 1966] puts it, the most violent collision is within Julian, with effects Aristotle declared necessary to complex tragedy. The tragedy is Julian's, in which he recognizes that he has destroyed that which he loved through his blindness. He has so carefully set himself off from his mother that, through the pretenses of intellect, he is as far removed from her as Oedipus from Jocasta. But the Christian implications of Julian's tragedy separate him from Oedipus. Guilt and sorrow come of knowing that one has spurned love. Already the possibilities of grace are present as he cries out to her with the voice of a child. Whether he will perform a more significant expiation on his own behalf than the childish gesture he pretends for his mother's sins—his sitting by the Negro man in the bus—is left suspended. What we do know is that, as if repeating an error of his namesake (St. Julian the Hospitaller of the Saints' legends), he has, through the childishness of intellectualism, made himself capable of a mistake of identity. And like Oedipus and St. Julian he has been an instrument in the destruction of his parent. As he goes crying to any person who might happen along in his dark night, the tide of darkness seems to sweep him back to his mother lying on the ground dead. But in his favor, he is opposing that tide of darkness which would postpone "from moment to moment his entry into the world of guilt and sorrow." He has at the least arrived, as Eliot would say, at the starting place, as Miss O'Connor's characters so often do, and has recognized it for the first time. He is now ready to profit from those words of Teilhard which give the story its title, but they are words which must not be read as Teilhard would have them in his evolutionary vision. For in Teilhard there is no place for guilt and sorrow since human existence has had removed from it that taint of original sin which this story certainly assumes as real. It is a Dantean reading of Teilhard's words that we are called upon to make:

> Remain true to yourself, but move ever upward toward greater consciousness and greater love! At the summit you will find yourself united with all those who, from every direction, have made the same ascent. *"For everything that rises must converge."*

Source: Marion Montgomery, "On Flannery O'Connor's 'Everything That Rises Must Converge,'" in *Critique*, Vol. XIII, No. 2, 1971, pp. 15–29.

Patricia Dinneen Maida

In the essay below, Maida discusses Julian's experience of convergence, comparing and contrasting O'Connor's use of the concept with Teilhard de Chardin's philosophy.

Flannery O'Connor's fiction continues to provoke interest and critical analysis. The title story of her posthumous collection of short stories, *Everything That Rises Must Converge,* has been among those stories that have received attention lately. But no one has yet examined the implications of the title. Robert Fitzgerald tells us [in his introduction to the collection] that Miss O'Connor got the idea for the title when she read Teilhard de Chardin's *The Phenomenon of Man* in 1961.

Typical of an O'Connor work, this story has meaning on several levels; especially, the allusion to Chardin's theory of "convergence" offers an enriching dimension to the story. Essentially, it describes an experience of a mother and son that changes the course of their lives. Measured against the background of Southern middle-class values, the mother-son relationship has social and also

> " Considering man's 'progress' in human development, Flannery O'Connor seems to be painting the most vivid picture possible to show mankind where his inadequacies lie and to open his eyes to some painful truth."

personal implications. But, on a larger scale, the story depicts the plight of all mankind. Furthermore, as one considers the allusion in the title, the universality of Miss O'Connor's message becomes even more evident—as does the intensity of her vision and her aesthetic.

The focus of the story is on the disparate values of Julian and his mother, epitomized by the bourgeois hat she chooses to wear on her weekly trip to an equally bourgeois event, a reducing class at the "Y." More provoked than usual because he considers the hat ugly, Julian sullenly accompanies her on the bus ride downtown. His mother, a descendent of an old Southern family, lives on past glories that give her a sense of self-importance. Thus as she goes to her reducing class, she tells Julian: "Most of them in it are not our kind of people, . . . but I can be gracious to anybody. I know who I am." In his retort Julian sums up the attitude of his generation: "They don't give a damn for your graciousness. . . . Knowing who you are is good for one generation only. You haven't the foggiest idea where you stand now or who you are." His mother, however, is convinced of her ability to communicate amiably: when boarding the bus, she "entered with a little smile, as if she were going into a drawing room where everyone had been waiting for her." In contrast, Julian maintains an icy reserve.

Integration emerges as the divisive issue. When Julian and his mother first board the bus, there are no Negro passengers. But when a Negro man enters shortly afterwards, the atmosphere becomes tense. As one might expect, Julian's mother does not see any value in integration, whereas Julian favors it.

He purports to be a liberal; yet he acts primarily out of retaliation against the old system rather than out of genuine concern for the Negro. We are told that ''when he got on a bus by himself, he made it a point to sit down by a Negro in reparation as it were for his mother's sins.'' His sense of guilt proves to be a negative force; for although he has tried to make friends with Negroes, he has never succeeded. Even during the bus ride when he attempts to converse with a Negro, he is ignored, his ingenuousness apparently sensed by those he approaches.

Julian's cynicism shuts him off from any human association. His chief asset, his intelligence, is misdirected: he freely scorns the limitations of others and assumes a superior stance. During the bus ride he indulges in his favorite pastime:

> Behind the newspaper Julian was withdrawing into the inner compartment of his mind where he spent most of his time. This was a kind of mental bubble in which he established himself when he could not bear to be a part of what was going on around him. From it he could see out and judge but in it he was safe from any kind of penetration from without. It was the only place where he felt free of the general idiocy of his fellows.

Ironically, he had convinced himself that he was a success—even though with a college degree he held a menial job instead of becoming the writer he had once hoped to be.

The bus and its passengers form a microcosm, and the events that occur in the course of the ride comprise a kind of socio-drama. As Julian's mother, bedecked in her new hat, chats with those around her, Julian remains distant and uninvolved. However, when a Negro woman and her son board the bus, the situation changes. Suddenly all eyes focus on the Negro woman, who happens to be wearing a hat identical to that of Julian's mother. Both women are shocked at first, but Julian is delighted: ''He could not believe that Fate had thrust upon his mother such a lesson. He gave a loud chuckle so that she would look at him and see that he saw.'' But she recovers and is able to laugh, while the Negro woman remains visibly upset. When the two pairs of mothers and sons emerge from the bus at the same stop, Julian's mother cannot resist the impulse to offer the Negro boy a coin—despite Julian's protests. This act provokes such anger in the boy's mother that she strikes Julian's mother with her handbag. As Julian attempts to help his mother up from the pavement, he realizes that the shock of the experience has caused her to suffer a stroke—thus she actually becomes victim to the outdated code by which she has lived. The patronizing act of offering

a coin is completely natural to her, yet offensive to the Negro. Her lack of touch with reality is dramatically exhibited after the stroke when she reverts to former times completely: ''Tell Grandpa to come get me.'' For Julian, however, the shock he experiences at his mother's condition seems to open his eyes at long last to ''the world of guilt and sorrow.''

Because Julian, unlike anyone else in the story, is distinguished by name, the story focuses on him and his development. Everyone else functions in relation to and for the sake of the learning experience that eventually becomes meaningful to him. On a larger scale, moreover, the story has mythic and universal proportions in terms of the treatment of how an individual faces reality and attains maturity. For Julian, maturity becomes a possibility only after his faulty vision is corrected. When he witnesses the assault on his mother and its subsequent effect, he experiences a form of shock therapy that forces him out of the ''mental bubble'' of his own psyche.

Julian's situation reflects the particular O'Connor combination of comedy and tragic irony. On the bus as he recalls experiences of trying to make friends with Negroes, his responses are genuinely funny. When he recounts his disillusionment in discovering that his distinguished looking Negro acquaintance is an undertaker, when he imagines his mother desperately ill and his being able to secure only a Negro doctor for her, when he dreams of bringing home a ''suspiciously Negroid'' fiancée—the comedy runs high.

But as one considers the bitter irony of the situation, the nature of the humor changes. The lesson that he had hoped his mother would learn turns out to be meant for him; the confrontation of the two women with identical hats is comical, but the comedy is quickly reversed. In a discussion of the author's unique comedy, [Brainard] Cheney contends [in his essay ''Miss O'Connor Creates Unusual Humor out of Ordinary Sin'' in the *Sewanee Renew* Autumn, 1963] that this kind of humor might be called ''metaphysical humor.'' He describes the effect in this way: ''She begins with familiar surfaces that seem secular at the outset and in a secular tone of satire or humor. Before you know it, the naturalistic situation has become metaphysical, and the action appropriate to it comes with a surprise, an unaccountability that is humorous, however shocking.'' It is metaphysical in the sense that such humor calls into question the nature of being: man, the universe, and the relationship of the two. The hat, a symbol of the self-image, and the convergence of the two women with identical hats poses several questions: What is the significance of the individual's self-image? What common qualities do all men share? How does one relate to the world and others in it?

The "convergence" of the hats and the personalities of the respective owners is a violent clash—unpredictable and shocking. Nevertheless, the timing and circumstances work together to produce a kind of epiphany for Julian. And this kind of epiphany seems to be conceived and produced by the author. The title of the story offers a key to a more complete understanding of the epiphany or convergence process in an O'Connor short story. From the structure of the story it becomes evident that the rising action culminates in a crisis, a convergence of opposing forces, causing a dramatic and decisive change.

In addition, an understanding of the origin of the title of the story reveals a link between content and form. In a commentary on *The Phenomenon of Man* [published in *The American Scholar* in fall, 1961], Miss O'Connor tells why the work is meaningful to her:

> It is a search for human significance in the evolutionary process. Because Teilhard is both a man of science and a believer, the scientist and the theologian will require considerable time to sift and evaluate his thought, but the poet, whose sight is essentially prophetic, will at once recognize in Teilhard a kindred intelligence. His is a scientific expression of what the poet attempts to do: penetrate matter until spirit is revealed in it. Teilhard's vision sweeps forward without detaching itself at any point from the earth.

Chardin's vision seems to correspond with her own vision as she attempts to penetrate matter until spirit is reached and without detaching herself from the earth at any point. Penetration of matter occurs in an O'Connor story at the moment of crisis. Thus in the scene in which Julian witnesses the assault of his mother, the effect of physical violence produces a spiritual equivalent—Julian is forced to take stock of his soul. In fact, the theme of the story might be considered "a search for human significance in the evolutionary process."

Chardin conceives of evolution as a constantly emerging spiral culminating at the center with God. In the tradition of the Christian humanist, he affirms the value of the individual by emphasizing his role as an intelligent being capable of cooperating with his Creator through grace—a term used for the communication of love between God and man. Chardin describes grace as "Christic energy," an illuminating force operative on the minds of men. The individual realizes his potential as a person through self-awareness, which is the ultimate effect of grace. In its entirety, Chardin's treatise is optimistic: he looks forward to the time when love will unite all individuals in the harmony of their humanity to produce a renewal of the natural order.

In contrast, Flannery O'Connor's view does not appear to be quite so optimistic: "Everything That Rises Must Converge" describes a bus ride in which there is no real communication between people, no understanding, and no harmony. How does this correspond with Chardin's prophecy of harmony between men at the point of convergence? The crux of the difference lies in perspectives: Chardin looks to the future; Miss O'Connor is concerned with the present and its consequences in the future. In other words, a mother and son boarding a bus in a Southern town at the present time are important individuals; the way they live their lives is also important. Why? Because, as Chardin would agree, each man has the potential to fulfill himself as a human being. In his introduction to *Everything That Rises Must Converge,* Fitzgerald says that Miss O'Connor uses the title "in full respect and with profound and necessary irony." The irony, however, is not directed at erring mankind or at Chardin's optimism; it is in the contrast between what man has the potential to become and what he actually achieves. For example, Julian deludes himself into thinking that no one means anything to him; he shuts himself off from his fellows and becomes the victim of his own egotism. In his immediate situation he is his own worst enemy and the cause of his own failure; but ultimately, he is less than a man—and, in this sense, his position is tragic. However, he does receive a revelation that may "redeem" him; that is, make him the man he could be.

The difference between the convergence described by Chardin and that which occurs in Miss O'Connor's story is ironic only in the contrast between the real and the ideal. Julian does experience a kind of convergence: his distorted vision is corrected (if not permanently, at least for a time): he does receive the opportunity to revamp his life. Consider how Julian arrives at his moment of truth: he does not seek it, nor does he achieve it himself through thoughtful deliberation. The means are external to him, gratuitous, though compelling. Chardin would call this a form of "Christic energy" or grace through which the individual is brought into closer communication with the source of truth. Miss O'Connor seems to be describing the same process, though in fictional terms. In discussing grace and its presentation in fiction [in "The Church and the Fiction Writer," *America*, LCVI (March 30, 1957)], she said, "Part of the complexity for the Catholic fiction writer will be the presence of grace as it appears in nature, and what matters for him here is that his faith not become detached from his dramatic sense and from his vision of what is." This statement explains her focus on the present; it also reveals the basis of her aesthetic.

In his study of Flannery O'Connor, [Stanley Edgar] Hyman contends that "any discussion of her theology can only be preliminary to, not a substitute for, aesthetic analysis and evaluation." Aesthetically, Miss O'Connor strived to produce a view of reality in the most direct and concrete terms. "Everything That Rises Must Converge" is a simple story told in almost stark language. But the combination of realism and the grotesque with simplicity and starkness effects a unique intensity. Consider, for example, the way realistic and grotesque elements form the imagery of the story. As mother and son begin their trip, "the sky was a dying violet and the houses stood out darkly against it, bulbous liver-colored monstrosities of a uniform ugliness, though no two were alike." Even the hat, which plays such a focal part in the conflict, is especially hideous: "A purple velvet flap came down on one side of it and stood up on the other; the rest of it was green and looked like a cushion with the stuffing out." Julian is hypersensitive: color and form possess an emotional equivalent for him. Thus when the Negro woman sits next to him on the bus, he is acutely aware of her: "He was conscious of a kind of bristling next to him, a muted growling like that of an angry cat. He could not see anything but the red pocketbook upright on the bulging green thighs." The correlation between color and emotion is also evident when he looks at his mother after she recognizes the hat on the other woman: "She turned her eyes on him slowly. The blue in them seemed to have turned a bruised purple. For a moment he had an uncomfortable sense of her innocence." But the ultimate horror awaits him after his mother has suffered the stroke: "Her face was fiercely distorted. One eye, large and staring, moved slightly to the left as if it had become unmoored. The other remained fixed on him, raked his face again, found

nothing and closed." Miss O'Connor does not flood her work with details; she is highly selective—choosing only those aspects that are most revealing. She does not cringe at ugliness; in fact, she seems compelled to highlight it when it is essential to meaning.

Julian has the potential to fulfill himself as a person and to be of use to a society in need of reform. Until his mother's stroke, he has no impetus to change his outlook; consequently, it takes a disaster to move him. The world in which he lives is grotesque, and perhaps the way in which he comes to his self-realization is appropriately grotesque. But the glimmer of hope shines only after he has been illuminated by the experience. Considering man's "progress" in human development, Flannery O'Connor seems to be painting the most vivid picture possible to show mankind where his inadequacies lie and to open his eyes to some painful truth. Through her keen, selective way of compressing the most significant material into a clear and simple structure, the message comes across with power and shocking clarity.

Source: Patricia Dinneen Maida, "'Convergence' in Flannery O'Connor's 'Everything That Rises Must Converge,'" in *Studies in Short Fiction,* Vol. VII, No. 4, Fall 1970, pp. 549–55.

Sources

Denham, Robert D., "The World of Guilt and Sorrow: Flannery O'Connor's 'Everything That Rises Must Converge,'" in *Flannery O'Connor Bulletin*, Vol. 4, Autumn, 1975, pp. 42–51.

Hicks, Granville, "A Cold, Hard Look at Humankind," in *Saturday Review*, May 29, 1965, p. 23–24.

Martin, Carter W., *The True Country: Themes in the Fiction of Flannery O'Connor*, Nashville, TN: Vanderbilt University Press, 1968.

McFarland, Dorothy Tuck, *Flannery O'Connor*, New York: Frederick Ungar Publishing, 1976.

O'Connor, Flannery, *Mysteries and Manners: Occasional Prose*, edited by Sally and Robert Fitzgerald, New York: Farrar, Straus and Giroux, 1969.

Schott, Webster, "Flannery O'Connor: Faith's Stepchild," in *Nation*, Vol. 201, No. 7, September 13, 1965, pp. 142–44.

Sullivan, Walter, "Flannery O'Connor, Sin, and Grace," in *Hollins Critic*, Vol. 2, No. 4, September, 1965, pp. 1–8, 10.

Further Reading

Bloom, Harold, ed., *Flannery O'Connor: A Comprehensive Research and Study Guide*, New York: Chelsea House, 1999.
This extensive collection of resources on O'Connor is an excellent starting point for in-depth projects on the writer.

Magee, Rosemary M., ed., *Conversations with Flannery O'Connor*, Jackson, MS: University of Mississippi Press, 1987.
Interviews with O'Connor over the course of her career. The selections cover a broad range of topics and offer readers a sense of her frank and clever persona.

McFarland, Dorothy Tuck, *Flannery O'Connor*, New York: Fredrick Ungar, 1976.
This short book is a useful introduction to O'Connor's life, career, and the central concerns of her fiction. McFarland includes close analysis of O'Connor's short stories and novels.

O'Connor, Flannery, *Mysteries and Manners: Occasional Prose*, edited by Sally and Robert Fitzgerald. New York: Farrar, Straus and Giroux, 1969.
After O'Connor's death, the Fitzgeralds collected her nonfiction in this volume. Includes unpublished essays, lectures, and previously published articles.

Teilhard de Chardin, Pierre, *The Phenomenon of Man*, New York: HarperCollins, 1980.
This challenging work of theology, which is the source of the story's title and the inspiration for its message, sheds light on O'Connor's ideas about religion and morality.

The Fat Girl

Andre Dubus

1977

In his lifetime, Andre Dubus was lauded for his highly realistic and captivating portraits of ordinary Americans. Honored throughout his long career by numerous and prestigious awards, his stories were often included in the pantheon of best American short stories.

His important role in the literary community was demonstrated in the late 1980s, after he was struck by a car while helping stranded motorists. The accident led to the loss of his leg and confinement in a wheelchair. In the ensuing years, Dubus came to see this accident as a transcendent experience, one that broadened his capacity for understanding human suffering and forgiveness.

''The Fat Girl,'' a story that was included in Dubus's 1978 collection *Adultery and Other Choices,* has been deemed one of his best short stories. Many reviewers praised his depiction of a young woman, Louise, torn between conflicting desires. Her plight has a universal quality in her quest for self-love and understanding.

Author Biography

Born into a middle-class Southern family, Andre Dubus was born on August 11, 1936 in Lake Charles, Louisiana. He attended a Roman Catholic high school, and throughout his career he credited his lifelong Catholicism for his strong compassion for others. In fact, when asked how he would describe his writings, Dubus answered, "Catholic."

After attending a state college and earning a bachelor's degree in English, Dubus joined the Marine Corps. At the age of nineteen, he began writing short stories; in 1963, he resigned his military commission to enter the prestigious Iowa Writers' Workshop at the University of Iowa. Also that year, Dubus' first story, "The Intruder," was published.

After receiving his M.F.A., Dubus and his wife and children moved to Massachusetts, where he taught modern fiction and creative writing at Bradford College. He held this job until 1984. During his years as a professor, Dubus published his first novel, *The Lieutenant*, as well several collections of short fictions and novellas.

In 1970 his work was included for the first time in *Best American Short Stories*. Throughout the decade, he continued to garner a number of impressive reviews and awards, including a Guggenheim Fellowship, a National Endowment for the Arts grant, and inclusion in *Prize Stories: The O. Henry Awards*. In 1977 he wrote "The Fat Girl," considered to be one of his more significant short stories.

By the late 1980s, Dubus was widely considered to be an important contemporary writer, and his stories were studied in college literature classes.

In 1986, while helping a stranded motorist on a Massachusetts highway, Dubus was hit by car. His injuries led to the amputation of one leg and his permanent confinement in a wheelchair. In 1991 he wrote an account of the accident called *Broken Vessels*.

For several years after the accident, Dubus was unable to write fiction. The support of fellow American writers, such as Ann Beattie, E. L. Doctorow, and John Irving, helped Dubus during this difficult period. In the years afterwards, he came to see the accident as a transcendent experience that made him a more empathetic person and allowed him greater understanding of human suffering and forgiveness.

When he returned to fiction writing, his work again garnered impressive awards, including the prestigious MacArthur Fellowship. Dubus died in 1999 of a heart attack.

Andre Dubus

Plot Summary

"The Fat Girl" chronicles the story of a young woman named Louise as she searches for love and self-acceptance. As a young, fat girl, she feels like she is not accepted by friends and family. Her mother encourages her to watch what she eats, but Louise develops the habit of sneaking fattening foods, such as peanut butter or candy bars, at a young age.

Louise continues to binge in private when she goes away to college. Carrie, her roommate and only friend, encourages Louise to give up this habit. When the two young women are seniors in college, Carrie suggests that Louise go on a diet.

For the rest of the year, Louise follows a very strict diet to lose weight. As a result, she grows irritable and she feels hungry all the time; but she also loses seventy pounds. When Louise goes home for Christmas vacation, her mother cannot believe how much weight she has lost.

Louise returns home to Louisiana after college. Her mother takes her shopping for clothes to fit her new, slender body. She meets a young lawyer, Richard, who works at her father's firm; they get married the following spring. As a housewife, Louise fixes heavy meals for her husband, but she does not eat them herself.

Richard and Louise enjoy many material advantages: they have a nice house; a boat; and they take several lavish vacations. Despite all these comforts, Louise sometimes feels as if her life is out of balance.

In the fifth year of their marriage, Louise gets pregnant. However, she is afraid of getting fat again. She tells Richard of her childhood and adolescence as a fat girl, but he dismisses her fears. Louise feels alienated from him and the life she has made for herself.

While pregnant, Louise begins to snack at parties and eat sweets and the dinners that she prepares for Richard. Even more telling, she begins to hide candy from her husband. After her baby is born, Louise continues to eat. Richard criticizes her weight gain and loses sexual interest in her. One night after Richard cruelly ridicules her, Louise weighs herself at 162 pounds.

That summer, Louise stops going on boat rides with Richard and their friends. Instead she spends her time with her young son. Every day, she and Richard quarrel. Richard believes they are arguing about her weight, but Louise feels they are arguing about much more serious issues.

One night Richard is angry. He pleads with her to go on a diet and even claims that he will eat the same foods as she does in order to help her lose weight. Yet Louise realizes that he has no real compassion for her; he just doesn't want to be embarrassed by her weight gain anymore.

She puts the baby to bed and gets a candy bar, which she plans to eat in front of Richard. She knows that he will leave her soon. When she comes back downstairs, she is surprised to find that Richard is still there.

Characters

Carrie

Carrie is Louise's college friend and roommate. She has an unhappy home life—her parents fight and will likely divorce—and she is prone to fits of depression. Carrie urges Louise to go on a diet, and she does everything in her power to help Louise. She proves to be a compassionate and understanding friend.

Joan

Joan is one of Louise's high school friends.

Louise

Louise is the protagonist of the story. As a young girl, she gains weight and remains overweight until college. Under pressure from her mother, Louise soon develops the habit of eating secretly, a habit that she considers to be ''insular and destructive.''

At college, Louise becomes good friends with her roommate, Carrie. With Carrie's support, Louise sheds seventy pounds in her senior year in college. Yet with the weight loss, Louise feels like she is shedding more than fat—she is losing part of who she is.

Louise maintains her new body for several years, long enough to marry a young lawyer and have a baby. The emptiness of her life prompts Louise to overeat again. This time, however, she does not eat in secret. She accepts—and wants Richard to accept—that she is a fat girl. Soon, she has regained much of the weight she lost years ago. Even though this means she may lose Richard, she feels she has regained her identity.

Louise's Father

Louise's father is an affectionate, tolerant man. He accepts her for who she is. He defends Louise and argues with her mother about what she should be allowed to eat.

Louise's Mother

Louise's mother is the first person who warns Louise about her weight. She believes that her daughter needs to eat less than her brother and father in order to stay thin. A slender, attractive woman, Louise's mother puts a lot of emphasis on physical appearance. When Louise finally loses all the weight, she calls her daughter beautiful.

Marjorie

Marjorie is one of Louise's high school friends.

Richard

Richard is Louise's husband. He is a young, energetic lawyer who works in Louise's father's firm. He wants the finer things in life: a big house, a boat, vacations abroad, and a beautiful wife.

Richard is unaware of his wife's past struggles with her weight. When she tries to share her fears with him, he is unable to empathize with her; he only sees what he wants to see. As Louise gains weight, he criticizes her and loses sexual interest. He volunteers to go on a diet with her, but Louise doesn't feel that he truly loves her. At the end of the story, Louise is certain that Richard will soon leave her.

Themes

Identity

The theme of identity is perhaps the most important aspect of "The Fat Girl." Since the age of nine, when Louise began to overeat, people identify her by her weight. Her mother unsuccessfully tried to reinforce in Louise the idea that other people—particularly boys—would respond to her physical presence, not the girl inside.

Louise's most defining characteristic seems to be her habit of eating food secretly. She deems it a "ritual of deceit and pleasure," yet at the same time she realizes it was a "vice that was insular and destructive." Louise's self-perception demonstrates that by the time she is in high school, she identifies herself by what she eats and how much she weighs.

At times, Louise tries to forge an identity for herself that is not based on her weight. She acknowledges that she likes other parts of her body— her eyes, lips, nose, chin, and hair. Louise's list alludes to her "tender soul" and her "good heart," but does not actually enumerate these as among her positive characteristics. This demonstrates that by the time she is in college, when she makes this list, Louise believes that her identity is intrinsically linked to her physical appearance.

Louise also equates the loss of seventy pounds with losing her identity. "She felt that somehow she had lost more than pounds of fat; that some time during her dieting she had lost herself too." At this point, Louise's seems spiritually lost, noting that "her soul . . . was in some rootless flight."

Despite her inner doubts, Louise embraces her new lifestyle, for it opens up new possibilities— such as marriage. Indeed, when she returns home after college, she meets and marries a young lawyer named Richard.

However, Louise has not lost the sense of her "fat self." She tries to communicate with Richard, to make him understand what her life was like before she lost all the weight. However, he cannot understand.

By the end of the story, when Louise begins to gain weight, she feels herself couched within "layers of flesh and spirit." She reverts to what she perceives to be her true identity—the fat girl.

Change and Transformation

Change and transformation are important themes in the story. When Louise goes to college, she goes on a diet and loses seventy pounds with the help of her friend Carrie. Carrie's acceptance of Louise establishes a solid friendship between the women.

With the tremendous weight loss comes a dramatic change in how people perceive her. Louise's mother calls the new, thin Louise "so *beau*tiful," while family and friends congratulate her. Yet there is also change in Louise's attitude and demeanor. She becomes cranky and ill-tempered, even snapping at Carrie.

However, Louise's weight loss also leads to a greater life change—her marriage to Richard. When she becomes pregnant, however, she loses the hard-earned control she gained during college. Soon, she has started to transform back into "the fat girl."

With this transformation Louise realizes that her husband will leave her, because he is embarrassed, frustrated, and alienated by her weight gain. Yet this realization does not seem to bother her; instead, she seems to welcome the change because she believes being fat will return her sense of identity and security.

Friendship

The friendship between Carrie and Louise is essential to the story. They forge a close bond, one based on mutual loneliness and dissatisfaction. The girls live together for four years at college, writing letters over the summer and joyfully reuniting in the fall. It is Carrie's support and compassion that enables Louise to undergo the arduous process of losing weight.

Carrie wants Louise to lose weight because she worries about what her friend's life will be like after graduation, not because she finds anything intrinsically wrong with Louise's weight. Carrie doesn't want her friend's weight to hinder her happiness in life.

Topics for Further Study

- By the time Dubus wrote ''The Fat Girl,'' the concept of the ideal American family was changing. Increasing numbers of women exerted their independence by working outside of the home. In response to the women's liberation movement, however, some women urged a return to more traditional family values. Do you think that Louise accurately represents a woman of her generation and time period? Why or why not?

- Does the Louisiana setting of the story matter? Why or why not? Do you think the fact that Louise goes to Massachusetts for college has any significance? Why or why not?

- Find out more about binge eating. How prevalent is this practice and how is it linked with other disorders, especially bulimia? What does the prevalence of eating disorders in the United States say about contemporary society?

- Conduct research to find out why the number of overweight Americans is on the rise. What health risks do overweight people have?

- Dubus abruptly shifts to the present tense for his presentation of the story's final scene. What affect does this shift have on you? Rewrite the scene in the past tense and compare the two versions. Which is the more effective? Why?

The importance of this friendship is made clear after Louise begins to get fat again. As she grows larger, her friends do not support her and make her feel uncomfortable. More importantly, she sees none of Carrie's love and compassion in Richard's face, which makes her realize that her marriage is based on superficiality, not on true love.

Style

Narration

''The Fat Girl'' is told chronologically and covers a period of seventeen years, which is unusual for a short story. However, Dubus deftly handles this span of time and gives readers a full sense of Louise's life.

Steve Yarborough considers ''The Fat Girl'' a ''compressed novel''—or a story in which years or even decades are compressed into one paragraph. Dubus alternates between summary sections—still filled with vivid details—and scene sections. The summary sections allow Dubus to give the reader all the necessary information, while the shorter scenes hone in on key points in Louise's life.

Point of View

The point of view of *''The Fat Girl''* is the third-person omniscient perspective. This means that the narration relates what Louise, as well as some of the other characters, think and feel. The primary focus, however, is on Louise.

The story never explicitly expresses a great deal of Louise's inner life. The reader must infer much of why Louise takes certain actions, such as going on the diet or allowing herself to regain the weight. Though Louise's reflections are few, they are important, and they relate her overwhelming sense of loss of self. By the end of the story, the focus on Louise makes it clear that she believes she should be loved for herself, not for what she looks like.

Ending

''The Fat Girl'' is not an experimental story, yet at its end, the tense abruptly switches to the present tense from the past tense. This shift makes the story more vivid, grounding it in Louise's present reality. Instead of remaining simply a story about something that has already happened, the reader realizes that the conflict—between Louise and society—is still going on and that Louise is currently in the process of regaining her own identity.

Setting

The setting of the ''The Fat Girl'' is a small Louisiana town. This town guarantees that Louise will not escape the scrutiny of her community. When Louise is fat, their eyes register disappointment; ''their eyes would tell her she was still fat Louise, who had been fat as long as they could remember, who had gone to college and returned as fat as ever.''

After Louise slims down, however, they look at her with pride and give her a true sense of belonging. Louise becomes friends with some of her former childhood acquaintances, but none of them seem to remember her when she was fat. Such a detail demonstrates their constant judgment of Louise. The people from home embrace her because she is thin, not because she is Louise.

Historical Context

The Carter Years

Jimmy Carter was elected to the presidency in 1976. His administration faced immediate challenges: the American economy was in flirting with recession and the country was on the brink of an energy crisis. Despite Carter's efforts, inflation and unemployment increased and the economy further stagnated. The energy crisis, which led to a sharp rise in the price of imported oil, only deepened the country's economic problems.

In foreign affairs, Carter called for a new commitment to human rights, using diplomatic and economic pressure on countries that violated the rights of their citizens. Some American diplomats opposed Carter's policy, warning that U.S. interference in other country's domestic affairs might lead to international tensions.

Carter's biggest victory in international affairs was his assistance in negotiating the Camp David Accords, a peace treaty between Egypt and Israel. Carter's greatest failure was his inability to free fifty-three American hostages who had been seized by Iranian militants in Tehran, the capital of Iran.

These hostages were held for 444 days before their eventual release in 1981.

The Women's Movement

In the 1970s, the women's movement made significant progress. The National Organization for Women, a women's rights group, was formed in 1966. Throughout the 1970s, more and more women joined the organization to gain equal rights for women.

The National Women's Political Caucus, founded in 1971 with the help of feminist Gloria Steinem, encouraged women to run for political office. It was believed that women in public office would support women's issues, such as equal pay for equal work, domestic abuse legislation, sexual harassment law, and pro-choice protections. Steinem also founded a new magazine for women, *Ms.*.

In 1972, Congress passed the Education Amendments Act, which outlawed sexual discrimination in higher education. Many all-male educational institutions began to allow women to enroll, and many universities established women's studies courses.

One great failure of the women's right movement was the inability to pass the Equal Rights Amendment, or ERA, a constitutional amendment barring discrimination on the basis of sex. Although Congress passed the ERA in 1972, not enough states ratified the bill, therefore it never became a law.

While many women supported the women's movement, some middle-class women felt that it devalued the family and condemned women who chose to be homemakers. These women also believed the women's movement threatened traditional family life. Other women who felt alienated by the women's movement included working-class women and women of color. These women felt that the leaders of the women's movement addressed issues more important to privileged white women.

A Changing American Population

American society experienced significant changes in the 1970s: the birthrate was dropping sharply to an average of two births per woman; the divorce rate continued to rise; and Americans moved around more than they had in the past. Throughout the 1970s, a growing number of Americans moved from the North and the East to the South and the West. Population grew in states such as California, Texas, and Florida.

Compare
&
Contrast

- **1970s:** In 1978, there are 1,130,000 divorces among the American population—or 5.2 divorces for every 1,000 Americans. This number reflects an increasing divorce rate from past eras.

  Today: In 1990 there were 4.7 divorces for every 1,000 Americans—or 1,182,000 total divorces among the American population. If this trend continues, younger Americans marrying for the first time have a 40–50 percent chance of divorcing in their lifetime. By the mid-1990s, around eighteen million Americans have gone through a divorce.

- **1970s:** Around five percent of all children and adolescents are overweight. Approximately 25% of American adults, and 27% of all American women, are overweight.

  Today: Studies show that one of three American adults aged twenty through seventy-four (fifty-eight million people) are overweight. This number has increased over the past decade. Eleven percent of all children and adolescents (4.7 million children) are overweight.

- **1970s:** The diet industry earns ten billion dollars in 1970.

  1990s: By the mid-1990s, the diet industry generates revenue of $33 billion. Two-thirds of all high school students claim to be on a diet, but only twenty percent of these teenagers are actually overweight. Fifty percent of all American women are on a diet at any one time.

- **1970s:** In 1978, there are thirty-eight million working women in America. Of these women, twenty-one million are married with a spouse present.

  Today: In the early part of the decade, just over forty-six million women are employed, out of a total workforce of 130 million. Seventy-one percent of married women hold jobs outside of the home.

- **1970s:** In 1976, approximately one percent of female high school and college students suffer or have suffered from the eating disorders anorexia and bulimia.

  Today: Anorexia nervosa afflicts approximately three percent of all teenagers. The number of bulimics, however, has increased faster than the number of anorexics; between three percent and ten percent of all women in college suffer from bulimia at some time during their college career. Only ten percent of teenagers with eating disorders are boys.

Critical Overview

"The Fat Girl" was published in 1977 as part of Dubus's short story collection *Adultery, and Other Choices*. It has become one of Dubus's best-known works.

Throughout Dubus's career, critics have praised his writing for his sensitive treatment of topical issues, such as abortion, infidelity, drugs, racism, and eating disorders. In fact, his stories have included characters like single mothers, divorced husbands, and abused wives.

Many of Dubus's stories focus on the turbulence of male-female relationships. Edith Milton, writing for the *New Republic*, viewed *Adultery, and Other Choices* as an exploration of the relationships between men and women. "I can think of no one," she writes, "who has drawn a more precise map of that no-man's land between the sexes than he has in this collection."

Other reviewers lauded the collection for its deft portrayals of the individual's search for identity. For example, J. N. Baker of *Newsweek* asserted that Dubus examined this familiar theme with "fresh perception and style."

Mary Soete, writing for *Library Journal*, also noted Dubus's knack for picking significant moments in the lives of his characters. "He presents moments of necessity and choice," she wrote, "in the inner lives of his men and women with precision, truth, and love."

Frances Taliaferro, who called Dubus a "skillful and temperate writer," acknowledged that *Adultery, and Other Choices* "takes some getting used to," but that "Dubus invites us into a world of quiet melodies. Gradually the ear learns to hear them." Taliaferro particularly liked Dubus's depiction of small-town America.

With his story entitled "The Fat Girl," Dubus raised complex issues of body image and identity. Critics generally praised the story. Milton asserts that Louise emerges "triumphantly human" in her understanding that anyone who truly loved her would find her true self underneath her layers of fat.

Baker also deemed the story as "the collections' exquisite prize." This reviewer saw Louise's actions at the end as an example of her "rebellious resolution" against the "charade of her existence."

Anatole Broyard, writing for the *New York Times,* also considered "The Fat Girl" to be the most successful story in the collection. He alludes to Louise's loss of identity when he writes that when thin, Louise is "only a mannequin of other people's expectations."

Steve Yarborough, writing in *Critique: Studies in Modern Fiction*, further discussed the story in terms of its narrative style, not its emotional content. Yarborough maintains that "The Fat Girl" was one of the "notable stories" in Dubus's "compressed novels." He writes,

> The compressed novel seems to be the ideal form for Dubus. . . . It allows him to probe . . . deeply into the characters . . . and . . . forge a dramatic narrative, something the shorter, 'formless' stories do not do.

Criticism

Rena Korb

Korb has a master's degree in English literature and creative writing and has written for a wide

Women's rights activists Gloria Steinem (left) and Mary Chung lead 15,000 marchers in a National Organization for Women parade.

variety of educational publishers. In the following essay, she discusses Louise's search for her identity.

In 1986 Andre Dubus, who for the past decade had so perceptively wrote of the "moment of truth" in the lives of ordinary Americans, was himself caught in just such a pivotal moment. Dubus, who had been driving on a Massachusetts highway, stopped to help a distressed car. While in the road, he was struck by an oncoming car, and his subsequent injuries led to the loss of one leg and his confinement to a wheelchair.

He came to view the accident, in the words of scholar James E. Devlin, "as a transcendent experience that has allowed him to understand more deeply the nature of human suffering, forgiveness, and love."

Certainly Dubus's "philosophy" seemed to be present in his later writing; for instance, the deeply moving "A Father's Story" chronicles the story of a man who helps his daughter flee the scene of a hit-and-run and his subsequent attempts to find comfort through religious ritual.

What Do I Read Next?

- Andre Dubus's "A Father's Story" (1983) chronicles the story of a man who helps his daughter escape from the scene of a hit-and-run accident.

- Dubus's work has often been compared to the stories of Raymond Carver, another realistic contemporary writer. In "Where I'm Calling From" (1981), Carver tells the story of a man searching for meaning in life.

- "In the Garden of the North American Martyrs" (1981), by Tobias Wolff, depicts a professor's attempts to regain her identity and her independence.

- Ernest Hemingway's "Hills Like White Elephants" (1927) is considered a classic short story. It focuses on the relationship of an American couple waiting for a train in Spain.

- *Life Size* (1992), a novel by Jenefer Shute, narrates the story of a young woman who has been hospitalized for anorexia. The novel switches between the past and the present, detailing the woman's recovery while showing the factors that led to her eating disorder.

Readers and critics of his pre-accident body of work, however, still find these same qualities; in fact, they seem to be intrinsic to Dubus. In his depiction of common Americans, Dubus realistically evokes their problems, pain, and efforts to find peace. He delves into the core of humanity and emerges with a key kernel of truth.

"The Fat Girl," first published in 1977 and one of Dubus's most well-known pieces of short fiction, demonstrates what Devlin has called Dubus's attempt to "impose order on chaos." The protagonist, Louise, is one such character trying to impose such order on her life. In "The Fat Girl," Louise is unable to find societal acceptance until she loses more than seventy pounds.

However, her attempt to change her life does not last; some five years after her marriage to a handsome, ambitious lawyer, Louise's food cravings return. As she piles on the pounds, she pushes her husband further and further away.

Though Louise is successful in severing her relationship with a man who seems too intent on physical appearances, she fails overall. Instead of finding a new meaning for her life, she reverts to the one that sustained her throughout her childhood—the solitary pleasures of food, which she herself once called "a vice that was insular and destructive."

Louise's odyssey begins when she is only a little girl. Her mother, warning that "in five years you'll be in high school and if you're fat the boys won't like you," won't let Louise eat potato chips and deserts. Louise compensates for this denial through secret bingeing.

From a young age, Louise defines herself through her weight and the food she eats. The girlfriends she chooses are always thin, because she didn't want anyone looking at herself and a friend "'to see two fat girls.'"

At college, she doesn't eat much in the cafeteria because not eating in public "had become as habitual as good manners." She attends a school for girls back East so she won't have to "contend with" boys. Yet Louise understands it is not only boys who judge her based on her appearance. She knows that at her new school "she would get not attention" from her teachers and fellow students. By the time she is a young adult, Louise too readily understands the way people look right through her.

Carrie is the first person who perceives Louise's weight as an obstacle that will keep her from enjoying life. Carrie's acceptance of Louise for who she is, not what she looks like, is demonstrated when she asks Louise to eat in front of her instead of secretly. Even when she urges Louise to diet, it is not because she has a problem with Louise's weight; rather, she worries for Louise's future.

For Louise, however, losing seventy pounds seems to change her personality too. She finds that she becomes irritable when "all her life she had never been afflicted by ill temper." After losing close to forty pounds, she still "did not feel strong, she did not feel she was committed to and within reach of achieving a valuable goal." Instead, she felt she "had lost more than pounds of fat; that some time during her dieting she had lost herself too."

With her new habits and eating routines, Louise gives up every vestige of her former life. She eats sparse meals—dinner is a piece of meat and lettuce and breakfast is an egg and black coffee—instead of candy bars and other sweets. She no longer eats secretly; instead, Carrie monitors every piece of food that goes in Louise's mouth.

In fact, Louise's body—one which "she liked most when she was unaware of it"—becomes common property. It is shared with Carrie, who charts Louise's progress via the scale. Everyone she knows comments on it: her parents, friends, and acquaintances. They all seem to be more comfortable and accepting of the new Louise. After she returns home from college, she becomes friends with people she knew as a child "and even they did not seem to remember her when she was fat." The overarching message is that Louise, the fat girl, is a person unworthy of knowing and loving; but Louise, the slender young woman, is acceptable.

Louise's relationship with Carrie is also affected by the diet. Since Carrie is monitoring the diet, Carrie is not only Louise's friend but also her enemy. Louise speaks sharply to Carrie, and she snaps at her about lettuce. In this way their relationship becomes permeated with talk of food. Louise later recalls her final year in college, the diet year, as "the worst year of her life."

The diet year is underscored by her feeling that "she was going to another country or becoming a citizen of a new one." This country seems to be populated by Louise's relatives and acquaintances, and at first Louise loves "the applause in their eyes."

Her transformation is officially established by her marriage to Richard. At times during her marriage, Louise tries to embrace her new identity. On the plane returning from Europe, "she thought of the accumulated warmth and pelt of her marriage, and how by slimming her body she had bought into the pleasures of the nation." At this point, Louise is

> " Whether or not she regains weight for any of these reasons--whether she is simply meant to be fat, or is gluttonous, or wants to drive Richard away, or even wants to find her own self-- the fact remains that in giving herself up to food, Louise finds peace again."

equating her slenderness with her ability to fit into society and thus partake of all it has to offer—a large lakefront house, expensive vacations, a boat.

Yet these are only possessions, and Louise's "moments of triumph were sparse." Sometimes she "was suddenly assaulted by the feeling that she had taken the wrong train and arrived at a place where no one knew her, and where she ought not to be." This sentence is immediately followed up by a scene between Louise and Richard, in bed, where she talks to him about having been fat. Such positioning seems to indicate that part of the feeling of being in the wrong place stems from her relationship with Richard—perhaps he is the wrong man for her.

Indeed, the narration states:

> she knew the story meant very little to him . . . She felt as though she was trying to tell a foreign lover about her life in the United States, and if only she could command the language he would know and love all of her and she would feel complete.

Louise's desire for completeness and for reconnecting with her own soul, which had gotten lost "in some rootless flight" during her diet years, leads her to regain the weight she so arduously took off. Part of Louise's transformation back into a "fat girl" may stem from the fact that she has become a mother. During her childhood, Louise's mother made her daughter feel unworthy and unattractive because of her weight.

When Louise becomes a mother, she is gratified that her son responds to her despite "the folds of fat at her waist.'' Perhaps Louise sees an opportunity to find someone who will love her for what she is and what she looks like. Louise also may feel that she doesn't want her own child to grow up as she did: judged and criticized.

As Louise derives pleasure from eating and she regains the weight, she also retreats back to her solitary world. She knows that her weight gain and her refusal to try and lose weight will make Richard leave her. The words, ''[i]t has been in his eyes all summer,'' implies that Louise not only expects his rejection, but will be relieved by it. In this way, she will discover his true feelings for her.

All her life, no one really has *seen* Louise except for Carrie. Although her father's eyes were filled with ''the lights of love,'' they were also filled with ''pity.'' His attempts to defend Louise to her mother are ineffectual and contribute to Louise's secret bingeing.

To her mother, Louise has been a constant source of disappointment. The only time her mother approves of Louise is after she has dieted to a slender 113 pounds. Her mother ''cried and hugged her and said again and again: You're *beau*tiful.''

Richard seems to care little about the woman inside and only covets her slender exterior. '''Have you *looked* at yourself?''' he asks Louise after she has gained back fifty pounds. Louise finds none of Carrie's ''compassion and determination and love'' in her husband, even after he volunteers to diet with her.

Readers have grappled with why Louise regains weight. Anatole Broyard, in the *New York Times*, says that Louise ''has dieted away her appetite for life, that, in some way, her fatness was part of her essence and now she is only a mannequin of other people's expectations.''

Edith Milton contends in the *New Republic* that ''fat is what she is, and . . . any love worth the name can find her under the blubber.''

J. N. Baker for *Newsweek* calls out the ''charade of her existence,'' which ''inspires a rebellious resolution.''

Whether or not she regains weight for any of these reasons—whether she is simply meant to be fat, or is gluttonous, or wants to drive Richard away, or even wants to find her own self—the fact remains that in giving herself up to food, Louise finds peace again.

''She knows Richard is waiting,'' the story ends, ''but she feels his departure so happily that, when she enters the living room, unwrapping the candy, she is surprised to see him standing there.'' So order for Louise comes with a tall price—the retreat back into the world of childhood, where food could satisfy all her basic needs. It is up to the reader to decide, then, if Louise is a success or a failure.

Source: Rena Korb, for *Short Stories for Students*, Gale, 2000.

Liz Brent

Brent has a Ph.D. in American Culture, specializing in film studies, from the University of Michigan. She is a freelance writer and teaches courses in the history of American cinema. In the following essay, Brent discusses themes of identity and spirituality in Dubus's story.

Dubus's short story ''The Fat Girl'' is about a young woman, Louise, who, from the age of nine, is seen by everyone around her as a ''fat girl.'' In order to get around her mother's insistence that she diet, Louise develops the habit of sneaking food which she secretly eats in her bedroom or in the bathroom.

When Louise is in college, her best (and only) friend Carrie puts her on a strict diet, as a result of which she loses some seventy pounds over the course of a year. When she was considered a ''fat girl,'' Louise felt she could never even dream of being asked out by a man; but once she has lost weight she dates and marries Richard, a young man who works in her father's business.

However, when Louise becomes pregnant, she begins to revert back to her old eating habits and quickly gains weight. After the baby is born, she continues to overeat. Her husband becomes increasingly angered by her weight gain until, at the end of the story, she defiantly eats a piece of pie and then a candy bar in front of him, almost relieved with his inevitable departure from her life.

Louise's struggle with being a ''fat girl'' is characterized by her struggles with her sense of identity. Early in life, Louise is convinced that it is her God-ordained fate, or destiny, to be a ''fat girl.'' Fate being a concept born of religious conviction, Louise believes that ''God had made her that way.'' She imagines that her two high school friends, both of them thin, would always remember her as ''a girl whose hapless body was destined to be fat.''

As Louise's sense of herself includes the firm belief that it is her God-ordained destiny to be a "fat girl," the practice of eating takes on religious implications. Eating for Louise is repeatedly referred to as a "ritual"—a term normally used to describe a sacred spiritual practice; for instance, "her creeping to the kitchen when she was nine became, in high school, a ritual of deceit and pleasure."

When Carrie puts her on a diet, this new regimen of eating replaces her old "ritual": "That was her ritual and her diet for the rest of the year, Carrie alternating fish and chicken breasts with the steaks for dinner, and every day was nearly as bad as the first."

Nonetheless, Louise's old eating "ritual" battles for prominence over her new "ritual" of eating: ". . . those first weeks of the diet . . . she was the pawn of an irascibility which still, conditioned to her ritual as she was, could at any moment take command of her."

Louis's struggle with her eating "ritual" and her identity as a "fat girl" are further expressed in spiritual terms, through reference to her "soul," and her "spirit," as well as to demons and morality. When Carrie first puts Louise on a diet, her struggle with hunger is described as a battle for her soul:

> In all her life she had never been afflicted by ill temper and she looked upon it now as a demon which, along with hunger, was taking possession of her soul.

However, Louise also considers the diet as inherently "immoral." At one point, Louise lashes out at Carrie, complaining of her hatred of lettuce; Louise concludes that, "'We shouldn't even buy it, it's immoral.'" This again suggests that Louise's accustomed "ritual" of eating takes on spiritual, religious implications—as if it were a veritable sacrament for her to eat as she always has.

Flying back to school after the Christmas vacation of her first year dieting, Louise is struck by the sense that, in the course of the diet, her very "soul" has been lost, her "spirit collapsed," and she likens the loss of her old eating habits to "lost virtues." From the airplane,

> She looked down at the earth far below, and it seemed to her that her soul, like her body aboard the plane, was in some rootless flight. She neither knew its destination nor where it had departed from; it was on some passage she could not even define.

For Louise, the struggle with eating and not eating, gaining and losing weight, is also a struggle with her sense of identity. From the age of nine, she

> It is as if 'flesh' and 'spirit' are one and the same for Louise, as if gaining weight were, for her, equivalent to feeding her spirit, just as losing weight feels to her like draining her spirit."

identifies herself as a "fat girl." When she loses the weight, she loses part of herself.

The day before embarking on her college diet, Louise is told to spend one day eating "as though it were the last day of her life." In some sense, Louise does experience this as the last day of her life; the loss of self begins immediately the next day with the loss of her eating "ritual."

When, after months of dieting, her weight plateaus, she is quick to suggest that maybe that weight is *who she is*—not just some arbitrary number that can be changed at will:

> During the next few weeks she lost weight more slowly and once for eight days Carrie's daily recording stayed at a hundred and thirty-six. Louise woke in the morning thinking of one hundred and thirty-six and then she stood on the scales and they echoed her. She became obsessed with that number, and there wasn't a day when she didn't say it aloud, and through the days and nights the number stayed in her mind, and if a teacher had spoken those digits in a classroom she would have opened her mouth to speak. *What if that's me,* she said to Carrie. I mean what if a hundred and thirty-six is my real weight and I just can't lose anymore. Walking hand-in-hand with her despair was a longing for this to be true, and that longing angered her and wearied her, and every day she was gloomy (emphasis mine).

While everyone around her views body weight as a fluid and malleable thing that may be altered at will, Louise struggles for a stable sense of identity, which includes a stable weight.

Louise's struggle for a stable sense of identity is also conceptualized in terms of national identity. When, after her first year of dieting, Louise's mother buys her new clothes and hires a photographer to document Louise's weight loss, Louise expresses her sense of alienation in terms of feeling like a foreigner in a foreign country: "The new clothes and the photographer made her feel she was going to another country or becoming a citizen of a new one."

When she meets Richard, Louise once again expresses herself in terms that suggest that only by losing weight is she able to become a legitimate citizen of her own country: ". . . she thought of the accumulated warmth and pelf of her marriage, and how by slimming her body she had bought into the pleasures of the nation."

At the same time, Louise still feels out of place in the world, as if being thin were not her desired, or legitimate, "destination" in life:

> But there were times, with her friends, or with Richard, or alone in the house, when she was suddenly assaulted by the feeling that she had taken the wrong train and arrived at a place where no one knew her, and where she ought not to be.

In trying to explain to her husband what it was like to be a "fat girl," Louise again expresses her frustration in failing to adequately communicate her experience in terms of national identity, as she feels like a foreigner in her own body and her own life: "She felt as though she were trying to tell a foreign lover about her life in the United States, and if only she could command the language he would know and love all of her and she would feel complete."

After having her baby, Louise returns to her old "rituals" of eating; her return to these rituals feels like a return of her "spirit." As her husband criticizes her weight gain, Louise "remained calm within layers of flesh and spirit, and watched his frustration, his impotence." It is as if "flesh" and "spirit" are one and the same for Louise, as if gaining weight were, for her, equivalent to feeding her spirit, just as losing weight feels to her like draining her spirit.

In the final moments of the story, Louise becomes resigned to the knowledge that Richard will soon leave her because of her weight gain. In holding the baby to her body, Louise again equates her body with her soul, as she "carries the boy to his crib, feels him against her large breasts, feels that his sleeping body touches her soul."

Source: Liz Brent, for *Short Stories for Students*, Gale, 2000.

Sarah Madsen Hardy

Madsen Hardy has a doctorate in English literature and is a freelance writer and editor. In the following essay, she discusses Louise's evolving attitude toward her weight in the context of 'fat acceptance.'

"Her name was Louise." So opens Andre Dubus's short story "The Fat Girl." But before readers even learn the protagonist's name, they have already learned the most important aspect of her identity from the story's title. The frank adjective "fat" is a powerful label. The story outlines how Louise negotiates this identity, focusing on her relationships with her parents, female friends, and men. Louise sees herself as a fat person in a double way—in terms of her own, private self-image, which includes self-love and pleasure, and in terms of how others see her, which centers on pity, worry, and disgust. Even when she succeeds in losing weight, fatness remains a dominant part of how she sees herself. Louise's struggle to come to terms with her identity as a fat girl reflects a larger cultural debate about the way obesity should be understood and dealt with.

As a nation, Americans are obsessed with weight and are chronically fat. According to medical researchers at the 1998 annual meeting of the American Association for the Advancement of Science (AAAS), "obesity is a public health epidemic and should be treated like one" reports Maggie Fox, who covered the conference for Reuters. Medical experts see obesity as an illness rather than a personal issue, attributing to it a host of health risks running from diabetes to heart disease. Despite evidence that obesity is largely attributable to genetics, research has shown that most Americans associate thinness not only with beauty, but with character and virtue as well. Fat people are often perceived as unattractive and asexual. Furthermore, they are often held responsible for their condition and labeled as undisciplined, lazy, even stupid. American culture stigmatizes fat people to the point that obesity often has stronger detrimental effects on their social and emotional lives than it does on their physical health.

According to fat-acceptance advocacy groups such as the National Association to Advance Fat Acceptance (NAAFA), in light of such discriminatory attitudes, obesity should be seen primarily as a human rights issue, not a medical one. They advocate for fat people who are routinely subjected to discrimination in employment, housing, and other arenas. They oppose weight-loss diet programs (which, NAAFA claims, have a collective 95–98 percent failure rate over a three-year period), speaking out against a diet industry that funds obesity research and exploits fat peoples' psyches and pocketbooks. Fat-acceptance advocates claim that it is years of off-and-on dieting, not obesity in itself, that leads to health problems among the fat.

Perhaps the most important part of NAAFA's mission, however, is to offer social and emotional support for fat people, many of whom are depressed and isolated. Because the mainstream culture looks so unfavorably on obesity, they strive to create a subculture where it's okay to be fat, offering fat-friendly social events, pen pals, and dating services. One recent internet search retrieved over seventy fat-acceptance groups, as well as a range of online magazines such as *Abundance Magazine, BBTeen E-zine, Fat?So!, Big Times* and *Fat and Fabulous*, which address issues including health, fashion, romance, and sex in the fat person's life. Such forums help foster self-acceptance and social ties among the obese.

In ''The Fat Girl'' Louise vacillates between a mainstream perspective—seeing her weight as a weakness and the source of her problems—and an accepting one—seeing it as no more than an incidental aspect of who she is. From a young age she seems to understand that ''she was fat because she was Louise. Because God had made her that way.'' But she is the only fat person in the story (at one point she explains, ''I was always thinking what people saw when they looked at me and I didn't want them seeing two fat girls'') so she also internalizes the ideas about fatness that thin people tend to have. Describing this double perspective on her weight, Louise says, ''When I was alone I didn't mind being fat, but then I'd have to leave the house again and then I didn't want to look like me.''

. The thin people in the story—with the notable exception of Louise's father—cannot imagine simply accepting her for who she is. They assume that Louise's weight is preventing her from leading a happy, fulfilled life. From a young age Louise is encouraged to lose weight for the specific purpose of attracting the opposite sex. ''If you're fat the boys won't like you; they won't ask you out,'' Louise's mother tells her bluntly. But Louise does not find this very powerful incentive. Her single sexual experience, being kissed by a drunk boy, is not pleasurable or affirming: ''He jammed his tongue into her mouth.'' By contrast, she takes such great pleasure in eating that Dubus describes it in sexual terms. Likening the chocolate that Louise keeps hidden in her drawer to ''lewd photographs,'' he describes how Louise ''thought of the waiting can-

> '' As a thin, beautiful woman Louise must live in denial of her physical and emotional appetites, suffering a dislocated sense that those around her do not know who she really is. . . . It is not until she gains weight back and loses Richard's love that she begins to see others' intolerance toward her weight as <u>their</u> problem or weakness rather than hers.''

dy with near lust.'' The candy seems to offer her the solace of love that is otherwise missing from her life. According to this way of thinking, Louise would stop lusting for candy when she finally found a fulfilling love relationship, which would therefore make it possible for her to give up food and be forever thin.

This is, indeed, what her friend Carrie seems to believe when she encourages Louise to go on a diet. Thin, chronically depressed Carrie has recently fallen in love for the first time. As she rides the bus from her boyfriend's place back to the dorm room she shares with Louise, she starts worrying about Louise's prospects for the future. ''I was thinking about when we graduate. What you're going to do. What's to become of you. I want you to be loved the way I love you. Louise, if I help you, *really* help you, will you go on a diet?'' The context of Carrie's concern suggests that she believes that Louise will be alone—without friends and also without the chance to find romantic love—if she doesn't lose weight.

While Carrie's response to Louise's weight is based on concern and sympathy, and her mother's response is more judgmental and hostile, both of them tie happiness and love—and, significantly, the love of men—to being thin. But, as the narrative unfolds, it becomes clear that what makes Louise unhappy, angry, and resentful is being *hungry*, not being fat. When, with Carrie's help, Louise sheds enough weight to no longer be seen as a fat girl by those around her (including her new husband, Richard), her new attractiveness and social acceptance do not bring her real happiness. "She felt that somehow she had lost more than pounds of fat; that some time during her dieting she had lost herself too." She later reflects on the year of dieting as "the worst year of her life."

As a thin, beautiful woman Louise must live in denial of her physical and emotional appetites, suffering a dislocated sense that those around her do not know who she really is. She occasionally feels "cunning" and "triumphant," but "there were times, with her friends, or with Richard, or alone in the house, when she was suddenly assaulted by the feeling that she had taken the wrong train and arrived at a place where no one knew her, and where she ought not be." It is not until she gains weight back and loses Richard's love that she begins to see others' intolerance toward her weight as *their* problem or weakness rather than hers. She has feelings of happiness and fulfillment when she is eating and nurturing her infant son. She is not heartbroken to lose Richard, whom she understands as crippled in his incapacity to love her truly, as herself, the way God made her.

Since Louise has never had a social network to support her in accepting her size, where does this emerging sense of self-esteem and self-acceptance come from? Throughout the story, Dubus describes Louise's father as somewhat weak but loving. He offers her love unconditionally and "kissed her often." He is the only character in the story that encourages her to eat and the only one to express ambivalence when she eventually loses weight, commenting, "But now there's less of you to love." Though he too pities her, he is the one figure from whom she receives a message that she is lovable just as she is, as a fat girl.

Another origin of Louise's eventual self-acceptance is the fat actresses with whom she was fascinated as a teenager. These women, who had "broad and profound faces," reflect for Louise an alternative affirmative vision of herself and her future—one that doesn't involve dieting, self-denial, and transformation. She imagines that "they were fat because they chose to be." In our thin-worshiping culture, this is a radical idea. "And she was certain of something else too: she could see it in their faces—they did not eat secretly." They are not ashamed of who they are. By the end of the story, Louise, too, is finally able to eat openly and without shame, despite her mother's silent disapproval and her husband's resentful rejection. "She is remained calm within layers of flesh and spirit," Dubus writes, suggesting that Louise's body and soul are at last in harmony. She is free to feed her hungers and this—rather than the approval of the thin mainstream—is what brings her true happiness and peace.

Source: Sarah Madsen Hardy for *Short Stories for Students*, Gale, 2000.

Sources

Baker, J. N, Review of *Adultery and Other Choices*, in *Newsweek*, December 5, 1977, p. 100B.

Broyard, Anatole, "Some Good Moments," in *The New York Times Book Review*, November 20, 1977, p. 14.

Devlin, James E., "Andre Dubus," in *Dictionary of Literary Biography*, Vol. 130, Gale, 1993, pp. 142–49.

Milton, Edith, Review of *Adultery and Other Choices*, in *The New Republic*, February 4, 1978, p. 33.

Soete, Mary, Review of *Adultery and Other Choices*, in *Library Journal*, January 15, 1978, p. 191.

Taliaferro, Frances, Review of *Adultery and Other Choices*, in *Harper's*, January, 1978, p. 87.

Yarbrough, Steve, "Andre Dubus: From Detached Incident to Compressed Novel," in *Critique: Studies in Modern Fiction*, Vol. XXVIII, No. 1, Fall, 1986, pp. 19–27.

Further Reading

Dubus, Andre, *Meditations from a Movable Chair*, Thorndike, MN: Thorndike Press, 1999
    A collection of Dubus's essays.

Kennedy, Thomas E., *Andre Dubus: A Study of the Short Fiction*, Boston: Twayne Publishers, 1988.
    Critical study of Dubus's most important short stories.

La Grande Bretèche

Honore de Balzac

1842

Originally published in France in 1842, "La Grande Bretèche" is set in 1830 and describes events that happened in the year 1815 to 1816. This was a turbulent period in France. After the Revolution in 1789, the bourgeoisie, or middle class, struggled to consolidate its power and to retain the political and economic victories it had won over the nobility and the church. By the time of the events of the story, the reign of Napoleon Bonaparte had come and gone, but the old class divisions remained beneath the surface of a new, freer, France.

A member of this new business class himself, Balzac has been praised for his keen insight into the daily lives and inner thoughts of characters not traditionally thought worthy of literary fiction. In "La Grande Bretèche," Balzac's alter ego is the physician Dr. Bianchon. His worldly tone is perfectly suited to Balzac's purposes, and as a member of the new professional class, he blends well with members of the aristocracy (the unseen rich patient he is caring for), as well as with servants and peasants like Madame Lepas and Rosalie.

"La Grande Bretèche" is part of a group of stories called *Another View of Woman* in English, which is itself part of Balzac's encyclopedic work of fiction, *La Comedie Humaine*, or *The Human Comedy*. This group of stores is set at a party, after dinner, where different narrators take turns telling stories. Dr. Bianchon's contribution belongs to his "collection of appalling stories," and its gothic

setting and suspenseful structure casts a spell over his listeners.

Balzac's story "La Grande Bretèche" represents a miniscule portion of the great author's fictional output. Nonetheless, its narrative momentum, rich detail, and penetrating look into the human condition are characteristic of the prolific nineteenth-century French writer who continues to confound critics even today.

Author Biography

Born in southwestern France in 1799, Honore de Balzac was a man whose temperaments and habits were perfectly suited to the changeable and exuberant age in which he lived. After completing his early education at boarding schools, Balzac studied for law and worked in a notary's office in Paris. Meanwhile, he was also studying literature at the Sorbonne. With his parents' somewhat reluctant support— they paid for a garret for him—he tried his hand at writing. This period, 1819 to 1824, produced a number of unsuccessful and undeveloped philosophical and literary works, but it also proved to be a valuable apprenticeship.

Around the time Balzac was finding his novelist's voice, he also formed the first in a series of close relationships with women from whom he received warmth—and sometimes passion, critical response, and the gift of insight into the female psyche. Balzac met Laurie de Berny when he was 22 years old and she was twice that. Their love affair lasted eight years, but their friendship endured until her death in 1836. He also formed a close, if platonic friendship with a schoolmate of his sister, Zulma Carrud, from whose military officer husband he gathered material about life in the Napoleonic campaigns. The third woman to influence the developing novelist during this period was the Duchess of Abrantes. From her, he gathered entertaining anecdotes on life inside the Imperial court and was introduced to the salons of nobility, which would be reproduced later in *La Comedie*.

After a period of newspaper and hackwork necessitated by financial need, Balzac finally published his first literary worked, *Le Dernier Choan*, which would later become the first volume of *La Comedie Humaine*. This book, though commercially unsuccessful, impressed the literary establishment with its rich rendering of details from ordinary life and its fully drawn characters. "La Grande Bretèche," first published as in a volume of *La Comedie Humaine* title *Autre Étude de Femme*, or *Another Study of Women* in 1842, shows the full flowering of the new Romantic Movement in Balzac's fiction.

Balzac died a newlywed in his Paris apartment in August of 1850. Despite humble origins, constant financial difficulties, and his irrepressible appetites, he left behind an impressive and lasting literary legacy. His rich personal life informed his fiction, which is still read today.

Plot Summary

The story opens *in media res*, or in the middle of things. Doctor Bianchon is conceding to the other dinner guests' requests that he tell one of the "appalling stories in [his] collection." Noting that the audience had been primed by a previous story, and that the late hour of 2:00 a.m. seemed ideal, the "obliging doctor bowed and silence reigned." The dinner guests then disappear from the story until the final sentences, and Doctor Bianchon tells the story in which he features as much as a listener as a narrator and lets three other storytellers relate the story of "La Grande Bretèche" to his listeners.

Setting the scene, Bianchon describes a dramatically ruined estate just on the outskirts of the town of Vendome, where he was staying to care for a rich patient. Revealing his sensitive, even poetic, nature the doctor reveals that he is so drawn to the "unwritten poetry" and "unrevealed thought" of the ruins that he frequently broke in and sat in the garden where he "wove delightful romances, and abandoned myself to little debauches of melancholy which enchanted me." These romantic reveries are called to a halt, however, when he is visited in his rooms one evening by a mysterious stranger, who introduces himself as Monsieur Regnault.

Regnault is a lawyer, the local notary, whose job is to inform Bianchon that he may longer trespass on the grounds of la Grande Bretèche. Far from dampening Bianchon's curiosity, Regnault's prohibition inspires the doctor to learn more about the decaying house's secret. He does learn from Regnault that the terms of the late Comtesse de Merret's will, delivered to Regnault on her deathbed, forbid any alteration to the property for 50 years following her death. The notary's vivid description of the scene at the lady's deathbed only fuels the doctor's quest to learn more, but Regnault professes ignorance and says ''with comical reticence, 'I never allow myself to criticize the conduct of a person who honours me with the gift of a diamond.''' One of the details of the notary's story, the crucifix that the dying woman clutched in her last moment, will prove to be significant when all the elements of the story are revealed.

With his appetite whetted, Bianchon turns to his next storyteller, the wife of his innkeeper, Madame Lepas, and she tells a different part of the story, the beginning. She relates the arrival of the Spanish prisoner, whose name she thinks she remembers as Bagos de Feredia, ''a handsome young fellow for a Spaniard, who are ugly they say.'' She mentions his devotion to his Catholic faith and his silver and ebony crucifix, as well as his mysterious disappearance and the stash of gold left behind (which she and her husband appropriated). She allows that she has always believed ''that he had something to do with the business about Madame de Merret.''

Madame Lepas's mention of Rosalie, Madame de Merret's former maid who now works for Lepas, leads Bianchon to the brink of discovering the truth. The girl then becomes to him ''the very centre of the interest and of the truth; she appeared to [him] to be tied into the knot of it.'' To get her to give up her secrets, however, he must first seduce her. Apparently Bianchon succeeds (which is revealed in the single line ''one evening, or rather one morning''), because Rosalie does fill in the remainder of the story of Madame de Merret's affair with the young Feredia.

Rosalie tells of the night Monsieur returned home unexpectedly and caught his wife with her lover. Turning the key to enter his wife's room, he thinks he hears the door shut to the closet. When he discovers that Rosalie is not in the closet, as he had at first thought, he realizes what his wife is up to. When his wife denies that there is anyone in there he makes her swear on her crucifix that she is telling the truth. Noticing the unusual craftsmanship of the piece he asks her where she got it. She lies again, claiming she bought it form the jeweler Duvivier, who had in turn bought it from a Spanish monk the prior year.

Having caught his wife in a web of lies, Monsieur de Merret plots his revenge. He summons the servant Gorenflot to arrange for a mason. To his wife's horror, he orders the door to the closet walled

Honore de Balzac

up with the Spanish lover trapped inside. Next he pretends to leave the house on an errand and catches his wife in an attempt to free Feredia. And finally, he produces the jeweler from who she claims to have purchased the crucifix. He then remains in his wife's room for the next 20 days while Feredia dies slowly and unaided.

When Bianchon finishes telling his tale, the dinner guests rise and disperse. The effect appears to be most pronounced on the ladies present, as there ''were some among them who had almost shivered at the last words.''

Characters

Bianchon

Doctor Bianchon is the narrator of this after-dinner tale and the character in the story to whom all the other narrators tell their tales. As the opening of the story reveals, he is known to his dinner companions to have ''some appalling stories in [his] collection.'' He also discloses in his tale that he is a man of refined sensibilities and is susceptible to the romantic powers of certain places and settings.

Duvivier

He is the jeweler from whom Madame de Merret claims to have purchased the distinctive Spanish silver crucifix (which her lover has given her). Monsieur de Merret summons Duvivier to his wife's bedroom and asks him in her presence if he had purchased some Spanish crucifixes, which of course he had not.

Jean Gorenflot

A minor character who performs a major role, Gorenflot is the servant who accepts Monsieur de Merret's bribe to seal the doorway to the closet in which his wife's lover is hiding. He engages the mason and accepts Monsieur's offer of a passport and sufficient cash to marry Rosalie and start a new life.

Madame Lepas

The narrator's landlord and the second narrator in the frame tale, Madame Lepas, supplements Regnault's story about Madame La Merret by introducing the idea that the Spanish nobleman may have been involved somehow. She also mentions the distinctive sliver and black crucifix that eventually unravels the Comtesse's deception.

Monsieur Regnault

He is the local notary and the first of the narrators within the frame tale. He visits Bianchon in his rooms to tell him that he has been trespassing on his occasional visits to the ruined gardens at la Grande Bretèche. When Bianchon asks why, Regnault explains that he late Comtesse de Merret had given him explicit instructions on her death-bed that the estate was to remain untouched and uninhabited for fifty years after her death.

Rosalie

Rosalie is the third narrator from whom Bianchon learns the full story of the mysterious la Grande Bretèche. A former maid for Madame de Merret, Rosalie now works for Madame Lepas and thus is available for Bianchon's inquiries. Though she is ''a good girl,'' according to Monsieur Regnault, Bianchon is apparently able to seduce her in order to elicit more information from her about her former mistress.

Bagos de Feredia

He is the Spanish nobleman who is dead before the story begins. A prisoner of the Napoleonic wars, he was being kept under house arrest in the same inn where Bianchon is now staying. Madame Lepas describes him as handsome and charming, if a little mysterious. When he disappeared inexplicably, she and others assumed that he had drowned. By the end of the story, however, Bianchon, discovers the much more gruesome cause of his death: slow starvation in Madame de Merret's closet.

Comtesse de Merret

Also refered to as Madame de Merret, she is the late inhabitant and last owner of la Grande Bretèche, and the woman whose secrets Bianchon seeks to find out from the storytellers he engages in the story. As the narrative finally reveals, she went to her death with the terrible secret that she had betrayed her husband with her lover, the Spanish nobleman, and then betrayed her lover when she allowed her husband to have him mortared into the closet rather than confess.

Monsieur de Merret

The Comtesse's husband, Mousier de Merret is said to have died in Paris due to the consequences of his excessive living. Bianchon learns later why he would have left his wife and estate in despair: he discovers his wife's adultery with the young Spaniard and cruelly condemns the man to a slow and agonizing death while he and forces his wife to listen or confess.

Themes

Betrayal

One of the most pronounced themes in ''La Grande Bretèche'' is betrayal. But Balzac resists the impulse to portray the act of betrayal as black and white. Instead, the story offers a complex and nuanced consideration of what it means to betray a vow or another human being. The primary act of betrayal occurs between Madame and Monsieur de Merret, but careful readers will notice how this act spawns several other betrayals as well.

Even the original betrayal is not as simple as it seems at first. Yes, Madame de Merret betrays her husband and her marriage vows by taking the Spanish lover. But it quickly becomes more complicated than that. She betrays her religious faith by making a false vow on the crucifix. Finally, in what is the most horrifying act of betrayal in the story, she betrays her lover by allowing her husband to imprison him in the closet. Ironically, Monsieur de Merret uses the sacredness of his wife's pledge on the cross to silence her efforts to confess her lie and free Feredia, reminding her when she tries to speak during the twenty days it takes for the man to die that she "swore on the cross that no one was there."

From this original betrayal there are many others. Madame Lepas and her husband betray Feredia's last wishes by keeping the money he had asked be donated to the church. Bianchon betrays Rosalie by seducing her just to get information from her. Rosalie betrays the confidence of her former employees by spilling the story to Bianchon. Finally, Bianchon, the dinner guests—and the readers— all betray the wishes of the late Madame de Merret when we trespass on her property both literally in the case of the narrator and figuratively in the case of the listeners.

Men versus Women

Since "La Grande Bretèche" belongs to the group of stories linked together under the title *Another View of Woman*, it is necessary to consider how the theme of men versus women is articulated through the narrative. At the center of the story is the adversarial relationship between Madame and Monsieur de Merret. Their fierce struggle (which almost certainly has a history we cannot know) results in both their deaths as well as the death of the Spanish nobleman. The scene in which the vengeful husband tries to force his wife to give up her secrets is repeated symbolically throughout the story. First, Monsieur Regnault, the notary, describes his encounter with a cryptic and secretive Madame de Merret who reluctantly tells him just enough information to get what she wants from him. Next, the narrator cajoles Madame Lepas into revealing more about the story and more about herself than she had intended.

The most troubling instance of this motif occurs in the exchange between Bianchon and Rosalie, all of which is hidden from the readers. Because he cannot get direct access to the secret of La Grande Bretèche and Madame de Merret, Bianchon must pursue indirect routes and proxies. Having discovered that Rosalie "was at the very centre of the interest and the truth," he launches a campaign to seduce her. Not only does he succeed in his goal of possessing what she knows, he also appropriates her right to tell her own story. Whereas Bianchon has allowed the other narrators, Regnault and Lepas, to speak for themselves, when he gets to Rosalie's part of the tale he intercedes and tells his listeners that he's summarizing what she told him.

Topics for Further Study

- What is the significance of Monsieur Regnault's diamond pin? Why does he mention it to Dr. Bianchon?

- What other stories have you read that remind you of the opening of *La Grande Bretèche* with its description of the ruined house and garden? Why do you think the place has such an effect on Bianchon?

- What is your judgement of Madame de Merret's choice to let her lover die in the closet rather than go back on her oath to her husband? What other options did she have? Who is ultimately responsible for Feredia de Bagos's death?

- Why do you think the ladies shivered at the end to Bianchon's tale?

The story ends with a final instance of the theme of men versus women. When Bianchon finishes the story, it appears that it has affected the women differently from the men. A new omniscient narrator explains that "all the ladies rose form the table, and thus the spell under which Bianchon has held them was broken." The narrator also mentions that "there were some among them who had almost shivered at the last words," as if this other view of women were too horrifying to contemplate.

Style

Narration: The Frame Tale

"La Grande Bretèche" is a frame tale, a story in which one narrative frames at least one additional narrative. Further complicating matters for the reader is Balzac's penchant for interlocking stories and recurrent characters in the many volumes of work that came to be known as *La Comedia Humaine*. The outer frame of "La Grande Bretèche," part of the structure of the group of stories in *Another View of Woman*, is the scene of a dinner party in which a series of narrators are asked to entertain the group. Dr. Bianchon, who is known to the group as an exceptional storyteller, presents his tale of the secrets of la Grande Bretèche.

Bianchon, though a character in his tale, has no direct access to the story itself. He must rely on three more narrators to reveal the secrets that he pursued during his stay in Vendome. In order for this device to be successful, Bianchon must establish his prowess not just as a teller of tales, but also as a listener or reader of them. In this way he serves as a model of the ideal listener for the members of his audience at the dinner table and as a model reader as well. Two somewhat contradictory features characterize Dr. Bianchon's listening style. On the one hand, as a scientist, he privileges a relentless inquisitiveness that never doubts the knowability of the truth. On the other hand, he reveals a susceptibility to romanticism as well as a tendency to be governed as much by desire as by reason.

Setting: The Gothic Imagination

It is significant that what starts Bianchon on his quest for the truth about the ruined gatehouse and its last living inhabitants is not the spirit of scientific inquiry, but the way the spirit of the place works on his emotions and imagination. In placing at the center of the story a ruined mansion, Balzac establishes a gothic tone which in turn sets up certain expectations in the minds of Bianchon's listeners as well as Balzac's reading audience.

A variety of Romanticism, gothic literature contains certain immediately recognizable features. Readers familiar with Edgar Allan Poe's classic gothic tale "The Fall of the House of Usher" will see the similarities to Balzac's (and Bianchon's) description of the house in "La Grande Bretèche." With its "dreadfully dilapidated" roof, paths "overgrown with purslane," and "balconies hung with swallows' nests," Bianchon hardly has to tell his audience that he felt like "an invisible has written over it all: 'Mystery.'" The scene inspires him to weave "delightful romances" and "little debauches of melancholy," and he claims to find it the ruined garden a source of "unwritten poetry." The gothic image of the ruined mansion which hides a mysterious—even hideous—secret is meant to convey a sense of the limits of human endeavor in the face of nature's relentless entropy and to remind readers of the fleetingness of mortal existence and to hint at the existence of a supernatural realm beyond.

Historical Context

France after the Revolution

Inspired in part by the American Revolution, the French Revolution in 1789 overthrew the oppressive class and economic structures of the old order. Absolute monarchy, unchallenged power, and privilege of the ruling class, or aristocracy were swept away by the revolution. Though they enlisted the help of the rural peasantry and the urban artisans in the challenge to the aristocracy, the bourgeoisie rather than the poor were the beneficiaries of the revolution. Contemporary historians like Roger Magraw point out, however, that the "triumph of the bourgeoisie was both incomplete and precarious." Much of the land and power that the aristocracy and the church conceded, was regained in subsequent years of governmental change and instability. In Magraw's words: "Yet if the nobles were, along with the clergy, the clear losers from the revolution, French history in the nineteenth century is incomprehensible if one fails to appreciate the strength which they retained."

Though the Revolution accomplished the goal of social change and increased economic opportunity (at least for some), political stability remained elusive. Since the goal of the revolution was to destabilize and decentralize power, revolutionary leaders found it difficult to decide on and install alternative systems of government. Though they had in mind the British model of a constitutional government controlled by a parliament, the current monarch (Louis XVI) proved to be unreceptive to the idea of a constitutional monarchy. Furthermore, continuing unrest among the peasants and artisans who still had not seen many benefits from the revolution, convinced the leading bourgeoisie to consolidate their power. Magraw noted, their "quest for law and order drove them into the arms of a man-on-horseback," General Napoleon Bonaparte. Napoleon had outlasted his welcome and been defeated and banished by 1812, three years before the events in the tale that Dr. Bianchon tells his listeners in "La Grande Bretèche."

Balzac and the Rise of the Middle Class

The first half of the nineteenth century in France was a period of turbulent social and political change. As revolution gave way to counter revolution and then military dictatorship, members of both the old aristocracy and the peasantry found themselves losing ground to an increasingly visible middle class, or bourgeoisie. These new class dynamics are well illustrated in "La Grande Bretèche."

Balzac is well known for portraying the rich texture of the daily lives of the newly visible middle class and for capturing the tensions from below (the peasantry) and above (the aristocracy). In La Grande Bretèche the aristocracy is represented by the morally bereft Madame and Monsieur de Merret and the misguided Feredia Bagos. Dr. Bianchon and his dining companions occupy the roles of the upwardly mobile bourgeoisie. The peasantry and artisan class is represented by several servants, most prominently by Rosalie, the maid who surrenders her secrets to the doctor.

Critical Overview

Criticism of "La Grande Bretèche" is usually incorporated in the extensive body of work about *La Comedie Humaine* in general. As editor and critic Martin Kanes observes, initial scholarship focused on the details of Balzac himself, on his "headlong, heedless plunging through life." Soon, however, biographical criticism ran its course and more substantive questions about his work began to emerge. This is not to say that critics agreed with each other. Rather, from the moment of Balzac's death in 1850 until the present, critics and readers have argued about the same questions. Kanes suggested that the essential questions about Balzac are these: "Was the master storyteller a brilliant social analyst? A philosophical thinker? A political commentator? A historian? A cultural anthropologist of sorts? Was he a realist? A Romantic? A visionary? A pre-Marxist Marxist? A pre-Freudian Freudian?" Though Kanes concedes that "In the end, Balzac criticism is paradoxical and suggestive because it is a response to a body of work that is itself paradoxical and suggestive," he still identifies several major periods of Balzac criticism.

The first period of criticism on Balzac's work began as soon as he began publishing under his own name and continued until his death. The chief concern of critics and readers of this period was, besides biographical details, whether Balzac was primarily a realist, a chronicler of his times, or primarily a philosopher whose fiction, in Kanes's words, "was merely the vehicle by which he expressed a metaphysical view of man and the world." This division among critics became consolidated during the second major period of Balzac scholar-

ship. The period 1850 to 1900 is dominated by the Great Debate, as it has come to be known.

The third major period of Balzac scholarship, 1900 to 1950, departed from the two-sided debate of the previous era. Critics of this age became more concerned with the political dimensions of Balzac's work and with its explicit literary qualities. By this time Balzac's work had gained the attention of academics in America, and these scholars were often as interested in Balzac's ability to render reality as they were in his adherence to literary standards.

The fourth major period of Balzac criticism extends from the 100th anniversary of his death to our own age. With the publication of a volume of critical essays to mark to centenary of Balzac's death, the old debate over whether he was philosopher or a realist resurfaced. But new ways of thinking about literary texts in recent decades has enriched Balzac scholarship by adding feminist, marxist, and psychoanalytical perspectives as well, to name a few. Furthermore, as Kanes notes, a kind of metacriticsim has also developed: "criticism and analysis of Balzac scholarship and criticism itself."

Balzac's contribution to literature goes beyond academic criticism. He has also influenced and inspired other major writers of fiction. In French literature, his obvious successor is Marcel Proust, and he inspired a whole school of realists such as Emile Zola and Gustave Flaubert. Students of American literature will be interested to know that Balzac was a powerful influence on landmark American novelists Henry James and William Faulkner.

Criticism

Elisabeth Piedmont-Marton

Elisabeth Piedmont-Marton teaches American literature and directs the writing center at Southwestern University in Texas. She writes frequently about the modern short story. In this essay, Piedmont-Marton discusses how Dr. Bianchon's narrative is driven by a cycle of seduction and betrayal.

The last lines in "La Grande Bretèche" close the frame of the narrative by returning to the scene of the dinner party where the narrator, Dr. Bianchon, has graciously complied with requests to tell one of his infamous tales. In the closing lines of the story, an omniscient narrator intrudes to mention that at the conclusion of Bianchon's tale ''all the ladies rose from the table,'' and ''some among them . . . had almost shivered at the last words.'' As readers of Balzac's tale, we are also present, by proxy, at that table. Even as we rise from our seats at the ''table,'' however, questions linger: why does Bianchon's tale have such a chilling effect on his listeners, and why does it seem to have affected the women so much more intensely? A close reading of the story suggests that it's not only the nature of the secret of ''La Grande Bretèche'' (Madame de Merret's adultery and her husband's cruelty), but also the manner in which our narrator uncovers and discloses that secret—a dynamic of seduction and betrayal—that causes the women to shiver and ''the spell under which Bianchon had held them'' to be broken. Not only is the story about seduction, betrayal, and their consequences, but also the structure of the narrative itself depends upon a similar cycle of seduction and betrayal.

The reader plays a very important role in Balzac's fiction, and especially in ''La Grande Bretèche.'' Literary critic Mary Susan McCarthy explains that in this story ''the audience is represented in the narration itself.'' Balzac, she goes on to explain, ''has projected between himself and his reader several other readers who form links in a chain connecting the author to us through his text. The complicated structure of the tale constructs an axis, at the poles of which are narrator and narrataire, speaker and listener, performer and audience, and, by extension, Balzac and his reader.'' But these categories are unstable, however, as Bianchon acts as both teller of the tale and listener to other narrators. ''Bianchon's position in the narration is problematical,'' Peter Lock cautions, ''On the one hand he is the sender, insofar as he is recounting one of the stories from his repertoire to a group of listeners; on the other hand he is the receiver of three narratives which he does no more than repeat, although he admits there has been some editing, some 'abridgement.''' Readers of the tale, similarly, become more than passive listeners; instead, like several of the characters in the story, they are enlisted—or seduced—into helping shape and frame the tale.

Following Bianchon's example of the ideal listener, readers of ''La Grande Bretèche'' find themselves drawn into a dynamic of desire. From the first glimpse (through Dr. Bianchon's eyes) of the ruined house upon which ''an invisible hand has written all over it: 'Mystery,''' readers share the narrator's desire to penetrate its secrets. The engine

that drives the story is desire. In McCarthy's words, ''The movement of ''La Grande Bretèche'' hinges upon the desire of the recipients represented in the text, and the structure depends on this element for its effectiveness.'' The key to the story is Bianchon's insatiable and unscrupulous desire and our complicity in it.

Bianchon regards the ruined house itself as an object of desire, and when he is denied its pleasures directly he must seek other means of possessing it and entering into its inner chamber. Describing the effect the house and garden had on him, Bianchon uses the language of romance and seduction. The sight of the house becomes one of his ''keenest pleasures,'' and it's where he invents ''delightful romances'' and indulges in ''debauches.'' When Monsieur Regnault turns up one night to inform him that he has been trespassing—that his advances have been unwanted, the notary soon takes on the role a fellow suitor. When he realizes that he will never be able to compete with Regnault's claim to possess Madame de Merret's intimate secrets—the notary proudly wears the diamond she gave him on her deathbed after all—Bianchon adopts a different tactic: flattering or seducing the notary into giving up what he knows. Having appealed to Regnault's inflated sense of his own importance, Bianchon succeeds in loosening ''the tongue of the discreet notary of Vendome.'' But when he relates this story to his listeners (and readers) he doesn't disguise his manipulation of Regnault in pursuit of his own aim to possess the secret of la Grande Bretèche. Though Regnault seems to derive pleasure from having a willing audience despite the fact that he's being used, this scene establishes Bianchon's own pattern of seduction and betrayal in pursuing the secrets of seduction and betrayal hidden in the ruins of la Grande Bretèche.

Having gotten all he could from Regnault, Bianchon then turns his attention to Madame Lepas. As the second narrator in the tale within a tale, Madame Lepas's job is to relate the events that happened prior to the deathbed scene described by Regnault. Madame Lepas's tongue is more easily loosened, but Bianchon is not above manipulating her into divulging more than she thinks she should. Bianchon is able to take advantage of her by recognizing that she wants something from him. Madame Lepas comes to his room to find out what Regnault has told him. Her demeanor is a ''happy compromise between the instinct of a police constable, the astuteness of a spy, and the cunning of a dealer.'' What she wants is to determine if the notary knows anything about the fifteen thousands francs she stashed away after the disappearance of the Spanish nobleman, which ultimately brought about the death of both de Merrets and the ruin of la Grande Bretèche. She also wants to confess, and believes that the socially superior Dr. Bianchon possesses the kindness and moral gravity to put her conscience at ease. Dr. Bianchon, of course, is all too willing to give her what she wants in exchange for more pieces of the story, all the while making her feel like he's doing her a favor. With Madame Lepas he strikes a deal: she gets reassurance that no one knows about the stolen money and he gets one step closer to the secret of Madame de Merret's bedroom.

From Madame Lepas, Bianchon learns one more crucial piece of information: Rosalie used to work for Madame de Merret. Therefore she comes to represent for the doctor, "the very centre of the interest and of the truth," she contains "the last chapter of a romance." Bianchon decides to use his skills at seduction to compel Rosalie to give up what she knows. In this case, however, he realizes that he'll need to literally seduce her. To his scheming eyes, she "was soon possessed of every charm that desire can lend to a woman in whatever rank of life." Significantly, however, Bianchon chooses to obscure the details of this the most important of his conquests. Listeners and readers alike only know about Bianchon's means of acquiring Rosalie's confidence by the allusive aside in this sentence: "A fortnight after the notary's visit, one evening, or rather one morning, in the small hours, I said to Rosalie. . . ." Bianchon's appropriation of Rosalie's body is completed and symbolized in his appropriation of her voice. Whereas he has allowed his other two narrators to tell their tales directly, he silences Rosalie, claiming that it's only necessary for him "to relate it in as few words as may be." Thus Bianchon ultimately claims the story as his own, casting new light on his claim at the opening of the tale to *possess* a "collection" of "appalling stories."

Dr. Bianchon's story is as much about his ability to get what he wants as it is about the tragedy of "La Grande Bretèche." Balzac shows that the machinery of narrative is driven by the engine of desire, but he also suggests, through the character of Bianchon, that desire can sometimes become its own end. Readers are left to wonder why some of the ladies at the table "shivered" when the doctor finishes telling his tale. Is it out of sympathy for Madame de Merret? For the martyred Spanish lover? Or perhaps because they recognize this "other view of woman" is an all too familiar pattern of

> "Bianchon decides to use his skills at seduction to compel Rosalie to give up what she knows. In this case, however, he realizes that he'll need to literally seduce her. To his scheming eyes, she 'was soon possessed of every charm that desire can lend to a woman in whatever rank of life.'"

seduction, betrayal, and silencing of women by men who wish to possess and appropriate them.

Source: Elisabeth Piedmont-Marton, for *Short Stories for Students*, Gale, 2000.

Liz Brent

Brent has a Ph.D. in American Culture, specializing in film studies, from the University of Michigan. She is a freelance writer and teaches courses in the history of American cinema. In the following essay, Brent discusses narration in Balzac's story.

Balzac's short story "La Grande Bretèche" is as much about storytelling itself as it is about the content of the story it tells. "La Grande Bretèche" is structured by multiple layers of *embedded narratives*. The *frame narrator,* who introduces and concludes the story, is an unnamed guest at a dinner party during which the central story is told. The *central narrator* is the doctor Monsieur Bianchon, who tells his story to the other dinner guests. Within Bianchon's story, however, are three embedded narratives: that of the executor, that of the innkeeper, and that of the maid at the inn. Through this layering of narratives, Balzac's story focuses on the human passion for telling stories and revealing secrets, the pleasure and art of storytelling, the role of mystery in inspiring the weaving and telling of tales, and the individual narrative style of each storyteller.

> In contrast to the three less-than-scintillating storytellers embedded in his narrative, Bianchon's storytelling style is represented by the frame narrator of Balzac's story as eminently skillful and effective. Bianchon demonstrates a fine sense of the importance of atmosphere to the effective telling of tales; he twice expresses the opinion that stories are best told late in the evening, and preferably over dinner."

A. W. Raitt has noted that Balzac's short stories tend to be similarly structured around the introduction of a mystery or enigma and the gradual revelation of the cause of that mystery or enigma: "Mystery and suspense are essential ingredients of almost all Balzac's tales, and his favourite method of constructing a short story is to propose some enigma at the outset, develop it so as to increase the tension, and then suddenly reveal the solution." "La Grande Bretèche" is a prime example of this story structure. Furthermore, the existence of a mystery, enigma or secret are demonstrated in this story to be precisely the seed from which stories grow. In this case, the central narrator, Bianchon, is inspired to spin a variety of narrative webs from his observations of the grand and mysterious Grande Bretèche house and garden which have been abandoned and left to overgrow. The narration ties the writing of stories to the presence of mystery in Bianchon's summation of his description of la Grande Bretèche: "An invisible hand has written over it all: 'Mystery.'" Bianchon describes the process by which the discovery of a mystery leads to speculation as to the *story* behind that mystery: "What fire from heaven can have fallen there? By what decree has salt been sown on this dwelling? Has God been mocked here? Or was France betrayed? These are the questions we ask ourselves. Reptiles crawl over it, but give no reply. This empty and deserted house is a vast enigma of which the answer in known to none." Bianchon revels in the opportunity which enigma provides for the workings of the imagination to create stories in order to explain its mystery. In fact, the pleasure of storytelling (even to oneself) is dependent on the existence of mystery; as Bianchon points out, an excess of factual knowledge limits the imagination's potential for creating stories.

Bianchon states that, "the sight of this strange dwelling became one of my keenest pleasures." He notes, however, that a historic building or site which suggests "indisputable authenticity" does not make for good storytelling: "Was it not far better than a ruin? Certain memories of indisputable authenticity attach themselves to a ruin; but this house, still standing, though being slowly destroyed by an avenging hand, contained a secret, an unrevealed thought." Thus, it is the indication of a "secret" which provides the storyteller with the raw material for building a narrative. Bianchon even asserts that he pointedly avoided asking any of the local inhabitants, "any gossiping native," for an explanation of the house's mystery; for such information would have cost him "the price of the story to which this strange scene no doubt was due." Without the limitations of any further information, the storyteller is free to "enchant" himself by "weaving delightful romances," out of the "unwritten poetry" afforded by the presence of the enigma. As it is, the storyteller is free to imagine a variety of "dramas," as Bianchon describes his imagining of "a gloomy drama to account for this monumental woe."

The central role of "mystery" to storytelling is again referred to when the first of three narrators whose stories are embedded in Bianchon's enters his room at the inn "with an air of mystery." Monsieur Regnault, the executor of the will of the former owner of la Grande Bretèche, offers Bianchon "the truth on official authority" of the abandoned house. Fearing the loss of mystery will ruin the drama of la Grande Bretèche, Bianchon is reluctant to "bid farewell to my beautiful reveries and romances." However, Bianchon fully appreciates the exquisite pleasure of the storyteller when given (or taking) the opportunity to tell his tale. Bianchon describes this pleasure in terms of the "passion" and "delight" afforded by the "hobby" of storytelling. When he invites Monsieur Regnault to tell him about the house:

> "At these words an expression, which revealed all the pleasure which men feel who are accustomed to ride a hobby, overspread the lawyer's countenance. He pulled up the collar of his shirt with an air, took out his snuffbox, opened it, and afforded me a pinch; on my refusing, he took a large one. He was happy! A man who has no hobby does not know all the good to be got out of life. A hobby is the happy medium between a passion and a monomania."

While Bianchon compiles his own version of the story from the fragments provided by the three embedded narrators, each narrator has her or his own *style* of storytelling, which is suited to individual personalities and occupations. As Raitt has pointed out, "La Grande Bretèche plays off three styles one against another: the pompous legalistic phraseology of the lawyer, the familiar, homely accents of the hostess, and the lively but acutely observant narrative of Bianchon." Monsieur Regnault, for instance, catches himself lapsing into a form of "legalese" in his explanations of Madame Merret's will. As he is explaining to Bianchon what became of the household items at la Grande Bretèche, Regnault states that, "Some people even say that she had burnt all the furniture, the hangings-in short, all the chattels and furniture whatever used in furnishing the premises now let by the said M.— (Dear! what am I saying? I beg your pardon, I thought I was dictating a lease.)" In describing what was left of the furniture of the house by the time Regnault saw it, he again describes the contents of the house in terms of an official "inventory": "That was all the furniture; not enough to fill ten lines in an inventory." And again, in explaining to Bianchon the contents of Madam Merret's will, Regnault uses legalese: "Otherwise la Grande Bretèche reverts to the heirs-at-law, but on condition of fulfilling certain conditions set forth in a codicil to the will, which is not to be opened till the expiration of the said term of fifty years." Bianchon, nonetheless, makes a point of complimenting Regnault on his storytelling skills, and particularly the effect of his description of Madame Merret on her deathbed: "'Monsieur,' I said in conclusion, 'you have so vividly impressed me that I fancy I see the dying woman whiter than her sheets; her glittering eyes frighten me; I shall dream of her to-night . . .'" However, Bianchon describes to the listeners of *his* story, the boring quality of Regnault's narrative style:

> However, I soon loosened the tongue of the discreet notary of Vendome, who communicated to me, not without long digressions, the opinions of the deep politicians of both sexes whose judgments are law in Vendome. But these opinions were so contradictory, so diffuse, that I was near falling asleep in spite of the interest I felt in this authentic history. The notary's ponderous voice and monotonous accent, accustomed no doubt to listen to himself and make himself listened to by his clients or fellow-townsmen, were too much for my curiosity. Happily, he soon went away.

The widespread urge to tell stories, and universal pleasure humans take in storytelling are indicated by Bianchon's mention of the local "gossip" inspired by the mystery of la Grande Bretèche. Gossip is a form of condensed storytelling shared among a community of people, whose passion for telling tales is equally inspired by the presence of mystery. Regnault explains that, almost as soon as he was summoned by Madame Merret to execute her will, "That very night, though it was already late, all the town knew that I was going to Merret." Rumor, like gossip, is equally inspired by the passion for telling "tales"; as Regnault explains, "From the rumours that were current concerning this lady (Monsieur, I should never end if I were to repeat all the tales that were told about her), I had imagined her a coquet."

The second narrator embedded within Bianchon's narrative is Madame Lepas, the landlady of the inn. Bianchon captures both the passion for telling stories, and the urge to reveal "secrets" which inspires storytelling in his description of Madame Lepas's countenance at the prospect of revealing to him her piece of the mystery; "your eyes are big with secret," he tells her.

Balzac wonderfully illustrates what seems to be a universal storytelling technique; the art of initiating the telling of a story is characterized by the storyteller's pretense to withholding the very story she or he is bursting to tell. This art, or artifice, is aptly demonstrated by Bianchon, in arousing the interest of his fellow dinner guests, causing them to virtually beg him to tell them the story of la Grande Bretèche, which he clearly takes no end of delight in telling. As Balzac's story opens, one dinner guest has just finished telling a story, and Bianchon artfully introduces his own story by teasing his listeners with the implication that this is not necessarily the proper time or occasion for him to tell such a story:

> "Ah! Madame," replied the doctor, "I have some appalling stories in my collection. But each one has its proper hour in conversation . . ." "But it is two in the morning, and the story of Rosina has prepared us," said the mistress of the house. "Tell us, Monsieur Bianchon!" was the cry on every side.

As do each of his three embedded narrators, Bianchon makes a ceremonial gesture of preparation in order to focus the attention of his listeners before launching into his tale: "The obliging doctor bowed, and silence reigned."

Just as Bianchon teases his fellow dinner guests with the false expression of reluctance in order to arouse their interest in his story, so does Madame Lepas pretend to a reluctance to reveal the secret she claims to guard so closely, but which she clearly delights in telling. When asked by Bianchon what she can tell him about the mystery of la Grande Bretèche, she first declares that, "'I know nothing about it.'" When Bianchon replies that, "I am sure you know everything," she does not hesitate to give in, responding that, "I will tell you the whole story." She further demonstrates both her skill in the art of storytelling, and her eagerness to tell such a story, in her artifice of protest against the revelation of the secret, and her assurance that he is being given exclusive knowledge of the mystery:

> "Up to now I have never dared to say a word to people of these parts; they are all chatter-mags, with tongues like knives. And never till now, sire, have I had any traveller here who stayed so long in the inn as you have, and to whom I could tell the history of the fifteen thousand francs—"

But Bianchon comments to his listeners that, "Her eagerness made me suspect that I was not the only person to whom my worthy landlady had communicated the secret of which I was to be sole possessor, but I listened."

The human passion for hearing, as well as for telling, tales is wonderfully expressed through Bianchon's focus upon Rosalie, the maid at the inn whom he suspects can reveal to him, "the heart of this solemn story, this drama which had killed three people." His desire to hear the end of the tale is metaphorically expressed through the desire he focuses upon Rosalie. He states that, "Rosalie became in my eyes the most interesting being in Vendome." His desire to learn "the whole history of la Grande Bretèche" is so strong that he will go so far as to "make love to Rosalie if it proves necessary" to "achieve this end." Bianchon's statement that the "last chapter" in the "romance" of the story of la Grande Bretèche is "contained" in Rosalie equates the human passion for stories with the passion of a man set on seducing an attractive young woman: "It was not a case for ordinary love-making; this girl contained the last chapter of a romance, and from that moment all my attentions were devoted to Rosalie." As representative of the

"romance" of the story, Bianchon finds that Rosalie for him "was soon possessed of every charm that desire can lend to a woman in whatever rank of life."

When Bianchon finally does induce Rosalie to tell him "the last chapter" of the story, she, like all of the other narrators, makes a pretense of reluctance to reveal the "secret," and, just as quickly, launches into the telling of her tale with dramatic ceremony and unabashed passion. When Bianchon first asks her, she immediately replies, "'do not ask me that, Monsieur Horace!'" However, without so much as a word of encouragement from Bianchon, she agree to tell him, but with the understanding that he will "'keep the secret carefully.'" Like all of the storytellers in Balzac's tale, Rosalie pretends to be revealing a well-kept secret to an exclusively privileged listener; and, as do all of the listeners (and potential storytellers), Bianchon swears to keep the secret, all the while knowing that he will reveal it with little provocation to the next potential listener. As do all of the narrators, Rosalie ceremoniously prepares to launch into her story: "Thereupon she set her head-kerchief straight, and settled herself to tell the tale; for there is no doubt a particular attitude of confidence and security is necessary to the telling of a narrative." Rosalie's narrative style in turn differs from each of the previous narrators. Bianchon describes her narrative in terms which befit the storytelling style of an eager young woman:

> "If I were to reproduce exactly Rosalie's diffuse eloquence, a whole volume would scarcely contain it. Now, as the event of which she gave me a confused account stands exactly midway between the notary's gossip and that of Madame Lepas, as precisely as the middle term of a rule-of-three sum stands between the first and third, I have only to relate it in a few words as may be. I shall therefore be brief."

In contrast to the three less-than-scintillating storytellers embedded in his narrative, Bianchon's storytelling style is represented by the frame narrator of Balzac's story as eminently skillful and effective. Bianchon demonstrates a fine sense of the importance of atmosphere to the effective telling of tales; he twice expresses the opinion that stories are best told late in the evening, and preferably over dinner. In introducing Rosalie's segment of the narrative, which Bianchon has pointedly elicited late at night, or, rather, in the "small hours" of the morning, Bianchon asserts that, "The best tales are told at a certain hour—just as we are all here at table. No one ever told a story well standing up, or fasting." Finally, the frame narrator indicates the effectiveness of Bianchon's storytelling style in the final lines of *his* story; he describes Bianchon's effect on his listeners among the fellow dinner guests as that of holding them under a ''spell'' during the course of his narration.

Source: Liz Brent, for *Short Stories for Students*, Gale, 2000.

Peter Lock

In the following article, Lock examines the psychoanalytic approach to literature and the need for critics and readers to find meaning in stories that often have meaning imposed on them by the author.

Readers of modern authors (Joyce, Kafka, Borges) are accustomed to becoming Egyptologists, undergoing what Deleuze has called ''an apprenticeship in signs.'' We have been initiated into the impenetrable and interminable through the decoding of modern texts. In *The Genesis of Secrecy* Frank Kermode suggests that all great works have about them an air of the opaque, the enigmatic and the unknowable, and that it is *we* who are tempted to confer upon them some structure and meaning without which our lives would be unendurable: ''This is the way we satisfy ourselves with explanations of the unfollowable world—as if it were a structured narrative, of which more might be said by trained readers of it, by insiders. World and book, it may be, are hopelessly plural, endlessly disappointing; we stand alone before them, aware of their arbitrariness and impenetrability, knowing they may be narratives only because of our imprudent intervention, and susceptible of interpretation only by our hermetic tricks.'' Such scepticism is salutary, particularly for readers of early nineteenth-century fiction where rhetoric and narration tend to *impose* meaning on the world and thence on the reader, and to represent the past as followable and knowable. A Balzac, for example, wills to present total meaning as accessible to a single consciousness, that of the omniscient narrator, and transmissible to the reader who comes to live the world as a transparently knowable totality—replica of a unity and mirror of a continuity which he himself possesses. ''[Balzac] ne cache rien, il dit tout,'' writes Proust impatiently; but this quick reaction is at once contested: ''Aussi est-on étonné de voir que cependant il y a de beaux effets de *silence* dans son oeuvre. ... 'Vous connaissez Rastignac? Vrai?. . . .'''

Acting on Proust's astonishment (itself astonishing to traditional Balzac readers accustomed to paying their money in exchange for the Whole Truth), I propose, through the reading of one of Balzac's short texts, *La Grande Bretèche*, to inves-

> ''. . .the reader may well feel somewhat let down by the solution; it is as if the critic-detective knew the answer all the time and, like James himself, rather enjoys titillating only to deceive.''

tigate the question of the *secret* and its troubling, silencing effect on narrative. Recent theorizing by the psychoanalysts Nicolas Abraham and Maria Torok (in *Le Verbier de l'Homme aux loups* and *L'Ecorce et le noyau*) compels us to become attentive to modes of encoding secrets in discourse and to strategies of *defense* which a text may adopt in order to mislead the reader. Particularly suggestive for readers of fiction is an elaboration of Melanie Klein's views on phantasy which Abraham and Torok interpret as a defensive ''language'' whereby the subject plots, narcissistically, to protect the ego against the exigencies and pressures of psychic conflict. Phantasy, in this reading, far from revealing the ''truth'' of psychic reality, blocks its working out, and is opposed to introjection and symbolization—those processes by which the subject re-situates and re-presents conflict with a view to resolution. At issue is the Janus-like stance of representation with respect to origin of conflict and articulation in language. In brief, what can discourse take in and how does it go about ''taking in'' the reader?

Although at first glance there seems nothing that the Balzacian text cannot comprehend, organize and totalize, the reader of the *Comédie humaine* becomes increasingly aware that the resolute forward march of Balzac's writing, motivated (in the words of one of his titles) by the Quest for the Absolute, seems frequently driven onwards by the presence of a *secret* which, as prior occurrence, haunts the text and causes its insistent, even frenzied, forward movement to be doubled by anxious recursions towards the past. The form of the Balzacian text is often akin to that of the detective story where narrative retraces or re-enacts an event which is presumed already to have taken place; the plot is the effect of an unknown cause, some act or story already encountered. Todorov, finding a similar figuration in the novellas of Henry James, describes it as *"the quest for an absolute and absent cause"*; the narrative strategy consists of "the search for, the pursuit of, this initial cause" which Todorov finally names, vaguely, as "this primal essence." In James' case the "essence" in question is usually death which is both sought and masked by the process of narrative; and since death can never be known or represented, the meaning of the story lies not in revelation but in the quest itself, a quest in which "the essential is absent, the absent is essential."

Although Todorov's analysis of individual texts is instructive, the reader may well feel somewhat let down by the solution; it is as if the critic-detective knew the answer all the time and, like James himself, rather enjoys titillating only to deceive. Readers of Balzac would certainly not be content with such a refined pleasure; they like to think their man isn't going to let them down: the omniscient author (or a privileged stand-in like Dr. Bianchon), acting like some precursive amalgam of Sigmund Freud and Sherlock Holmes, watchful, waiting, secure in a place of knowing, knowing his place, will surely, by means of some incisive flash-back or some melodramatic unmasking, reveal the truth of the enigma, the riddle's *mot.* And often it is just so. Very frequently, unmaskings and revelations take place with great dispatch; and the *speed* of Balzac's endings (*Facino Cane, Le Chef d'oeuvre inconnu, La Fille aux yeux d'or, L'Enfant maudit,* for example), contribute to the air of finality, the sense of proper execution. Yet the reader may, as so often with the detective story, be left with that vague malaise which accompanies one of Hercule Poirot's conjuring tricks: the act is too crisp, too conclusive; the thing is devoured too swiftly, eliminated too completely. One may think with Julien Sorel: "Ce n'est que ça?" and the very thought betokens some doubt, some dissatisfaction, some feeling that the portentous build-up had promised more, even threatened more: something is missing in the links between the Cause (in Balzac's case upper case) and the Effect.

"Secret," "mystery," "enigma": once one takes note of it, Balzac's writing seems riddled with references to the unknown, the unresolved, the unaccountable. The secret may concern a *question of identity:* in *Le Colonel Chabert* the central character is a "missing person," taken for dead, whose position has been usurped, exploited; a *relationship:* in *Ferragus* the virtuous Madame Jules is connected with a mysterious and violently threatening stranger with whom she appears joined in kinship; a *crime:* in *Un Drame au bord de la mer* the absent drama concerns some unspeakable act of murder; *jouissance:* in *L'Enfant maudit* the writing circles around some Absolute of gratification shared between lovers. In each case what is in question is some missing information or opaque encounter, essential for sense to be posited, owned, mastered … though what is missing, or missed (missing *because* missed?) is often sought with increasing apprehension, as if the desire, the rage to know is fraught with some anguished fear, some dread of knowing, against which the writing, while manifestly working towards some solution, deviously defends itself. Identity, relationship, *jouissance,* crime: these mysteries seem to suggest that their uncovering in narrative may reactivate some memory unable to be borne, and call radically into question unruffled fictions of continuity, totality and resolution.

Exemplary in this respect is a short work enigmatically titled *La Grande Bretèche,* in which the narrative obsessively insists on a "pensée inconnue," a "secret," a "Mystère," setting itself up as an "immense énigme dont le secret n'est connu de personne." The story (which is often published as a complete text in anthologies) is in fact part of a longer work, *Autre Etude de femme,* in which are related a series of narratives concerning violent events apparently connected in each case with a woman's infidelity. The narrators are all men, and the *effects* of the narratives are described predominantly insofar as they affect the women among the listeners. In *La Grande Bretèche* the narrator is Horace Bianchon, a man of passionate curiosity and great learning, whose psychological perspicacity is frequently relied upon to analyze some physical or mental symptom, and to provide for all of us, with Balzac's implied approbation, a quite conclusive interpretation.

In *La Grande Bretèche* he is baffled. In spite of restless curiosity and relentless interrogation he succeeds only in arriving at a confused apprehension of the events which supposedly took place in the abandoned house known as "La Grande Bretèche," to which he comes as a stranger, an outsider. That there took place some unspeakable event is certain; but the event, described as a violently catastrophic separation, can only be reconstructed out of three different narratives and given a tentative (and fearsome) interpretation which Bianchon passes on, with some complacency, to his listeners, the women among whom react with a chill of horror.

The three narrators, each of whom relates a different segment of the story, are a lawyer (Regnault), an innkeeper's wife (Mme Lepas), and a servant girl (Rosalie). All were involved in the gruesome events which involved three other persons: Mme de Merret, her husband and a mysterious stranger, a Spanish prisoner named Bagos de Feredia. Regnault, the man of the law, forbids Bianchon to trespass in the ruins of "La Grande Bretèche," and relates the terrible suffering and death of the countess. Mme Lepas reluctantly tells the beginning of the story—the arrival of the Spanish prisoner who swims in the river opposite the house of the countess, and one day mysteriously disappears. Rosalie, equally reluctant but finally seduced by Bianchon, leads him toward the "center" of the story: M. de Merret, returning one evening unexpectedly, hears a noise in his wife's closet; in spite of her denial (sworn on a crucifix) that anyone is there, the count sends for a mason and orders the closet to be bricked up, and sadistically compels his wife to remain in the room for twenty days until no further sounds are to be heard. Shortly afterward the count dies, and his wife, after ordering "La Grande Bretèche" to remain closed and untouched for fifty years, dies after a long period of suffering. In her final moments a fierce joy blazes from her eyes, a joy which remains startlingly present, "gravé sur ses yeux morts," even beyond her death.

Curiously, Bianchon is the (initially anonymous) narrator of the whole sequence entitled *Autre Etude de femme,* a first-person narrator who is, notwithstanding, indistinguishable from an omniscient narrator, relaying the various anecdotes and exchanges but also intervening with insights, comments and generalizations, demonstrating the unlimited privilege of the usual Balzacian narrator. Yet immediately before beginning to recount, again in the first person, *his* story (*La Grande Bretèche*), the text makes of him the *object* of a narrative voice which exceeds him: "'Ah! répliqua le docteur, j'ai de terribles histoires dans mon répertoire . . .' A un geste du complaisant docteur, le silence régna." This abrupt shift from omniscience, combined with a gloss on "complaisant" as describing "a person who closes his eyes to amorous intrigue," gives rise to the paradoxical figure of a master analyst (Bianchon expresses his desire not to give up his search before learning "toute l'histoire de la Grande Bretèche"), whose optic is limited, who cannot or does not choose to see, and who also, although apparently dispassionate and objective, is *implicated* (the word "complaisant" suggests as much) in the narrative. Certainly this immediately raises the question of the position of the subject in the text and the relationship between narrator and narrated; such a shift suggests a displacement which implies the narrator's identification with at least parts of the narrated. The text does in fact indicate a strong emotional reaction, as Bianchon recalls the mixture of lively pleasure and involuntary terror which accompanied his relentless search for knowledge. The events become endowed with uncanny significance if we interpret them as being connected with Bianchon himself.

Certainly, Bianchon's position in the narration is problematical. On the one hand he is the sender, insofar as he is recounting one of the stories from his repertoire to a group of listeners; on the other hand he is the receiver of three narratives which he does no more than repeat, although he admits that there has been some editing, some "abridgement." Throughout are raised problems of position (analyst or analysand?), repetition, resistance, and transference, and above all, the question of the relationship between Bianchon's relentless curiosity, his passionate desire to know and the constructions he confers upon the events. It becomes increasingly evident that his interpretation comes up sharp against the mysterious resistance of the story being pursued, a resistance as redoubtable as the fortress-like house whose presence commands the tale.

The first few pages describe Bianchon's passionate yet circumspect endeavor to penetrate the secret of the mysterious abode, *La Grande Bretèche,* whose devastated garden and crumbling ruins—described with Poe-like apprehension—attract and repel him. The narration recoils from its own title-object in horror ("terreurs involontaires," "j'ai frissonné"), estranged as from some "cloister," "cemetery," "leper colony," "house of Atreus"; yet at the same time it is drawn towards it with a certain lustful pleasure ("poésies inédites dont je m'enivrais," "débauches de l'imagination"), which uncannily suggests a satisfaction once familiar. In Kleinian, rather than in Freudian terms, the ambivalence signaled by the uncanny sends back to a scenario of fearsome anxiety and violence. For Melanie Klein, the mother's body is the locus of the child's initial experiencing and exploration of the world. In Lacan's words: "Through Melanie Klein we know the function of the imaginary primordial enclosure formed by the imago of the mother's body; through her we have the cartography, drawn by the child's own hands, of the mother's internal empire, the historical atlas of the intestinal divisions in which the *imagos* of the father and brothers (real or virtual), in which the voracious aggression of the subject himself, dispute their deleterious dominance over her sacred regions.'' Central to Melanie Klein's view of the development of the psyche is the primacy of the mother's body as the origin of the child's quest for knowledge—a lustful drive which takes the inner space of the mother's body as the source of sexual gratification, and which also, sadistically, aims to invade, plunder and destroy that same body which contains hated and feared signs of hostility or loss, in particular the phalluses of the father or of the brother, detested rivals in the search for absolute possession. The child's imagined attacks lead to phantasies of a poisoned body mutilated and destroyed by acts of sadistic aggression; and this fragmented body becomes, through projective identification, an image of the child's own body and of his ego. Dramatically countering this image of the body ''in bits and pieces'' is the phantasy of the perfect body, the body once again whole—which the child constructs from the idealized portrait of the mother or from his own image, jubilantly discovered and re-discovered in the mirror reflecting his phantasy of Oneness.

The house in *La Grande Bretèche* is likened to ''the house of Atreus,'' recalling a history of bestiality (Zeus and Europa), adultery (Clytemnestra and Egisthus), incestuous love (Phaedra and Hippolytus), enemy brothers (Atreus and Thyestes), inter-familial murder (Egisthus and Agamemnon), and matricide (Orestes and Clytemnestra). Pre-dominant throughout the myth is the drama of a *family* and the violence and sexual rivalries within blood relationships. Curiously, in the MS of *La Grande Bretèche* (and again in the Introduction to the *Etudes de moeurs* published in 1835) Madame de Merret's name is spelled MÉRÉ, and Feredia appears as Heredia—the name of a lover of Balzac's mother. Heredia is often supposed to be the father of Balzac's brother Henry—Henry ''le bien aimé'' towards whom Balzac had unremitting feelings of hostility and jealousy. The third person, the intruder, the rival the mother's lover (man or child), sign of dispossession, object of hatred and aggression—this is the figure whose brutal death forms the climax of *La Grande Bretèche.*

Bianchon's uncanny narrative can be read as the obsessive return to the scene of a crime in which he himself is implicated and which his narrative attempts to analyze and, in recounting, in iterating, to master. His journey backwards in time takes him towards the mother and her body as origin and source of pleasure and discontent. One of the narrators, Regnault, the man of the Law, taunts him with an incestuous lure: '''Etes-vous allé à Merret (MÉRÉ), Monsieur?' 'Non,' dit-il, en faisant lui-même sa réponse.'' And again: '''Ah! mais vous n'êtes pas allé à Merret!'.'' The fearful movement of the text seems anxiously to be repeating a scenario once experienced—a scenario involving both pleasure and crime (pleasure *as* crime, crime *as* pleasure, perhaps)—seeking to unravel the knot and to supply or supplement some missing information: '''J'essayai de pénétrer dans cette mystérieuse demeure [la Grande Bretèche] en y cherchant le noeud de cette solennelle histoire . . .'.'' The search takes Bianchon to the servant Rosalie who is mysteriously implicated in the drama, indeed apparently at its *center* wherein lies the *truth:* ''Elle était au centre même de l'intérêt et de la vérité.'' Throughout, the narrative has been suggesting that the place of the secret, the place where sense is secreted, is the *center* (both of the other narrators are also positioned at the center: Regnault is associated with ''milieu précis,'' Mme Lepas with ''juste milieu''). Discovery of the center would bring the narrative to a halt at a final point, arresting the play of language at a fixed position, a place of ultimate knowing at which the writing would come to rest.

But the position of the center as locus of truth is called into question: Rosalie's crucial position is compared to that of the central square on a chessboard (''la case qui se trouve au milieu d'un damier''), a space which of course doesn't exist. The displaced center is replaced by the figure of the *knot* in which Rosalie, apparently a mere spectator, is herself implicated (''elle me semblait nouée dans le noeud''). The knot is what analysis is called upon to wrestle with; and, in Lacan's reading of Freud, the knot implies the prior existence of a ''bad'' encounter, an encounter ''forever missed''—an encounter which, if unsymbolized, keeps on repeating itself as an absent, yet unwelcome cause which produces anxious, painful and inexplicable effects. Bianchon's own narrative is clearly a repetition in a different, hence novel form of the original scenario involving the murder of Feredia. But the crucial sexual encounter between Bianchon and Rosalie ''takes place'' in an ellipsis (''un soir, ou plutôt un matin''), an ellipsis which indicates a repetition of the encounter as missed; and the coital act in which the truth is quested leads only to a magical ''theft'' resulting in what Bianchon himself calls "une confuse connaissance" and in the reinterment of the secret.

Of transference Lacan writes: "If the transference is only repetition, it will only be of the same missed encounter." And the same may be said of *reading*. In seducing Rosalie Bianchon acts indeed like the impatient reader who wills to penetrate the text's secret by forcing a repetition rather than by essaying a reconstruction. And in seeking the truth from the one who apparently knows ("il y avait dans cette fille le dernier chapitre d'un roman"), he behaves like the analysand who demands knowledge through "seduction" of the other while ignoring the implication of the other in the act of exchange. The test insists that Rosalie's involvement in the psychic drama goes well beyond her roles of servant and spectator: she bears on her features "les traces d'une pensée intime" bespeaking the existence of some "secret" which is astonishingly linked to that of "la fille *infanticide* qui entend toujours le dernier cri de son enfant" (my italics). The text has already set up the murdered Feredia as *infans*, the one who does not speak ("si on lui parlait, il ne répondait pas"); and a reading of his swimming across to Merret, naked, "nageant comme un poisson," via the equation fish-phallus-child/water-womb, set alongside the double evocation *infans, infanticide,* suggests that the unconscious drama to be reconstructed has to do with a psychic reality whose scenario implicates the dual relationship binding child and mother, a relationship which here is associated with some mysterious crime.

The "reality" which is quested (and occulted) by a cryptic text like *La Grande Bretèche* must be presumed, in a psychoanalytical reading, to lie in the conflict of incompatibilities waged between unconscious desire—whose "realization" represents the text's impossible utopia—and the counterforce of some (equally unconscious) obstacle, contrary wish or interdiction. Nicolas Abraham has suggested a more precise and potent definition of psychic reality which can prove productive in reconstructing such enigmatic texts as *La Grande Bretèche*. For Abraham, Reality (the capital R signifies its "anasemic" nature) is that which comes into existence through the insistence that it remain . . . denied, hidden, inadmissable, unnamable. Just as desire is intricated with the interdiction which founds it, so Reality comes into play associated with what makes its realization unthinkable and its articulation impossible. The unthinkableness of Reality derives from its incompatible, heterogeneous, warring components—"jouissance" and crime, "jouissance"

associated in the psyche with crime, "jouissance" in its very affirmation experienced *as* crime. In their re-reading of the Wolfman case, Abraham and Torok posit a duplicity of sense in which the Wolfman affirms "jouissance" through his relationship with his father-as-ideal while denying in paralyzing fashion its very possibility because of the father's betrayal and degradation through his incestuous relationship with his daughter. The Wolfman's secret locks together in a puzzle of tessera the absolute contradictions attendant on his desire—tessera whose fragmentation betokens the radical impossibility of any processes of introjection, sublimation, symbolization: the very ground, the "given" of symbol-formation is fractured by the subjacent conflict and by its association with a crime which precludes identification and shatters the coherence of the ego. Yet the secret must be preserved—retained and hidden in enigmatic form—if the "idyllic" outcome quested by desire is to continue to exist within the bounds of possibility. Foreclosure would condemn the subject to oblivion; preservation is achieved through a magical act which encrypts the conflict within the ego in a fetishistic and non-sensical key-word, itself blocking the motion of desire and halting any symbolic process—yet indirectly, enigmatically productive of sense. *Le Verbier de l'Homme aux loups* is the analysis of the taboo words, the "cryptonyms," the fetish-words, and the "allosemes," whose peculiar figurations and interactions disguise (and finally betray) the Wolfman's Reality.

The problem being posed by *La Grande Bretèche* (and by such other Balzacian texts as *Un Drame au bord de la mer, L'Enfant maudit* and *La Fille aux yeux d'or* in which the conjuncture of *jouissance* and crime is central) is how does writing contain embodied within it an unbearable Reality which it cannot *be* or *do* without? And how does it attempt to fortify itself (to what extent and with what counterforces of resistance, distortion, phantasy and duplicity—and with what success?) against Reality's *effects* as they traverse the text with their ineluctable reminders of separation, defect, lack, and loss, derivative representations of some primordial crime? One might suppose, simply, that a text "takes in" what it can deal with and leaves outside what is hostile or alien to its functioning, conducting itself in this like the primitive ego, either "introjecting" or "ejecting." In Kleinian terms, objects are introjected as signs affecting both ego-structure and object-relations; the process of introjection may be doubled by phantasy acts of appropriation whereby intolerable objects are magically relegated to the deepest layers of the unconscious. Working from this distinction, Abraham and Torok have developed the notion of ''incorporation'' to describe a phantasmatic act of magical ingestion and violent entombment which merely *mines* the expansive process of normal introjection. Incorporation usurps a place (in the psyche, in writing) where an object, event or person may be *retained*, because needed (as reminiscence of *jouissance*), while at the same time it is *excluded* from the scrutiny of consciousness, ''encrypted'' within the ego.

For Freud, the ego is an organization characterized by compulsion to synthesize, binding energy in the form of representation; ego, like a well-made plot in narrative, is formed out of what has been taken in, introjected. *Introjection* is defined in opposition to rejection and expulsion. In Freud's words: ''Expressed in the language of the oldest—the oral—instinctual impulses, [the subject says]: 'I should like to eat this,' or 'I should like to spit it out'; and, put more generally: 'I should like to take this into myself and to keep that out.''' This definition of the oral stage implies either/or: either ''inside'' or ''outside,'' ''good'' or ''bad,'' with the two first terms allied against the two second terms. Introjection, first defined by Ferenczi in 1909, is ''an extension to the external world of the subject's original autoerotic interests, by including its objects in the ego.'' Ferenczi stresses the expansive and unifying force of introjection: *Einbeziehung,* pulling in, integrating. ''I put the emphasis on this 'including' and wanted to show thereby that I considered every sort of object love or transference as an extension of ego . . . that is of introjection.'' Introjection attempts to overcome separation and loss by integration and symbolization; ideally, the dynamic, expansive process of introjection would dispense with phantasy, constituting the ego by means of repetition, transference (*Ubertragung*: retranscription), and symbolization.

But what of the object or event which cannot be introjected *or* rejected, for example a lost or missed object whose ''presence'' is simultaneously desired or prohibited, needed and feared, associated with a *jouissance* once experienced or hallucinated, but marked and marred by the stigma of crime—an object which the subject cannot do or be without, yet which must remain *without*, and yet not abolished? Ego's offensive-defensive strategy here is the phantasmatic act of incorporation, a silent, omnipotent act of magical, secretive and protective appropriation which simulates or mimes the for-

ward process of introjection, to which it is related . . . nostalgically. Because of the object's association with Reality (as that secret force which demands an intolerable modification of the ego and poses a threat to narcissistic integrity and omnipotence), the object must be delivered of its existence and violently occulted, and yet in some cryptic form must be accessible (but only to the subject), because the *jouissance* associated with it has become essential. Ego's response to this dilemma is to encrypt the object, to bury it alive, as object and yet as language, as monstrous object-language which defies symbolization (and hence communication and exchange), and which is nonetheless ''readable'' by the subject as a message signifying the contradictions associated with it (*jouissance* and crime). This enactment is named by Nicolas Abraham as ''conservative repression,'' implying exclusion *and* retention, the words encoding the object being lodged inside the split ego, buried, ''encrypted,'' yet accessible.

This conservative repression has a paralyzing and stunting effect on the subject, since the crime associated with *jouissance* has caused the forbidden word to be withdrawn from circulation, isolated and sealed with the virulent hatred associated with the crime which cannot be mourned. The result is that the analyst (or the reader) is faced with that duplicity of discourse which Freud associates with fetishism and splitting of the ego, except that here the language of denial, although indisputably fetishistic in its phantasmatic protectiveness, is even more enigmatic than usual, since it contains echoes of an imaginary scenario composed of contradictory and utterly irreconcilable elements.

In *La Grande Bretèche jouissance* is represented by the longed-for fusion (or ''dual unity,'' to use Nicolas Abraham's term) between Feredia and Mme de Merret, in which each seeks complementarity in the other. This utopian phantasy is articulated in the repeated phrase, involving Bianchon as well as Feredia, ''aller à Merret.'' For Nicolas Abraham such utopian phantasies are represented in the *id*, where the mother and the child's desire for her are kept alive; this universal unconscious phantasy causes the mother to project onto her child *her* wish to rediscover the lost dual unity with her own mother. Longing for fusion is the insistent, magical, omnipotent demand which traverses the *Comédie humaine* and which finds expression in the desire to be re-united with the Other in a state of absolute Oneness. Thus Louis Lambert writing to Pauline: ''Je voudrais me glisser dans tous les actes de ta vie, être la substance même de tes pensées, *je voudrais être toi-même. . . .* Aucun sentiment humain ne troublera plus notre amour, infini dans ses transformations et *pur comme tout ce qui est un*; notre amour vaste comme la mer, vaste comme le ciel! Tu es à moi! toute à moi!''

In the Balzacian text, the source of absolute *jouissance* is located in the Other, and, in the apprehension of the child, initially in the ideal figure of the mother (''La Femme dans la perfection de ses attributs,'' as Louis Lambert's mother is represented). Attainment of desire is rendered by phantasmatic invasion and possession of the Other (''En effet, le désir ne constitue-t-il une sorte de possession intuitive,'' in Balzac's words). Non-attainment is experienced by the Balzacian character as catastrophic separation, a sudden fall into anxiety caused by a longed-for encounter missed, a gratification denied. Denial of absolute gratification leads to vulnerability and a return of infantile helplessness (thus Louis Lambert, isolated in his madness, comes to resemble ''a child in his cradle''). In Freudian terms, non-satisfaction, caused by the loss of a once known or, rather, hallucinated gratification, leads to anxiety because of unanticipated ''growing tension due to need, against which (the infant) is helpless.'' This tension is felt *by the ego* as a threat to its constant ''striving for binding and unification.'' For Melanie Klein such a condition is best described as ''a tendency towards disintegration, a falling into bits,'' as if the ego is undergoing violent persecution from the Other.

The drive towards fetishistic idealization and perfectionism of the Balzacian text is frequently interrupted or succeeded by scenarios of sadistic violence including mutilation and murder. In *Un Drame au bord de la mer,* the monstrous child Jacques assaults and stabs his mother, Jacquette, whose refusal to gratify his voracious desires thwarts and frustrates him. In *La Fille aux yeux d'or,* de Marsay's inability to achieve total gratification with Paquita Valdès leads to a brutal act of murder: Paquita's body is ripped and slashed in a scene of incredible violence. In *La Grande Bretèche,* the violence of the unrepresented encounter between Feredia and Madame de Merret is suggested by the play of names (Fer/Mer; Brette/Bretèche) and by the scars and gashes on the body of the mutilated building (''désordre,'' ''dévorée,'' ''disloquée,'' ''démolie,'' ''rongé,'' ''trous nombreux,'' ''lézardes [qui] sillonnent les murs''), reiterated in the description of the body of Madame de Merret (''décharnée,'' ''rongé,'' ''abattu,'' ''violet pâle.'' Bianchon's language, couched in the rhetoric of curiosity and quest for truth, suggests that conjunction of the scoptophilic and epistemophilic drives which, for Freud, are derivatives of the sexual instinct (''thirst for knowledge [being] inseparable from sexual curiosity,'' and connected, as attempted mastery, with sadism). Melanie Klein insists on the presence of the mother's body as focus of this drive: ''The first object of the instinct for knowledge is the interior of the mother's body. . . . [The child] wants to force its way into the mother's body in order to take possession of its contents and destroy them. . . . Thus the instinct for knowledge becomes linked at its source with sadism when it is at its height, which [explains] why the instinct for knowledge should arouse so much guilt in the individual.''

In *La Grande Bretèche* the secret, encrypted Reality of the text consists of the absolute contradiction between what must be preserved at all costs (that hallucinated *jouissance* uniting the *infans* Feredia and Mme de Merret) and what cannot in any way be acknowledged (phantasies of mutilation of the mother's body and the retaliatory act of infanticide). The emmurement and death of the child can be read as unconscious projections of punishment merited by infantile acts of aggression—a scheme akin to those incredible scenarios outlined by Melanie Klein in her discussion of the child's phantasies of attacking and sadistically entering the mother's body: ''Unconscious phantasies of forcing the whole self into the inside of the object [to obtain control and possession] lead, through the fear of retaliation to a variety of persecutory anxieties such as claustrophobia. These fears are connected with the unconscious 'catastrophic' phantasies of being dismembered . . . and torn to pieces, and of total internal disruption of the body and personality and loss of identity—fears which are an elaboration of the fear of annihilation.'' The ''catastrophic separation'' of which Bianchon speaks, and the mutilated appearance of the bodies of ''La Grande Bretèche'' and Mme de Merret, together with the incarceration and death of the child, are the disruptive, fragmenting elements of the text which threaten its coherence and hegemony. The writing as narration strives to present continuity, concatenation and control, and to represent a series of scenarios which place the subject (Bianchon) in the fictitious position of spectator, merely curious observer, Master. Denying the subject's implication, attempting to overcome conflict and contradiction, the narratives aim to provide a movement towards homogenization and totalization and to present a formal, abstract, closed perfection, sealing off, and bricking up the violent, forceful, random, heterogeneous drives which inhabit the figure of the *infans* Feredia, Bianchon's double, the other stranger. The narration, here as elsewhere in Balzac (in *Le Colonel Chabert, Ferragus, La Recherche de l'absolu,* for example) submits its own ambivalent Reality to a rigorous and imperious restructuring, feigning omniscience, establishing authority, and magically, omnipotently attempting to deny and conceal what threatens its mastery. It is here that we see the totalitarian aspect of Balzac's writing which comes into being out of desire, randomness and violence and which responds by repression, murder and violent emmurement.

Yet its own enactment is its own undoing. Not, one should say, as a result of any narrative process of introjection which might lead to transference: Bianchon's rape of the secret only leads to its reincarceration, and he does no more than pass on to his listeners, sadistically, the message he cannot bear. The text's undoing is through the very language which would contain its fracture. As in the dream where fragmentation is contained in the rebus only to be again fragmented; as from the crypt where the secret, buried in code, re-surfaces in indirect forms of language, so in *La Grande Bretèche* does the compressed enigma force its way through—*as writing,* in the letters of the writing itself, in the name of the stranger which the text would deny. Denial takes the form of emphatic negation: Mme Lepas asserts that there is nothing to tell, that she knows ''nothing''; Mme de Merret swears that there is ''nobody'' in the closet, the narrative closes on the echo of this *nobody:* '''Vous avez juré sur la croix qu'il n'y avait *personne*'.'' This ''nobody'' is the outsider, the mysterious third party, the one who does not speak, whose name is at first given as no more than an approximation: Mme Lepas recalls only that the name contains ''os'' and ''dia,'' that it is something like ''Bagos de Feredia.'' It is a name that can be read, if one wishes to do so; Mme Lepas has it written down in her register. Interpretation is clearly a matter of *reading,* and Bianchon resists; ''Mastery'' is achieved at the expense of reading, indeed here Mastery is in *not* reading, refusing involvement: Bianchon evidences his resistance in his response to Mme Lepas: ''Si votre confidence est de nature à me compromettre, pour tout au monde je ne voudrais pas en être chargé.'' The burden of Bianchon's Reality is one he will not assume.

The stranger is marked as an indeterminate figure (''figure indécise''), and the writing draws attention to the possibility of interpretive duplicity by reference to ''paroles à double entente.'' Bagos de Feredia, though real enough, seems to resist symbolization absolutely; *said,* his name says nothing, just as he himself says nothing. The foreign, alien letters are there—but excluded from interpretation, incorporated into the writing, sealed in the text, but making no sense, dumbfounding the reader. In ''Bagos de Feredia'' sense, as a whole, is mocked; we are left merely with the figure of a ''stranger,'' an ''unknown'' quantity. The name itself is the unknown, the unknowable: the text is right to have the last word as ''nobody.'' The name itself draws attention to the difficulty of making sense out of the random and the disparate: *Bagos* derives from the Spanish *vago,* synonymous with *indefinido, vacio* (indistinct, void—of sense); to be deciphered, as is, *en vago*: in vain (*en vago:* ''without succeeding in arriving at the goal of one's desires''; ''being deceived in one's judgment''). The name, like the figure, makes knowledge and judgement difficult, yet excites deciphering. And the name itself, fragmented already by Mme Lepas into *os* and *dia*, does suggest circulation, vagabonding; another sense of *vago* is ''shifting from place to place to place without stopping at any point.'' The signifier, fragmenting, fragmented, forces its way through the writing as the cryptic ''proper'' name disintegrates into its diacritical marks, unstable and duplicitous: FereDIA: DIA (according to the O.E.D.) twice, a-two, through, thorough, thoroughly apart. The name itself as signifier suggests absence of unity and a process of doubling echoed by BI-anchon, the other stranger. And the conjunction of OS and DIA (day) suggests death intricated with life, unpresentable yet percussively active in the writing in the substitutes and supplements of its mark (for example Feredia's cross which, in the possession of Mme de Merret, becomes the sign of their conjunction, separation and death—fissuring sign, mocking fusion). Death *in* life, not here, as in *La Peau de chagrin,* a longed-for state of suspension of motion, but an active, potent force. But also *life in death,* the desire for *jouissance* continuing into death (Feredia's *regard de feu* echoing the joy engraved upon the dead eyes of Mme de Merret). The narration attempts to separate life and death by fortifying itself against its own secret and by incarcerating the random figure of the stranger; but the writing, repeatedly, divisively inscribes their conjunction.

Here, in *La Grande Bretèche,* as so often in the *Comédie humaine* and in nineteenth-century fiction, narration and phantasy collaborate in a forcible attempt to banish contradiction, conflict, randomness and heterogeneity (represented by the unstable, wanton, violent figure of the child), and present the final version of events (in this case Rosalie's narrative) as a solution to the enigma and as a resolution. The solution here is in fact presented by Bianchon in his own words—as an abridgment: he admits that he has condensed, abbreviated Rosalie's diffuse eloquence ("j'abrège donc" [p. 108]), "Abréger" suggests not only condensation but also omission . . . of letters, as in abbreviation. And indeed in the final part of the narration there is no mention of the name Bagos de Feredia; there is a reference only to "l'étranger," to "l'inconnu": the proper name is erased from the writing—a strategy which recalls the manner in which, according to Freud, we attempt to eradicate the intolerable from out histories: "Almost everywhere noticeable gaps, disturbing repetitions and obvious contradictions have come about—indications which reveal things to us which it was not intended to communicate. In its implications the distortions of a text resemble a murder: the difficulty is not in perpetrating the deed, but in getting rid of its traces. . . . Accordingly, in many instances of textual distortion, we may nevertheless count upon finding what has been suppressed and disavowed hidden away somewhere else, though changed and torn from its context. Only it will not always be easy to recognize it." In *La Grande Bretèche* I would argue that the "detective" Bianchon is also the murderer—murderer of those parts of himself which he cannot abide. In tracking down the crime he attempts to abolish his own traces, by banishing, eliminating, emmuring the double of himself, the child he will not assume. In approaching Rosalie he claims to be questing "le noeud de cette solennelle *histoire*" (my italics), but he finds there the merest fiction ("il y avait dans cette fille le dernier chapitre d'un *roman*" [my italics]), which turns out to be a phantasy of his own making. The distinction between "histoire" and "roman" in this context can be connected with that between the terms Reality and phantasy as we have been using them throughout. Here "roman" seductively attempts to phantasize away "histoire"; as so often in Balzac, the romancing text masks and spirits away the unbearable knot of its conflictual origin.

But for the reader, the knot is in language, *is* language, in the signs which compose and decompose the name Bagos de Feredia—signs of that "nobody" whose unstable name inscribes the random, duplicitous, heterogeneous, violent play of the *infans* who finally becomes seen as the pressuring force of the text—desire, *jouissance,* violence, death—a monstrous sign, sign of the monstrous, breaching the repressive fortification of the narration. In this writing, the secret is not an absent center, or an absence at the center, or (as Todorov would have it) an impenetrable essence, but always already an imprint of that Reality which though incorporated, vomited into the crypt, maintains the continuous pressure of an occult force, an inexplicable and monstrous Thing which, buried alive in code, is nonetheless active and actively signifying: an enigma whose decipherment is up to the reader— if the reader is up to it. If the reader refuses to be tyrannized into silence and accepts the transferential activity of reading as the de-crypting of the writing and as the perilous re-enactment of the text's unconscious. As the text itself puts it: "Vous pouvez le lire si vous voulez."

Source: Peter Lock, "Text Crypt" in *MLN,* Vol. 97, No. 4, May 1982, pp. 872–89.

Sources

Kanes, Martin, ed., *Critical Essays on Honore de Balzac*, Boston: G. K. Hall & Co., 1990.

Lock, Peter, "Text Crypt," in *MLN*, Vol 97, No. 4, May, 1982, pp.872–889.

McCarthy, Mary Susan, *Balzac and his Reader*, Columbia: University of Missouri Press, 1982, pp.1–145.

Raitt, A.W., ed., *Balzac: Short Stories*, London: Oxford University Press, 1964, pp. 10, 16.

Further Reading

Bertault, Philippe, *Balzac and the The Human Comedy*, New York: New York University Press, 1963.
  An approachable but somewhat dated overview of Balzac's major work. Contains a useful biographical sketch as well as a chronology of the major works that comprise *The Human Comedy*

Festa-McCormick, Diana, *Honore De Balzac*, Boston: Twayne Publishers, 1979.
  As usual, the Twayne series provides a comprehensive introduction to the author's life and career. The chapters are organized chronologically and focus on individual works.

Lukacher, Maryline, *Maternal Fictions: Stendahl, Sand, Rachilde, and Bataille*, Durham: Duke University Press, 1994. Though Balzac is not one of the principle authors that she focuses on, her introduction contains an interesting discussion of how Balzac's relationship with his mother is reflected in his writing.

The Hitchhiking Game

Milan Kundera

1963

"The Hitchhiking Game" was first published as part of a collection of Milan Kundera's stories entitled *Laughable Loves*. The story centers on a young couple on the first day of their vacation together. Driving along in the young man's sports car, they spontaneously engage in a "game" whereby the young woman takes on the pretend "role" of a seductive hitchhiker, and the young man takes on the role of the stranger who has picked her up along the side of the road. But the fantasy element of the "game" bleeds into the reality of the relationship, with dire emotional and psychological consequences for both parties.

"The Hitchhiking Game" picks up on a recurring theme in the work of Milan Kundera, which concerns the ways in which sexual relationships become power struggles between individuals in a political and social climate in which the individual has no power over a repressive socialist state. This story also concerns a common theme in Kundera's work whereby jokes, humor, and games have serious implications. As Philip Roth has characterized the story in his introduction to *Laughable Loves*: "simply by fooling around and indulging their curiosity, the lovers find they have managed to deepen responsibility as well as passion—as if children playing doctor out in the garage were to look up from one another's privates to discover they were administrating a national health program, or being summoned to perform surgery in the Mount Sinai operating room." The meaning and implica-

tions of the "game" for both the young man and the young woman are also based on the traditional virgin/whore dichotomy, whereby women are categorized according to their sexual behavior as either "good girls" or "bad girls."

Author Biography

Milan Kundera was born in Brno, Czechoslovakia, on April 1, 1929. In addition to studying music, he attended Charles University in Prague. In 1948, he went to study scriptwriting and directing at the Film Faculty at the Academy of Music and Dramatic Arts in Prague. Beginning in 1952, he taught cinematography a the Prague Academy. From 1958 to 1969 he was an assistant professor at the Film Faculty at the Academy of Music and Dramatic Arts. From 1963 to 1969 he was also a member of the central committee of the Czechoslovak Writers Union. Kundera began writing his first novel, *The Joke,* in 1962, but, due to conflict with the national censors, it was not published until 1967. In June, 1967, Kundera gave a speech at the Fourth Czechoslovak Writers Congress, criticizing censorship and encouraging greater freedom of expression for Czech writers. Many writers followed his example in giving similar speeches. As a result, the government increased oppression of those writers who had spoken out. By 1968, however, in a briefly more permissive atmosphere referred to as "Prague Spring," Kundera was one of the most prominent writers of his nation. However, after Russian tanks rolled into Prague in the summer of 1968, initiating a repressive occupation, Kundera's books and plays were banned and removed from libraries and bookstores. He was also fired from his job and forbidden to publish any of his work in Czechoslovakia. In 1975, he was given permission to move to France in order to accept a position as Invited Professor of Comparative Literature at the Universite des Renne II, in Rennes, which he held until 1979. When his novel *The Book of Laughter and Forgetting* was published in 1979, his Czechoslovakian citizenship was remanded. Beginning in 1980 he became a Professor in the Ecole des Hautes Etudes en Sciences Sociales, in Paris, France, and in 1981, he became a naturalized French citizen. His novel, *The Unbearable Lightness of Being* (1984), was made into a movie in 1988. *Immortality* (1990) was his first book set in France. *Slowness* (1996) was his first novel originally written in the French language, as was *Identity* (1998).

Plot Summary

The story begins with a young couple, on the first day of their vacation, driving along the road in the young man's sports car. Although they have been together for a year, the young woman is still shy around her boyfriend and is even embarrassed whenever she has to ask him to stop the car so she can go to the bathroom. The young man has had casual sexual relationships with many women, but likes this young woman because she seems to him to be "pure," as compared to other women he's encountered. The young woman wishes she were not so self-conscious about her body, and envies the kind of women who are more comfortable with their sexuality. She is especially jealous of the young man's attentions to other women, because she feels that other women can offer him a type of seductiveness which she is incapable of. She fears that she will one day lose the young man to such a woman.

At a rest stop, she gets out of the car to go to the bathroom, and he makes a point of embarrassing her by asking where she is going. When she comes out, the young man pulls up at the side of the road to let her back in the car. Because the scenario resembles that of a stranger picking up a hitchhiker along the road, they both spontaneously pretend that this is the case. As they ride along, they continue to act out this "game" of role-playing, whereby she pretends to be the hitchhiker who has gotten into the car of a strange man in order to seduce him. By taking on this "role," the young woman begins to behave in overtly sexual ways which are in stark contrast to her usual self-conscious, embarrassed behavior. The young man, in turn, takes on the role of the stranger who has picked up this hitchhiker with the intention of seducing her. This role is easy for him to assume, for he has in fact had many such relations with women.

While it begins lightheartedly, the "game" begins to have an affect on the reality of how the young man and the young woman feel about each other. For the young woman, it is a liberating experience that, under the cover of her "role" as seductive woman, she is able to shed her sexual inhibitions and express her sexuality more freely. She also finds that her jealousy of other women slips away, since she feels that she is finally giving her boyfriend what she had always feared he could only get from other women: "lightheartedness, shamelessness, and dissoluteness." The young man, on the other hand, begins to see the young woman in a different light. When he sees how naturally she seems to be able to take on this role of seductive woman, he begins to think that maybe she is not the "pure" girl he had perceived. He thus becomes jealous at the thought of her behaving seductively toward men other than himself. Furthermore, he begins to lose respect for her, as he imagines that she is just like all of the other women with whom he has had casual sexual relationships.

At a crossroads, the young man spontaneously decides to take a road in another direction than that which they had originally planned. They end up at a hotel, where they check in and have dinner. During dinner, she becomes increasingly engaged in her "role" as seductive woman, thinking that she is at last able to please him the way other women have. He, on the other hand, begins to hate her for behaving like other women, and begins to treat her with disrespect. He even goes so far as to call her a "whore." At the same time, however, the more he finds himself repulsed by her as a person, the more he finds himself sexually attracted to her. In their hotel room that night, he treats her callously and disrespectfully, refusing to kiss her and speaking to her coldly and heartlessly. By the time she realizes that he now truly sees her, it is too late. She bursts into tears, pleading with him to see her as the same young woman he had loved and treated with respect. But, once having seen her as a sexual woman, he hates her, and dreads the next 13 days of their vacation together.

Characters

The Girl

The "girl," as she is referred to in the story, is on vacation with her boyfriend, whom she has been with for a year. In the beginning of the story, she is shy and embarrassed about her body, and is full of sexual inhibitions. She is extremely jealous of other women, because she knows that the young man has had many casual sexual relationships with women

Milan Kundera

more overtly sexual than herself, and she fears that she will one day lose him to such a woman. When they begin to pretend that she is a hitchhiker he has picked up along the road, she finds herself slipping easily into the role of seductive woman, and, under the cover of this pretend "role," her sexual inhibitions slip away. She finds this experience liberating, as she feels she is finally able to be the type of sexually free woman she envies. She feels she is finally giving the young man what she was afraid only other women could give him: "lightheartedness, shamelessness, and dissoluteness." When they check in at a hotel and have dinner, she continues in the role, becoming more and more bold. Although she is not aware that he has begun to hate her for this behavior, she perceives, once they are in their hotel room, that he is treating her like a "whore." He becomes completely cold and callous toward her, to the point where she bursts into tears, pleading with him to acknowledge that she is still the same woman he loved.

The Young Man

As the story opens, the young man is driving with his girlfriend in his sports car, on the first day of their vacation. Although he has had casual sexual

Media Adaptations

- *The Unbearable Lightness of Being* was made into a movie released in 1988, and starring Daniel Day-Lewis, Juliette Binoche and Lena Olan.

- *The Unbearable Lightness of Being* was recorded on audiocassette in 1988 by Books on Tape (Newport Beach, CA). It is read by Christopher Hurt.

- *Identity* was recorded on audiocassette in 1998 by Books on Tape (Newport Beach, CA). This unabridged version of the novel is read by Barrett Whitener.

relationships with many women, the young man likes the young woman because her thinks of her as "pure" in contrast to all of the other women whom he has encountered. When they begin the "hitchhiking game," of pretending she is a hitchhiker he has picked up along the road, he is eager to drop the role playing, and go back to interacting as their usual selves. But the young woman continues to talk and behave in her newfound role as seductress, and so he continues to behave toward her the way he is used to behaving toward all other women *except* her. When they come to a crossroads, he spontaneously decides to turn in a direction other than that in which they were originally headed. When they check into a hotel and have dinner, his irritation with her newly seductive behavior turns to hatred of her as a person. Nonetheless, he becomes more and more sexually attracted to her in this "role." He begins to treat her more and more crudely, calling her a "whore." In their hotel room, he treats her as nothing more than a "whore," speaking to her in a cold, callous way, and forgoing any signs of intimacy, affection or tenderness. He is deaf to her crying and sobbing, and unresponsive to her pleas that he acknowledge her as the woman he had loved, and treat her with his usual warmth. But it is too late once he has perceived her to be a sexual woman, he

hates her and dreads the rest of their vacation together.

Themes

Virgin/Whore Dichotomy

Central to the relationship between the young man and the young woman in "The Hitchhiking Game" is the historical way in which women have been categorized as either "virgins" or "whores." Through art, literature, and other elements of Western or European culture, women have often been judged based on their sexual behavior as either "virgins," and therefore "pure," or "whores," and therefore shameful, dirty, and sinful. In more colloquial terms, this "virgin/whore dichotomy" has been referred to as the "good girl"/"bad girl" split.

Both the young man and the young women view all women in terms of these categories. At the beginning of the story, they both see the young woman as falling into the category of "good girl." Although she is not technically a virgin, her shyness, embarrassment and general sexual repression place her in this category. For the young woman, this is a source of insecurity, as she fears she is not sufficiently sexually exciting to please her boyfriend. For the young man, on the other hand, this characteristic is what draws him to her, as he distinguishes her from all other women he's encountered as "pure." Based on this central theme, "The Hitchhiking Game" explores the consequences for their relationship when the young woman takes on the "role" of "bad girl," in the context of a playful "game." Through this story, Kundera seems to confirm the criticism launched by many feminists that the "virgin/whore" dichotomy is an unfair way to categorized women, with dire consequences for male-female relationships.

Jealousy

Jealousy is a central theme in the relationship between the young man and the young women. As a result of their role-playing "game," however, the role of jealousy in their relationship shifts dramati-

Topics for Further Study

- Many of Kundera's stories are set in Czechoslovakia in the second half of the Twentieth Century. Learn more about the political history of Czechoslovakia (now the Czech Republic) since World War II. What major political and social upheavals has the country experienced? How has the country's political climate affected the life and work of Kundera? How are the social, political, and economic conditions of the nation different now from the time in which "The Hitchhiking Game" was first written and published?

- The greatest Czech fiction writer of the first half of the Twenthieth Century was Franz Kafka. Learn more about the life and work of Kafka and the social and political climate in which he wrote. Like Kundera, Kafka's work was also banned in his own country—although not until years after his death. Pick one of Kafka's short stories to read. How can his life and work be illuminated by understanding the historical context in which he lived and worked?

- Vaclav Havel and Miroslav Holub are both well-known Czech writers of Kundera's generation. Learn more about the life and work of either Havel or Holub. How were his experiences and choices as a writer in the same political climate as Kundera different from, or similar to, those of Kundera? In what ways did these experiences affect his poetry?

- The government-sanctioned style of literature during much of Kundera's lifetime was "socialist realism." What are the basic aesthetic and political principles of the "socialist realist" style in writing? In other art forms? What is the history of the "socialist realist" style?

- Read another one of Kundera's stories in the collection *Laughable Loves,* (in which "The Hitchhiking Game" appeared). It what ways does it explore similar themes to those explored in "The Hitchhiking Game"?

---

cally. In the beginning of the story, the young woman is jealous of other women because she knows that her boyfriend has had many casual sexual relationships. She fears that, because she is not as sexually expressive as other women, she cannot offer him the excitement he finds in these women. She fears she will one day lose him to a woman he finds more sexually alluring. For the man, at the beginning of the story, this sexual jealousy is an irritation.

As the "game" progresses, however, the young woman's jealousy slips away, while the young man's increases. Because she is taking on the "role" of a seductive woman looking for a casual sexual encounter, the young woman feels that she can finally give her boyfriend the sexual excitement she thought he could only get from other women. She therefore loses her jealousy of other women. From the young man's perspective, on the other hand, seeing his girlfriend in the role of seductress brings feelings of jealousy he had not had before. He imagines that if she can behave seductively toward him, she must be capable of doing so with other men. His increasing jealousy at the thought of her seducing a man other than himself in part builds his growing sense of disdain toward her, as the "game" progresses.

Games

A central theme of "The Hitchhiking Game" is the "game" itself. The "hitchhiking game" begins spontaneously when the couple jokingly pretend that she is a hitchhiker he has picked up along the road. Kundera explores the ways in which "games" between people can become expressions of hidden thoughts and feelings that structure a relationship. For the young woman, the "game" allows her to get in touch with her own repressed sexuality by giving her an excuse to behave in seductive ways she would normally find embarrassing and uncomfortable. For the young man, the ''game'' places him in a role he has often occupied, that of a man seeking out a casual sexual relationship with a woman he does not know, respect or care about. While this role-playing ''game'' is at first liberating to the young woman, it ultimately reveals the deep hatred the young man feels for female sexuality. When he sees his girlfriend in this new light as a sexually expressive woman, he considers her no better than a ''whore'' and treats her as such.

Style

Narrative point-of-view

This story is told from a third person limited perspective. This means that the narrator is not a character in the story but is not necessarily omnipotent in its perspective. The point-of-view of the story alternates between the internal thoughts and feelings of the young woman and those of the young man. This alternating perspective is central to the meaning of the story, because it is the discrepancy between the meaning and significance of the ''game'' to the young woman and to the young man, which has such dire consequences for their relationship. This narrative technique heightens the effect of the story in that the reader is all the more aware of the extent to which the young woman is *not* aware of the negative affect of her behavior in terms of the young man's opinion of her until it is too late. This narrative perspective makes the ending of the story that much more sad because, while the reader is aware that the young man now hates his girlfriend, and is dreading the remaining days of their vacation, the young woman still has not realized the magnitude of his changed feelings for her. One can only imagine that she is going to spend the next 13 days attempting to win back his affection, unaware that his newfound hatred for her is irrevocable.

Setting

''The Hitchhiking Game'' is set in Czechoslovakia in the 1960s, and the story was first published in 1963. During this time, Czechoslovakia, under Communist rule, first enjoyed a period of democratic reform, and then suffered invasion and occupation by Soviet troupes. This setting is important because a central theme of Kundera's stories is about the ways in which an oppressive society affects intimate interpersonal relationships. This context affects the young man's decision to take a different road from that which he had originally planned. Spontaneously choosing to take a turn away from the direction he had planned six months ahead of time represents to the young man a rebellion against ''the omnipresent brain that did not cease knowing about him even for an instant.'' In other words, the societal pressures of the workplace which seemed to leave him with no privacy and no sense of spontaneity or personal freedom. The ugly power play which emerges from the ''game'' between the young man and woman is thus an expression of the young man's sense of powerlessness in his societal circumstances.

Irony

The concept of the ''game,'' as emphasized by its use in the story's title, creates a strong sense of irony. While a ''game'' is something that is supposed to be fun, trivial and playful, this ''game'' turns out to be cruel, significant and devastating for the young couple. In many of Kundera's stories, games and humor often turn out to expose a dark, evil underbelly, with dire consequences for the lives of his characters. In this story, the ''game'' ironically turns into something ugly as it exposes deep-seated attitudes which structure the relationship between the young man and the young woman.

Metaphor

The ''road'' in this story functions as a metaphor for one's path in life in the atmosphere of a repressive society. For the young man, his ''road'' in life seems to be planned, controlled and watched down to the last detail, for ''the main road of his life was drawn with implacable precision.'' Kundera tells us, ''He had become reconciled to all this, yet all the same from time to time the terrible thought of the straight road would overcome him—a road along which he was being pursued, where he was visible to everyone, and from which he could not turn aside.'' It is this metaphor of the road as applied to his life which leads the young man to spontaneously decide at a crossroads to turn in a direction other than what he had planned—for him, taking a different turn symbolizes an act of individual defiance against the controlled circumstances of life in a repressive Communist society: ''Through an odd and brief conjunction of ideas the figurative road became identified with the real highway along which he was driving——and this led him suddenly to do a crazy thing.'' While his decision to spontaneously change plans is motivated by the desire to veer from the ''straight and narrow'' road prescribed to him by society, it results in a decision to change the manner in which he treats his own girlfriend.

Historical Context

History of the Czech Region

The Czech region has undergone many political upheavals throughout the 20th century. Before World War I, the area now known as the Czech Republic was a part of the Austro-Hungarian empire, ruled by the Hapsburg monarchy. In 1918, not long after the War ended, the Czech and Slovak regions declared independence, forming the Republic of Czechoslovakia. This democratic regime lasted until 1938, when Prague suffered occupation by Germany under Adolf Hitler. In 1945, Soviet forces invaded Prague, and, with the defeat of Hitler, a provisional government was established from 1945 to 1948. After the war, a popular Communist movement had arisen, and Czechoslovakia came under Communist rule as a result of both democratic elections and pressure from mass demonstrations by Communist-led workers. Soon after, Czechoslovakia adopted a Soviet-style government, due to pressure from Joseph Stalin in Russia. In this spirit, the 1950s were characterized by purges of politicians accused of bourgeois nationalism. The 1960s, however, enjoyed a period of reform, whereby an attempt was made to show ''socialism with a human face.''

Prague Spring

Key events of 1968, known as the ''Prague Spring,'' mark a major event in the history of Czechoslovakia. As a result of democratic reforms begun in the early 1960s, citizens expressed a desire for even more rapid reform. A public statement known as the ''Two Thousand Words,'' signed by many citizens, called for further measures toward democracy. This did not sit well with surrounding Communist nations, however, and, two months later, the Soviet Union and several allies invaded and occupied Prague.

The Czech Republic

Popular uprisings, in the form of pro-democracy demonstrations and strikes, eventually lead to the collapse of Communist rule in Czechoslovakia in 1989. The first free elections in 45 years were held in 1990, and in 1991 the last Soviet troupes withdrew from Czechoslovakia. In 1992, Czechoslovakia was dissolved as a nation, leading to the formation of the Czech Republic.

Socialist Realism

With a socialist government running Czechoslovakia, a Marxist literary and artistic standard referred to as ''socialist realism'' became the standard by which all Czech literature was judged by the state-sponsored censors. ''Socialist realism'' is essentially an artistic aesthetic that supports a socialist cultural analysis and socialist ideals. Because of its propagandistic nature, ''socialist realism'' requires ''realistic'' representation (in art and literature) in keeping with the values of socialist society.

Socialist realism was the only officially sanctioned aesthetic in the U.S.S.R. from 1932 through the mid-1980s. Thus, the practice of state-sponsored censorship in Czechoslovakia under socialist rule, and under Russian occupation, functioned to repress the work of many writers and artists attempting to break away from the dictates of socialist realism. The works of such great Czech writers as Kundera, Miroslav Holub, Vaclav Havel and even Franz Kafka (who died in the 1920s) were therefore banned from publication, sale or library circulation in their own country until the mid-1980s.

Czech Cinema

Kundera studied script-writing and filmmaking in Prague. Like that of Czech literature, the history of the Czech film industry is largely dictated by state-sponsored censorship. Nonetheless, influenced by the ''Polish School'' of filmmakers working in the 1950s to 1970s, Czech filmmakers developed a fresh, new cinematic style referred to as the ''Czech New Wave'' cinema, which briefly flourished during the period of reform from 1962 to 1968. Although widely praised and appreciated by international audiences, however, these filmmakers were considered ''subversive'' inside their own country, and many of them were suppressed. After the Soviet invasion of 1968, the films created by the Czech New Wave were banned, and many filmmakers sent into exile.

Dissident Czech Writers

Two prominent Czech writers, contemporaries of Kundera, lived through similar experiences of censorship and oppression in their own country.

Compare & Contrast

- **1960s:** Under Communist rule since 1948, the Czechoslovakian government institutes a period of democratic reform in 1962, culminating in the Prague Spring of 1968. Several months later, however, Soviet troupes invade and occupy Czechoslovakia, instituting a severe crackdown on writers and politicians considered "dissident."

   1990s: In 1989, Communist rule collapses throughout much of Eastern Europe, as characterized by the tearing down of the Berlin Wall. Czechoslovakia becomes the Czech Republic. The first democratic elections were held in 1990, and the last Soviet troupes withdraw from the country in 1991.

- **1960s:** The Cold War, characterizing the ideological antagonism and the arms race between the United States and the U.S.S.R. since the end of World War II, is in full swing.

   1990s: The fall of Communism in many Eastern European countries in 1989, and the tearing down of the Berlin Wall, signify the end of the Cold War, which had lasted more than 40 years.

- **1960s:** The conditions under which Czech writers write is characterized by state-sponsored censorship and the idealized "aesthetic" of socialist realism in art and literature. The works of novelists and poets such as Kundera, Vaclav Havel and Miroslav Holub are censored and banned in their own country, and the writers themselves often imprisoned, fired from their jobs, prevented from leaving the country, or sent into exile.

   1990s: With the collapse of Communist rule in 1989, the fate of many writers formerly considered "dissident" changes drastically. Most notably, Vaclav Havel, writer and political leader who had spent four years in prison for his "dissident" activities, is elected leader of the newly formed Czech Republic three times between 1989 and 1993. Books by writers whose work had been banned for decades are finally made available in their native country.

- **1960s:** Kundera is living in Czechoslovakia, where the publication of his work, is restricted by state-sponsored censorship, and later banned from publication, sale or circulation in his own country. Eventually, in 1979, his citizenship is revoked. Nevertheless, his stories and novels are written in the Czech language, and set in Czechoslovakia

   1990s: Kundera lives in France, where he became a naturalized citizen in 1981. His first novel set in France is published in 1990, and his subsequent novels were originally written in the French language.

Miroslav Holub (1923–1998) was a celebrated poet who also maintained a profession as clinical pathologist and immunologist, publishing more than 150 research papers in his field. In the 1950s, Holub became associated with other writers who opposed the dictates of "socialist realism" in literary production. Consequently, from 1970 to 1980, Holub's work was banned from publication or circulation in his own country.

Another contemporary of Kundera, Vaclav Havel, experienced similar repression, due to his politics and writing. Havel, a poet and playwright, was politically active during the brief period of reform culminating in the Prague Spring of 1968. With the Soviet invasion of Czechoslovakia several months later, Havel's plays were banned and his passport was taken away from him. In subsequent years, he was arrested several times and spent four years in prison, from 1979 to 1983. Havel was, nevertheless, a leader in the protests against the Communist regime in Prague in 1989, and was subsequently elected President of the newly formed Czech Republic three times between 1989 and 1993.

Critical Overview

Kundera's writing career has in large part been determined by the political circumstances of Czechoslovakia under which he wrote. Before becoming a novelist, for which he has won international critical acclaim, Kundera was a poet and playwright His first book of poetry, published in 1953, was denounced by the censors. Nonetheless, he published two more books of poetry, in 1955 and 1957. His first play, written in 1962, was staged both in Czechoslovakia and abroad. His first novel, *The Joke*, was delayed in publication for several years, due to conflict with the state-sponsored censors. As Czechoslovakia was under Communist rule, any literature not conforming to the strict standards of "socialist realism" was suspect. Socialist realism as a literary standard requires that a story or poem support the principles of Marxism within a realistic setting. *The Joke* questions Communist society, as it centers around a young man who, as a result of a humorous post-card sent to his girlfriend, is denounced as subversive. Nevertheless, during the brief period of democratic reform in Czechoslovakia, from 1962 to 1968, Kundera's novel was finally published in its original form in 1967.

During the period of reform, Kundera was a member of the central committee of the Czechoslovak Writers Union (from 1963 to 1969). In June of 1967, Kundera gave a memorable speech at the Fourth Czechoslovak Writer's Conference, criticizing censorship, and calling for freedom of expression for writers. Many writers followed Kundera's example, echoing similar speeches at this same conference. As a direct result, repressive measures against these outspoken writers, and censorship of their work, became harsher. However, by the winter of 1968, increased efforts at reform were in part attributed to the influence of these same writers. During the "Prague Spring" of 1968, which culminated the height of the reform era, *The Joke* enjoyed enormous popularity.

In 1968, however, after Soviet troupes invaded and occupied the country, the period of reform was followed by a crackdown on writers considered to be dissident. Kundera was among those whose books were banned from publication and removed from bookstores and libraries. In addition, Kundera was fired from his teaching position at the Prague Academy and forbidden to publish any of his work in Czechoslovakia. Similar censure and censorship were imposed upon other prominent writers

of his generation, such as Miroslav Holub and Vaclav Havel.

As a consequence of his censure, Kundera was also forbidden to travel in the West, until, in 1975, he was given permission to move to France in order to accept a post as Invited Professor of Comparative Literature at the Universite des Rennes II. When his novel, *The Book of Laughter and Forgetting,* was published in 1979, his Czechoslovakian citizenship was revoked. Although a novel, it focuses on a variety of characters whose stories intersect thematically, but not literally. It is set in the context of Communist Czechoslovakia, and the real historical circumstances under which Communist propaganda operated by "forgetting" historical occurrences inimical to its ideology.

The Unbearable Lightness of Being was published in 1984, garnering international praise. Set around the time of the Russian invasion, this novel focuses on two couples and concerns relationship issues such as sex and fidelity in the context of a repressive society. In 1988, *The Unbearable Lightness of Being* was made into a movie directed by Phil Kaufman and starring Daniel Day-Lewis, Lena Olan and Juliette Binoche. The film includes a dramatic reenactment of the citizen protests surrounding the invasion of Prague by Soviet forces.

Immortality, Kundera's first novel set in France, is characterized by an authorial voice which breaks from the narrative to comment upon the writing process itself. The central characters of the story form a love triangle. *Slowness,* his first novel originally written in the French language, focuses on three different stories, all of which take place on a single night at a French Chateau (although set in different time periods). The three stories include the narrator (Kundera himself) and his wife on the way to the Chateau; a liason between an eighteenth century couple; and three characters attending a conference at the chateau. His 1997 novel, *Identity*, was also originally written in French. Of his two works of literary criticism, *The Art of the Novel* (1986) outlines his theory of the development of the European novel, and *Testaments Betrayed* (1993) discusses humor in the novelistic tradition, with particular focus on the great Czech writer Franz Kafka.

Kundera has won many writing awards, and his novels and stories have been internationally lauded. Critics have noted his style of combining fictional characters and storytelling with historical fact. He has been particularly critical of the social and political climate of Czechoslovakia under Communist rule. The structure of his novels tends to be non-linear, often structured episodically, whereby the stories of different characters are more thematically than narratively linked. Kundera's narrative style is often characterized by authorial intrusions, in which the narrator comments on the process of storytelling. His recurrent themes include a playful eroticism in the context of repressive societal and political circumstances. Humor, games and play, however, have a dangerous edge in his stories, through which his characters act out power struggles in a world in which they feel fundamentally powerless.

Criticism

Liz Brent

Brent has a Ph.D. in American Culture, specializing in cinema studies, from the University of Michigan. She is a freelance writer and teaches courses in American cinema. In the following essay, she discusses the effect of the "hitchhiking game" and the relationship between the two main characters.

In Milan Kundera's short story "The Hitchhiking Game," a young couple, on vacation, spontaneously find themselves engaged in a fantasy "game," in which they pretend that she is a hitchhiker he has picked up along the road. This "game," which begins playfully, turns out to have dire consequences in irrevocably transforming the relationship between the young man and the young woman. The fantasy begins to bleed into reality, leaving both parties feeling completely different about another by the end. But the meaning of the "game," and its ultimate effect on each of them, is very different for the young woman than for the young man. Through this story, Kundera explores the implications of the virgin/whore dichotomy in Western culture for male-female relationships.

The Virgin/Whore Dichotomy

In order to understand this story, it is important to see the dynamics between the young man and the young woman in terms of the ways in which women have traditionally been perceived in Western culture. To be more specific, in Western culture, women have often been categorized in two distinct categories, based on their relative sexual behavior. This dichotomy has been referred to as the "virgin/whore" split. In more colloquial terms, this di-chotomy can be referred to as the "good good/bad girl" dichotomy, whereby the "good" girl is one who is perceived as sexually pure and the "bad" girl is perceived as sexually active. In a similar vein, Western culture tends to perceive humans in terms which assume the mind (or soul, or spirit) is a distinct realm from the physical body (especially sexuality). Clearly, the "virgin" woman is thought of as spiritually and morally pure, devoid of all sexuality. The "whore," by the same token, is perceived as sinfull, dirty, earthly and devoid of all spiritual value.

Both the young man and the young woman in "The Hitchhiking Game" perceive women in terms of these two categories. According to this perspective, the young woman, at the beginning of the story, is certainly a "good" girl. Her sense of herself as uncomfortable with her sexuality is expressed through her embarrassment about her own body, and her discomfort with any reference to her bodily functions. For instance, she is overly embarrassed about having to tell her boyfriend when she is going to the bathroom.

> The girl really didn't like it when during the trip—she had to ask him to stop for a moment somewhere near a clump of trees. She always got angry when, with feigned surprise, he asked her why he should stop. She knew that her shyness was ridiculous and old-fashioned. Many times at work she had noticed that they laughed at her on account of it and deliberately provoked her—.She often longed to feel free and easy about her body, the way most of the women around her did.

The young man's perception of the young woman as a "good" girl, at the beginning of the story, is also central to his attitude toward her. His relationship with her is based on the distinction he makes in his own mind between her sexual repression and the sexual expressiveness of other women with whom he has had meaningless sexual affairs. "In the girl sitting beside him he valued precisely what, until now, he had met with least in women: purity." It is this perception of her as "pure" which arouses his love and affection for her, and her shyness about having to go to the bathroom is in fact endearing to him: "he had known her for a year now but she would still get shy in front of him. He enjoyed her moments of shyness, partly because they distinguished her from the women he'd met before . . ." In keeping with the virgin/whore dichotomy in Western culture, the young man mentally places her on a pedestal, whereby he expects her to be almost a spiritual being, rising above the material world of sexuality.

What Do I Read Next?

- *The Joke: The Definitive Version Fully Revised by the Author* (1992), Kundera's first novel, was originally published in 1967, after several years' delay by the censors. It concerns a young man who, as a result of a humorous post-card sent to his girlfriend, is chastised by the Communist government for expressing rebellious sentiments.

- *The Book of Laughter and Forgetting* (1981), by Milan Kundera, concerns fictional characters in the context of real historical events which took place in Czechoslovakia under Russian occupation. Kunera's citizenship as a Czech was taken away from him upon publication of this novel.

- *The Unbearable Lightness of Being* (1984), by Milan Kundera, focuses on two couples in the context of the Russian occupation of Czechoslovakia. It was made into a movie in 1986.

- *Slowness* (1996), by Milan Kundera, was Kundera's first novel originally written in the French language. It focuses on three separate fictional stories which take place in the same Chateau over the course of one night, and concerns a central theme of the speeding up of modern life, as compared to the slowness of pre-modern culture.

- *Milan Kundera: A Voice from Central Europe* (1981), by R. C. Porter, discusses Kundera's literary career in the historical context of the political circumstances of Central Europe.

- *Writing At Risk: Interviews in Paris with Uncommon Writers* (1991), by Jason Weiss, includes an interview with Kundera, as well as interviews with such writers as Albert Camus, Julio Cortazar, Eugene Ionesco, Carlos Fuentes and others.

- *Milan Kundera and the Art of Fiction: Critical Essays* (1992), edited by Aron Aji, is a diverse collection of essays by different critics, discussing Kundera's literary style.

- *Milan Kundera and Feminism: Dangerous Intersections* (1995), by John O'Brien, explores the feminist implications of Kundera's stories.

- *The Novel: Language and Narrative from Cervantes to Calvino*, by Andre Brink, explores the uses of language and literary style in the development of the novel through history, and includes a chapter on Kundera's *Unbearable Lightness of Being*.

Although the young woman is clearly not technically a virgin, her sexual relations with her boyfriend are still characterized by her shyness about her sexuality. She experiences "anxiety even in her relations with the young man, whom she had known for a year . . . " Yet, while the young man seems to value in the young woman her embarrassment and shyness about her sexuality, she envies those women who are more sexually expressive. She knows that the young man has had many sexual affairs with such women, and so fears that she lacks a certain sexual appeal to him.

> For instance, it often occurred to her that the other women (those who weren't anxious) were more attractive and more seductive and that the young man,

who did not conceal the fact that he knew this kind of woman well, would someday leave her for a woman like that. She wanted him to be completely hers and she to be completely his, but it often seemed to her that the more she tried to give him everything, the more she denied him something: the very thing that a light and superficial love or a flirtation gives a person.

The Game

The "hitchhiking game" begins spontaneously between the young couple when, at a rest stop, after she has gone to the bathroom, he pulls up in his sports car so that she can get back in and they can continue their journey along the road. Because the scenario resembles that of a car stopping to pick up a strange hitchhiker, they both lightheartedly banter

> The story also suggests that it can be damaging to men to categorize women as either 'pure' or 'sexual,' because it can cut them off from the possibility of a relationship with a woman that is both loving and sexual."

as if they were strangers and he had just picked her up by the side of the road. The man pretends that he is trying to seduce this strange woman, a role that comes naturally to him, as he has done it many times with other women, but which is completely contrary to his usual treatment of his girlfriend. The young woman, likewise, takes on the part of a woman who is used to having casual sexual affairs, a role which she has never taken on in real life, and certainly not with her boyfriend. The "game," however, begins to effect the reality of their relationship, at first in subtle ways, and then in very disturbing ways. It becomes "dangerous," as it brings out feelings in each of them which, in the year of their relationship, have never before been expressed. The consequences of the "game" in its effect on the reality of their relationship are devastating to each of them but in very different ways.

For the young woman, the opportunity to take on the "role" of a woman who is comfortable with her sexuality, and comfortable with the idea of casual sex with a stranger, is in some ways liberating. Because it is just a "game," she feels comfortable expressing the repressed elements of her own sexuality. She also takes pleasure in the thought that she is, for once, embodying the type of sexual woman with whom her boyfriend has had affairs. Because she is imagining that she herself is one of these kind of women, she is able to (temporarily) let go of her jealousy and fear of losing him to that type of woman. She imagines that, for the first time, she is giving him the sexual satisfaction she had feared only other women could give him. Furthermore, the young woman is surprised to find that, under the cover of the "game," the role of seductress seems to come naturally to her. It seems that all she needed

was this excuse not to be her usual shy self in order to express the repressed sexuality within her, as "the girl could forget herself and give herself up to her role."

Her role? What was her role? It was a role out of trashy literature. The hitchhiker stopped the car not to get a ride, but to seduce the man who was driving the car. She was an artful seductress, cleverly knowing how to use her charms. The girl slipped into this silly, romantic part with an ease that astonished her and held her spellbound.

For the young man, however, the affect of the game on his perceptions of his girlfriend, and his behavior toward her, is more ominous. Because he had loved the young woman based on his perception of her as "pure," once he sees her behaving seductively, he begins to regard her as he does all other women, i.e., as a slut who deserves only his disdain. Whereas he had treated her with respect because she was shy and self-conscious about her sexuality, he now treats her cruelly—as if punishing her for her sexuality.

When the young couple arrive at a hotel for the night, the "game" changes from a trashy romance to a tragedy. It is partly the discrepancy between the young woman's pleasure in her newfound role as sexual being, and the young man's growing disdain for her in this light, which makes it tragic.

The young woman, at this point, is completely unaware of the negative feelings her "role" in the game are arousing in her boyfriend. She continues to imagine that she is finally giving him what he wanted from other women, and so she imagines that she no longer needs to be jealous of such women.

"she smiled at the thought of how nice it was that today she was this other woman, this irresponsible, indecent other woman, one of those women of whom she was so jealous. It seemed to her that she was cutting them all out, that she had learned how to use their weapons; how to give the young man what until now she had not known how to give him: lightheartedness, shamelessness, and dissoluteness. A curious feeling of satisfaction filled her, because she alone had the ability to be all women and in this way (she alone) could completely captivate her lover and hold his interest.

As the game continues, however, and the young man sees his girlfriend in this new light, he begins to hate her for it. Because she is now expressing herself sexually, in the "game" of seducing her own boyfriend as if he were a stranger, he begins to imagine her as actually capable of seducing a strange man other than himself. Thus, while her jealousy slips away as she imagines that she is embodying the type of woman whom she envies, he becomes jealous for the first time, imagining her as such a woman seducing another man. Because he can only see women as either "pure" or as "whores," he begins to think that, since this role seems to come to her so easily, she must, deep down in her soul, really be a "whore." He is incapable of imagining that his girlfriend is both the woman he has known all along, and a sexual being. Because of this, he begins to treat her cruelly, with disdain and disrespect, calling her a "whore," and distancing himself from her emotionally. At the same time, as his feeling for her as a human being slips away, he becomes more sexually attracted to her. His limitations make it impossible for him to be either sexually attracted to the woman he loves, or to love the woman to whom he is sexually attracted. Because he has now seen her in this sexual light, he comes to hate her and dread the remaining thirteen days of their vacation together.

When, after it is too late, the young woman perceives that her sexual behavior has caused him to distance himself from her emotionally, she pleads with him to recognize her as the same woman he has loved. When he is unresponsive, she cries repeatedly, "I am me, I am me, I am me," trying to convince him that she is both the woman he has always known and a sexual being, not just the "whore" he has determined her to be.

Kundera in this story explores the negative implications, for male-female relationships, of the ways in which Western culture categorizes women as either sexual, and therefore "bad," or sexually "pure," and therefor "good." The story illustrates the ways in which this dichotomous way of categorizing women according to their sexuality is unfair to women, because it implies that there is something inherently shameful, evil and despicable about female sexuality. The story also suggests that it can be damaging to men to categorize women as either "pure" or "sexual," because it can cut them off from the possibility of a relationship with a woman that is both loving and sexual.

Source: Liz Brent, for *Short Stories for Students*, Gale, 2000.

Rena Korb

Korb has a master's degree in English literature and creative writing and has written for a wide variety of educational publishers. In the following essay, she explicates the text of "The Hitchhiking Game" and then briefly links it to Kundera's philosophies and the political background of Czechoslovakia.

Milan Kundera's international reputation rests on his novels, not the handful of short stories he wrote in the six years leading up to the Prague Spring of 1968, when Czechoslovakia experienced a brief period of independence before being invaded by Soviet tanks. Kundera's short stories, collected in *Laughable Loves*, nevertheless demonstrate some of his important ideas and techniques. Robert A. Morace writes in *Reference Guide to Short Fiction* that the stories "are in style, structure, and substance clearly the work of an already mature writer who conceives of writing as a series of exploration in form and theme." In "The Hitchhiking Game" in particular, Morace finds a "miniature" version of "Kundera's characteristic philosophical playfulness, classically precise anti-Romantic style, and the theme and variation approach. The story is less a conventional short fiction than it is an aesthetic and existential inquiry, a search for a new literary form to understand the human situation in the modern. . . world."

The title "The Hitchhiking Game" boldly connotes to the reader what lies at the core of Milan Kundera's story—a game with a dangerous twist. The anonymous characters in the story, referred to merely as "the young man" and "the girl," play out a drama that masquerades a deeper search for human meaning. The lovers are beginning their two-week vacation. Though the lovers are only at the start of their journey, the games they will play have been defined by previous experiences. As succinctly summed up by Morace: "The game he [the young man] plays is this: he drives until the car runs out of gas and then, hidden, watches as she [the girl] hitches a ride from another man to the nearest petrol station, during which time he fantasizes about what she and driver may be doing. Alternatively, he drives until she, despite her shame, must ask him to stop so that she can urinate."

The girl, however, likes neither of these games, which favor her boyfriend. "She always got angry" when he asked, with "feigned surprise," why he should stop the car, seeing that he relishes her embarrassment. The girl also complains about his allowing the car to run out of gas. Although the young man protests that "whatever he went through with her had the charm of adventure for him," the

> The young man and girl's role-playing, their experimentation with other identities and personas, stems from the repressive nature of communist Czechoslovakia. In such a state, no one is truly 'me.' Though the political aspects of the country and the story are not directly referenced, the young man and girl's actions are a direct result of it."

---

girl points out that the adventure is "only for her." She must "make ill use of her charms" in order to get a ride to the nearest gas station.

These games are set up right away in Sections 1 and 2 of the story. Section 1 also shows the girl's attempt to play the young man's game. When he asked "whether the drivers who had given her a ride had been unpleasant. . . She replied (with awkward flirtatiousness) that sometimes they had been *very* pleasant but that it hadn't done her any good as she had been burdened with the can and had had to leave them before she could get anything going." This exchange shows that the girl undertakes a role that is difficult for her in the hopes of pleasing her boyfriend.

The girl and the young man clearly have an unequal relationship. The young man is older, 28 to her 22. The titles given to the characters, like the title of the story, have deeper symbolic meaning—he is a *man* but she is only a *girl*. In fact, in Section 1, the young man acknowledges his belief that "he was old and knew everything that a man could know about women." The girl, for her part, defers to him. Despite being with her boyfriend for a year, she is still uneasy in his company—as the narration notes, "In solitude it was possible for her to get the greatest enjoyment from the presence of the man

she loved." She is jealous, shy, and anxious, all traits that show the instability she feels in their relationship.

Along with the history of the game-playing, the characters are established by the end of Section 2, when the direct action of the story begins. The couple stop for gas, the girl gets out and walks to the woods, but instead of returning to the car she walks down the highway. When the car comes down the road, she "began to wave at it like a hitchhiker waving at a stranger's car." The girl gets in the car, and the two begin to role-play.

Almost immediately, however, the young man and the girl begin to confuse their roles—he as "the tough guy who treats women to the coarser aspects of his masculinity" and she as "the artful seductress"—with their own identities. The young man flatters her "and at this moment he was once again speaking far more to his own girl than to the figure of the hitchhiker." The girl, however, caught up in her jealousy at seeing how he would react to an attractive stranger, "felt toward him a brief flash of intense hatred" and refuses to acknowledge him. Although at that moment, the young man "longed for her usual, familiar expression" and tries to stop the game, she refuses and rebuffs him as if he were a stranger behaving inappropriately. The young man, in turn, becomes "furious with the girl for not listening to him and refusing to be herself when that was what he wanted." The young man becomes angry both with the *girl*—who is defying him—and with the *hitchhiker*—who deserves rough treatment because of her very character.

As the two more fully embrace their roles, this shift brings freedom. For his part, the young man becomes spontaneous, driving to Nove Zamky instead of the Low Tatras, where they have a room reserved. The import of this action is underscored both by the narrator's acknowledgement that in Czechoslovakia it is necessary to book a room months in advance and by the narrative statement that the young man "was moving from himself and from the implacable straight road, from which he had never strayed until now." The girl responds to the new situation by drinking vodka when she normally does not enjoy alcohol, and flirting and talking frivolously. The ultimate symbol of her renunciation of her "girl" self is when she excuses herself to the bathroom. When the young man asks where she is going, she responds, "'To piss.'"

The roles that the young man and the girl play affect them differently. The girl relishes her new persona. Inhabiting the hitchhiker's body brings her self-awareness and freedom from the usual shame she feels about her body as a sexual object. The young man, however, even though he is aware that he is playing a role, cannot help but see his girl as the hitchhiker. Seeing her revel in her new sexual freedom, he treats her rudely, like a prostitute, and soon he longs to humiliate the girl and not the hitchhiker. He no longer can separate the girl from the hitchhiker.

Inevitably, the game goes too far. "The game merged with life," and there was no getting out of it. As the narration states, "A team cannot flee from the playing field before the end of the match... The girl knew that she had to accept whatever form the game might take, just because it was a game." The game leads to the bedroom, where the young man forces her to strip naked and dance for him. The two have sex in their roles of strangers, which initially disturbs the girl but eventually his "furious passion gradually won over her body, which silenced the complaint of her soul." She, who "had scrupulously avoided... love-making without emotion or love," feels more pleasure than she ever has before. Through sex, the girl crosses beyond the metaphoric boundaries of the playing field—she leaves the game. After sex, the young man, too, knew that "it was all over," meaning both the end of the game and the players' perceptions of one another.

Afterwards, the young man and woman return to their own selves, but with greater knowledge and without their previous security in each other. The girl, upset by her ability to view her body as "impersonal," a "ready-made borrowed thing," cries over and over in "pitiful" fashion, "'I am me, I am me, I am me...'" Her assertion, however, contains only a "sad emptiness." The young man, in contrast, does not rebel against his new state of mind and actually fears returning to their relationship. He resists the girl and is forced to call the compassion necessary to calm her down "from afar, because it was nowhere near at hand." His motive for helping her is selfish: "[T]here were still thirteen days' vacation before them."

The young man and girl's role-playing, their experimentation with other identities and personas, stems from the repressive nature of communist Czechoslovakia. In such a state, no one is truly "me." Though the political aspects of the country and the story are not directly referenced, the young man and girl's actions are a direct result of it, as many critics have pointed out. The lives of the two

protagonists are hardly their own. The girl "had a quite tiresome job in an unpleasant environment, many hours of overtime without compensatory leisure and, at home, a sick mother." The young man has a job that "didn't use up merely eight hours a day, it also infiltrated the remaining time with the compulsory boredom of meetings and home study, and... it infiltrated the wretchedly little time he had left for his private life as well," a private life that "never remained secret and sometimes even became the subject of gossip and public discussion." The lovers commence the vacation in an attempt to find freedom in a sports car and the open road, away from prying eyes but "[E]ven two weeks' vacation didn't give him a feeling of liberation and adventure."

Morace writes of the ending, "It ends with the realization that in pursuing freedom the young man and the girl have come to embody the very tyranny they sought to escape, becoming as it were the mirror of the larger political situation." Kundera has said that the modern world has become one of totalitarian tyranny and absolute skepticism, both of which are part of the hitchhiking game. As such, the story reflects a basic philosophy of Kundera. Writes Roger Rosenblatt in the *New Republic*, "For Kundera massive confusion is the essential human state... Stalinism was more dangerous than fascism because [according to Kundera] 'it began as the advocate and gradually converted it into the opposite: love of humanity into cruelty, love of truth into denunciation....'" The actions of the young man and girl, who take their love and twist it into hate and debasement, demonstrate this fundamental belief.

Source: Rena Korb, for *Short Stories for Students*, Gale, 2000.

Joyce Hart

With a background in English/Creative Writing, Hart has taught writing, been a director of a national writers' conference, and an editor of a literary magazine. She discusses the psychological and feminist implications in "The Hitchhiking Game."

Issues of power and identity are recurring themes in most of Milan Kundera's writings. Having been expelled by a communist regime from his homeland, Czechoslovakia, after his novel *The Joke* was published, Kundera often writes about these issues within a political framework. Just as often, Kundera also plays out these themes while exploring the personal and sexual relationships between his main characters. A good example of this occurs in his short story "The Hitchhiking Game."

> The absurdities deepen as the story progresses. The young girl begins to feel trapped once again, this time by the rules of their game. The young man is humiliated and then angered because the girl has become so free and flirtatious. Lashing out, he does his best to humiliate, not the hitchhiker, not the role that the girl is playing, but the girl herself."

The story, much like the road down which the characters travel, twists and turns around questions of authority, sexuality, and self, stopping not at conclusive answers, but rather stopping only out of sheer exhaustion and a need for sleep. It is the questions that are important, Kundera says over and over again in interviews and essays as he attempts to explain his work. In a *New York Times* interview with author Philip Roth, Kundera upholds his right as an author to pose these questions and leave them unanswered. He says that it is the purpose of the writer to teach ''the reader to comprehend the world as a question. There is wisdom and tolerance in that attitude.'' In ''The Hitchhiking Game'' it is definitely the questions that push the story forward. It is also the questions that both bind and alienate the story's characters as they try on variations of themselves, and play out different roles.

So leave the need for answers at the gas station and climb on board for a wild ride. Take a back seat and observe in silence and with an open mind, as Kundera's hitchhiking couple game their way through equally absurd identity crises. When those questions start banking up on one another, remember that another one of Kundera's aims as stated in his book *Testaments Betrayed* is to teach ''the reader to be curious about others and to try to comprehend truths that differ from his own.''

Being curious about one another does not seem to be one of the aims of either the boy or the girl (no names are given to these characters) in this short story. Rather they each think they already know one another very well. The boy knows that the girl is insecure, but he forgives her. ''Jealousy isn't a pleasant trait,'' he thinks, ''but if it isn't overdone (and if it's combined with modesty), apart from its inconvenience there's even something touching about it.'' The girl, on the other hand, believes that her modesty is ''ridiculous and old-fashioned.'' She thinks the young man wants a woman who can give him more ''. . .light-heartedness, shamelessness and dissoluteness.'' Their knowledge of one another is limited, and neither foresees the transformations that lurk at the next crossroads.

As they become entrenched in their make-believe roles in their invented road game, they discover hidden and somewhat contradictory aspects not only of one another, but also of their own personalities. According to Freudian theory, these hidden aspects are called repressions, or parts of the personality that have been formerly denied. In this story the repressions are related to both sexual and authoritarian drives. The girl, in the guise of anonymity as the hitchhiker, slips easily into a mirror image of her former self—a kind of shadow, as Carl Jung, another psychoanalyst and student of Freud, would say. In Jung's book *Man and His Symbols* he states, ''Sometimes, though not often, an individual feels impelled to live out the worst side of his nature and to repress his better side.''

This leads to some of the first questions in Kundera's story: Is this role, this guise that the girl puts on, an enactment of her worst side? The boy definitely believes it is not her better side, but the girl is not so assured. No more than three paragraphs into the story, the girl is already questioning her identity. ''Many times at work she had noticed that they laughed at her on account of it [her modesty] and deliberately provoked her. . . . She often longed to feel free and easy about her body, the way most of the women around her did. . . . She was too much at one with her body; that is why she always felt such anxiety about it.''

Since she cannot do it for herself, the girl seeks a unity of body and soul through the boy. However the relationship with the boy also causes anxiety because, in her mind, women who are less anxious and more carefree with their bodies are also more attractive. So she is caught in her own trap—a trap that she has obviously been living in for some time.

Her self-consciousness makes her react awkwardly. Her awkwardness makes her feel more self-conscious. Like most traps, this one has a release, and it is unexpectedly sprung when the girl puts on the mask of the hitchhiker.

Again from *Man and His Symbols* Jung says there are times when the shadow should not be repressed. "Sometimes the shadow is powerful because the urge of the Self is pointing in the same direction, and so one does not know whether it is the Self or the shadow that is behind the inner pressure. . . . If the shadow figure contains valuable, vital forces, they ought to be assimilated into actual experience and not repressed. It is up to the ego to give up its pride and priggishness and to live out something that seems to be dark, but actually may not be." The girl in Kundera's story decides to follow her shadow. She refers to it as a role "from trashy literature." When she does slip into this role, she is surprised at how easily she does it, and she finds herself becoming "spellbound."

The boy, in the meantime, is dealing with issues of power. He is obviously used to being in the metaphorical driver's seat in this relationship as well as in all his relationships with women. In the beginning of the story, the boy is aware of the girl's shortcomings. He deals with her moodiness, her lack of energy and self-confidence, her fears and her jealousies. When she becomes upset, he soothes her with a "gentle kiss on the forehead." He is, after all, twenty-eight years old and knows "everything that a man could know about women." He loves her in spite of her shortcomings. She is modest and pure. What more in a woman could a man ask for?

Not very long into the game, the boy gets his first hint of trouble. "The young man looked at the girl. Her defiant face appeared to him to be completely convulsed. He felt sorry for her and longed for her usual, familiar expression (which he considered childish and simple). He leaned toward her, put his arm around her shoulders, and softly spoke the nickname he often used and with which he now wanted to stop the game. But the girl released herself and said: "You're going a bit too fast!""

Reading this story with feminist theory in mind, the young man would be said to be playing out the patriarchal, or father role. He wants his girlfriend to reflect the qualities of a child, and is sickened when he witnesses her rebellion. He desires to control her like he controls the car. "He was furious with the girl for not listening to him and refusing to be herself when that was what he wanted." So he

retaliates. He decides that he, too, can play the game and takes up his mask of the "coarser aspects of his masculinity: willfulness, sarcasm, self-assurance."

At this point the story takes a literal turn. For the first time in his life the boy does something spontaneous—he changes the direction of his well thought-out course. When he does this, everything begins to fall apart: the road on which they are driving is torn up; there are long-delaying detours; and when they arrive at the only hotel in this unfamiliar town, every room inside is filled with smoke, noise, dirt and darkness.

Kundera is too intelligent to tell a story that is strictly black and white. He loves ambiguities. It is, of course, from ambiguities that the questions arise. So he has the young man, who at one point is disgusted with the new role that the girl is playing, reflect on the changes that he is witnessing. "The more the girl withdrew from him psychically, the more he longed for her physically; the alienation of her soul drew attention to her body; yes it turned her body into a body; as if until now it had been hidden from the young man within clouds of compassion, tenderness, concern, love, and emotion. . . ." Oh, such sweet reversal! In the beginning the girl is too conscious of her body. As she takes on the game, she frees herself from her body-consciousness. And it is in the freeing of her self that the boy all of a sudden notices her physically. In addition, how absurd it is that all the girl wants is to please her young man, but the more she tries to win his love, the more he pulls away his emotions. What are we to think about this?

The absurdities deepen as the story progresses. The young girl begins to feel trapped once again, this time by the rules of their game. The young man is humiliated and then angered because the girl has become so free and flirtatious. Lashing out, he does his best to humiliate, not the hitchhiker, not the role that the girl is playing, but the girl herself. Thus the shadow part of the boy's personality comes to the front, out into the light, and he finds he likes neither aspect of the girl: neither the angel nor the devil. In his mind they have coalesced into one. "Now he longed only to treat her as a whore. But the young man had never had a whore, and the ideas he had about them came from literature and hearsay."

As the story turns back on itself with the boy taking on a role from literature as the girl had in the beginning, the two characters turn their personalities inside out in what Jung might analyze as a step toward better defining their identity. "When dark figures turn up—and seem to want something—we cannot be sure whether they personify merely a shadowy part of ourselves, or the Self, or both at the same time. Divining in advance whether our dark partner symbolizes a shortcoming that we should overcome or a meaningful bit of life that we should accept—this is one of the most difficult problems that we encounter on the way to individuation.''

The story ends on an inconclusive note, in other words, it ends with unanswered questions. The boy fears a 'return' to their old relationship. The girl feels ''horror at the thought that she had never known such (sexual) pleasure.'' As the girl moans, ''I'm me, I'm me,'' the young man ponders the ''sad emptiness of the girl's assertion, in which the unknown was defined by the same unknown.'' So the characters put clear definitions of their emotions, their relationship and all their shadowy identities on hold. After all, there are still ''thirteen days of vacation before them.''

Source: Joyce Hart, for *Short Stories for Students*, Gale, 2000.

Sources

Morace, Robert A., An overview of ''The Hitchhiking Game,'' in *Reference Guide to Short Fiction*, 1st ed., edited by Noelle Watson, St. James Press, 1994.

Rosenblatt, Roger, A discussion of *Laughable Loves*, in *The New Republic*, September 6, 1975, pp. 29–30.

Roth, Philip, Introduction to *Laughable Loves*, a collection of short stories by Milan Kundera, New York: Penguin Books, 1974, p. xvi.

Further Reading

Kundera, Milan, *The Art of the Novel*, New York: Grove Press, 1986.
  Kundera's non-fiction work exploring his theories of the development of the European novel.

———, *Testaments Betrayed: An Essay in Nine Parts*, New York: HarperCollins, 1995.
  Kundera's non-fiction essay critiquing the ways in which the modern novel has been perceived by many critics. Focuses particularly on his view that the humor of the Czech writer Franz Kafka has been overlooked.

Misurella, Fred, *Understanding Milan Kundera: Public Events, Private Affairs*, Columbia, SC: University of South Carolina Press, 1993.
  Explores the recurrent theme in Kundera's work in which political circumstances affect the power dynamics of personal relationships.

Pillai, C. Gopinathan, *The Political Novels of Milan Kundera and O. V. Vijayan: A Comparative Study*, New Delhi: Prestige, 1996.
  Compares the political implications of Kundera's novels with those of the Indian writer Vijayan.

Podhoretz, Norman, *The Bloody Crossroads: Where Literature and Politics Meet*, New York: Simon & Schuster, 1986.
  Treats a small selection of writers, such as Camus, Orwell and Henry Adams. Includes a chapter entitled, ''An Open Letter to Milan Kundera—the terrible Question of Aleksadr Solzhenitsyn.''

Jeeves Takes Charge

P. G. Wodehouse's "Jeeves Takes Charge" was first published in 1919 in England in a collection of stories entitled *My Man Jeeves*. Wodehouse wrote dozens of stories and several novels detailing the comical misadventures of Bertie Wooster, a befuddled young Englishman, and his resourceful butler, Jeeves. "Jeeves Takes Charge" is one of the earliest stories in the series. Bertie recounts how he came to hire Jeeves in the story. In "Jeeves Takes Charge," as in all the "Jeeves and Wooster" stories, Bertie foolishly gets himself into a difficult predicament and it is up to Jeeves to save him. Wodehouse's stories were very popular when they were published, and they are still widely read today. His particular brand of humor continues to amuse many people as the numerous fan clubs that are found on the Internet demonstrates.

Pelham Grenville Wodehouse

1919

Author Biography

P. G. Wodehouse was born on October 15, 1881, in Hong Kong, where his father was stationed as a member of the British civil service. He was sent to England along with his older brothers for his schooling in 1884. He attended Elizabeth College and Malvern House, a naval preparatory school. At the age of 12, he began his most important educational experience at Dulwich College. His six years at Dulwich were a major influence on his life and

work. His first payment for writing came during his last year there when one of his essays was published in the *Public School Magazine.*

Wodehouse knew early that he wanted to be a writer, but his father did not believe that writing was a sensible occupation. He was forced to become a bank clerk at the London branch of the Hong Kong and Shanghai Bank. However, he wrote during the evening and sold 80 stories and articles while he worked at the bank. Ultimately, he quit working there and became a journalist for *The Globe* in 1903, first writing and then editing the *"By the Way"* column. In 1904, he made the first of frequent visits to the United States and immediately fell in love with American culture. On one of his visits, he met the widow who would become his wife, Ethel Newton Rowley. They were married on September 30, 1914.

Wodehouse began writing lyrics for the musical stage in 1904. In1906, his first collaboration with Jerome Kern, *The Beauty of Bath*, was produced for the Aldwych Theatre. Kern introduced Wodehouse to Guy Bolton in 1906. The three men worked together to revolutionize the musical comedy. Wodehouse was a gifted lyricist with a breezy wit and he teamed with Bolton and Kern to write several hit plays, including *Have a Heart* (1917) and *Oh, Lady! Lady!* (1918). One of their plays, *Leave it to Jane* (1917) had a successful revival Off-Broadway in the early 1970s. Wodehouse also worked periodically in Hollywood during the 1930s, making what he believed was an outrageous amount of $2,000 per week as a script doctor for Samuel Goldwyn. However, he experienced greater success with his plays and his fiction. The theater had a tremendous influence on his fiction; he once commented that his books were musical comedies without the music.

Wodehouse's fiction was popular because of the absurd yet complex plots and zany characters. His stories were formulaic, but his formula allowed for a wide variety of situations and characters. His tales of Mr. Mulliner, Blandings Castle, and Jeeves and Wooster shared many of the same plot elements: silly young men seeking or avoiding marriage, mistaken identities, the purloining of some object by successive characters, etc. Many of the characters cross over from one story or novel to another, and the characters make frequent references to events that take place in other stories or novels. Another reason Wodehouse's formula was successful was his masterful command of the English language. He used metaphors, puns, slang, and literary references in his fiction to great effect.

In 1940, Wodehouse was captured by the Germans while living in France and spent much of the war interned in Berlin. He unwisely made a series of radiobroadcasts sponsored by the Germans from Berlin to America in 1941. Although the broadcasts subtly ridiculed the Germans, many right-wing publications in England branded him a traitor. Writers such as George Orwell and Evelyn Waugh, however, defended Wodehouse by pointing out that he was politically naive. Wodehouse did not realize that the broadcasts were valuable propaganda for the Germans. Wodehouse, who dearly loved England, was deeply wounded by the charges and ended up emigrating to the United States, becoming a citizen in 1955. The scandal ultimately blew over, and Wodehouse, to his great satisfaction, was knighted shortly before his death in 1975.

Plot Summary

The story takes place in England sometime between 1910 and 1920. Narrator Bertie Wooster, an idle and rich young man, opens "Jeeves Takes Charge" by admitting that he is much too dependent on his butler Jeeves. However, he is unashamed; after all, in Bertie's opinion, Jeeves is a genius. "From the collar upward he stands alone," says Bertie, and he proceeds to detail how he came to trust the butler with all of his affairs.

During a visit to Easeby, his Uncle Willoughby's estate, Bertie catches his original butler, Meadowes, stealing silk socks. He is forced to return to London to hire a new valet. Bertie is attempting to read a dull book given to him by his fiancée, Florence Craye, when Jeeves first arrives. Bertie, who is nursing a hangover, is immediately impressed when Jeeves concocts a remedy for him. During their conversation, Bertie learns that Jeeves was formerly employed by Florence's father, Lord Worplesdon. Jeeves resigned because he disapproved of Lord Worplesdon's fashion sense. Bertie senses that Jeeves does not approve of his engagement to Florence. Bertie receives a telegram from Florence urgently requesting that he return to Easeby, where she is staying as a guest. He orders Jeeves to pack, and discovers that Jeeves dislikes the suit he is wearing. Bertie disregards the butler's disapproval.

Upon arriving at Easeby, Bertie determines the nature of the emergency. His Uncle Willoughby has been writing his memoirs, ''Recollections of a Long Life.'' It seems that the old man has read some of the manuscript to Florence, and she is appalled. The book details Sir Willoughby's wild adventures with his friends during their youth. Her father is one of many respectable gentlemen who, she feels, will be scandalized if the book is published. She proposes that Bertie pilfer the manuscript before it can be published. Bertie, who is financially dependent on his Uncle Willoughby, is extremely reluctant. He suggests that maybe Florence's younger brother Edwin, who is also a guest at Easeby, might be better suited for the task. After all, Edwin is a Boy Scout who is always looking for ''acts of kindness'' to perform. Florence threatens to break off their engagement if Bertie does not steal the book. Bertie, flustered, agrees to the wacky scheme. As he leaves the room, he runs into Jeeves, who informs him that someone has used black polish on his brown shoes.

Bertie lurks near his uncle's library waiting for an opportunity to filch the book. Sir Willoughby leaves the manuscript on a hall table for his butler, Oakshott, to take to the post office the next morning. Bertie snatches the book up and returns to his room. He arrives to find Edwin snooping about his things under the pretense of ''tidying up.'' Bertie attempts to hide the book behind his back. Edwin informs him that one of his recent ''acts of kindness'' was to polish Bertie's shoes. Bertie sends the boy off to trim some cigars and immediately locks the manuscript in a drawer.

Bertie is fearful of trying to destroy the manuscript while he is still at Easeby. He determines that leaving it the drawer for the time being is the best solution. Sir Willoughby is concerned because the publishers have not yet received his book. Bertie attempts to pin the blame on his former butler, but his uncle points out that Meadowes was not present when he finished the manuscript. Bertie becomes nervous and walks around the estate chain-smoking. While passing the library window, he overhears a conversation between Edwin and his uncle. Edwin knows that Bertie has the book and he convinces Sir Willoughby to search Bertie's room. Bertie dashes back to the room only to meet his Uncle Willoughby and Edwin. Sir Willoughby uses the story Edwin has contrived as an excuse to search Bertie's room. The drawer where the book is hidden remains locked and Bertie, to his relief, cannot find the key. Suddenly, Jeeves, to Bertie's horror, appears with the key. The drawer is opened, but Bertie is sur-

P. G. Wodehouse

prised to see that the manuscript is no longer there. After Edwin and Sir Willoughby leave the room, Bertie questions Jeeves and learns that the butler had overheard his conversation with Florence regarding the book. Jeeves determined that it would be more prudent if he took possession of the parcel. Bertie is pleased with his butler's performance and is satisfied that he has done his duty for Florence.

Florence returns from a dance and Bertie tells her that, although he hasn't exactly destroyed the manuscript, he has fulfilled his obligation. At that moment, his happy uncle appears to tell them that the manuscript has arrived at the publisher. Florence, infuriated, breaks off their engagement. Bertie angrily confronts Jeeves. Jeeves tells Bertie that he thinks they overestimated the effect the book would have on the people in it. Bertie fires Jeeves, and Jeeves takes the opportunity to tell him that he believes that Florence and Bertie are a mismatch. Bertie orders him to leave the room. After a nights sleep, Bertie begins to think about what Jeeves has said. He attempts to read the book Florence gave him and realizes that Jeeves was right. He rehires the butler and, in an effort to win his approval, he tells Jeeves to get rid of his checked suit. Jeeves informs Bertie that he has already given the suit to the under-gardener.

Characters

Aunt Agatha

Although Bertie Wooster's Aunt Agatha never actually appears in "Jeeves Takes Charge," the details Bertie reveals about her as he narrates the story suggest that she disapproves of him. Bertie mentions in the beginning that his Aunt Agatha thinks that he is too dependent on Jeeves, going so far as to call the butler Bertie's "keeper." After Florence discovers that Bertie was unsuccessful in preventing his Uncle Willoughby's book from being mailed to the publisher, she breaks off their engagement and informs him that his Aunt Agatha discouraged her from marrying him.

Mr. Berkeley

Mr. Berkeley is an unseen character who leaves Sir Willoughby's estate before Bertie arrives. Edwin convinces Sir Willoughby to pretend that Mr. Berkeley has left a cigarette case in Bertie's room as an excuse to search for the stolen book.

Edwin Craye

Edwin is Florence's devious 14-year-old brother. He is a mischievous tattletale who feigns innocence as he torments Bertie throughout the story. Bertie describes him as a "ferret-faced kid, whom I had disliked since birth." Nine years earlier, young Edwin led Lord Worplesdon to the spot where Bertie was sneaking a cigar, which caused "unpleasantness." Bertie suggests to Florence that Edwin is a perfect candidate for the role of thief in her scheme, but she won't allow it. Edwin, ever the diligent Boy Scout, uses black polish on Bertie's brown shoes. He catches Bertie trying to hide the stolen book. Bertie nearly loses his inheritance when Edwin tries to convince Sir Willoughby that the book is in Bertie's room.

Florence Craye

Florence Craye is Bertie's pushy, snobby fiancee. Bertie has grown up around her family. She forces Bertie to read boring volumes of philosophy in an effort to "mold" him properly. She is staying as a guest of Bertie's uncle, Sir Willoughby, while Bertie is in London hiring Jeeves as his new butler. She is shocked when Sir Willoughby reads her his memoirs, mainly because the book details the boisterous, drunken follies of her father, Lord Worplesdon, in his youth. She fears embarrassment for her family and bullies Bertie into stealing his uncle's manuscript before it can be mailed to the publisher. Ultimately, Jeeves sabotages her scheme as well as her engagement plans.

Lord Emsworth

Lord Emsworth is one of several people Florence thinks will be scandalized by being mentioned in Sir Willoughby's memoirs.

Lady Florence

See Florence Craye

Aubrey Fothergill

Aubrey is Bertie's unseen friend in the story. At the beginning of the story, Bertie proclaims that, unlike his friend Aubrey, he will not let his valet run his life. The irony is that he does indeed end up like Aubrey when he lets Jeeves take charge.

Sir Stanley Gervase-Gervase

Sir Stanley is another person Sir Willoughby gossips about in his book.

Jeeves

Jeeves is the sly and droll butler of the title. Jeeves is hired by Bertie Wooster after Bertie catches his old butler, Meadowes, stealing socks. As Bertie is narrating the story after the fact, he has already learned his new butler's value. He claims that Jeeves is a genius—"From the collar upward he stands alone." It seems that Jeeves instinctually knows what Bertie needs; he immediately proves his worth after he first arrives when he fetches Bertie a hangover remedy without being asked. However, Jeeves is unafraid to show when he disapproves of Bertie—if not vocally, then in his tone and manner. Bertie is at first suspicious and defiant, but Jeeves twice saves him in the story. First, he removes Sir Willougby's manuscript from Bertie's drawer to cover up the theft and saves Bertie's inheritance. However, he promptly mails the manuscript despite Lady Florence's wishes. Bertie fires Jeeves when she cancels the engagement. Although Bertie doesn't immediately realize it, Jeeves has saved him again, this time from a miserable marriage. Bertie rehires Jeeves after some consideration. He finally gives in to the same impulse that guides his friend Aubrey, allowing the butler to take charge and graciously disowning the suit that Jeeves has already given away.

Meadowes

Meadowes is the thieving butler replaced by Jeeves. He is fired when Bertie catches him stealing socks. Bertie tries to blame him for his uncle's missing book, but Sir Willoughby points out that he was already gone when the book disappeared.

Oakshott

Oakshott is Sir Willoughby's butler.

Sir Willoughby

See Uncle Willoughby

Uncle Willoughby

Bertie Wooster is financially dependent on his uncle, Sir Willoughby. The old man is insistent on publishing his memoirs, "Recollections of a Long Life." He and his friends, now respectable gentlemen, were apparently quite rowdy in their youth. The stories scandalize Lady Florence and she devises a scheme in which Bertie reluctantly steals his uncle's manuscript. Florence's bratty brother Edwin spies Bertie with the book and informs Sir Willoughby. Bertie's uncle is at first skeptical, but Edwin convinces him to search Bertie's room. Jeeves removes the book before Sir Willoughby can find it and sends it to the publisher.

Bertie Wooster

Bertie Wooster is the likable but hapless narrator of "Jeeves Takes Charge." Bertie is a young man of the leisure class who is financially dependent upon his Uncle Willoughby. The story is an introduction to his remarkable butler, Jeeves. Bertie admits at the very beginning that he has become hopelessly dependent on his valet. Jeeves displays his ingenuity soon after he arrives and saves Bertie from his fiancée Florence and her ridiculous schemes. Bertie is seemingly oblivious to what Jeeves recognizes immediately: Florence is a shrew. She is a snob who forces him to read dry philosophy that makes no sense to him, and she puts him in a difficult predicament when she insists that he steal his uncle's manuscript. Bertie foolishly agrees to her plot, even though he knows that it could lead to financial ruin if he is caught. Bertie is not only helpless against Florence; he is bedeviled by her sneaky younger brother, Edwin. The boy leads Sir Willoughby to the scene of the crime, but Jeeves removes the evidence before they can find it. Bertie's

Media Adaptations

- Stephen Fry and Hugh Laurie played *Jeeves and Wooster* in Granada's production of several Wodehouse stories on British television from 1990 to 1993. Many episodes were broadcast in the United States on PBS as part of the *Mobil Masterpiece Theatre* series. All of the episodes are available on videotape.

- There have been more than 50 audio-tape versions of P. G. Wodehouse's stories recorded, including a tape featuring eight stories from *Carry On, Jeeves* read by Martin Jarvis.

admiration quickly goes sour when Florence breaks off their engagement after the manuscript is published despite his efforts. Jeeves has of course determined that it was in Bertie's best interests if the manuscript was published. Bertie fires Jeeves, but after some thought, he realizes that Jeeves was right. Bertie, although somewhat dim, is modest enough to admit his dependence upon Jeeves.

Lord Worplesdon

Lord Worplesdon is the eccentric father of Florence and Edwin Craye. Sir Willoughby writes of his youthful friendship with Lord Worplesdon in his "Recollections of a Long Life." Florence is scandalized by the revelation that her father, after consuming a quart and a half of champagne, and Sir Willoughby were booted from a music-hall in 1887. This leads to the theft of Sir Willougby's manuscript. Bertie notes that a few years after the events of the story, Lord Worplesdon leaves his family for France after one too many servings of eggs.

Themes

Engagement and Marriage

One of the sub-plots of "Jeeves Takes Charge" is Bertie's engagement to Florence Craye. Readers,

Topics for Further Study

- Study and discuss the titles and rankings of English nobility. By what process does one become a "Sir" or "Lord?"

- Compare other well-known satirical writers, such as Mark Twain or Kurt Vonegut, to P. G. Wodehouse. Discuss the similarities and differences in their styles and subjects.

- Research the history of England during the early 1900s. Discuss the economy and society of the period. Describe the fads and fashions of Edwardian England.

- Study the role of the butler or valet in the Nineteenth and Twentieth centuries and write an essay comparing the reality of the position with the way that it has been portrayed in popular media such as film and television.

- Read several of the "Jeeves and Wooster" stories. Once you are familiar with the various characters and plots, attempt to write a scene (or story) of your own using the characters of Wodehouse. You could also attempt to create contemporary versions of the characters; use your imagination.

---

like Jeeves, immediately recognize that Florence would make Bertie miserable if they were to marry. Bertie, even though he somewhat dimly realizes that she is a shrew, is too charmed by her "wonderful profile" to fight her attempts to "improve" him by forcing him to read dull works of philosophy. She bullies him into stealing his uncle's manuscript by threatening to break their engagement. Perhaps her greatest offense is that she is in league with his horrid Aunt Agatha. In many of the "Jeeves and Wooster" stories, Bertie finds himself engaged to the wrong girl; some are sickeningly sentimental ninnies, others snare him in wild schemes. Jeeves, of course, always saves Bertie from the clutches of the wrong girl.

Role Reversal

An important and amusing theme running through all of the "Jeeves and Wooster" stories is the reversal of roles in the master/servant relationship between Bertie and his butler. Although Jeeves is the quintessential gentleman's gentleman, ready to serve Bertie at a moment's notice, Bertie is just bright enough to realize that his butler possesses a superior intellect. "Jeeves Takes Charge" establishes a formula that is familiar throughout the "Jeeves and Wooster" stories. When Bertie hires

Jeeves, the butler wastes no time in showing subtle disapproval for Bertie's choice in women and suits. Bertie is initially defiant, but in the end, after Jeeves has extricated him from his predicament, the young fop gives in to the butler's quiet demands when he tells Jeeves to get rid of the distasteful suit. Jeeves has of course already disposed of the suit by giving it to the under-gardener. Later stories find Bertie changing his behavior or appearance (even once shaving off a mustache) in order to gratify Jeeves in the same manner. Thus, Jeeves actually has the upper hand in their relationship despite his lower social status as Bertie's servant.

Social Class and Wealth

Bertie Wooster is a young man who has never worked a day in his life. In "Jeeves Takes Charge" and other stories in the series, it is revealed that Bertie lives on allowances and inheritances from his rich aunts and uncles. This type of lifestyle, while it may seem unusual now, was common for young men in the upper class in England during the Edwardian era. Bertie is 24 years old, yet he has his own valet to serve him. Because of his class, he is able to live frivolously on the wealth of others. He spends much of his time drinking with his friends; in the opening of this story, as in many others, he is recovering from a hangover. His life is a pursuit of pleasure. This is one reason why Bertie is threatened by Florence's scheme to steal his uncle's manuscript: if he is caught, Sir Willoughby would probably disinherit him. This would definitely disrupt an ideal situation for Bertie.

Style

Satire

P. G. Wodehouse is recognized as one of England's great light satirists of the twentieth century. The "Jeeves and Wooster" stories delicately tweaked the wealthy lords and ladies of Great Britain and their society. The plot of "Jeeves Takes Charge" revolves around the memoirs of Sir Willoughby, Bertie Wooster's rich uncle. The various vignettes in the manuscript ("Recollections of a Long Life") detail embarrassing moments in the youths of several prominent Englishmen. Here, although it is obvious in most of his fiction that he looks favorably upon the wealthy, Wodehouse gently mocks the idea that the upper class is without flaw. One does not have to actually read Sir Willoughby's autobiography to realize this; the events and characters in "Jeeves Takes Charge" are evidence enough. For example, Lord Worplesdon (although he never physically appears) is an eccentric blowhard. His daughter, Florence Craye, is a pushy, conceited snob. Edwin Craye, supposedly a model young boy, is a sneaky and mischievous troublemaker. Meadowes, Bertie's original butler, is a kleptomaniac. However, it is the relationship between Bertie and Jeeves that serves as Wodehouse's main ironic punch. Bertie, in a position of power because he is rich (although it is through no effort of his own), is forced to recognize that Jeeves, his butler and therefore of a lower class, possesses a superior intellect.

Narration

Bertie Wooster is the narrator of "Jeeves Takes Charge." Although Bertie often seems clueless, much of the flavor of this story, as in all the "Jeeves and Wooster" stories, is derived from his narration. Wodehouse uses a variety of devices to make Bertie an amusing narrator: slang, exaggeration and understatement, mixed metaphor, and literary refererence. Bertie is a fool, but through his narration Wodehouse

demonstrates that he is an endearing and likable fool because of his innate modesty and eagerness to please.

Plot

Wodehouse is famous for the complex plotting of his stories. In Jeeves Takes Charge, the action revolves around Sir Willoughby's memoirs. Each of the characters are struggling for control of the manuscript and their efforts result in pandemonium. Florence wants it destroyed because she is embarrassed by it. Bertie is bullied into stealing it so Florence won't break their engagement. Edwin wants Sir Willoughby to find it so that Bertie will be branded as a kleptomaniac. Poor Sir Willoughby simply wants it published. Finally, it is the clever Jeeves who finally wins possession of the book, thereby saving Bertie from both disinheritance and a disastrous marriage.

Setting

The story is set in England sometime soon after the Edwardian period. The action takes place at Easeby, the estate of Sir Willoughby. Many of Wodehouse's stories and novels take place at large estates or in castles. These settings lend themselves to the type of farce that he writes. Many rooms exist where characters can hide, and many windows where characters can spy or eavesdrop on each other. For example, while standing outside the library window, Bertie overhears Edwin tell Sir Willoughby about the stolen manuscript. One of the reasons Wodehouse's stories are so popular is that he so brilliantly describes the lavish settings where the stories of his privileged fools take place.

Historical Context

Edwardian England

In his essay "P. G. Wodehouse: The Lesson of the Young Master," published in the 1958 annual edition of *New World Writing*, John Aldridge notes that Wodehouse "belongs exclusively to Edwardian times. . . ." Aldridge is referring to the era of England's King Edward VII, who reigned from 1901, until his death in 1910. This decade marked a remarkably quiet transition from the Nineteenth to the Twentieth Century. At the time, England was one of the most powerful, advanced countries on

Compare
&
Contrast

- **1910:** King Edward VII dies at Buckingham Palace on May 6 after a reign of nine years.

  1999: Queen Elizabeth, crowned in 1952, is the monarch leading England into the 21st century. Her 51-year-old son, Prince Charles, is Heir apparent. Prince Charles has two sons, Prince William and Prince Henry, which virtually guarantees that the next person to take the throne will be the first male monarch in 50 years.

- **1917:** The House of Commons grants suffrage to most women 30 years of age and older.

  1990: After 11 successful years, Margaret Thatcher, the first female Prime Minister (PM) in English history, is succeeded by John Major. Thatcher, as well as being the first woman to become a PM, is also the first to win three consecutive general elections.

- **1914:** World War I begins when a member of the Austrian royal family, Archduke Ferdinand, is assassinated by a Serbian nationalist in the Balkans.

  1999: Civil strife in the Balkans threatens to engulf Europe in war. The North Atlantic Treaty Organization (NATO) intervenes in a conflict between a sovereign nation (Yugoslavia) and its citizens for the first time since the treaty's inception. NATO's air-strikes, beginning March 24, lead to a tentative peace agreement between Serbs and ethnic Albanians on June 9.

---

earth. England was an industrial giant, and the British Empire stretched into Africa and Asia. Certainly, England had problems, including terrible poverty in the wretched slums of the larger cities. But the first decade of the Twentieth Century in England was an idyllic time, especially for the rich, in comparison to the tumult of the following decades. Wodehouse idealized the period; his characters spent evenings at "the club" and weekends at sprawling country estates. Although his later stories sometimes made references to contemporary culture, his fiction always remained firmly rooted in the values of Edwardian England.

Women in Early 20th Century England

Wodehouse, consciously or not, may have recognized the changing role of women in British society when he created the assertive (though unlikable) Florence Craye. Throughout the Nineteenth Century, women in England had been fighting for political power and social reform. The Kensington Society, eleven women who were seeking careers in medicine or education, brought a petition asking for women's suffrage to Members of Parliament John Stuart Mill and Henry Fawcett in 1865. John Stuart Mill favored universal suffrage and added an amendment that would grant women the right to vote to the Reform Act that was before Paliament. It was soundly defeated. The women went on to form the London Society for Women's Suffrage. In the 1890s, over a dozen suffrage societies from across England consolidated as the National Union of Women's Suffrage Societies (NUWSS) to bring pressure on Parliament to grant women the vote. A radical spin-off of the NUWSS, the Women's Social and Political Union (WSPU), formed in 1903. The battle for suffrage intensified over the next decade; many women were imprisoned, and hunger strikes were common. By the time Wodehouse was writing his first Jeeves and Wooster stories, Parliament was under an enormous amount of pressure to enact reform. In June, 1917, the House of Commons voted 385–55 to grant women over the age of 30 the right to vote. The archaic nineteenth-century notion of a "women's sphere" was beginning to crumble.

World War I

Wodehouse began writing the "Jeeves and Wooster" stories during World War I. The lack of any reference to the war is almost astonishing; again, his characters are forever part of Edwardian England. However, Wodehouse wisely knew that his strength was in writing light comedy. Many people were no doubt thankful for the slight relief that Wodehouse's absurd little stories gave them during one of the most horrible conflicts in mankind's history. "The Great War" began when Archduke Franz Ferdinand of Austria-Hungary was assassinated by Serbian nationalist Gavrilo Princip on June 28, 1914. Austria-Hungary declared war on Serbia and a chain of alliances were activated. Germany and Turkey joined Austria-Hungary to become the Central Powers. France and Russia began to build up their armies, and Germany declared war on both countries. Great Britain joined France and Russia against the Central Powers on August 4, 1914, when Germany invaded Belgium. Later in the war, Italy, the United States, and Japan would join the Allies against the Central Powers. World War I marked the first time many modern weapons were used and the results were devastating. Germany, France, Russia, and Great Britain lost almost an entire generation; 8.5 million were killed during the war. The entry of the U.S. into the war (April 4, 1917) served as a turning point. Ultimately, the Central Powers were overwhelmed and they were forced to sign the Armistice on November 11, 1918.

England's King Edward VII, who ruled from 1901 to 1910. Edwardian England is the setting for most of Wodehouse's fiction, including 'Jeeves Takes Charge.'

Critical Overview

By the time *Carry On, Jeeves*, the collection of stories containing "Jeeves Takes Charge," was published in 1925, Wodehouse had already firmly established himself as one of England's leading humorists. His books were usually well-received, and *Carry On, Jeeves* was no exception. An unidentified reviewer in the December 3, 1927 edition of the *Saturday Review of Literature* wrote:

> We frankly admit our fondness for all the Wodehouse comics, and our especial delight in Bertie and the peerless Jeeves. The broad, rich, hilarious humor of the book places it, in our opinion, among the author's best.

Most reviews of the book were similar. However, the *New York Times* was somewhat more reserved in its praise:

> Mr. Wodehouse's humor, diverting though it is at first, seems to be drawn too much to formula after one has read beyond a certain point. Many of the stories taken singly are nothing short of delightful. But one cannot avoid the feeling that an entire book of Wodehouse stories is an overabundance.

This was a fault that several critics found in Wodehouse's fiction. No doubt a recognizable and somewhat repetitious formula earmarks the Jeeves and Wooster stories. For example, in "Jeeves Takes Charge," Jeeves disapproves of a particular suit Bertie favors. Bertie is initially hesitant to part with the suit, but eventually he gives in to Jeeves. This situation is repeated, with slight variances, in almost all the Jeeves and Wooster stories. Another frequent plot device is the presence of pesky aunts and uncles. Thus, some critics found his writing tedious. Familiarity did not, however, breed contempt with the general public. Wodehouse's books enjoyed tremendous popular success.

Early in his career, Wodehouse was not granted the same sort of critical attention reserved for more serious writers of fiction. In the 1958 edition of *New World Writing*, John W. Aldridge writes that he knows of ''no critical discussion of [Wodehouse's] work which attempts at all seriously to investigate the peculiar quality of his comic gifts or to account for the phenomenally high favor in which they have been held for all these years by the reading public.'' Aldridge argues that Wodehouse is one of the finest comic writers of the twentieth century. Since Aldridge's essay was published, there have been many scholarly articles and books written on Wodehouse's work. An essay published in the autumn 1959 *Arizona Quarterly* by Lionel Stevenson traces Wodehouse's antecedents in English literature from Ben Jonson to Oscar Wilde. In an introductory essay written for *P. G. Wodehouse: A Comprehensive Bibliography and Checklist* (1990), Anthony Quinton continues in the same vein. Quinton compares to relationship between Bertie and Jeeves to several other master/servant relationships in literature, such as Don Quixote and Sancho Panza, Mr. Pickwick and Sam Weller, and Phineas Fogg and Passepartout. Several biographies of Wodehouse have been published in the last three decades as well. Although Wodehouse wrote light comedy, a great deal of respect is held for his brilliant use of language and his well-crafted stories.

Criticism

Don Akers

Akers is a free-lance writer whose work has appeared in college journals and educational publications. In the following essay, Akers discusses the influence of P. G. Wodehouse's ''Jeeves and Wooster'' stories on the film and television of the late twentieth century.

In 1917, P. G. Wodehouse first introduced the characters of Bertie Wooster, the young, rich, and endearing English nitwit, and Jeeves, his cool and ingenious butler. More than 70 years later, the critical and popular success of the early 1990s British television series, *Jeeves and Wooster*, clearly demonstrates the enduring influence of Wodehouse's fiction on popular culture. Wodehouse's ''Jeeves and Wooster'' stories have been adapted many times for the stage and screen through the years, perhaps most regrettably for a pair of ''Jeeves'' movies starring Arthur Treacher in the 1930s. (These films had no trace of

Wodehouse's actual stories; Jeeves is portrayed as an idiot and, unbelievably, there is no Bertie Wooster character!) However, the 1990s *Jeeves and Wooster* television series benefited from faithfulness to the original stories, sharp writing, and brilliant characterizations by Stephen Fry (Jeeves) and Hugh Laurie (Wooster). A frequent criticism of Wodehouse is that his fiction has always been oblivious to contemporary culture; although he wrote ''Jeeves and Wooster'' stories for over 50 years, the characters seem to be in a time-warp, circa Edwardian England. In another wise favorable essay published in the 1958 annual edition of *New World Writing*, John Aldridge writes:

> One does have to suspend one's sense of the contemporary world, either through physical isolation or an act of the imagination, while reading Wodehouse, for he belongs exclusively to Edwardian times and has apparently chosen to remain unaware of just about every important development which has occurred in the world since those times. All efforts, including his own, to up-date his work must end in failure: his characters, even when they strike out with brave allusions to Clark Gable and Gatsby, betray in their every gesture, action, and assumption their helpless allegiance to the past.

Grumpier critics, such as the solemn Edmund Morris, found this type of fiction superficial and tedious. But as Aldridge explains in his essay, Wodehouse was simply a product of his era. Wodehouse's fiction was no doubt formulaic; but what an ingenious and effective formula! The familiarity of the characters and settings somehow facilitates a variety of situations in Wodehouse's stories. Thus, the *Jeeves and Wooster* television series is an almost perfect *situation* comedy. Here it is seen just how much Wodehouse's admittedly light, yet influential, fiction has permeated even today's culture. Perhaps the person who coined the television word ''sit-com'' never read Wodehouse's stories, but there is a Wodehousian element to the term nonetheless.

Wodehouse had great early success writing lyrics for the musical theater. His collaborations with Jerome Kern and Guy Bolton revolutionized American musical comedy. Today, the plots of these plays resemble those of television situation comedy. He later commented that his fiction was musical comedy without the music. He created two vibrant characters in Jeeves and Wooster and placed them in absurd situations in dozens of stories and novels. The writers of television's comedy series do the same thing every week (and Wodehouse was

What Do I Read Next?

- *Carry On Jeeves* (1925) is the short collection of "Jeeves and Wooster" stories containing "Jeeves Takes Charge." It is a good introduction to the dozens of misadventures of the young dolt and his butler.

- Wodehouse also wrote several novels about Jeeves and Wooster. One of the best is *Code of the Woosters*. Like "Jeeves Takes Charge," the characters all chase after a ridiculous object, in this case a cow creamer.

- The works of the great British author Charles Dickens were a huge influence on Wodehouse. Dickens wrote several masterful novels concerning life in England during the 19th century. One of the best is *Oliver Twist* (first serialized 1837–39). It is the story of an orphan taken in by a gang of pickpockets on the streets of London.

- A completely different take on England's upper class can be found in Evelyn Waugh's classic novel of moral disillusionment, *Brideshead Revisited* (1945). The novel is the story of Charles Ryder, a middle-class man obsessed with a wealthy, dysfunctional family in the years leading to World War II.

- *A Butler's Life: Scenes From the Other Side of the Silver Salver* (1996), written by Christopher Allen and Kimberly K. Allen, is based on Christopher Allen's expererience as a butler in Europe and the United States. The book is filled with anecdotes of a butler's life, as well as instructions for those who wish to become the perfect gentleman's gentleman.

---

almost as prolific). The 1990s television adaptation of his stories, *Jeeves and Wooster*, is only the most obvious evidence of the influence of his fiction on the popular media of the late twentieth century. There are several other examples.

One example of Wodehouse's influence, as suggested above, is the very form of the television situation comedy series, which has existed since the 1950s. The ten stories in the 1957 Penguin edition of *Carry On, Jeeves* average 21.3 pages. Even the slowest of readers should be able to finish one of these stories within 30 minutes (including a break for the privy, of course). Perhaps Wodehouse was unable to leave the comfort of Edwardian England himself, but his formula was perfect for the half-hour television comedies of the last half-century. Television's most successful comedy series, regardless of their relative quality (compare *Three's Company* to *Taxi*), derive their success from placing characters familiar to the audience in absurd situations that are quickly resolved, either accidentally or through a particular character's cleverness. (The characters themselves, of course, may be as absurd as the situations.) The "Jeeves and Wooster" stories operate in the same manner. One can watch an episode of almost any contemporary situation comedy on television and find a "Jeeves and Wooster" plot to match it. Mistaken or deliberately falsified identities, mis-placed or stolen objects, practical jokes gone awry, abject and utter humiliation; all of these are prime plot ingredients for both Wodehouse and the writers of today's television situation comedies. This is not to say that these plot elements originated with Wodehouse; he claimed to read the entire works of Shakespeare every year, and Dickens was a great influence on him. It was his style that was original and, despite the anachronisms in some of his work, somewhat ahead of its time.

The character of Jeeves is another example of Wodehouse's influence on pop culture. While it might be argued that the similarities between Wodehouse's fiction and situation comedy are coincidental, there can be no debate that Jeeves, Wodehouse's most brilliantly conceived character, has become an archetype. The resourceful, loyal, yet acerbic, butler has become a familiar character

> " The 1981 film Arthur, written and directed by Steve Gordon, featured Dudley Moore as the title character, a ridiculously rich, drunken playboy. . . . Although the perfectly cast Moore was hilarious in the role, John Gielgud, who played Arthur's butler Hobson, steals many scenes. . . . any reader of Wodehouse can see the similarities between the characters of Jeeves and Hobson. Both butlers serve their 'masters' diligently; however, they are quick to show their disapproval through sarcasm."

to stage, film, and television audiences of the late twentieth century. There are many examples, but two stand out especially over the last 20 years.

The 1981 film *Arthur*, written and directed by Steve Gordon, featured Dudley Moore as the title character, a ridiculously rich, drunken playboy. Moore was nominated for an Oscar for best actor in 1982. Although the perfectly cast Moore was hilarious in the role, John Gielgud, who played Arthur's butler Hobson, steals many scenes. In fact, Gielgud won the Academy Award that year for best supporting actor in the film. The story itself is a throwback to the screwball comedies of the 1930s. The plot concerns Arthur's decision to marry a lower-class woman against his mother's wishes, but audiences warmed to the close relationship Arthur has with Hobson. This writer doesn't know if Gordon actually read Wodehouse (Gordon died tragically just one year after the film); however, any reader of

Wodehouse can see the similarities between the characters of Jeeves and Hobson. Both butlers serve their ''masters'' diligently; however, they are quick to show their disapproval through sarcasm. For example, in ''Jeeves Takes Charge,'' Bertie persists in wearing a suit that Jeeves finds distasteful. At the end of the story, Bertie is reluctant to give up the suit, even though he knows he must because Jeeves has saved him from disaster. This leads to the following exchange:

[Wooster] Oh, Jeeves, 'I said; about that check suit.'

[Jeeves] Yes, sir?'

'Is it really a frost?'

'A trifle too bizarre, sir, in my opinion.'

'But lots of fellows have asked me who my tailor is.'

'Doubtless in order to avoid him, sir.'

In *Arthur*, Hobson is equally sarcastic when speaking to his ''master'':

[Arthur] ''Do you know what I'm going to do? I'm going to take a bath.''

[Hobson] ''I'll alert the media, sir.''

Jeeves and Hobson may cut their respective employers to the bone with wit, but they are protective. They often show disgust with their employers, but still they act as caring, parental figures. Jeeves fixes Bertie a special drink for his hangover; Hobson bathes Arthur. Hobson would probably not exist without Jeeves.

Neither would the character of Benson. Robert Guillame won a supporting actor Emmy playing the role of the caustic butler on the situation comedy series, *Soap*. (He later won a best actor playing the same role in the spin-off series, *Benson*.) *Soap* premiered on ABC in 1977. It was a controversial (at the time) satire of soap operas. The program, in the early years, had excellent satirical writing, and some of the best performers, on television. Several performers on the show, including Guillame and Billy Crystal, went on to even greater success. Guillame's Benson shares several traits with Jeeves. Benson, like Jeeves, is sarcastic; however, he is not quite as subtle. Benson's classic line: the doorbell rings, everybody looks at him . . . pause . . . ''You want me to get that?'' The role-reversal in the ''Jeeves and Wooster'' stories and *Soap* takes on even more importance in the case of Benson in obvious ways (considering our country's history) because he is an African American. Benson, despite his acid tongue, is extremely protective of several (almost) innocent characters on the show, much in the same way that Jeeves is protective of Bertie. Both butlers are supposedly members of the ''lower-class'' because they are servants, but both men are more intelligent than their employers. Yet they still do everything in their power to protect them.

Critics have complained that Wodehouse's fiction reeks of antiquity. There is some truth to this; however, it is ironic that his fiction has had such an impact on contemporary culture as demonstrated by Wosehouse's influence on on the characters and form of television and film comedy of the last 50 years. Regardless of the era, Wodehouse was a master of the English language, and his sparkling wit has aged well.

Source: Don Akers, for *Short Stories forStudents*, Gale, 2000.

William F. Love

In this essay Love compares the similarities of the characters of P. G. Wodehouse, Dorothy L. Sayers, and Ian Fleming, and argues that there exists literary continuity from Wodehouse to Sayers to Fleming.

In writing this essay (which started out to be a study of Lord Peter Wimsey), I was struck by the parallels between the novels of Dorothy L. Sayers and those of two other—hugely popular—British writers: P. G. Wodehouse and Ian Fleming. The more deeply I looked into it, the more interested I became. As a result, I will try to show that Sayers is a centerpiece joining the other two.

Wodehouse, Sayers, and Fleming were three of the more popular novelists to come out of Britain in the twentieth century. Wodehouse (pronounced ''Woodhouse'') had an almost unbelievable longevity as a published author. His first novel, *The Pot Hunters,* was published in 1902; his last (and ninety-sixth), *Aunts Aren't Gentlemen* (U.S. title: *The Cat-Nappers*), in 1974. Dorothy L. Sayers's Lord Peter Wimsey mysteries covered the 1920s and 1930s. And Ian Fleming's James Bond series ranged from 1953 to 1964, ultimately topping the bestseller charts. All three continue to be read widely throughout the English-speaking world. In addition, the BBC productions of the Lord Peter stories have been seen by millions; and every year or so Hollywood brings out another James Bond movie. I believe these writers have more in common than simply their popularity and nationality. I think literary dependency can be traced: from Wodehouse to

> " Is some of Lord Wimsey in James Bond? I think so..."

Sayers; and from Sayers to Fleming. Jeeves to Wimsey to Bond, if you will.

First, Jeeves to Lord Peter. It's a simple matter to prove that Sayers read Wodehouse. No less a Sayers authority than James Sandoe takes it for granted. But we needn't rely on Sandoe: in the early pages of *Murder Must Advertise* Sayers mentions Wodehouse twice.

First, Pym's Publicity's new copy-boy (Lord Peter Wimsey) is compared to Bertie Wooster, one of Wodehouse's major characters: ''I think I've seen him,'' says Miss Meteyard. ''Tow-coloured, supercilious-looking blighter.... Cross between Ralph Lynn and Bertie Wooster.'' (A good indication of Wodehouse's popularity this: Sayers felt no need to explain to her readers who Bertie Wooster was.) A page later we read about ''a bulky, dark youth in spectacles, immersed in a novel by P. G. Wodehouse and filching biscuits from a large tin.'' Obviously, Sayers was conversant with Wodehouse.

But Wodehouse achieved more than mere mention. He clearly left his mark on Sayers. (I suspect he leaves his mark on everyone who reads him. In researching this essay I discovered, to my surprise, clear evidence of dependency on Wodehouse in my own books—despite a thirty-year gap between the last time I read him and the beginning of my writing career.)

As evidence of Wodehouse's influence on Sayers, consider Wimsey's self-description in *The Nine Tailors:* ''I'm a nice wealthy bachelor. Fairly nice, anyway. And it's fun to be rich. I find it so.'' Such a self-description would be just as appropriate on the lips of Bertie Wooster.

Or take the way Wimsey occasionally strikes others: ''I met [Lord Peter] once at a dog show. He was giving a perfect imitation of the silly-ass-about-town.'' Later in the same book, another character says, ''If anyone asked, 'What is ... the Oxford manner?' we used to show 'em Wimsey of Balliol. ... One never failed to find Wimsey of Balliol planted in the centre of the quad and laying down the law with exquisite insolence to somebody.... Afterwards, the Americans mostly said, 'My, but isn't he just the perfect English aristocrat?'" Each of these descriptions would fit Bertie Wooster at least as accurately as it fits Wimsey.

Wooster and Wimsey are both bachelors. (Lord Peter's life on the printed page would end shortly after his marriage to Harriet Vane.) Both are hard-drinking, fast-talking party animals with a penchant for finding and losing pretty women. Both have faithful, ingenious butlers. Both, finally, are upper-class, with an unquestioned, albeit unspoken, loyalty to the class system.

But Wimsey moves far beyond Wooster, as the leading character in a series of crime novels should, as opposed to the centerpiece in a set of humorous entertainments. Lord Peter is venturesome, daring, and self-reliant: qualities totally alien to Bertie.

But if Bertie knows nothing of these qualities, that doesn't mean they are absent from Wodehouse's stories. This brings us to the character who is more truly Wimsey's—and therefore Bond's—literary antecedent than Wooster: Wodehouse's supreme creation, Jeeves. Bertie's butler may not be venturesome or daring, but he is supremely self-reliant.

"Jeeves!"

"Sir?"

"I'm sitting on the roof."

"Very good, sir."

"Don't say 'Very good.' It's nothing of the kind. The place is alive with swans."

"I will attend to the matter immediately, sir."

"All is well," I said. "Jeeves is coming."

"What can he do?"

I frowned a trifle. The man's tone had been peevish and I didn't like it. "That," I replied with a touch of stiffness, "we cannot say until we see him in action. He may pursue one course, or he may pursue another. But on one thing you can rely with the utmost confidence—Jeeves will find a way . . ."

Jeeves is an expert on fashion, on cuisine, on horse racing, on literature, on politics, and, of course, on *le grand jeu:* he knows precisely the way to a woman's heart.

There are, of course, striking differences as well. Jeeves is primarily concerned with saving his master's onions; Lord Peter is concerned with solving murders. Lord Peter is a master (of Bunter, his butler) and Jeeves a servant. Nonetheless, I maintain, the difference between the characters is far less than the difference between the genres of their stories.

Wodehouse's stories rely on an inverted master-slave relationship as old as Plautus: the servant, for all his social inferiority, is the brains of the pair. Sayers's stories, though they contain an element of irony and self-deprecation (the Egotists' Club, for instance) depend finally on the cleverness of Lord Peter, who, after all, has Jeeves's trick of showing up at exactly the right time and place. (Though Bunter is a faithful servant and a delightful companion, his contributions to Wimsey's crime-fighting tend to be minimal.) Like Jeeves, Lord Peter is omniscient, omnipotent, and always right.

Now to the second point: if Jeeves, the superior servant, is literary antecedent to Lord Peter, the wealthy aristocrat, Lord Peter, with even more justice, can be said to have been the same for Ian Fleming's James Bond.

Not that Bond is either aristocratic or rich. He, first of all, is far from rich—*Moonraker* lists his salary as 1,500 pounds a year taxable, plus 1,000 pounds a year in tax-free income. But (like Jeeves) Bond enjoys elaborate perks, including travel to exotic locales and stopovers at luxury hotels. Furthermore, he never seems to lack for money with which to gamble, occasionally at very high stakes.

As to Bond's place within the British hierarchy of class, he is definitely a commoner. Or is he? Observe him on an outing at M.'s prestigious club, the Blades. We find another inverted master-servant relationship in the two men's dining habits: M., the aristocrat, dines on such items as deviled kidney, bacon, peas, and new potatoes—decidedly proletarian fare—while Bond orders smoked salmon, lamb cutlets, asparagus with Hollandaise. Bond, the commoner, has the upper-class tastes his boss lacks. And though he technically takes his orders from M., he is also shown to be the brains as well as the class of the partnership.

Is some of Lord Wimsey in James Bond? I think so, despite the complete lack of reference to Sayers in any of Fleming's biographies.

First of all, take the following description of Wimsey in *Gaudy Night:* "height of the skull; glitter of close-cropped hair . . . minute sickle-shaped scar on the left temple. . . . Faint laughter-lines at the corner of the eye and droop of lid at its outer end. . . . Gleam of gold down on the cheekbone. Wide spring of the nostril . . . an oddly amusing set of features." Compare this passage, in its wealth of minute detail, to the way Ian Fleming frequently describes James Bond. Ironically, the best of these descriptions is in *The Man with the Golden Gun,* in a passage that describes not Bond but the assassin Scaramanga—who looks enough like Bond to be able to impersonate him successfully:

> Age about 35. Height 6 ft. 3 in. Slim and fit. Eyes, light brown. Hair reddish in a crew cut. Long side-burns. Gaunt, sombre face with thick pencil moustache, brownish. Ears very flat to the head. Ambidextrous. Hands very large and powerful and immaculately manicured.

(Note both writers' use of elaborate detail. Wodehouse, by contrast, is extremely sparing in his descriptions. Virtually all we are ever really told of Jeeves's appearance is that he is a "darkish, respectful sort of Johnny.")

Another connection between Lord Peter and James Bond may be seen in the two men's use of cardsharping to foil villains. Lord Peter's behavior in Sayera's short story "The Unprincipled Affair of the Practical Joker" provides a basis for considering similar activities of James Bond.

In the Sayers story, a parasite named Paul Melville has stolen a diamond necklace from Mrs. Ruyslaender. She is unable to bring charges because along with the diamonds he also stole a small portrait with a highly compromising inscription.

Melville likes to play poker. Lord Peter, knowing of Mrs. Ruyslaender's predicament and wishing to help her, engages the thief in a game. During Melville's deal Lord Peter catches him by the arm, and a card falls from Melville's sleeve. Melville protests his innocence—correctly if vainly—because by adroit sleight of hand Lord Peter had planted the incriminating card on him. Having forced the thief into a corner, Wimsey offers him a way out: if he will return the necklace to its rightful owner he will be allowed to slink away.

This idea of cheating a cheater was used by Ian Fleming more than once, first in *Moonraker.* The initial premise of this book (published in 1955) is that a guided missile capable of reaching any capital in Europe has been developed. The missile is being financed privately by the fabulously wealthy Sir Hugo Drax. The British government is worried that Sir Hugo's propensity to cheat at cards might constitute a risk to national security. For his own good as well as for the defense of the realm, Sir Hugo must be stopped. James Bond, of course, is just the man to catch Sir Hugo out.

Bond is a trained cardsharp: he has learned to handle such tricks as how to drop cards from his sleeve—shades of Lord Peter! M., Bond's superior, invites Bond to the Blades Club, where he engages Sir Hugo in a bridge game and relieves him of fifteen thousand pounds.

But this was not Bond's last dustup with a cardsharp. In *Goldfinger,* the book that constitutes the strongest proof for my contention that Ian Fleming drew inspiration from the works of Dorothy L. Sayers, Bond encounters Auric Goldfinger, money launderer for the evil SMERSH organization. At their first meeting, Goldfinger is cheating at a canasta game at a Caribbean resort: he has positioned a woman in a hotel room behind his opponent to observe his hand through binoculars. She then transmits her findings through a radio disguised as Goldfinger's hearing aid. Bond funds the woman, calls Goldfinger's bluff through the radio, and forces him to make restitution to his victim.

But this byplay between Bond and Goldfinger—so reminiscent of that between Wimsey and Melville—is only the beginning. As the book proceeds, Fleming borrows a murder device employed by Sayers in her short story "The Abominable History of the Man with Copper Fingers."

The narrator of that story, Varden, relates an incident that occurred in the home of the fabulously rich sculptor Eric P. Loder, who lived there with his favorite model, Maria Morano. Loder's specialty as a sculptor was silver castings and "chryselephantine" (gold-and-ivory) overlays. Following a period during which Loder and his model were secluded (ostensibly for artistic work), Loder showed Varden a cast-silver Roman couch in the shape of a nude woman.

Shortly thereafter, while Loder was away, Lord Peter came on the scene and pointed out to Varden that the nude was the silvered body of the model. Loder had silver-plated her as punishment for an affair he imagined her to have carried on with Varden, for whom Loder had planned a similar fate. Thanks to Wimsey's intervention, Varden escaped, and Loder tumbled into a vat of his own cyanide solution.

Goldfinger imitates Loder. Goldfinger has a kinky taste for making love to women coated in gold paint. He leaves unpainted only a strip along their spines, to allow their skins to breathe. When Jill Masterson, Goldfinger's partner with the binoculars, betrays him with Bond, Goldfinger has her painted—entirely—so that Jill dies coated in gold, just as Maria Morales died coated in silver.

Conclusion: Wodehouse influenced Sayers; Sayers influenced Fleming. Jeeves to Wimsey to Bond.

What drove these three popular authors to write? Similarities can be found. According to Paul Gallico, Ian Fleming originally wrote *Casino Royale* as an escape from the ''terrifying'' prospect of matrimony. As to Wodehouse, reading between the lines of his biographies, we see the lonely child, Plum, passed from boarding school to distant relative, happy only in an imaginary world of comfort and security. These two authors created their own worlds: Wodehouse, a world of comfort and security; Fleming, one of danger and intrigue.

When we ponder Dorothy L. Sayers's career as a scholar and her less than ideal marriage, we may see a certain similarity to Fleming's escape into a world of danger and excitement. Her project, indeed, seems to be encoded in the very name of her hero. Lord Peter is, indeed, an expression of Sayers's *whimsy*.

We are fortunate to have Sayers's own words to guide us, for the following quotation has the ring of a deeply personal sentiment, for all the irony in the second sentence: ''Mysteries . . . comfort [a person] by subtly persuading that life is a mystery which death will solve, and whose horrors will pass away as a tale that is told. Or is it pure perversity?'' This snippet suggests that Sayers found life a horror; a horror her mystery writing may have mitigated.

A number of critics believe that Sayers, whether knowingly or not, created Lord Peter Wimsey as her beau ideal: the ideal man she could never find in real life. In this connection a line in *Have His Carcase* is revealing: Harriet [Vane] felt she had never fully appreciated the superb nonchalance of her literary offspring.'' For ''Harriet'' might we not read ''Dorothy''?

Finally, how does Sayers rank as a writer against these other two giants of English literature? I concede she cannot be put in their class when it comes to name recognition of their major characters. ''Jeeves'' and ''James Bond'' have become synonymous, among English-speaking people everywhere, for ''the proper English butler'' and ''the quintessential British spy.'' ''Lord Peter Wimsey,'' resonate though it will for mystery-lovers, is not as recognizable to the public at large.

But popularity is not synonymous with quality; and it is with the quality of the writing I am here concerned. Comparing Sayers with Wodehouse is extremely difficult, since their genres are so different. Wodehouse, it must be said, was a master stylist. Making allowance for the firm and constant placement of his tongue within his cheek, his dialogue and descriptive passages rank high among the masters of the language. If readers are unfamiliar with him, I respectfully suggest they reread the brief passage of dialogue quoted earlier in this paper. The reader whose funny bone is not tickled by that passage is not the Wodehouse type.

In my opinion, Sayers is the finer writer of the two, but I can respect those of the opposite persuasion. What I will not countenance is the opinion that Fleming was Sayers's equal as a writer.

In his preface to the anthology *Gilt-Edged Bonds,* writer Paul Gallico expressed the view that Fleming was a ''master of detail.'' Gallico could not have been more wrong. Fleming's genius lay in expressing certain broad tendencies in the politics and public rhetoric of his day, not in careful craftsmanship. He was a boxer, not a chess player. He didn't write ''so that he who reads might run''; rather, he wrote while he ran! Evidence of Fleming's haste can be found throughout his books in numerous errors and inconsistencies.

First, compare James Bond's pharmacology (an important area of his expertise) to Sayers's careful research. His is frequently faulty. In *Moonraker,* in which Bond stirs a dose of Benzedrine into his champagne: '''It doesn't taste,' said Bond, 'and the champagne is excellent.''' ''In fact, Benzedrine has an appalling taste, rather like quinine mixed with insecticide. The *Encyclopaedia Britannica* calls it ''very bitter and numbing.'' But Bond doesn't find it so. Nor does the Benzedrine set him off the dinner he is in the process of eating— lamb cutlets with all the trimmings—despite the fact that one of Benzedrine's principal uses is as an appetite *suppressant.*

Bond's understanding of marijuana is even weaker. Later in the same book, he learns of a new Japanese narcotic, addiction to which, ''as in the case of marijuana . . . begins with one 'shot.''' [!] And as *Goldfinger* opens, Bond reminisces about a Mexican assassin with pupils tightly *constricted* from the deadly marijuana. [!!] Unfortunately for Fleming, he was writing just prior to a veritable explosion of marijuana information. Had his career been delayed a few years he might have been spared howlers like these.

Bond's French (unlike Sayers's) is little better than his pharmacology: ''It was eight o'clock. The

Enzian, firewater distilled from gentian that is responsible for Switzerland's chronic alcoholism, was beginning to warm Bond's stomach and melt his tensions. He ordered another double and with it a choucroute and a carafe of Fondant.'' Leaving aside the imputation that the Swiss are a nation of chronic alcoholics (I more often hear them referred to as workaholics!), Bond has made a rather odd selection from the menu: a *choucroute* is an order of sauerkraut. I presume Bond meant to order a *cassecroute,* or snack (usually some variation on a grilled ham-and-cheese sandwich).

Arithmetic is another chink in the Fleming armor. Consider the incident wherein Leiter complains of receiving short measure from a bartender in his martini. He complains of the large olive, the false bottom in the glass, then notes, '''One bottle of Gordon's gin contains sixteen true measures—double measures, that is, the only ones I drink. Cut the gin with three ounces of water and that makes it up to twenty-two. . . .'''

Three ounces equal six double measures? Mr. Leiter had shorted himself long before any bartenders had the opportunity to do so.

Not that Ian Fleming can't write. Passages like ''a bustle of waiters round their table'' or ''leashed in by the velvet claw of the front disks, the engine muttered its protest with a mild back-popple from the twin exhausts'' show an expertise in the use of vivid metaphors.

I believe Fleming's weakness (and his popularity?) stems from that fact that he eschewed detail work in favor of painting in broad strokes, mythologizing the 1950s and early 1960s, when the headlines were filled with stories of international intrigue.

Double agents Fuchs, Burgess, Philby, Blunt, and Maclean had compromised MI5 (Military Intelligence 5) and even the palace (Anthony Blunt was art historian to the queen). Worse yet, George Blake, imprisoned for fingering forty-two British agents assassinated by the KGB, managed a daring escape from Wormwood Scrubs and was in Moscow almost before his guards knew he was gone. Then in 1963 the John Profumo/Christine Keeler scandal brought down the government.

The British public, frustrated and angered by such blunders and incompetence, needed a distraction. Enter the superhero: ever-competent, never-blundering James Bond.

The Christine Keeler affair is a case in point. It had all the elements of a James Bond story—beautiful women, fantastic wealth, global power, international intrigue: all that's missing is James Bond himself. But compare the Christine Keeler story to a James Bond novel and one begins to see most clearly Ian Fleming's process of mythologization. His purpose was not to analyze or criticize events but to make them larger than life.

Keeler, only nineteen at the time of the Profumo affair, went to prison for two years on rather dubious charges, and lives today in public housing. For James Bond also, beautiful women are expendable, but their ruin is accomplished spectacularly: they are gilded, zapped, shot, stabbed, or exploded; not railroaded—and always in the vital interests of the realm, never for such tawdry, real-life motives as selling newspapers or winning an election.

Fleming's lack of irony is, in fact, characteristic of all his writing. SMERSH, ''Smiert Spionam'' (= ''death to spies''), is described as ''the Soviet organization of vengeance and death.'' Bond himself has a ''license to kill.'' M. (and Bond) react with an outrage completely out of proportion (compared to the matter at hand—the construction of the Moonraker rocket) when they learn of Drax's ungentlemanly cardsharping. And although Bond himself doesn't indulge in racial stereotyping, he accepts such stereotyping without question, as when he is told that Koreans ''are the cruellest, most ruthless people in the world,'' or that Jamaican ''Chigroes'' (of mixed African and Chinese ancestry) ''have inherited some of the Chinese intelligence and most of the Negroes' vices.'' Fleming's lack of irony, like his carelessness with details, is characteristic of his emphasis on myth.

Sayers's books are much more interesting. Her background is realistic, her characters are three-dimensional, her sense of evil realistic and true to life, her research far more exhaustive than Fleming's.

No better example could be given than the extensive and careful study that went into the descriptions of the ancient art of change ringing in *The Nine Tailors*. This novel has received much praise—some of it from experts in the field—for the accuracy and thoroughness of those descriptions.

Next, I would also call attention to the meticulously plotted and, within the context of the plot, important time sequences in *The Five Red Herrings*. One cannot read that book without being struck by the care with which Ms. Sayers handles those sequences.

As to her overall abilities as a prose stylist, we should start with a concession. She was capable of self-indulgence. Witness the extreme length of *Have His Carcase,* which Sayers can fairly be accused of padding. I personally find none of the Wimsey books tedious, but *Have His Carcase* is not the first, or even the second, book I'd recommend to a budding Sayers enthusiast.

Nonetheless, if Sayers wasn't perfect, she was still a very fine writer, and capable of some bravura turns. The following monologue (from *The Nine Tailors*) is evidence of an ear finely attuned to the nuances of local dialect. The speaker is the gravedigger Harry Gotobed telling how he and his son came upon a corpse in a grave where it had no business being.

> ''Dick drives his spade down a good spit, and he says to me, 'Dad,' he says, 'there's something in here.' And I says to him, 'What's that?' I says, 'what do you mean? Something in here?' and then I strikes my spade hard down and I feels something sort of between hard and soft, like, and I says, 'Dick,' I says, 'that's a funny thing, there *is* something here.' So I says, 'Go careful, my boy,' I says, 'because it feels funny-like to me,' I says, 'that's a boot, that is.' . . . So we clears away very careful, and at last we sees him plain. And I says, 'Dick, I don't know who he is nor yet how he got here, but he didn't ought to be here.'''

Another delightful passage, of a totally different type, is the description of Wimsey's heroics in the cricket match in *Murder Must Advertise*.

Mr. Simmonds' third delivery rose wickedly from a patch of bare earth and smote [Wimsey] violently upon the elbow.

> Nothing makes a man see red like a sharp rap over the funny bone, and it was at this moment that [Wimsey] suddenly and regrettably forgot himself. . . . The next ball was another of Simmonds' murderous short-pitched bumpers, and Lord Peter Wimsey, opening up wrathful shoulders, strode out of his crease like the spirit of vengeance and whacked it to the wide. . . .

> Mr. Simmonds . . . was replaced by a gentleman who was known as ''Spinner.'' Wimsey received him with enthusiasm . . . till Brotherhood's captain moved up his fieldsmen and concentrated them about the off-side of the wicket. Wimsey looked at this grouping with an indulgent smile, and placed the next six balls consistently and successfully to leg. When, in despair, they drew a close net of fielders all round him, he drove everything that was drivable straight down the pitch.

If Sayers was the better writer, how then account for Fleming's greater popularity? The sensa-

tionalism of his stories could be part of the reason, as well as the public's known proclivity for soft-core porn. But I think the primary reason is the power of myth and Fleming's ability to tap into it. Sayers's type of book is aimed at a smaller, more select audience. Jeeves, Lord Peter, James Bond: no one would ever confuse them, but I hope I've shown that they (and their authors) have more in common than meets the eye.

Source: William F. Love, ''Butler, Dabbler, Spy: Jeeves to Wimsey to Bond'' in *Dorothy L. Sayers: The Centenary Celebration*, edited by Alzina Stone Dale, Walker, 1993, pp. 31–43.

Eberhard Spath

Friedrich Nietzsche's concept of the superman—a self-created hero and a natural leader—influenced a number of British writers during the early twentieth century, most notably D. H. Lawrence and George Bernard Shaw. In the following essay, Spath argues that Jeeves represents one of the best examples of the superman in popular literature.

There can hardly be any doubt that the most intriguing character created by P. G. Wodehouse is that of butler Jeeves, even though, as the clever servant who, episode after episode, proves superior to his master, he is anything but original. From the viewpoint of literary history he is indeed of as ancient a family as that hopelessly inefficient rich young man whom he serves. The extraordinary fascination Jeeves has held for a vast number of readers invites some investigation of how his author made use of one of the stock figures of comedy.

But, as we hope to demonstrate, Jeeves is not only the traditional sly servant; he is also one of the supermen of popular literature, who may be considered in relation to, for instance, the hero of the detective novel— a genre which gained the peak of its popularity at about the same time as Wodehouse. Furthermore, there is the well-known fact that in the early twentieth century interest in the superman was expressed by several English writers of recognized literary importance, notably by Shaw and Lawrence. The corresponding developments of political history hardly need mentioning here. It seems worthwhile then to analyse the function of Jeeves in this context.

George Orwell, always a sensitive critic of popular writers, noted in 1936:

> [. . .] it was a great day for Mr. Wodehouse when he created Jeeves, and thus escaped from the realm of

comedy, which in England always stinks of virtue, into the realm of pure farce. The great charm of Jeeves is that (although he did pronounce Nietzsche to be 'fundamentally unsound') he is beyond good and evil.

At first this may seem a little surprising since, superficially, Jeeves appears to be as genuinely Victorian as any average middle-class reader might have wished, especially when we compare him to the traditional servant of comedy whose morals are notoriously low. Jeeves knows neither financial greed nor sexual desires; it is, in fact, impossible to think of him as having erotic inclinations. He does like to collect any pecuniary rewards that may come his way, but what he enjoys in such cases is the success of his stratagems rather than the material gains. He would never do anything improper; his language is as immaculate as his manners or his appearance.

What strikes us about Jeeves is that he is not essentially interested in either doing good or doing well. The only guideline for his actions is contained in the phrase he frequently uses: ''I endeavour to give satisfaction, Sir.'' It might be said that as a moral being Jeeves will be nothing but a butler. However, this sole ethical rule of loyalty to his master is interpreted by him as he thinks fit, not as the latter might wish. Jeeves's methods include a little blackmail now and again, or the occasional use of knock-out drops, but never anything as undignified as actual violence. The point about him is that he does not need it. He does not labour for success; it comes to him as the result of artistic endeavour.

Characteristically, he is a virtual dictator in questions of taste, whereas his ethics do not permit him to criticize morally any of Bertram's enterprises. However obstinately the young gentleman may behave at first, Jeeves inevitably gets his way when there are dissenting opinions about ties and suits. From time to time Bertram feels he ought to express an employer's righteous indignation about this, but his mood softens quickly, when he recalls some of his man's superhuman feats:

> More than once, as I have shown, it has been my painful task to squelch in him a tendency to get uppish and treat the young master as a serf or peon.
>
> These are grave defects.
>
> But one thing I have never failed to hand the man. He is magnetic. There is about him something that seems to soothe and hypnotize. To the best of my knowledge, he has never encountered a charging rhinoceros, but should this contingency occur, I have no doubt that the animal, meeting his eye, would check itself in mid-stride, roll over and lie purring with its legs in the air.

> "What strikes us about Jeeves is that he is not essentially interested in either doing good or doing well. The only guideline for his actions is contained in the phrase he frequently uses: 'I endeavour to give satisfaction, Sir.' It might be said that as a moral being Jeeves will be nothing but a butler."

At any rate he calmed down Aunt Dahlia [. . .]

In most cases there is a perfectly rational explanation for Jeeves's charismatic powers: he has wide experience, common sense, and psychological insight. But some of his achievements are so impressive that not only the feeble-minded Bertram is inclined to credit him with superhuman abilities. Jeeves, for instance, is able to mix a ''magic'' drink which instantly cures his master's hangovers. He moves noiselessly, and Bertram even believes that he can walk through walls. Often Jeeves is referred to as ''the higher powers,'' and on several occasions his actions are described in the words of Cowper's hymn: ''[he] moves in a mysterious way his wonders to perform.''

It appears to be appropriate, then, to call him a superman, and also a true genius, who, as genius ought to be, is bounded only by his own laws: the laws of butlering. This means that he uses his giant brain to no other effect than to steer a not too bright young man gently past the pitfalls, which threaten a life devoted to innocent pleasure. It also explains that he has high standards of taste, which he autocratically imposes on his employer.

Turning our attention to Bertram Wooster we recognize some features of the dandy in him, but they are less prominent than he himself would have liked. The general impression is one of an overgrown schoolboy with plenty of pocket money. He likes drinking in his club, where he and his pals have a great time throwing bread at each other. He is very happy playing with a toy duck in his bath. Unfortunately, he is repeatedly torn from such joys and called upon to undergo testing adventures. One of his friends observes aptly:

> We are as little children, frightened of the dark, and Jeeves is the wise nurse who takes us by the hand.

Happily, Jeeves is not only a wise nurse, but a male one, or else his protegés would be very unwilling to put so much trust in him. Women often strike fear in the hearts of Wooster and his friends:

> I've said it before, and I'll say it again—girls are rummy. Old Pop Kipling never said a truer word than when he made that crack about the f. of the s. being more d. than the m.

Bertram is particularly terrified of aunts, as he sees in them a highly repressive type of authority. Wodehouse who, by the way, was brought up mostly in boarding schools and by relatives, very rarely shows us parent-child relationships, and if he does, they are of a rather detached nature. The role of mothers in his books is an especially small one, while aunts are in abundance, and where there are aunts, there is trouble. Invariably they tyrannize their nephews, husbands or brothers. They begrudge them their favourite pleasures and seek to diminish their liberty; they want them to put on proper clothes and to be a social success; they make it their constant concern to prevent unsuitable matches and to bring about desirable ones; they are snobbish and parsimonious. Aunts have morals, of course, but these are such as to suit entirely their own inclinations while interfering grossly with the wishes of others. There is very little a Wooster-aunt would *not* do in pursuit of what she considers her right or duty. The title of a late Wodehouse novel, *Aunts Aren't Gentlemen* (1974) sums up Bertram's lifelong experience with that kind of relative. The fact that Dahlia, to whom this verdict refers, is the aunt he dislikes least, fits in with her being rather masculine in appearance and habits: she hunts, swears, gambles, and spends more money than is good for her husband's digestion.

Young women make no less trouble for Bertram than aunts. According to the different dangers they represent, they can be divided into two types, both of which we find in *The Code of the Woosters*. There is Madeline, a dreamy, sentimental girl, who reveals to Bertram on more than one occasion that he is in love with her and that she will accept him. This poses a paralyzing problem for the young hero, as his code of honour forbids him to tell a lady that he would do anything rather than marry her. On the other hand, there is Stiffy Byng, who capriciously exploits the cavalier code by demanding of her lover, a young curate, that he steal the local policeman's helmet. One is reminded of *Salomé,* when, later on, the helmet is brought in by a butler ''on a silver salver.''

There are male persons, too, of whom Wooster is afraid, older men of high professional or official authority, like the psychiatrist Sir Roderick Glossop, and Sir Watkyn Bassett, a judge, who fined him once and would love the opportunity of sending him to prison. In the absurd Wodehouse world it is not at all surprising that both gentlemen are also potential fathers-in-law for Bertram, since their daughters are determined to marry him. In the presence of persons like Sir Watkyn he is reminded of childhood fears, such as he experienced before punishment by his headmaster:

> I was feeling more as I had felt in the old days of school when going to keep a tryst with the headmaster in his study. You will recall my telling you of the time I sneaked down by night to the Rev. Aubrey Upjohn's lair in quest of biscuits and found myself unexpectedly cheek by jowl with the old bird, I in striped nonshrinkable pyjamas, he in tweeds and a dirty look. On that occasion, before parting, we had made a date for half-past four next day at the same spot.

The aged judge, though not exactly a *senex amorosus,* and possibly for some quite practical purpose, wishes to marry into the family of Roderick Spode, founder and leader of a fascist organization, called ''Saviours of Britain'' or ''Black Short.'' Roderick is the other type of man of whom Bertram is terrified, the male bully. He is of giant size, wears an impressive moustache, and, for the sake of his mission, which requires him to remain single, refrains from marrying the judge's daughter.

We are now able to take stock of the problems, fears and enemies besetting our young gentleman. At one level he is the child afraid of grown-ups, of their power and authority; he is the weak boy afraid of those who are stronger. At a second level he is an adolescent male afraid of the other sex. Girls frighten him because they do not behave according to the rules that he himself accepts; so they appear to be unpredictable, unscrupulous, and dangerous:

> I stared at the young pill, appalled at her moral code, if you could call it that. You know, the more I see of women, the more I think there ought to be a law. Something has got to be done about this sex, or the whole fabric of Society will collapse, and then what silly asses we shall all look.

Furthermore, Bertram has learnt that girls imply the threat of married life. Presumably he was once told that women wait for men to ask the relevant question, but he has found that ladies who decide to make him their husband take immediate steps to that effect, caring little whether and how he has made up his mind. And worse, the girls who go for him, are intelligent, strong-willed persons; they want to "mould" him according to their wishes. The culmination of all threats is an aunt, since she combines semi-parental authority with female unscrupulousness.

All in all, the enemy side stands—capricious girls excepted—for an orderly middle-class way of life which includes marriage, money, and a career. Judged by this standard, Bertram is bound to receive a very poor rating, as he does, for instance, from Aunt Agatha:

> It is young men like you, Bertie, who make the person with the future of the race at heart despair. Cursed with too much money, you fritter away in idle selfishness a life which might have been made useful, helpful and profitable. You do nothing but waste your time on frivolous pleasures. You are simply an anti-social animal, a drone. Bertie, it is imperative that you marry.

Marriage, it appears, is the first social obligation of man, and the sole road to a tolerably virtuous life. In the eyes of his aunt, Bertram's neglect of this duty is not only morally reprehensible and even sinful, but downright unpatriotic. The naughty nephew, on the other hand, tenaciously clings to his freedom to live a playful life of leisure. This liberty is vaguely associated with the upper classes, to which he belongs in some unspecified way. He does feel responsible for his pals, who seem to have an unlimited claim to his assistance, and for any lady who can make a credible pretence of being in distress.

Bertram might be called a strictly innocent playboy. Life, for him, is a game, interspersed with occasional test matches, which, with his blend of boy-scout and knight-errant mentality he would not have the slightest chance of winning—were it not for Jeeves.

In *The Code of the Woosters* the invincible butler is involved in a fight against Roderick Spode, who as a pseudo-superman, could be regarded as his direct antitype. Even Bertram recognizes the dictator in him at first sight:

> I don't know if you have ever seen these pictures in the papers of Dictators with tilted chins and blazing eyes, inflaming the populace with fiery words on the occasion of the opening of a new skittle alley, but that was what he reminded me of.

It is remarkable that a judge, Sir Watkyn, is Roderick's friend and ally. In combination, the fascist's physical strength and the force of the law are hard to beat. In order to help Wooster, Jeeves makes use of information received through the intelligence network of his butlers' club. There, in the headquarters of the good spirits, Spode's dark secret is known: he earns his living as a designer of ladies underwear—an occupation clearly unfavourable to the ambitions of an aspiring dictator. Jeeves tells the name of Spode's business to Bertram, who is to mention it in times of danger. The latter, equipped with what to him is a completely mysterious weapon, confidently confronts the enemy, only to find that he has forgotten the magic word. However, just in time he remembers, and the bully is reduced to a cringing coward, while Bertram is able to cast himself in the role of a stern teacher:

> 'I have not been at all satisfied with your behaviour since I came to this house. The way you were looking at me at dinner. You may think people don't notice these things, but they do.'
>
> 'Of course, of course.'
>
> 'And calling me a miserable worm.'
>
> 'I'm sorry I called you a miserable worm, Wooster. I spoke without thinking.'
>
> 'Always think, Spode. Well, that is all. You may withdraw.'

Since *The Code of the Woosters* was published in 1939, the political allusion implied by the character of Spode is obvious enough. It would be wrong, however, to emphasize the importance of such direct references to contemporary political affairs in the novels of P. G. Wodehouse. Basically Spode is just one type of evil person in Wooster-land. By making him a potential dictator Wodehouse adds topicality to an essentially timeless character, and thus connects his fairytale-world with the reader's experience. Fiction and reality, despite their apparent disparity, are shown to be related to each other, as indeed they always are, even though in popular literature such relatedness is normally of a less obvious kind. The character of Spode, when contrasted to Jeeves, points to the fact that the latter may be seen in connection with the question of leadership, which at that time was widely discussed in politics and literature.

Collaboration between Wooster and his butler began in 1917, from which time until 1941, the year of his ill-advised Berlin broadcast, the popularity of Wodehouse grew continuously. There is no need to describe at any length the social and political problems that marked Britain in those decades. Certainly the threat of another war, the struggles for power, and the hunt for jobs and money led to an acute consciousness of change—of change for the worse. In David Thomson's *England in the Twentieth Century* the chapter on the years after the First World War is given the heading "Into the Waste Land". Thomson writes:

> It seems likely that public life at all levels suffered a deterioration of standards, and a decline of taste. [. . .] and there was a propensity [. . .] to see pre-war conditions in a rosier hue than they had ever merited.

In this context the author also describes the changing role of women in society:

> The emancipation of women took a multitude of forms: from lighter clothing and shorter hair and skirts to more open indulgence in drink, tobacco, and cosmetics, from insistence on smaller families to easier facilities for divorce.

If we set against this the essentially Victorian views on women of Bertram Wooster, we can perhaps understand that he was frightened, that he feared the collapse of society and called for anti-feminine legislation, whereas, in real life, women were about to be granted equal suffrage.

In the United States depression and unemployment signalled the end of the American Dream. There, at least, the usefulness of the inherited constitution was never seriously questioned, while in Europe, not excluding Britain, the capacity of democracy for dealing with the problems that had arisen was doubted by a considerable number of people, some of whom expressed the wish for a kind of political superman.

D. H. Lawrence, for instance, believed that since hereditary aristocracy had spent its strength, and since democracy was based on a false assumption of equality, people would eventually seek their "natural" leaders:

> At last the masses will come to such men and say: "You are greater than we. Be our lords. Take our life and our death in your hands, and dispose of us according to your will. Because we see a light in your face, and burning on your mouth."

Earlier, in 1903, a writer whom Lawrence disliked, George Bernhard Shaw, had argued similarly that the "overthrow of the aristocrat has created the necessity for the Superman." He expected nothing but the worst from what he called "Proletarian Democracy," as such a government would inevitably share the low mental and moral standards of its voters: "You cannot make a silk purse out of a

sow's ear," is Shaw's caustic verdict. Therefore progress must remain an illusion, until it is given a biological basis:

> The only fundamental and possible Socialism is the socialization of the selective breeding of Man: in other terms, of human evolution. We must eliminate the Yahoo, or his vote will wreck the commonwealth.

Man, according to Shaw, must consciously develop himself into superman. The ultimate purpose of this process is not a new type of individual leader, but the breeding of nations of supermen, of "King Demos."

The Irish dramatist nearly always gave the public a chance not to take his provocative ideas seriously, and usually they were not taken seriously. Lawrence, on the other hand, left no such loop-hole to his readers, and, consequently, was received with considerable hostility. And if we look for a superman in what was popular fiction at the time, in the detective novel for instance, we do not find heroes whom we might give such a title without unduly stretching the meaning of the word. The fictional detectives are gentlemen rather than supermen; they certainly cannot be said to be "beyond good and evil."

Bertram Wooster, too, adheres strictly, if somewhat naively, to a gentleman's code, but it is this attitude that often brings him close to disaster. In both the works by Shaw and Lawrence from which the above quotations were taken there is also a typical gentleman who fails to achieve his main object, *because* he is a gentleman. Octavius, in *Man and Superman,* is a sincere, chivalrous and kind man, deeply in love with Ann, who drops him for the radical revolutionist Tanner. In "The Ladybird," Basil, a good-looking, courageous officer, adores his wife Daphne, but she is drawn irresistibly to the "natural aristocrat," the Bohemian count Psanek.

Shaw and Lawrence, though for different reasons, attack both the ideal of a gentleman and the Victorian idea of a lady. Ann is described as a person, who will "commit every crime a respectable woman can"—an attitude that with equal justice might be attributed to the typical aunt in a Wodehouse novel. And like some of the young women there, Ann is, where men are concerned, the hunter, not the prey.

So, while there is in early twentieth-century English literature a tendency to be critical of traditional standards of behaviour as regards the two sexes, as well as of the liberal belief in progress and democracy, the detective novel, on the other hand, affirms the validity of pre-War concepts of social order, justice, morals, and manners; it presents as hero a perfect gentleman in a milieu essentially unaffected by historical change.

At a superficial glance, the fictional world of P. G. Wodehouse, who was said by Orwell to have remained "mentally in the Edwardian age," seems to belong to the past in a similar way. However, strange as it may seem, his novels, quite unlike other popular fiction of the period between the Wars, reflect current issues in a remarkable degree. In this, and also in the psychology on which their characterization is based, they are closer to what is generally regarded as the mainstream of English fiction of that time. There, for instance, the influence of childhood traumata on later life is frequently pointed out and analysed. Bertram Wooster, too, is shown to suffer from the imprint left on him by adult authority when he was a boy:

> To people who don't know my Aunt Agatha I find it extraordinarily difficult to explain why it is that she has always put the wind up me to such a frightful extent. I mean, I'm not dependent on her financially or anything like that. [. . .] You see, all through my childhood and when I was a kid at school she was always able to turn me inside out with a single glance and I haven't come out from under the influence yet.

Such inhibitions are closely connected with his imagining women to be both mentally and physically stronger than he is. So he suspects that Honoria Glossop, while she was educated at Girton, was a selection for the college boxing team. One of his verdicts on modern women in general is that they are "thugs, all lipstick and cool, hard, sardonic eyes."

An error often to be found in critical opinion on Wodehouse is that he ignores the economic and social troubles of his age. In fact, the quest for money and the anguish caused by the lack of it, are recurrent motifs in his works. Wooster, it is true, lives on a secure financial basis, but several of his friends are hampered by an acute shortage of cash needed either to open a small business and get married, or, just as likely, for some utterly absurd project. Even members of wealthy aristocratic families, like the relatives of the Earl of Emsworth are sometimes forced to resort to the meanest schemes to balance their budgets.

These problems, admittedly, always affect individuals, not society as a whole. However, the stately homes of these novels seem to be pervaded by a veiled threat of change, and, at times, people have to be reminded not to forget their station, be they footmen, or secretaries, or upstart millionaires. One of the earlier Wodehouse heroes, the impecunious R. P. Smith, goes as far as to join the Socialists, but apart from his calling everyone "comrade," he does not exhibit any sign of left-wing inclinations. When Bertram's pal Bingo Little joins the Communists, he does so from purely personal motives, as the object of his devotions at the time happens to be a member of that party. The one extremist politician of any importance in a Wodehouse novel is the Fascist Spode, who, much like his counterparts of the opposite persuasion, is a violent and basically insincere person, without either taste or manners. It is because of their crudeness, mainly, that these enemies of democracy are felt to be even more disagreeable than the bourgeois aunts.

Obviously, some of the topics which aroused general interest between the Wars found their way into this fictional world, which otherwise reminds us so much of Edwardian England. Bertram's life seems to consist of repeated efforts to reconcile the troubled present with that mythical past, when gentlemen were still free and unencumbered, bound only by their honour, and when ladies still were ladies. Left to himself, he would be doomed to fail, not only through lack of strength and intelligence, but because, in order to succeed, he would have to be untrue to his code. Clearly, he needs someone able to combine in an aesthetically satisfactory way the demands of modern life with the ideals of the past. What is needed, this appears to be the message of P. G. Wodehouse, is a butler, not a Hitler.

Butlers seem to have been a specifically English upper class institution, highly esteemed as distinguished members of the household staff. They were assigned to the master of the house rather than to the lady and were, for instance, in charge of the wine cellar and responsible for the plate. They would be able to advise their masters on questions of etiquette or clothes, but would never attempt to be on familiar or intimate terms with them. They would have to be tactful, discreet, and, above all, loyal. A butler, therefore, was a person of considerable authority, and Wodehouse tells us that, as a youth, he used to be in awe of these "supermen," who "passed away with Edward the Seventh." In a country in which language and manners are regarded as distinctive of class their being able to speak like gentlemen would put them in a unique position between the separate worlds of upstairs and downstairs. This, at a time when Europe was seething with social turmoil, must have made the butler a figure of some literary potential. Was not there a type of character whom one could well imagine turning into a working class hero and strip the idle rich of their wealth and power?

Indeed, if we watch Jeeves continually solving Bertram's problems—outwitting bullies, extracting money for his friends from their tight-fisted relatives, saving him from conjugal slavery—we may wonder how the relationship between master and butler is to remain stable. Is it credible that this superman should not attempt to become ruler of him who has enlisted his help, since it is in the nature of a superman to dictate? Is it not inevitable that he should dictate in order to help? In 1902 a stage butler, created by James Matthew Barrie, actually deposed his aristocratic employers. In *The Admirable Crichton,* the hero turns out to be a "natural aristocrat," who, as the only capable person, assumes the role of leader when their ship is wrecked on a desert island. After their return to civilization the previous hierarchy is restored. Thus, this Shavian comedy of ideas demonstrates that artificial traditions are of greater weight than natural abilities in determining a person's place in English society.

Bertram, as we have seen in an earlier quotation, does feel that he has to assert himself against Jeeves and he cannot help asking himself occasionally,

> [. . .] why a man with his genius is satisfied to hang around pressing my clothes and what not. If I had half Jeeves's brain I should have a stab at being Prime Minister or something.

Thus, in an unobtrusive way, the question of the potential political ambition of a superman is raised. However, Jeeves is too complete a butler to wish to be anything else. Loyalty is essential to his character, rebellion outside the scope of his existence. Furthermore, his mental superiority makes it unnecessary for him to seek a position of dominance. His ultimate perfection consists in the fact that he does not have to become a dictator.

The relationship between Jeeves and Bertram, therefore, is beautifully balanced, neither of them wishing to alter it. One might even consider it to be an exemplary case of co-operation for their mutual benefit between capital and brains, rendering superfluous every social dispute. The butler leads without dominating, while the master is led and, yet, retains his status. The reader can safely turn his mind to Bertram's agonies and rejoice with him over his victories, knowing that he has put his trust in a reliable, unambitious superman.

So, when the novels of P. G. Wodehouse mix with the timeless material of comedy some current problems, the solution offered is of current interest too; it is also absurd and specifically English: Wodehouse advances the paradoxical idea of a 'constitutional superman,' i.e. a superman who by virtue of his inherent constitution will be ever loyal and benevolent. Psychologically, this was probably a more satisfactory way of dealing with this question in literature than the provocative attempts of Shaw and Lawrence or the conservative approach of the detective novel. Jeeves, indeed, gave satisfaction! It seems appropriate that, when in 1939 Oxford conferred upon him the honorary degree of D. Litt., Wodehouse was hailed in *The Times* as "Ruler unquestioned of the Land of Laughter."

Source: Eberhard Spath, "P. G. Wodehouse's Jeeves: The Butler as Superman" in *Functions in Literature: Essays Presented to Erwin Wolff on His Sixtieth Birthday*, edited by Ulrich Broich, Theo Stemmler, and Gerd Stratmann, Max Niemeyer Verlag, 1984, pp. 269–281.

Richard J. Voorhees

In the following essay, Voorhees recounts the long and successful career of Wodehouse and his most popular creations, the characters of Jeeves and Bertie.

The cynical and witty W. Somerset Maugham once remarked that to be a grand old man of letters it was necessary to do two things: write a great many books and live a very long life. By Maugham's law, P. G. Wodehouse (1881–1975) was a grand old man of English letters, for he published about a hundred books and lived to be nearly ninety-four. The fact is that Wodehouse was obviously one of the masters of English comedy when he was still in his thirties.

Beside Wodehouse, many British and American comic writers who flourished between World War I and World War II now look like figures in a museum or an old scrap book. The "brittle" sophistication of Noel Coward has cracks through which sentimentality is embarrassingly visible, and some charter members of the Algonquin Round Table look less like great wits than high-school wiseacres. They did what Oscar Wilde only *said* he did: they put their talents into their writing and their genius, such as it was, into their lives. Coward did most of his acting on the stage, but they did most of theirs off it. Wodehouse was not an unclubbable man, but his idea of a writer was a man who sat at his desk and wrote. Of all the Algonquins, Robert Benchley holds up best, in part perhaps because his comedy, like Wodehouse's, is without malice and without posturing.

Wodehouse did not begin as a comic novelist. He wrote boys' books with a public-school background, he wrote light romantic novels, he wrote (when he was still a struggling young author) anythings that he thought popular magazines would publish. All of the earlier work, however, was in one way or another a preparation for the pure comedy which is his contribution to English literature. This includes not only the great Blandings Castle and the Bertie and Jeeves cycles but also several other series and cycles. One features Pongo Twistleton's aged but unsinkable uncle, another the raffish Ukridge, another the innumerable nephews of Mr. Mulliner, still another a cast of mad golfers. (By the chart bound into his book *The Comic Style of P. G. Wodehouse,* Robert A. Hall, Jr. demonstrates the full extent and complexity of Wodehouse's creation.) It is remarkable that Wodehouse, having reached a rare height of comedy so soon, kept the height for such a long while. *Something Fresh* (American title, *Something New*), his first comic country-house novel, was published in 1915. *Jeeves and the Feudal Spirit* (American title, *Bertie Wooster Sees It Through*) appeared in 1954, and Wodehouse professed to write its dedication from Colney Hatch (he was always willing to make jokes about himself), but it is one of his very best books. *Aunts Aren't Gentlemen* came as late as 1974, and it can hardly be regarded as a great falling off.

Wodehouse created a fictional world as authentic in its way as that of Trollope or Balzac or Faulkner. To read his novels and short stories is to encounter again and again old acquaintances and familiar places: Bingo Little and the Drones Club, Aunt Dahlia and Market Snodsbury, Lord Emsworth and Blandings Castle, Bertie Wooster and Berkeley Mansions. Unlike the worlds of the other three writers, however, Wodehouse's is perfectly innocent; there is not a Slope in it or a Rastignac or a single Snopes. Life is pastoral even in the centre of London: there are no whores in Piccadilly Circus, no rakes in the clubs of the West End, no adulterers in Mayfair. The great English country house is a haven for the naive: the storm of life blows through it in the shape of whirlwind farce, and beyond its grounds there lie those involvements which are hazardous only by the conventions of Wodehouse's comedy: school prize-givings, village concerts, and bonny baby contests. Even the tough old explorer Plank steers clear of the last of these, knowing that

> " Wodehouse makes little attempt to keep up with the world. On the contrary, one of his distinctions is to have made anachronism a fine art."

mothers the world over become thirsty for judges' blood when their infants do not win.

Wodehouse makes little attempt to keep up with the world. On the contrary, one of his distinctions is to have made anachronism a fine art. He was born early enough to have spent his first twenty years in the Victorian Age, and he had published a dozen books before the death of Edward VII. Not only the prevailing atmosphere but also various details of all the novels and short stories that followed are those of Victorian and Edwardian times. The books also abound in anachronisms from less remote periods. In a novel published in the fifties, a nightclub entertainer sings through a megaphone, like the young Rudy Valee, and in one published in the sixties, a girl drives a "roadster." The anachronism of the novels is part of the charm and part of the comedy. (A great joke, not in the novels but begotten by them, is that in World War II the Germans, taking Wodehouse literally, parachuted into the Fen Country an agent who was instantly apprehended because he was wearing spats.)

For Wodehouse's characters, time has been arrested. They are placed once and for all at some point of youth or age, like figures in a comic strip (or gods on Olympus), and forever tied to special pursuits. Bertie Wooster toddles off to the Drones Club or tools down to the country to be caught up in some comic imbroglio. The impossible Ukridge incessantly contrives schemes for getting rich quickly, every one of which falls flat. Golfers go round and round golf courses without end.

Of all the works of Wodehouse, those about Bertie and his extraordinary valet Jeeves are the best. To begin with, they have the best characters. Bertie and Jeeves were as happy an invention for Wodehouse as Sherlock Holmes and Doctor Watson were for Arthur Conan Doyle, and Wodehouse did what Doyle could not or did not trouble to do: he surrounded his main characters with platoons of well developed subordinate ones. The young men constitute a marvelous muster roll of eccentrics and nitwits. Bingo Little, after a fatheaded bachelorhood, marries the sentimental novelist Rosie M. Banks. Gussie Fink-Nottle retires to the country and devotes himself to raising newts, though he visits other country houses occasionally and once, in pirate's costume, goes to a fancy-dress ball in London. (''There is enough sadness in the world,'' Bertie says, ''without fellows like Gussie going about in sea boots.'')

Tuppy Glossop loses Bertie's friendship for a time by betting Bertie that he cannot swing across the Drones Club swimming pool by the rings and then looping back the last ring, so that Bertie is immersed in full evening dress. Roderick Spode is no friend of Bertie's but an evil genius resembling ''those pictures . . . of dictators with tilted chins and blazing eyes, inflaming the populace with fiery words on the occasion of the opening of a new skittle alley.'' All the girls whom Bertie knows are beautiful, like those in a musical comedy, but dangerous. Roberta Wickham is discontented if she is not forcing Bertie into some lunatic enterprise. Florence Craye is determined to make him stop smoking and drinking and start reading serious books. Madeline Bassett believes that the morning mists on the meadows are the bridal veils of the elves. Worse, she believes that Bertie loves her. One of his recurrent fears is that, labouring under this delusion, she will insist on marrying him.

Most older characters are figures of authority, and aunts (as they are in Wodehouse's other books) are of special significance. Aunt Agatha, the one who, Bertie says, eats broken glass and turns into a werewolf at the full moon, is an older Florence Craye. Aunt Dahlia is his ''good and deserving aunt,'' yet she blackmails him into dreadful adventures, not, as Roberta often does, just for the hell of it, but for ends to which she is quite willing to sacrifice him. Madeline's father, a magistrate in whose court Bertie has been fined, is authority in the legal sense. Sir Roderick Glossop, a ''nerve specialist'' convinced through most of the cycle that Bertie is certifiably insane, is authority in the medical sense.

The world of Bertie and Jeeves is also populated by a number of characters who would be, without Wodehouse's variety and vivacity, mere stereotypes. One is Wodehouse's variation on the American woman grown rich by a succession of mar-

riages. Mrs. Spottsworth says to Captain Biggar, who offers to look for her lost necklace: ''I wish you would. It's not valuable—I don't suppose it cost more than ten thousand dollars—but it has a sentimental interest. One of my husbands gave it to me, I never can remember which.'' Captain Biggar is a variation on the virile outdoor man, a good-natured joke on Kipling, Haggard, and their imitators. He is a great white hunter who lives by a strict code, loves the Empire, fears nothing, masters numerous African dialects. (Having become engaged to Mrs. Spottsworth, he hums a Swahili wedding march.) The explorer Plank is a variation on the same type, not a modest fellow like Biggar, but a blusterer.

Wodehouse can be as frugal as he is prodigal, and a few characters are so many interchangeable parts. Madeline Bassett appears in *The Mating Season* (1949) and Phyllis Mills in *Jeeves in the Offing* (1960), but it would scarcely matter if they changed places. Stephanie Byng is not much more than an alias for Roberta Wickham, and Harold Pinker is Reginald Herring again with one difference: on the football field, Pinker is a marvel of dexterity, but he cannot cross a room without overturning furniture. D'Arcy Cheesewright and Orlo Porter are clones of Roderick Spode.

There is nobody like Bertie. At the start of the cycle he is, as Wodehouse himself remarked, a fairly standard model of the ''knut,'' the dandy and silly ass of the Victorian and Edwardian music hall. Wodehouse developed him in some of the early stories and then deliberately fixed his character when he discovered that he was on to a good thing. Though fixed, Bertie has contradictions that make him more than a ''humour'' character and a decency and sweetness that make him always likeable. The narrator of all but one of his adventures, he quotes right and left from the great literature of the Western World, but he frequently remarks that he ''was made to read'' at school a writer whom he quotes. He now concentrates on thrillers, racing papers, and detective stories, on which he considers himself an expert. He dislikes people who write serious books. Lady Melvern is ''a pal of my Aunt Agatha . . . . A very vicious speciment. She wrote a book on social conditions in India when she came back from the Durbar.'' (Wodehouse probably has in mind *Mother India,* the best seller by Katherine Mayo, which purports to be an exposé of the ignorance and squalor of India. Evelyn Waugh made jokes about it in two of his novels, and Norman Douglas wrote an indignant reply to it called *How About Europe?*)

Though he is the narrator of more volumes than there are in *The Music of Time,* Bertie is ''a spent force'' after writing a short article on the well-dressed man for Aunt Dahlia's magazine. Indeed, he is, whenever he is allowed to be, as languid as any fop who ever wore a wig in a Restoration comedy. In *The Inimitable Jeeves* (1923) he sits ''in the old flat one night trying to muster up enough energy to go to bed.'' His summum bonum is a quiet life with plenty of sleep and plenty of good food, drink, and tobacco. He suffers ''agony'' when, visiting Aunt Agatha, he must go without cocktails and lie on the floor in his bedroom to exhale cigarette smoke up the fireplace chimney. Without Jeeves, he could not get through the routine of an ordinary day, much less get out of the predicaments into which he is repeatedly thrust. Each time Jeeves extricates him, Bertie must pay, usually by surrendering a piece of wearing apparel of which Jeeves disapproves: an unorthodox dinner jacket, a cummerbund, a blue Alpine hat with a pink feather.

But Bertie's indolence, self-indulgence, and incompetence are allied with innocence, with vulnerability, with nostalgia for times more decorous than his own. In one of his favourite clichés, he calls women ''the delicately nurtured,'' but he is more sensitive than most of the women he knows. The food crank Laura Pike shocks him by talking clinically about the organs of digestion, and he dislikes The Palace of Beauty at the British Empire Exposition at Wembley, where girls portray famous women through the ages. A beautiful woman ''loses a lot of her charm if you have to stare at her in a tank. Moreover, it gave me a rum feeling of having wandered into the wrong bedroom of a country house.''

Bertie has contradictory visions of himself. In one he is the total loss that Aunt Agatha thinks him, but in the other he is the hero of high adventure. He has the ''keen intelligence'' of a Sherlock Holmes, ''broods'' much, sometimes ''tensely,'' and ''muses,'' like Tennyson's Lancelot. There is something of Sabatini's Captain Blood in him: ''. . . though my voice was suave, a close observer in a position to watch my eyes would have noticed a steely glint.'' Bertie is like a boy who knows pretty well what he is but likes to live a fantasy life derived from his reading. He cannot be blind to the disparity between his style and his matter: ''Those who know Bertram Wooster best are aware that he is a man of sudden, strong enthusiasms and that, when in the grip of one of these, he becomes a remorseless machine—tense, absorbed, single-minded. It was

so in the matter of this banjolele-playing of mine.'' Jeeves objects to the banjolele, and Bertie has to give it up.

The vast differences between Bertie and Jeeves do not include one of age. There is merely a vague impression to the contrary, fortified by a few book jackets. Some picture Jeeves as a haughty major-domo, others as a kindly elder statesman. On the jacket of *Jeeves and the Tie that Binds* (1971) Osbert Lancaster draws him florid, portly, virtually bald, which is to say that he draws him as Wodehouse's classic *butler.* Bertie says that Jeeves is tall and slender and dark, and there is no more reason for Jeeves to be much older than Bertie than for Crichton to be much older than Lord Loam. Still it is easy to understand why, for many readers, Jeeves should appear to be at least twice the age of Bertie. In the first place, he knows more and thinks better. Whereas Bertie is addicted to detective stories, Jeeves is devoted to Spinoza (somewhere Bertie says that Jeeves has probably got to the point in Spinoza where one discovers that the butler did it). He has a wide acquaintance with other philosophers and with literature and is equipped with a jeweller's knowledge of precious stones. He knows the technical term for the Roman gladiator who fought with net and trident (*retiarius*) and the exact distance between London and Harrogate (two hundred and six miles).

Jeeves' manner and speech are the reverse of Bertie's. Bertie says, ''Right ho,'' and Jeeves says, ''Very good, sir.'' Quoting Henley's ''Invictus,'' Jeeves begs Bertie's pardon just before coming to the word ''bloody.'' Yet Jeeves is not all propriety. He has a strong strain of the gamester in him and bets as readily on the sack race at a village sports as he does on the horses at Ascot or the roulette wheels at Monte Carlo. Furthermore, he is capable of great physical violence, at least twice knocking people out, once with a putter and once with a cosh. He recovers the confidential records of his club by slipping a Mickey Finn into the thief's drink and tells Bertie that he never travels without one or two.

The long association of Bertie and Jeeves is only half plausible, since Bertie needs Jeeves but Jeeves does not need Bertie. Why, then, does Jeeves not leave? Indeed, how does it happen in the first place that a superman like Jeeves (not Nietzsche's kind: Jeeves once tells Bertie that Nietzsche is ''fundamentally unsound'') is unengaged just when Bertie has been obliged to dismiss his valet? Such questions are hardly to the purpose, for the relationship of Bertie and Jeeves depends not upon plausibility but on convention. Wodehouse's comedy descends from the ''artificial comedy'' of the seventeenth- and eighteenth-century stage, and the figures of the clever servant and the stupid master descend from more distant sources in classical comedy. Wodehouse adapted them, but luckily he did more than that; he invented his own version of an archetype and created a new myth.

Some works of Wodehouse are an ingenious mixture of modes, but the Bertie and Jeeves books are pure comedy. Their plots are better than those of most of the other books, and Wodehouse was one of the great plot-makers of literature. He composed rapidly (Guy Bolton said that to save time Wodehouse fed a continuous roll of paper into his typewriter, later cutting it into eleven-inch pages), but he plotted slowly. (At a manuscript sale at Sotheby's, Richard Usborne saw seventy pages of pencilled notes for *Jeeves in the Offing*.) He once remarked that his brain almost ''came unstuck'' as he created complication upon complication.

Wodehouse finds plenty of scope for farce in a big house in Wimbledon, and he contrives excellent foolery in a small cottage with a potting shed, but he discovers the ideal theatre in the stately home of England. With its numerous rooms and extensive grounds, it becomes under his direction a labyrinth, an obstacle course, and a huge booby trap. With its large staff of servants and its many guests, it is also a great playhouse for the disguise, impersonation, and mistaken identity which are staples of farce. On Wodehouse's stage, beards and moustaches are properties as common as umbrellas and muffins. Sir Roderick Glossop (of all people) impersonates a butler, and Jeeves impersonates Inspector Witherspoon of Scotland Yard. In a single novel Bertie impersonates Gussie Fink-Nottle, and Gussie impersonates Bertie. In another novel Bertie thinks that Plank is an old labourer on his own estate, and Plank thinks that Bertie is, first, a reporter come to interview him about his Brazilian expedition and, second, a cook named Alpine Joe.

Into the fabric of farce Wodehouse weaves threads from types of literature vastly different from farce, conspicuously the sentimental fiction which he called ''bilge.'' Madeline Bassett tells Bertie the plot of *Mervyn Keene, Clubman,* a novel by Rosie M. Banks, which sounds as if it were inspired by Ouida. Keene is a handsome officer in the Coldstream Guards. He loves the beautiful Cynthia Grey but cannot declare himself, since she is engaged to

another. He takes the blame for a crime committed by her brother and, released from prison, becomes a beachcomber in the South Seas. He breaks into Government House to get a rose which Cynthia has worn in her hair, and she tells him that her brother made a deathbed confession. Her husband, thinking Keene a burglar, shoots him. When the Governor rushes in to ask whether anything is missing, ''Only a rose,'' says Cynthia, in a nearly inaudible voice.

Wodehouse finds it profitable to be in debt to Rosie M. Banks. Before Bingo Little marries Rosie, he has, as it were, enacted a score of her novels in goofy versions of his own. Other Wodehouse clowns slog through bilge, and Catsmeat Potter-Pirbright, more cynic than clown, recommends the most abominable brand of it. He proposes to write letters to Madeline Bassett for Gussie Fink-Nottle and say that Gussie has dictated them because of a broken wrist: ''He gave it a nasty wrench while stopping a runaway horse and . . . saving a little child from a hideous death. A golden-haired child if you will allow yourself to be guided by me, with blue eyes, pink cheeks, and a lisp.''

For purposes of burlesque and parody, Wodehouse also borrows from crook stories and racetrack melodramas. Village sports include footraces for boys ''whose voices have not broken before the second Sunday in Epiphany,'' girls entered in egg and spoon races are bribed and disqualified, mysterious voices are heard in the shrubberies, and there are fears that the favourite in one event will be drugged.

Such happenings as these, like all others in Wodehouse, are related in a prose that Hilaire Belloc called the best of his time. The basis of it is Wodehouse's public-school education at Dulwich, where the Bible, Shakespeare, and nineteenth-century writers were emphasized, together with the usual Latin and Greek. Belloc must have admired the grace and lucidity of it, and perhaps he admired the complexity that makes it inimitable. Wodehouse lays tribute upon great writers, but (just as he exploits clichés of character and plot from subliteratures) he also exploits vocabularies and idioms from a great range of written and spoken English: not only bilge and thrillers but also popular science, newspaper editorials, the argot of trades and professions, slang, sermons, the talk of schoolmasters and schoolboys. The style is not altogether unlike the talk of a bright schoolboy newly aware of language, fascinated by great poetry and archaic expressions and fascinated as well by slang and technical terms. But it is, of course, a Platonic form of that talk: sophisticated, widely informed, skillfully controlled in all its incongruities.

The style suits Wodehouse as narrator. Properly adapted, it suits most of his comic characters. And it suits Bertie best of all, for Bertie is a hero educated but not intellectual, of wide reading but erratic memory, enthusiastic but puerile. Bertie, however, has Wodehouse's excellent ear, and at his very vaguest his speech may have the rhythm of a good nursery rhyme or riddle. With misty recollections of Keats' "On First Looking into Chapman's Homer," he asks, "Jeeves, who was the fellow who looking at something felt like someone looking at something?" In grammar and diction he is a purist, though fallible, and argues points of usage with Aunt Dahlia even at farcical crises.

Bertie's style incorporates some devices of Restoration comedy and later forms of the comedy of manners. For example, with an adverbial construction like "quite an indecently large stock of money," he transforms an objective statement into a subjective one, adding an emotional dimension and a fop's flourish. One thing that he does not use is obscenity. As Orwell said, he is remarkable for the purity of his language, since a comic writer sacrifices a great source of comedy when he refrains from obscenity. In the later novels, however, there are occasional *hells* and *damns* and a rare *bastard* or *bitch*. Now and then Bertie gets halfway across the frontier of vulgarity: "I shouldn't be at all surprised if Jeeves' three aunts shut him up when he starts talking, remembering that at the age of six the child Jeeves didn't know the difference between the poet Burns [whom Jeeves has just quoted] and a hole in the ground."

Wodehouse's figures of speech are like those of no other writer in English. One character stands "scrutinizing a safe and heaving gently like a Welsh rarebit about to come to the height of its fever," and another looks like "a halibut which has just been asked by another halibut to lend it a quid until next Wednesday." Wodehouse is endlessly inventive, and for the speech of Bertie he invents a particularly exuberant and lunatic kind of poetry. Bertie's mind is less literal than metaphorical, but his metaphors are often marvelously mixed. The commotion that Roberta Wickham is always starting, he says, is very amusing to her but not to the unfortunate toads beneath the harrow whom she ruthlessly plunges into the soup.

Bertie employs such learned devices as the transferred epithet, repeatedly taking grave sips of coffee and smoking meditative cigarettes, and his hyperboles and understatements are probably the best in Wodehouse. Sometimes he appears to forget that there is a singular in English, and if two constables enter a room, he says that the place is filling up with rozzers. At the other extreme, drawing upon the Biblical knowledge for which he won a prize at school, he refers to "that time when there was all that unpleasantness with the cities of the plain" and speaks of the French Revolution as "the time when there was all that unpleasantness over in France."

In the Wodehouse novels there are more quotations and allusions than in those of Aldous Huxley and Anthony Powell combined. They may involve Sir Isaac Newton (Newton's sad words to his dog Diamond, who had eaten a manuscript), a movie actress, or an obscure fact (for example, that William Gladstone was a disciple of the quack Fletcher and chewed each mouthful of food thirty-two times). Bertie often relies on a basic stock which Wodehouse got at Dulwich. There is a good deal from the Bible and still more from Shakespeare. Bertie has met a schoolmistress named Miss Mapleton: "'Twas on a summer evening in my tent, the day I overcame the Nervii." He declares, like other characters in Wodehouse, that he will meet someone at Philippi. (Evelyn Waugh admired Wodehouse greatly. Is it a coincidence or a tribute and inside joke that in *Men at Arms* Guy Crouchback says to Frank De Souza, "Well, we shall meet again," and De Souza says, like the ghost of Caesar to Brutus, "At Philippi?") Bertie draws upon Tennyson and Browning but also on minor poets of the nineteenth century like Thomas Moore and even Felicia Hemans. He remembers the peri "who stood disconsolate at the gate of paradise" and notes that the laugh of Honoria Glossop sounds "like waves breaking on a stern and rock-bound coast." (He also says, in other places, that it sounds like a train going through a tunnel or a troop of cavalry crossing a tin bridge.)

The rightness of the formulas on which Wodehouse constructed the world of Bertie and Jeeves is proved by his comparative failures when he departs from the formulas. He makes Jeeves, not Bertie, the narrator of "Bertie Changes his Mind," and by doing so he changes the whole nature of the world. It is one thing for Bertie to tell how Jeeves extricated him from a scrape and another for Jeeves to tell how he deliberately got Bertie *into* a scrape. It is one thing for Bertie to admit cheerfully that he is a chump and another for Jeeves to confide cooly that Bertie has no intellect. To prevent Bertie from inviting his sister and her children to live with him, Jeeves traps him into making a speech at a girls' school. The speech is a disaster, and Bertie drops the notion of an enlarged household. Jeeves rescues Bertie from the school but takes some pleasure from Bertie's distress. The story is, in effect, advice to beginning valets about keeping the upper hand, and it introduces into the stories what Bertie never introduces, the practical politics and cruelty of the real world. Moreover, the speech of Jeeves, amusing when contrasted with Bertie's, is not so amusing in itself. One may call it *Times* Augustan, as Richard Usborne does, or bogus Augustan, as Evelyn Waugh called the prose of Winston Churchill. Instead of the Wooster music, the wild Wooster poetry, it has order, dignity, irony; instead of amiability, it has a somewhat stuffy reserve.

In *Ring for Jeeves* (1953) the departures and failures are greater; the hard facts of social change have invaded Wodehouse's idyllic country-house world. Though he is Chief Constable of the county, Colonel Wyvern cannot get the kind of servants who once graced the stately homes of England. His butler is not well-stricken in years, corpulent, and nicely soaked in port from the pantry but a whipper-snapper of sixteen, and his cook is an impudent fifteen. The ninth earl of Rowcester, the hero of the novel, is obliged to sell Rowcester Abbey because he cannot pay the taxes on it. To Captain Biggar, long out of the mother country, Jeeves explains: "Socialistic legislation has sadly depleted the resources of England's hereditary artistocracy. We are living now in what is known as the Welfare State, which means — broadly — that everybody is completely destitute." Wodehouse loved the England of his earlier years and, though he did not live in England after 1940, he evidently could not in his later years refrain from a kind of commentary which he had never made before.

Worse for *Ring for Jeeves,* Bertie is absent from the novel. Jeeves has not left him but serves Bill Rowcester as butler, not valet, while Bertie attends a school designed to teach the aristocracy to fend for itself, m'lord. Mr. Wooster, though his finances are still quite sound, feels that it is prudent to build for the future, in case the social revolution should set in with even greater severity." The absence of Bertie leaves a vacuum which cannot be filled, since his character, style, and point of view are vital to the Bertie and Jeeves books. Wodehouse relates *Ring for Jeeves* in the style of his other comic novels, and

that style is one of his great accomplishments, but the style of Bertie is a greater one. Without Bertie, Jeeves is diminished, for his character needs the dialogue between him and Bertie more than Bertie's does and, having no one to trade quotations with, he quotes too much.

With the loss of Bertie goes the loss of other important characters in the cycle like Bertie's aunts, Sir Roderick Glossop, Gussie Fink-Nottel, etc., and Wodehouse replaces them with characters modeled on those of his earlier comic romances. Jill (a favourite name in the earlier books) Wyvern moves "with a springy step" and once was "a flashy outside right in the hockey field," but she is inclined to great good news with squeals of delight. Wodehouse brings her up to date by making her a licensed veterinarian, the first professional woman in the novels. The impoverished Bill (another favourite name) Rowcester becomes a bookie with insufficient capital and a disguise of eye patch, false moustache, and loud checked coat. Bill's brother-in-law, an aristocrat compelled to go to work at a big London department store, talks of the place as if it were a military organization and is intended as a comic character, but he is only a mischievous fool. Mrs. Spottsworth and Captain Biggar save the novel, but it barely survives a major calamity. Jeeves becomes assistant to Bill on the racecourse and wears a dreadful checked suit and false moustache. The authentic Jeeves might have wished these on Bertie, but he would never have worn them for Bertie, much less for Bill Rowcester.

In virtually all the other Bertie and Jeeves novels, Wodehouse obeys the bylaws that he enacted for his world, with happy results for the commonwealth of literature. Given the word *valet* in an association test, thousands of readers would think of Jeeves. (Given the word *butler,* they would be less likely to think of James Barrie's Crichton than to think of Beach or another of Wodehouse's butlers.) Bertie is a character of almost Dickensian vividness and a narrator whose voice is unmistakable.

Wodehouse's farce has the ingenuity and speed of Feydeau's, but none of the sex. Visiting country houses, Bertie goes into a girl's bedroom only by accident, and bedroom farce is a business of practical jokes, of puncturing hotwater bottles and making apple-pie beds. Like the Sherlock Holmes stories, the Bertie and Jeeves books evoke a nostalgia for the Victorian-Edwardian world. But the Holmes stories are, after all, crime stories and, as Gavin Lambert has shown, there is a sense of evil in them that grows greater as Doyle grows older. In the entire world of Bertie and Jeeves, however, Holmes himself could not discover the slightest trace of wickedness. Anyone who dismisses that world as a bauble because it is buoyant makes a great eror. For it is in fact the creation of an artist whose adroitness is one of the distinctions of English comedy.

Source: Richard J. Voorhees, ''Wodehouse at the Top of His Form'' in *The University of Windsor Review*, Vol. XVI, No. 1, Fall-Winter 1981, pp. 13–25.

Sources

Aldridge, John W., ''P. G. Wodehouse: The Lesson of the Young Master'' in *New World Writing*, 1958 annual, p.186.

Quinton, Anthony, ''P. G. Wodehouse and the Comic Tradition,'' introduction to *P. G. Wodehouse: A Comprehensive Bibliography and Checklist*, ed. Eileen McIlvaine, Detroit: Omnigraphics, 1990, p. xiv.

———, Review of *Carry On, Jeeves*, in *New York Times*, October 23, 1927, p. 28.

———, Review, *Carry On, Jeeves*, in *Saturday Review of Literature*, December 3, 1927.

Further Reading

Hall, Robert A., *The Comic Style of P. G. Wodehouse*, Hamden, CT: Archon Books, 1974.
    A study of the comedic form, plots and characters in the fiction of Wodehouse.

Olson, Kirby, ''Bertie and Jeeves at the End of History: P. G. Wodehouse as Political Scientist,'' in *Humor: The International Journal of Humor Research*, Vol. 9, No. 1, 1996, pp. 73–88.
    An ironic reading of politics in Wodehouse's ''Jeeves and Wooster'' stories.

Voorhees, Richard J., *P. G. Wodehouse*, New York: Twayne, 1966.
    A literary biography by an eminent Wodehouse scholar.

———, ''Wodehouse at the Top of His Form,'' in *University of Windsor Review*, Vol. 16, No. 1, 1981, pp. 13–25.
    An analysis of Wodehouse's best writing.

Wodehouse, P. G., *America, I Like You*, New York: Simon & Schuster, 1956.
    Wodehouse's autobiographical account of his life in the United States.

Lullaby

Leslie Marmon Silko

1981

Leslie Marmon Silko is one of the most celebrated Native American writers of her generation. Her short story ''Lullaby'' first appeared in *Storyteller* (1981), a book in which she interweaves autobiographical reminiscences, short stories, poetry, photographs of her family (taken by her father) and traditional songs. The book as a whole is concerned with the oral tradition of storytelling in Native American culture. Through a variety of formats, Silko attempts to reproduce the effect of oral storytelling in a written English form. She is also concerned with the transformative power of storytelling in the lives of her characters and the role of storytelling in maintaining cultural traditions and intergenerational ties, particularly in a matrilinear line from grandmother to granddaughter.

''Lullaby'' is one of the most noted pieces in *Storyteller.* It is told from the perspective of an old woman reminiscing about some of the most tragic events of her life, all of which seem to be precipitated by the intrusions of white authority figures into her home. She recalls being informed of the death of her son in war, the loss of her children taken by white doctors, and the exploitative treatment of her husband by the white rancher who employs him. Furthermore, these events seem to have led to a long-term alienation between the old woman and her husband. Yet she also recalls strong ties with her own grandmother and mother.

While much of the story is told in terms of these reminiscences, the present tense of the story finds the old woman searching for her husband at the local bar. The lullaby she sings to her husband at the end of the story, as he lies dying in the snow, brings the oral tradition full circle, as she recalls this song that her grandmother sang to her as a child. In addition to appearing in the *Chicago Review* and *Yardbird Reader*, ''Lullaby'' has been anthologized in *The Best American Short Stories* of 1975, edited by Martha Foley.

Author Biography

Leslie Marmon Silko was born on March 5, 1948, in Albuquerque, New Mexico. Silko was raised on the Laguna Pueblo Reservation in northern New Mexico, her cultural and ethnic heritage a mix of Laguna Pueblo, Plains Indian, Mexican, and Anglo-American. She attended schools run by the Bureau of Indian Affairs (BIA) and Catholic schools in Albuquerque. Also central to her education were several generations of women in her family, such as her grandmother and aunt, from whom she learned much about her cultural traditions. In 1969, she received her B.A. from the University of New Mexico, where she graduated summa cum laude. Her short story ''The Man to Send Rain Clouds'' was first published while she was still in college, and has since been reprinted in several anthologies. She briefly attended law school, but left in order to pursue a career in writing. Silko has taught at Navajo Community College in Tsaile, Arizona; the University of New Mexico; and the department of English at the University of Arizona, Tucson. She spent two years living in Alaska, where she wrote her first novel, *Ceremony* (1977).

Silko's writing emerged from the revival of Native American literature in the 1970s referred to as the Native American Renaissance. It was the positive critical response to *Ceremony* which first established Silko's place as one of the most celebrated Native American writers of her generation. *Ceremony* established her characteristic literary style of incorporating the oral tradition of storytelling in Native American culture into the novelistic, poetic, and short story form. As a result, some of Silko's earlier short stories garnered renewed attention, and many of them have since been anthologized in collections of Native American literature. Her collection *Storyteller*, in which ''Lullaby'' appears, combines fiction and non-fiction stories with poetry and photographs taken by her father, a professional photographer.

Upon receiving a distinguished MacArthur Foundation grant in 1981, Silko was able to use her time working on her epic-scale novel *Almanac of the Dead* (1992). *Almanac of the Dead* focuses on a mixed-race family over five centuries of struggle between Native American and European American cultures. The work took her ten years to write, and has received mixed critical response. Her series of films based on Laguna oral traditions was made possible by a grant from the National Endowment for the Humanities. Silko has since taken up the production of books made by her own hands, under her own imprint Flood Plains Press, in addition to publishing a collection of essays on contemporary Native American life. Her novel *Gardens in the Dunes* was published in 1999.

Plot Summary

''Lullaby'' begins with Ayah, an old Native American woman, leaning against a tree near a stream, reminiscing about some of the most tragic events of her life, as well as about the role of her grandmother in some of the most happy events of her life: ''She was an old woman now, and her life had become memories.'' She recalls watching her mother weaving outside on a big loom, while her grandmother spun wool into yarn. She remembers her mother and the old woman who helped her give birth to her first child, Jimmie. Yet she also recalls the time the white man came to her door to announce that Jimmie had died in a helicopter crash in the war. Because Ayah could not speak English, her husband, Chato, had to translate the tragic news to her.

Even more devastating, however, is her memory of the time her two young children, Danny and Ella, were taken away from her. White doctors came to her house, trying to get her to sign some piece of paper. Because she did not know English, and could not read, she signed the paper simply out of fear, in hopes that they would go away. After she signed it, however, they attempted to take her children away with them. She grabbed the two children and ran up into the hills. She waited there all day, until Chato came home. The doctors had chased her at first, but gave up and left. When the doctors came back the

Leslie Marmon Silko

next day, with a policeman from the Bureau of Indian Affairs, Chato spoke to them, and then explained to her that the paper she had signed gave them permission to take the children away. Their grandmother had died of tuberculosis, and they claimed the children had contracted it as well. After this, Ayah blamed Chato for the loss of the children, because he had taught her how to sign her name. This created a rift in their relationship, and they began to sleep apart.

The first time the children were brought back to visit, they are accompanied by two white women. Ayah recalls that the white women were nervous and anxious in her home, were perturbed when the children spoke to her in their native language, and judged her to be an unfit mother for them. The last time the children were brought to visit, they could no longer even speak to their mother in her own language, and Ella, who was taken away as an infant, did not seem to recognize her.

She also remembers when, years later, the white rancher said Chato was too old to work any more, and threatened to evict them. After the couple began receiving federal assistance checks in order to survive, Chato would cash the check and immediately go spend it at the bar. In the present tense of the story, Ayah goes there to look for him. When she

does not find him there, she goes out in the snow to search for him, and comes upon him walking toward home. When they stop to rest, he lies down in the snow, and she realizes that he is dying. She tucks a blanket around him and begins to sing a lullaby her grandmother had sung when she was little: ''And she sang the only song she knew how to sing for babies. She could not remember if she had ever sung it to her children, but she knew that her grandmother had sung it and her mother had sung it.''

Characters

Ayah

Ayah is the main character and narrator. In the present tense of the story, Ayah is an old woman reflecting on her personal history: memories of her grandmother weaving outside, the birth of her first child, the death of her child Jimmie in war, and the loss of her two young children, who were taken away by white doctors. Ayah also recalls her husband, Chato, who, because he could speak English, served as the go-between in many of her significant interactions with white authorities. In the present time of the story, Ayah goes out to look for Chato, who has not yet come home for the evening. She looks for him at the bar, where he can usually be found on the days he receives and cashes their small assistance check, but he is not there. Leaving the bar, she eventually comes upon him walking home. They stop to rest, and Chato lies down in the snow. Seeing that he is about to die, Ayah wraps a blanket around him and sings him a lullaby she learned from her grandmother.

Chato

Chato is the husband of the story's narrator, Ayah. Because he speaks English and she does not, Chato serves the role of go-between in the family's interactions with white authority figures. When white people come to the door to inform them that their son, Jimmie, has died in the war, it is Chato who must translate the devastating news to Ayah. Chato works for the white rancher, who shows no sympathy when his leg is injured on the job. When the white doctors, and then the BIA police, come to take their two young children away from them, it is again Chato who must communicate to Ayah that she has unknowingly signed the children away to the white people. Because she blames him for the loss of their children, Ayah no longer sleeps with her husband after that point. As an old man, during the present tense of the story, Chato sometimes becomes confused, and she finds him walking toward the ranch, as if they still needed him to work there. On the days when their assistance check arrives, Chato cashes it and heads straight for the bar. After Ayah finds him walking in the snow, Chato lays down to rest. He dies, as Ayah sings him a lullaby.

Danny

Danny is Ayah and Chato's young son who is taken away from them by the white doctors.

The Doctors

The white doctors come to take Ayah and Chato's children away from them, because they have contracted tuberculosis from their grandmother. The doctors intimidate Ayah into signing a piece of paper which gives them permission to take the children away forever. Although she has no idea what she is signing, she does so because she is afraid of them and wants them to go away. When they try to take the children, she grabs them and runs for the hills. They give up on chasing her, but come back later with a police officer and take the children, after which she rarely sees them again.

Ella

Ella is Ayah and Chato's young daughter who is taken away from them by the white doctors.

Grandmother

Ayah's grandmother does not appear in the present time of the story, but only in Ayah's reminiscences. Ayah recalls her grandmother spinning yarn from wool and passing on traditional songs. The grandmother is significant as the generational link in the matrilinear culture whereby women pass on tradition in the form of stories. When Chato is dying, Ayah sings him a lullaby her grandmother had sung to her.

Jimmie

Jimmie was Ayah's first-born child. When he died in a helicopter crash in the war, a white man came to the door to inform the family. The army blanket Ayah wraps around herself at the beginning of the story, and her dying husband Chato at the end of the story, had been sent to her by Jimmie while he was in combat.

Media Adaptations

- *Running on the Edge of the Rainbow: Laguna Stories & Poems* is a videorecording made in 1978 in which Leslie Silko shares stories and poems with friends and discusses the role of storytelling in Laguna culture. It is directed by Denny Carr in cooperation with the University of Arizona, Radio-TV-Film Bureau.

- *Native American Novelists* is a videorecording of interviews with four Native American novelists, including Leslie Silko, N. Scott Momaday, James Welch, and Gerald Robert Vizenor. It was produced in 1995, directed by Matteo Bellinelli and written by Andrea Belloni.

The Policeman

The B.I.A. (Bureau of Indian Affairs) policeman appears the second time the white doctors come to claim Ayah and Chato's children. This character is significant in that he represents the Native American who helps the white authorities in the oppression and exploitation of other Native Americans.

The Rancher

The white rancher is Chato's employer. The rancher is another figure of white authority who contributes to the most tragic events in Ayah's life. When Chato injures his leg on the job, the rancher does not pay him. When he determines that Chato is too old to work, he evicts them from their house.

White Women

On the few occasions when Ayah's children are brought back to visit her, they are accompanied by white women, presumably teachers or social-worker-type figures. On the first visit, there is a blonde white woman and a thin white woman. They both seem to Ayah to be anxious and nervous in her home, and appear to be judging it as an unfit environment for raising the children. The white

Topics for Further Study

- Many of Silko's stories address the issue of the role of tradition in contemporary Native American culture, and particularly the role of the storyteller. Read a short story by a different contemporary Native American writer such as Paula Gunn Allen, Louise Erdrich, or Sheman Alexie. In what ways does this author address similar or different issues within Native American culture? What role does tradition play in the story, as compared to Silko's story? How do the characters in the story reconcile Native American tradition and history with the conditions of contemporary Native American life?

- There are hundreds of Native American tribes on the North American continent (such as Navajo, Cherokee, Chippewa, Pueblo, etc.), yet one complaint many Native Americans have is that mainstream American culture does not recognize the tremendous diversity of cultures among these tribes. Find out more about the history, traditions, and contemporary conditions of one particular Native American tribe. In what ways is it different from or similar to that of other tribes?

- In addition to fiction, Silko and other writers of the 1970s Native American literary renaissance wrote collections of poetry. Pick one Native American writer and read several of her or his poems. In what ways do they address similar or different concerns from those addressed in Silko's fiction? In what ways does the poetic form communicate ideas differently from the fictional prose form?

- Learn more about contemporary Native American visual art forms, such as drawing, painting, jewelry-making, and other crafts. In what ways do these visual forms grapple with similar concerns about the role of tradition in contemporary Native American culture? To what extent are the forms, process, and use of this art different from or similar to that of traditional Native American culture? What role does art play in contemporary Native American culture?

- The 1970s, during which Silko's short story ''Lullaby'' was first written, were a significant time in the history of Native American struggles with mainstream American culture. Learn more about the political, cultural and economic struggles of Native American tribes from the 1960s through the 1990s. What national organizations of Native Americans are active today? What has changed as a result of these struggles? Was has not changed?

---

women also seem perturbed when Ayah's children speak to her in their native language.

Themes

Storytelling

The role of storytelling in Native American culture is a theme central to all of Silko's work. ''Lullaby'' appears in a collection entitled *Storyteller,* which is especially concerned with ways of translating the oral tradition of storytelling into a written English format. Ayah, the old woman who is the main character, does not tell a story directly to another person; however, the story is comprised of her reminiscences, which function as a form of internal storytelling. This written story captures the structure of an oral story, in that it weaves past memories and present occurrences through a series of associations, rather than in a set chronological order.

Tradition and Change

In all of her writing, Silko is concerned with the ways in which Native American traditions can be adapted to the contemporary circumstances of Native American life. Her characters are often caught between a traditional and a modern way of life. In this story, Ayah recalls such traditions as her mother weaving blankets on a loom set outside, while her grandmother spun the yarn from wool. This memory is evoked by Ayah's use of the old army blanket her son Jimmie had sent home from the war. Looking down at her worn shoes in the snow, she recalls the warm buckskin moccasins Native Americans had once worn. At the point of her husband's death, Ayah falls back on the singing of a traditional lullaby sung by her grandmother. The story suggests that, at such a profound event as the death of a loved one, such traditions such serve an important purpose, even in modern life.

Matrilinear Relationships

Silko's stories are often concerned with the granddaughter-grandmother relationship as a link between modern and traditional Native American culture. Silko herself learned much about her own tribal traditions from her grandmother and older female relatives. In this story, Ayah, as an old woman, recalls traditional forms of blanket-weaving, as practiced by her mother and grandmother. She also recalls giving birth to her first child with the aid of her mother. When her husband is dying, she turns to a traditional lullaby sung by her grandmother in order to comfort him through the process of death.

Death and Loss

Ayah's reminiscences focus mainly on the major losses in her life. The strong sense of nostalgia in the story expresses a sadness over the loss of traditional culture and ways of life, as well as pain and bitterness over the loss of all three of her children. Ayah had lost two infants already, but only to natural causes, and was comforted by burying them in the land surrounding her home. The loss of her other children to white authorities, however, she finds more traumatizing. Her first child, Jimmie, dies in a helicopter crash during the war. She learns that his body may have been burned, so she does not have the opportunity to mourn his loss in a more traditional way. She later loses her two young children, Danny and Ella, to the white doctors who intimidate her into signing an agreement allowing them to take the children to a sanitarium. Ayah's final loss comes at the end of the story, when her husband Chato lies down in the snow, and she realizes that he is dying. In this story, Silko is concerned with the ways in which storytelling can heal and transform the experience of loss—both personal and cultural.

Racial and Cultural Oppression

All of the major tragedies of Ayah's life are precipitated by the intrusion of white authorities into her home. The cultural oppression of Native Americans in general is indicated through the personal losses Ayah has suffered at the hands of white culture. It is a white man who informs Ayah and Chato of this loss, symbolizing the larger racial issue of Native Americans dying in service to a nation that has oppressed them. Ayah's coercion into signing away her children also has much deeper implications in the context of Native American history. The near-genocide of Native Americans by the U.S. government in the nineteenth century was in part characterized by the practice of tricking Native Americans into signing ''treaties'' that worked to their disadvantage. Finally, the rancher who employs Chato is another symbol of oppressive white authority. When Chato breaks his leg on the job from falling off a horse, the rancher refuses to pay him until he is able to work again. And when he determines that Chato is too old to work, he fires him and kicks the old couple out of their home to make room for new workers. These actions add class oppression onto the conditions of racial oppression from which Ayah and her family suffer.

Language Barriers

The language barrier caused by her inability to understand the English- or Spanish-speaking white people adds to Ayah's experience of being taken advantage of by white people. When a white man comes to the door to inform them that their son Jimmie has died in the war, Ayah is unable to understand him; her husband Chato has to translate for her. The white doctors take advantage of Ayah's inability to understand English by bullying her into signing a piece of paper that gives them permission to take her children away. Although the children are occasionally brought back to visit Ayah, they eventually forget their native language, and can only speak English. The loss of their native language signifies the complete alienation of the children from their traditional Native American culture, as well as from their family.

Style

Narrative

"Lullaby" is told from the third-person-restricted point of view. That means that, although the narrator is not a character in the story, the perspective of the story is entirely from that of the main character, Ayah. An old woman in the present tense of the story, Ayah thinks back on key events in her life. The story thus interweaves the present time of the old woman sitting outside, then going to look for her husband at the local bar, with her memories from childhood through old age. The story is told in non-chronological order, jumping from one time period or incident to another and back again, reproducing the old woman's thought patterns rather than a standard narrative flow of events from beginning to end.

The Oral Tradition

In all of her work, Silko is interested in representing the storytelling style of the Native American oral tradition in the form of written English. Silko's narrative style of interweaving the old woman's memories of the past with her present circumstances creates a non-linear narrative, in which thoughts and memories circle back on one another. Silko also represents elements of the oral tradition in the story's ending; when she perceives that her husband Chato, lying curled up in the snow, is dying, Ayah sings a lullaby that her grandmother used to sing to her. This is an important element of the story, because Silko is particularly interested in the ways in which the oral tradition is passed on from grandmother to granddaughter.

Recurring Motif

A motif is a minor theme or element that recurs throughout the story, gathering significance with each new appearance. The blanket is a key motif in this story, as it links Ayah with her grandmother and her dead son Jimmie, in addition to associations with both life and death throughout her life. The blanket also reminds Ayah of happier times, sitting outside while her mother wove blankets on a big loom and her grandmother spun the yarn from raw wool. Here, the traditional handwoven blanket made from scratch by the women in the family serves as a metaphor for the passing of the oral tradition between generations of women—just as her mother and grandmother wove blankets in a traditional way, so Ayah carries on the tradition of weaving a tale in the style of the oral tradition. The old army blanket becomes even more significant at the end of the story, when Ayah wraps it around her husband as he lies curled up to die in the snow. The motif of the blanket is an important element of this story because it expresses Silko's concern with the ways in which Native Americans can combine traditional with contemporary culture in order to create meaning in their lives.

The Lullaby

The lullaby that lends the story its title, and ends it, is central to the story itself. The lullaby represents the passing of oral tradition from generation to generation of women in the Native American family: "She could not remember if she had ever sung it to her children, but she knew that her grandmother had sung it and her mother had sung it." When her husband is dying, this lullaby is the first thing that comes to her mind to sing to him as a means of comfort. The lullaby itself combines images of nature and family to affirm both in eternal unity.

Historical Context

The Native American Literary Renaissance

A new generation of Native American writers emerged in the 1970s in what has been termed the Native American Renaissance in literature. Prominent writers of this generation include Leslie Silko, Paula Gunn Allen (b.1939), Louise Erdrich (b. 1954), Scott Momaday (b. 1934), James Welch (b. 1940), and others. Silko was in fact the first Native American woman ever to publish a novel. Erdrich's novel *Love Medicine* and Allen's novel *The Woman Who Owned the Shadows* have been compared to those of Silko in terms of their perspective on tradition and their portrayal of issues around gender in Native American culture.

Sherman Alexie

Sherman Alexie (b. 1966) has become one of the most prominent Native American writers of the generation following that of Silko. Alexie's output includes collections of poetry (*The Business of Fancydancing*), short stories (*The Lone Ranger and Tonto Fistfight in Heaven*), and novels (such as *Indian Killer*). Alexie adapted his short story collection to the screen, in a 1998 film production entitled *Smoke Signals*. *Smoke Signals* was directed by

Compare
&
Contrast

- **1970s:** Silko's novel *Ceremony* (1977) was the first novel by a Native American woman ever to be published.

  1990s: Several Native American women novelists have risen into prominence, including Paula Gunn Allen, whose first novel, *The Woman Who Owned the Shadows,* was published in 1983, and Louise Erdrich, whose first novel *Love Medicine,* was published in 1984.

- **1970s:** The Native American rights movement, first formally organized in 1968 as the American Indian Movement (AIM), was still in its early stages. Native Americans were concerned with such issues as the return of land stolen from them by the U.S. government, the return of cultural artifacts and human remains pillaged by white anthropologists and collectors and placed in museums; and the right to practice spiritual traditions on sacred ground, among many other concerns.

  1990s: Although AIM was disbanded in the early 1980s, Native Americans in North America have met with some success realizing their civil rights demands.

- **1970s:** Up until 1978, the U.S. government made little effort to protect the freedom to practice traditional religious ceremonies among many Native American tribes.

  1990s: A number of federal acts aimed at protecting and preserving Native American cultures have gone into effect, including the Native American Graves Protection and Repatriation Act of 1990.

- **1970s:** There had never been a major motion picture written and directed exclusively by Native Americans, and casting Native Americans in all significant roles.

  1990s: In 1998, *Smoke Signals,* adapted by writer Sherman Alexie from his own collection of short stories, became the first major motion picture written and directed by Native Americans, and features an (almost) all-Native American cast.

Native American Chris Eyre and features the Native American actor Gary Farmer. It was the first major film exclusively written and directed by Native Americans and featuring an exclusively Native American cast in all major roles.

The American Indian Movement

Silko's story was written in the wake of significant political activism among Native Americans. Inspired by the Civil Rights movement led by African Americans, Native Americans in the 1960s began to exert increasingly organized efforts to overcome cultural oppression. The American Indian Movement (AIM) was founded in Minneapolis, Minnesota, in 1968 by four Native American men. AIM organized three highly publicized protests during the early 1970s, including the occupation of Alcatraz Island (in the San Francisco Bay) for nineteen months in 1969–1971; a march on Washington, D.C., in 1972; and a protest at the historical battle site at Wounded Knee on the Pine Ridge Reservation in South Dakota, in 1973. Wounded Knee is the site at which over 200 Sioux Indians were massacred by U.S. troops in 1890, and represented the ultimate defeat of Native Americans by the United States. From February 27 to May 8, 1973, 200 members of AIM took over the reservation hamlet by force, in protest against U.S. policy toward Native Americans. The protest turned violent when the AIM members were surrounded by federal marshals, and a siege ended with the surrender of the Native Americans after two of the Indians had been killed and one of the federal marshals badly wounded. The AIM members did, however, win a promise of attention to their concerns by the

U.S. government. AIM was disbanded in the early 1980s.

Native American Languages

One theme of "Lullaby" is the language barrier between the Native American woman and the white authorities whose language she cannot understand. Silko's concern with Native American culture and tradition in the modern world encompasses a desire to preserve Native American speaking styles, if not the language itself. According the *Encyclopaedia Britannica Online,* there were originally as many as 300 different Native languages spoken in North America, before the arrival of the Europeans. In 1962, estimates accounted for about 200 of those still spoken. Although there is no clear understanding of the roots of native North American languages, linguists have categorized them into about 60 different language families.

Pueblo Indians

Silko's cultural heritage is part Laguna Pueblo Indian. Pueblo culture has been traced as far back as the first millenium A.D. The Pueblo Indians are known for the ancient living structures they built into the sides of cliffs, starting in the sixth century, and located in what is now the area of intersection of Arizona, New Mexico, Colorado, and Utah. The most famous of these are located in Mesa Verde National Park, Colorado. According to *Encyclopaedia Britannic Online,* Cliff Palace, the largest of the remaining structures, housed as many as 250 people in 217 rooms. These were inhabited from the eleventh through thirteenth centuries, after which most Pueblos migrated South into what is now New Mexico. Silko's family are probably descendants of this original tribe. The total population of Indians in New Mexico, where Silko was born, is less than ten percent, and includes a large Navaho reservation, as well as Pueblo Indians living on land grants.

Native American rights

In 1978, The American Indian Religious Freedom Act was passed by the federal government as a commitment to protecting and preserving tribal rituals, which are often tied to sacred ground in specific locations. In 1979, Congress passed the Archaeological Resources Protection Act, which protects Native American cultures from the removal of cultural artifacts by archaeologists and other collectors. In 1990, the Native American Graves Protection and Repatriation Act (NAGPRA) called for the return of thousands of sacred objects and human remains to their rightful tribal owners.

Critical Overview

Silko is widely recognized as one of the most important Native American writers of her generation. With her first novel, *Ceremony* (1977), she was the first Native American woman ever to publish a novel. Paula Gunn Allen followed in her footsteps, with the publication of *The Woman Who Owned the Shadows* in 1983, as did Louise Erdrich with her novel *Love Medicine* in 1984. Silko is associated with a generation of Native American writers which emerged in the 1970s, in what has been called the Native American Renaissance in literature. Silko has been associated with other writers of this renaissance such as Scott Momaday, James Welch, and Gerald Vizenor.

Silko's first significant publication, while she was still in college, was the short story "The Man to Send Rainclouds," which has since been anthologized several times. Her first book of poetry, *Laguna Woman,* referring to her heritage as part Laguna Pueblo Indian, was published in 1974. But Silko's first significant critical attention came after the publication of Kenneth Rosen's anthology of Native American literature, *The Man to Send Rain Clouds,* which took its title from Silko's story. In addition to the title story, several other of her works were included in the anthology.

The publication of her first novel, *Ceremony*, in 1977 brought her widespread critical attention and acclaim. *Ceremony* follows the central character Tayo, who, returning from combat in World War II, must reconcile his personal experiences in the war with his traditional Native American heritage. Silko's collection *Storyteller,* published in 1981, includes some of her earlier poems from *Laguna Woman,* as well as autobiographical reminiscences, short stories, songs, and newer poems, as well as photographs of her family and ancestors taken by her father, who is a professional photographer. In this interweaving of various literary forms, Silko attempted to capture the storytelling forms of the oral

Ancient cliff dwellings built by Pueblo Indians at Mesa Verde, Colorado.

tradition in Native American culture. The short story ''Lullaby'' is one of the most noted of the *Storyteller* collection, and has been anthologized in *The Best American Short Stories of 1985,* as well as the *Norton Anthology of Women's Literature.* Also in 1985, Silko's personal correspondences with the poet James A. Wright, whom she met only twice before he died, were published in a book entitled *With the Delicacy and Strength of Lace.*

In 1983, Silko received the distinguished MacArthur Foundation award of $176,000. This allowed her to devote herself full time to her next novel, *Almanac of the Dead,* which took almost ten years to write and was published in 1991. It is of epic proportions, and includes a wide range of characters. It covers five centuries of conflict between Native American and European cultures, focusing on a mixed-race family. *Almanac of the Dead* has received a mixed response from critics. While some have rated the novel highly for its mythical elements, others have criticized it for its sprawling structure and underdeveloped characterization. In 1996, Silko published a collection of her own essays entitled *Yellow Woman and a Beauty of the Spirit: Essays on Native American Life Today,* which includes discussion of Native American tradition, philosophy, and politics. Her novel *Gardens*

in the Dunes was published in 1999. It focuses on the character of Indigo, a Native American woman who runs away from a white government school and ends up traveling throughout Europe, England and Brazil.

Silko's body of work has been noted for the ways in which her characters incorporate Native American tradition and ritual into a context of experiences in contemporary Native American life. She has been particularly interested in the role of the storyteller in Native American culture, and the transformative power of the act of storytelling itself. Her writing style has attempted to represent the Native American literary tradition in a written English form by interweaving memoirs, songs, poems, and photography into non-linear narrative. Of mixed Anglo and Native American heritage herself, Silko's characters are often of mixed race, and must struggle to reconcile their dual cultural heritage. Having learned much about her Laguna Pueblo cultural heritage from her grandmother and other female relatives, Silko often focuses on themes of the ways in which native culture is passed on through the matrilinear generations. She has explained that Pueblo Indian culture is in many ways matriarchal, and that women and men do not suffer the kinds of gender inequalities present in Anglo culture.

Criticism

Liz Brent

Brent has a Ph.D. in American Culture, specializing in cinema studies, from the University of Michigan. She is a freelance writer and teaches courses in American cinema. In the following essay, she discusses the theme of cultural loss in "Lullaby."

Leslie Marmon Silko's short story "Lullaby" depicts Native American culture in collision with a white culture that has dominated and oppressed it. Silko's story illustrates the sense of loss experienced by one Native American woman at the hands of white authority figures. As the main character, Ayah, looks back on the most devastating events of her life, she mourns the loss of tradition, language, and family experienced by many Native Americans in the twentieth century. At the same time, however, Ayah, as many of Silko's characters, is able to combine traditional with modern cultural elements in order to make meaning in her life.

Language as a bearer of culture is central to Ayah's sense of loss throughout her life. The language barrier between Ayah and the white doctors who eventually take her children away is an important factor in Ayah's experience. Because she does not speak their language, she has no idea why they have come to her home. It is mentioned in the story that this was "back in the days before they hired Navajo women to go with them as interpreters." This highlights the fact that the doctors did not bother to find someone who could have translated for them in order to explain to Ayah exactly what it was they wanted. Furthermore, she is unable to read the contract they want her to sign. She sees only that it is being thrust upon her in an intimidating way, and that they are regarding her children as an animal does its prey: "They were wearing khaki uniforms and they waved papers at her and a black ball-point pen, trying to make her understand their English words. She was frightened by the way they looked at the children, like the lizard watches the fly."

Ayah has, however, learned from her husband how to write her name in English. It is in part because she is proud of this new ability that she signs the papers they put before her. "Ayah could see they wanted her to sign the papers, and Chato had taught her to sign her name. It was something she was proud of. She only wanted them to go, and to take their eyes away from her children." The ability of the doctors to essentially trick her into signing away her children thus hinges on a language barrier in several ways. It turns out to be worse for Ayah to know a little bit of English (only enough to sign her name) than not to know any English at all.

This incident becomes a rift between Ayah and her husband, Chato. Chato has learned to speak English, presumably as a means of fairing better in a world dominated by whites, and so she blames Chato for the theft of her children by the white authorities: "She hated Chato, not because he let the policeman and doctors put the screaming children in the government car, but because he had taught her to sign her name." To Ayah, learning English, or any attempt at assimilation into a white world, does more harm than good: "Because it was like the old ones told her about learning their language or any of their ways: it endangered you." Ayah's anger toward her husband for learning English, and her self-righteousness in the belief that assimilation carries no rewards, is expressed by her response to Chato being fired by the white rancher and kicked out of their house when he is deemed too old to work: "That had satisfied her. To see how the white man repaid Chato's years of loyalty and work. All of Chato's fine-sounding English talk did not change things."

The strong association with language as a bearer of culture—and the loss of language as loss of culture—is most poignant in Ayah's few brief visits with her children after they have been taken away from her. When Danny and Ella are first brought to visit her by the white woman, Danny is still fluent in his Native Navajo, and is able to maintain a sense of connection with his mother. The Native American home, as well as the Navajo language, however, is seen by the white woman as a negative influence, an unfit environment for the raising of children. The white woman "was frightened by what she saw inside (the strips of venison drying on a rope across the ceiling and the children jabbering excitedly in a language she did not know." The last time the children visit, the almost complete loss of their native language signifies that they have become so assimilated into white culture that they cannot even communicate with their own mother. While Ella, the young child, stares at her as if she were a stranger, Ayah speaks "cheerfully" to Danny. But, "When he tried to answer her, he could not seem to remember and he spoke English words with the Navajo." With this language barrier, Ayah's sense of alienation from her own children is so strong that she does not even say goodbye to them.

What Do I Read Next?

- *Ceremony* (1977) by Leslie Marmon Silko. Interweaves free verse poetry with narrative prose. Tayo, a World War II veteran of mixed Anglo-Indian heritage, returns to the reservation after the war, psychically wounded by his war experiences. Rejecting alcohol and other diversions, Tayo must come to terms with his cultural heritage in a process of spiritual and psychological healing.

- *Storyteller* (1981) by Leslie Marmon Silko. A collection of autobiographical reminiscences, stories, poetry, songs, and photographs concerning the role of storytelling and the storyteller in contemporary Native American culture.

- *The Lone Ranger and Tonto Fistfight in Heaven* (1993) by Sherman Alexie, a Native American writer. A collection of short stories about growing up on the Coeur d'Alene Indian Reservation in Washington. Concerns the role of both popular mainstream American culture and Native American tradition in the formation of contemporary Native American identity.

- *Love Medicine* (1984) by Louise Erdrich. One of the best known novels by one of the most prominent Native American writers of the Native American literary renaissance. Erdrich won the National Book Critics Circle Award for this, her first novel, which is comprised of fourteen interconnected stories told by seven different members of the Turtle Mountain Chippawa community.

- *The Woman Who Owned the Shadows* (1983) by Paula Gunn Allen. A novel in which the main character, of mixed Anglo-Indian heritage, grapples with her ethnic heritage and her sexual identity as a lesbian.

- *Leslie Marmon Silko: A Collection of Critical Essays* (1999) by Leslie Marmon Silko. Silko's most recent non-fiction work of critical essays.

- *Song of the Turtle: American Indian Literature, 1974–1994* (1996) edited and with an introduction by Paula Gunn Allen. A collection of contemporary American Indian poetry and short stories, including ''Tony's Story,'' by Leslie Marmon Silko.

- *Yellow Woman and the Beauty of the Spirit: Essays on Native American Life Today* (1997) by Leslie Marmon Silko. Includes essays on Native American philosophy, folklore, and social conditions.

- *With The Delicacy and Strength of Lace: Letters Between Leslie Marmon Silko and James Wright* (1986) by Leslie Marmon Silko and James Wright. A collection of the personal correspondences between Silko and the poet James Wright, who met each other in person only twice before Wright died.

- *Carriers of the Dream Wheel: Contemporary Native American Poetry* (1975) edited by Duane Niatum. A collection of poetry by contemporary Native American writers, including Leslie Marmon Silko.

- *The Man to Send Rain Clouds: Contemporary Stories by American Indians* (1974) edited by Kenneth Rosen. An early collection of stories by the writers of the Native American literary renaissance of the 1970s. Includes Silko's early story ''The Man to Send Rain Clouds,'' after which the book was titled. Critical attention to this book helped to gain early recognition of Silko's work.

The loss of tradition which Ayah experiences at the hands of whites is conveyed in part through the motif of the blanket, which she wraps around herself at the beginning of the story, and around her dying husband at the end of the story. A motif is a minor theme or element which recurs throughout a

> " The death of Jimmie, and the removal of Ella and Danny from her home, thus, are her most painful losses because they represent not just the loss of loved ones to death, but the loss of an entire culture to the hands of white culture."

story, gathering significance with each new appearance. The blanket is a key motif in this story, as it links Ayah with her grandmother as well as her dead son Jimmie. The blanket mixes images of traditional Native American culture with modern American culture in a way that becomes meaningful to Ayah. Silko's work has often been noted for the ways in which her characters create meaning in their lives through such amalgamations of traditional and modern culture.

As she sits leaning against a tree watching the snow in the beginning of the story, Ayah wraps an old army blanket around herself for warmth. The blanket is a reminder of her son Jimmie, who had sent it to her while serving combat in war. Ayah recalls the day the white man came to their door to inform them that Jimmie had died in a helicopter crash. Although the blanket comes from the U.S. government, which is responsible for Jimmie's death, as well as the death of thousands of Native Americans in the nineteenth century, it takes on great significance for Ayah. The army blanket comes to hold great sentimental value, as it is a tangible reminder of Jimmie, whose body was never recovered. When she goes to look for her husband in the white man's bar, an environment clearly unwelcoming toward her, Ayah finds comfort in the old blanket: ''The wet wool smell reminded her of new-born goats in early March, brought inside to warm by the fire. She felt calm.''

Jimmie's army blanket also reminds Ayah of happier times, sitting outside while her mother wove blankets on a big loom and her grandmother spun the yarn from raw wool. Ayah's recollections

of the making of these traditional blankets is expressed through rich, colorful imagery: ''She watched them dye the yarn in boiling black pots full of beeweed petals, juniper berries, and sage.'' The blankets themselves are described in terms of the warmth and comfort they provided: ''The blankets her mother made were soft and woven so tight that rain rolled off them like birds' feathers. Ayah remembered sleeping warm on cold windy nights, wrapped in her mother's blankets on the hogan's sandy floor.'' The traditional hand-woven blanket made from scratch by the women in the family also serves as a metaphor for the passing of the oral tradition between generations of women—just as her mother and grandmother wove blankets in a traditional way, so Ayah carries on the tradition of weaving a tale in the style of the oral tradition.

The old army blanket becomes even more significant in the end of the story, when Ayah wraps it around her husband as he lies curled up to die in the snow. Wrapping him in the army blanket given to her by Jimmie, while singing a traditional lullaby taught by her grandmother, Ayah combines elements of Native American tradition with important personal associations from modern culture in comforting her husband as he dies. In singing the lullaby, Ayah carries on an important element of Native American culture, as embodied in language. The singing of the lullaby while wrapping Chato in the blanket also clinches the metaphor of traditional blanket-weaving with the oral tradition of song and storytelling. Ayah symbolically weaves the modern white culture (represented in the army blanket) with traditional Native American culture (the lullaby, and, by association, the tradition of blanket-making). The motif of the blanket is an important element of this story because it expresses Silko's concern with the ways in which Native Americans can combine traditional with contemporary culture in order to create meaning in their lives.

Ayah's life is characterized by a series of traumatic losses of her family members at the hands of white culture. Loss of traditional culture, loss of native language, and loss of family are each brought about by her encounters with white culture. Her son Jimmie dies in a war, fighting for the U.S. government, the very government responsible for the destruction of his native culture. Ayah loses her two younger children, Danny and Ella, when they are taken away to a government institution. Their removal from the family home ultimately leads to their alienation from their native culture and language, as well as their family.

Juxtaposed against these traumatic losses is the burial of two of Ayah's babies who did not survive. For Ayah, it was easier to accept the death of two of her babies when she was able to bury them in a traditional way on their native land than to accept the theft of her children by white culture: "It was worse than if they had died: to lose the children and to know that somewhere, in a place called Colorado, in a place full of sick and dying strangers, her children were without her." By contrast, the burial of the two babies becomes an enactment of tradition and ritual that allows Ayah to heal from the loss:

> She had carried them herself, up to the boulders and great pieces of the cliff that long ago crashed down from Long Mesa; she laid them in the crevices of sandstone and buried them in fine brown sand with round quartz pebbles that washed down the hills in the rain.

The death of Jimmie, and the removal of Ella and Danny from her home, thus, are her most painful losses because they represent not just the loss of loved ones to death, but the loss of an entire culture to the hands of white culture.

While the story ends with Chato's death, this is not the most crucial loss Ayah experiences in her relationship with her husband. Rather, it is their encounters with white culture which lead to alienation between them. After her children are taken away, and Ayah blames Chato for teaching her to sign her name, she no longer sleeps in the same bed with him. She even sleeps outside until winter sets in, her only comfort being the army blanket given to her by Jimmie. Ayah's feelings for Chato never recover from the trauma caused by the loss of Danny and Ella. Shortly before Chato dies, as they are walking together in the snow, Ayah looks upon him as a stranger, her sense of alienation from him is so great: "this man is a stranger; for forty years she had smiled at him and cooked his food, but he remained a stranger." Nevertheless, Chato's death at the end of the story becomes the final episode in a series of losses Ayah has suffered at the hands of white culture: the loss of tradition, the loss of language, and the loss of family. As the old couple sit together in the snow, shortly before he curls up and dies, Ayah invites her estranged husband into the fold of the army blanket, symbolically inviting him back into the warmth of tradition and family that the blanket represents to her: "She offered half of the blanket to him and they sat wrapped together." When Chato lies down and curls up in the snow, wrapping him in Jimmie's army blanket and singing a lullaby learned from her grandmother,

Ayah symbolically reconciles all of these losses through a continuation of the oral tradition.

Source: Liz Brent, for *Short Stories for Students*, Gale, 2000.

Erika Taibl

Taibl has a master's degree in English writing and has written for a variety of educational publishers. In the following essay, she discusses multiple voices and the ritual of reading as a means of creating meaning in "Lullaby."

As one of the foremost authors to emerge from the Native American literary renaissance of the 1970s, Leslie Marmon Silko is challenged to blend Western literary genres with the oral tradition of her Laguna Pueblo roots. The result is a narrative grounded in two literary worlds, that of the Native American tradition and that of contemporary America. In her work, the past world meets the present in creative if not conflicting ways. Her collection of poems, short stories and non-fiction, *Storyteller*, uses mixed genres and voices in an attempt to put an oral tradition on the page. The resulting narrative mimics the give and take of oral storytelling and creates a unique reading experience. Silko strives to teach readers how to read this type of work, which is multi-voiced and culturally diverse. The second story in the collection, "Lullaby" harbors many examples of this multi-voiced, mixed discourse. In "Lullaby," the stories and memories of the protagonist, Ayah, enter into dialogue with the reader and initiate the creation of meaning through the act or ritual of reading.

Leslie Marmon Silko's main character, Ayah, in her story "Lullaby," watches "wide fluffy snow fill in her tracks, steadily, until the direction she had come from was gone." In real time, the snow's falling spans only a few hours, the capsule of the story, yet in these hours we come to experience a Native American woman's grief process. In the western critical tradition, a reader might experience Ayah's stages of grief as formulated by psychologist, Elizabeth Kubler-Ross in her book *On Death and Dying*. Ayah follows Kubler-Ross's grief theory in the cycle of denial, anger, despair and finally reconciliation. Silko's special talent in "Lullaby" and the entire *Storyteller* collection is in drawing the reader into the text through an anticipated discussion, one that is grounded in a western tradition, such as the Kubler-Ross theory of the grief process, and then turning that discussion around so that it might express cross-cultural goals. The resulting voice is a "mixed" discourse, blending a unique

> Ayah travels through her stories to her death. She dies, and readers travel to the end of her story, which becomes, in the words of the poem, a universal story. The song is a song of continuity sung by a dying woman about the living story of which she is simply one small part."

Native American voice and a Western Anglo voice that engages readers on many levels. As Ayah's tracks are filled in with snow until she no longer knows where she has come from or where she is going, so are the readers', as they disengage from a strict Anglo, or traditionally western, interpretive tool and encounter the text as both Native American and contemporary American.

Silko, in a talk entitled "Language and Literature from a Pueblo Indian Perspective," said that "a great deal of the story is believed to be inside the listener, and the storyteller's role is to draw the story out of the listeners." In the case of "Lullaby," the listener is the reader and must fabricate his or her own meaning for the text. The mixed discourse as a tool enables meaning making in a diverse population of readers and initiates the great challenge for Native American writers, which is to teach readers how to read this kind of work, both on traditionally Anglo and Native American levels. The ritual of reading, or the interaction of the reader with the written words, is likened to the storytelling event and is the event that creates meaning. Silko strives to help that meaning-making experience along in the entire *Storyteller* collection and in "Lullaby."

In order to grasp the idea of a "mixed" discourse in "Lullaby," or one that engages and encourages readers on a variety of cultural levels, readers may enter the text at the end of the story with the poem or lullaby. The voice of the ending poem is not the protagonist's nor the narrator's. The voice is one of tradition, the great story of the world. In many ways, it is representative of everyone's story. Readers locate the story of Ayah within the universal story of the poem, and as they do, they discover that the voice also leaves room for the reader to read him or herself into the poem. In this act of discovery, readers are undertaking the journey Silko most wants for them. They are experiencing the narrative as ritual.

Reading as ritual is not an easy concept to understand. Paula Gunn Allen, herself a celebrated Native American writer, is quoted by Linda Krumholz in "Native Designs: Silko's *Storyteller* and the Reader's Initiation," saying, "Ritual can be defined as a procedure whose purpose is to transform someone or something from one condition or state to another." Readers can use this definition of ritual to describe the stages of grief through which Ayah travels as well as what happens to themselves as they experience Ayah's losses. Through Ayah's progression of memories, readers experience stories as self-renewing acts of imagination, designed to keep cultures and identities from the tragic fate of being lost to memory. Ayah's children return to her and their home without their memory. They don't know their Native language; they have forgotten their history. They have been transformed in dangerous and negative ways. Their transformation elicits transformation for the reader. Krumholz, a Silko scholar, writes in *To Understand This World Differently': Reading and Subversion in Leslie Marmon Silko's "Storyteller,"* that ritual "is the arena of the 'other' where the power of mystery supersedes the power of the social structure." In other words, that which is foreign, in this case Native American, is given meaning through ritual. Readers experience Ayah's losses and her children's loss and discover something about themselves and the world. Silko's power as author is through emphasizing not the story but the ritual of storytelling and of reading as the way of creating meaning for the Native American story. Ayah can journey through the stages of grief and arrive at reconciliation because of the stories she actively relives in her few hours in the snow. Her act of remembrance is ritual, and through this ritual her life has meaning. The reader's act of reading becomes ritual as well, which has the power to initiate deep cultural survival as he or she understands the necessity of the story's stories as avenues to preservation and survival of real culture.

As a part of *Storyteller*, "Lullaby" is in what has been called the "survival" section. The section deals with the need for stories as a means of survival. In "Lullaby," Silko asks for an interpretation of white culture from the reader on conflicting levels. On one level, the English-speaking white community uses a language that takes away, that results in the loss of her children. Yet, this is the same language Silko chooses for *her* story. She uses English as a creative tool to comment on English as a destructive tool. Stories told or written in English are the ultimate tools of survival for the "other," or foreign one, as they use the oppressor's language to actively create meaning for marginalized lives. Mixing Native American voices and different genres with traditional western theories and writing in English allows the ritual of reading to shape multiple and rich meanings for the text.

The ability to glean differing and sometimes conflicting interpretations from the ritual of reading is what Silko relies upon in her narrative. According to Andrew Wiget in his article, "Identity, Voice, and Authority: Artist-Audience Relations in Native American Literature," Silko can't write tradition because it will be misrepresented, misunderstood; neither can she create something utterly "Other," or foreign, from "her historical and cultural entanglements, because that space is occupied by Euro-American voices." How does Silko navigate these challenges, which would seem utterly paralyzing? She denies a commanding narrative voice, which Wiget says, almost disengages her from a Western notion of authorship or author's authority, and allows the act of storytelling, not simply the stories themselves, create the narrative. She relies on a theory of reading, writes Krumholz in "Native Designs: Silko's *Storyteller* and the Readers' Initiation," "in which ritual bears similarities to certain reader response theories that describe novels as sites of change." Silko's multiple genres and voices require that the reader read as ritual or fail to understand the goal of any storytelling which is the integration of action and change within the thread of commonality.

The narrative becomes an exciting and fertile place for Silko's readers. The readers' response to the text may be as simple as storytelling and the sacred act of memory preservation. This is ritualistic transformation, when the text becomes a time and place of possibility, where, in "To Understand the World Differently," Krumholz says, a reader "may take imaginative risks that may transform his or her perception of the world." Krumholz writes that the stories told in *Storyteller* and in "Lullaby," "depict the determination of Native Americans to resist the forces that are dismantling Native Ameri-

can families, traditions and interpretations." The transformative goal of the text is to reveal this resistance and perhaps invite a reader, Native American or non-Native American, to actively take part in that resistance.

The transformation initiated through the ritual of reading takes different forms for Native American and non-Native American readers. Krumholz writes, "What serves as an act of transformation for a non-Indian reader may serve as an affirmation for an Indian reader." In other words, as the reader creates meaning for the text, the meaning can and will be different for each reader. This, perhaps, is the finest example of the success of a "mixed" discourse; it is a text which allows the creation of meaning for a diversity of readers. A non-Native American reader may discover that English is an oppressor's language as Ayah, who prides herself in her ability to sign her name, then signs away her children. What should, conventionally speaking, be empowering, the utilization of language, becomes an instrument of oppression. For the Native American reader, the same illustration may simply affirm what the reader already knows and has experienced. The story offers a community to the Native American reader, as the non-Native American reader is simultaneously offered a new perspective.

The verb that is storytelling, that is the interaction of text and reader, is where meaning is made. The beginning of "Lullaby" describes Ayah as an old woman whose life had become stories. This is what the text wishes upon readers, a life comprised of stories with which the reader constantly interacts. Ayah travels through her stories to her death. She dies, and readers travel to the end of her story, which becomes, in the words of the poem, a universal story. The song is a song of continuity sung by a dying woman about the living story of which she is simply one small part. Though Native American stories are rendered meaningless or simply unheard by traditional Anglo interpretive structures, the song is a great hope. As it embodies a multi-leveled discourse, it addresses a collective you, who is Ayah, who is Silko, who is every storyteller, every character, and every reader encountering and experiencing the text. "The earth is your mother, she holds you. The sky is your father, he protects you." With the poem, readers are placed in space, the space in which stories are created and recreated. English, which has been the oppressor's language is taken back by the "other," or the foreign one, as means of empowerment. Language is honored as having the power to create and transform reality, a power Brian Swan in his introduction to "Smoothing the Ground: Essays on Native American Oral Tradition," describes as "generative," a "sacrament." The power of the word translates to the reader and effects change in his or her own perspectives. The readers' perspectives are then freed in the literary dialogue.

The discourses, ethnicities, and various "I's" that are carried to the story as author, character and reader, are, as the ending poem promises, "together always." Readers are warned and encouraged to believe in the power of the story, which is echoed in Silko's affirmation that these voices and stories were always enmeshed, that "there was never a time when this was not so." The great hope of the entire *Storyteller* collection is that there will never be a time when this is not so as readers learn to read themselves toward a deeper meaning of texts written in multiple and rich voices.

Source: Erika Taibl, for *Short Stores for Students*, Gale, 2000.

Sarah Madsen Hardy

Madsen Hardy has a doctorate in English literature and is a freelance writer and editor. In the following essay, she discusses the relationship between language and power in Silko's story "Lullaby."

In Leslie Marmon Silko's lyrical short story "Lullaby," Ayah, an aged Navajo woman, reflects back on her life as she trudges through a snowstorm to retrieve her husband Chato from the bar where he is drinking away their monthly welfare check. Silko's writing balances tragedy against beauty; loss and bitterness scar Ayah's life, but she is sustained by a spiritual connection with nature and its cycles of generational continuity. In "Lullaby," as in many of her works, Silko celebrates the strength of Native American cultures through mixing genres and including aspects of traditional oral forms in her writing. "One of Silko's purposes . . . is to stress the continuity of her literary work with the oral tradition that she had absorbed" from her grandmother and other family members, writes William C. Clements in his entry on Silko for the *Dictionary of Literary Biography*. "Lullaby" celebrates the purity and power of Ayah's connection to her Navajo heritage even as it reveals the costs of her powerlessness in the context of the larger Anglo-American society.

Silko is herself an unapologetic "half-breed." Of white, Mexican, and Native American (Laguna) descent, she has always occupied two cultural worlds

and negotiated between them. Raised on a reservation, she was educated at a Bureau of Indian Affairs school and a private Catholic one. Even as these non-Natives trained her mind, she was equally influenced by the stories and traditions passed down by her family and the Laguna community around her. In several of her works, most notably her acclaimed novel *Ceremony,* blending between Anglo and Native cultures is represented as a strength and a form of survival. It makes sense that someone with Silko's personal history would reflect this view, and her work itself offers an example of such cultural blending. In *Ceremony* she transforms the Western literary form of the novel by injecting Native American concepts of non-linear plot and by integrating examples of Native American oral culture. *Storyteller,* the collection in which "Lullaby" appears, is another example of multi-generic blending—it mixes poetry, fiction, and photographs and melds Anglo and Native forms and aesthetics.

In *Ceremony* the protagonist is, like Silko, of mixed ethnic heritage and reflects a hybrid cultural consciousness, capable of understanding both Native American and Anglo sensibilities. But in "Lullaby" Silko lets English-speaking readers inside the mind of a woman who is thoroughly enclosed within traditional Native American belief systems and is highly suspicious not only of the mainstream Anglo society, but of those, like her husband, who try to straddle the two worlds. The majority of the story involves the sundering of Ayah's connections to her family members by the intrusion of a larger and more powerful Anglo-American culture. At each point, the English language is significant in breaking the bond that ties Ayah and her family together through their Navajo cultural heritage. In Ayah's mind, the destructive force of Anglo culture is represented most clearly by English. "It was like the old ones always told her about learning their language or any of their ways: it endangered you." While Chato is proud of his mastery of English, thinking that it will bring him power in the white man's world, Ayah sees that it is otherwise. She sees that while it gets him a job, it does not protect him from his white employer's exploitation of him as a worker or prevent his betrayal and their poverty once Chato becomes too old to work. Even the government welfare check leads only to Chato's drunkenness. "All of Chato's fine-sounding English talk didn't change things."

Language is also pivotal in the Ayah's experience of the loss of her children. When her first son, Jimmie, dies in war, the news comes by means of "a man in a khaki uniform trimmed in gold" who "gave them a yellow piece of paper" and told them—in English, of course—that Jimmie was dead. Chato translates for his wife, saying "'Jimmie isn't coming home anymore,' and when he spoke, he used the words to speak of the dead." The report of Jimmie's death reveals the chasm between Native and Anglo ways of speaking—and, thus, thinking—of the dead. Because of the way he died and the way the news reached her, the death doesn't feel real to Ayah. Mediated by distance, government institutions, and a foreign language, it isn't part of the rhythm of life and death that she knows and has a spiritual way of coping with. "It wasn't like Jimmie died. He just never came back."

English is even more central to Ayah's loss of her two remaining children, Danny and Ella, who are taken into custody by a government agency when they test positive for tuberculosis. She is afraid of the doctors who come "wearing khaki uniforms and they waved papers at her and a ball-point pen, trying to make her understand their English words." In an attempt to get them to leave her alone, she signs her name on the forms that give them the legal right to take the children away. She blames Chato for having taught her to write her name and refuses to sleep next to him for many years thereafter. The children both survive the sickness, but they are never returned to Ayah's care. Due to prejudice and poverty, she is quietly deemed unfit. Meanwhile, during their brief visits, she feels her children slip away from her and from the land and language that give Ayah's life meaning. "She knew they were already being weaned from these lava hills and this sky," she thinks after their first visit home. On their last visit, when Ayah speaks to him, Danny "could not seem to remember and he spoke English words mixed with the Navajo." This loss to Anglo culture is "worse than if they had died" for Ayah. She had lost babies in infancy and buried them in the nearby hills. "She had carried them herself . . . [and] laid them in the crevices of sandstone and buried them in fine quartz pebbles that washed down the hills in the rain. She had endured it because they had been with her. But she could not bear this pain."

For Ayah, life is a cycle. At the beginning of the story she reaches out to the snow "like her own babies did"—an old woman, near death, becoming like a baby again. This snow reminds her of "new wool-washed before the weaver spins it" and carries her back in memory to the wool that she watched her grandmother spin long ago, when she

> **English is even more central to Ayah's loss of her two remaining children, Danny and Ella, who are taken into custody by a government agency when they test positive for tuberculosis."**

was young. Nature, the earth and sky, represent continuity with the past—with her heritage, the generations before her, and the beloved dead. Thus death, for her, is not an absolute loss. The English-speaking world—which her husband partially inhabits—robs her of this sustaining continuity, bringing about losses that are more profound than even death.

The story ends with the lyrics of a traditional lullaby, which Ayah sings to her estranged husband as he, passed out in drunkenness, freezes to death under the transcendently beautiful night sky. This lullaby has simple lyrics but a complex status in the context of the story that proceeds it. The lullaby is, at once, a sincere tribute to Native American cultural continuity and an ironic statement about all that Ayah has lost. Intended to lull a baby to sleep, it lulls a man to death. "The earth is your mother, / she holds you. / The sky is your father, / he protects you," it begins. On the one hand, this is true. In death, Chato is not lost to Ayah as radically as Jimmie, Danny, and Ella are. He is with her. The earth on which Chato lies and the freezing sky above him, with the "purity of the half moon and the stars" and the "strength of the stars in Orion" usher him gently beyond his hopeless life, so compromised by his concessions to Anglo ways. His death is, thus, a kind of return to her.

"We are together always / We are together always / There was never a time / when this / was not so." These words are both true—in a spiritual sense, Chato and Ayah have reconciled—and heart-wrenchingly false. Ayah has lost all of her family and is now alone in the world, a world in which being "together always," through the perpetual cycle of birth, life, and death, is no longer so. Mother and child, husband and wife, people and land, are wrenched apart by the belief systems and power associated with the English language. Even as Silko reaches toward a sense of continuity and resolution by closing the story with the lullaby, the lyrics' ironies underscore the story's themes of discontinuity and loss. And, given Ayah's feelings toward the treacherous nature of the English language, it is even more ironic that Silko translates the Navajo lullaby into English for the benefit of her largely Anglo reading public. While many readers and critics—Anglo and Native American alike—may appreciate Silko's cultural translation of Ayah's experience and her literal translation of the lovely Navajo lullaby, it is just this kind of translation that Ayah would believe has broken her family and her heart.

Source: Sarah Madsen Hardy for *Short Stories for Students*, Gale, 2000.

Sources

Krumholz, Linda, "Native Designs: Silko's Storyteller and the Reader's Initiation," in *Leslie Marmon Silko: A Collection of Critical Essays*, edited by Louise Bernett and James Thorsen, Albuquerque: University of New Mexico Press, 1999, pp. 63–86.

———, "'To Understand this World Differently': Reading and Subversion in Leslie Marmon Silko's Storyteller," *Ariel*, Vol. 25, No. 1, January, 1994, pp. 89–113.

Kubler-Ross, Elizabeth, *On Death and Dying*, New York: MacMillan, 1969.

"Mesa Verde National Park," *Encyclopaedia Britannica Online*, Checked 3/22/00.

"New Mexico," in *Encyclopaedia Britannica Online*, Checked 3/22/00.

"North American Indian Languages," *Encyclopaedia Britannica Online*, Checked 3/22/00.

Silko, Leslie Marmon, "Language and Literature from a Pueblo Indian Perspective," *Beauty*, Vol. 50.

Swann, Brian, Introduction, *Smoothing the Ground: Essays on Native American Oral Literature*, edited by Brain Swann, Berkley: University of California Press, 1983, pp. xi–xix.

Wiget, Andrew, "Identity, Voice, and Authority: Artist-Audience Relations in Native American Literature," in *World Literature Today*, Vol. 66, No. 2, Spring, 1992, pp. 258–263.

Further Reading

Brown, Wesley, and Amy Ling, eds., *Imagining America: Stories from the Promised Land*, New York: Persea Books, 1991.

A collection of short stories by immigrant and minority authors that present alternative visions of America. Includes "American Horse," by Leslie Marmon Silko.

Coltelli, Laura, ed., *Winged Words, American Indian Writers Speak*, Lincoln: University of Nebraska Books, 1990.

A collection of interviews with contemporary Native American writers, including Leslie Marmon Silko. This book is part of a series entitled American Indian Lives.

Gattuso, John, ed., *A Circle of Nations: Voices and Visions of American Indians / North American Native Writers & Photographers*, Hillsboro, OR: Beyond Words Publishers, 1993.

A collection of Native American literature and photography. Includes a forward by Leslie Marmon Silko.

Jaskoski, Helen, *Leslie Marmon Silko: A Study of the Short Fiction*, New York: Twayne Publishers, 1998.

Critical essays that focus on Silko's short stories in terms of her representations of gender and the Southwest in the context of twentieth-century Native American history.

Nelson, Robert M., *Place and Vision: The Function of Landscape in Native American Fiction*, New York: Peter Lang, 1993.

Discusses the works of N. Scott Momaday, James Welch, and Leslie Marmon Silko in terms of their representations of landscape. Covers Silko's novel *Ceremony*.

Ortiz, Simon J., ed., *Speaking for the Generations: Native Writers on Writing*, Tucson: University of Arizona Press, 1998.

A collection of essays by Native American writers on Native American identity and the writing process. Includes a chapter by Leslie Marmon Silko entitled, "Interior and Exterior Landscapes: The Pueblo Migration Stories."

Roalf, ed., *Strong Hearts: Native American Visions and Voices*, New York, NY: Aperture, 1995.

Described on the book jacket cover as "the first comprehensive collection of contemporary Native American photography." Includes a photographic essay by Leslie Marmon Silko entitled "An Essay on Rocks."

Salyer, Gregory, *Leslie Marmon Silko*, New York: Twayne, 1997.

Includes biographical information on Leslie Marmon Silko, as well as critical essays on each of her major works.

Trafzer, Clifford E., ed., *Earth Song, Sky Spirit: Short Stories of the Contemporary Native American Experience*, New York: Doubleday, 1993.

A collection of short stories by Native American writers that focus on the contemporary experience of Native Americans. Includes "The Return of the Buffalo," by Leslie Marmon Silko.

Velie, Alan, R., ed., *The Lightning Within: An Anthology of Contemporary American Indian Fiction*, Lincoln: University of Nebraska Press, 1991.

A collection of contemporary Native American short stories. Includes "The Man to Send Rain Clouds," by Leslie Marmon Silko.

My First Goose

Isaac Babel
1926

''My First Goose'' appeared in *Red Cavalry*, Babel's first collection of vignettes and stories—none longer than four pages. This interconnected cycle of stories, considered by many critics to be Isaac Babel's best work, is also considered one of the most important contributions to twentieth-century Russian literature. The stories showcase Babel's gift for disturbing imagery and complex philosophy. Containing his signature moral and religious ambiguity, they are characterized by an ironic and exaggerated tone. *Red Cavalry* initially gained popularity in serialized newspaper form and commanded international critical attention. The public was quick to respond to these new and shocking tales that were simultaneously beautiful and brutal, traditional and contemporary. However, Babel had political detractors as well as religious ones. The government became uneasy with his work, which did not appear to present exclusively socialist thought. ''My First Goose'' typifies the kind of writing that gained Babel this kind of varied and emotional response. The story contains the violence and passion typical of most of his work and concerns a deeply emotional narrator of ambiguous political, religious, and moral sentiment. Indeed, throughout his body of work and in his dealings with the government, Babel remained elusive about his actual political views.

The story contains a meticulous shape and acutely particular language. ''My First Goose'' contains one of Babel's famous and suggestive descrip-

tions—that of the Commander's legs, "like girls sheathed to the neck in shining riding boots." This detail, the first the reader encounters, is echoed in the story's end, when the unnamed narrator sleeps with his legs entwined in the other soldiers' legs, dreaming of women. The narrator, whose job as Propaganda Officer is to educate the troops on Leninist thought, tells of his first day of assignment to a Cossack troop. Babel makes much of the narrator's physical frailties, including his eyeglasses. In fact this narrator resembles the author himself physically, and appears in many of *Red Cavalry*'s tales. In the story's crucial moment, the previously weak narrator proves his strength by killing a helpless goose. Themes of violence run throughout the story, as well as erotic and religious themes. Swift, unsettling, and strangely elevated, "My First Goose" remains one of Babel's most widely read and variously interpreted stories.

Author Biography

Russian writer Isaac Babel was born on July 13, 1894, and given the full name Isaac Emmanuilovich Babel. Though some of his writing implies that he was raised in a Jewish ghetto by a crazy family of drunks and criminals, Babel was in fact raised middle class in Odessa, which, nearly 50 percent Jewish by 1917, had no legal restrictions on Jewish living quarters. Babel's father, who managed an agricultural warehouse, was not particularly observant of Jewish religious tradition. Babel attended the competitive Commercial School and studied violin. Anti-Semitic sentiment remained strong in the early part of the twentieth century in Russia, and it is believed that the young Babel witnessed violent anti-Jewish demonstrations, though not necessarily the pogroms he claimed to have seen. He was small, fragile, needed glasses, and suffered from asthma. Acutely aware of these weaknesses, Babel believed them to be caused by nerves—nerves further grated upon by persecution. Later in life, Babel once wryly excused his small literary output with a physical explanation, claiming that his asthma only allowed him to say so much with words.

After graduating from The Institute of Finance and Business in Kiev, a mediocre college he attended only because of limits on Jewish attendance at better Odessa schools, Babel moved to St. Petersburg (the city later known as Leningrad). There he published his first story, "Old Shloyme," which

was about a suicidal Jew, a character type he explored in many later works. In 1916 Babel met the influential revolutionary writer Maxim Gorky, who published two more of Babel's stories in his journal *Letopis*. Early on, Babel's writing contained shocking images and sexual overtones, and included vague details about the characters' histories. Babel's own personal history is equally vague, as he often told stories about himself that were later contradicted, either by himself or some revelation of fact. However, some details are known. Upon Gorky's advice to gather material for his writing, Babel volunteered for the Russian army during World War I, serving on the Romanian front. He returned to Odessa after becoming ill. There Babel met his first wife, Evgeniya Gronfein, with whom he had a child. He did not live with his wife throughout much of their marriage, and he later had a child with Antonina Nikolaevna Pirozhkova, a Soviet engineer.

In a gesture central to much of his fiction, Babel volunteered to serve in the Red Army in 1920 on the Polish front—a strange choice for a Jewish intellectual. The Cossacks were a brute, illiterate force, known to hate Jews. Yet Babel survived the fronts much like the narrator of "My First Goose," working as a propagandist and spreading the socialist word. During that time and in the years immediately following, Babel published work under the pseudonym "K. Lyotov," and gave the name "Lyotov" to his narrator as well, suggesting that much of his fiction may be largely autobiographical. These publications established him as a writer popular with the Russian public. *Red Cavalry* (the collection in which "My First Goose" appears) was published in 1926, and is considered by many critics to be the most artistically significant Babel work. In this book he displays a remarkable gift for startling images ("Blue roads flowed past me like streams of milk spurting from many breasts") and an ability to portray sensitively even the ugliest scenes. For example, in "The Story of a Horse," Babel famously ends a tale of a man driven mad by war with the line "Both of us looked on the world as a meadow in May—a meadow traversed by women and horses." Yet this story, like most of those from the Polish front, are full of blood and death.

After his next publication, a series of autobiographical sketches entitled *Odessa Tales*, Babel's literary output slowed. He defended this silence with various excuses. He did not want to write only propaganda, as writers were increasingly pressured to do. He also claimed he was no genius, like his literary predecessor Tolstoy. He wrote two plays that were produced (*Sunset* and *Maria*), and one final story, ''The Trial.'' Many additional facts about Babel's life remain uncertain even to this day. In part this is because he was evasive about his own history. He presented himself as a socialist yet there is no evidence that he ever joined the Communist party. His work was considered pornographic and not propagandistic enough by the Soviet regime.

Babel was arrested by the Soviet regime for unclear reasons in 1939. For many years it was believed that he was taken to a labor camp, where he died either from suicide or a heart failure. His second wife later revealed, however, that he had been beaten in prison until he confessed to spying against the Soviet regime. No proof exists that Babel in fact did spy; he did have anti-Fascist associations, which under Stalin's regime were deemed a threat to Russia. Babel later recanted his confession, but in 1940 his fate was sealed: sentenced to death, he was shot.

Isaac Babel

Plot Summary

The simple plot follows a narrator, whose name the reader does not learn, through the afternoon and evening of his assignment as a Propaganda Officer to a Cossack Division of the Red Army. The story takes place during the civil war which began in Russia in 1918. The narrator's job is to spread Leninism throughout the Russian division at the Polish border. The story opens with the introduction of the narrator to Commander Savitsky, a man of significant military power. The narrator, small and bespectacled, finds himself transfixed by Savitsky's commanding physique, from his long legs to his chest and even his perfumed scent. While signing a document ordering destruction of the enemy, Savitsky strikes his riding whip on his desk and smiles at the narrator. He commences to grill the narrator on his background, and, upon learning that the narrator is educated, mocks him, calling him a ''nasty little object.'' The narrator replies simply ''I'll get on all right.'' A quartermaster then leads the narrator to a Cossack yard, carrying his trunk full of books and papers. Along the way, the quartermaster sympathizes with the narrator and offers him advice: to gain respect of the division, he says, the narrator ought to ''mess up a lady,'' that is, rape one. The narrator, typically, makes no comment.

Once at the yard, Cossacks immediately pick on the narrator, shaming him with toilet sounds and tossing his belongings out the gate, including all his papers. Yet the narrator remains unruffled, and admires the very lad who tossed his trunk (and made mocking toilet noises) with his ''long straight flaxen hair'' and ''handsome face.'' The Cossacks are the opposite of the narrator, who is Jewish, learned, and physically weak. While he cannot be one of them, he envies them. The remainder of the story concerns how he wins over the Cossacks.

He does so easily, in fact. Encountering the landlady upon whose property they are camped, the narrator begins to demonstrate his peculiar will. Though she seeks his help, confessing suicidal thoughts, he shoves her in the chest, exclaiming ''Christ!'' Seeing a goose nearby, he stomps its head beneath his boot. The goose dies surrounded by dung, its white wings twitching. The narrator again exclaims ''Christ!'' over its body; he notes the Cossacks as ''stiff as heathen priests at a sacrifice'' as they avert their eyes from the dead goose.

In this brief interlude the narrator accomplishes the task of winning over the Cossacks, without having had to rape a woman. The oldest Cossack acknowledges him, saying he's all right. Ignoring Jewish custom, the narrator shares the Cossacks' pork. Thus stripped of the stigmas of his education and religion, the narrator has cleared the way for work. He reads them Lenin's speech from *Pravda*, the Russian newspaper. They rejoice, as does he, in the "straight line" of this writing. Entwined together they sleep, the narrator dreaming of women, his heart "stained with bloodshed." The narrator has passed the test and proven muster, yet he, like the landlady, is depressed. His admiration of the army grows tainted with guilt and self-disgust. He knows he will have to kill again.

Characters

The Landlady

The near-blind landlady whose property the Cossacks infest approaches the narrator to tell him she wants to die. Weak and depressed, she sees the frail narrator as potentially sympathetic to her ugly predicament—hosting an unruly force of men. The narrator, however, shows no pity for her at all. He shoves her in the chest and steps on the head of her goose, which splatters. The landlady shuffles off to cook the goose, saying pathetically, "I want to go and hang myself." Her pitifulness is loathsome to the narrator, who, though equally depressed, must display no affiliation with her at all. She is the narrator's female foil, representing weakness in the face of war.

The Quartermaster

The unnamed quartermaster, who has been assigned to take the narrator to his squadron, is sympathetic to the narrator's tough task ahead with the Cossacks. He knows the Cossack life is no "life for a brainy type," or Jew. He suggests that the narrator "mess up a lady"—rape her—in order to win the Cossacks' respect. This suggestion foreshadows the narrator's killing of the goose. The quartermaster, seeming nervous, makes a hasty exit from the scene.

Savitsky

Savitsky is the Cossack Commander of the VI Division to which the unnamed narrator of the story has been assigned. His "giant's body" emanates power and beauty. The description of Savitsky contains one of Babel's most famous images: "His long legs were like girls sheathed to the neck in shining riding boots." Savitsky exemplifies the strange allure violence holds for the narrator. In a brief verbal exchange, Savitsky takes great pleasure in mocking the narrator's relative weakness. Upon discovering the narrator not only attended law school but can also read and write, Savitsky says, "Oh, are you one of those grinds?" Critics point out that this is a comment on the narrator being Jewish, though the narrator's religion is not referred to explicitly in the story. Savitsky also calls the narrator "a nasty little object," yet despite his own nastiness, Savitsky is depicted as enviable, containing the "flower and iron" of youth. The narrator admires his strength, which personifies the Red Army's glory.

Surovkov

Platoon Commander of the Staff Squadron, Surovkov is the first Cossack to acknowledge the narrator kindly. After the narrator kills the goose, the "older" Surovkov winks at him and invites him to join the group. His wink at the narrator indicates the wry humor in the situation of an educated Jew among the brute Red Army. Surovkov listens avidly as the narrator reads a speech of Lenin's from *Pravda*, the Russian newspaper. Just like the narrator, Surovkov is impressed with Lenin's words, how he strikes at the truth "like a hen pecking at a grain!"

Unnamed Male Narrator

The narrator and protagonist of "My First Goose" remains nameless. He has recently been appointed to the Staff of the Division. The narrator is educated and Jewish, and a "Propaganda Officer," or reporter. It would be unusual for a Jewish man to join the Cossack force, though not unusual for one to support the socialist cause. On the evening of this story, the narrator goes to the village to join the Cossack division to which he has been assigned. At first he is mocked by the soldiers. The narrator knows he must win them over in order to educate them on Leninism. To impress them, he kills a goose violently. Thus the outsider—a bespectacled, emotional Jew—gains the shallow confidence of the Cossacks. When the narrator goes to sleep that night, he warms his legs against those of the Cossacks. Dreaming of women, he sleeps. Yet his admiration of beautiful force is complicated by a gnawing sense of moral justice. The story ends as he states that his "heart, stained with bloodshed, grated and brimmed over" with the knowledge that he will have to kill again.

Themes

Ignorance and Knowledge

The physically small narrator of "My First Goose" possesses a law school education; he reads, writes, and wears glasses. Representing knowledge and culture, he is set in opposition to the Cossacks, who cannot read or write. Yet in this story Cossacks possess the greater power. Though the narrator knows Leninist politics, the very reason for the war, it is he who must prove his worth to those fighting for it. This theme relates to the complex political moment during which the story is set. The revolutionary cause for which the Red Army is fighting is not a factor on the front lines, populated by illiterate Cossacks merely willing to plunder. It is the narrator who must gain power and learn to kill and survive on the front. The narrator must suppress his intellectual and emotional sensibilities to have the power to forward the socialist cause. He must equalize the distance between knowledge and ignorance, power and weakness. This he achieves by bullying a near-blind old woman and stomping a goose to death. The contrast between brain-knowledge and body-power echoes the aims of this war, which was fought both for ideology (Communism) and physical boundaries (Russia's border with Poland).

Religion

In other stories in *Red Cavalry*, the cycle of stories in which "My First Goose" appears, Babel reveals the Jewish faith of this unnamed narrator. However, the narrator of this particular story does not mention his own religion, nor does he mention that the Cossack army is primarily Russian-Orthodox Christian. Nevertheless, strong themes of Christianity, Judaism, and in fact paganism run throughout the story. The language is imbued with religious images and a certain religious tension. The Cossacks, who made up the Red Army, traditionally were anti-Semitic and often violent toward Jewish populations. Some critics have interpreted the Commander's derogatory remarks about the narrator ("nasty object") to be anti-Semitic. Yet the narrator envies him and tries throughout the plot to conceal or to downplay his Jewishness. The narration also presents Christian and pagan images. "Christ!" the narrator twice exclaims upon sacrificing the goose. Whether this is blasphemy or prayer remains unclear. The narrator also describes the Cossacks "stiff as heathen priests at a sacrifice." Babel explores the connections between primitive

Media Adaptations

- "Jewish Short Stories from Eastern Europe and Beyond," hosted by Leonard Nimoy, was produced by National Public Radio with the goal of preserving a rich and diverse tradition of modern Jewish life through short stories. Authors whose work is read in this cassette series include Isaac Bashevis Singer, Cynthia Ozick, Isaac Babel, Grace Paley, and Philip Roth. The stories are read by Walter Matthau, Lauren Bacall, Alan Alda, Eli Wallach, Elliot Gould, Jeff Goldblum, Carol Kane, and other noted actors. The cassettes also feature music composed and conducted by Hankus Netsky, founder of the acclaimed Klezmer Conservatory Band. Available from NPR and the National Yiddish Book Center.

and Christian rituals, and draws parallels between these and the rituals of war. Socialist philosophy also cast doubt on God's ability to save. Babel's striking religious images, paired with the ambivalent religious ideas of the narrator, contribute to the political ambiguity of this story.

Innocence

Innocence as a theme is most starkly symbolized by the "white" (thus clean or pure) goose in "My First Goose." The only inoffensive creature in this story, it dies at the boot of a formerly innocent narrator. With the title Babel reveals that the narrator's fall from grace will continue. Though initially presented as harmless, the narrator becomes increasingly cold. Even an old blind woman irritates him. He kills the innocent goose, a shocking thing. Immediately after killing the goose, the sullied narrator eats Cossack pork. This would contradict traditional Jewish dietary laws, indicating the narrator has become godless. His fall looks necessary and inevitable in the plot, because he *must* win over the Cossacks to do his work. Since the narrator believes in the war, he must become corrupt. The inevitability of this fall makes his heart bleed.

Topics for Further Study

- At the beginning of the story the narrator wonders at the beauty of the Commander's legs and body; later he admires a handsome soldier's face. From the way other characters comment on the narrator's appearance, what does he look like? Is his envy of the Cossacks based only on his physical shortcomings?

- Babel ends "My First Goose" with a complicated series of images—legs, women, and blood. What do these images symbolize? Where else are these images found in the story, and how do they relate to the story's theme of war?

- Research Lenin's ideas during the Russian civil war and find a speech by Lenin from this time. Does the narrator present typical socialist views in this story? What do you think the Cossacks and the narrator mean when they praise the "straight line" of Lenin's writing?

- During the initial walk to the Cossack camp, the quartermaster suggests to the narrator that he "mess up a lady," which has been interpreted by most critics to mean he is suggesting the narrator commit rape. Research the treatment of women during the Russian civil war. Does this suggestion fit in with what you discover? From other details in the story, do you think Babel is actually advocating this kind of violence against women? Would you describe the story as sexist or not, and why?

Style

Point of View

Told from the first-person ("I") point of view of the unnamed narrator, this story remains very close to the action. The narrator offers his immediate reactions to the events of his day and little background information. The narrator of "My First Goose" withholds information from the reader, who learns only what the narrator wants to reveal—in this case, a limited amount of information. He tells that he attended law school and can read and write, and of what his job consists. He does not state whether he is Jewish or Christian. The narrator does not say exactly why he admires the Cossacks, though he does comment several times on their physical beauty. This kind of ambiguous narrator often appears in Babel's stories, particularly those included in *Red Cavalry*. Critics often point out that even in his own diaries, Babel did not always tell the whole truth about his life, though this evasion could have been an act of self-protection as a writer and a Jew. Had Babel said what he really thought, he risked being censored or arrested. From a literary perspective the vague, yet intimate, first-person narrator of "My First Goose" helps to create a feeling of confusion and non-comprehension in the story. This kind of narrator is also sometimes referred to as "unreliable," a form demonstrated in many works of fiction, and exemplified in British author Ford Maddox Ford's novel *The Good Soldier* and American author F. Scott Fitzgerald's *The Great Gatsby*. This unreliable narrator complicates Babel's story's themes and effect.

"My First Goose" contains a simple plot. The narrator, also the story's main character, recites the events of one day in his life, like a diary. The plot unfolds logically: The narrator is assigned to a Cossack division by a skeptical Commander. Once at the army camp he earns the Cossacks' trust by shoving an old woman and killing her goose. He does this so he can try to spread political propaganda in the form of a speech by Lenin, which he reads to the troops at the end of the tale, full of pride. He goes to sleep sad and dreaming of women. This bare plot contrasts with the story's complex themes. Although the plot is simple, the final moral or political ideas in the story remain difficult to pin down, even for accomplished literary critics. Babel tricks the reader a little with the "straight line" of his plot, which is like the "straight line" of Lenin's speech, so highly praised by both narrator and Cossacks alike.

Figurative Language

Critics consider Babel to be one of the great masters of figurative language—language that uses metaphors and suggestive imagery to convey ideas and emotions. "My First Goose" is packed with description. It also contains some of Babel's most famous images, like that of the Commander's "long legs" like "girls sheathed to the neck in shining riding boots." This example of simile, when a writer compares one thing to another for effect, is particularly disturbing to critics, as it has a sadistic tone. Another famous example of Babel's use of figurative language is when the narrator describes "the dying sun, round and yellow as a pumpkin" and "giving up its roseate ghost." This sentence uses a simile as well as a religious reference—to the roseate ghost, or the ghost of Christ. This is what is known as a "mixed metaphor," in which the sun is a pumpkin, but also has a ghost. This kind of entangled metaphor marks much of Babel's prose. Later in this story, the soldiers are described as "stiff as heathen priests"—again a religious simile. Babel favored colorful language and surprising details, which complicated his stories in order to deepen the thematic weight of the tale. He remains well known for this, though some critics suggest he overused this sort of descriptive flourish merely for shock effect, and risked writing flowery prose.

Historical Context

The Russian Revolution

Babel used his experiences in the Red Army, the socialist force that began to take power in Russia in 1917, as the basis for much of his fiction, including the story "My First Goose." The socialist revolution emerged out of an already volatile political situation. After a revolution in 1905, Nicholas II, Russia's last Czarist emperor, had been forced to establish a parliament. But the initial promise of freedom did not last at all, and the government quickly reverted to its repressive ways. Unrest bred revolutionary murmurs, which then caused backlash by a violent police force. Waves of anti-Semitism resounded, as non-revolutionary forces associated revolution with intellectual Jews. The revolution of 1917 led directly to a civil war and the socialist growth to power, so crucial to Babel's writing.

A long Russian history contributed to the growth of the socialist cause. The revolution in 1905 had shifted the social structure in agricultural regions so that individual workers no longer were "owned." But wealth did not redistribute, and hunger and poverty grew in agricultural regions. Additionally, populations increased in cities such as Moscow, newly industrialized, creating a labor force amenable to Social Democracy with its original ideals of shared wealth and intellectual freedom. The revolution of 1917—with intellectuals such as Babel behind it—led to the official proclamation of Russia as the Russian Soviet Federated Socialist Republic. This new, Leninist government was championed as holding great promise for Russia's impoverished and ignorant masses, as well as its intellectuals. The unlikely partnership of the populace with the Bolsheviks worked for a time. Yet by March 1918, forced to sign the humiliating Treaty of Brest-Litovsk, a result of its actions in World War I, Russia lost land and lost face. In May 1918, a violent civil war broke out, and on July 16th of that year Czar Nicholas II and the royal family were executed.

Lasting from 1918 through 1920, the war between the Czarist Whites and the Bolshevik (Socialist) Reds was bitterly violent. Eventually the Reds prevailed, with the military guidance of Leon Trotsky. The exaggerated, shifting alliances of Russian politics were good fodder for the kind of irony and satire Babel used in his stories, even stories as "realistic" as "My First Goose." When Stalin took control of the government and it grew increasingly controlling and censorious, Babel's work, deemed not quite propagandistic enough, was suppressed. Arrested in 1939 for unclear reasons, Babel was first thought to be imprisoned, then to have died of either natural causes or suicide. finally, it was revealed that he had been executed after only the briefest trial. This kind of ambiguity marked much of his life and was not uncommon particularly in Stalinist Russia, which maintained a political atmosphere of distrust and fear.

Odessa

On July 13, 1894, Babel was born in Odessa, and raised there after the age of eight. By the time he

Compare & Contrast

- **1920s:** After the Revolution of 1917, Nicholas II, sets up a constitution and a parliament. However, his repressive government quickly ceases offering new freedoms to Russian citizens. This leads to the civil war in 1918. This civil war between the Bolsheviks, or ''Reds,'' who espoused socialist views, and the Czarists, or ''White Czars,'' who favored Russia's old authoritarian regimes, ends in 1920. Believing violence to be necessary to establishing socialism, the Reds gain control, setting up the Russian Soviet Federated Socialist Republic. The country remains rife with conflict between the Czarists and the Reds, the two primary political groups.

  1990s: Though hard-line socialism initially held great promise for a country rife with internal conflict and widespread poverty, it has not succeeded in eliminating Russia's troubles. Repressive and corrupt government activities continue, breeding distrust within and among the Soviet nations, now known as the Russian Federation. While liberal leaders such as Boris Yeltsin espouse idealistic views, human rights violations persist under the current Socialist government. A range of political parties now co-exist in Russia, though Socialists maintain deep control. The parties include a special interest party called ''Women of Russia'' and several democratic groups. The Socialist party is divided among liberals and traditionalists.

- **1920s:** Though Russia has a strong Jewish population, the Russian government and its predominantly Russian Orthodox people persecute Jews and others of non-Christian faith. Jews are prohibited from some educational institutions, positions of political power, and even from living in certain places. Pogroms flare up, continuing a tradition of violence against Jews and other ''unpopular'' ethnicities in Russia. Though often forced to work in support of the socialist movement, many writers are censored, arrested, or otherwise punished if they express even mildly unpopular views, just like other Russian writers also projecting opinions deemed ''undesirable''

  by the government. Most of the population, except an elite, remains illiterate.

  1990s: Anti-Semitism and other forms of ethnic discrimination remain great problems in Russia. In February of 1998, the Russian Constitutional Court abolished the need for residence permits, known as the *propiska* system. Police continue to detain individuals, particularly those of ethnic minorities, for not having such a permit. Some Jews, sponsored by American temples, emigrate to the United States to enjoy religious freedom. Demonstrations against Jews in Russia continue. In publishing, *Samizdat*, or ''underground writing,'' flourishes internationally as a forum for writing which would otherwise be censored. Ninety-eight percent of the population can read and write.

- **1920s:** The civil war is fought by a male army, who also hold all positions of recognized power in the government. Socialist writings speak broadly of liberation of laborers, yet do not explicitly speak of the freedom of women. Along with the majority of Russia's population, since education is a privilege of the financial elite, women are not educated beyond grammar school. It is not a crime to rape a woman. Rape is sanctioned as a necessary aspect of war and is a widespread practice.

  1990s: Although women do hold political positions and continue to make advances for women's rights, violence against women still persists in Russia. Some government statistics cite that 11,000 women reported rape or attempted rape, both now considered crimes, in 1996. Yekaterina Lakhova, President Yeltsin's advisor on women's issues, has estimated that 14,000 women in Russia are killed by husbands or family members each year. The government fails to afford victims of violence the protection of the law required by the international human rights treaties to which Russia is a party. During war times, major newspapers report that rape continues as a sanctioned ''right'' of soldiers.

began writing, Odessa had a large Jewish population: nearly 50 percent. Though during his formative years there was no legal ghetto in Odessa most of the Jewish families lived in a neighborhood known as the Moldavanka, which had close quarters and a family atmosphere. That Jews were banned from Odessa for a time, and that pogroms and anti-Semitic protests did take place in and around Odessa, certainly influenced Babel's writing. His exploration of these themes in fiction contributed to the government's extreme caution about his work. While not overtly critical of Russia's anti-Semitic tendencies, it still did not conceal some of Russia's harsh realities.

Fellow Travellers

Known in Russian as *Poputchick*, "Fellow Travellers" consisted of writers in the Soviet Union who, while not opposed to the Bolshevik Revolution of 1917, did not actively support it with cookie-cutter socialist plots. This group recognized the artist's need for intellectual freedom and maintained a strong respect for Russian literary tradition. Though Fellow Travellers were given official sanction in the early Soviet regime, they later became criticized for avoiding strict proletarian themes in their writing. In the 1920s some of the most gifted and popular Soviet writers, such as Osip Mandelshtam, Leonid Leonov, Boris Pilnyak, Isaac Babel, and Ilya Ehrenburg, were considered Fellow Travellers. The period during which they dominated the literary scene is now regarded as the brilliant flowering of Soviet literature. According to the *Encyclopedia Britannica*, the term was employed during the Cold War era as a political label to refer to any person who, while not thought to be an actual "card-carrying" member of the Communist Party, was in sympathy with its aims and supported its doctrines.

Social Realism and Structuralism

A movement begun by Maxim Gorky, the first person to publish Babel's work, writing of the Social Realism movement asked that a piece of literature present exclusive socialist ideals. Its body of work was overseen by the Congress of Writers. Babel was not a social realist, though his writing bore some resemblance to their work. Babel also had no ties with his contemporaries in the Structuralist movement. Structuralists experimented with form, believing language to be writing's most important feature, beyond description or plot. Babel stands out in Russian literature as anomalous in many ways—a socialist of ambiguous morality who maintained a distinct, personal voice.

Critical Overview

After his first publications in Maxim Gorky's Petrograd-based journal *Letopis*, Babel next wrote as a war correspondent. Following the Red Army, he wrote the stories and reports that were collected as *Red Cavalry*, published to an enthusiastic Russian audience in 1926. The first English edition came out in 1929. His next collection, *The Odessa Tales*, was published in 1931, but the English edition in which these appear, *The Collected Stories of Isaac Babel*, did not come out until 1955, after Babel's death. Babel's work has received a complicated critical reception. Considered exemplary from a literary standpoint, his work was not strictly propagandistic. As a war correspondent, or "propaganda officer," Babel was expected to use literature to spread socialist views. While full of political and moral motifs, the stories remain ambiguous as to any final opinion. Instead, they are atmospheric, intense and confusing; their narrators present an amalgam of seemingly contradictory ideas and emotions. Some have interpreted this as a cagey way for Babel to avoid speaking his true feelings as an unconventional Jew. The evasiveness strikes a peculiar emotional chord, as well. In his ambiguity, Babel seems to take the advice of one of his own characters in a very early sketch, a grandmother, who advises a young boy, "Don't give them your heart." In a later story, "In the Basement," he describes himself as "untruthful . . . inflamed."

Because of a failure to pursue the "straight line" of socialist ideology in his writing, Babel became unpopular with the Russian government and faced criticism and pressure from above. Rather than bend to restrictions on his work, Babel instead censored himself and ceased to produce for long periods of time. He had his defenders: Gorky championed Babel's complexity from the beginning of his beleaguered career. In an early letter responding to a harsh newspaper critique by Cavalry commander Semyon Budyonny, Gorky wrote, "It is impossible under these conditions to make very strict demands of ideological consistency" upon writers such as Babel, that is, writers bearing

A Cossack cavalry unit 1914. The narrator in Babel's story is a Russian propaganda officer assigned to educate Cossack troops on Leninist thought.

witness to the vast and violent. He also was referring to the ''condition'' of Babel's acute sensitivity. Other critics have marveled at Babel's strange ability to convey the dark passion of war without romanticizing it, and his ability to take an ironic stance without seeming unsympathetic. Revered literary critic Irving Howe, in an essay for *The New Republic*, recognized in 1955 that Babel was ''the master of his genre.''

After the publication of his second collection, Babel entered a self-imposed silence, choosing to remain unpublished though he continued to write plays, sketches, and stories, and to keep a personal diary. Continued refusal on his part to comply with government demands on his writing, and accusations of espionage which have never been confirmed as true, led to Babel's arrest. Though conflicting stories of his death still circulate, ranging from suicide to pneumonia, it is now known that he was executed after a short trial.

While his small literary output is in part the result of his resistance to spouting political dogma, it also reflects Babel's fragile nature. In late interviews and speeches he explained his silence by claiming that he had little to say, adding that he did not want to punish his readers with bad writing.

Critics noted that while giving these speeches, he appeared weak and resigned. Yet many contemporary writers continue to lament his fate and consider his writing some of the most important and haunting Russian literature. He continues to influence writers today. As facts about his life and eventual arrest continue to unfold and as new works are discovered and translated, Babel remains of serious interest to literary scholars worldwide.

Criticism

Kate Bernheimer

Bernheimer has a master's degree in creative writing and edited Mirror, Mirror on the Wall: Women Writers Explore Their Favorite Fairy Tales *(Anchor/Doubleday 1998). In the following essay, she discusses symbolism in ''My First Goose.''*

When the disconsolate narrator kills a goose in Babel's story ''My First Goose,'' he is not merely getting himself a nice supper. It is true that the narrator is miserably hungry, and that the Cossacks have denied him a share of their food. And the goose, waddling about innocently, makes an easy

What Do I Read Next?

- *Russian Fairy Tales*, collected by Aleksandr Afanas'ev and translated by Norbert Guterman (1945), is a collection recommended by respected Jewish author Isaac Bashevis Singer that includes 200 traditional folk and fairy tales and is full of important Russian literary motifs that were influential on Babel's work.

- *Enormous Changes at the Last Minute* (1979) by Grace Paley, an American writer, is a short story collection marked with irony and wit that sketches tales in the lives of several characters, most particularly Faith, a young woman getting divorced. The stories draw upon a Yiddish tradition of humor and tragedy. This collection was adapted into a popular film of the same title, which stars Ellen Barkin.

- *The Collected Stories* (1983) by Isaac Bashevis Singer, a Yiddish writer, contains magical elements and a deeply moral sensibility and explores the Jewish immigrant experience in America.

- *Arrested Voices: Resurrecting the Disappeared Writers of the Soviet Regime* (1996) by Vitalii Shentalinskii is a non-fiction book that looks at the KGB (Russian police) files on Russian writers repressed during Stalin's reign. Until glasnost, the fates of Soviet Russia's most prominent writers were not known. Shentalinskii inspects detailed KGB reports describing how these writers—including Babel and his friend Maxim Gorky—were arrested, tortured, falsely accused of crimes, imprisoned, and even executed.

- *The Oxford Book of Jewish Stories* (1998), a collection of stories by 52 Jewish writers and edited by Ilan Stavans, begins with a tale by the Hasidic Rabbi Nakhman (1772–1811) of Bratzlav, Poland. This collection includes the writing of such celebrated authors as Franz Kafka, Isaac Babel, Saul Bellow, Isaac Bashevis Singer, Grace Paley, Cynthia Ozick, and Philip Roth. The stories were written originally in about a dozen languages, and the authors are from around the world. The variety of themes include anti-Semitism and the Holocaust, but also domestic affairs, biblical subjects, and interreligious and ethnic relations.

---

enough meal. Nonetheless, this goose serves several other functions in the story. Significantly, the goose is the story's very first image, found at the very beginning—in the title. Even in the title, the image of the goose is symbolic and exceeds the boundaries of Babel's plot. It is only the *first* goose; there will be others after the story ends. And by the end of the story, we can guess that those "others" will not be only geese. Babel makes the goose stand for several other things, through the use of symbolism. Charles Baudelaire, a nineteenth-century French writer of the Symbolist literary movement, defined symbolism as the use of "evocative bewitchment"—language that elevates details to mean more than just their physical parts. One of Babel's favorite literary devices, symbolism, appears prominently throughout this short, disturbing tale.

The goose is central to the story's plot, in which a weak narrator wins over the brute Cossacks, whom he must educate on socialism. Bespectacled, Jewish, learned, and small, the narrator demonstrates his own kind of strength by crushing the head of the goose to win over the brute Cossacks. According to *The New Princeton Encyclopedia of Poetry and Poetics*, a widely used resource that defines critical literary movements, one of the most popular symbols in literature was the swan, "a code word with shifting frames of reference representing pure beauty and the poet's alienation from his surroundings." Babel's goose, a sort of ugly and awkward swan, works this way. Babel describes the unfortunate goose as "inoffensive," while all the other characters—even a pathetic old woman—irritate the narrator. The goose, white and preening,

> More explicitly, at one point in the story, as the narrator walks to the Cossack camp, the old quartermaster advises him to 'mess up a lady.' Yet the bespectacled narrator does not choose to rape. Instead, he shoves an old woman and stomps on her goose.... Throughout this sequence of exchanges, the goose comes to stand in for 'a lady' and symbolizes the female. The goose and the feminine thus become associated with weakness or victimhood...."

stands in contrast to the nasty military camp, but eventually dies in "dung." Its innocence cannot survive the filth of the camp on the physical level, or the "dung" of war on the symbolic level. Likewise, the narrator, identified with the goose and alienated from his surroundings, will lose his innocence to the war.

At the beginning of the story, the narrator admires the boots of Savitsky, the Cossack Commander, which are described as threatening yet seductive. When the narrator encounters the goose, he crushes its head beneath his own boot. Thus he identifies himself with the Cossacks in his violence.

The narrator's difference from the Cossacks is crucial to the story's symbolic weight. Other characters often mention the narrator's spectacles and his frailty. Critics have agreed that the narrator of this story is Jewish, based on descriptions from other Babel stories in which this character appears. The fact that the narrator will not kill a human or rape a woman can be interpreted as symbolic of the morality of his Jewish faith. His faith prevents him

from partaking in the kind of human cruelty required in this socialist, godless war. Instead, the narrator performs a symbolic sacrifice—the killing of the the goose. Just before killing the goose, the narrator exclaims "Christ!" and he shouts "Christ!" again immediately afterward, connecting the death of the goose with the sacrifice of Christ. The meaning of this connection, however, is unclear. Is the narrator embracing the ideal of Christian sacrifice, or does he reject the notion of Christian sacrificial beauty, stomping it with his boot? The ambiguity of this moment typifies the story and much of Babel's prose.

Drawn throughout the plot, in an equally complex manner, is an association between eroticism and brute force. The narrator tells of the Commander's legs, sensuous "like girls sheathed to the neck in riding boots." Later in the story, the narrator sleeps with his legs entwined in other men's legs, "dreaming of women." More explicitly, at one point in the story, as the narrator walks to the Cossack camp, the old quartermaster advises him to "mess up a lady." Yet the bespectacled narrator does not choose to rape. Instead, he shoves an old woman and stomps on her goose. (The landlady confesses to the narrator her suicidal thoughts, which would be considered a crime under Russian Orthodoxy. In this way the narrator becomes a sort of priest, in fact a "heathen priest," as he is a non-Christian.) Throughout this sequence of exchanges, the goose comes to stand in for "a lady" and symbolizes the female. The goose and the feminine thus become associated with weakness or victimhood, yet the narrator also glorifies femininity and dreams of women romantically. In this way, the story strikes a disturbing but sensuous chord.

Babel's use of the goose in "My First Goose" shares historical literary significance with William Butler Yeats's famous poem "Leda and the Swan," which was written at nearly the same time. In that poem, using the swan as the central symbol, Yeats also explores the themes of war and religion. Yeats begins the poem with following lines:

> A sudden blow: the great wings beating still
> Above the staggering girl, her thighs caressed
> By the dark webs, her nape caught in his bill
> He holds her helpless breast upon his breast.

In this poem, Leda is raped by the god Zeus, who has taken the guise of a swan. Leda gives birth to Helen of Troy: consequently, this act leads to the sack of Troy, and the foundation of Greek civilization, and, according to some critics, the establishment of Christianity. In Babel's story, one also finds images of thighs, twitching wings, and women. Yet while Yeats's swan is unequivocally "great," though violent, Babel's goose cannot survive. Rather, the goose, despite its goodness, is actually completely helpless, like its blind female owner. As a Jew in a country where Jews were traditionally persecuted, Babel's narrator identifies with this victim. He cannot brutalize anything without disturbing his conscience. Thus the goose can here be seen as yet another symbol—a Jew. Yeats's swan is his poem's protagonist, masculine and terrible. Babel's goose is his story's victim, feminine and hapless.

Russian folklore had a great influence on Babel's writing, both syntactically and formally. The story of "My First Goose" bears resemblance to a well-known Russian folktale called "The Wondrous Wonder, The Marvelous Marvel." In the folktale, an unhappy husband finds a magical goose. Whenever the goose is killed and roasted, it comes back to life, symbolizing eternal wealth. However, the goose also contributes to the destruction of the marriage. In the husband's absence, the goose witnesses the wife's infidelity. The goose sticks the wife to her lover and drags them to the town square. There they are discovered by the disillusioned husband, who beats his wife. The goose is finally crushed. Here the goose symbolizes goodness and an inevitable fall from grace. The sad husband in the folktale exclaims, "How can I help being sad?" Likewise, the narrator in "My First Goose" is "depressed," and his heart brims over.

The goose bears the weight of eternal sadness just as it embodies eternal beauty. Such is the way of socialism, which is so glorified, flying a straight and lovely line, yet causes violence and cruelty in the war. The propaganda officer knows this, and folds into himself with fear. The goose will come to life in other forms, and meet a similar fate.

Source: Kate Bernheimer, for *Short Stories for Students*, Gale, 2000.

Rena Korb

Korb has a master's degree in English literature and creative writing and has written for a wide variety of educational publishers. In the following essay, she discusses the narrator's dual personality in "My First Goose."

Red Cavalry, Isaac Babel's 1926 collection of 35 stories, drew on the author's experience as a war correspondent for the Red Army during the tumultuous Russian Civil War. From the start, Babel conceived the collection as a larger whole composed of individual parts. In fact, he referred to the stories as "excerpts" or "chapters" of a book. Writes David McDuff in the *Reference Guide to World Literature*, *Red Cavalry* "marks the pinnacle of Babel's literary achievement." In his study *Isaac Babel*, Milton Ehre further commends the collection, finding it the "most important fiction to come out of the Russian Revolution." Most of the stories are told from the point of view of Lyutov, a Jewish war correspondent, as he travels with the Cossack army on their 1920 campaign in Poland. Lyutov, educated and possessing a poet's sensibility, is juxtaposed against the violent backdrop of war and the coarseness of the soldiers.

McDuff further writes that *Red Cavalry* "demonstrates the duality of his [Babel's] nature most forcefully and vividly. . . his personality splits in two." Lyutov wavers between what he is—the "bespectacled, bookish, and sensitive" war correspondent—and what he wants to become—"a true revolutionary and Bolshevik solider with no fear of blood and killing." Indeed, "My First Goose", which Babel placed eighth of 35 stories, depicts a Lyutov drawn to the trappings of the war and wanting the respect of its major players. Savitsky, Lyutov's new commander, becomes an object of admiration that appeals to Lyutov on multiple sensory levels. Lyutov views "the beauty of his gigantic body" and notes the details of his costume—the purple breeches, the raspberry cap, the medals on his chest. Savitsky assails Lyutov on an olfactory level as well as a visual one. Lyutov smells Savitsky's "unobtainable scent and the sickly sweet coolness of his soap." These few words are meaningful, for they demonstrate at the same time that Lyutov inherently understands he will never truly be like the Cossacks ("unobtainable"), he also recognizes that their characteristics are not those to which a person such as himself should aspire ("sickly sweet"). Yet, Lyutov concludes the opening paragraph by affirming again the attractiveness of Savitsky in his comparison of the commander's "long legs" to females. Lyutov's inner conflict, succinctly set up in these opening sentences, is at the core of "My First Goose" and many of the stories in *Red Cavalry*.

Savitsky's ensuing actions immediately demonstrate his masculinity. Even before uttering a word, he hits his riding-switch against the table. Only after such physical assertion does Savitsky return to everyday matters, pulling Lyutov's order toward him and completing it. Savitsky's initial and

"The goose is Lyutov's stand-in for the pure woman whose rape the billet officer had advised would alter the men's opinion. Indeed, Lyutov describes his killing of the goose in sexually violent and degrading terms. 'I caught up with it and bent it down to the ground; the goose's head cracked under my boot, cracked and overflowed. . . .'"

accurate assessment of Lyutov is recognized in this order, for Savitsky allows Lyutov to serve anywhere the army goes except at the front. Savitsky's assessment of Lyutov must be based solely on Lyutov's physical appearance. Lyutov's glasses immediately symbolize his sensibility; Lyutov is not a true soldier. Savitsky is even more derisive when he finds out that Lyutov studied law at the university and calls him a "milksop."

Savitsky turns Lyutov over to the billeting officer, who sums up the prevailing attitude that Lyutov is sure to face: "'Our lads here have a stupid thing about glasses, and there's nothing to be done about it. Your man of distinction—he's not to be found here." The officer further illuminates that the Cossacks value violence and pillage; "'But lay a finger on a lady,'" he says, "'the properest lady that ever there was, and our fighting lads will give you a fond caress. . .'"

Lyutov, however, cannot hide his true self. The Cossacks immediately dislike him. A young soldier even picks up his trunk and hurls it through the air. When it spills open, further, if unnecessary, evidence of Lyutov's nature reveals itself in the form of manuscripts that fall on the ground. The young soldier then "turned his posterior to me and. . . began to emit some disreputable sounds." Although Lyutov recognizes the crudeness of the action—and that the soldier's only real accomplishment is just a

"simple knack," not really a "special" one—Lyutov's inner harmony is still disturbed. His attempts to calm himself by reading a speech of Lenin's in the newspaper do no good, for "the Cossacks tripped over my legs, the lad mocked me tirelessly, and the welcome lines of print approached me by a thorny road and were unable to get to me."

Seemingly without thought, Lyutov takes definitive action that will win him a place among the Cossacks. Significantly, he "put down his newspaper" before demanding of a peasant woman that she feed him, an action that symbolizes his rejection of his truer refined self. When she ignores his request, he "gave her a shove in the chest with [his] fist" and then grabs a *white* goose from the yard. The goose is Lyutov's stand-in for the pure woman whose rape the billet officer had advised would alter the men's opinion. Indeed, Lyutov describes his killing of the goose in sexually violent and degrading terms. "I caught up with it and bent it down to the ground; the goose's head cracked under my boot, cracked and overflowed. The white neck was spread out in the dung, and the wings began to move above the slaughtered bird." Then Lyutov sets about "delving into the goose with the sword." Lyutov's actions mimic on a minute level those of the Cossack soldiers, feared in Eastern Europe for their destruction of Jewish villages as well as their attacks on the women who live there. He chases the fleeing goose, harshly subdues it, forces it to open itself to his superior physical presence, and then penetrates it with a sword, or phallus. That the sword does not belong to Lyutov—who, it must be remembered, is a Jew—demonstrates that he is only *borrowing* the violence of the Cossack soldier, but that he does not *own* such a characteristic. Indeed, to become a Cossack would be to act against his own people.

At first, the Cossacks seem not to notice him, for they "sat unmoving, straight as priests, and had paid no attention to the goose." One Cossack, however, shows that they did witness Lyutov's actions. He says, "'The lad will do all right with us,'" and winks Lyutov's way. Despite this gesture of acceptance, Lyutov demonstrates his unease with what he has done. He "wiped the sword dry with sand," but he can't wipe away his actions or his guilt. He remains "in torment" and views the tawdriness of his physical surroundings. Yet, his interior debate is ever present. At the same time that he sees the moon hanging in the sky "like a cheap earring," he also watches the Cossack eat their supper with "restrained elegance."

Lyutov is soon rewarded for his behavior. All of a sudden, the "most senior of the Cossacks" invites Lyutov to join the men and share their supper until the goose is ready. Surovkov extends his welcome to Lyutov along with the spare spoon stowed in his boot. Earlier, Lyutov had experienced "loneliness without parallel," but now the men set about "making a place" for Lyutov, both literally and physically. The young soldier who had previously mocked Lyutov moves over so Lyutov can sit down and the men listen eagerly as Lyutov reads Lenin's speech aloud. Now the men value his literacy. It can be assumed from Savitsky's previous words that the men cannot read themselves, and this inadequacy on their part shifts the balance of power. Lyutov reads "loudly, like a deaf man triumphant," asserting his new sense of belonging, even his superiority. The night also welcomes him, tucking him up "in the life-giving moisture of its crepuscular sheets" and placing "its motherly palms on my burning forehead." Significantly, Lyutov's acceptance comes with twilight, and the blackness of the sky seemingly reflects the dark turn of his soul. Lyutov, however, ignores the symbolism inherent in his own narrative.

Lyutov also deliberately rejects the obvious differences between himself and the Cossacks. While his pleasure at his acceptance is reflected in his ability to enjoy Lenin's speech, he again takes pleasure in its intellectual puzzle; "I read and rejoiced and watched out, as I rejoiced, for anything crooked in the Lenin straightness." The Cossacks, by contrast, admire the directness of Lenin's words. "'The truth tickles every nostril,' said Surovkov, when I had finished, 'and how is a man to pull it from the pile, yet Lenin hits it at once, like a hen pecking a grain of corn. . .'" The importance of Surovkov's statement—the indication that it reflects the Cossacks' unquestioning view of the world—is underscored by Lyutov's narration: "Surovkov, *platoon commander* [italics mine] of the staff squadron, said *this* [italics mine] about Lenin."

At the end of the story, Lyutov joins five other men sleeping in the hayloft. There, though "our legs tangled together," Lyutov is still not one of them. For he "had dreams and saw women in my dreams." What happens in these dreams is not made clear, but it would seem that continued violence takes place, for Lyutov narrates "*only* [italics mine] my heart, stained crimson with murder, squeaked and overflowed"—the implication being that his brain, the organ of intelligence, rejects any notions of compassion; no matter how he tries, he will remain at *heart* a sensitive, thoughtful person. The end of the story, however, forecasts the ongoing anxiety that will meet Lyutov's attempts to insert himself into the Cossack regime.

Source: Rena Korb, for *Short Stories for Students*, Gale, 2000.

Joe Andrew

In the following essay Andrew compares the first impressions drawn on reading Babel and themes that evolve from a closer examination of the story.

I

Babel's short stories provide excellent material for structural analysis. He is a self-conscious, cerebral writer, often to the point of opaqueness. The story chosen, *My First Goose* is particularly dense in texture and on first reading may well mystify the reader as regards its meaning. It is hoped that the daylight shed on the story in the following pages will remove this obscurity. *My First Goose* now forms part of the *Red Cavalry* cycle of stories which deal with the Civil War period of Soviet history, but was originally published separately. It can quite legitimately be studied in isolation, as can most of the stories of the cycle. Nevertheless reference will naturally be made to the overall themes and conflicts of the cycle, where necessary.

II

First impressions of any work of art involve a perception of the totality of the overall themes of the work, and these will be considered first. In *My First Goose* the central theme concerns a kind of initiation into a group, into a new world. This theme implies two main themes: the individual in relation to the group (with the specifically Russian variation of the intelligentsia and the people) and the fate of innocence and beauty in a harsh world. Among other side issues are the latent sexuality of many of the actions, and the violence inherent in the everyday world. (These themes can be derived from a 'first-reading' response to this particular story but are of course common themes in the *Red Cavalry* cycle). The analysis will be an attempt to see to what extent these first impressions are correct, and at the same time to discover how far Babel was concerned to make us aware of these themes.

III

As we have seen in the Introduction, the three main Formalist concepts for structural analysis are fable, plot and narrative structure. In certain types of

"The basic function of the structure of any work is both to motivate the action, to reveal why things happen, and, even more importantly to dispose the material of the work for the maximum effectiveness."

fiction, for example, detective and mystery stories the contrasts between fable (the actual events) and the plot, or *syuzhet* (the way the reader learns of the events) may be highly important to the structure and effectiveness of the work. Here there is no such disjunction. The fable is deceptively simple: from a mere retelling of events we learn little of what 'really' happened. It seems to be, quite simply as follows: a (presumably) newly-arrived officer is roughly treated, firstly by his divisional commander and then by his new 'comrades'. He wanders off disconsolately, decides he wants to eat, attacks an old woman, kills a goose, and now is accepted by those who had treated him so brutally before. Clearly we must look more deeply. This is the *disposition* of events, but it is their *exposition* that will perhaps reveal rather more.

Indeed, an analysis of the plot does indicate rather more. Neverthless, whereas from an analysis of the plot elements we normally discover the chain of causes and effects, that is, what the story is all about, here we learn remarkably little, as will be seen. This is perhaps principally because the narrator almost never reflects or comments on what is happening—and we will have to look to other levels of analysis to tell us more fully the truth about this particular work. Nonetheless, it is useful to interpret the story on this level: we do discover important aspects of the theme, but perhaps even more importantly it highlights the curiously oblique way in which Babel creates his effects.

The story, then, considered in more detail, opens with a description of the Divisional Commander Savitsky. There are odd notes in this description, with emphasis laid on physical details.

Savitsky welcomes the narrator though in a very ambiguous way, and then sends off his order using rather violent terms. Physical violence is further *suggested* (but no more) in a short conversation between the two, and the narrator is sent off to meet his comrades. On the way there is again a seemingly unmotivated reference to the impending fate for such an intellectual. It should be noted that after none of these suggestions is there the conventional aside of 'I was disturbed', 'This struck me as odd', as for example Lermontov's hero Pechorin comments in a similar situation in *Taman*. By the very mode of narration Babel creates a certain atmosphere. The narrator then meets the other Cossacks, and is totally, and physically rejected. For the first time he is alone, and also for the first time he reflects on his situation, summing up as it were what has happened, although there is nothing like an explicit statement of why he feels as he does.

The second part of the story continues in a similarly enigmatic fashion. The narrator approaches an old woman, asks for food, and receives a bewildering and unexpected answer; he then pushes her away, sees the goose and kills it. No reason is given. Suddenly, his Cossack enemies become friendly: he joins them, eats with them, reads to them, and is relatively happy at the unexpected reversal of his situation. They all fall asleep and he sees bittersweet dreams: the last two lines recapitulate the overall ambiguous, unexplained quality of the story.

Such then is the plot, the 'structure of causation'. The above account is not an excessively 'naive' recounting of events: it does seem that from the actual *events* we learn only this much—that is rather less than we might expect from such an analysis. However, the very ambiguity is revealing, and there are various clues as to the central meaning, which can be more fully discerned from the other levels of analysis. Moreover, what the plot analysis does reveal is that the killing of the goose *is* the central episode (as we suspect from the title). This is the point of peripeteia, after which there is a reversal of the previous situation. Just how complete this reversal is can be seen from a discussion of the narrative structure.

IV

There are a number of aspects to such a discussion. The basic function of the structure of any work is both to motivate the action, to reveal why things happen, and, even more importantly to dispose the material of the work for the maximum effectiveness. Oulanoff succintly expresses this idea: 'The narrative structure is the totality of motives present-ed in the very sequence which appears in the work. What matters is the introduction of a given motive at the moment when this motive achieves the greatest aesthetic effect'. Also important, however, is the arrangement of the material to disclose the theme more clearly and fully to the reader. In the present instance a close examination of the narrative struc-ture enables us to see that Babel was extremely careful to place the killing of the goose structurally (as well as thematically) at the very centre of the work, and thereby he seems to imply all the more strongly that we should look to this event for the meaning of the work.

The killing of the goose is formally marked off in a very clear fashion. Immediately before, and immediately afterwards, two phrases occur: 'I wish to hang myself' (the old woman) and 'Oh Mother of God!' (the narrator) which serve as a simple fram-ing device to isolate the killing off from the rest of the story. This mirror-image effect is highlighted by two references, immediately before and after the killing, to the woman's blindness, and perhaps even more significantly by the fact that the woman ap-pears only immediately before the killing, and dis-appears immediately afterwards. The formal sym-metry is not only satisfying aesthetically, but clearly serves a vital structural function: we are to treat the killing separately, as something set apart. Else-where, the narrative structure serves the function of comparing the narrator's situation before his central experience, and the new state of affairs. The paral-lels are striking and most successful in Babel's concentration on unity of effect. For example, at the beginning stress is laid on the fact that the author is literate: both Savitsky and the quartermaster point out the potential dangers of such a condition, yet is it precisely because he is an intellectual, and reads to the Cossacks, that he has his greatest success with them. (This is further deepened by the two referenc-es to Lenin's speech in *Pravda:* immediately before the killing the words mean nothing to him—after-wards he is exultant as he reads to them.) Originally, the Cossacks as a *group* (while shaving each other) reject him; later it is precisely in the group activity of a meal that they welcome him. This parallel, too, is underscored by the twin references to the Cossack with flaxen hair it is he who emits the obscene noises which so crush the narrator and it is precisely he who asks for the reading. Clearly, *any* of them could have performed the second function, but Babel highlights the dramatic change by using the same character twice.

The change is indeed *dramatic,* involving as it does the crucial, central peripeteia. In general the story follows the traditional pattern of exposition - complication - crisis - dénouement, each of which takes place principally on the psychological level of the narrator's changing experience of the situation. The sequence is: exposition - narrator introduced to Cossack milieu, which is simultaneously sketched in; complication - he is rejected by them; crisis - his feelings of desolation, the killing of the goose; dénouement - acceptance by the Cossacks. As has been shown, the dénouement symmetrically matches the complication, which adds greatly to the power of the central episode. This power is also deepened by the absence of any general prologue or epilogue. As Oulanoff points out, this is typical of the short story, because it only has one 'knot' to be unrav-elled in order to end dramatically or unexpectedly.

However, one must beware of oversimplifica-tion. The actual moment of peripeteia here may seem obvious enough (the killing of the goose), but perhaps the *real* turning point is a little earlier—that is when the narrator lays aside the newspaper and approaches the old woman. It is then that he makes a decision even more crucial than to kill the goose. Indeed, one can point to several 'turning-points' in the story. When the narrator leaves Savitsky's of-fice, he enters the wider world to meet his test; the threatened violence builds up, and then becomes actual violence (when the Cossacks throw him out), and immediately afterwards he is alone, for the first time. Then comes the psychological peripeteia: he lays aside the newspaper, and speaks and acts like the others had done, brutally and cruelly, which leads immediately to the actual killing. So, in one sense this event is only the culmination of a whole series of climaxes, each marked off by being a particular 'first-time' event. The extremely skilful use of the narrative structure by Babel not only serves to emphasise the reversal element, but marks off the series of climaxes leading to the central one.

V

A closely connected level of analysis is the use of recurrent 'key-words', which often play an im-portant structural role. For example, if the same adjective is used to describe two characters, it seems that some thematic link is being made between them; the same is true, of course, if contrasting adjectives are used. In ''My First Goose'' the recur-rent words are mainly terms of violence. Clearly these create a particular atmosphere, but also serve a structural function, of binding certain characters or events together, making certain inferences about their relationship to one another which otherwise would not be so apparent.

Savitsky is described by, and uses, a whole series of terms of violence. All of them are verbs, which reinforces still further his brutal dynamism. They are:

> 'he cut the hut in two'; 'struck with his whip'; 'I'll crush it on the spot'; 'yelled'; 'but here they'll cut your throat for wearing glasses'

The narrator also says of him: 'he yelled, laughing' and a little later we read: 'The elder Cossack shouted to him, and began to laugh'. This close textual similarity binds the two together as an aggressive, threatening unit. Even more significant are the words used of the narrator's first aggressive action: 'I pushed the old woman with my fist'. The construction and words remind us of Savitsky's action 'struck with his whip' and the narrator is clearly linked with Savitsky. Again the change is noted for us by Babel, but the specific link with Savitsky is particularly interesting. Another significant point about the use of semantically identical or related words as a structural device is that no words of violence occur after the apotheosis of violence in the killing of the goose. Once again this central event is marked off as being special. There is, however, one last repetition of the words 'cracked and *bled*' (when the narrator kills the goose) and 'creaked and *bled*' (about his own heart), at the very end. This is a kind of 'lyric recapitulation' of the whole mood of the story, recalling as it does the central episode. Recapitulation is perhaps a more apt assessment of the dénouement of this story than the term 'epiphany'. Many writers indicate the use of this device in *Red Cavalry*, but as has been constantly shown, there does not seem to be here a *single* point of 'revelation', of something that was unknown before. The ending is rather a *reminder* of the awareness reached in the killing, but the specific psychological truth is implicit almost from the beginning.

VI

Because we have to look for the meaning of the central theme in indirect elements, the analysis of setting and of the similes used to convey it is particular important. N. Stepanov described the general tendency to exoticism in Babel's landscapes, the fact that everyday things seem to take on a new appearance, without however, attempting to reveal what structural or thematic function such descriptions play in the Babel short story. In *My First Goose* the treatment of setting not only has the typical function of creating or deepening a particular atmosphere, but plays a vital structural, thematic part in the revelation of the narrator's experience. The role of setting is clear from its very absence at the opening of the story: there is no conventional 'setting of the scene'; the first reference to the setting comes only after the narrator has left Savitsky's office, after he has already been exposed to the latter's verbal assaults. That is, the description of the setting is *reactive,* it acts as a kind of lyrical commentary to the narrator's emotions.

The first reference is even more revealing if we consider it in detail: 'The village street lay before us, round and yellow like a pumpkin, while in the sky the dying sun gave up its pink ghost'. This description is foregrounded against the surrounding narrative background because after the relatively bare prose preceding this (apart from the description of Savitsky) the double image strikes us very forcibly. The first simile, of the street scene, is extremely opaque and cannot be fully interpreted on a realistic level: that is, the street is 'made strange'. More importantly, Babel not only reveals to *us* the new vision of a dirty street, but, because it is described through the narrator's eyes, it reflects his feelings of alienation and spiritual distortion. The image of the setting sun further reveals the essential purpose of the setting in this story. It is another dense image, each part of which is precisely chosen. The very fact of setting, of decline, reflects feelings of depression, but the actual image of 'giving up the ghost', that is, of death, not only reflects the emotional atmosphere but also hints at the later killing. A third layer of meaning emerges from the precise wording of the idea of death. That is, these are the words used to describe the death of Christ on the cross. There is, in fact, a later reference to Christ's agony: 'The lines came to me along a road of *thorns*' an image suggesting the crown of thorns. Through the imagery, then, Babel suggests to us ideas of martyrdom and religious suffering, which is further exploited on other levels, as we shall see.

The next reference to the setting is also in simile form: 'It [the pork] was smoking like one's home in the village, when seen from afar.' This is a much more straightforward simile, perhaps a deliberate cliché: again it serves as an indication of how the narrator feels, precisely because the landscape is seen through his eyes. The setting is the main mode through which we understand his experience: at the same time setting acts as a key structural element in that descriptions of it are placed at crucial moments

—after his 'rejection' by Savitsky, now after his rejection by the Cossacks (and the same later) and reflect his changing experience more exactly than any other element. Moreover, because the setting is foregrounded by being almost always in simile form (in a story where there is little imagery) Babel asks us to pay particular attention to the setting, and therefore it has particular importance in the story.

The last reference to the setting before the killing of the goose is not a simile, yet still has an odd ring: 'The sun was falling *upon me*.' Perhaps Babel deliberately reverts to a more simple description to convey the nadir of the narrator's fortunes. The whole world does indeed seem to be falling in on him. The killing now occurs, and one might expect the description of the setting to change— from the narrative structure we have seen to what extent the killing marks a turning point: the Cossacks immediately gather the narrator into their fold. However, the next reference to the setting is very revealing: 'The moon hung over the courtyard like a cheap ear-ring.' Again a simile reveals the disturbed perception of reality: all is not yet well in our narrator's heart, he is not yet at one with himself or the universe. It is particularly important to use the word 'universe' here: almost all references to the setting involve celestial bodies—the sun twice, now the moon, and later the stars. Babel's choice is, I feel, deliberate, and is meant to show precisely that the narrator feels the whole cosmic order is out of joint as yet. (Incidentally, this also serves as a shorthand reference to the passing of time.)

The two final descriptions of the setting reveal to us more precisely the moment of change. When the narrator has read to the Cossacks, nature absorbs him in a womblike embrace: 'The evening enfolded me in the life-giving moisture of its dusky sheets, the evening pressed its motherly palms to my flaming brow.' The images are still extravagant, exotic, and distorted, but nevertheless reveal a shift in the narrator's response to the external world, in that the image reflects that the narrator has at least regained his former well-being. This change is confirmed in the final paragraph when the Cossacks and the narrator sleep together, 'beneath a roof, full of holes, which let through the stars.' This, then, at the very end is the first undistorted representation of the outside world, the first which reveals a 'normal' perception of reality. The implication of the last three descriptions of, or references to, the setting would seem to be that it is not so much the killing of the goose, the ability to act which restores the narrator's sense of reality: nor even is it the Cos-

sacks' invitation to dinner. Only when he performs his own independent role, as an intellectual, and reads to them does he feel that the world looks kindly on him. One could perhaps extend this process even further: the final image of the evening enveloping him still acts as an extension of his inner state: that is, he is not yet fully integrated into himself, not yet fully autonomous. Only at the very end, when he establishes *physical* contact with the Cossacks can he describe nature *as itself* and not as part of himself. Be that as it may, it remains clear how important the setting is in this story: firstly as a lyrical commentary, and secondly as a structural element, revealing again the very gradual assimilation of the narrator into the Cossack milieu. It reveals the complexity of the story: the main turning point at first seems to be quite obviously and dramatically the moment when the narrator kills the goose, and thereby acts like the Cossacks. The narrative structure, however, indicates that a more important point is his *decision* to act (when he discards the paper). But now the setting reveals two further moments of peripeteia: after the narrator has read to the Cossacks (thereby acting as an intellectual), and when he sleeps with them (sexual fulfilment?). A final statement of theme (or themes) can really only be made when all levels of analysis are completed.

VII

Symbolism in modern literature is rather more problematic than in, say, medieval literature when often one knows the function of Christian (or pagan) imagery. As Wellek and Warren point out it is often possible to work out a symbolic system for certain modern writers, and this undoubtedly exists for Babel, if one examines the cycle of stories as a whole. In the context of the present story, however, what is most striking is the use, admittedly the non-explicit use, of traditional symbolism. This level of analysis is rather more susceptible to subjective intuitions than others, but there seems to be sufficient evidence, both internal and by wider reference, to suggest that Babel means us to see certain actions or things in symbolic terms. Such an analysis illuminates, in fact, events which otherwise would remain obscure or inconsequential.

Reference has already been made in the discussion of the setting to overtones of Christian symbolism. Many of the events seem to reinforce this element, in particular the *ritualisation* of the process of rejection and acceptance. When the narrator first meets the Cossacks they are shaving one another—an irrelevant detail of 'local colour' perhaps. However, it is important to realise that this is, firstly a *communal* activity, which establishes their identity as a social group from which the narrator is excluded, and secondly that it can be seen as a ritual event. This implicit suggestion is immediately reinforced by the narrator's reaction to them—he gives a correct salute, which in the circumstances is somewhat ludicrous (certainly the Cossacks hardly appreciate it); but in itself, it can be interpreted as a ritualised response. Later, when he is accepted by them the ritual aspect is even more apparent: they share a meal together (a very common cultural ritual of acceptance and community, as in the Catholic Mass). This time Babel not only makes the ritual aspect more explicit, but reinforces the specifically religious connotations, already implied in the imagery. He describes the Cossacks: 'They sat motionless, erect as *high-priest*.' They are the high-priests of his initiation into the world of violence and experience. The implication is clear: although the killing itself is not ritualised, the overall pattern is. The narator has to undergo certain initiation rites, fulfil certain rituals in order to join their exclusive world. And when he is finally integrated, at the end of the story, Babel is again very careful to describe the event in terms of a communal activity—they all sleep together. Once more one must look at the precise formulation: 'We slept there, the six of us, warming ourselves from each other, with out legs intermingled.' They do not simply sleep in the same room, they all *share* the activity. Analysing the action in terms of the symbolism adds an important element to the understanding of the action. For the narrator the experience is profound enough to be perceived of as an intensely religious sensation. Furthermore in such an analysis, we are able to appreciate, firstly the power of the experience, and, in aesthetic terms, the remarkable integration of all the various elements on Babel's part to create a unity of effect. As one proceeds with the analysis one is increasingly aware of how one level deepens another, how everything is interconnected to quite an extraordinary extent.

VIII

In the discussion of setting one of the main factors that was stressed was the role it played in revealing the narrator's inner life: that is, everything was seen from his point of view. As is generally recognised, point of view is an essential element in understanding how we perceive and interpret any piece of fiction. Carden emphasises Babel's search, from his earliest stories, to find the right 'voice' for each story. It is precisely the point of view that provides the unity of the individual stories, and of the *Red Cavalry* cycle as a whole. As she says: 'The voice becomes the story. We attend to its tone more than to what it is saying. It is the cement that holds the fragments together, that gives a surface to the story'. It is perhaps generally true that with a 'first-person narrator' type of story point of view must be regarded as a key factor in understanding the story. How far is he objective, how clearly does he see things, what does the way he describes other characters and events tell us about him? As we have already seen, the way he describes the setting tells us at least as much about the narrator as it does about the object described, if not rather more. That is, the narrator reveals his point of view precisely by his manner of description indirectly rather than by explicit statements. The same is true of character description: the representation of Savitsky, for example, tells us more about the narrator than about the proud Cossack. Because everything is so coloured by the narrator's subjective experience, we apprehend the power of events all the more intensely, because we feel a clearly identified human psyche undergoing, suffering these emotions. There is something of a paradox here: as already indicated the story is curiously oblique and impersonal in its mode of narration and we are really never told *explicitly* what it feels like to be in this situation. But this is surely proof of the power of Babel's concise art. He never needs to be explicit because, if we read his words carefully, they tell their own story, and perhaps this gives the story greater power—Babel is acting on our nerves and sensations without our quite realising what he is doing. As Trilling indicates, the sensation on reading *Red Cavalry* is almost one of shock: partly because of the nature of the subject matter, but also because of the mode of narration. It is intense and *ambiguous*, and we can only attempt to resolve this ambiguity by examining the stories in great detail. But to return to the present discussion: the stories are so ambiguous because of the handling of point of view, which enables Babel to leave so much unexplained, and yet to imply so much by the way in which his narrator describes events.

IX

Another important point concerning the narrator is his role in the story as a character, which is at least as importnat as his role as narrator: he is both the 'sentient centre' and the main character. His importance as a character will be more fully discussed in an analysis of the structural relationships between characters. For the moment certain details may be usefully emphasised. He is at first curiously passive, even inert, but then attempts to take his fate into his own hands. He wears glasses, he is *gramotnyy*, he is interested in politics and is isolated from the milieu in which he finds himself. All these details are commonplaces of Babel criticism, but their precise function in this story has nowhere been fully discussed. For the moment they are merely mentioned, to be returned to later.

There would seem to be three central elements in Babel's use of characterisation: the way in which it reflects point of view, the methods of description used, and the recurrent motifs. As a general principle one must first state the fairly obvious: virtually the only approach to character found in the stories is physical description. All the characters are approached from the outside and as with all else in the story we have to look most carefully at the precise formulation of description in order to discover what Babel is attempting to do.

The description of Savitsky opens the story (and is strikingly foregrounded). Although he is to play no active part in the story, far more attention is paid to his description than to anyone else's. We are to take note. In his description his beauty in particular is mentioned and it is a curiously feminine sort of beauty, with his perfume and long shapely legs. The comparison here is of great interest: 'His long legs were *like girls,* encased up to their shoulders in gleaming boots.' In any simile or term of comparison the second element obviously implies something about the first; it is not a simple comparison but implies something qualitative or evaluative. Savitsky's legs are like girls, not like girls' legs as one might have expected. Again there would seem to be strong sexual overtones in the narrator's attitude to him. Savitsky's behaviour is also important as part of his character description. He is aggressive, almost violent, as the verbs used for him clearly imply—*udaril, shylopnu, brosil* (*struck, will crush, threw*). He produces a very strong impression on the narrator who, for once, makes an explicit comment on his feelings: he answers Savitsky's question: 'Envying the iron and flowers of this youthfulness.' This reaction is typical of the narrator in many of the *Red Cavalry* stories. The narrator, as an intellectual feels the power and vitality in the Cossacks, responds to it, envies it, and ultimately tries to emulate it. Furthermore, as Maguire has pointed out the violence has an almost sexual hold over the narrator, and in the remark quoted above

the sexuality of Savitsky, and specifically this aspect, attracts the narrator.

The young Cossack, although only briefly sketched, also strikes the narrator by his physical beauty: we are told only of his flaxen hair and fine face. All men, or at least all Cossacks, seem to appear physically beautiful to the narrator, and the sexual overtones are clearly reinforced by the obscene behaviour of the Cossack. On the other hand, the old woman, as the first *female* character is presented in a strikingly different way. For the first time physical ugliness enters the story: she is not described directly, but only *en passant* when the narrator remarks on her blindness. The shift in approach and emphasis is slight, but in this story we have to notice even the most inconsequential detail, and the change is significant. The old woman is even more emblematic and mask-like than the other characters, and she fulfils a purely symbolic role in the story. It is rather difficult to be precise as to what she symbolises, but we can point to one or two significant details. She appears immediately before the killing, and then vanishes; she is central to the narrator's fate, almost as if she were a supernatural being, meeting the hero at the symbolic cross-roads of his life. Moreover she represents some sort of archetypal victim figure—even the weak, passive, inert narrator pushes her around.

In a sense the goose must also be seen as a *dramatis persona*. Certainly it is presented in a manner strikingly similar to the terms used for the more human characters; that is, through purely physical description. Precise details are again important: the goose is *strogiy* (severe); it has a white neck. Both details seem to echo back, to link up with the previous remarks. Its 'severity' in some ways recalls the majestic, stern Savitsky, while the *belaya sheya* ('white neck') seems an obvious reference to the advice given to the narrator on how to succeed among the Cossacks: 'And if you despoil a lady, a *most pure* lady. . .' (p. 54). The goose is his purest of ladies, and in these terms too the killing takes on obvious sexual implications.

X

But what exactly do all these links and hints at cross-reference tell us? The overall themes of the story now seem obvious and generally accord with the accepted critical opinion of the conflicts involved in the *Red Cavalry* stories as a whole. However things are rather more complicated in Babel than is generally recognised, even if most critics do indicate an awareness of his ambiguity.

Ultimately it is perhaps impossible to know all the levels of meaning together, to discover the 'final truth' about this exceeding complex story, but an examination of the structural use of characters, an unravelling of the various links in the chain should enable us to see more clearly what "My First Goose" is all about.

There exists many ways of forging thematic links between characters in fiction, the most common being kinship, or identity of life situation. In this story all the Cossacks can be seen as one group because of their ethnic identity, but as always we have to look below the immediate surface to see what inferences Babel is making about structural or thematic links between characters. Some of these are obvious but other less so. The important aspects of these links are that the narrator is faced with a series of choices, between opposite ideals or modes of being, although it is not quite as simple as the Jew/Cossacks confrontation. All the important characters can be divided into 'static' and 'dynamic' characters. Savitsky is the most obvious static character, but another is Lenin, to whom five references are made in the story: in a subtle way the two seem to be connected, by their very 'stasis' by standing outside the action. The narrator, the young Cossack, the old woman, the goose are the principal 'dynamic' characters. What structural links, then, are made between and among these various groups, and what are the implications of these links?

Savitsky as we have seen, is linked with the goose: he is described in terms of *straight-lines* (he cuts the room like a standard), he is stern—the goose is 'severe'. The narrator, then, in killing the goose is implicitly 'killing' Savitsky. The narrator and the old woman are quite clearly linked: they both wear glasses, they are both pushed around, the narrator is rejecting what he sees of himself in her, he is deciding that *he* will not be an eternal victim. The narrator and the goose are also linked. Savitsky describes him as *parshiven'kiy* ('mangy'), an attribute usually applied to animals; when the Cossacks throw his case out, he *crawls* on the ground like an animal. Most directly they are linked by the use of lexical repetition. As already mentioned, when the narrator kills the goose, its neck 'cracked and bled': later when the narrator sleeps and dreams, his heart, bloodied by the 'murder' (as he terms it himself) 'creaked and bled.' In killing the goose, then, he is also by virtue of these structural links killing part of himself. That is, he breaks his own 'white neck', his virginal innocence. If he is to join the Cossacks he must reject his past, his 'softness' and this he

attempts to do. Savitsky and Lenin, as we have seen, are linked structurally by being the two main static characters: a further structural link would seem to be made in the curious ambiguous remark the narrator makes about himself while reading Lenin's speech: 'I read, and rejoiced, and caught, as I rejoiced, the mysterious curve of Lenin's straight line'. It is perhaps difficult to elucidate fully this highly elliptical remark, but for present purposes it is important to note the reference to Lenin's 'straight line'—a covert allusion, or linking to Savitsky's 'straight lines'? However, Savitsky has no mysterious curve, and just what this means we can see in a moment. Let us first sum up what now appear to be the implications of the killing, implications made specifically by these structural links. The narrator kills the goose, and thereby he kills a symbol of purity (the white neck), because this has no place in this world; he rejects the elements in himself which had linked him to the old woman, because he is not going to be an eternal victim; he becomes like Savitsky, acting with aggression and brutality (the *sabre* perhaps echoing Savitsky's 'iron'). That is, he reluctantly accepts the need for the iron hand, the 'straight line', rather than the glasses of the old woman. However, because of the structural links made in the story, the theme implies more than initiation, attainment of psychological maturity. Here the link between Savitsky and Lenin is important: the narrator becomes a 'straight-line' man, like Savistky and Lenin, but like Lenin, and unlike Savitsky, the narrator too, has a 'mysterious curve', by the very fact of being an intellectual. Clearly, even after he has acted, he remains an intellectual, by reading politics to the Cossacks; in a sense he does not finally reject his intellectual 'softness' but tries to integrate the two values of action and reflection. This, then, would seem to be the meaning of the 'mysterious curve' which Lenin too retained, despite his ability to act. In this story, at least, the 'irremediable rift' between the two worlds, which Terras describes is bridged, in the symbol of Lenin.

And so the killing of the goose, at first an ambiguous and startling action, can be interpreted on four major levels. In psychological terms it acts as a kind of sexual initiation, the narrator loses his virginity. In religious terms, he is initiated into the secret rites and mysteries of life. In human terms, the outsider joins the group, and finally, and perhaps most significantly, the story has an essentially political 'message'. The intellectual joins the people, he takes power into his own hands, he throws off his oppression, without descending into sheer brutalism, without losing the power to reflect and interpret events and his own actions. Ultimately, perhaps, the narrator tries to emulate Lenin, at least by implication, rather than Savitsky, as it first appears. Yet in the final analysis the ambiguity remains. The conclusion is optimistic in that the narrator acts and overcomes his alienation, but the underlying sadness remains. We remember the goose's white neck lying crushed in the dung (indeed Babel reminds us of it with the final word of the story) 'teklo' (bled), referring back to 'potekla'. The last lines to indeed act as a 'lyric recapitulation': the narrator is happy, yet guilty.

Source: Joe Andrew "Babel's 'My First Goose'" in *The Structural Analysis of Russian Narrative Fiction*, edited by Joe Andrew, Keele University Press, 1984, pp. 64–81.

Sources

Amnesty International Report 1998, Amnesty International Publications, 1998.

Ehre, Milton, A discussion of *Red Cavalry*, Isaac Babel, *Twayne's World Authors Series Online*, G. K. Hall & Co., 1999.

Gorky, Maxim, Letter dated 1928 to Semyon Budyonny, translated by Andrew R. MacAndrew, *Isaac Babel: The Lonely Years, 1925–1939*, edited by Nathalie Babel, translated by Andrew R. MacAndrew and Max Hayward, Farrar, Straus and Giroux, 1964, pp. 387–89.

Hallett, Richard, *Isaac Babel*, quoting "Childhood: At Grandmother's," an early Babel sketch, Frederick Ungar Publishing Co., 1973, p. 15.

Howe, Irving, "The Right to Write Badly," in *The New Republic*, Vol. 133, No. 1, July 4, 1955, pp. 16–18.

McDuff, David, A brief overview of the major themes expressed in *Red Cavalry*, in *Reference Guide to Short Fiction*, 2nd ed., Edited by Lesley Henderson, St. James Press, 1995.

Yeats, William Butler, "Leda and the Swan," in *The Norton Anthology of Poetry*, 3rd ed., Edited by Alexander W. Allison et al., W. W. Norton and Company, 1983, p. 523.

Further Reading

Babel, Isaac, *1920 Diary*, New Haven: Yale University Press, 1997.

    A much-awaited translation of Babel's diary, which contains many sketches that helped form the content of *Red Cavalry*. The diary contains the kind of surprising and contradictory details that are often seen in Babel's fiction.

Carden, Patricia, *The Art of Isaac Babel*, Ithaca and London: Cornell University Press, 1972.

    A well-regarded critical study of Babel's fiction, offering a substantial look at the historical, cultural, and personal influences on his work, as well as acute literary analysis of the writing.

Hallett, Richard, *Isaac Babel*, New York: Frederick Ungar Publishing Co., 1973.

    A thorough, brief introduction to the life and work of Babel, which serves to sort through many conflicting stories about his life and the history of his time.

Pirozhkova, A. N., *At His Side: The Last Years of Isaac Babel*, Grace Paley, foreword. New York: Steerforth Press, 1996.

    A memoir by Babel's second partner, one of the first woman engineers in Russia who helped build the Moscow subway. Like Babel, Pirozhkova remains vague about certain details from his life. Yet this well-written, lyrical memoir does shed light on the socialist perspective and personality of the time during which Babel wrote. While it is not full of definitive biographical or historical information, it offers an emotional portrait of an elusive man

The News from Ireland

William Trevor

1986

"The News from Ireland" hearkens back almost 150 years, to a cataclysmic event in Ireland's history: the Great Famine, which left over a million Irish dead from hunger and drove as many as two million to leave their country of birth. Many Irish peasants were dependent on the potato as their only source of food, and the blight that struck in the 1840s virtually wiped out the country's potato crop. Yet as the Irish author George Bernard Shaw pointed out in his play *Man and Superman*, the term "famine" was a misnomer: throughout the entire period, food products were being exported from Ireland instead of being made available to the starving population.

In "The News from Ireland," Trevor demonstrates the disparity between the starvation of the poor Irish and the comfort of Anglo-Irish who profit from their labor. He evokes the situation through the viewpoint of outsiders who feel no real effect of the famine. Hs characters are all Protestants, the majority from England. The Pulvertafts, who have inherited an English estate in Ireland, have over the years learned to accept the inequities inherent in Ireland and no longer feel uncomfortable about the position of privilege and ease that they occupy. Their new governess, however, has some difficulty acclimating to her new surrounding and accepting such "unintentional wickedness." The story chronicles her shift to complacency, and in so doing, it raises more universal themes: the greater issues of personal and social responsibility.

Author Biography

William Trevor Cox was born in 1928 in County Cork, Ireland, to Protestant parents. His family moved frequently, and Trevor spent his childhood in many different towns throughout the south of Ireland. Because he belonged to the minority religious group, Trevor says he developed early on a sense of being on the "outside looking in." Despite his "outsider" status, however, Trevor described himself as a young man who was "very, very nationalistic, intensely Irish."

Trevor attended Trinity College in Dublin, where he earned a bachelor's degree in history. After his graduation in 1950, Trevor spent the next several years teaching history and art in Northern Ireland and in England. He also spent several years working as a copywriter for a London advertising agency, a job he did not enjoy. Around this time, he began to pursue work as a sculptor; he had first become interested in this art as a teenager. Trevor became known for his church sculpting, and earned his living through his artwork.

Trevor had been writing short stories since his youth, and eventually he decided to write a novel; he later stated that his motivation was the need to earn money. The novel *A Standard of Behaviour*, published in 1958, was generally dismissed as imitative and pretentious. Despite these harsh reviews, in 1960 Trevor gave up sculpting and turned all of his artistic energy into writing. *The Old Boys*, published in 1964, won the Hawthornden Prize for literature. This prize marked the auspicious beginning of Trevor's career as a successful writer.

In 1967, Trevor published his first collection of short stories, *The Day We Got Drunk on Cake*. The title story of his next collection, 1972's *The Ballroom of Romance, and Other Stories*, established his reputation as a talented short-fiction writer. Critics drew comparisons between Trevor and other important contemporary British writers, such as Evelyn Waugh, Graham Greene, and Muriel Spark. His short fiction has even been likened to James Joyce's *Dubliners*. "The News from Ireland" is the title story from a 1986 short-story collection. By the time of its publication, Trevor was generally considered a master of the genre.

Over the years, Trevor has won many prestigious awards, including the CBE (Commander to the Order of the British Empire) in recognition of his valuable services to literature. Universities in Ireland and England have awarded him honorary doctorates in literature. He is recognized as a contemporary short-story master, and he is particularly known for his portrayals of ordinary people.

Plot Summary

"The News from Ireland" opens with the reflections of Fogarty, a butler in the home of the Pulvertafts, an English family who came to Ireland to claim an estate left to Mr. Pulvertaft by an uncle. The Pulvertafts came to Ireland eight years ago, in 1839. Over the years, the Pulvertafts have cleared the overgrown estate grounds and, in general, learned "to live with things." Fogarty wishes they had left the estate unclaimed. Like Ireland's other "visitors," they have taken what is not theirs.

A new English governess has recently arrived at the Pulvertaft estate. Anna Maria Heddoe fascinates Fogarty because she is another visitor who does not truly belong in Ireland. His obsession leads him to read her diary and correspondence.

Anna Maria's diary records her homesickness and her confusion at the place in which she now resides. She understands that outside the walls of the estate, the poor Irish people, suffering the effects of the potato famine, die of hunger. Within the walls, however, the Pulvertafts seem unaware of this tragedy. Even the news that a child has been born with the marks of the stigmata on his hand and feet does not interest them. The Irish people consider the stigmata to be a sign from God in these difficult times, but the Pulvertafts remain engrossed in their own business: piano recitals, weddings, and the construction of a road that encircles the property. The road goes nowhere, but Mr. Pulvertaft supports its construction because it allows him to employ the Irish men who have no work.

The narration switches, exploring the family's and Fogarty's thoughts about Anna Maria. Mr. and Mrs. Pulvertaft think she is settling in, while the daughters, past the age of having governesses, are not concerned with her at all. George Arthur, the son, compares her to the last governess, and Fogarty thinks that she will make the Pulvertafts face the issue of the child with stigmata. Fogarty and his sister, the cook, discuss Anna Maria. Fogarty shares with her the Legend of the True Cross, which Anna Maria told him. The legend says that a seed fell into

William Trevor

the mouth or ear of Adam, the first man. After he died, a tree grew from the seed. The tree was then used to make the cross upon which Jesus Christ was crucified.

Meanwhile, Mr. Pulvertaft and his estate manager, Erskine, oversee work on the road. Erskine had his military career cut short by the loss of an arm. He tells Mr. Pulvertaft that the men working on the road are dissatisfied and ungrateful. While speaking with his employer, Erskine thinks about Anna Maria and how he will propose marriage to her.

In the house, Mrs. Pulvertaft thinks about her plans for her children. Charlotte will marry Captain Coleborne, Adelaide will remain a spinster at home, Emily will travel to foreign countries, and George Arthur must be dissuaded from making a career in the military so he will stay at home and care for the estate. She briefly thinks about the plight of the Irish people, but knows that no one could be blamed for the failure of the potato crop.

The narration returns to Anna Maria's diary. She reports that Fogarty has told her that the child with stigmata has died and the people are anxious; they feel that Christ has been crucified again. Fogarty says that the Pulvertafts believe that the markings on the child were inflicted by the parents, as do

Fogarty and his sister. Anna Maria wonders why the parents would do such a thing, and Fogarty says that hunger and death made them do so: they thought they would be saved if they were considered a holy family.

Life for the Pulvertaft family continues. The workers, attaching an omen to the death of the child, do not show up to build the road, but Mr. Pulvertaft knows they will come back—their hunger will require it. Emily goes on her trip, Charlotte accepts her beau's proposal, George Arthur begins to agree with his family about giving up a life in the military, and Fogarty believes that Anna Maria will leave the house.

Five months after her arrival, Anna Maria still thinks about the plight of the Irish people; they are starving, men haven't the strength to work on the road, and the babies die. The next month, however, her thoughts turn to different issues when she becomes aware of Erskine's interest in her. By the time the road is completed, they have become friends. The following year Charlotte's wedding is celebrated with champagne.

Come September, Anna Maria is still debating Erskine's proposal. At the beginning of November, however, Fogarty advises her not to marry Erskine. He confesses to reading her diary. Then he tells her that it would have been better if the Pulvertaft estate had been left untended to fall into a natural state of decline; it could have been returned back to the people from whom it was taken hundreds of years ago. Fogarty speaks of the "wickedness" that "is not intentional." He says that Anna Maria, as well as Mr. and Mrs. Pulvertaft and Emily, all sensed the wickedness of the dispossession of the Irish people but have come to ignore it. Anna Maria denies this and asks Fogarty to leave. Instead he tells her that the Pulvertaft line should end with George Arthur, and he speaks of a future "that's withering now." He tells her of a dream he had in which the Irish peasants attack the estate. They burn and destroy the buildings and shoot the son of George Arthur. The estate falls into disrepair.

Fogarty's conversation with Anna Maria is to no avail. She marries Erskine. Miss Fogarty speaks to her brother of her belief that Anna Maria will befriend them, but Fogarty says the Erskines will ally themselves with the Pulvertafts instead. Fogarty thinks of how he tried to warn Anna Maria from becoming like the Pulvertafts—accepting and ignorant of what goes on in their new home. He considers Anna Maria a stranger and visitor, but like the Pulvertafts, "she has learnt to live with things."

Characters

Erskine

Erskine, a former English soldier, is the Pulvertafts' estate manager. He is not happy with how life has turned out—ending up in a country that is not his own and having his military career destroyed by the loss of his left arm. He doesn't trust the Irish Catholics, although his job brings him into daily contact with them as he supervises their work on the road and collects their rents. Instead of lapsing into melancholy, however, he sets his sights on Anna Maria, who eventually accepts his proposal of marriage.

Fogarty

Fogarty is the butler to the Pulvertafts. He is a poor Irish Protestant, but an educated man, and he occupies a middle ground between the starving Irish Catholic masses and the rich Anglo-Irish family he serves. In many ways, he is the link between the devastated world outside the estate walls and the idyllic world inside of them. For instance, Fogarty brings the family the news of the child with the marks of stigmata. Fogarty appears to be half-crazed; his obsession with Anna Maria-indicated by his reading of her journals and letters as well as his over-zealous interest in her life—is just one manifestation of his unstable mental state. He also resents the Pulvertafts' takeover of the estate, for he believes it would have been better for the estate to return to nature, and then it could be of use to all the people.

Miss Fogarty

Miss Fogarty, Fogarty's sister, is the cook for the Pulvertaft family. She is a critical woman and she believes that her brother is too solicitous of Anna Maria. Although at first she appears to dislike Anna Maria, after the governess marries the estate manager, she hopes to develop a friendship with her.

Anna Maria Heddoe

Anna Maria Heddoe is the English governess who has newly arrived at the Pulvertaft estate. She is unhappy in her employment, both with the family and the servants and with being away from home. At first, she does not understand the Pulvertafts. For instance, she does not comprehend why they are they not interested in the child born with stigmata, or why they discount the markings. Her emotional discomfort with her surroundings is indicated explicitly through her journal entries as well as implicitly by her physical state, such as her inability to eat much of the food which is served to her. By the end of the story, however, she seems to adopt the Pulvertafts' disinterest. When she marries Erskine, she indicates her acceptance of the Pulvertafts and their isolation from the world around them—the world of the poor starving Irish.

Adelaide Pulvertaft

Adelaide is the plain daughter. She wears glasses, plays poorly at the piano, and seems fated to spend her life on the family estate as the spinster sister. Adelaide is secretly in love with her sister's beau.

Charlotte Pulvertaft

Charlotte is the petite and pretty daughter. She marries Captain Coleborne, although she does not love him. Instead, she is won over by his adoration of her.

Emily Pulvertaft

Emily is the beautiful daughter. Her aesthetic sensibility is more developed than that of others in her family. For instance, she imagines the estate when it was a monastery hundreds of years ago. She persuades her father to send her on a tour of the cities of Europe, where she can absorb their art and architecture. The following year she returns to Ireland, and it seems she will marry in the near future. According to Fogarty, Emily alone of her siblings once sensed the dispossession of Ireland.

George Arthur Pulvertaft

George Arthur is the only son of the Pulvertafts. He is drawn to the romance and intrigue offered by a career in the military, but he is persuaded to forsake his dreams in order to stay at home and learn how to manage the family estate.

Mr. Pulvertaft

Mr. Pulvertaft inherited the estate in Ireland from a distant relative. Although he had not wanted to move overseas, he felt it was his duty to accept the responsibility. Similarly, Mr. Pulvertaft feels he has a duty to employ as many of the Irish peasants as possible to work on estate improvements, and he even makes the road construction a more lengthy procedure than it need be.

Mrs. Pulvertaft

Mrs. Pulvertaft occasionally gets nostalgic for England, but after eight years in Ireland, she has become somewhat accustomed to it. Her discomfort, however, manifests itself through her abdominal pain, which she experiences every day. She has learned to live with the pain by ignoring it, as she has learned to live in Ireland by isolating herself and her family.

Themes

Poverty and Wealth

The differences between poverty and wealth figure strongly in ''The News from Ireland.'' The difficult life of the poor Irish—though they are not seen—is sharply contrasted with the ease of the Pulvertafts' life. The Pulvertafts are a wealthy English family. They enjoy the means to maintain a large estate with several servants. They have the money to provide food for the poor, donations to beggars, and even to employ a number of men to build a road that will encircle their property. The road is essentially an act of charity: it goes nowhere and is unnecessary, but it gives some of the local men a way to earn money. Mr. Pulvertaft acknowledges this truth with his orders to Erskine: ''We must continue to occupy these men.'' Despite a superficial understanding of the plight of their less-fortunate neighbors, the Pulvertafts continue to live in luxury, and their point of view influences their perceptions. For instance, they see the road as an act of benevolence for the community because it provides work; they never understand that for their impoverished community it may symbolize excess and waste.

In contrast, the majority of the Irish Catholics in the community have not even enough money to buy food to stave off starvation. With the failure of the potato crop, they have lost their primary food source. There is little work or food to be had, and people are dying in seemingly countless numbers. Parents feed their babies grass and roots in a futile attempt to provide nourishment. Their monetary poverty also leads to emotional and spiritual poverty, as indicated by their perception of the stigmata child. The Great Famine has made the Irish peasants feel as if they have been forsaken by God; thus they see the child as a sign that God has at last recognized them. If the child's parents actually inflicted the marks on him, however, such an action would also indicate a moral poverty. The sum of the poor Irish experience in the story is one of physical and spiritual emptiness.

God and Religion

By the time the story opens, the Great Famine has been devastating Ireland for about two years; all the Irish peasants have left is their Roman Catholic faith. The child with the marks of stigmata is considered by the people as a ''miracle, a sign from God in these distressful times.'' For a time, this event transforms the community: the priests give sermons about it, the bishop pays a visit to see the child, a letter is sent to Rome. The Irish people in the community believe in the validity of the stigmata, but the child dies. Subsequently the Irish grow discontent, attaching ''some omen to this death.''

In contrast to the faithful Irish, the protagonists of the story, all of whom are Protestant, do not believe that the child was born with stigmata. Fogarty and his sister believe that the parents did it themselves, as a means of saving their lives by becoming a ''holy family.'' The Pulvertafts also come to that same conclusion. Anna Maria is astonished when Fogarty tells her this. ''I could not believe what he was telling me,'' she writes in her diary, ''that all these people had independently dismissed, so calmly and so finally, what the people who were closer to the event took to be a miracle.'' But Anna Maria comes to accept this explanation for the marks on the child, thus indicating her alliance with the other Protestants, all of whom negate the Irish Catholic experience. As Erskine says, the Irish do not think the stigmata child is a fraud ''any more than they believe that the worship of the Virgin Mary is a fraud perpetrated by the priests. Or that the Body and the Blood is. Fraud is grist to their mill.'' Such a statement not only degrades the Catholic religion, but also demonstrates the lack of understanding the plight of the poor Irish people. In trying times, people often rely on their faith to sustain them, but the Protestants in the story would take even that away from the Irish Catholics.

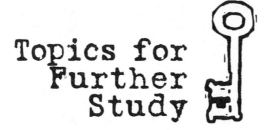

Topics for Further Study

- Find out more about the role of the Anglo-Irish in Ireland during the famine years. Do you think the Pulvertafts reflect a typical Anglo-Irish family? Why or why not?

- Read "The News from Ireland" as if it were your introduction to the cataclysmic famine that devastated the Irish population in the 1840s, then compare it to a history of that time. How does the story portray the famine? Do you think it is an accurate portrayal?

- Imagine that a portion of the story is told through another character's diary entries. Who would you choose to best convey the story, and why?

- Find out what caused the devastation of the Ireland's potato crop in the 1840s, and how

scientists managed to prevent such devastation from occurring again.

- Conduct research to find examples of Irish literature written during the famine years. How do these portrayals differ from or resemble Trevor's?

- Find out more about the efforts taken by the British government to improve the situation of the Irish during the famine. Do you think the government took enough action? What solutions might you propose to alleviate the starvation?

- Do you think the multiple points of view and narrative styles render "The News from Ireland" a more effective story? Explain your answer, using specific examples from the text.

Change and Transformation

The themes of change and transformation are crucial to the story. Fogarty opens the story by presenting the idea of the transformation of Ireland itself. He "thinks of other visitors there have been: the Celts whose ramshackle gypsy empire expired in this same landscape, St. Patrick with his holy shamrock, the outrageous Vikings preceding the wily Normans, the adventurers of the Virgin Queen." All of these people came to Ireland over the centuries and changed it: The Celts dominated the region for over a thousand years. St. Patrick, a Romano-British missionary, brought Christianity to the pagan region. The Viking conquerors attacked in the 700s and 800s but eventually assimilated with the Irish people. The Normans invaded Ireland in 1170 and soon gained great wealth and land, and Queen Elizabeth I sent soldiers to Ireland, which effectively brought Ireland under English control. Fogarty's list indicates that the nature of Ireland has changed over the centuries as "strangers and visitors" have come to dominate the region.

On a more personal level, Anna Maria's transformation into an Anglo-Irish person is demonstrated in the story. When she first arrives, she keenly feels the inequity of the situation. Even five months after her arrival in Ireland, she is still "thinking of the starvation, of the faces of the silent women when they come to the gate-lodge for food." By the end of the story, however, her marriage to Erskine allies her with the other, more callous Protestants. She has come to accept the imbalance that is Ireland.

Style

Setting

The setting of "The News from Ireland" is an unidentified location in Ireland, but the Pulvertaft estate is most likely in a county in southern Ireland, as indicated by the profusion of poor Irish Catholics in the community. At the time the story opens, Ireland has been in the throes of the Great Famine for around two years. Over a million Irish people leave their homes during this period, heading for harbor towns and, with hope, America. They have little choice but to leave their homeland, for they have neither food for their families nor money to purchase food.

The Pulvertafts are English and have been settled on their estate for eight years. Despite this length of time, they do not actively engage with their community, except by giving away food and hiring men to build their road. Instead, they maintain their isolation behind the walls of their estate, demonstrating that they are not really of their community, but rather, exist apart from it. What goes on outside of their walls does not strongly affect them or their actions and decisions.

Point of View and Narration

Trevor uses multiple points of view in "The News from Ireland," allowing the story to explore the innermost thoughts of his characters. The voices of Fogarty and Anna Maria, however, are given prominence throughout. Thematically, this makes sense, for the Pulvertafts have already come to accept their role as "strangers and visitors" to Ireland, but Anna Maria is still working through her feelings about the events in Ireland and the place of the English there. Fogarty is also deeply concerned with Irish history and the relationship between the Irish and the English. He focuses on Anna Maria because she is the newest arrival, thus a person he hopes to influence.

The story is told chronologically, beginning a few weeks after the arrival of Anna Maria and ending shortly after her marriage to Erskine, more than a year later. Though this is a straightforward narrative style, the narration itself is varied, as indicated by the shifting points of view. The narrative itself also plays with various forms. Some of it employs traditional storytelling technique, such as use of dialogue and description, but Anna Maria's point of view is solely expressed through her diary entries.

Symbols and Symbolism

The most important symbol in the story is the child born with the marks of the stigmata. For the Irish peasants, this child symbolizes that God has not forgotten them; God has sent His message to them through the child. For the Protestants and the English, however, the child is seen as a symbol of both the desperation of the Irish people and their desecration of human life. Fogarty expresses the prevailing opinion that the family inflicted the marks

on their infant in the hopes that being a "holy" family would save them in a time of famine. For the Protestants, the stigmata also serves as a symbol of the superstitious nature of the Catholic religion. Erskine vocalizes these thoughts when he talks about the fraud inherent in Catholic religious beliefs.

Other aspects of the story function symbolically. Details emphasize the Pulvertafts self-imposed isolation from their community: the maids shuttering the windows, the wall that surrounds the property. The road also has a symbolic property, both one that is formally recognized in the text and one that is more subtle. Mr. Pulvertaft readily acknowledges that construction of the road is primarily undertaken to provide work for the Irish men in the community. However, the form of the road also has a symbolic content, for it merely encircles the property, essentially going nowhere. Thus the road further reinforces the insular nature of the Pulvertaft family while demonstrating the wasteful excess of the wealthy while others are starving.

Historical Context

The English in Ireland

England first gained control of Ireland in the late 1100s. The English conquerors initiated a program of seizing land belonging to Irish owners and giving it to English settlers, most of whom were Anglican. These landowning Anglo-Irish became the upper class and controlled most of the countries wealth. Over time, much of the land came under the control of these absentee landlords. The majority of native Irish were Roman Catholics and worked as laborers and as tenant farmers on the English estates. They formed the lowest social and economic class. The English brutally repressed the Irish, and at times over the centuries, the Irish rebelled.

In 1801, the Act of Union joined Ireland and Great Britain to form the United Kingdom of Great Britain and Ireland. This act disbanded Ireland's Parliament, but the Irish had little representation in Britain's Parliament. The Irish resented their lack of representation, as well as the use of their tax dollars to support the Anglican Church.

During the 1800s, the British government struggled with Irish nationalists over the issue of home rule for Ireland. In 1916, Irish nationalists revolted

Compare
&
Contrast

- **1840s:** In 1847, one quarter of a million Irish people leave their country. About 75 percent of these immigrants go to the United States.

  1990s: Between 1985 and 1995, more than 150,000 Irish citizens leave their country. The majority of these immigrants go to the United Kingdom. The United States is the next most popular destination; between 1991 and 1994, 47,800 arrive in the United States.

- **1840s:** During the Great Famine, as many as 1.5 million Irish people die as a result of starvation and disease. From 1845 to 1851, the population drops from 8.5 million to 6.6 million, or 23 percent.

  1990s: The population of Ireland by 1999 is around 3.6 million. The death rate is 9 per 1,000 people, and the natural increase of population is .50 percent. The population of Ireland, on the decline since the 1840s, did not begin to rise again until the 1970s.

- **1840s:** Half the Irish population learn the Irish language before they learn English. In 1841, 4 million, or about half the population, spoke Irish, but within ten years only 25 percent of the population could speak Irish.

  1990s: Today, the Irish language is spoken by a distinct minority. Schools teach Irish, but classes are conducted in English.

- **1840s:** It takes at least twelve hours to get from London, England, to Dublin, Ireland, via boat and railway.

  1990s: Plane travel between London and Dublin takes under an hour and a half.

- **1840s:** In 1841, 7 percent of land holdings are over 30 acres, while 45 percent of holdings are under five acres. Over two-thirds of the Irish people depend on agriculture for their livelihood. Despite the Great Famine, by 1850, the area of cultivation has increased by over a million acres.

  1990s: In the 1990s, 12 percent of the Irish workforce is employed in agriculture, which makes up 90 percent of the gross national product. The service industries dominate the Irish economy, and 40 percent of Irish industry is foreign owned.

- **1840s:** In 1841, Daniel O'Connell launches a political movement to repeal the union of Ireland and Britain. Of the 100 Irish representatives in the British Parliament, 39 support this measure.

  1990s: Most Irish citizens (in Southern and Northern Ireland) have come to accept the division. In 1998, an overwhelming majority of voters—94 percent in Southern Ireland and 71 percent in Northern Ireland—voted in support of the Good Friday peace accords, which ceased hostilities between the two factions.

---

in the Easter Rising. The British suppressed the rebellion and executed its leaders. Two years later, fighting broke out between the Irish Republican Army and British troops. Finally, in 1922, a treaty divided Ireland, with the 26 counties of Catholic southern Ireland becoming the Irish Free State. It was a self-governing dominion with ties to Britain. The remaining six northern counties, which were mainly Protestant, remained part of the United Kingdom. Many Irish nationalists refused to accept the arrangement, and civil war again broke out. In 1949, the Irish Free State, now the Republic of Ireland, became completely independent.

Protestants in Northern Ireland came to dominate the government and economy. In the late 1960s, Catholics in Northern Ireland began to demonstrate for an end to discrimination. These demonstrations soon turned violent, and the British government sent in troops. The Irish Republican Army wanted to drive the British out of the north and unite all of Ireland. In the ensuing decades, Northern Ireland was fraught with violence.

Ireland in the 1980s and 1990s

By the mid-1980s, the British government was trying to end the violence in Northern Ireland through political means. The Anglo-Irish Agreement of 1985 gave the Republic of Ireland a voice in the affairs of Northern Ireland, but in time, both Catholics and Protestants denounced the agreement.

In 1993, the British and Irish prime ministers pledged their commitment to the principle of self-determination in Northern Ireland. The IRA declared a cease-fire the following year. The British, however, demanded that the IRA disarm before talks began. The IRA refused and in 1996 renewed its fighting. Peace talks resumed the following year, and the Good Friday peace accords were signed in 1998.

The Irish Potato Famine

In 1845, a fungus struck Ireland's potato crop, the mainstay of Irish agriculture. Irish peasants subsisted on their small potato plots; many worked in return for a plot of land instead of money. At least two million people—one quarter of the total population—depended on the potato for survival. Afflicted plants wilted overnight and yielded potatoes that quickly rotted. By February 1846, only five months after the fungus first struck, the potato disease had struck every county in Ireland and three-quarters of the country's potato crop had been destroyed.

Irish peasants immediately suffered as a result of the destruction of the potato crop. Unable to work or pay their landlords, thousands of Irish families were evicted from their homes. Food prices rose dramatically, and riots to obtain food took place in several cities. A year after the blight was first discovered, the first deaths from starvation were reported. Soon, epidemics and diseases took their hold on the starving human population.

As a partial response, the British Parliament repealed the Corn Laws, which limited the importation of cheap foreign grain, in 1846. While this helped the English population, it made little difference in Ireland, where people could hardly afford to buy bread at any price. In 1846, after another potato crop was destroyed by blight, the British government reinstated a public works program. Local landlords were required to pay for most of the work, but the government would advance them the neces-

sary money as a loan. This program, however, was hard to organize. By December, 400,000 persons were thus employed, but there were still not nearly enough jobs for all the people who needed them.

While the British government continued to make other food items available to the Irish, the prime minister refused to lower the prices or to give food away, fearful that such actions would ruin the United Kingdom's economy. Some private organizations did run charities to feed the starving, and Queen Victoria even donated money to this cause. Under public pressure, and after the deaths of thousands of people, the government decided to distribute free soup and other basic rations. By the middle of July 1847 over three million Irish adults and children were receiving relief. This program, however, ceased in September of the same year. The British government made no more efforts to help the Irish people survive the famine. Throughout the famine years Irish farmers did produce foodstuffs, but these were for import or for those residents who could afford to buy them. Thus bacon, oats, flour, cattle, butter, eggs, and other such provisions were exported from the country while the Irish poor starved to death.

More than two million Irish people left the country between 1845 and 1855. Many left for the port cities of England, and those who could raise the money for passage emigrated to the United States, where they faced great prejudice. The famine lasted until 1849. All told, famine and disease killed over one million people.

Critical Overview

By the time "The News from Ireland" was published in 1986, as part of a collection of short stories, William Trevor was already a highly renowned writer of fiction. As they had done in the past, reviewers acclaimed Trevor's clear style, subject matter, and character evocation. While Trevor continued his trend of exploring the lives of ordinary people, he also expanded his scope to focus on the historical and political turmoil that Ireland has suffered over the centuries.

Reviewers almost unanimously admired the collection. Overwhelmingly, reviewers preferred the stories set in Ireland to those set in England or Italy, where Trevor has also lived. Elizabeth Spencer, writing for the *New York Times* Book Review, believed that his English stories were ''strangely 'produced,' planned instead of crying to be written.'' But she continued, ''It is the news from Ireland that, wander where he will, [Trevor] is always returning to give voice to—and these are the stories with flow and power.'' T. Patrick Hill also lauded the authenticity of Trevor's Irish stories in a review for *America:* ''This book serves as a strong reminder of how authoritatively [Trevor] can hold up a mirror of fiction to reveal a real face of Ireland that many of us . . . cannot fail to appreciate.''

John Dunne was one of the few exceptions to the laudatory reviewers. He wrote in *Books Ireland*, ''generally [Trevor's] work ambles along in a pleasant nondescript manner which, for me at any rate, seldom elicits any emotional response at all.'' Dunne, however, acknowledged the subjectivity of the genre of book reviewing and did not fault Trevor stylistically.

Surprisingly, other criticism stemmed from Trevor's already proven artistry. Geoff Dyer wrote in the *New Statesman*, ''Of Trevor's skill, his understanding of human foibles and weakness—of his stature as a writer, in other words—there is no question. Each of these stories is extremely impressive in its own right; taken as a whole though one wonders what this collection *adds* to his reputation.'' John Fowles, on the other hand, took exception to those who faulted Trevor for his past achievements: ''Everyone conceded that he is a very accomplished writer and then argues that such accomplishment is not enough.'' Fowles opened his *Atlantic* review stating that ''William Trevor is one of the finest writers in English today and that his new collection of short stories equals the best of his past ones,'' and he closed his review by adding, ''I pray my American readers will join the circle round [Trevor's] sad and fastidious but ever seductive Irish voice.''

Most reviewers particularly enjoyed the title story. Wrote Spencer, ''For its grasp of a historical moment, penetration of character and dramatic force, [the title story,] less than 40 pages long, comes close to creating the resonant effect of a full novel.'' A few reviewers, however, saw the story's length and wide-ranging content as a drawback. Fowles believed that Trevor was guilty of ''trying to smuggle the would-be short novel into the short story.'' However, he concludes his discussion of the story with this positive declaration: ''It is a story that needs to be read more than once to be fully savored.'' Veronica Geng, writing for the *New Repub-*

lic, called ''The News from Ireland'' Trevor's ''primal story.'' She explained, ''From it has flowed all his earlier fiction—five volumes of stories, twice as many novels—and he's needed 20 years to be able to write it.'' Overall, many reviewers shared Geng's opinion that Trevor's ''are still the best stories around.''

Criticism

Rena Korb

Korb has a master's degree in English literature and creative writing and has written for a wide variety of educational publishers. In the following essay, she explores the process by which the privileged characters in ''The News from Ireland'' learn to shirk responsibility for the devastation of the Great Famine.

The prolific writer William Trevor is one of the modern masters of the short story. He turned to writing after he had already developed a successful career as a sculptor, and his talent for the written word quickly propelled him to fame. Despite his long-term residence in England and other locations in Europe, Trevor considers himself to be a wholly Irish author. As scholar Kristin Morrison points out, ''Just as Trevor wrote about England from the vantage point of an outsider [in his earliest works], so later he began to write more and more about Ireland only after the years spent in England, Switzerland, and Italy had provided necessary distance, allowing him [in his words] 'to look back from someplace else.''' Indeed, it was several decades into his career before Trevor's fascination with Irish history began to manifest itself, starting with two novels from the 1980s: *Fools of Fortune* and *The Silence in the Garden*. Those novels are now considered masterpieces of Irish fiction, as is Trevor's short story ''The News from Ireland.''

''The News from Ireland'' immediately distinguishes itself in its length; some of the story's first reviewers dubbed it a would-be novel. However, the length of the story mirrors its breadth of scope. In this story, Trevor hauntingly evokes the Ireland of the 1840s, when the nation was caught in the midst of the Great Famine that led to the deaths of as many as 1.5 million Irish, or almost 18 percent of the estimated population of 8.5 million. However, Trevor also raises issues that extend beyond the tragedy of the famine, particularly ideas of personal and social

What Do I Read Next?

- Trevor's fiction has been compared to that of the Irish writer James Joyce. Joyce's short story collection *The Dubliners* (1914) explores facets of life in Ireland from the viewpoints of children and adults, and raises political, artistic, and religious concerns. The final story of the work, "The Dead," is considered a masterpiece of fiction worldwide.

- Graham Greene's novel *Brighton Rock* (1938) explores sin and redemption through evocation of a British teenage gang leader and his young wife. Both are Roman Catholics, and their religious background plays a major role in their thoughts if not their actions.

- British writer Elizabeth Bowen's novel *The House in Paris* (1935) reveals the inner workings of an upper middle-class family through the narration of two children. Against the backdrop of a house in Paris, the family's infidelities and tragedies are revealed.

- Trevor's short story "Beyond the Pale" (1981) explores the political turmoil in contemporary Ireland through the plot device of English tourists exposed to terrorist violence in Northern Ireland. The vacationers are forced to confront their own roles in the Anglo-Irish conflict.

- Seamus Deane's novel *Reading in the Dark* (1996) chronicles an Irish Catholic family in the 1950s and 1960s, relating how the family tragedies hearken decades back and have their roots in the Anglo-Irish conflict.

- Irish writer Sean O'Faolain, known for his carefully crafted, lyrical short stories, presents historical views of the Irish people in 1940s *An Irish Journey* and 1949's *The Irish, A Character Study*. His short stories have also been collected in *The Collected Short Stories of Sean O'Faolain I* (1980), many of which examine the decline of the Irish nationalist struggle and the oppressive provincialism of Irish Roman Catholicism.

- Irish writer Liam O'Flaherty recreates the effects of the Great Famine on the individuals of a small Irish community in his 1937 novel *Famine*.

- Frank O'Connor's stories have been collected in 1981's *Collected Stories*. These stories use mundane incidents to illuminate Irish life.

---

culpability. Though the characters in "The News from Ireland" attempt to escape responsibility, Trevor shows that all people have a moral obligation—a human responsibility.

"The News from Ireland" uses one Anglo-Irish family and their household to draw these universal themes from the famine experience in Ireland. The wealthy and Protestant Pulvertafts arrived in Ireland in 1839, only eight years before the story begins, to claim the estate left to them by a distant relative. Although they aid the Irish peasants with food, monetary donations, and even work projects, they evidence little true understanding of the plight of the people who live outside their walls; thus they belong to the private and protected world.

Fogarty, their half-mad butler, who is also Protestant, recognizes them as foreigners who "belong here now," yet he actively resents their ignorant intrusion. "The wickedness here is not intentional," he says of the Pulvertafts, yet it is wickedness nonetheless. At the same time, however, he recognizes that he "belonged neither outside the estate gates with the people who had starved nor with a family as renowned as the Pulvertafts"—neither in the private world of privilege nor in the public world of poverty. Another member of the household who has no clearly defined place is the English governess, Anna Maria Heddoe, who has recently arrived in Ireland. Her fresh perception is a focal point of the story: as a newcomer, Anna Maria—a "young woman of principle and sensibility" but more importantly, a "stranger and visitor"—still has the ability to see the inequities in Ireland.

Fogarty accuses the Pulvertafts of "perpetrat[ing] theft without being thieves." By this he means that the Pulvertafts have, by virtue of an inheritance handed down among English families since the days of Queen Elizabeth, assumed that their estate is actually *theirs*. Their acts of charity are based on a sense of feeling that they *should* do so, not that they must. Through his litany of those other "visitors" who have overrun Ireland-Celts, Vikings, Normans—Fogarty demonstrates the Pulvertafts' lack of true claim to the land. He would prefer the estate to have gone unclaimed and revert back to its natural overgrown state. The Irish peasants would have eaten the wild fruit that grew there, fished in the lake, and trapped rabbits as game. Fogarty's dream shows his belief that the land should not be usurped and transformed by the conquerors but should belong to those people who would use it most equitably. This vision contrasts strongly with the Pulvertafts' plans, which include improving the land. "Much undergrowth has yet to be cleared and burned," Mr. Pulvertaft says; the natural order of the land must be demolished in order to make the estate habitable for the newcomers.

When Anna Maria arrives on the estate, she instantly senses the disparity between the public and private spheres, the domains of those who have long been in Ireland and those who are newly arrived. Although only in Ireland for a few weeks, she sincerely prays for the Irish peasants, asking for God's mercy. Mrs. Pulvertaft, in contrast, although repeating the reverend's prayer each Sunday "that God's love should extend to the hungry at this time," believes the Irish only deserve as much charity and prayers as she sees fit to disperse. She agrees with the "[J]ust and sensible laws [that] prevent the wholesale distribution of corn," subscribing to the English propaganda that providing food to the starving would destroy the British economy. Thus she shows her agreement with the British government's policy of essentially doing nothing to ease the hunger in Ireland.

Among the actions the British government did take on briefly were work programs to employ the unemployed, and Mr. Pulvertaft hires as many of the local Irish peasants as possible to construct a road that encircles the estate. The Pulvertafts feel they are doing a great service in hiring the Irish men, and Mr. Pulvertaft even creates more work in order to employ more men for a longer period of time.

> "Although Anna Maria continues to despair of the plight of the starving Irish . . ., she is slowly becoming incorporated into the landscape: the world of the Pulvertafts, not the world of the Irish. . . . Yet the transition is slow. Her discomfort with her surroundings and the situation of Ireland is evidenced by her inability to eat the food served by the Irish Catholic cook. . . . Interestingly, Anna Maria, so cognizant of the starvation of the Irish, never faults her own wasteful habit."

Pulvertaft, however, fails to recognize the injustice of spending so much money to build a road that essentially goes nowhere, while people do not even have the means to feed themselves and their families. That the road only traverses the Pulvertaft property also serves to enforce the private, privileged aspect of the estate; along with the wall, it acts as another barrier to protect the family from the outside world of death and devastation.

Mrs. Pulvertaft, like Anna Maria, gives voice to the supposed reason for the famine: God's wrath. Erskine best expresses the Protestant view of the Catholic religion: "Fraud is grist to their mill." Thus, when the village reports a Catholic child born with the marks of stigmata, the Protestants—the Pulvertafts and the Fogartys-believe the parents to have inflicted the injury in order to be considered a "holy" family and be saved from starvation. Anna Maria listens, "astonished," as Fogarty tells her this.'' I could not believe. . .,'' she thinks, ''that all these people had independently dismissed, so calmly and so finally, what the people who were closer to the event took to be a miracle.'' That night she cries before going to sleep, ''hating more than ever the place I am in, where people are driven back to savagery.'' With these words, Anna Maria shows her acceptance of the idea that the Irish parents did mutilate their own child, although it goes against her first instincts. Like the other Protestants, she is ''learn[ing] to live with things'' as they are in Ireland.

Although Anna Maria continues to despair of the plight of the starving Irish and of the ''infant tortured with Our Saviour's wounds,'' she is slowly becoming incorporated into the landscape: the world of the Pulvertafts, not the world of the Irish. Yet the transition is slow. Her discomfort with her surroundings and the situation of Ireland is evidenced by her inability to eat the food served by the Irish Catholic cook. Soon, however, she will more closely resemble Mrs. Pulvertaft, who also manifests physically her discomfort in Ireland. Just as Mrs. Pulvertaft ''has become used to [the discomfort], arriving as it does every day in the afternoon and then going away,'' Anna Maria comes to accept that Fogarty will dispose of her meals—in a sense, making the problems go away. Interestingly, Anna Maria, so cognizant of the starvation of the Irish, never faults her own wasteful habit.

Anna Maria draws closer to the Pulvertafts when she and Erskine, the estate manager, spark up a courtship. The two speak of the Pulvertaft son, who has been persuaded by his family to forsake a career in the military in order to learn to care for the estate. ''He is reconciled now,'' Anna Maria says of George Arthur, but in reality, she is also speaking of herself. When Erskine proposes to her, she ends in accepting his offer and, as Fogarty points out, ''pulling herself up by marrying him.'' At last, she has found a place for herself, and indeed, the marriage seems more out of desire for position than for love. When she first arrived at the estate, she recognized that she belonged with neither the Pulvertafts nor with the servant Fogartys, but once she is Erskine's wife she will sit in church with him ''in the pew behind the Pulvertafts, not at the side of the Fogartys.'' In allying with Erskine, Anna Maria ultimately rejects the public world of the Irish. She no longer is concerned with the difficulties that lie in the country, for after a year residing with the Pulvertafts, her world has already shrunk to the goings-on inside of the estate walls.

Still, Fogarty tries to prevent her alignment with Erskine, and hence the Pulvertafts. He tells her that it would be better if the Pulvertaft line should expire with George Arthur. When Anna Maria exclaims that is a wicked thing to say, Fogarty admits that ''It is wicked, miss, but not untrue. It is wicked because it comes from wickedness, you know that. Your sharp eye has needled all that out.'' ''I do not know these things,'' Anna Maria protests, thus negating her former interest in understanding the situation in Ireland and everyone's place in it—both English and Irish. As the story sums up, ''Stranger and visitor, she has learnt to live with things.''

Source: Rena Korb, for *Short Stories for Students*, Gale, 2000.

Liz Brent

Brent has a Ph.D. in American Culture, specializing in film studies, from the University of Michigan. She is a freelance writer and teaches courses in the history of American cinema. In the following essay, Brent discusses themes of invasion and homesickness in Trevor's story.

The characters in William Trevor's story ''The News from Ireland'' are preoccupied with their place in the world. As the story presents the perspective of several different characters, themes of history, nostalgia, and foreignness emerge as dominant in the thoughts of these characters.

History is a central theme of this story. Particularly, Irish national history. The story, first published in the 1980s, is set in the 1840s, during the potato famine in Ireland. The author thus demonstrates an interest in history through setting his story in the context of a historically real era in Irish history which took place some one-hundred-and-forty years earlier. Several characters in the story are equally preoccupied with the history of Ireland. Fogarty, the butler at the home of the Pulvertafts, is keenly aware of Ireland's long history of being invaded by foreign forces. Fogarty resents the presence of the ''Pulvertafts of Ipswich,'' an English family, on the Irish estate of their deceased ancestors. In Fogarty's thoughts about the Pulvertafts, as well as about their newly arrived English governess, Anna Maria Heddoe, he ironically refers to them as ''visitors,'' quickly making the connection of their presence in Ireland to previous ''visitors,'' who were in fact series of ''invaders'' in the history of Ireland: ''Fogarty is an educated man, and thinks of other visitors there have been: the Celts, whose ramshackle gypsy empire expired in this same land-scape, St Patrick with his holy shamrock, the outrageous Vikings preceding the wily Normans, the adventurers of the Virgin Queen.'' For Fogarty, the series of foreign invasions which characterize Irish history are as much a factor in his perspective as if they had occurred in his own life time. Fogarty adds the Pulvertafts to his litany of invaders, following mention of the Normans: ''His present employers arrived here also, eight years ago, in 1839.'' Fogarty even marks the exact year of their arrival, in a similar fashion as one would note the date of an important historical event. Even the fact the Fogarty still thinks of the family in residence as the Pulvertafts ''of Ipswich'' expresses his opinion of them as a people who come from, and rightly belong, elsewhere than in Ireland. Fogarty is particularly preoccupied with the latest ''visitor'' to the estate, Miss Heddoe, the governess, whom he views as ''another of the strangers'' who have accompanied the Pulvertafts, as ''such visitors, in the present and in the past, obsess the butler.'' Miss Heddoe confirms this preoccupation with history, as she writes in her diary that, ''I was not here long before I observed that families and events are often seen historically in Ireland—more so, for some reason, than in England.''

Fogarty's preoccupation with Irish history includes a strong sense of resentment toward all ''visitors,'' past and present. In addition to his preoccupation with Ireland's history of invasions, Fogarty has a strong sense of *nostalgia* for the past. In fact, this nostalgia is warped and distorted to the point that he hopes for the decline and decay of the Pulvertaft's estate, by means of returning to its natural, prehistoric, primitive state, returning ''back into the clay it came from.'' In other words, Fogarty's nostalgia for a past free of invaders goes all the way back to the beginning of time. When in possession of old Hugh Pulvertaft, ''House and estate fell away under the old man, and in Fogarty's opinion it is a pity the process didn't continue until everything was driven back into the clay it came from.''

The new family of Pulvertafts—new to Fogarty, although they have occupied the estate for eight years at the opening of the story—are also interested in the history of their inherited land. Fogarty muses that they have done much to the grounds, ''in their endeavor to make the place what it had been in the past, long before the old man's time.'' The Pulvertafts, however, view the history of their estate as a legitimization of their rightful ownership; as Mr. Pulvertaft remarks, '''There have been

> ''Mrs. Pulvertaft is also 'homesick' for England, haunted by dreams which express her feelings of foreignness and displacement in Ireland. In contemplating the possible dangers of her daughter Emily's plans to travel throughout Europe, Mrs. Pulvertaft thinks nostalgically of England as the only 'safe' place in the world. . . .''

Pulvertafts here, you know, since Queen Elizabeth first granted them the land.'''

But, clearly, for Fogarty, the desire to return the estate to its past state goes infinitely further back in history than what the Pulvertaft's have in mind. Again, from Fogarty's perspective, the Pulvertafts are simply one of many invaders, whose offense against his person, and against Ireland, lies in the fact that they ''did not stay where they were.''

> He wishes to speak the truth as it appears to him: that their fresh, decent blood is the blood of the invader though they are not themselves invaders, that they perpetuate theft without being thieves. He does not dislike the Pulvertafts of Ipswich, he had nothing against them beyond the fact that they did not stay where they were. He and his sister might alone have attended the mouldering of the place, urging it back to the clay.

Fogarty's desire for the departure of these English ''invaders'' is so extreme that he even delights in the fantasy that Miss Heddoe will leave in dismay, that Erskine, the English grounds keeper, will be killed in anger by the Irishmen Mr. Pulvertaft has employed to build the estate road, and that the Pulvertafts will ''return to their native land.'' Fogarty hopes that ''the governess might leave,'' and that: ''Erskine might be knocked from his horse by the men in a fit of anger. . . . Erskine might lie dead himself on the day of the governess' departure, and the two events, combining, would cause these Pulvertafts of Ipswich to see the error of their ways and return to their native land.''

The perspective of the English characters in this story, the Pulvertaft family, the grounds keeper Erskine, and the governess, Miss Heddoe, is contrasted with that of Fogarty. While from Fogarty's perspective, these English ''visitors'' are in fact ''invaders,'' from the perspective of the English characters, their experience on the Pulvertaft estate is that of foreigners in a foreign land. The English are similarly concerned with history and nostalgia, but of a very different nature from that of the Irish Fogarty. As foreigners in Ireland, these characters struggle to find a secure sense of place in their new environs.

Miss Heddoe states in her diary at one point that she is ''homesick'' for England: ''I am homesick, I make no bones about it. I cannot help dwelling on all that I have left behind, on familiar sounds and places. First thing when I awake I still imagine I am in England: reality comes most harshly then.'' In addition to her sense of being misplaced nationally, Miss Heddoe does not have a stable sense of place in terms of her socioeconomic status within the Pulvertaft household. As she writes in her diary, ''I had not thought a governess' position was difficult in a household, but somehow I am finding it so. I belong neither with the family nor the servants.'' Miss Heddoe's distress over her sense of displacement worsens over time. As the famine worsens, and Miss Heddoe learns that the child supposedly born with a stigmata has probably been intentionally marked by its own parents, she comes to despise ''the place I am in'': ''I wept before I went to bed. I wept again when I lay there, hating more than ever the place I am in, where people are driven back to savagery.''

Erskine, the English grounds keeper who eventually proposes marriage to Miss Heddoe, is also aware of his status as a foreigner in Ireland: ''He has ended up in a country that is not his own, employing men whose speech he at first found difficult to understand, collecting rents from tenants he does not trust, as he feels he might trust the people of Worcestershire or Durham.''

Mrs. Pulvertaft is also ''homesick'' for England, haunted by dreams which express her feelings of foreignness and displacement in Ireland. In contemplating the possible dangers of her daughter Emily's plans to travel throughout Europe, Mrs. Pulvertaft thinks nostalgically of England as the only ''safe'' place in the world: ''Only England is not like that: dear, safe, uncomplicated England, thinks Mrs. Pulvertaft, and for a moment is nostalgic.'' Dozing in her room one afternoon, Mrs. Pulvertaft drifts into a dream which expresses her anxiety over occupying an ''unfamiliar landscape,'' and the disjunction between her sense of vulnerability (in the dream she is ''naked''), as a foreigner, and the feelings of comfort and familiarity she experiences inside her home with her family: ''She dreams that she runs through unfamiliar landscape, although she has not run anywhere for many years. There are sand dunes and a flat expanse which is empty, except for tiny white shells crackling beneath her feet. She seems to be naked, which is alarming, and worries her in her dream. Then everything changes and she is in the drawing-room, listening to Adelaide playing her pieces. Tea is brought in, and there is ordinary conversation.''

By the end of the story, these foreigners in Ireland, these ''visitors,'' ''strangers,'' accept their uncomfortable status on the Pulvertaft estate, just as Fogarty has no choice but to accept the perpetual presence of ''invaders'' to his country. In the final lines of the story, Fogarty, probably based on his clandestine reading of her diary, reflects that, although Miss Heddoe is ''sick at heart,'' and ''has wept on her pillow,'' she will remain, and, although she ''has learnt to live with things,'' she will always be a ''stranger and visitor'' in Ireland.

Source: Liz Brent, for *Short Stories for Students*, Gale, 2000.

Richard Bonaccorso

In this essay, Bonaccorso illustrates how Trevor employs his characters to evoke the author's view of historical truth.

What is history? Is it a kind of truth that transcends our individual lives, and, essentially, our understanding? Or is it our creation, an external manifestation of our lives together, of relationships that begin at the level of intimacy? Here, at this base point, we often find the wisdom of fiction.

A prevalent device for the revelation of truth in William Trevor's fiction is his characters' evasion or subversion of it. When these characters are seen in their social contexts, it is historical truth that often emerges like an uninvited guest, insinuating itself into collective experience and individual lives. Amorphous and mainly perceptible in shapes of family, class, and culture, history is ultimately revealed as a moral force adhering to the inheritances and destinies of Trevor's people.

In the story form Trevor does not so much write historical fiction as fictional portraiture in the context of history. And yet in Trevor's hands such group and individual portraiture is an interpretation of history. He envisions Irish history along the lines of Stephen Dedalus' definition, of a "nightmare" from which few awake. Certainly, in Trevor's stories, the recognition of history as nightmare precedes any possible wakefulness. And yet to be sure, there is pain in such an enlightenment.

"Beyond the Pale" and "The News from Ireland," two title stories of the collections published in 1981 and 1986, evidence Trevor's development of historical context as a short story device. In both stories that context moves into the reader's focus from the outer edges of the narrative, paralleling Trevor's vision of the infiltrating effects of history into people's lives. The suggestion is that it moves so subtly that many fail to comprehend it, or, because it seems so sinister in its pervasiveness, willfully avoid contemplating it.

In "Beyond the Pale" the historical element is at first contained almost entirely in one person's (Cynthia's) mind, and, after she receives an external shock, she becomes the medium through which it essentially explodes upon the other characters. Yet Trevor ironically mutes and distances that explosion by writing the story in the first person from the perspective of the emotionally smug and intellectually indifferent Milly. Furthermore, as in the Cassandra myth, Milly and the other characters react to the oddities of Cynthia's behavior rather than to the verities of her message.

"Beyond the Pale" is one of Trevor's many tourist stories. Four middle-aged people from Sussex arrive on their fourteenth annual trip to Glencorn Lodge in County Antrim. The bridge-playing foursome includes Cynthia's husband, Strafe, his old bachelor schoolmate Dekko, and the widowed narrator Milly, with whom Strafe is having an affair. "To Milly," as Ted Solotaroff states, "this is but another aspect of their longstanding comfortable arrangements." Indeed, all four are aware of the relationship, but tactfully wrap it into their complacent cocoon. We begin to sense the story's historical linkage when we notice that this group also insulates its sensibilities from the political violence taking place in Northern Ireland. "We'd come to adore Co. Antrim, its glens and coastline," remarks Milly:

> A prevalent device for the revelation of truth in William Trevor's fiction is his characters' evasion or subversion of it. When these characters are seen in their social contexts, it is historical truth that often emerges like an uninvited guest, insinuating itself into collective experience and individual lives."

Since first we got to know it, in 1965, we'd all four fallen hopelessly in love with every variation of this remarkable landscape. People in England thought us mad of course: they see so much of the troubles on television that it's naturally difficult for them to realize that most places are just as they've always been. Yet coming as we did, taking the road along the coast, dawdling through Ballygally, it was impossible to believe that somewhere else the unpleasantness was going on.

As Gregory Schirmer comments, Milly's euphemistic tone "both perfectly characterizes and ironically undermines" her as one whose "willed innocence . . . rules out any understanding of the world beyond that of the self." But indeed, Trevor also shows that her failure to seek external understanding corrupts her self-awareness.

The small, bookish Cynthia stands in relative isolation within the group, however, and on this occasion suffers a shock of recognition about Ireland and about herself that all but consumes her and causes her to violate the group's placid code. An uncouth young Irishman, "not at all the kind of person one usually sees at Glencorn Lodge," appears as a one-night guest. He is in a distracted state, and finding Cynthia alone, singles her out to have her hear his tragic story. As a youth he had lived in the area near Glencorn Lodge. A young woman he had loved became an I.R.A. bomber in England. In utter despair over her crimes and shattered personality, he has sought her out and killed her. He makes a clumsy attempt to physically touch Cynthia, then goes down to the sea and, with her as an only witness, drowns himself.

When the others return to the lodge they find Cynthia teetering between hysteria and collapse. Their initial sympathy for her is tempered by her insistent protestations over what has happened and its meaning. Wishing to shunt off this new "unpleasantness," they prefer to think that the drowning was an accident and that the man's having touched Cynthia has set her mind astray. "All's well that's over," states Dekko, speaking for the three of them. But Cynthia does not acquiesce as she usually does to their refusal to listen to her, and she slips into a state that seems on one hand deranged and on the other clairvoyant, emerging as one of those manic menaces, those unwelcome truth-tellers that populate Trevor's works: "Can you imagine," she embarrassingly asked, "our very favorite places bitter with disaffection, with plotting and revenge? Can you imagine the treacherous murder of Shane O'Neill the Proud?"

She has been a reader of Irish history, and she mixes old events with present ills. Of course the others cannot and will not imagine such things. But we do, and we begin to sense a link between hysteria and history. Sibylline, she makes a wild but telling connection between the sexual guilt of her companions, their indifference to the day's tragedy, and a history of English colonial abuses in Ireland. Never before has she conceived a unity between these levels of selfish indifference, "the active principle," observes Ted Solotaroff, of their "privileged life." Up to this moment, her reading knowledge of Ireland has served to spice the tourist curiosities of the others. Now and in this form it becomes threatening, and her husband angrily proclaims it "rubbish."

The fear that she inspires in the others convinces us that Cynthia is at least partially right. Her associates certainly generate an atmosphere of hypocrisy that squares with her sense of historical wrongdoing. Though they do not exactly perpetrate imperialism, they perpetuate its spirit by clutching their well-wrought complacency. Whether they are historically guilty by association is another matter. One may wish to apply Kristin Morrison's general point when she argues that ". . .in Trevor's world, the immoral behavior of individuals necessarily wounds the whole social fabric." It seems, however, that Trevor is content in "Beyond the Pale" to show a correspondence rather than a causality. He comes closer to causality in "The News from Ireland."

Although this story, set in mid nineteenth-century Ireland, brings historical event to the doorstep in the form of the Great Famine, history enters tangentially as it does in "Beyond the Pale." The famine's horrible realities are spoken of (and indeed, mythologized) rather than shown, and only gradually do they dominate the feeling of the story. There is an oracular voice to match that of Cynthia in "Beyond the Pale" (that of the butler Fogarty), but in this work even the less emphatic characters seem to express history's manifestations. Active or passive, conscious or unaware, the characters in this story all move within a symbolically-defined historical context. There is no single dramatic crisis as in "Beyond the Pale," but this story more ably bears its historical weight.

The Pulvertafts of Ipswich have come to restore and live in their inherited Big House on an estate ceded to their ancestors during the Elizabethan plantation. It is 1847, and while starvation ravages the native population, the Pulvertafts carry on their renewal of grounds and house within their estate walls and plan an uncomplicated future for their children.

This family inhabits a complacent position similar to that of Milly, Strafe, and Dekko in "Beyond the Pale." Yet its intentions seem benign. Mr. Pulvertaft performs as master steward of his family's traditional succession. In this vein he considers his generation's "contribution to the estate" to be embodied in the construction of a road that is to encircle it. He is quite unaware, however, of how ironically the road symbolizes the Pulvertaft relationship to Ireland. It is a meaningless project, a circle that goes nowhere. It does not connect the estate with the outer world, but rather reenforces and actually extends the old barrier walls that it runs around. It is thought to be constructed as "an act of charity," employing destitute men for miles around, but as such it shows how the Pulvertaft position continues to be empowered by the people's disadvantage. Furthermore, and in spite of his apparent good will, Mr. Pulvertaft has hired a harsh and unscrupulous manager named Erskine to oversee the labor, who will send the men off one by one as gradual starvation makes them too weak to work. For the peasants the road involves heavy, boulder-moving effort; for Mr. Pulvertaft, it represents an aesthetic proposition: "Now, what could be nicer," he resumed, "than a picnic of lunch by the lake, then a drive through the silver birches, another pause by the abbey, continuing by the river for a while, and home by Bright Purple Hill?'' Robert Rhodes calls attention to the story's drawing-room symbolism of ''the Irish maids fastening the shutters and drawing the blinds, further isolating and insulating the family.'' The road becomes another curtain drawn between the powerful and the helpless.

The Pulvertafts hide themselves as a way of coming to terms with the unruly, unencouraging reality of Ireland. Perhaps they also intuit the injustice of their powerful position and the moral compromise that inheres to their acceptance of it. Kristin Morrison comments succinctly: ''The lie that they live is quite simply their assumption that the estate is theirs, that they can live safely within its walls, that their obligations outside are a matter of charity and not justice.'' Theirs is a ''polite'' self-deception, and their avoidance of truth approaches an art form. But the main characters in this moral drama are not the Pulvertafts. Rather they are two household retainers to whom the truth matters greatly: Fogarty, the poor Irish Protestant butler whose residence in the house precedes that of the Pulvertafts, and Anna Maria Heddoe, a principled young Englishwoman who is the newly-arrived governess. Through these two characterizations Trevor respectively separates the visionary and humanistic qualities that were embodied in Cynthia in ''Beyond the Pale.'' This is an effective piece of strategy, for Trevor here wishes to challenge a purely humanistic version of truth.

The unpleasantly insinuating but accurate Fogarty considers the Pulvertafts unwitting meddlers in a world that is not rightfully theirs, ''not themselves invaders'' but perpetuators of a ''theft without being thieves.'' Indeed, although Fogarty is himself devious and ungenerous, he alerts Heddoe to the grand irony of this well-fed family living easily in the midst of famine, assuming ownership while failing to acknowledge responsibility (for indeed, the Great Famine is partially a product of the colonial system that also produced the Big House).

The humanitarian Heddoe, on the other hand, is deeply troubled by the people's suffering and by the Pulvertafts' moral evasions. The story (much of it told through excerpts from her diary) mainly concerns the process of her Irish initiation. Fogarty hopes that she will become rebellious and throw outrage at the Pulvertafts. Ultimately, however, she is more repelled than moved by Fogarty's words and by the horrors beyond the estate walls. Robert

Rhodes observes that this ''desensitization process'' leads to her acceptance of the marriage proposal of Erskine, in effect moving her ''closer to the company of the Pulvertafts.'' Her goodness is compromised in turn, even as that of the Pulvertafts was by their inherited situation.

If such an inertia can overcome Anna Maria Heddoe, one wonders if all is not preordained by past events. What then is this powerful thing we call history? On the one hand it seems a manifestation of startling correspondences—such as a report of a peasant child born with the stigmata. On the other hand, history seems entirely inscrutable (''We live with His mistakes,'' says Fogarty.) Fogarty loves history's revelations. Heddoe is horrified by them. The Pulvertafts avoid them. Erskine manipulates them. Divine or hellish, the force of history seems a monolithic emanation from the beyond. Nevertheless, history is by definition human. In both stories, forces beyond the characters enter into their makeup and destiny, yet most of them fail to notice or willfully dismiss that connection. And yet Trevor shows us that their complacency or moral evasion is part of history itself, that they unknowingly perpetuate the forces they fail to recognize, or perpetrate their evil effects without taking responsibility for doing so. In the later ''The News from Ireland,'' the apparent conversion of the most morally responsible character into the perpetrators' camp lends a more sinister aspect to Trevor's tragic view of history itself.

Source: Richard Bonaccorso, ''Not Noticing History: Two Tales by William Trevor'' in *Connecticut Review*, Vol. XVIII, No. 1, Spring 1996, pp. 21–27.

Sources

Dunne, John, *Encounter*, September, 1986, as quoted in Bruce Allen, ''William Trevor and Other People's Worlds,'' in the *Sewanee Review*, Vol. CI, No. 1, Winter, 1993, pp. 138–44.

Dyer, Geoff, Review, in *The News from Ireland and Other Stories*, *New Statesman*, August, 1986, p. 89.

Fowles, John, Review, in *The News from Ireland and Other Stories*, *Atlantic*, September/October, 1986, p. 57.

Geng, Veronica, Review, in *The News from Ireland and Other Stories*, *New Republic*, June 9, 1986, p. 28.

Hill, T. Patrick, Review, in *The News from Ireland and Other Stories*, *America*, May 2, 1987, p. 371.

Hulse, Michael, Review, in *The News from Ireland and Other Stories*, *Encounter*, September/October, 1986, p. 57.

Morrison, Kristin, *William Trevor*, New York: Twayne Publishers, 1993, a critical study of Trevor's writings.

Spencer, Elizabeth, Review, in *The News from Ireland and Other Stories*, *New York Times Book Review*, June 1, 1986, p. 14.

Further Reading

Course of Irish History, ed., F.X. Martin and T.W. Moody, Dublin: Roberts Rinehart Publishers, 1994.
  A collection of essays by renowned scholars sketching out the history of Ireland.

Foster. R. F., *Modern Ireland, 1600–1972*, New York: Penguin Books, 1993.
  This historical work focuses on Ireland in the past four centuries.

Schirmer, Gregory A., *William Trevor: Study of His Fiction*, London: Routledge, 1990.
  An examination of Trevor's fiction in terms of its fictional technique and moral vision.

Wandering Willie's Tale

Sir Walter Scott

1824

"Wandering Willie's Tale," by Sir Walter Scott, first appeared in Scott's 1824 novel, *Redgauntlet*. The tale is not directly part of the action of the novel; it is simply a story told by one of the characters to another, and in fact is merely the most developed of such stories contained in the novel. Several other times in *Redgauntlet* the action stops while one character tells another the story of his life or of one specific event. In this case, Wandering Willie, a blind fiddler, tells Darsie Latimer, a young man traveling in the Border region of Scotland, a cautionary tale to warn him to be wary of whose company he accepts on his travels, for even a friendly traveler may turn out to be the devil in disguise.

Later in the novel it is revealed that the story Willie told concerns some of Darsie's ancestors, but Darsie and the reader do not know this at the time, and so the story seems at first to be something almost entirely separate from the rest of the novel. Indeed, some early readers of the novel and some later commentators regarded the tale as being quite distinct from the larger work, sometimes praising it at the expense of the novel. Later commentators, however, have tended to see thematic connections between the two. Critics have noted that they both reflect Scott's ambivalent interest in Scottish traditions, and have drawn a parallel between the tale's account of a trip to hell and the novel's depiction of Darsie's encounter with his dark, mysterious uncle. Commentators new and old have praised Scott's

handling of Scottish dialect in the tale, and in general have described the story as one of the best ever written.

Author Biography

Born in Edinburgh in 1771, Scott was interested all his life in Scottish history, folk tales, and the supernatural, three of the major components of "Wandering Willie's Tale." As a child, he listened to stories and songs about the Jacobite rebellions in which some of his distant relatives had fallen, and he developed a lifelong sympathy for the lost cause of Jacobitism, writing about it in several of his novels, including *Redgauntlet*, the novel in which "Wandering Willie's Tale" is found. However, his attitude to Jacobitism and the old feudal and heroic ways was ambivalent; he became a lawyer like his father, and was very much a part of the modern world of law and commerce, in opposition to the old feudal Scotland symbolized by the Jacobites.

In a sense, Scott took it upon himself to seek some sort of incorporation of the old Scotland into the new by writing extensively about Scottish history, notably in his Waverley novels, beginning in 1814 with *Waverley* itself, a story set at the time of the 1745 Jacobite rebellion. Other titles in the Waverley series include *Guy Mannering*, *The Heart of Midlothian*, and *Old Mortality*, the latter being set during the religious struggles involving the Presbyterian Covenanters in the late seventeenth century, the same setting found in "Wandering Willie's Tale." Scott's Waverley novels became very influential in the nineteenth century as a model and an inspiration for the historical novels of William Makepeace Thackeray, Robert Louis Stevenson, and others.

Scott's interest in folk traditions led him to make a series of expeditions to the Border country (where Scotland meets England) in the 1790s in search of folk songs and poems, many of which he eventually published in *The Minstrelsy of the Scottish Border* in 1802. His interest in such folk material, especially any such material with supernatural overtones, continued all his life; most of the incidents in "Wandering Willie's Tale" come from folk legends about ghosts, devils, and hell.

Scott's interest in the supernatural was also stimulated by the influence of German romantic writers and the English writer Matthew Lewis, known as Monk Lewis because of his popular Gothic novel of horror, *The Monk*. Scott made Lewis's acquaintance and contributed to his *Tales of Terror* in 1799. He later wrote about ghosts and demons in such ballads as "The Eve of St. John" and "The Gray Brother" and used supernatural elements in such stories as "The Tapestried Chamber," "My Aunt Margaret's Mirror," "The Highland Widow,", and "The Two Drovers." Supernatural elements can also be found in his novels, notably in *The Bride of Lammermoor*. In 1830, just two years before his death, he produced a nonfiction work on the supernatural, entitled *Letters on Demonology and Witchcraft.*

Plot Summary

"Wandering Willie's Tale" opens with an account of Sir Robert Redgauntlet and one of his tenants, narrated by a character, Wandering Willie, who does not appear in the tale himself. Sir Robert, a strong supporter of bishops, is much feared as a persecutor of Presbyterians during the political and religious struggles in Scotland after 1660. Sir Robert's tenant, Steenie Steenson, has no strong political or religious convictions himself, but he accompanies Sir Robert as a loyal follower on his persecuting expeditions. He also plays the bagpipes for him.

After the 1688 Revolution, Sir Robert's party loses power, and he cannot continue his persecutions. Although he is not punished by the new government, he loses the income he used to receive from the fines imposed on the Presbyterians. As a result, he becomes more strict about collecting his rent from tenants like Steenie, who falls two payments behind and is threatened with eviction.

By borrowing from his neighbors, Steenie is able to raise the rent money and brings it to Redgauntlet Castle, where he finds Sir Robert with his pet monkey, named Major Weir after a notorious wizard. Sir Robert is ill, in part because he has been fretting over having to evict his long-time tenant, and he looks ghastly. He sends Steenie off with the butler, Dougal MacCallum, to have a drink while he counts the money, but Steenie and the butler are hardly out of the room when they hear Sir Robert crying out in agony. Steenie takes fright and runs off, not waiting for a receipt, and word goes round that Sir Robert is dead.

Sir Robert's body is put in his old room in preparation for his funeral. Dougal the butler makes the arrangements, but looks like a corpse himself and finally confides in Hutcheon, another servant, that he has heard Sir Robert calling him on his whistle every night, just as he used to before he died. Dougal says that if he hears the whistle again he will answer the summons as long as Hutcheon goes with him. The whistle sounds that night, Hutcheon and Dougal go to Sir Robert's room, and Hutcheon faints when he sees the devil on Sir Robert's coffin. Dougal is later found dead beside the coffin.

After the funeral, Sir Robert's son and heir, Sir John Redgauntlet, calls Steenie in about the rent. Sir John, a lawyer, will not believe Steenie's claim to have delivered the rent money, since there is no evidence of payment. Steenie has no receipt, the payment is not recorded in the rent book, and the money itself has disappeared. The only witnesses to the payment, Sir Robert and Dougal, are both dead. Sir John accuses Steenie of trying to cheat him and demands to know where the money is. Desperate and angry, Steenie says the money must be in hell with Sir Robert, then runs out of the castle while Sir John calls out for someone to stop him.

Steenie rides off to see one of the men he borrowed money from, hoping he can get some more from him, but the two of them end up arguing, and Steenie rides off through a dark wood to an inn, where he has a drink, curses Sir Robert, and calls for the devil's assistance. On riding away from the inn, Steenie encounters a stranger who offers to help him by taking him to Sir Robert. Steenie is frightened but follows the stranger to a place that looks like Redgauntlet Castle, but is ten miles away from where the real castle is. Dougal, the dead butler, opens the castle door and ushers Steenie into the parlor, where Sir Robert and numerous other dead men, all notorious persecutors of Presbyterians, are carousing. They seem to be enjoying themselves, but their contorted smiles and wild laughter frighten Steenie, who feels like a man in a dream. Sir Robert (or his ghost or a devil in his shape, as the narrator puts it) asks Steenie to play the pipes and offers him food and drink, but following the warnings of Dougal, Steenie refuses and simply insists on getting his receipt. Sir Robert finally gives it to him and tells him the missing money is in the Cat's Cradle. He then asks Steenie to return in a year to pay him

Sir Walter Scott

homage, but Steenie says he serves God, not Sir Robert, at which point everything becomes dark and Steenie faints.

Steenie awakes in the parish churchyard, then goes to Sir John to present the receipt and his story. Sir John at first seems angry at the suggestion his father is in hell, but calms down and wants to look for the money. Hutcheon says that one of the castle's turrets is known as the Cat's Cradle, so Sir John climbs up there, pistol in hand, and shoots when attacked by something coming from the turret. The attacker turns out to be the pet monkey; Sir John flings its dead body aside and announces that the missing money is indeed there. He later apologizes to Steenie for doubting him and asks him to keep quiet about the whole incident, for although it shows Sir Robert to be concerned about justice even after death, it also suggests unpleasant things about where Sir Robert is now. Sir John even offers to reduce Steenie's rent and agrees to let Steenie tell the story to the parish minister, who says that though Steenie has gone far into dangerous matters, he should be safe as long as he lives a careful life from now on. Sir John tries to destroy the receipt, but when he tosses it in the fire it flies up the chimney without burning. He then circulates a story saying that the monkey was to blame for all the strange goings-on; he says the monkey stole the money and blew the whistle, and it was the monkey Hutcheon saw on the coffin. But Steenie insists on his own version, and the narrator says that Heaven knows the truth.

Characters

Tibbie Faw

The female innkeeper who serves Steenie a drink on his way into the dark wood.

Horseman

See Stranger

Hutcheon

A servant in the Redgauntlet household, Hutcheon loyally accompanies Dougal the butler when the latter answers the call of the dead Sir Robert. Later, because he knows the traditions of Redgauntlet Castle, he is able to explain what the Cat's Cradle is, which perhaps suggests the importance of preserving one's connections with the past.

Laurie Lapraik

Laurie Lapraik, a neighbor of Steenie's who lends him money for his rent, puts himself forward as a Presbyterian now that the Presbyterians are in power, but the narrator says he is actually a sly fox who adjusts his beliefs according to what is popular. He refuses to help Steenie a second time, instead unfairly blaming him for persecuting Presbyterians. Through him Scott may be suggesting disapproval of the Presbyterians and a preference for their opponents, the old rough knights like Sir Robert Redgauntlet.

Dougal MacCallum

Dougal is Sir Robert Redgauntlet's loyal butler, ready to follow him even into death. He is friendly to Steenie and gives him important advice in the haunted castle. His relationships with Steenie and Sir Robert suggest something of the close ties that could develop in the old feudal world, in contrast with the purely monetary relationships associated with new men like Sir Robert's son.

Minister

The minister disapprovingly tells Steenie that he was "tampering with dangerous matters" in his adventure, but adds that he will probably be in no further danger from Satan as long as he leads a prudent life from now on. He thus acts as a force for pulling Steenie back from the world of his adventure. On the other hand, he does help spread the story of the adventure by telling it to his wife, who repeats it after he dies.

Sir John Redgauntlet

Sir John is very different from his father. He carries a small rapier, unlike the huge broadsword Sir Robert used to wear, suggesting that violence is less important to him. He is a smooth-talking Edinburgh lawyer who will not believe Steenie about the rent without some supporting evidence for his story. He even accuses Steenie, falsely, of trying to cheat him, and unlike his father, he seems to have no qualms about pressing for his rent and threatening eviction. He is also very much concerned about his reputation, making sure that Steenie does not tell people that Sir Robert is in hell. He does resemble his father at times, for instance, when he swears at Steenie and when he shoots the monkey in the castle turret. But mostly he presents a contrast with his father, being concerned with law, money, and reputation in a way his father was not.

Sir Robert Redgauntlet

On the surface, Sir Robert Redgauntlet looks like the villain of the story. He is a violent persecutor of Presbyterians and is said to be in league with the devil. When his income is reduced, he squeezes his tenants and threatens to evict Steenie. However, he seems to be upset about the eviction threat, as if he would rather not be resorting to such measures; and before his income problems led him to become strict about the rent, he was kind to his tenants and his followers. He inspires loyalty in Steenie and in his butler, and when his son replaces him, the tenants think they would have been better off with Sir Robert. He does end up in hell, perhaps a fitting end for a "rough auld Knight," but he seems to be enjoying himself there in his revels with his companions, and even in hell he is honorable enough to give Steenie the receipt he asks for. He is representative of the good and bad of the old ways, both the violence and the loyalty. Money does not come first for him, as it seems to for his son.

Steenie Steenson

Steenie is the protagonist of the story, but in some ways is quite passive for a protagonist. In part, his social position as a tenant and follower of Sir Robert Redgauntlet creates this passivity. He is not a leader, that is not his role in life; it is his job to support his master even in doing such villainous things as persecuting Presbyterians. The story itself also puts Steenie in a passive position. He does not seek to do great deeds or to go out on adventures; he is pushed into action by external forces: the demand for rent payment and the urgings of the mysterious stranger. However, once embarked on his adventure, Steenie acts bravely and wisely, standing up to the ghost of Sir Robert and not letting himself be lured into taking part in hellish activities. Steenie is no saint—he argues, curses, and calls for the devil's help in the course of the story—but he has been a loyal follower, he has many friends, he ends up declaring his service to God, and overall he is the character with whom the reader is asked to identify.

Willie Steenson
See Wandering Willie

Stephen Stevenson
See Steenie Steenson

Willie Stevenson
See Wandering Willie

Stranger

The mysterious stranger appears out of nowhere as Steenie rides through a dark wood. He has a strange effect on Steenie's horse and frightens Steenie by telling him he can take him to see the dead Sir Robert. Neal Frank Doubleday, in his book *Variety of Attempt*, suggests that the stranger is the devil in disguise, a suggestion also made by the narrator, Wandering Willie, in the passage in *Redgauntlet* preceding the tale. Supporting this view is the fact that the stranger appears just after Steenie calls for help from "Man's Enemy." If he is the devil, however, he is, as Doubleday suggests, in quite a helpful mood. He will not make Steenie bargain his soul away (he comments that Steenie might not like his terms if he gave him money), but he will help him with his financial difficulties.

Major Weir

Major Weir, Sir Robert's pet monkey, is cantankerous like Sir Robert and appears at one point wearing a coat and Sir Robert's own wig, as if he were Sir Robert's alter ego. On one level, his role in the story is to provide an alternative, non-supernatural explanation for some of the strange events at Redgauntlet Castle. He himself is associated with the supernatural, however, through his name, which

Media Adaptations

- The French Romantic poet and dramatist Alfred de Musset adapted "Wandering Willie's Tale" into a French stage play called *La Quittance du Diable* [The Devil's Receipt] in 1830, but the play was not produced owing to revolutionary disturbances that year in Paris. A production was mounted in Avignon, France, in 1998.

- There have been several stage and operatic adaptations of *Redgauntlet*, the novel containing "Wandering Willie's Tale," including English stage productions in 1824, 1825, and 1872, the last named being in Dundee, Scotland (adaptation by A. D. McNeill). A French musical called *Le Revenant*, based on the novel, was put on in 1834 at the Paris Opera-Comique. A French opera called *Redgauntlet* was produced in 1843 (words and music by Paul Foucher and Jules Alboise de Pujol).

is that of a famous wizard. And his resemblance to Sir Robert may be meant to suggest that Sir Robert has something of the animal about him: a wild naturalness, in contrast with his more civilized city-dwelling son the lawyer.

Wandering Willie

The narrator reveals little about himself as he tells the tale, except that he is the grandson of Steenie Steenson, the protagonist. Elsewhere in *Redgauntlet*, however, the reader learns that Wandering Willie is a blind fiddler who travels around the country with his wife, playing his fiddle at dances. He is a wild-looking elderly man with a long gray beard, and he fascinates Darsie Latimer, a young man traveling in the Border region who is seeking to discover his true identity. Though blind, Willie serves as Darsie's guide both literally and figuratively: he leads him to a cottage where a dance is taking place, and he gives him advice, in part through the story he tells him: "Wandering Willie's Tale."

Topics for Further Study

- How well does "Wandering Willie's Tale" fit the pattern of the quest story as outlined by Joseph Campbell in *The Hero with a Thousand Faces*? In what ways, if any, does it differ?

- Compare "Wandering Willie's Tale" with its main source, the folk legend reprinted in Joseph Train's 1814 book, *Strains of the Mountain Muse* (pp. 191–95). Discuss how Scott altered the legend, pointing out specific instances. What did he add or change or leave out? What effect did his alterations have?

- Read the rest of *Redgauntlet* and see to what extent "Wandering Willie's Tale" fits in with the novel of which it is a part. Some commentators have said the tale has little to do with the novel. Others say its themes parallel those of the novel. What is your view? Explain, using examples from both texts.

- Compare the characters of Sir John Redgauntlet and Sir Robert Redgauntlet. Which one does the story seem to favor? Why?

- Research the landlord-tenant relationship in the sixteenth and seventeenth centuries. What were the advantages and disadvantages for both tenant and landholder? Based on your research, do you think most landholders tended to feel kind toward their tenants or did they take advantage of their superior status? Is the character of Sir Robert representative of actual landholders from that era?

- Research the Jacobites and loyalty to James II after the Glorious Revolution of 1688. What kind of reputation did the Stuart family have with their detractors and supporters? From what social groups did they draw their support?

Themes

The Clash of Old and New Worlds

One of the themes of "Wandering Willie's Tale" is the clash between the old and the new. The story begins with a description of the old rough ways of Sir Robert Redgauntlet, his violent attacks on Presbyterians combined with his kind treatment of his tenants and followers. Now, however, the world has changed; the persecutions have ended, and Sir Robert does not ride out on violent expeditions anymore. At the same time, he is forced to be more strict with his tenants about their rent. This upsets him—it may even be what kills him—but he does it, and his son has no qualms at all about continuing the process.

In days gone by, there was more than a monetary relationship between Sir Robert and his tenants; Steenie went out riding with him and played the bagpipes for him and in effect had a friendly relationship with him. The story suggests that Sir Rob-ert's much more modern son will have no time for any of that and will look to his tenants solely for their rent. The feudal days of loyalty and service (and violence) are being replaced by a world focused much more on money and the law.

Nostalgia

Associated with the theme of the clash of old and new is the suggestion that something good has been lost with the passing away of the old world. Early in the story the narrator comments that his grandfather's house is deserted now and in a sorry state. Things have deteriorated; they are not what they were. He also notes that the tenants preferred their old landlord to their new one. In general the story suggests that there was something better about the days of old, despite all their violence: they were a time of fellowship and festivity that seems now to have been lost. Some of that festivity can be seen in the phantom castle, where there is much drinking and singing, but of course all the participants in those revels are dead. In effect, such festivities are dead too; they will not be seen in the real Redgauntlet Castle now that Sir John has replaced his father.

The Role of the Supernatural

One question the story raises is whether to believe in the existence of the supernatural. Did Steenie visit hell? Did the devil appear on Sir Robert's coffin? Did the dead Sir Robert first summon Dougal and then write out a receipt for Steenie? Sir John tries to provide rational explanations for all the events, blaming his father's pet monkey for some of them and suggesting that Steenie's visit to the phantom castle was a dream or the result of too much brandy. One thing Sir John cannot explain away, however, is the rent receipt signed by his dead father; perhaps that is why he tries to burn it. The story seems to suggest that even in a mundane everyday life focused on raising money to pay the rent, there is a place for mystery and the supernatural.

Ambiguity

The uncertainty over whether the supernatural is at work is just one example of ambiguity in the story. A minor example of the same thing is the narrator's statement that he does not know whether the firs in the wood are black, as everyone says, or white. Readers of the whole novel in which the story is found can understand the narrator on a literal level here: he is blind, so how can he tell what color the trees are? But the statement fits into the larger sense of uncertainty in the story, also reflected in uncertainty about the existence of the supernatural and about whether the old rough days were good or bad.

Trusting Strangers

Wandering Willie says the point of his story is not to trust strangers. He says as much when he finishes recounting his tale to Darsie Latimer, in the paragraph of *Redgauntlet* that immediately follows the story. Darsie, however, contests this interpretation, saying that it was because Steenie trusted the stranger in the dark wood that things turned out well for him.

Although Willie is the narrator—and therefore perhaps the one who should know—Darsie seems to be right. It is true that the stranger appears to have been the devil in disguise, but in this case the devil was trustworthy, and so the explanation that Wandering Willie proposes for his own story seems to be false.

Dealing with Dark Forces

Whereas Willie suggests that the theme of his story is that one should be wary of strangers, the story actually suggests that it is necessary to engage with the dangerous aspects of life. The mysterious stranger may have taken Steenie to hell, but that is where he has to go to solve his problem. He has to travel through the dark wood, enter the phantom castle, and confront the ghost or demon who looks like his dead master. At the same time, he must not be lured into staying in hell; he is not to join the devil's party. But he must confront the hellish company in the phantom castle in order to get the receipt that will save him from eviction back on earth.

This theme is a symbolic one having to do with the need to engage with the darker side of life in order to achieve one's ends. One must sometimes wrestle with demons, or at least make demands of them, while at the same time remembering that one's place is not with the demons but back at home. Another way of stating this theme is to say that it is sometimes necessary to go on a heroic quest, like Steenie's visit to his dead master, in order to complete a task in a strange environment and then return to the everyday world strengthened by one's accomplishment.

Style

Point of View and Narration

"Wandering Willie's Tale" has an unusual point of view that combines elements of first-person and third-person narration. On the one hand, the narrator is not a participant in the events; he is not telling his own story in the manner of Huckleberry Finn or one of Edgar Allan Poe's murderers. For the most part, he functions as an objective third-person narrator, recounting the actions of all the characters without entering the minds of any of them, except to comment occasionally that the protagonist is frightened.

On the other hand, the narrator does identify himself as the grandson of the protagonist and refers to his own activities at times. For instance, he tells of recently visiting his grandfather's house and mentions his own knowledge, or lack of knowledge, of the color of the trees in Pitmarkie wood. Readers of the novel in which the story appears know the narrator as a character in his own right (Wandering Willie) who takes part in the action of the novel. Still, this is primarily a story told from an objective third-person point of view, although clearly the narrator must be distinguished from the author; it is Wandering Willie, not Sir Walter Scott, who tells the story.

Folk Tradition, Dialect, and Setting

Wandering Willie mentions at one point that he has heard this story told many times, and the impression conveyed is that of a folk tale handed down through the generations. The story presents itself as part of an oral tradition among ordinary folk, not the work of an individual author. That the story is told in Scots-English dialect reinforces its folk nature and helps transport the reader from the modern rationalistic world to a world of legend in which mysterious, supernatural events can occur.

The story is set in the Border region of Scotland, away from any city, contributing to its folk quality. It is also set in the past; Willie is telling a story of days gone by, further distancing the events from modern rationalism and creating a setting in which the reader is more likely to accept supernatural events. The use of a historical setting, especially the historical overview that begins the story, also enables Scott to draw a contrast between past and present.

Dramatic Form

Scott does something unusual partway into the story, abandoning the normal dialogue conventions of fiction to present the encounter between Steenie and Sir John in dramatic form, that is, with speech headings as if this were a play instead of a story. It is also this particular dialogue that Wandering Willie says he has heard so many times. That comment of his, along with the use of the unusual dramatic form, lets the reader know that this encounter is a crucial one, representing the clash of worlds central to the story.

Flash Forward

Scott uses another unusual device at one point: a brief flash forward into the future, in which Wandering Willie mentions that Sir John in later years voted for the Union between Scotland and England, an action that would have horrified his father. This brief look ahead helps Scott draw the contrast between father and son and between the old ways and the new—between traditional Scotland as a separate country and modern Scotland as a part of the United Kingdom.

Gothic Elements

The story employs many of the techniques of Gothic fiction: supernatural elements including ghosts and demons, wine that turns to blood, and cold water that suddenly boils; Gothic settings such as an old castle and a journey through a dark wood; a mysterious stranger; and moments of terror. However, unlike the traditional Gothic story, the purpose here is not to create terror for its own sake, or to show characters succumbing to supernatural forces, but to show how the protagonist succeeds despite being in a frightening situation.

Symbols and Other Devices

Scott uses the different sort of swords carried by the two Redgauntlets (a small rapier for Sir John, a huge broadsword for his father) to symbolize the two men's different attitudes toward violence. The image of Sir Robert's rent book being propped open by a book of indecent songs also suggests something larger than itself: that Sir Robert is at least as interested in partying as in collecting his rents. And the decay of Steenie's house, as reported by his grandson, is another symbol, this time of how things have deteriorated in general over the years.

The anthropomorphic treatment of the pet monkey (dressed in human clothes, wearing Sir Robert's wig) is part of the eerie, Gothic nature of the story and also functions as a symbol of the eccentric, rough character of Sir Robert.

Historical Context

Scotland in the Late Seventeenth Century

The story begins with an account of Sir Robert Redgauntlet's involvement in actual historical events of the second half of the seventeenth century, including the mid-century civil wars and the persecution of the Covenanters after 1660. The Covenanters were the supporters of the Presbyterian National Covenant of 1638, which had aimed at abolishing bishops in the Church. During the civil wars of the 1640s, the Presbyterians succeeded in removing the bishops. After Charles II regained the throne in 1660, however, the bishops were restored, the Epis-

Compare & Contrast

- **Seventeenth Century:** In the seventeenth century, the old feudal relations involving service and protection, though passing away, still survived to some extent in Scotland, especially in the northern Highlands region.

  Modern Day: Feudal tenure was legally abolished in Scotland in 1748, and by the nineteenth century, when Scott was writing, it was only a memory. Today it is hardly even that; the notion of landlord-tenant relations involving military service or any other sort of relationship beyond rent payment is hard even to grasp.

- **Seventeenth Century:** Scotland in this century still had a lawless, violent aspect; violent persecutions took place, as did fighting between clans. The central government was not always able to assert its control.

  Modern Day: In some ways, the situation in old Scotland resembles the American frontier of the nineteenth century, a region where the rule of law did not always extend and violence was common. Similarly, Scott's writings about the old rough days in Scotland have a certain similarity to twentieth-century Westerns; both describe a violent, lawless past in a romanticized way.

- **Seventeenth Century:** Religious persecution, including laws against Presbyterians and violent acts against them by individuals with or without government sanction, was common.

  Modern Day: Although religious toleration is common today, religious conflict is far from eradicated. For instance, Catholics and Protestants have engaged in violent clashes against each other in Northern Ireland for many years.

- **Seventeenth Century:** Old Scotland was an independent country until the Union with England in 1707. In the years after that, especially after the final defeat of the Jacobites in 1746, Scottish national feeling was a romantic sentiment but little more. It is this sentiment that Scott brings to life in his novels without seriously advocating a return to Scottish independence.

  Modern Day: In the late twentieth century, especially after the collapse of Communism, old national feelings revived around the world. Countries like Czechoslovakia split in two, the old Soviet Union broke up into smaller units, and Yugoslavia tore itself apart in civil war. In Scotland itself, nationalist feeling has increased. At the very end of the twentieth century, though remaining part of the United Kingdom, Scotland got its own Parliament back for the first time in nearly 300 years, along with a limited amount of autonomy.

---

copalian opponents of the Presbyterians took over control of the national Church of Scotland, and many Presbyterian ministers lost their positions. Some of these ejected ministers took to preaching at open-air field-meetings, which the government tried to suppress. Open warfare broke out in 1679, resulting in the defeat of the Covenanters and the imposition of punitive measures on Presbyterians, such as fines, torture, and arbitrary trials and executions, especially during the "killing time" in the 1680s. However, the 1688 Revolution removed the Stuart king (then Charles's brother James II) from the throne and led to the restoration of Presbyterian control of the Church of Scotland. The Church has remained Presbyterian ever since.

In the story, Sir Robert is on the side of the Episcopalians and the Stuarts, both of whom lost in the long run. Similarly, he is associated with the old-fashioned feudal organization of the countryside, in which tenants and landlords had more than just a monetary connection: certain tenants held their land in return for military service and other service in addition to monetary payment. In return, the landlord owed them protection and served as their leader in military activity. This system was dying out in the seventeenth century and was finally abolished by legislation that took effect in 1748.

Scott was sympathetic to lost causes and traditions like those associated with Sir Robert Redgauntlet. In *Redgauntlet* and other novels in his Waverley series, he writes sympathetically of the Jacobites, who fought for the lost cause of restoring the deposed Stuart monarchy, and who were basically the eighteenth-century version of Sir Robert. As Wandering Willie says, Sir Robert was a "Tory, as they ca' it, which we now ca' Jacobites." For Scott, the Jacobites were associated with the past glories of Scotland, which fired his imagination, though at the same time he recognized that the passing away of those glories had been necessary to allow Scotland to develop into a modern, prosperous nation. This ambivalence towards the legacy of the past can be seen in the story: Sir Robert is dead and gone, and in any case was excessively violent, but there is a life to him even in hell which seems missing from his modern lawyer son.

Literary Influences

Colman Parsons, in his book *Witchcraft and Demonology in Scott's Fiction*, traces the sources that Scott drew on for "Wandering Willie's Tale," notably a folk legend published in an 1814 work called *Strains of the Mountain Muse* by Joseph Train. This legend includes many of the elements of Scott's story: a landlord's sudden death which prevents a tenant from getting a receipt for a late payment, the refusal of the landlord's son to believe the payment was made, a stranger who conducts the tenant on a trip to a phantom castle in a wood, the discovery of the dead landlord and other dead men in the castle, and the dead landlord's willingness to provide a receipt. Scott also drew on accounts of anti-Covenanters, which described them as being in league with the devil.

More generally, Scott had a lifelong interest in the supernatural, stimulated by his early reading of German romantic literature, some of which he translated, and by his association with the Gothic novelist Monk Lewis. He also read the Gothic novelist Ann Radcliffe, best known for the novel *The Mysteries of Udolpho*. Scott criticized Radcliffe for providing non-supernatural explanations for the apparently supernatural occurrences in her fiction, something that he has Sir John Redgauntlet do (but not entirely unsuccessfully) in "Wandering Willie's Tale."

Critical Overview

Redgauntlet, the novel in which "Wandering Willie's Tale" first appeared, was not an immediate success when it came out in 1824. One reviewer complained that there were too many villains in the novel and that the heroes were too passive. Others complained that Scott was repeating himself by writing again about the eighteenth-century Jacobites (a group who wanted to return the throne of England to the heirs of James II). However, though the novel as a whole did not win praise, Wandering Willie's story within it did. The *Westminster Review* called Willie's tale the best thing in the book, and Scott's friend Lady Louisa Stuart (quoted in W.M. Parker's preface to the Everyman edition of the novel) wrote Scott to say that "the legend of Steenie Steenson . . . [was] in the author's very best manner." She added that she wished there had been more of Willie in the novel.

At times, the tale has been praised at the expense of the novel. In 1948, the noted critic F.R. Leavis wrote in his influential study *The Great Tradition* that Willie's tale was "the only live part" of *Redgauntlet*. However, critics in the last half of the twentieth century have had a more positive view of *Redgauntlet*. Although some have criticized its eclectic structure (its use of a variety of narrative techniques, including letters, a diary, and objective narration), most have seen it as Scott's last serious novel. They have also rejected the notion that the story is alien to the novel; even though the novel as a whole is realistic and the story is a fantasy, they see thematic connections between the two having to do with the importance of quests and master-servant relations in both. Critics have also noted that both the story and the novel deal with historical conflicts: the seventeenth-century Covenanter struggles (over the Scottish Presbyterian Covenants) in the story and the eighteenth-century Jacobite struggle in the novel.

Scott's overall reputation declined dramatically in the twentieth century. In the nineteenth century, he was celebrated as the "Wizard of the North," and his Waverley novels helped create the genre of historical fiction, but beginning as early as the 1870s he began to fall out of favor and was seen as boring and lacking in seriousness. The last decades of the twentieth century have seen a revival of academic interest in him, but he still has not recaptured the preeminent rank he held during his lifetime. Yet although Scott's reputation and that of

Redgauntlet have fluctuated over the years, "Wandering Willie's Tale" has always won praise. The Victorian poet D. G. Rossetti spoke highly of it, as did the twentieth-century writer John Buchan, who called it one of the best half-dozen stories ever written. Later writers have been somewhat more restrained, saying it is only one of the best 25 or 50, but there is general agreement that it is an excellent story, Scott's best in the supernatural short story genre. In the last two decades of the twentieth century alone, it has appeared in at least five anthologies of supernatural fiction.

Commentators on the story praise Scott for his handling of the Scots dialect, his feeling for the historical period, and his control of his folk sources. Julia Briggs, in her book *Night Visitors: The Rise and Fall of the English Ghost Story*, says "Wandering Willie's Tale" has "a tightness of structure, a logic in its retributive workings, and a careful equilibrium between natural and supernatural elements" that sets it apart from some of Scott's other ghost stories. Neal Doubleday, in his book *Variety of Attempt*, says Scott succeeds so well in this story because he has actual folk materials to work with. H. P. Lovecraft, himself a well-known writer of horror stories, praises Scott's combination of the supernatural and the everyday. In his study *Supernatural Horror in Literature* he says that in Willie's story "the force of the spectral and the diabolic is enhanced by a grotesque homeliness of speech and atmosphere." James L. Campbell, in his article on Scott in *Supernatural Fiction Writers*, sums up the reactions to the story by saying it is "universally admired by readers and critics alike."

Criticism

Sheldon Goldfarb

Goldfarb has a Ph.D. in English and has published two books on the Victorian author William Makepeace Thackeray. In the following essay, Goldfarb discusses the interaction of the themes in "Wandering Willie's Tale" and the connection of the tale to the novel in which it appears.

At first glance, "Wandering Willie's Tale" seems like an odd combination of the supernatural and the mundane. On the one hand, it is the story of a visit to what seems like hell. On the other hand, the point of the visit is to obtain a rent receipt. This odd combination may be what led one commentator (A. O. J.

Cockshut in his book *The Achievement of Walter Scott*) to deny that the story is a tale of the supernatural. And it may be what led another commentator, David Daiches, in his essay on *Redgauntlet* in *From Jane Austen to Joseph Conrad*, to say that the supernatural elements are brought into the story simply to give the feel of a folk tale to what is actually a realistic story about master-servant relations.

However, as Colman Parsons points out in *Witchcraft and Demonology in Scott's Fiction*, Scott's story derives from a real folk tale about a visit to hell; that is, the supernatural elements are not some extra frills stuck on by Scott, but are embedded in the heart of the story. Moreover, the rent payment is also at the heart of the story. Both elements are there in the original folk tale, which in fact is the way with folk tales: they combine the otherworldly with the down-to-earth in an artless fashion, reflecting a time when there was a stronger sense of connection between everyday reality and the world of ghosts and demons.

Indeed, it may be that one of the reasons Scott sets this story, like so much of his fiction, back in the past is to get back to a time when ghosts and demons seemed more real, or at least a time when there were "rough auld Knights" like Sir Robert Redgauntlet, who were so terrifying that one might think they were the "deevil incarnate" or at least had a compact with him.

Sir Robert is a terrifying presence in the story, and yet also a compassionate and just one. He wreaks havoc against the Covenanters, but is kind to his own followers, at least until the changing times force him to start squeezing his tenants for the rent and threatening to evict them if they cannot pay. Similarly, in the novel outside the story, Hugh Redgauntlet, the grandson of Sir Robert, terrifies his nephew Darsie, and yet is a noble and inspiring presence even in defeat. What is more, he provides Darsie with the thing he is looking for: the key to his identity. In the same way, Sir Robert in the story provides Steenie with what he is looking for: his receipt.

There are multiple messages in all this. First, there is the traditional message of quest literature: the hero must confront dangerous forces to obtain what he is looking for. Wandering Willie is quite wrong to tell Darsie that the moral of his tale is that one should avoid strangers. On the contrary, the story suggests that it is important to follow strangers even to hell if one wants to achieve what is neces-

What Do I Read Next?

- *Redgauntlet* (1824) by Sir Walter Scott, the novel in which "Wandering Willie's Tale" is found, is a tale of a young man's quest to discover the secret of his identity told against the background of a failed Jacobite rebellion.

- *Old Mortality* (1816) by Sir Walter Scott is a novel about the struggles between the Covenanters and anti-Covenanters in seventeenth-century Scotland.

- *The Bride of Lammermoor* (1819) by Sir Walter Scott is a love story set against the backdrop of Scottish history and events that may or may not have supernatural explanations.

- *The Supernatural Short Stories of Sir Walter Scott* (1986), edited by Michael Hayes, includes Scott's other supernatural tales.

- "Young Goodman Brown" (1835) by Nathaniel Hawthorne is a short story about a young man who may or may not have attended a witches' sabbath.

- "The Devil and Daniel Webster" (1937) by Stephen Vincent Benet is a story about a struggling American farmer who accepts the devil's help and then regrets it.

- "Thrawn Janet" (1882) by Robert Louis Stevenson is a horror story told in Scots dialect involving the devil.

- *Dr. Faustus* (1594) by Christopher Marlowe is one of the earliest versions of the story of making a deal with the devil.

- *The Odyssey* (8th century BC) by Homer is the original quest story. Odysseus encounters various supernatural beings during his attempt to sail home to Greece.

- *The Hero with a Thousand Faces* (1949) by Joseph Campbell is a non-fiction study of the various heroes and quest motifs found in world folklore and literature, suggesting that all the heroes are just variants of one archetypal hero in one archetypal quest story.

---

sary. At the same time, it is important not to get stuck in hell; in the traditional quest story, the hero must return from his journey with the magic potion or golden fleece or rent receipt, not stay with the sorcerers who gave it to him—or else all his efforts will be in vain. Thus Steenie has to avoid eating and drinking or playing the bagpipes in the haunted castle, and in the novel beyond the story, Darsie has to refrain from joining his uncle's Jacobite conspiracy.

On a less symbolic level, the reason Darsie has to hold back from the Jacobites is that they represent a lost and hopeless cause. They are representatives of a past that cannot return, of an older, more primitive Scotland that has given way to a more modern world. Similarly, in the story, the world of fighting associated with Sir Robert has passed away. He has hung up his pistols and sword, and no longer rides off to slaughter Covenanters. Of course, the violence associated with Sir Robert cannot really be approved; the peace that follows the Revolution is surely better in some ways. And yet there is an ambivalence in the story, as there is in the novel—as indeed there is in all of Scott, according to Daiches.

Scott, says Daiches, had a complex attitude towards tradition and progress. He recognized the benefits of living in a modern, commercial society free of the lawlessness of old Scotland; yet old Scotland, with its heroism and its national pride, had a great appeal for him. He knew the Jacobites had been doomed to lose, and that it was good that they lost, but he sighed for their cause and wrote about them repeatedly.

In the novel, modern society is not particularly appealing. It is represented by, among others, a

Quaker named Joshua Geddes whose efficient modern fishing methods threaten the livelihoods of the old-fashioned spear-fishermen. It is also represented by Peter Peebles, who has foolishly pursued an incomprehensible law case for years, and who is also responsible for having evicted an old woman for not paying her rent, an action that leads indirectly to her death.

The threat of eviction for non-payment of rent is central to "Wandering Willie's Tale" as well. The threat begins when Sir Robert is still the landlord, but the story suggests that Sir Robert is reluctant to carry it out. This would be only natural, for Sir Robert is of the older, feudal world that placed less emphasis on money. In Sir Robert's world, status derived less from wealth than from the number of followers one had; it thus would be foolish to expel tenants. But the changing times have forced Sir Robert to change too; however, he does so with great reluctance. In fact, having to change seems to have made him ill, and symbolically one could say that the change kills him: the idea of evicting Steenie, or even pressing him for money, is too much for him. It is as if he cannot stand to adopt these new commercial ways; he will seek to stick to the old ways or die. Indeed, the next time we see him he is dead, in hell, but carousing and enjoying himself in his raucous old fashion, surrounded by companions.

The point is that the old feudal ways of protection and service can exist now only outside of this world. Thus when Dougal the butler seeks to follow Sir Robert and continue in service to him, he has to die too.

Sir John Redgauntlet, in contrast to his father and Dougal and Steenie, is a representative of the new world. He is a lawyer and has no qualms about pressing for his rent or threatening eviction. He comes across as cold and unfeeling, though no doubt he is less murderous than his father. Those impulses are still there, however, even in this Edinburgh lawyer; they can be seen when he erupts in anger at Steenie, "swearing blood and wounds behind him, as fast as ever did Sir Robert," and when he shoots the monkey.

The death of the monkey further demonstrates the end of the old ways. Named after a famous wizard, Sir Robert's pet seems eerily associated with the powers of darkness, all the wild, animal-like forces that can no longer exist in Sir John's world of law and order. No wonder Sir John is the one who shoots him.

> " The two major themes of the story are the need to confront dangerous, even hellish, forces if one wants to achieve one's ends and the appeal of the old dead Scotland. In a way they connect. The dangerous forces that used to ride abroad in Sir Robert's day, in the days of old Scotland, are dead and gone; if you would seek them now, you must go out of this world, to hell or to haunted castles."

Scott of course is not recommending some sort of return to the violent feudal world of Sir Robert, nor to the world the Jacobites tried to bring back. But he does seem to be suggesting that for all its violence, there was something about the old Scotland that is worth remembering and preserving. There is life in Sir Robert even after death: even in the haunted castle he and his companions seem livelier than Sir John could ever be. And there is honor in Sir Robert too: he will give Steenie his receipt, unlike his legalistic son, who insists on proof from Steenie and will not accept his word.

The two major themes of the story are the need to confront dangerous, even hellish, forces if one wants to achieve one's ends and the appeal of the old dead Scotland. In a way they connect. The dangerous forces that used to ride abroad in Sir Robert's day, in the days of old Scotland, are dead and gone; if you would seek them now, you must go out of this world, to hell or to haunted castles. But you *should* seek them, Scott seems to say. You should not seek to live in some other, unearthly world, but you should journey to such a world, in some symbolic way, to gather some of the strength that is there, some of the strength that has gone out of this world. In "Wandering Willie's Tale" and in the novel in which it appears, Scott himself achieves this feat. In them Scott brings the old powerful world to life again, and he invites his readers to venture into that world for a while so that they may emerge reinvigorated and better able to deal with the more humdrum world in which they live, the world where they must cope with such mundane problems as having to pay the rent.

Source: Sheldon Goldfarb, for *Short Stories for Students*, Gale, 2000.

Lois Kerschen

Kerschen has a master's degree in Creative Writing and a doctorate in literature and has taught English on the secondary and college levels as well as writing for a variety of media. In the following essay, she points out the sources for the storyline in "Wandering Willie's Tale."

During the early 19th century, Sir Walter Scott was considered the greatest European writer, first for his poetry and then for his novels. His income from writing and the anticipation with which the public awaited each new work is comparable to the stature of Stephen King or John Grisham today. Scott largely achieved his success by following the first basic rule of writing: Write what you know. Of course, part of what one knows is what one has read, and good writers draw upon this background. In Scott's case, "Wandering Willie's Tale" is an interesting blend of personal experience and literary study.

Scott spent a great deal of time as a child at his grandfather's home in the country. Away from his middle class life in the city, Scott was exposed to the common people of the Border lands. He saw how they lived, learned their vernacular, and listened to their stories. Eventually, Scott would become a serious collector of folk ballads and tales, not only for their historical value to the Scottish culture, but also as a source of material for his own writing. As if to prove his belief that writers are affected by their environment and the climate of their age, these influences can be seen over and over in a variety of the books that Scott produced.

For example, "Wandering Willie's Tale" is a masterpiece in the use of the vernacular. Scott captures perfectly the language of the characters in his story, thus making the story more realistic and

giving it the "local color" that would become such a popular literary device later in the century, especially in the stories of writers such as Bret Harte and Mark Twain who traveled the American West and South and lived among the people of these regions. By copying the vernacular and describing the style of dress and settings, they shared their experiences, just as Scott did by copying the speech and customs of the Scottish country folk in his story.

Scott's talent also involved his ability to retell an old story in his own creative way. The gist of "Wandering Willie's Tale" was published in 1810 in a version that was only a few pages long. Scott elaborated on the basic story and incorporated into it the above-mentioned elements of local characters and language. In addition, he gave the story familiarity to the reader by including common themes from mythology, devil lore, and fairy tales. Scott was heavily influenced by Germanic and Gothic literature, which was the most fashionable literary trend in Scotland when Scott was a young man studying the law. Germanic and Gothic literature are rife with fairy tales, fantasy adventures, and folk stories of the preternatural. In fact, Scott's first book was a verse translation of two German supernatural ballads.

It is not a big leap from the genre of Grimm's fairy tales and the literature that produced Faust to Willie's tale. The same elements of the dark, the mystical, and the "stranger in the forest" appear in both the fairy tales and Scott's story. The tragedy of Faust, the magician who enters into a contract with the devil, has been copied countless times. The present-day Broadway musical "Damn Yankees" is just another version of the same basic story. In Scott's fantasy tale, Steenie Steenson reports that Sir Robert was thought to have "a direct compact with Satan" and we are led to believe that he is condemned to live his same raucous life throughout eternity in hell as the price of his compact.

In "Wandering Willie's Tale," Steenie Steenson is well aware of the tricks of the devil and is careful not to get tricked into bargaining his soul. He is wary of everything that is offered to him because he has been taught that tasting any food in the underworld could lead to the spirits having a claim on you. These beliefs go as far back as the ancient Greeks and Romans whose mythology holds that Persephone had to stay in the land of the dead for six months of every year with her abductor, Pluto, because she swallowed six seeds from a pomegranate that she ate there. Similar injunctions can be found in Oriental religions and in Homer when Ulysses is warned about the Land of the Lotus Eaters.

One of the most common symbols for the devil or the preternatural in literature is that of the monkey. Various strange animals can be used, such as a glowing-eyed cat, a snake, or a raven, but an exotic creature like a monkey adds mystery to the story. Most students are familiar with the bizarre powers of "The Monkey's Paw." In keeping with this assumed relationship, Scott casts the monkey in "Wandering Willie's Tale" as the evil culprit and it is the monkey's image that is seen sitting on Sir Robert's casket. While the monkey and its image may have been borrowed from common superstition, the creature gets its name from a wizard executed at Edinburgh in 1670 for sorcery. Another of Scott's additions to the original 1810 tale was an element that he borrowed from himself. In his book *The Antiquary,* Scott described another servant who dies while trying to answer the call of the dead mistress that she thinks she hears calling to her. Furthermore, a note on that passage indicates that Scott got the idea of the scene from a report on the death of a servant to the Duke of Roxburghe. On the day of the Duke's burial, the servant thought he heard his summons bell and died trying to get out of bed to answer it.

In creating his description of Sir Robert Redgauntlet, Scott got the idea of the horseshoe mark on Sir Robert's forehead from a couple of sources. One was from a famous poem that referred to a lord having an image on his brow, and the other was from the legend that a certain notorious witch had a horseshoe mark on her forehead. Superstition has long held that a horseshoe mark is a sign of the devil because the devil has hooves. If Sir Robert has the devil's horseshoe mark on his forehead, that means he has been branded as the devil's property. The details about water seething when Sir Robert's gouty feet were plunged into it and wine turning into blood when Sir Robert takes the goblet are taken from published descriptions of two of the men who were condemned as political enemies by the Scottish society to which Scott belonged.

Further superstitions are woven into the story that may have been commonly known or were borrowed from fairy tales. The toasts that Steenie Steenson drinks to Sir Robert supposedly cause the subsequent events to happen. Such consequences remind one of the superstition: Be careful what you

> **"Further superstitions are woven into the story that may have been commonly known or were borrowed from fairy tales. . . . The sympathetic stranger is a character found in fairy tales and is usually someone who has already fallen under an evil spell and is trying to spare a fellow human from the same fate."**

wish, for it may come true! The stranger's offer to buy Steenie's horse may be the devil's first attempt at a favor which must be repaid with Steenie's soul. The stranger seems to be helpful, though, when he advises Steenie not to eat, drink, or accept anything offered to him in Sir Robert's unearthly castle. The sympathetic stranger is a character found in fairy tales and is usually someone who has already fallen under an evil spell and is trying to spare a fellow human from the same fate.

Finally, Steenie's clever retort that he will return in a year as ordered only if it be "God's pleasure" is a well-known device for getting the devil to go away. Ever since Christ said "Begone, Satan," people have believed that invoking Christ's or God's name, or holding up a cross, will drive away the devil. A similar superstition believes that a cross will hold back a vampire. Having called upon God, the castle and its occupants vanish, and Steenie faints. In every such tale, the protagonist has to lose consciousness at a critical point so that everyone, including the protagonist, is left to wonder if anything he saw was real or just imagined in a dream. But there is usually some clue left as evidence that the event was real. In this case, Steenie has the receipt.

Just as Scott copied from his predecessors, others have copied from him. Several new forms of literature evolved from Scott's efforts. We study the author when we study a story because writers like Scott developed the genre of literary biography and established in the practice of criticism that one must understand the author to understand the work. Scott invented the ballad-epic form of poetry, caused the romantic novel to be considered a serious form of literature, and established the historical novel as the dominant narrative genre of nineteenth-century literature. In addition, Scott's use of the first person in "Wandering Willie's Tale" is an antecedent of the modern-day detective story—how I solved the mystery as told by Steenie Steenson or Sam Spade or any of a number of famous sleuths. In the Sherlock Holmes stories, the first-person narrator is his associate, Dr. Watson, but the effect is the same: disassociation of the author from the story. This way, the reader will focus on the tale and not the author. This is supposed to be Willie's tale, not Scott's, to the reader. Successfully achieving the illusion is a hallmark of good writing and Scott's mastery of the technique adds to his greatness.

Writing what you know is often autobiographical, and that is definitely true of Scott's works. He embedded into his stories his political leanings, his education, his morals, and his worries. The element of debt in Wandering Willie's Tale probably stems from the fact that Scott, despite his great wealth, was nonetheless heavily in debt for years. Like so many celebrities, he lavishly outspent his income and became involved in some bad business deals. But Scott's strong sense of honor caused him to work hard to pay his creditors. He churned out book after book not only from genius, but from necessity. Scott's courage and character in adversity evoked admiration even into the later years of the nineteenth century from the Victorian readers who were always looking for moral examples in their public figures and in their literature. There is a lesson in Willie's experience—The reader knows that Willie has probably not been a stranger to the devil in his wayward life, and that may be why he suffers a trip to hell that teaches him to call upon God for salvation.

Scott wrote stories that would have popular appeal, and thus big sales, but still managed a remarkable quality. Part of the appeal and the quality comes from Scott's ability to share his Scottish world in a universal way. Scott may have been influenced by his country upbringing, by his associates, and by the literature and climate of his times, but like all great writers, he knew how to control these influences and use them to achieve his purpose as a writer of masterfully crafted tales.

Source: Lois Kerschen, for *Short Stories for Students,* Gale, 2000.

Jennifer Bussey

Bussey holds a Master's degree in Interdisciplinary Studies and a Bachelor's degree in English Literature. She is an independent writer specializing in literature. In the following essay, she examines Scott's presentation of the battle between good and evil on Earth in Wandering Willie's Tale.

Sir Walter Scott's short story *Wandering Willie's Tale* is considered his greatest achievement in supernatural writing. Although Scott's reputation rests on his novels, his few short stories are well respected, if often overlooked. *Wandering Willie's Tale* appears in the novel *Redgauntlet: A Tale of the Eighteenth Century,* a work of historical fiction that relates the stories of the Redgauntlet family. Set in Scotland, the story is told by a blind traveler to another person who is significant to the novel in its entirety, but not to this story as a freestanding piece of short fiction.

Although the eighteenth century was marked by a sharp turn away from the supernatural and divine, and toward the natural and rational, Scott had a lifelong love of the folk literature of his native Scotland. He wanted to preserve the folktales and legends that had been kept alive by oral tradition. He also understood that the allure of ghost stories is part of human nature, regardless of literary and intellectual movements of the period. As a result, he continued to write fiction such as this eerie, supernatural story-within-a-story, which contains many elements common in Scottish folk literature. These elements include a traveling storyteller; a visit to hell; and dark miracles such as wine turning to blood and water boiling upon contact with an evil person.

Wandering Willie's Tale is squarely within the tradition of ghost stories and tales of the supernatural in that the interaction between earthly and otherworldly characters is intentional. Ghost stories generally involve some motivation on the part of the ghost or supernatural figure (unfinished business, revenge, deep sorrow, etc.); or, in some cases, the person or place being haunted deserves or needs the ghostly intervention, as in Dickens' classic *A Christmas Carol.* In this tale, Steenie Steenson, the story's protagonist (he is the grandfather of Willie, the storyteller) chooses to visit the dead Sir Robert Redgauntlet to obtain a much-needed rent receipt. On the other hand, the reader also is led to believe that Steenie is summoned by Redgauntlet, who wants to tempt Steenie into losing his soul to the devil. In this story, it seems, both parties desire a meeting; good and evil are equally drawn to the battlefield.

On the surface, *Wandering Willie's Tale* appears to be a simple story in the manner of a folktale about the eternal struggle between good and evil. To an extent, this is the case; but Scott creates a story that is more complex and fascinating than that. Certainly, Redgauntlet is depicted as a truly evil man with no apparent virtue. A fanatical Tory, he prowls the countryside in search of Whigs and Covenanters to kill them without mercy. Willie says that Redgauntlet's name was known all over the land for his harshness and coldness, and that he killed countless people. The very name Redgauntlet evokes a sense of what kind of man he was. A gauntlet was a piece of armor worn over the hands in battle, so the addition of "red" to "gauntlet" elicits an image of a bloody, armored hand in combat. Describing the power of Redgauntlet's evil, Willie says, "Men thought he had a direct compact with Satan—that he was proof against steel—and that bullets happed aff his buff-coat like hailstanes from a hearth...." After the revolution, Redgauntlet could no longer terrorize his enemies and was resigned to life as a landlord. In that position, he was strict and uncaring toward his tenants, interested only in acquiring money. Redgauntlet also had a jackanape, which is a type of monkey or ape. The jackanape's name was Major Weil (after a warlock), and he was a mischievous and disagreeable beast that ran around the castle screaming and biting people.

Redgauntlet's death is a horrible scene in which he has a seizure. When he yells for his feet to be placed in water, it boils, and when he demands a sip of wine, it turns to blood. His dramatic death and the ensuing ceremony show that Redgauntlet was a tortured and depraved person with no attachment to religion whatsoever. Willie gives the reader no reason to believe that there was any kindness or piety at all in him, so it is not surprising when Steenie later sees him in hell. In fact, Redgauntlet's presence as the host of a great banquet in hell, surrounded by profane and hedonistic figures, affirms that Redgauntlet has been in league with the devil all along. When he tempts Steenie three times, the reader knows that the stakes are very high for Steenie, and even when Redgauntlet agrees to write the rent receipt "for conscience-sake," it is clear that his agreeableness is a ruse.

> " The gravity of Steenie's experience weighs heavily on him, and he agrees to give up some of his vices until one year has passed and he is sure that Redgauntlet will not return to claim his soul for the devil. . . . In letting the reader know that Steenie is abandoning his vices only temporarily, until danger seems to be at bay, Scott no doubt makes reference to the fact that human attempts at virtue are often short-lived."

Turning to Scott's portrait of good, we find it painted in strokes less bold. Although Steenie is basically good, he has a number of flaws that prevent him from appearing pure and angelic to Willie, his listener, or the reader. Willie describes Steenie as a carefree man who bears no grudge against anyone and who delights everyone with his skillful pipe-playing. When the great conflict between the Tories and the Whigs breaks out, he had no strong feelings one way or the other, but since he lived on Redgauntlet's land, he joined him. Willie says that Steenie wished no harm to anyone, but riding with Redgauntlet, "he saw muckle mischief, and maybe did some, that he couldna avoid." It is implied that, because Steenie was Willie's grandfather, the "mischief" Willie casually mentions may well be a euphemism for violence and even murder. The outlines of Steenie's sins begin to emerge on Scott's canvas.

Later, after the misunderstanding about Steenie's rent payment, he was angry and afraid, and made two sinister toasts when he stopped to rest in the woods. First he toasted Redgauntlet, saying, "and might he never lie quiet in his grave till he had righted his poor bond-tenant." Second, he toasted the devil, invoking him to return the missing rent money or reveal where it was. Finally, the stain of sin deepens when Steenie recalls learning a tune on his pipe from a warlock as they were worshipping the devil. These episodes make clear that Steenie is far from a heroic and innocent protagonist. On the contrary, the reader may wonder for a time exactly what Steenie's soul's orientation truly is. His ability, ultimately, to resist Redgauntlet's temptations indicates an untapped source of strength. When he is finally able to invoke God's name, the entire scene of hell drops away, leaving only the darkness of the woods. The scene is a powerful one that illustrates that even a sinner such as Steenie can access the power of God's grace—though not without a harrowing struggle. The gravity of Steenie's experience weighs heavily on him, and he agrees to give up some of his vices until one year has passed and he is sure that Redgauntlet will not return to claim his soul for the devil—something Redgauntlet has given him reason to fear. In letting the reader know that Steenie is abandoning his vices only temporarily, until danger seems to be at bay, Scott no doubt makes reference to the fact that human attempts at virtue are often short-lived. Steenie, by this time, has been painted as everyman.

At the close of the tale, Willie claims that the moral of the story is that one must be careful about following strangers on unknown roads. The fact that a mysterious stranger led Steenie to the hellish version of Redgauntlet's Castle seems a minor point in the story, so the reader must wonder why Willie offers such an unusual moral. Critics debate over the identity of the stranger. Some maintain that he is the devil himself, offering Steenie over to Redgauntlet in the hope of claiming him for an eternity in hell. Other critics note that the stranger is amiable and does not conform to the popular notions of the devil at the time the story was written. Further, he turns away an opportunity to take advantage of Steenie's desperation for money and strike a deal for his soul. Scholars add that while Scott's presentation of hell is somewhat in line with that of Dante in *The Inferno* (where sins become their own punishments), it does not comply with the common perception of hell at the time. The unusual portrayal of hell, therefore, casts doubt on the idea that the stranger was the devil.

Whether or not the stranger was the devil, the story is clear about the facts that Redgauntlet is in hell and that he attempts to trick Steenie into surrendering his soul. The story is also clear that the role of the mysterious stranger is to meet Steenie in the woods and guide him to Redgauntlet, and then to vanish. Steenie's decision to go with the stranger, knowing that he is being taken to see the deceased Redgauntlet, is the turning point in the story. The story takes on its supernatural and menacing dimension at this moment, which explains why Willie tells his listener to beware of dark and unknown figures who approach when one is feeling lost, desperate, and alone. Steenie trusted the man and found himself led into a struggle for his very soul.

The fact that Willie is telling the tale about his grandfather gives the story a sense of history that would be absent if it were about Willie or a contemporary. By dipping into the past, Scott gives the story a universal flavor that suggests that the battle between good and evil is ever and always being waged.

In *Wandering Willie's Tale* Scott offers a frightening portrayal of the struggle between good and evil. It is frightening because Scott paints evil as truly, wholly evil. Although Redgauntlet is suffering in hell—his strained signature on the receipt is proof—he does not try to warn Steenie against such a fate, but instead embraces his own corruption and attempts to lure Steenie, too, into an eternity in hell. And it is frightening, too, because even good is impure and tainted with evil. Steenie's soul bears streaks of evil; the good in him is barely adequate to keep him out of hell. The reader can identify with Steenie, and can also imagine things having gone the other way. This reminds the reader that his own soul, undoubtedly, is painfully imperfect and faces tests it is not guaranteed to pass; and leaves one feeling that it is wise, indeed, to beware of mysterious strangers on dark roads, who may very well be calling souls to immortal battle.

Source: Jennifer Bussey, for *Short Stories for Students*, Gale, 2000

Sources

Briggs, Julia, *Night Visitors: The Rise and Fall of the English Ghost Story*, London: Faber, 1977.

Campbell, James L., Sr., ''Sir Walter Scott, 1771–1832,'' In *Supernatural Fiction Writers: Fantasy and Horror*, edited by E. F. Bleiler, Vol. 1, New York: Scribner's, 1985, pp. 169–76.

Cockshut, A. O. J., *The Achievement of Walter Scott*, London: Collins, 1969.

Daiches, David, ''Scott's Redgauntlet,'' in *From Jane Austen to Joseph Conrad*, edited by Robert C. Rathburn and Marin

Steinmann, Jr., Minneapolis: University of Minnesota Press, 1958, pp. 46–59.

Doubleday, Neal Frank, *Variety of Attempt: British and American Fiction in the Early Nineteenth Century*, Lincoln: University of Nebraska Press, 1976.

Leavis, F. R., *The Great Tradition*, London: Chatto and Windus, 1948.

Lovecraft, H. P., *Supernatural Horror in Literature*, New York: Abramson, 1945.

Parker, W. M., Preface to the Everyman edition of *Redgauntlet* by Sir Walter Scott, London: Dent, 1958.

Parsons, Coleman O., *Witchcraft and Demonology in Scott's Fiction*, Edinburgh: Oliver & Boyd, 1964.

Scott, Sir Walter, *Redgauntlet*, edited by G. A. M. Wood and David Hewitt, Edinburgh: Edinburgh University Press, 1997.

Further Reading

Boatright, Mody C., "Scott's Theory and Practice Concerning the Use of the Supernatural in Prose Fiction in Relation to the Chronology of the Waverly Novels," in *PMLA*, Vol. 50, 1935, pp. 235–261.
   In this book, Boatright explores Scott's inclusion of supernatural themes in his writings in general and in relation to the Waverly Novels.

Brown, David, *Walter Scott and the Historical Imagination*, London: Routledge & Kegan Paul, 1979.
   A study of Scott's Waverley novels.

Cowan, Ian, *The Scottish Covenanters, 1660–1688*, London: Gollancz, 1976.
   A study of the religious struggles in seventeenth-century Scotland.

Daiches, David, "Scott's *Redgauntlet*," in *From Jane Austen to Joseph Conrad*, edited by Robert C. Rathburn and Martin Steinmann, Jr., University of Minnesota Press, 1958.
   Daiches' review of the great English writers provides an overview of notable figures and important literary movements.

Harris, Wendell V., *British Short Fiction in the Nineteenth Century: A Literary and Bibliographic Guide*, Wayne State University Press, 1979.
   This book provides an overview and guidelines for researching Britain's nineteenth-century short story writers.

Hewitt, David, ed., *Scott on Himself: A Collection of the Autobiographical Writings of Sir Walter Scott*, Scottish Academic Press, 1981.
   Through letters, essays, and other personal writings, this book offers the reader insight into Scott's life and times.

Johnson, Edgar, *Sir Walter Scott: The Great Unknown*, 2 vols., New York: Macmillan, 1970.
   A detailed biography of Scott containing corrections of the errors in Lockhart's biography.

Lockhart, J. G., *Memoirs of the Life of Sir Walter Scott*, 6 vols., Edinburgh: Cadell, 1837.
   A detailed biography of Scott by his son-in-law. Includes an autobiographical memoir by Scott himself.

Mitchison, Rosalind, *A History of Scotland*, 2nd ed., London and New York: Methuen, 1982.
   A standard political history containing a critical perspective on the Covenanters.

Parsons, Coleman O., "Demonological Background of 'Donnerhugel's Narrative' and 'Wandering Willie's Tale,'" in *Studies in Philology*, Vol. 30, 1933, pp. 604–617.
   Folklore, superstition, and belief in the supernatural are examined as they appear in literary work in the early nineteenth century.

———, *Witchcraft and Demonology in Scott's Fiction with Chapters on the Supernatural in Scottish Literature*, Oliver and Boyd, 1964.
   In this book, Parson discusses popular beliefs about evil powers in Scottish culture, specifically as they relate to the writings of Scott.

Scott, Sir Walter, *Letters on Demonology and Witchcraft*, George Routledge and Sons, 1887.
   Scott discusses the origins of black magic and expands his treatment to include fortune tellers, apparitions, witches, charms, and immortality. There is specific commentary on Major Weir, after whom the jackanape in "Wandering Willie's Tale" was named.

Smout, T. C., *A History of the Scottish People, 1560–1830*, London: Collins, 1969.
   Focuses on social and economic developments.

The Way We Live Now

Susan Sontag

1986

Susan Sontag's "The Way We Live Now" first appeared in the *New Yorker* in 1986. Narrated almost exclusively through dialogue, it tells of an unnamed man's struggle with the AIDS through the reactions of his large circle of friends.

Sontag began writing the story on the night she learned that a close friend had been diagnosed with AIDS. Very upset and unable to sleep, she took a bath; it was there that the story began to take shape. "It was given to me, ready to be born. I got out of the bathtub and started to write very quickly standing up. I wrote the story very quickly, in two days, drawing on experiences of my own cancer and a friend's stroke," she told Kenny Fries of the *San Francisco Bay Times.*

Selected for the collection *The Best American Short Stories of 1987* and also included in *The Best American Short Stories of the Eighties,* "The Way We Live Now" was written at the time that the impact of the AIDS epidemic was felt throughout America and the rest of the world. As such, critics maintain that it truly represents the spirit of its time. The characters reflect on the sudden omnipresence of death in their community and dissect their own changing attitudes about morality and mortality.

"The Way We Live Now" is also viewed as a dramatic rendering of some of Sontag's most important ideas about attitudes about sickness, as discussed in her infamous essays *Illness as Metaphor* and *AIDS and Its Metaphors.*

Author Biography

Sontag was born on January 16, 1933 in New York City. She grew up in Tucson, Arizona and Los Angeles, California. A serious and precocious child, Sontag began to read when she was three and wrote her first stories and plays at age seven. Her interest in literature and philosophy began early in childhood.

Sontag finished high school at fifteen and enrolled at University of California, Berkeley for one year. She continued college at the University of Chicago, placing out of most courses and graduating at age seventeen. That same year she married Philip Rieff, a sociology professor at the University of Chicago, only two weeks after meeting him. She followed Rieff to Harvard, where she earned masters degrees in literature and philosophy.

At age nineteen Sontag gave birth to her son, David, who was to be her only child. After eight years, her marriage to Rieff ended in divorce, and for the first time in her life she explored beyond her academic interests. "I had a very enjoyable adolescence from age 27 to 35," she told the *Washington Post*'s Paula Span.

She has held positions at various universities and, beside a brief foray into filmmaking, has devoted her life to writing. She began publishing essays and book reviews in the early 1960s, making a name for herself as a prolific intellectual. Her works, which borrow heavily from a Western European tradition and take up broad modernist themes, range from philosophy and politics to art and cultural criticism. Her best known works of nonfiction, the novels *Against Interpretation* and *Styles of Radical Will,* provoked both controversy and renown.

In 1975 Sontag was diagnosed with cancer. She struggled with the disease for two-and-a-half years before she was finally cured. In response to the experience she wrote *Illness as Metaphor,* which explores the cultural myths surrounding disease. While writing "The Way We Live Now" she drew on her experiences as a cancer patient, as well as her friendships with many people afflicted with AIDS.

Sontag was primarily known as an intellectual until the surprise success of her 1992 novel *The Volcano Lover.* She has been the recipient of numerous awards, including a National Book Critics Award for criticism in 1978 for *On Photography* and a MacArthur fellowship from 1990 to 1995. Sontag lives in New York.

Susan Sontag

Plot Summary

"The Way We Live Now" is comprised of a series of conversations as a large network of friends share information and express concern about one of their friends, an anonymous character who is showing symptoms of an unnamed disease. The story opens with several characters describing these symptoms. They also point out that he must be frightened because he has quit smoking and put off a doctor's appointment. They discuss the panic that has spread among their circle of sophisticated gay, straight, and bisexual Manhattanites about the spreading AIDS epidemic.

In the next scene, the friends visit the man in the hospital. He has been diagnosed with AIDS, and they talk about how best to keep his spirits up in light of the devastating news. Most of the friends visit him frequently. They discuss his need for visitors, and one of them admits her feelings of fear and awkwardness about seeing him.

The friends notice his drop in spirits and discuss a diary he has just started to keep, theorizing that it helps him think about his future. They discuss the side effects of his medications and, referring to their constant presence and new group identity, one of them jokes, "*We* are all side effects." The friends reflect on how the man's illness has changed their lives and relationships to one another.

The man improves enough to return home, and a close friend and former lover moves in to take care of him. The friends worry about the sick man's state of mind and discuss the possibilities of new experimental drug treatments. Several of them suggest therapies that are alternatives to traditional medicine. The man is accepted into the protocol for a new drug. His friends think it is a good sign that and has started to talk less about being sick and also that he says the word *AIDS* "often and easily, as if it were just another word."

They compare the conditions of living with AIDS to what it was a few years earlier, when less was known about the disease and there was more prejudice and hysteria. A friend from out of town says that the "utopia of friendship" that they have formed around the man in his illness is "rather beautiful." Another friend comments, "We are the family he's founded, without meaning to." A third objects to this collective identity, and they all discuss the differences between the man's responses to various visitors.

The man improves and informs the friend staying with him that he no longer needs his help. The friends hear about two other acquaintances that have been stricken with AIDS. They think it is best to keep the news from him. They talk about how life has changed for all of them, how none of them do the same things or take life for granted since the spread of .AIDS. Soon after, another member of their immediate social circle is diagnosed, a fact that they also withhold from him.

The man's health appears relatively stable. Tensions and competition among his friends increase. The man takes their attention for granted. He begins to have fewer visitors.

The man has a relapse. Facing death, he talks about his feelings of fear and exaltation. One of his friends comes up with the idea of a "visiting book" with a schedule for visitors, limiting the number to two at a time. The tension between the friends eases up in the face of the man's latest brush with death. His condition stabilizes and he is out of danger of not recovering from this particular downturn. Friends observe that he has become more detached. His

death from the disease seems inevitable, but as the story ends he is still alive.

Characters

The AIDS Patient

The unnamed AIDS patient is the focus of the story. Diagnosed with AIDS, he is the subject of his friends' concern. His struggle with the illness is narrated exclusively through their observations and descriptions.

The man is described as a sophisticated urbanite, a collector who lives in the penthouse of a pretentious apartment building in Manhattan. He lived a "risky" lifestyle before his illness—smoking, using drugs, and having unprotected sex with men and women. His circle of friends becomes a "family he's founded without meaning to."

Aileen

Aileen has a close but somewhat ambiguous relationship with the AIDS patient. She rarely visits him and considers herself as a coward because of her behavior. She speculates that he is attracted to her, but others speculate that she is in love with him.

Betsy

Betsy is a friend of the AIDS patient. She recommends a diet specialist to help him fight the disease, but he declines her offer.

Clarice

Clarice is Zack's widow and part of the AIDS patient's larger social circle.

Donny

Donny is a close friend of the AIDS patient.

Ellen

Ellen is a close friend of the AIDS patient.

Frank

A close friend of the AIDS patient, Frank is a gay man who volunteers at an AIDS crisis center. He has a falling out with Lewis, which signals the rise of tensions among the man's friends and visitors.

Greg

Greg is a friend of the AIDS patient.

Hilda

Hilda is a close friend of the AIDS patient.

Ira

Ira is a close friend of the AIDS patient.

Jan

Jan is a close friend of the AIDS patient.

Kate

Kate plays a "big sister" role in the AIDS patient's life.

Lewis

An ex-lover of the AIDS patient, Lewis "still has the keys to his apartment." He is at the fringe of the circle of friends. Once he finds out that the AIDS patient is sick, he starts to visit him regularly.

Max

Max is a friend of the AIDS patient. He is described as one of the circle of friends "most at risk" and, during the course of the man's illness, he too is diagnosed with AIDS.

Nora

Nora is the estranged ex-lover of the AIDS patient. The only woman the AIDS patient ever loved, she now lives far away, and he has not told her about his diagnosis.

Orson

Orson is a friend of the AIDS patient.

Paolo

A friend and ex-lover of the AIDS patient, Paolo is described as one of the people most at risk of getting sick.

Quentin

Quentin is both a close friend and ex-lover of the AIDS patient. He is fiercely protective of his ill friend and, according to some, keeps a tally of who does most for him. Quentin moves in with him to help him when he gets out of the hospital and comes up with the system of a "visiting book" to regulate the stream of visitors when he returns to the hospital.

Robert

Considered a friend of the AIDS patient, Robert has only visited him twice since the man's diagnosis.

Stephen

Stephen is a close friend of the AIDS patient. Out of the circle of friends, he has the most knowledge about medicine and the treatments for AIDS. He asks the doctors "informed questions."

Tanya

Tanya is a close friend and ex-lover of the AIDS patient.

Ursula

Ursula is a friend of the AIDS patient.

Victor

A friend of the AIDS patient, Victor recommends a "visualization therapist," a kind of alternative medicine based on the mind-body connection.

Wesley

Wesley is a friend of the AIDS patient.

Xavier

Xavier is a close friend of the AIDS patient. He brings a statue of Saint Sebastian to him at the hospital as a protection against pestilence.

Yvonne

A friend of the AIDS patient, Yvonne flies to New York from London for business and spends the weekend visiting him. She tells his friends that the attitude towards AIDS in the United States is less fearful and hysterical than it is in Britain.

Zack

Zack was an acquaintance of the AIDS patient. He died of AIDS the previous year.

Themes

Life and Death

The title of the story, "The Way We Live Now," refers to the lifestyle of a group of friends and of a wider community of people like them who have made a fundamental change in their attitudes and worldviews in light of the AIDS epidemic. The characters reflect on their growing intimacy with death, as their friend's health declines and other friends fall ill from the disease.

It is significant that Sontag chooses to end the story with the words "he's still alive," countering

Topics for Further Study

- Why do you think that Sontag chose to tell the story from the perspective of the AIDS patient's many friends? How would the story be different if it were narrated from the perspective of only one friend or of the man with AIDS himself? Write your own version from another point of view.

- One of the characters, Stephen, states that "to utter the name [of the disease] is a sign of health, a sign that one has accepted being who one is, mortal, vulnerable, not and exception after all, it's a sign that one is willing, truly willing, to fight for one's life." In the story, Sontag never names the disease. Why do you think that she never writes the word *AIDS*?

- Research the Stonewall uprising of 1969 and the gay liberation movement that followed it. How does this historical context enhance your understanding of the story?

- Sontag is known as a theoretician as well as a fiction writer. How are the main concerns of her essay *AIDS and Its Metaphors* reflected in the story? Take one of the main ideas from *AIDS and Its Metaphors* and explain how Sontag explores it in "The Way We Live Now."

---

expectations that a story about a man with AIDS will end with his death. Sontag does not imply that the man will not die—which would be historically inaccurate given the treatments available at the time when the story is set—but makes a point of closing the story while his battle with the disease is still underway. This underscores her point that AIDS had become a way of *life*, not only for those who contracted it, but for the community at large.

Language and Meaning

In "The Way We Live Now," Sontag suggests that there is a connection between language and survival. The AIDS patient begins to keep a diary after he becomes ill; in addition, Quentin speculates that writing is a way of "slyly staking out his claim to a future time." The story closes with Ursula's observation that the difference between a story and a photograph is language's ability to move beyond the present tense: "In a story you can write, He's still alive. But in a painting or a photo you can't show 'still.'"

Sontag again connects the use of language to survival when Paolo and Stephen discuss the sick man's use of the word *AIDS*. They see it as a good sign when he begins to name his illness freely and casually, which is ironic, given that the word *AIDS*

never appears in the story. The fact that the disease is left unnamed suggests that "the way we live now" is not healthy or honest. In her book *AIDS and Its Metaphors* Sontag seeks to demystify the disease by revealing the cultural myths that attach themselves to the medical condition, obfuscating its reality. In "The Way We Live Now" she shows such mythologizing at work among the patient's closest friends.

Friendship

The story illustrates the way that friendship grows and changes in the face of a crisis. The AIDS epidemic is represented through its impact on a group of friends that forms a collective identity when one of them is diagnosed with the disease. Moreover, the story shows how AIDS brings not only death, but changes in life. Yvonne describes the circuit of communication and caring that springs up around the AIDS patient as a "utopia of friendship," which Kate modifies as a "pathetic utopia," as if to remind her of limits to how much their friendship can help him.

Sexuality

Sexuality is an important underlying theme of the story, a crucial element in the connection that holds the group of friends together. In the course of the story, they assume a group identity in caring for the man with AIDS; yet previously they had all been part of a circle of friends and lovers. Several of the characters—both male and female—are named as ex-lovers of the man with AIDS. He is bisexual, indicating a link between gay and straight worlds. Several members of the group have had affairs with one another, creating further links of love and risk between men and women, gay and straight.

In the words of one character, "everyone is at risk, everyone who has a sexual life, because sexuality is a chain that links each of us to many others, unknown others, and now the great chain of being has become a chain of death as well." The freedom to view sexuality as safe and positive is something that has been destroyed by the onslaught of AIDS. While homosexuality is closely associated with this phase of the AIDS crisis, Sontag is deliberate in representing sexuality *in general* as an important aspect of the disease and its impact.

Style

Point of View

The story's point of view is the most striking stylistic element of Sontag's story. It is told in the third person, through the voices of a large group of friends as they share information about a friend who has AIDS. No one character's perspective dominates the narration and the large number of characters creates a kaleidoscope effect. Within a single sentence, the perspective often shifts several times. The characters frequently disagree with each other and one of them, Quentin, objects to the constant references to the group as "we."

However, the experience forges a collective identity. The many individual voices that make up the group create a constantly shifting point of view, but the collective identity that they share lends the multiple points of view a certain unity. The fact that the friends are speaking to each other is more important than which particular friend is talking to another.

Dialogue

The story is narrated almost entirely through dialogue, with nearly all information expressed through the spoken words of the characters to one another. Sontag's use of dialogue is unusual not only because it plays such a large role in her telling of the story, but because it is presented in an idiosyncratic format, which means that she does not use the conventional paragraph breaks and quotation marks to distinguish between different speakers. Instead, she runs the dialogue of different speakers together, often using extremely long sentences to capture the flow of conversation. The very first sentence runs eleven lines and includes the comments of four different people. This has the effect of melding the identities of the different speakers and suggests the merging of their identities, as well as the urgency of their communication with each other.

Symbolism

In "The Way We Live Now" Sontag uses language, for the most part, in a realistic way. The conversations that make up the narration mimic the natural intonations and patterns of speech. The story represents a real situation and offers concrete historical details.

However, it can also be viewed as an allegory, where the characters and events represent larger ideas about the AIDS crisis. The story's symbolic quality is most clearly illustrated in Sontag's use of naming: she uses names in a manner that is intentionally unnatural, calling attention to fact that the story is an artistic construct. The AIDS patient is never named and neither is his illness. While the way the characters talk is largely naturalistic, it is highly unlikely that real people would fail to mention the man's name in the course of their many conversations about him. The omission is symbolic of the absence of his perspective in the story, and his underlying isolation from the friends that surround him.

The rest of the twenty-six characters are given distinctive first names, each beginning with a different letter of the alphabet. These friends, as represented by the alphabet, suggest the universal scope of the disease. The characters themselves are all part of a narrow sector of society—well-educated, liberal, urban sophisticates—but their alphabetical naming suggests that AIDS touches every kind of person, from A to Z. However, it also suggests that the man who has AIDS is left out of the collective experience. Sontag's use of naming suggests that he is not one of the "we" that react in response to the illness, but one of the "them" who becomes irrevocably "other" when he contracts it.

Historical Context

Gay Liberation in the 1970s

The story takes place in the mid-1980s, after AIDS had begun to decimate the gay population of Manhattan and other large urban centers. The lifestyle referred to in the title of the story stands in implicit contrast to "the way we used to live" before the AIDS epidemic. Sontag is careful to include characters of every sexual orientation, but gay history is a particularly pertinent context for her story.

In 1969, the Stonewall riots occurred to protest the police harassment of a bar in the New York neighborhood of Greenwich Village. Many gay men and women were inspired by the solidarity exhibited at the uprising, and several historians point to that moment as a defining one in the burgeoning gay rights movement.

The free, often promiscuous sexual attitudes of gay liberation were in some ways an outgrowth of the more widespread and mainstream sexual revolution of the 1960s, which resulted from women's access to abortion and birth control. Yet sexual freedom had special meaning to homosexuals, who, before their "liberation," had lived either without a community or in a highly secretive one, and who often and regarded their own sexuality as a sickness, sin, or shame. (It was not until 1973 that the American Psychiatric Association removed homosexuality from its list of mental illnesses.)

After Stonewall brought pride and attention to the homosexual community, gay men regarded promiscuity as a celebration of the unhampered male libido. While there were always people who saw this behavior as sordid and immoral, those who participated in the lifestyle viewed it as the reflection of a positive, optimistic, and even innocent time.

AIDS in the 1980s

In 1981 reports of a mysterious and deadly disease affecting homosexual men first hit the mainstream press. By 1983 it was acknowledged as an epidemic. That year the Assistant Secretary of Health announced that AIDS was the country's number one health priority. Haitians, hemophiliacs, and intravenous drug users were also identified as populations at high risk for AIDS, but it was still widely perceived as a "gay disease." There was public hysteria and a backlash against gay people in the face of false reports that casual contact might spread AIDS. This is the attitude Yvonne refers to when she calls the man in the story with AIDS "fortunate" because "no one's afraid to hug him or kiss him lightly on the mouth."

There was no medical explanation for the disease and no clear understanding of how it was spread until 1984, when French and American teams of doctors simultaneously discovered Human Immunodeficiency Virus (HIV) as the most likely cause of AIDS. As it became clear that AIDS was spread by intimate sexual contact or blood, there was further hostility and moral judgment directed toward gay culture. The gay community itself responded with grief, shock, and denial.

Because sexual freedom was so closely associated with political liberation for this generation of gay men, many initially refused to change their risky behaviors. In the story Kate remembers asking the central character if he is being "careful, honey, you know what I mean," one night at a disco before he gets sick. He responds by saying, "No, I'm not, listen, I can't, I just can't, sex is too important to me." Safe sex guidelines were not initially effective, but as the AIDS crisis wore on, and gay men became more involved in organized AIDS prevention, safe sex became a community standard.

In the early and mid-1980s AIDS was concentrated in a few urban gay communities, with New York and San Francisco particularly hard hit. In 1984 more than a third of all reported cases were in New York City. By 1987, one in 25 gay men in Greenwich Village had AIDS. Shops in that neighborhood started to close earlier and pedestrian traffic was down forty percent. The disease had profoundly transformed what once had been the wild and thriving center of gay liberation.

Critical Overview

Sontag is a writer of amazing range, writing on subjects from photography to politics to the my-

Compare
&
Contrast

- **1984:** There are 4,177 reported AIDS cases in the United States, with 1,600 of these in New York City. Homosexuals, Haitians, hemophiliacs, and intravenous drug users are the populations at highest risk for contracting AIDS.

  Today: AIDS is on the decline in New York City. There are more than thirty million people infected with AIDS worldwide, the majority of them in sub-Saharan Africa. Heterosexual sex is the main method of transmission in the United States and worldwide.

- **1984:** There is no effective treatment against AIDS until 1985, when the Federal Drug Administration (FDA) approves a drug called AZT.

  Today: AZT is still used to fight AIDS. When combined with a class of drugs called protease inhibitors, it is effective in delaying the onset of full-blown AIDS among people infected with HIV. The treatment entails taking costly and carefully timed "cocktails" of different drugs. The treatment dramatically increases the life expectancy of those infected.

- **1980s:** The concept of "safe sex" is introduced by public health officials, bringing a new and explicit vocabulary of sexual acts into public discourse. The gay community is initially slow to accept safe sex guidelines, but as the decade wears on and the disease exacts its toll, gay men organize their own effective and innovative public health campaigns.

  Today: "Safe sex" has become a standard in the gay community. It is acknowledged that no sex is completely "safe," so public health officials adopt a vocabulary of "safer sex" and "harm reduction."

- **1985:** In July Rock Hudson announces that he has AIDS, making him the first national public figure to admit to suffering from the disease. On October 2, 1985 Hudson dies of the disease.

  Today: In 1991 NBA basketball star Earvin "Magic" Johnson announced that he was HIV-positive and retired from the game. He remains in good health, is considered a role model for young people, and remains a popular public figure.

thology of illness. Though her first novel *The Benefactor* appeared in 1963, her role as an intellectual has always overshadowed her career as a fiction writer.

In the 1960s Sontag published two maverick works of art criticism, *Against Interpretation* and *Styles of Radical Will.* These works, as well as her 1977 *On Photography,* made her one of the most recognizable and controversial intellectuals in American public life.

As she was finishing *On Photography* Sontag was struck with near-fatal cancer, an experience that inspired her to write *Illness as Metaphor,* which examines the cultural symbolism surrounding can-

cer. This book won her a new audience and more critical esteem.

Began as a three-page epilogue to *Illness as Metaphor, AIDS and Its Metaphors,* became the subject of her next book. Having lost a very close friend to the disease, Sontag applied the critical approach of the earlier book to the AIDS epidemic. Published in the midst of both hysteria and activism regarding AIDS, *AIDS and Its Metaphors,* was received with mixed reactions.

Sontag's interest in the AIDS epidemic also inspired one of her most successful works of fiction. "The Way We Live Now" first appeared in the *New Yorker* in 1986. The following year editor Ann Beattie selected it as the lead story in *The Best American Short Stories of 1987,* a popular series

A crowd gathers in front of Greenwich Village's Stonewall bar, a site considered the birthplace of the gay rights movement.

ties. Though these four publishing venues are all highly prestigious, the story was reviewed infrequently, mostly because Sontag never published it as part of a collection.

The few reviews of the story were uniformly positive. The *New York Times Book Review*'s Gardner McFall compares the story to Trollope and Camus, adding that "its haunting effect belongs entirely to Ms. Sontag."

In this and several other short reviews, critics quote or paraphrase Sontag extensively in order to catch the flavor of her unusual narrative style, which they agree is uniquely suited to her subject matter. Barbara A. MacAdam of *ARTnews* praises Sontag's "fluid, stream-of-consciousness style, describing the way we come gradually to acknowledge AIDS and accommodate it in our own style of living, loving, joking, and just plain coping."

Rosemary Dinnage of the *Times Literary Supplement* characterizes the story as "a brilliant and chilling account of AIDS" and "a complete, minutely scaled dissection of attitudes toward death at its starkest." Both Dinnage and Leon S. Roudiez of *World Literature Today* point out connections between the story and Sontag's essay on the cultural myths surrounding AIDS, *AIDS and Its Metaphors*. Roudiez describes the story as "a remarkable, moving book" that also has a "eerie uncertainty . . . that draws one toward death while also refusing to accept the inescapable outcome."

In *Susan Sontag: Mind as Passion,* Liam Kennedy compares "The Way We Live Now" to *AIDS and Its Metaphors,* deeming the former "more successful in giving powerful and poignant expression to the 'universe of fear in which everyone now lives.'" He goes on to describe the story as a "daring application of the aesthetic of silence which renders the reality of AIDS more immediately personal than *AIDS and Its Metaphors*."

featuring fiction from the best literary and general readership magazines. At the decade's end, the story was also included in *The Best American Short Stories of the Eighties.*

In 1991 Noonday Press issued the story as an expensive and beautifully produced thirty-page paperback, with the addition of abstract etchings by British artist Howard Hodgkin. Sontag and Hodgkin donated the proceeds from the book to AIDS chari-

Criticism

Sarah Madsen Hardy

Madsen Hardy has a doctorate in English literature and is a freelance writer and editor. In the following essay, she addresses the question of why the story's characters are so hard to keep straight.

If you had trouble keeping track of the characters in "The Way We Live Now," consider yourself in

What Do I Read Next?

- *I, etcetera* (1978), a collection of witty and inventive short stories by Sontag, concerns human behavior in the modern world.

- In Sontag's *AIDS and Its Metaphors* (1989), she considers how society regards AIDS as a metaphor for invasion and pollution and argues against such symbolic ways of thinking about the disease.

- *The Plague* (1913), a classic novel by French existentialist Albert Camus, is an account of an Algerian town leveled by the bubonic plague. It explores the themes of death and illness from a psychological and philosophical approach.

- *Borrowed Time: An AIDS Memoir* (1988) is Paul Monette's moving memoir of his lover's two-year struggle with AIDS. It offers an intimate glimpse into the author's confrontations with love and loss.

- *Tales of the City* (1976) is the first volume of a six-book series by Armistead Maupin chronicling the life and times of the residents of a San Francisco apartment building. Maupin's colorful novels reflect the spirit of the times in the 1970s and 1980s.

- Written by David Leavitt, *The Lost Language of Cranes* (1986) portrays the life of a young gay man living in New York.

---

good company. Reviewers at two prestigious publications confused the unnamed man at the story's center with one of the friends who gather around him. Barbara A. MacAdam of *ARTnews* refers to the AIDS patient as Stephen, who is, instead, one of his closer friends. Gardner McFall of the *New York Times Book Review* calls him Max, who is actually member of the circle of concerned friends who, late in the story, is himself diagnosed.

I point this out not to mar the reputations of two fine critics, but to call attention to an unusual and challenging aspect of Sontag's style. If reviewers—professional readers and writers—can't keep the characters straight, how are the rest of us expected to? The short answer is, we aren't.

Most short stories are about distinct, individual characters and how they interact with one another. Most have a protagonist, in addition to an array of other characters of varying importance. ''The Way We Live Now,'' has no protagonist. The AIDS patient at its center is silent and nameless. The story represents the lifestyle and mentality of a large group of people who have been forced to respond to AIDS and treats them as minor and, to a certain degree, interchangeable characters.

Either Sontag has done a very bad job attempting to portray conventional characters, or she has chosen to portray them in an unconventional way for particular reasons. The fact that she includes twenty-six characters and names each of them beginning with a different letter of the alphabet is a clue that readers are not intended to consider each character as an individual person, but to step back and view them more abstractly—as the expression of an idea about life in the age of AIDS.

In her introduction to ''The Way We Live Now'' in *The Best American Short Stories of the Eighties,* editor Shannon Ravenel observes that ''here the story's form is truly wed to its content.'' In this essay I will consider how Sontag's form relates to the social dynamics surrounding AIDS by looking at her techniques for representing character.

For the most part, Sontag simply withholds information about the relationships among the various small groups of characters who gather to share news and engage in the rambling, speculative talk that makes up the narrative. The story's characters are defined only in terms of what they say about the man who is ill and how they react to his illness. She doesn't mention what they do, where they live, and with whom they are closest.

> " The merging between characters, which creates, at its best, a communion of concern, also has a deadly flip side: in the AIDS crisis love and death get mixed up. As one character muses, 'now the great chain of being has become a chain of death as well.'"

Furthermore, she deliberately obfuscates who is speaking by writing in long sentences that run the speech of different characters together. For example, this mouthful:

He didn't want to be alone, according to Paolo, and lots of people came in the first week, and the Jamaican nurse said there were other patients on the floor who would be glad to have the surplus flowers, and people weren't afraid to visit, it wasn't like the old days, as Kate pointed out to Aileen, they're not even segregated in the hospital anymore, as Hilda observed, there's nothing on the door of his room warning visitors of the possibility of contagion, as there was a few years ago; in fact, he's in a double room and, as he told Orson, the old guy on the far side of the curtain (who's clearly on the way out, said Stephen) doesn't even have the disease, so, as Kate went on, you really should go and see him, he'd be happy to see you, he likes having people visit, you aren't not going because you're afraid, are you.

This passage offers a useful illustration of how the form of Sontag's writing de-emphasizes and even obscures the significance of individual characters in favor of evoking the mood and dynamics of the group. The passage describes some of the details of the sick man's first stay at the hospital and broaches the phobic fear of people with AIDS reflected in both hospital policies and the attitudes of friends. This information is communicated through the spoken words of four different speakers—Paolo, Kate, Hilda, and Stephen—in a single run-on sentence.

Speech is usually closely identified with individuality and carefully labeled to indicate which character is speaking. Yet Sontag eschews the conventional punctuation marks that would offer readers visual cues for distinguishing between one character's words and that of another character. There are no paragraph indents or quotation marks to separate the speech of different characters.

Because sentences are often so long, readers must gloss over the clauses that describe who is speaking to whom in order to follow the gist of the conversation: He didn't want to be alone . . . so lots of people came . . . there were other patients on the floor who would be glad to have the extra flowers . . . people weren't afraid to visit anymore, etc.

These choices about how to present the speech of different characters shape the reader's whole concept of character. You cannot linger on what one particular person says, or sort it out clearly from what another says, all while trying to reach the end of an eleven-line sentence.

Instead, the sentence carries you along with its momentum. You hear a chorus of panicked, reassuring, argumentative, joking, and despairing voices that interrupt each other and continue each other's thoughts. So why does Sontag use this stylistic technique for writing about the AIDS crisis? What does Ravenel mean when she says that Sontag's form is "truly wed to her content"?

Sontag compares the AIDS crisis to London during the Blitz of World War II and refers to the disease as "an exaggeration." To a certain extent, her style can simply be understood as a representation of the pressured kind of conversation that takes place in an emergency. Sontag's long sentences express the friends' compulsion to communicate about the situation that is on their minds all of the time.

It seemed that everyone was in touch with everyone else several times a week, checking in, I've never spent so many hours at a time on the phone, Stephen said to Kate, and when I'm exhausted after the two or three phone calls made to me, giving me the latest, instead of switching off the phone to give myself a respite I tap out the number of another friend or acquaintance, to pass on the news." The characters are in crisis and do not rest when they would normally rest. Likewise, the sentence goes on and on when it really should stop.

The style also expresses the changed sense of priorities that emerge when a person is seriously ill. The individual identities of each friend and their separate interests become less important than their relation to the patient and his condition. They are "side effects," "the well," "at risk." Compared to the patient, whose situation is so extreme, the friends begin to think of themselves as a "we."

Yet this is not to say that AIDS brings a leveling of identity, that all characters become somehow the same as soon as one of them falls gravely ill. Some characters are more closely allied with each other than others. Some relationships are intimate, others cold.

Yet, depending on the example, it's either difficult or impossible to keep track of which is which: Quentin and Ira compete; Lewis and Frank have a falling out; Kate is a mediator. Yet this is revealed only because it relates to everyone's central concern: the AIDS patient. Sontag's style suggests that the specific details of what links various people is less relevant than the fact that they *are* linked. The long sentences that merge the speech of many characters emphasize the connection between various speakers—forged by their vehement reason for talking—even as it causes confusion.

Xavier comments that the man's illness sticks the friends "all in the same glue." This image of merging and mixing has specific meaning in the context of AIDS, which is spread through only the most intimate bodily contact. In the story, it has both positive and negative connotations.

There is much past and present intimacy within the circle of friends. The bonds of loyalty, caring, and closeness that form the patient's intimates into a "utopia of friendship" are, in some cases, potentially lethal. The AIDS patient has had sex with Lewis, Quentin, Tanya, Paolo, and Nora, "among others." The timing and nature of these relationships is unknown, but these characters are presumably at some risk of having contracted the virus from the man. Quentin, Lewis, Frank, Paolo, and Max are gay men and thus, demographically speaking, at higher risk than the rest of the population.

Yet Ellen notes that "everyone is at risk, everyone who has a sexual life, because sexuality is a chain that links each of us to many others, unknown others," a point Sontag stresses by including a full range of sexual preferences and orientations among the twenty-six characters. The characters are linked by various kinds of intimacy, which is the source of their strength and their weakness, their comfort and their fear.

A corresponding idea of intimacy may also be gleaned from Sontag's style: she makes her sentences into chains. The lack of punctuation links the individual speakers. The sentences also stick characters "all in the same glue."

The merging between characters, which creates, at its best, a communion of concern, also has a deadly flip side: in the AIDS crisis love and death get mixed up. As one character muses, "now the great chain of being has become a chain of death as well." I would therefore conclude that the confusion Sontag creates by linking so many characters in her epic sentences is both intentional and effective. Such confusion is part of the way we live now.

Source: Sarah Madsen Hardy, *Short Stories for Students*, Gale, 2000.

Liz Brent

Brent has a Ph.D. in American Culture, specializing in film studies, from the University of Michigan. She is a freelance writer and teaches courses in the history of American cinema. In the following essay, Brent discusses the theme of death in Sontag's story.

Sontag's short story "The Way We Live Now" is about a man who is dying of AIDS. Although AIDS and HIV are not specifically mentioned in the story, it quickly becomes clear to the reader that this is the dreadful illness the man has contracted. In fact, the disease is mentioned only in terms which assume that AIDS is such an ubiquitous and dreaded presence at this point that all one need say is: ". . . what makes you think the worst, he could be just run down, people still do get ordinary illnesses, awful ones, why are you assuming it has to be *that*."

However, the story focuses less on the experience of the man with AIDS than it does on the group response of his wide circle of friends to the progression of his illness. The story is also more broadly about "the way we live" as a culture "now" that the AIDS epidemic—and the potential of any given individual to contract the HIV virus—has become a fact of modern life since the early 1980s.

Critics universally recognize the social milieu of the dying man's friends as a group of young, professional, New York intellectuals—and so the story charts the response of this particular subculture to the presence of death in their lives. The style in which the story is written captures the dense texture of "discourse" generated by the infected man's friends in response to the fact that he is dying of AIDS. In other words, the story is written as a composite of the excess of *talk* and discussion by

❝ **. . . Sontag's tone seems to be ultimately compassionate toward the friends of the dying man. . . . All of the talk generated by the friends of the dying man is ultimately a symptom of the incomprehensible horror and tragedy of the death of a loved one--with its attendant reminder of one's own inevitable death--which has been made all the more present by the seemingly ubiquitous nature of AIDS.❞**

which this group of intellectuals attempts to deal with death.

Although death is an existential reality that all human beings throughout history have had to face, the advent of the AIDS epidemic has made death a more immediate and widespread presence in the lives of many young adults in the United States, forcing them to grapple early in life with a wide spectrum of possible responses to death. Furthermore, by focusing on the survivors, rather than the victim, of the disease (although, as the atmosphere of the story indicates, every survivor is a possible next victim of AIDS), Sontag highlights the effect of the dying man's disease on the social structure of his circle of friends and acquaintances.

Although Sontag has been accused by critics of focusing her writing only on a relatively small, privileged, educated, elite segment of society, "The Way We Live Now" consciously highlights an excessively intellectualized group response to death which interrogates the nuances of human pettiness, competition, and self-interest which invariably accompany such nobler (though no less valid) reactions as commitment, compassion, and self-sacrifice to the dying of a cherished soul.

Sontag's narrative technique in this story captures a dense matrix of conversation carried out among the members of the dying man's social milieu: Max, Ellen, Tanya, Orson, Frank, Jan, Quentin, Kate, Aileen, Greg, Donny, Ursula, Ira, Paolo, Hilda, Nora, Wesley, Victor, Xavier, Lewis, Robert, Betsy, Zack, Clarice, and Yvonne. Sontag intentionally confuses the reader with this complex and extensive web of voices precisely because she is not interested in the reaction of any one individual to the AIDS epidemic. Instead she explores the way "we," as a group, a society, a culture, attempt to make sense of something which is essentially incomprehensible—the end of a human life. Sontag thus weaves long, run-on sentences which reproduce the feverish pitch at which Stephen's friends attempt to talk their way through, or around, the presence of death at their doorstep. Note the opening sentence of the story:

> At first he was just losing weight, he felt only a little ill, Max said to Ellen, and he didn't call for an appointment with his doctor, according to Greg, because he was managing to keep on working at more or less the same rhythm, but he did stop smoking, Tanya pointed out, which suggests he was frightened, but also that he wanted, even more than he knew, to be healthy, or healthier, or maybe just to gain back a few pounds, said Orson, for he told her, Tanya went on, that he expected to be climbing the walls (isn't that what people say?) and found, to his surprise, that he didn't miss cigarettes at all and reveled in the sensation of his lungs being ache-free for the first time in years.

In addition to exploring their own responses to their friend's illness, his friends maintain an incessant dialogue regarding both his physical health and his psychological state. Sontag's concern primarily with the *talk* generated by the man's friends is indicated by the frequent references throughout the story to the *process* by which his condition is evaluated, discussed, speculated upon, argued, and debated. The story is thus riddled with phrases such as: "Max said to Ellen," "according to Greg," "Tanya pointed out," "said Orson," "Tanya went on," "as Max pointed out to Quentin," and so on.

The dying man's friends also continually report to one another what he has said to them, as they all compare notes in order to produce a composite picture of how he is doing:

> And when he was in the hospital, his spirits seemed to lighten, according to Donny. He seemed more cheerful than he had been in the last months, Ursula said, and the bad news seemed to come almost as a relief, according to Ira, as a truly unexpected blow, according to Quentin. . . .

The narrative is also riddled with references to whom he said what to, and who told whom what he had said to whom; this is captured in the third sentence of the story (emphases mine):

> And *he said to Frank,* that he would go, even though he was indeed frightened, *as he admitted to Jan,* but who wouldn't be frightened now, though, odd as that may seem, he hadn't been worrying until recently, *he avowed to Quentin,* it was only in the last six months that he had the metallic taste of panic in his mouth, because becoming seriously ill was something that happened to other people, a normal delusion, *he observed to Paolo,* if one was thirty-eight and had never had a serious illness; he wasn't *as Jan confirmed,* a hypochondriac.

A further layering of discourse is indicated through reference, not only who said what about the dying man, but also who said what about a third party, or even about what the AIDS patient has said to a third party; for example (emphasis mine):

> ... or maybe just to gain back a few pounds, *said Orson, for he told her, Tanya went on,* that he expected to be climbing the walls ...

In another example:

> But is there anything one can do, *he said to Tanya (according to Greg),* I mean what do I gain if I to the doctor; if I'm really ill, *he's reported to have said,* I'll find out soon enough.

The dying man's friends even comment on the excess of conversation among them:

> It seemed that everyone was in touch with everyone else several times a week, checking in, I've never spent so many hours at a time on the phone, Stephen said to Kate, and when I'm exhausted after the two or three calls made to me, giving me the latest, instead of switching off the phone to give myself a respite I tap out the number of another friend or acquaintance, to pass on the news.

Sontag is further interested in the ways in which the friends of the dying man find that the habit of concerned discussion generated by such a crisis takes on a life of its own. Aileen suspects her motives in focusing so extensively on the friend's illness, suggesting that there is a measure of "excitement" in the process of responding to crisis: "I suspect my own motives, there's something morbid I'm getting used to, getting excited by, this must be like what people felt in London during the Blitz."

As Sontag is concerned with the effects of illness on the social structure of the loved one's circle of friends, she focuses attention on the ways in which the crisis elicits petty feelings of competition and jealousy among the dying man's friends and acquaintances; the crisis seems to elicit in them

a desire to "jockey for position" in relationship to the dying man:

> ... but you could hardly expect him to have said the same thing to all his friends, because his relation to Ira was so different from his relation to Quentin (this according to Quentin, who was proud of their friendship), and perhaps he thought Quentin wouldn't be undone by seeing him weep, but Ira insisted that couldn't be the reason he behaved so differently with each, and that maybe he was feeling less shocked, mobilizing his strength to fight for his life, at the moment he saw Ira but overcome by feelings of hopelessness when Quentin arrived with flowers. ...

As the illness progresses, this "jockeying for position" among the dying man's friends becomes more intense; it is worth quoting the long passage which captures the complex dynamics of competition which arise from their sincere concern for his well-being:

> According to Lewis, he talked more often about those who visited more often, which is natural, said Betsy, I think he's even keeping a tally. And among those who came or checked in by phone every day, the inner circle as it were, those who were getting more points, there was still a further competition, which was what was getting on Betsy's nerves, she confessed to Jan; there's always that vulgar jockeying for position around the bedside of the gravely ill, and though we all feel suffused with virtue at our loyalty to him (speak for yourself, said Jan), to the extent that we're carving out time every day, or almost every day, though some of us are dropping out, as Xavier pointed out, aren't we getting at least as much out of this as he is. Are we, said Jan. We're rivals for a sign from him of special pleasure over a visit, each stretching for the brass ring of his favor, wanting to feel the most wanted, the true nearest and dearest, which is inevitable with someone who doesn't have a spouse or children or an official in-house lover, hierarchies that no one would dare contest, Betsey went on, so we are the family he's founded, without meaning to, without official titles and ranks (we, we, snarled Quentin); and is it so clear, though some of us, Lewis and Quentin and Tanya and Paolo, among others, are ex-lovers and all of us more or less than friends, which one of us he prefers, Victor said (now it's us, raged Quentin), because sometimes I think he looks forward to seeing Aileen, who has visited only three times, twice at the hospital and once since he's been home, than he does you or me; but, according to Tanya, after being very disappointed that Aileen hadn't come, now he was angry, while, according to Xavier, he was not really hurt but touchingly passive, accepting Aileen's absence as something he somehow deserved.

Although one could interpret Sontag's story as in part a depiction of the pettiness and self-absorption of a group of over-privileged intellectuals when faced with the reality of suffering and death, Sontag's tone seems to be ultimately compassionate toward the friends of the dying man—and, indeed, toward all of us in the late twentieth century. All of the talk generated by the friends of the dying man is ultimately a symptom of the incomprehensible horror and tragedy of the death of a loved one—with its attendant reminder of one's own inevitable death—which has been made all the more present by the seemingly ubiquitous nature of AIDS.

As one friend of the dying man puts it: "Well, everybody is worried about everybody now, said Betsy, that seems to be the way we live, the way we live now." The ultimate horror and tragedy of the presence of the epidemic is poignantly expressed by the character Ellen: ". . . everyone is at risk, everyone who has a sexual life, because sexuality is a chain that links each of us to many others, unknown others, and now the great chain of being has become a chain of death as well."

Source: Liz Brent, for *Short Stories for Students*, Gale, 2000.

Emily Smith Riser

Riser has a master's degree in English literature and teaches high school English. In the following essay, she discusses the theme and form in "The Way We Live Now."

It is not surprising that Susan Sontag's short story "The Way We Live Now" was published in 1987, the same year as Randy Shilts's journalistic work *And the Band Played On*, as well as the same year ACT UP, an AIDS activist organization, was formed. Shilts's groundbreaking book chronicles the AIDS epidemic in America, covering its political, scientific, and personal impact from the early 1980s, when AIDS was a little-known disease associated with the relatively small gay male community, to 1987, when practically all Americans perceived the threat of the disease looming over them or those they loved. ACT UP (AIDS Coalition to Unleash Power) was organized in response to the growing epidemic to increase awareness and force policy makers and researchers to give it their attention; the group did so through demonstrations and acts of civil disobedience. In contrast with Shilts's journalistic angle and ACT UP's activist approach, Sontag's response to the AIDS epidemic was through fiction. In her story "The Way We Live Now," Sontag develops the theme that, as a result of AIDS, "the way we live now" is in fear and isolation; to propel her message, she employs an unusual form as well as character voices and dialogue.

The initial impression of the story is of a cacophony of voices. The labyrinthine sentences (the first sentence is 133 words long), with names thrown around like confetti and no quotation marks despite the fact that many people are speaking, create a sense of confusion and chaos. This form reflects one of the aspects of "The Way We Live Now": life has become frantic and impersonal. The characters live in a fast-paced world where technology permeates every facet of life, and, despite surface appearances, technology ironically precludes them from actually connecting with each other. The character Stephen says, "I've never spent so many hours at a time on the phone." Later in the story, Yvonne flies in from London for a weekend to see her ailing friend. Tanya says to Lewis that "the thing I can't bear to think about . . . is someone dying with the TV on." Stephen and Yvonne may feel that they are using technology to enhance their friendships, but it really disconnects; it is too easy, too quick-Stephen has many brief conversations, and Yvonne comes in for only a weekend-while real human connections take time. The television, as Tanya observes, is a substitute for human interaction, and she mourns the idea of someone dying while watching it. Despite the fact that all of the characters who speak in the story seem to interact with each other, they do not really relate to each other in truly meaningful ways. Since none of the characters is developed fully, it can be assumed that they know each other only superficially. Furthermore, they do not know well the one person with whom they really need to connect-"him," the one suffering from the disease and obviously (at least to the reader) dying from it.

By the end of the first paragraph, which goes on for more than a page, it becomes clear that there is one person in the story who is *not* speaking, and ironically this person is the subject of everyone's conversations. "He," who in fact is *never* named in the story, is the one around whom the story revolves. Not only is "he" never named in the story, but also the name of the disease from which he suffers is never mentioned-though it becomes clear that the disease is AIDS. Interestingly, his friends say that he himself uses the name of the disease, and say that this is a good sign:

> From the start . . . he was willing to say the name of the disease . . . . As Stephen continued, to utter the name is a sign of health, a sign that one has accepted being who one is, mortal, vulnerable, not exempt, not an exception after all, it's a sign that one is willing, truly willing, to fight for one's life. And we must say

the name, too, and often, Tanya added, we mustn't lag behind him in honesty.

The fact that the friends never name either him or the disease indicates that the friends have not accepted that he is mortal and, by extension, that they are mortal as well. At the same time that his friends are congratulating him for living honestly, they themselves are in denial.

The friends continue to exhibit this reluctance to confront the truth throughout the story. To Ellen's question, "how is he *really*?" Lewis responds, "But you see how he is . . . he's fine, he's perfectly healthy." It is obvious to both of them that this is not true, and yet they cannot bring themselves to talk about how he is "*really.*" Quentin tells a story about Frank saying, in response to someone's comment that a man is dying, "I don't like to think about it that way." Frank, like the other friends, refuses to confront the reality of the situation. However, Quentin is not without blame in the reality-denial department: he intercepts the "bad news" about two acquaintances, and later about their friend Max, so that the unnamed "he" will not have to suffer the disheartening truths about the disease from which he suffers. All of these friends attempt to look out for their friend's best interests, but in doing so, they become guilty of dishonesty and denial. They seem really to be looking out for their own best interests.

A true postmodern story, "The Way We Live Now" has no reliable narrator. In other words, there is no single voice that the reader can trust to tell things the way they are. Instead, the story consists of many conflicting voices; this is a reflection of the many different types of friendships "he" has. The reader is told "You'd hardly expect him to have said the same thing to all his friends, because his relation to Ira was so different from his relation to Quentin (this according to Quentin, who was proud of their friendship)." In the same paragraph, Quentin says, "who wouldn't exaggerate at a time like this," throwing into question the trustworthiness of everything he, or any of the other friends, says. Even the title is an evasion: the story is really about the way we die today. Whereas once people had their family around them when dying from a terminal disease, now the reader is told that the mother in Mississippi is being kept "informed, well, mainly [kept] from flying to New York and heaping her grief on her son and confusing the household routine." When she finally does fly to New York, "he seemed to mind her daily presence less than expected." Everything is "according to" someone, or it is

> **The story ceases to be about how the one afflicted with the disease copes with it and evolves into a tale about how the friends are affected by it. At first, the friends are frantic with concern, but, in time, the disease brings out some rather unsavory aspects of their personalities, though it is difficult to blame them for their flaws since they are so self-aware that they are able to articulate their own failings."**

reported by one person who is reporting what somebody else has said. The story is made up of gossip and sound bites, and it is impossible to weed out the truth from the exaggerations from the evasions.

The story ceases to be about how the one afflicted with the disease copes with it and evolves into a tale about how the friends are affected by it. At first, the friends are frantic with concern, but, in time, the disease brings out some rather unsavory aspects of their personalities, though it is difficult to blame them for their flaws since they are so self-aware that they are able to articulate their own failings. For instance, Ellen says, "I suspect my own motives, there's something morbid I'm getting used to, getting excited by, this must be what people felt in London during the Blitz." Quentin asks whether it is possible that "being as close to him as we are . . . is a way of our trying to define ourselves more firmly and irrevocably as the well, those who aren't ill, who aren't going to fall ill, as if what's happened to him couldn't happen to us." Finally, Jan says, "I know for me his getting it has quite demystified the disease . . . I don't feel afraid, spooked, as I did before he became ill, when it was only news about remote acquaintances, whom I never saw again after they became ill.'' Intellectuals who stand back and observe themselves, all of the friends seem to be getting something out of his illness. This allows them to become removed from what is happening to their friend and to themselves-it is another tool for denial. As the friends discuss their own reactions to the disease, it becomes clear that the story is about them, and not about the one immediately afflicted with AIDS.

Yet, the friends are doing their best. They are human, and the disease brings out their humanity, with all its defects and its strengths. In this age of telephones, computers, fax machines, and airplanes, the disease, in contrast, is a biological force; though the disease is horrible and devastating, it brings these characters back into close contact with one another, forcing them to examine themselves and their relationships with others. The characters fail at accepting the reality of their friend's condition, but through the constant conversation of the community of friends, they do at least construct a network among themselves. At the end of the story, though the characters are still in denial-Tanya is shocked by the decline in his handwriting, Jan wonders ''where [is] his anger,'' and they send his mother home to Mississippi-they do at least take some joy from the fact that he is ''still alive.'' ''The way we live now'' is in fear and denial, but it is also in concern for others and in an attempt to make real connections-even if we are not successful in doing so.

Source: Emily Smith Riser, for *Short Stories for Students*, Gale, 2000.

Sources

Costa, Marithelma, and Adelaida Lopez, ''Susan Sontag: The Passion for Words,'' in *Conversations with Susan Sontag*, edited by Leland Poague, Jackson, MS: University Press of Mississippi, 1995, pp. 222–36.

Dinnage, Rosemary, ''Learning How to Die,'' in *Times Literary Supplement*, March 22, 1992, p. 19.

Fries, Kenny, ''AIDS and Its Metaphors: A Talk with Susan Sontag,'' in *Conversations with Susan Sontag*, edited by Leland Poague, Jackson: University Press of Mississippi, 1995, pp. 255–60.

Kennedy, Liam, *Susan Sontag: Mind as Passion*, New York: St. Martin's Press, 1995.

MacAdam, Barbara A., ''Speaking of the Unspeakable,'' in *ARTnews*, March, 1992, p. 20.

McFall, Gardner, Review, in *New York Times Book Review*, March 1, 1992, p. 20.

Ravenel, Sharon, ed., *Best American Short Stories of the Eighties*, Boston: Houghton Mifflin, 1990.

Roudiez, Leon S., *World Literature Today*, Vol. 66, No. 4, Fall, 1992, p. 723.

Span, Paula, ''Susan Sontag: Hot at Last,'' in *Conversations with Susan Sontag*, edited by Leland Poague, Jackson: University Press of Mississippi, 1995, pp. 255–60.

Further Reading

Andriote, John-Manuel, *Victory Deferred*, Chicago: University of Chicago Press, 1999.

Andriote offers a thorough and impassioned examination of the impact of AIDS on the image, culture, and politics of the gay community over the past two decades.

Lerner, Eric K., and Mary Ellen Hombs, *AIDS Crisis in America*, 2nd ed., Santa Barbara, CA: ABC-CLIO, Inc., 1998.

A clear and comprehensive overview of the rise of AIDS and its effects. Includes demographics, basic medical information, public policy, as well as reference materials and glossary.

Poague, Leland, *Conversations with Susan Sontag*, Jackson, MS: University Press of Mississippi, 1995.

This collection of twenty interviews with Sontag given between 1967 and 1993 offers insight into her views on arts and ideas, as well as some personal background.

Shilts, Randy, *And the Band Played On: People, Politics, and the AIDS Epidemic*, New York: St. Martin's Press, 1987.

Chronicles the AIDS crisis from its very beginning. The book focuses on the difficulties of forming an effective public health response and criticizes the government for its silence on the issue.

The White Horses of Vienna

Kay Boyle

1935

Kay Boyle wrote short stories and novels for almost half a century. In her fiction she consistently utilized her own experiences as well as her uncanny insights into human nature. She first won widespread critical acclaim in 1935 when ''The White Horses of Vienna'' won the O. Henry Award for best short story of the year.

Despite this honor, reviewers at the time held mixed opinions of the story, which examines the rise of Nazism in Austria. Many reviewers, however, did appreciate Boyle's obvious talent. The following year, the story was included in her fourth volume of short fiction. Today ''The White Horses of Vienna'' stands as one of Boyle's most renowned pieces of work.

The success of the story stems in part from Boyle's understanding of the chaos that engulfed Austria at the time. The author lived in that country for three years in the early 1930s and came to know Nazi sympathizers who were otherwise decent people. Boyle brought this realism and humanity to her work.

Author Biography

Kay Boyle was born to a wealthy family in St. Paul, Minnesota, in 1903. As a child, she traveled with her parents throughout the United States and Europe

Kay Boyle

Short Stories. She continued to write novels and poetry, and many of her best-known novels were published in that decade. She also worked on translations, a children's book, and edited a short story anthology.

Her experiences in Europe in the years before World War II influenced many of the short stories she wrote during this period, such as "The White Horses of Vienna." After the end of World War II, Boyle lived in West Germany and worked as a foreign correspondent for the *New Yorker*. Her short stories at this time were informed by her experiences living in the then-occupied, devastated nation.

In the 1950s Boyle was identified as a Communist sympathizer and as a result, she lost her job with the *New Yorker*. She returned to the United States to clear her name. At that time the *Nation* was one of the few magazines that would print her work.

From 1963 to 1979 Boyle taught at San Francisco State College and became a political activist, which included her arrest for protesting the Vietnam War. She died in 1992.

and developed an early appreciation for art and literature.

She moved to New York City while she was still a teenager. There she got a job as an assistant to the editor of *Broom* magazine. Within a short period of time, her work began appearing in that publication as well as in *Poetry: A Magazine of Verse.*

Also that year, Boyle married a French engineer and traveled to France. Out of money and unable to return to the United States, the couple moved to Paris where her literary contacts led to her acquaintance with many American expatriate writers living in France. Soon her literary associates were asking for her contribution to new publications. She also obtained work editing a journal called *This Quarter.*

In 1927 several of her short stories appeared in an avant-garde magazine called *transition*; she published regularly in that journal for the next several years. In her fiction Boyle created startling images, experimented with syntax, and employed a stream-of-consciousness technique.

By the 1930s, Boyle's work was appearing frequently in numerous American magazines, including the *New Yorker*. The stories from this period were collected in her first American book,

Plot Summary

The first part of "The White Horses of Vienna" takes place in the home of an unnamed doctor who lives with his wife and two sons at the foot of a mountain range in Austria. The doctor often climbs the mountain at night, and one night he sprains his ankle. The injury is severe enough that he will be unable to care for his patients for several weeks, so he writes to the hospital in Vienna for a student-doctor to come to his town and take care of his patients. While bedridden, the elderly doctor makes puppets.

Three days later, Dr. Heine arrives from Vienna. Realizing that the young man is Jewish, the elderly doctor's wife is stunned. She is unhappy about having to share their home with a Jew, and she knows that the rest of the townspeople also do not like Jews. However, as a doctor's assistant she has a responsibility to her husband's patients and she is needed to help Dr. Heine pull a tooth shortly after his arrival. She advises him to stand behind the patient, as the doctor always does. Dr. Heine acquiesces, but as he moves position, his coat catches the flame of the sterilizing lamp.

By the time the fire is noticed and extinguished, it has burned the back of his white jacket. Dr. Heine is upset because he is afraid his carelessness will cost him his job. The doctor's wife tells him the accident was her fault and that she will try and fix his new jacket. Then she suddenly feels awkward, remembering he is Jewish.

The second section of the story takes place at the supper table. Dr. Heine tells a story about the royal Lippizaner horses of Vienna. A maharajah had recently seen the horses perform. He wanted to take one of the horses back to India, and the impoverished Austrian government demanded an extraordinary sum for this privilege. The maharajah agreed to the price, but only if the rider came with the horse. The government then demanded an enormous salary for the rider, which the maharajah agreed to pay.

However, the government agents had forgotten about the young groom who cared for the horse. The groom did not want the horse to be taken from Vienna, so he cut the horse on the leg to keep the horse from traveling. After the horse healed, the groom cut the horse again. This time the horse's blood became poisoned and the animal had to be killed.

Throughout the story, the doctor's wife bitterly noted how often Dr. Heine seemed to talk about money. Now she emphasizes that the maharajah's money could not save the horse. Dr. Heine doesn't understand her point and continues with the story, saying that the government had not figured out how the horse came to be injured until the groom killed himself. At that point, they figured out what happened.

The police arrive to ask the doctor about the increase of burning swastikas on the mountainside. They want to know how to get there by the quickest path, but the doctor claims that he cannot move because of his leg. After they have gone, Dr. Heine talks bitterly of how all of Austria is ruined by the current political situation and he wonders who lit the swastika fires. The doctor answers that some people light them because of their beliefs.

One evening, the doctor gives one of his famous puppet shows for his family and neighbors. The puppet show features a grasshopper and a clown. The graceful grasshopper elegantly dances through a field. Then the clown comes on stage, awkward and tripping over his sword. The clown compares poorly to the grasshopper, with his faltering voice, stupid gestures, and obsequious manner.

The grasshopper and the clown talk about the artificial flowers the clown carries. The clown says he is going to his own funeral and wants to be sure he has fresh flowers.

Everyone is enjoying the puppet show immensely, but Dr. Heine starts to realize that the grasshopper is called "The Leader" and the clown "Chancellor" for no apparent reason. He laughs less and less. The Leader and the Chancellor continue to talk about religion, but the Leader always wins their arguments. To the roars of the children's laughter, the clown says "I believe in independence" and then promptly falls over his sword. The Leader says that the clown is relying on the help of the heavens, but implies they may not be strong enough to support him.

The last section of the story takes place sometime later. As Dr. Heine walks outside one night, he thinks that he is growing tired of his stay here and that he wants to be with the intellectuals he left behind in Vienna. The police arrive to arrest the doctor. Dr. Heine asks them why they must come for a man in the middle of the night. They explain that Dollfuss, Austria's chancellor, was assassinated that afternoon and they are rounding up all those people whose political sympathies lie against the Austrian leader. As the police take the doctor away, Dr. Heine asks if there is anything he can do to help. The doctor tells him he can throw peaches and chocolates through his prison window.

Characters

The Doctor
The unnamed doctor is an elderly man and a longtime Nazi sympathizer. He believes that people should actively express their political beliefs; he works with a band of men who burn swastikas atop the mountains to show their desire for Austria's allegiance with Nazi Germany.

Unlike his wife and despite his political leanings, he does not openly display any prejudice against Dr. Heine. When his wife complains about having a Jewish man in her house, he reminds her that Dr. Heine comes highly recommended and seems amiable. However, his fundamental disdain for the Jew reveals itself subtly throughout the story.

Superficially, the doctor seems to be a thoughtful, worldly, and artistic man. However, he uses his charm, good reputation, and obvious intelligence to promote Nazi ideology. For instance, his puppets are used to express his political beliefs in the form of a puppet show. His political demonstrations are known by the Austrian police; he has already been arrested for his activities, and at the end of the story is arrested again.

The Doctor's Wife

The unnamed doctor's wife is a capable woman. A former nurse, she assists her husband with his patients. She is also anti-Semitic and believes that all Jews are greedy and obsessed with money. She is disturbed to have Dr. Heine in her house, yet tolerates him.

Heine

Dr. Heine is a young Jewish student-doctor from Vienna. Not a political man, he is interested primarily in intellectual and artistic matters. He does not realize that the doctor's wife is anti-Semitic and that the doctor is a supporter of the Nazis. However, while he commends the doctor for the artistic aspect of his puppet shows, he does not realize that the play the doctor stages represents the political situation between Austria and Nazi Germany. On a larger scale, Dr. Heine does not understand the import of the Nazi activity in Austria and how it might affect his own life.

Dr. Heine

See Heine

The Student-Doctor

See Heine

Themes

Prejudice

One of the main themes in ''The White Horses of Vienna'' is prejudice; in this case, anti-Semitism. The doctor's wife immediately dislikes Dr. Heine simply because he is Jewish. She views him as alien and impure, someone who will try to poison the townspeople's ''clean, Nordic hearts.'' For one moment she empathizes with him—after his jacket burns and she offers to fix it—but then immediately recognizes her mistake and steps back ''as if she had remembered the evil thing that stood between them.''

She also subscribes to the stereotype that all Jews are greedy and obsessed with money. Thus when Dr. Heine tells the story of the Lippizaner horse, she attributes his interest to the exorbitant amount of money demanded by the government.

The prejudice held by the doctor's wife is not dissimilar to that of the townspeople. The doctor, the only character presented who is an active member of a Nazi group, shows the least amount of prejudice. The student-doctor even forges a bond with the older doctor.

Politics and Political Protest

The elderly doctor is a political activist: he protests the ruling Austrian government in favor of Nazi Germany's government. Apparently, he has been involved in political activities for some time. He has previously been arrested, and his willingness to go to jail for his beliefs evinces his ardent support for Nazi Germany.

In fact, the elderly doctor sustained his leg injury during one of his regular excursions up the mountaintop, presumably to light swastika fires. He is not secretive about his political beliefs and often dramatizes his political opinions through his marionette shows. Such actions show that political protest can be carried out on all levels of life—almost anything can be politicized.

The obtuse Dr. Heine points out this fact in his constant anguish over the political talk that has taken Austria. However, Dr. Heine does not recognize the extent of the elderly doctor's political involvement—thus, he doesn't recognize how prevalent the conflict is in Austria. Therefore he ignores the very real threat of Nazi ideology, especially for someone of his religious faith.

Nazism

Although not specifically mentioned by name, Nazism is a major theme in ''The White Horses of Vienna.'' Nazism, or the doctrines followed by the Nationalist Socialist Party, was initiated by Adolf Hitler. He outlined the main elements of the Nazi program in the 1920s with his book *Mein Kampf (My Struggle)*.

Hitler was nationalistic, anticommunist, antidemocratic, and expansionist. His nationalism derived from a major belief that Germans, or ''Aryans,'' were a biologically superior race. He identified the Jews as Germany's racial and cultural

Topics for Further Study

- Conduct research to find out more about Austria in the 1930s. Why did so many Austrians support Nazism? What kinds of people tended to be Nazi sympathizers? Who opposed these Austrian Nazis?

- Find contemporary accounts of the political situation in Austria and Germany in the 1930s by looking in magazines, newspapers, or books. How has public perception of these events changed over the years?

- The Nazis strongly believed in nationalism. Listen to a musical composition by the nationalist German composer Frederick Wagner. What is nationalism and how can it be expressed through music? What types of feelings does the composition evoke?

- Dr. Heine mentions his interest in science and art. Find out about the prevailing scientific thought and modes of artistic expression in Austria in the 1930s. How does this scientific and artistic situation relate to the developing political situation?

---

enemy, claiming that they kept Germany from reaching its greatness. As his power grew, Hitler initiated programs to deny German Jews of any of the basic rights of citizenship. His plan for the ''final solution'' to the Jewish problem was their systematic extermination in concentrations camps.

Hitler also believed that Germany needed more territory as the country's population rapidly grew. He looked toward Eastern Europe—particularly Russia—as a means to provide the German people with thousands of square miles of needed land. He envisioned the Germans enslaving the Slavs—also thought to be an inferior people—who already lived there. Acquiring Austria was a first step in this expansion, as it gave Hitler economic and military control of the transportation systems leading into Eastern Europe.

Style

Allusion

The doctor's marionette show functions as a satirical allusion for the political difficulties between Germany and Austria. Satire is the use of humor, wit, or ridicule to criticize human nature and societal institutions; the indirect satire employed by the doctor in the puppet show relies upon the ridiculous behavior of its characters to make its point.

In the doctor's puppet show, the clown—called the ''Chancellor''—represents Austrian leader Engelbert Dollfuss, while the grasshopper, or ''The Leader,'' represents German leader Adolf Hitler. The grasshopper, ''a great, gleaming beauty,'' is clearly the superior creature with its elegant dance and powerful voice. The grasshopper is also charismatic and has the power to reach the common people. As such, the doctor presents an accurate portrayal of Hitler, who was able to convince the majority of Germans to give him and his programs their allegiance.

In contrast, the clown is clumsy and foolish. The conversation between the two characters demonstrates the two leaders' beliefs and foreshadows what will come to pass—the clown is on his way to his own funeral. Towards the end of the show, the clown declares, '''I believe in independence,''' but then promptly trips over his sword and falls down. These actions show the doctor's belief that Dollfuss is on his way out and that members of the Austrian Nazi Party, men such as himself, will oust the ineffectual Dollfuss in favor of Hitler.

The satire comes into play through the sheer ridiculousness of the clown. He carries artificial flowers although the lush Austrian countryside is filled with beautiful wildflowers. He cannot manage to even walk properly, tripping constantly over his sword, which is the emblem of power.

Metaphor

Dr. Heine's tale about the Lippizaner horses from the Spanish Riding School in Vienna forms the central metaphor of the story. The horses are described as ''still royal . . . without any royalty left to bow their heads to, still shouldering into the arena with spirits a man would give his soul for, bending their knees in homage to the empty, canopied loge where royalty no longer sat.'' The elderly doctor is strongly identified with the horses. Like the horse purchased by the maharajah, the doctor suffers from an injured leg. Both the doctor and the horse are crippled, and both have poison running through their bodies; the horse's poison is on a physical level, and the doctor's on a symbolic level.

The doctor is further identified with the horse in his need for some kind of royalty or leader to follow. Thus he embraces Hitler and rejects the weak leadership of Dollfuss. The tale of the horses also symbolizes lost Austrian ideals and helps shed light on why so many Austrians were looking to Germany. The death of the horse can also be seen as forecasting the doctor's destruction, perhaps even the eventual demise of the Nazi Party.

Hero and Anti-Hero

In ''The White Horses of Vienna,'' readers must grapple with the question of who is a hero—or if there is even a hero in the tale. Typically, a hero is the principal sympathetic character in a literary work and usually exhibits admirable traits such as idealism, courage, and integrity. An anti-hero is a central character who lacks these traditional heroic qualities.

Dr. Heine and the Austrian doctor emerge as the central figures in the story. The doctor does demonstrate certain heroic qualities; he is self-sufficient, multitalented, and worldly. Interestingly, one of his most admirable qualities—his tolerance for Dr. Heine—is counter to his political and personal beliefs. Dr. Heine exhibits both heroic and anti-heroic qualities; as an anti-hero, he is extremely obtuse and feels alienated from the villagers. Yet neither of these men can truly be categorized in one category or the other.

Structure

''The White Horses of Vienna is divided into three parts. While these parts follow a linear order, each section presents different types of information. Part I provides pertinent information about the doctor and his wife as well as how a Jewish doctor fares in a thoroughly anti-Semitic community. Part II presents the central metaphor of the story as well as the doctor's puppet show. Part III includes the story of the doctor's arrest.

Historical Context

Austria in the 1920s

Knowledge of the political and economic situation in Austria in the 1920s and 1930s is essential to understanding ''The White Horses of Vienna.'' Austria greatly suffered as a result of the Treaty of Versailles, which had ended World War I and had carved out Austria from the former Austro-Hungarian Empire. Austria faced increasing economic problems; the treaty prevented economic growth, and the new republic could not grow enough food for its people or supply its industries with adequate raw materials.

Austria also suffered from social upheaval, particularly as urban socialists and rural conservatives weakened attempts to forge a democratic government. A third of the country's population lived in Vienna—including Jews who contributed to the city's rich cultural life and rose to respected government positions. The country split into two factions: Viennese and everyone else. As different political groups set up private armies, the desire for order made authoritarian rule more appealing. The country became progressively less democratic.

Austria in the 1930s

Austria's economy was further devastated by the Great Depression. In 1931 the leading Austrian bank, which had loaned money to nations throughout Europe, went bankrupt. This bank collapse contributed to the spread of the depression in Europe and resulted in further difficulties to Austria, already struggling with massive unemployment and rampant inflation. By the mid-1930s, an entire

Compare
&
Contrast

- **1930s:** Austria's government is ruled by a series of dictators: first Engelbert Dollfuss, then Kurt von Schuschnigg, and after the *Anschluss*—Germany's annexation of Austria—the German leader Adolf Hitler. By 1938, Austria has become part of the new German empire and no longer exists as an independent, sovereign nature.

  Today: Austria is a federal republic with an executive government made up of a chief of state, the president, and a chancellor who serves as the head of government. The president, who is elected by the Austrian voters to a six-year term, selects the chancellor. The chancellor, in turn, helps the president select a cabinet.

- **1930s:** Austria faces increasing economic hardship. Many people live in poverty, jobs are scarce, manufacturing is low, and inflation is high. The Austrian government is virtually bankrupt and can no longer provide necessities for all of its people.

  Today: Austria has a well-developed market economy, and its people enjoy a high standard of living. A member of the European Union (EU) since 1995, Austria's economy is linked to the economies of other EU member countries, especially with Germany's. Since joining the EU, Austria has attracted a number of foreign investors eager to gain access to the European market.

- **1930s:** By the beginning of the 1930s, Germany's Nazi Party has 180,000 members. Such support gives the Nazi Party a majority in Germany's government in 1933. Throughout the decade, the Nazis pass several discriminatory measures against Jews, homosexuals, gypsies, liberals, socialists, Communists, and other "undesirable" members of society.

  Today: The 1990s have seen a resurgence of Nazi ideology. Neo-Nazis can be found around the world, including Germany, Austria, Italy, Sweden, and the United States. Neo-Nazi and right-wing extremist behavior has increased in Germany since the reunification of West and East Germany. In 1997 official figures showed a national rise of fourteen percent in "extreme right-wing" offenses. In that year, the neo-Nazis who actively participated in demonstrations and other activities numbered 47,000 in East Germany alone.

---

generation of Austrians had grown up in poverty with little opportunity to better their economic circumstances.

The political strife deepened. By the 1930s Austria was led by the so-called Christian dictatorship of Engelbert Dollfuss. His government was made up of right-wing political and military supporters; in addition, it was anti-socialist and opposed the Nazi power growing in Germany. Dollfuss's government tried to curtail the German presence along its borders, but as Austrians grew more discontent, many believed Dollfuss to be incapable of leading the country out of its problems.

Many Austrians favored a union with Germany. A greater numbers of Austrians, some of whom had been members of Austria's Nazi party since the late 1920s, took part in pro-German groups and activities. In July 1934, Dollfuss was assassinated; a new dictatorship, led by Kurt von Schuschnigg, took over the government.

Unfortunately, this new government shared many of the same weaknesses as the old one. Increasingly, more and more Austrians looked to Germany and Adolf Hitler to solve their problems. Around this time, the Austrian Nazi party began demanding the union of Austria and Germany. By 1938 Hitler had forced the Austrian government to include Nazi members in its cabinet.

Austria's government was in favor of an *Anschlusss*, or union, with Germany. Austria's leaders, however, regretted the agreement and suggested the *Anschluss* be put to a vote to the Austrian people. Hitler refused to allow this. He wanted to control Austria's resources and he believed that controlling Austria would put Germany in a better position to expand in southeastern Europe. The chancellor resigned, and on the Austrian Nazi party took over the government, allowing the German army to march into Austria unopposed. In March 1938, Hitler proclaimed Austria to be part of Germany.

Hitler's Rise to Power and Nazi Germany

Germany also suffered greatly as a result of the Treaty of Versailles. The Kaiser had abdicated in 1918, and Germany's new democratic government faced both political and economic crises. Germany had difficulties implementing a stable, effective government, and inflation ran rampant until the mid-1920s.

Adolf Hitler first came to national prominence for the leadership role he played in a failed uprising in Munich in 1923. While in prison, he wrote *Mein Kampf (My Struggle)*. In this book, he outlined the major philosophies of the National Socialist, or Nazi, movement. The Nazis were rabidly nationalistic, anticommunist, and anti-Semitic.

Hitler captivated the disillusioned German people, many of whom felt humiliated by the Treaty of Versailles. Hitler's promises to restore German lands and power also appealed to many Germans.

The Nazis had few followers until the Great Depression led to increasing economic difficulties. By 1930 tens of thousands of German voters supported the Nazi Party. Nazism, with its anti-Communistic stance, strongly appealed to German conservatives. In 1933, Germany's leader appointed Hitler chancellor of the republic. Within a month, using the Nazis' private army, Hitler had effectively turned himself into a German dictator, outlawing opposing political parties.

The Nazi government increased spending programs, which helped Germany emerge from the depression; created a system of social and cultural education to train the German people in Nazi doctrine; and developed a brutal program of anti-Semitism, under which Jews lost their citizenship. Hitler also broke with the Treaty of Versailles in his rearmament of Germany and his recapturing of lost territory. In 1938, Germany attacked Poland, an action that led to the beginning of World War II.

Critical Overview

"The White Horses of Vienna" was initially published in *Harper's* magazine in 1935. It garnered much critical recognition when it won the O. Henry Award for best short story that year. In 1936 it became the title story for her short story collection. Altogether ten of the eighteen stories in *The White Horses of Vienna and Other Stories* attracted positive critical commentary, and Boyle's work consistently appeared on lists of the year's best stories throughout the decade.

Criticism

Rena Korb

Korb has a master's degree in English literature and creative writing and has written for a wide variety of educational publishers. In the following essay, she explores the different facets of Nazism and compares the protagonists in "The White Horses of Vienna."

In 1935, two years after she first moved to Austria, Kay Boyle told a friend about her experience listening to an illegal radio broadcast of an Adolf Hitler speech. She spoke of his "moving appeal" to Austrians to "return to the Fatherland," or unite with Germany. "I prefer the emotional thing," she wrote, "and the Germans have got it in Hitler anyway."

By that time, Boyle had come to grasp the economic and political woes that had plagued Austria since the end of World War I and had seen the serious ramifications they had on an entire generations of Austrians. She also became acquainted with Nazis and Nazi sympathizers—including her children's nurse, who described the swastikas fires blazing in the mountainsides and admitted to lighting them herself several nights a week. While Boyle stood against fascism herself—she lived in the only anti-Nazi hotel in her town—she also recognized the that the situation had literary potential.

When Boyle met a young doctor who was won over by Hitler's promises of bringing an economic revival to Austria, she used him as inspiration for the Nazi sympathizer she so keenly portrayed in

What Do I Read Next?

- Hugh Ford's *Four Lives in Paris* chronicles the lives of four American expatriates who lived in Paris in the 1920s: Boyle, the composer George Antheil, social and political critic Harold Stearns, and New York editor Margaret Anderson.

- Boyle's 1936 novel *Death of a Man* explores the love affair between an American woman and a Tyrolean doctor. The doctor is a Nazi who is torn between his love for the woman and his devotion to his cause.

- *Mein Kampf (My Struggle)* (American translation, 1943), written by Adolf Hitler while he was in prison for his role in an uprising against the government, outlines his Nazi program and plans for Germany.

- *Stones from the River*, Ursula Hegi's 1994 novel, explores the rise of Nazism through the story of a young girl growing up in a small German town. The novel, told from the viewpoint of a dwarf, deftly portrays the effect Hitler's policies had on Jewish families and examines the results of Hitler's actions on German culture and society.

"The White Horses of Vienna." "It was his character," she wrote, "and his political problems, which constituted a large part of my eagerness to write [about him]."

In 1935, "The White Horses of Vienna" was awarded the O. Henry prize for best short story of the year. This honor won the author $300 as well as the widespread critical recognition that had so far alluded her throughout her ten-year career as a writer. The following year, the story was chosen to title Boyle's fourth volume of short fiction.

Despite these honors, the story was criticized; reviewers from the 1930s expressed disappointment in the story, for they did not understand the political situation arising in post World-War I Europe and thus confused her message. Even more telling, one of the O. Henry judges disagreed with the rest of the panel, objecting to the story because it presented a sympathetic Nazi character.

What this judge and other readers could not comprehend, writes Sandra Whipple Spanier in *Kay Boyle, Artist and Activist*, was that although Boyle might admire "fervent commitment to a cause, she did not embrace that cause itself." Boyle herself believed that "the true artist presents; he does not judge." She countered critics: "In writing 'The White Horses of Vienna' . . . I was seeking to find out, on a human level, what the almost inexplicable fascination of Hitler was."

Boyle's attempt to integrate her emotional perceptions with the social and political situation in Austria, however, is considered successful by most contemporary critics. As Mary Loweffelholz writes in *Experimental Lives*, "the story does not demonize Nazi sympathizers; it instead grounds the evils of Nazism in particular and complicated social conditions."

"The White Horses of Vienna" chronicles the story of an Austrian doctor who is a Nazi sympathizer and his encounter with a young Jewish student-doctor. This unlikely pair meets after the older doctor, who has injured his leg setting swastika fires in the mountains, sends to Vienna for a replacement. The anti-Semitism of the doctor's town is revealed through the doctor's wife; cleverly, Boyle keeps hidden the doctor's own political agenda.

The major conflict in the story arises from the relationship between the older doctor and the student-doctor. From the onset, Boyle sets up the contrast between the two men. The older doctor is a "savagely clean man" with "well-scrubbed skin." He is a quintessentially blond Nordic, right down to the "pure white plaster wall" in his home. Dr. Heine, however, is introduced after climbing up

---

> The emotional backbone of the story derives from such missed communications as well as Boyle's multidimensional characters. No one is all good or all bad; rather, characters manifest elements of each."

from the village on foot. He has a "long, dark, alien face" and an "arch" to his nose. He is also dirty—his forehead is covered with sweat and his shoes are "foul with the soft mud of the mountainside."

However, the two men are dissimilar in more ways than the physical. The older doctor is a Nazi sympathizer who actively works with a group intent on promoting Nazi ideology; the student-doctor is a Jew who actively resents the way politics and political talk has overtaken Austria. As such, both men represent polar ways of dealing with difficult political and social situations: activism or avoidance. While Dr. Heine willfully ignores the significance of the events surrounding him, the older doctor takes his stand; yet, it is hard to commend him for supporting a racist dictator.

Despite this fact, the older doctor is depicted as an intelligent, tolerant man. In the first part of the story, Boyle develops the doctor's character aside from his political beliefs: he has built his own house; he makes puppets; he paints and draws; he has traveled throughout Europe. Boyle lulls the reader into appreciating the man for his talents before revealing his darker side.

By the end of the story, however, his political beliefs have overshadowed his accomplishments. Through his puppet show he displays his arrogance in his disrespect of the Austrian chancellor. He also ridicules Dr. Heine when he tells the younger man to throw peaches and chocolates at his prison window—he relies on the fact that Dr. Heine, who is so removed from the debilitating economic situation, will not know that it is virtually impossible to get such luxury items in stricken Austria. In this instance, the doctor's disdain for Dr. Heine is particu-

larly cutting as the younger man acts out of a genuine desire to help.

The most interesting exploration of the doctor's Nazism, however, is through his attitude toward Dr. Heine. Despite supporting Hitler—an icon of obscene racism—he never expresses any dislike for Dr. Heine based on his religious background. When the doctor's wife complains about having a Jew in their house, the doctor seems to be on Dr. Heine's side. It could even be suggested that the doctor's disdain for Dr. Heine arises, not because of his Jewishness, but because of his utter ignorance at the economic turmoil that grips Austria. A man as politically active as the doctor certainly would not respect someone like Dr. Heine, who deliberately avoids such a difficult situation.

In comparison, the younger doctor is so obtuse that it is difficult to empathize with him, although he is the victim of prejudice. He never comprehends the older doctor's political activities or his true sympathies, despite witnessing the police officers questioning the doctor about the swastika fires and watching the blatantly political puppet show. The student-doctor, instead, frets about the fact that Austria "is ruined by the situation . . . Everything is politics now." He doesn't question what devastating events would bring about such a condition.

Dr. Heine further demonstrates his lack of awareness in believing that the older doctor also avoids the political situation, basing this assumption solely on the doctor's interest in making puppets and staging marionette shows. Dr. Heine sees only the surface of things, never delving beyond the superficial.

Dr. Heine does understand on a general level how Germans and Austrians perceive Jews. He sees the swastika fires as "inexplicable signals given from one mountain to another in some secret gathering of power that cast him and his people out, forever upon the waters of despair." Yet he cannot make the crucial leap from the general to the specific. He prefers to hide in his card games and in his longing for the old days, when he and his friends discussed art and other intellectual matters.

The two central literary devices in the story—the older doctor's puppet show and Dr. Heine's tale of the Lippizaner horses—both function to more fully develop the two men's characters and their ideals and show their relationship to the current events unfolding in Austria. The doctor, earlier described as hopping and resembling a "great, golden, wounded bird,'' is allied with the grasshop-per of his show, ''a great, gleaming beauty.'' As the grasshopper represents Hitler, the doctor's alliance with the Nazis is at last made apparent.

The doctor uses the puppet show as a vehicle to further his own cause and to spread Nazi propagan-da. The ''monstrously handsome'' grasshopper is charismatic, possessing a voice that has a ''wild and stirring power that sent the cold of wonder up and down one's spine.'' According to the doctor's script, the grasshopper, also called ''The Leader,'' has the ability to reach the common people and to under-stand their needs. The Leader, perfectly at ease in an Austrian field of daisies, is presented as part of the natural order of things.

The foolish, ''faltering'' clown—also called ''Chancellor''—represents the Austrian leader, Engelbert Dollfuss. The puppet show demonstrates the doctor's disgust for this clown who is ''ridicu-lous in his stupidity.'' It also foreshadows the fall of the chancellor—which occurs at the end of the story through his assassination. Where the clown puts his faith in the church, a human-constructed entity, the grasshopper recognizes that ''the country is full of God.'' That the doctor shows his preference for the grasshopper cannot be denied; even Dr. Heine rec-ognizes that the clown is ''quite the fool of the piece.''

The chasm between the two doctors widens as it becomes apparent that the obtuse clown shares characteristics with Dr. Heine. Like the clown, Dr. Heine is uncomfortable in a natural setting and prefers to ignore what is going on around him. Hindsight shows that the Jews were already in great danger as Germans embraced Hitler, but even ana-lyzing the story in its own time frame would lead to a similar conclusion. As early as the 1920s, Hitler had outlined his racial beliefs in his book *Mein Kampf (My Struggle)*, and by the mid-1930s, his Nazis had already initiated harsh and discriminatory measures against German Jews.

Dr. Heine's story of the Lippizaner horses provides another vehicle for comparison and exami-nation. The doctor is identified with the injured horse from Dr. Heine's story—both the horse and the doctor suffer leg injuries and both have been poisoned, the horse physically and the doctor with Nazi rhetoric.

However, a deeper meaning can be construed from the metaphor. The doctor, like the horses, needs a powerful leader. Austria's dysfunctional governmental system has only provided the ineffec-tual Dollfuss, who has failed to solve the country's many social and economic problems. The doctor must find a strong leader—Hitler. The horses fur-ther represent all the Austrians who sharply feel their country's loss of prestige and glory.

By the end of the story, Dr. Heine is beginning to feel uncomfortable in his situation. He shows such signs during the puppet show, when he sud-denly ''found he was not laughing as loudly as before.'' The night the Heimwehr police officers arrive to arrest the doctor, Dr. Heine is walking outside the house, ''lost in this wilderness of cold'' despite the heat of the summer. He longs to be ''indoors, with the warmth of his own people, and the intellect speaking.'' Dr. Heine's feelings of alienation would seem to indicate a growing aware-ness of his anti-Semitic surroundings, yet when he sees the officers approach, his first instinct is to alert the doctor, whom he mistakenly perceives as his friend.

The emotional backbone of the story derives from such missed communications as well as Boyle's multidimensional characters. No one is all good or all bad; rather, characters manifest elements of each. The Nazi doctor swiftly shifts from feeling sorry for Dr. Heine to mocking him. Dr. Heine, who seems impervious to the problems of those around him, makes a real effort to help someone in need. Even the doctor's wife helps extinguish the flames when Dr. Heine's coat catches fire and offers to fix it. Spanier finds in such actions an expression of hope: ''even in the face of divisive social forces, the basic connections of compassion between individu-als might survive.''

In ''The White Horses of Vienna'' Boyle pre-sents diametrically opposed characters, both of whom represent ways of dealing with an uncomfortable situation. While many critics do not agree on all the story's symbolism, a number of them do find evi-dence of Boyle's humanism—a notable exception is Ray B. West, Jr., who asserted in *The Short Story in America* that the story is a ''study in decadence.'' These contemporary dissenting views mirror those that accompanied the story when it was first published.

It clearly is a story that defies easy categoriza-tion. The critics' quandaries mirror the complexity within the story itself. One thing is certain, howev-er: the story demonstrates both Boyle's keen under-standing of the chaotic world unraveling around her as well as her ability to forecast a grim future. With this story, Boyle opens the doors on the experience of Europe in the 1930s.

Source: Rena Korb, for *Short Stories for Students*, The Gale Group, 2000.

Liz Brent

Brent has a Ph.D. in American Culture, specializing in cinema studies, from the University of Michigan. She is a freelance writer and teaches courses in American cinema. In the following essay, Brent discusses the conflict between personal relationships and political perspectives in Boyle's short story.

Critics have long debated whether or not Kay Boyle's short story, "The White Horses of Vienna," is sympathetic to the Nazi-activist family with which the young Jewish doctor comes to stay. In the following essay, I examine the characters of the wife of the Nazi-activist doctor and Heine, the Jewish student-doctor, in order to discuss the relationship of each character to the political context in which the story takes place. I will first discuss the nature of the wife's anti-Semitic prejudice against Heine, and then discuss Heine's own response to the anti-Semitic sentiment which surrounds him. Through these characters, Boyle's story can be read as a successful portrait of the dilemmas created by each character's attempt to reconcile her or his political perspective with personal relationships.

Heine, the Jewish student-doctor, sent to stay with the Doctor and his family, represents an alien intrusion into their home and community in two senses: he is Jewish, and he is from the city. The wife's prejudice against the young Jewish doctor is intertwined with her perception of him as a "man from the city," and an outsider to their country life and peasant heritage. That the Jewish student-doctor is a fish out of water in the home of the Nazi-activist country doctor is indicated immediately upon his arrival by his city ways. Thinking of Heine's face, with its Jewish features, as "dark" and "alien," the wife first notices the inappropriateness of his city dress to the mountain setting: "his city shoes were foul with the soft mud of the mountainside after the rain, and the sweat was standing out on his brow because he was not accustomed to the climb." When Heine greets the doctor and his wife, even his speech marks him as a man of the city, not the country: "'Good day,' he said, as city people said it." His status as a man from the city, and outsider to the doctor's country milieu is

also indicated by his inability to recognize the pet fox as a fox: "'Is this a dog or a cat?'" he asks. Like her description of the young student-doctor's muddy shoes, the wife equates the city with that which is dirty, "foul" and alien, and the country with that which is clean and pure and familiar; her anti-Semitism thus causes her to view the young doctor's Jewishness in similar terms: "So much had she heard about Jews that the joints of his tall, elegant frame seemed oiled with some special, suave lubricant that was evil, as a thing come out of the Orient, to their clean, Nordic hearts."

The wife's disdain for Heine as both a Jew and a man from the city is further expressed through her internal response to the story he tells the family that evening over supper. She associates his Jewishness with a lack of attachment to any land, which she regards as an affront to the ways of her family's country peasant heritage, by which identity is strongly tied to land: "...the young wife sat giving quick, unwilling glances at this man who could have no blood or knowledge of the land behind him; for what was he but a wanderer whose people had wandered from country to country and whose sons must wander, having no land to return to in the end?"

The wife's internal response to Heine's story is completely colored by the anti-Semitic stereotypes she holds, whereby she expects the young Jewish man to be greedy and money-grubbing. As part of Heine's story concerns payment for a white horse, the wife thinks: "Oh, yes...you would speak about money, you would come here and climb our mountain and poison my sons with the poison of money and greed!" When Heine's story includes an uneven business exchange, the wife imagines that "their shrewdness pleased his soul." And again, her anti-Semitism against Heine is associated with her own identity as a peasant of the country; she views his urban sophistication as alien to the simplicity of country people, and an affront to their heritage and way of life: "The whole family was listening, but the mother was filled with outrage. These things are foreign to us, she was thinking. They belong to more sophisticated people, we do not need them here. The Spanish Riding School, the gentlemen of Vienna, they were as alien as places in another country, and the things they cherished could never be the same."

The wife's bitter prejudice against the young Jewish man seems additionally born of an awareness of the economic hardship of her own peasant community, against which she pits Heine's urbane interest in "art and science." When Heine expresses to the wife his admiration for the doctor's artistic projects, the wife interprets this as further reason for prejudice against Heine, as if his Jewishness and urbanity were to blame for the economic plight of the nation: "'Yes,' said the doctor's wife, saying the words slowly and bitterly. 'Yes. Art and science. What about people being hungry, what about this generation of young men who have never had work in their lives because the factories have never opened since the war? Where do they come in?'"

Only once does the wife's natural sense of human warmth and compassion momentarily override her seething bitterness toward the young Jewish man. When Heine's jacket is accidentally caught on fire, the wife's unthinking response is to save him, as she "picked up the strip of rug from the floor and flung it about him." This act leads to a moment of physical proximity between the wife and Heine, in which the wife spontaneously holds his body with a human warmth which seems almost affectionate, even bordering on the intimate. Upon flinging the rug around Heine to put out the fire burning his jacket, "She held it tightly around him with her bare, strong arms. . ." In this embrace-like gesture, the wife continues "holding him fast still in her arms," and begins to "beat his back softly with the palm of her hand." She then offers to patch the jacket, "touching the good cloth that was left"— meaning the part of the jacket still attached to Heine's body. But, when she becomes aware of her own warmth and kindness toward him, her prejudice causes her to again regard him as evil and repellant: "And then she bit her lip suddenly and stood back, as if she had remembered the evil thing that stood between them." The impulse to bite her lip implies a sense of shame or embarrassment at her own expression of affection toward the Jewish man.

Heine is caught between his desire to deny the significance of "politics" to his personal relationships, and his increasing awareness that he is defenseless against the intrusion of "politics" into his life. In the beginning of the story, Heine's character chooses to be oblivious to both the political turmoil around him and the prejudice which inflects his relationship to the Doctor's family. Heine's behavior toward the family is amiable and friendly, and he seems not to notice the various indications of the wife's prejudice against him. Heine prefers to retreat into a realm of "art" and "science," the aesthetic and the intellectual. As the story progresses, however, Heine becomes aware of the personal implications of his position as a Jew amidst a family and community of Nazi sympathizers.

> " As the doctor's wife equates Heine's Jewishness with his origins in the 'city,' Heine begins to equate the forces of anti-Semitism with the 'wilderness' of the mountain community to which he is an alien."

Heine's obliviousness to the wife's prejudice against him seems due to his naturally amiable nature, as well as his desire to deny the significance of politics to his own life and personal relationships. As he tells the tale of the white horses of Vienna, he does not notice when the wife gives him a "look of fury." Even when she misinterprets the point of the story in terms of the stereotype she holds of Jews as greedy, as she comments "bitterly" that "'Even the money couldn't save him, could it?'" Heine is merely "perplexed" by her meaning. Heine wishes to deny the significance of "politics" to his life, preferring to retreat into the realms of "art and science." He also wishes to regard his relationships with other people as unsullied by the intrusion of "politics." His admiration for the doctor, and guileless amiability toward the family indicate his complete disregard for the implications of the fact that this is a family of Nazi sympathizers and that he is a lone Jewish man in a community of Nazi sympathizers.

Heine resents the intrusion of politics upon his interest in aesthetics and intellectual pursuits, as well as upon his personal relationships. "'The whole country is ruined by the situation,' said the student-doctor. . .'Everything is politics now. One can't meet people, have friends on any other basis. It's impossible to have casual conversations or abstract discussions any more. . .'" Expressing his disdain for "politics," Heine prefers a retreat into the artistic and the social: "'Politics, politics,' said the student-doctor, 'and one party as bad as another. You're much wiser to make your puppets, *Herr Doktor.* It takes one's mind off things, just as playing cards does. In Vienna we play cards, always play cards, no matter what is happening.'"

Yet, while Heine admires the doctor for his artistic pursuits, the doctor, in contrast to Heine, is a pro-Nazi political activist who makes use of his hobby of creating puppets and putting on puppet shows for his community as a means of conveying a political message. The doctor's political activism as a Nazi-sympathizer, however, highlights Heine's political apathy as a Jew whose people are threatened by Nazi activities: "'There was a time for cards,' said the doctor, working quietly with the grasshopper's wings. 'I used to play cards in Siberia, waiting to be free. We were always waiting for things to finish with and be over,' he said. 'There was nothing to do, so we did that. But now there is something to do.'" Heine's desire to deny the significance of politics to his own life, however, seems in part born of a sense of helplessness—that, as a Jew in the face of Hitler's Nazi sympathizers, there may in fact be "nothing to do."

As Heine stays on with the doctor's family, however, he develops a growing awareness of the plight of his people—and his own inability to escape the forces of "politics" all around him. When he sees the swastikas of fire burning on the mountain, he feels hopeless and powerless against the anti-Semitic forces which surround him: "He felt himself sitting defenseless there by the window, surrounded by these strong long-burning fires of disaster. They were all about him, inexplicable signals given from one mountain to another in some secret gathering of power that cast him and his people out, forever out upon the waters of despair."

Heine's growing awareness of the menace of the "politics" which surround his presence in the mountain community of Nazi-sympathizers causes a change in his response to the doctor during the puppet show. While Heine at first admired what he took to be the Doctor's retreat into "art" in the face of political turmoil, he comes to realize, during the puppet show, that the doctor's efforts at entertaining his guests are in fact in the service of expressing political views which pose a threat to the young Jewish man. As this realization dawns on the student-doctor, he "found he was not laughing as loudly as before" at the antics of the Doctor's puppets.

Through his growing inability to deny the impact of "politics" upon his life and personal relationships, Heine begins to equate the mountains which surround him with the menace of anti-Semitism which resides in the mountain community of Nazi-sympathizers. As the doctor's wife equates

Heine's Jewishness with his origins in the "city," Heine begins to equate the forces of anti-Semitism with the "wilderness" of the mountain community to which he is an alien. The coldness of the mountains becomes for him a metaphor for the coldness of these peasant Nazi sympathizers toward "his own people." "He was lost in this wilderness of cold, lost in a warm month, and the thought turned his blood to ice. He wanted to be indoors, with the warmth of his own people, and the intellect speaking. He had had enough of the bare, northern speech of these others. . ."

Yet, even when the Heimwehr men come to arrest the Doctor for his pro-Nazi activism, Heine's personal affection for the man and his family overrides his awareness of the political implications of the Doctor's activities. At this point, his disdain for "politics" is based on his compassion for the Doctor. "'Ah, politics, politics again!' cried Dr. Heine, and he was wringing his hands like a woman about to cry." And, although Heine begs the doctor to tell him what he can do to help, even these efforts signify how defenseless he is against the forces of "politics," which surround him in all their enormity, for "his own voice sounded small and senseless in the enormous night."

The presence of the young Jewish student-doctor creates in the older doctor's wife a conflict between her personal impulse to compassion for other human beings and her deeply held prejudice against Jews; meanwhile, Heine's stay with the family of Nazi-sympathizers forces him to realize that the forces of "politics" have an undeniable impact on his personal relationships, his own life, and the lives of his fellow Jews. Boyle's characterization of the wife clearly represents the woman's anti-Semitism both without excusing it and devoid of any sentimentality indicating that Heine's presence has in any way caused her to question her prejudices. Her characterization of Heine, meanwhile, in a story written amidst the gathering storm of Nazism which lead to the Holocaust, comes across as an alarmist concern for the growing plight of Jews in a political context which posed an increasingly powerful threat to Jewish people.

Source: Liz Brent, for *Short Stories for Students*, The Gale Group, 2000.

Elizabeth S. Bell

In the following excerpt, Bell describes Austria's situation at the time Boyle wrote "The White Horses of Vienna" and shows how the story, "per-

haps more cogently and certainly more humanly than news reports of the day, outlines the forces at work in Europe in the decade preceding World War II.''

While most reviewers complimented the topical nature of ''The White Horses of Vienna,'' some did not understand the events in Europe that provided the backdrop for the story. For example, Sylvia Pass of the *Christian Century* finds the story obscure, but she mistakenly sets the story in Switzerland instead of Austria and—because she does not realize that the story grows from the particular situation brewing in Austria—naturally grumbles that the central piece of satire, the doctor's marionette show, fails to communicate. Howard Baker, writing for *Southern Review,* dismisses this central episode as well, failing to realize that it provides the underlying explanation for the story itself. Pass's and Baker's confusion points out a central feature of Boyle's relationship to her reader: she expects her reader to know the shape of world events; she refuses to mar her stories with explanations of events the reader jolly well should already know.

Briefly stated, Austria—and indeed most of Europe—suffered from massive unemployment and crushing inflation during the 1930s. Part of the problem, of course, was the worldwide Depression that began in the United States in 1929 and spread with some rapidity to Europe. Yet another element of the problem grew from the stringent treaties that ended World War I, designed to stifle economic growth for Germany and its allies. As Boyle points out in several of her stories, an entire generation of young people had grown up in poverty, with no opportunity to find productive employment in a moribund economy. By the 1930s, people found that ways of life that had sustained them for generations no longer worked. Most of the vanquished European countries developed strong nationalistic movements as a result of what they considered the humiliating conditions of the World War I treaties. These nationalistic movements flourished because they reestablished a sense of pride and worthiness that World War I had shaken, and they promised hope for rebuilding the prosperity of the land.

Austria in the 1930s was ruled by a so-called Christian dictatorship headed by Engelbert Dollfuss, made up of right-wing political and military supporters. Rabidly antisocialist, the government also fought to counter the growing German presence on its border, yet economic conditions throughout Austria became more and more desperate. A growing

> " Boyle objectively presents the perspectives of both: through the old doctor she suggests the desperation of a people crushed by economic instability and political humiliation, grasping at any promise, especially a political movement promising salvation. Through Dr. Heine she shows the deadly nature of the solution being promised and a naive reliance on the intellect as a saving power."

number of Austrians saw Dollfuss as incapable of providing the leadership they needed. In July 1934 Dullfuss was assassinated, and a new dictatorship headed by Kurt von Schuschnigg took charge. However, the new government shared many of the same weaknesses that marked the old one, and many Austrians began to look more favorably at what appeared to be a stronger, more promising government in Germany. Indeed, the Austrian Nazi party began demanding the union of Austria and Germany. This situation prevailed as Boyle wrote and published the stories she collected in *The White Horses of Vienna and Other Stories*, just after Dollfuss's assassination and during the four years' respite before Germany marched into Austria and made the Austrian nationalistic movement a moot issue.

''The White Horses of Vienna,'' set in Austria immediately before Dollfuss's assassination, develops the interplay between political movements and personal lives amid the confusion of a rapidly changing international situation. Its three parts are chronologically and narratively related, but intentionally offer different kinds of information about the people and situations of the central story. Part I provides the personal context of the story, the reason the fastidious doctor and his wife must deal with the young Jewish doctor whom the wife, at least, detests. Boyle mentions that in World War I, the older doctor was a prisoner of war in Siberia. He has studied throughout Europe, but has returned to the Tyrol as a kind of haven, a land that provides him with the distance from people and the vistas of mountains he craves. An injury to his knee occurring on one of his frequent nighttime trips into the mountains, where mysterious swastika fires burn, necessitates his calling for a student doctor to come help him in his practice until the knee heals. Boyle highlights the physical contrast between the two doctors, describing the older one as immaculate in white clothing and somewhat neurotically concerned with cleanliness, while young Dr. Heine is dark and alien, appearing on the doctor's property with mud on his shoes and sweat pouring from him.

The doctor's wife provides a barometer for the anti-Semitism of the community, first through her own distress at the doctor's obvious Jewish looks: she begins recoiling from him at first sight. She mentions that the community will feel the same way. The doctor agrees, but does not overtly join in his wife's distress. This section of the story ends with a scene between Dr. Heine and the older doctor's wife, as she offers to mend his coat for him, then realizes she has offered to help a Jew. With this episode, Boyle contrasts the nature of relationships forged between people responding to each other as individuals with those broken or truncated relationships that sometimes exist between groups of people.

Part 2 of the story deals with a more metaphorical kind of information. Boyle has both doctors present an analogue for reality as they see it. Dr. Heine tells of the royal Lippizaner horses of Vienna, still performing as if for a royalty that no longer exists. An incredibly wealthy Indian maharajah, seeing the horses, decides he must have the best for himself. The state, in chronic need of money, sells the horse to him, but on the day of the scheduled departure for India, the horse develops a mysterious cut on its hoof. The groom who has loved the horse from its birth cannot bear to see it leave Austria and has taken measures to delay the process. After the first cut heals, he makes another, this time causing blood poisoning. The horse must be destroyed; the groom commits suicide. Both have died senselessly for a way of life no longer possible.

The doctor's wife, accepting the stereotypical image of Jewish people, assumes Dr. Heine tells the story from his appreciation of the sharp deal the state made or of the marahajah's incredible wealth. She gloats on the moral she attaches to the story: money can't buy everything. But Dr. Heine recognizes the irony of the Lippizaner's training to please a royalty that will never exist again. He and the doctor's wife continue their mismatched conversation, with the young doctor asserting his belief in art and science, while the doctor's wife interjects her own disdain for art and her concerns for the people starving and unable to find productive work. The two speak on different planes, for although Dr. Heine is virtually apolitical, the doctor's wife is unable to view life on any terms except the political.

Austrian authorities come to ask the old doctor about the swastika fires and reveal he has been arrested previously for his pro-Nazi activities. In the face of his refusal to cooperate, they leave, indicating they always feel better when the doctor is safely behind bars. This exchange troubles Dr. Heine, but he fails to connect the doctor's political activities with anything that could possibly affect his own life.

The old doctor then presents his analogue with a marionette show, peopled by puppets he has made. He provides a thinly disguised satire of the ineffective Dollfuss, portrayed as a clown called "Chancellor" and a magnificent Hitler, embodied as an elegant grasshopper referred to as "The Leader." The clown bears artificial flowers in a setting of Austrian wildflowers, contributing to his ludicrous and lifeless character. The grasshopper, however, belongs in the setting and appears to uphold the natural order of things. While Boyle refers neither to Dollfuss nor Hitler by name, their characters are unmistakable. Dr. Heine, distinctly uncomfortable during the presentation, realizes that even the playfulness of the doctor is political.

This section of the story illustrates metaphorically the underlying philosophical conflict between the two doctors. Boyle objectively presents the perspectives of both: through the old doctor she suggests the desperation of a people crushed by economic instability and political humiliation, grasping at any promise, especially a political movement promising salvation. Through Dr. Heine she shows the deadly nature of the solution being promised and a naive reliance on the intellect as a saving power. She portrays his gentleness and his sensitivity, his love of art and learning, but also his virtual indifference to the political storm gathering around him. Both men, taken individually, have valid human concerns. Their choices, however, are mutually exclusive.

The third part of the story occurs on an evening in July, the evening after Dollfuss's assassination. The Austrian authorities come to arrest the old doctor. Dr. Heine asks what he can do to help the doctor, who responds with ironic humor that Dr. Heine can throw peaches and chocolates to him through the prison's window bars. Last time, he says, his wife was such a poor shot he could not catch all the oranges she threw to him. For that biting edge of irony, Boyle plays on the reader's knowledge of contemporary reality in Europe, for in the economic disaster of Europe, peaches, chocolates, and oranges are unobtainable luxuries. As the authorities carry away the doctor, Dr. Heine thinks in anguish of those Lippizaner horses and their bond to a way of life gone forever.

Both doctors use their analogues to shape their own choices, believing them to be true and accurate. The old doctor's worldview leads him to action that counters his personal experience, for as prisoner of war he has seen political movements fail; the young doctor's leads him to no action at all, but merely a philosophical musing on the conditions of the world. In 1935, at the time Boyle wrote this story, the full horror of Hitler's Reich was still incomprehensible. She accurately portrays the human concerns and frustrations rapidly coming to boil in central Europe and delves into the mind-sets that allowed Nazism to come to power. ''The White Horses of Vienna,'' perhaps more cogently and certainly more humanly than news reports of the day, outlines the forces at work in Europe in the decade preceding World War II. . . .

Source: Elizabeth S. Bell, ''Chronicling the Changing Age: *The White Horses of Vienna and Other Stories*,'' in *Kay Boyle: A Study of the Short Fiction*, Twayne Publishers, 1992, pp. 29–43.

Morris Renek

In the essay below, Renek praises the depth and power of Boyle's storytelling in ''The White Horses of Vienna.''

An entire culture is collapsed into the rich few pages of ''The White Horses of Vienna.'' The faint of mind might wish they had never read it. The story's powerful kernel is a psychological truth that is both open ended, thus haunting, and a denial of received wisdom so that you do not want to know the truth, this truth behind ''The White Horses of Vienna.''

You do not want to speculate on it, nonetheless be faced by it. The story goes deeply into the woods with a biblical simplicity.

Decades before the Nazis, Austria-Hungary Jews were murdered, beaten, segregated for being *German*. The German Nazis killed them for being Jews.

''The White Horses of Vienna'' can be taken as a hymn to people breaking through barriers to see the good in others, or a horror story of innocence. The story is harrowing, insightful, prophetic as a horror story: ''. . . books that make us happy we could, in a pinch, also write ourselves. What we need are books that hit us like a most painful misfortune . . . as though we had been banished to the woods. . . .''

An injured doctor writes from his mountain home to Vienna for a student doctor replacement while he recovers. The doctor is a savagely clean man, determined, compassionate and with a strong, humble pride in himself. He was a prisoner in Siberia for a year. His young, beautiful wife condemns Jews for looking amiable. Into their home comes an amiable young Jew from Vienna, Dr. Heine.

The young doctor is animated with the culture of Vienna: books, art, music, especially the ''royal, white horses of Vienna, still royal . . . without any royalty left to bow their heads to, still shouldering into the arena with spirits a man would give his soul for, bending their knees in homage to the empty, canopied loge where royalty no longer sat.'' Applause opens their nostrils wide as if a wind were blowing: ''. . . these perfect stallions who knew to a breath the beauty of even their mockery of fright.''

It is Dr. Heine's good-hearted intelligence that makes his cultural innocence so terrifying. His friendly, affirming nature is quite capable of surmounting the evil around him, if only blindly. His zest for living making him incapable of seeing.

The wife, nevertheless, sees the student doctor as an unclean thing oiled by an evil lubricant. But when Dr. Heine and the wife are working close together over a patient, his coat is accidentally set aflame. She instinctively puts out the fire by holding him in her strong arms.

What escapes Kay Boyle's eye is not worth mentioning. The burnt coat is ''scalloped black to his shoulders.'' The wife takes the blame for the accident, volunteers to redo the coat while holding him around. ''And then she bit her lip suddenly and

"'The White Horses of Vienna' can be taken as a hymn to people breaking through barriers to see the good in others, or a horror story of innocence."

stood back, as if she had remembered the evil thing that stood between them.''

Heimwehr arrive to ask the injured doctor to show them the way to the men burning a swastika fire on the mountain. They are convinced the doctor was injured coming down the mountain from a similar fire.

> The young doctor said nothing after they had gone, but he sat quiet by the window, watching the fires burning on the mountains in the dark. They were blooming now on all the black, invisible crests, marvelously living flowers of fire springing out of the arid darkness, seemingly higher than any other things could grow. He felt himself sitting defenseless there by the window, surrounded by these strong, long-burning fires of disaster. They were all about him, inexplicable signals given from one mountain to another in some secret gathering of power that cast him and his people out, forever out upon the waters of despair.

After Dollfuss is assassinated the Heimwehr return. Dr. Heine defends the doctor's character and protests his arrest in the night and cries out against politics. He comforts the injured doctor, presses his hand, asks how he can help. He stands in the night watching the doctor being carried down the mountain on a stretcher.

Before the Heimwehr arrive the young doctor was looking out on this scene with longings to be ''indoors with the warmth of his own people, and the intellect speaking.'' Dr. Heine was saying within himself at the sight of little lights moving up from the valley that he took for beacons of hope, but were the Heimwehr coming for the doctor, ''Come to me, come to me. I am a young man alone on a mountain. I am a young man alone, as my race is alone, lost here amongst them all.''

Calling after the injured doctor being carried away, Dr. Heine promises help. He thinks in ''an-

guish of the snow-white horses, the Lippizaners, the relics of pride, the still unbroken vestiges of beauty bending their knees to the empty loge of royalty where there was no royalty any more.''

The end.

But is it? No. What rises from the story is unbearable. Dr. Heine's cultural affirmation disconnecting him from the brutal reality closing around him. Caught up in the grandeur of Vienna he becomes hopelessly defenseless. Dr. Heine himself becomes a white horse of Vienna, only with a far worse fate in store.

The end?

No. There is no end to a story where the ending keeps following you about, and makes you live with it.

I suspect that people call Kay Boyle distinguished to acknowledge her worth and keep themselves from grappling with what she sees. An invaluable recognition has come from where it counts the most—the younger generation of poets who face the world they live in. A recent collection, *American Poetry Since 1970: UP Late*, chose Kay Boyle as ''an embodiment of courage . . . our link in the spirit of previous *avant-gardes*'' and wisely reprinted her memorable and classic poem *Poets* to begin their anthology.

It is one kind of Kay Boyle victory over the frozen sea to describe how an age was lived and a rarer victory to locate the pain of that age and give human endurance a moving, unforgettable voice, lean as time itself, to a pain all but unutterable.

Source: Morris Renek, ''Kay Boyle's Victory over the Frozen Sea,'' in *Twentieth Century Literature*, Vol. 34, No. 3, Fall, 1988, pp. 294–98.

Ray B. West, Jr.

In the following excerpt, West briefly examines the characters of the two doctors in ''The White Horses of Vienna,'' finding the older one a leaderless elitist, comparable to the Lipizzaner horses Heine so admires, and judging Heine a pitiable but nonetheless admirable romantic.

A good example, and also an example of Miss Boyle at her best, is her short story ''The White Horses of Vienna,'' which won the O. Henry Memorial Prize in 1935. The surface events of the story are slight, involving little more than the visit of a young Jewish doctor to the isolated office of an

Austrian Nazi, to substitute while the Nazi doctor is incapacitated by an injured leg. The Nazi doctor presents a puppet show which betrays his political sympathies at a time prior to the German-Austrian *Anschluss* and which also portrays his own attitude toward his young medical colleague. The young Jew betrays his own attitude by relating the story of the white Lippizaner horses of Vienna. Although the story is anti-Nazi in theme, the treatment is so far from being propagandistic that Clifton Fadiman, one of the O. Henry judges, wrote that he considered the Austrian doctor "much too heroic for his role." Actually, this character is not heroic at all. He is competent and cocksure. One does not pity him or even feel sympathy for him. Like the white horses of the vanished Austrian royalty, he arouses the admiration of the young Jewish doctor. In speaking of the horses, the young doctor indicates Miss Boyle's attitude toward his Nazi employer: "'Still royal,' he said, 'without any royalty left to bow their heads to, still shouldering into the arena with spirits a man would give his soul for, bending their knees in homage to the empty, canopied loges where royalty no longer sat!'" This is, in fact, a description of the Nazi doctor, a man of spirit who considers himself elite in a world which has no "leader" to pay homage to. One can admire his skill and his talents, but one is frightened by the sheer power they represent. In contrast, the young Jew is awkward and romantic, not a man to be feared certainly. He is like the clown in the Nazi doctor's puppet show, putting his faith in clouds, not in the realities which the doctor recognizes. But the young Jew is a man to be pitied because he is a human being. He is, as Miss Boyle suggests, "the Chancellor" compared to "der Fuhrer." He may die because he is too full of admiration and trust, and this is impractical; but it is admirable, and his spirit will survive.

Nazism, then, is seen by Miss Boyle as the survival of the elite in a world where it can no longer function except as a show of spirit and force. Her short story is a study in decadence, not heroism, and, except for its political subject matter, it is not too dissimilar from comparable studies by James and Faulkner. There is something to be admired in a past grandeur, the story seems to say, but such admiration must not lead us to mistake the past for the present. An easy romanticism may lead us to make this mistake, with serious political or social consequences. In the case of Miss Boyle's story, the consequences follow two directions: the easy persecution of one who puts too much faith in pure beauty disassociated from its function, or the arrogance of him who sets himself above others for the practice of pure power without regard for its human aims. . . .

Source: Ray B. West, Jr., "Fiction and Reality: The Traditionalists," in *The Short Story in America 1900–1950*, Henry Regnery Company, 1952, pp. 59–84.

Sources

Bell, Elizabeth S. *Kay Boyle: A Study of the Short Fiction*, Boston: Twayne Publishers, 1992.

Hart, Elizabeth. Review of *The White Horses of Vienna and Other Stories*, in *Books*, February 9, 1936, p. 5.

Loeffelholz, Mary. *Experimental Lives: Women and Literature, 1900–1945*, Boston: Twayne Publishers, 1992.

Rothman, N. L. Review of *The White Horses of Vienna and Other Stories*, in *Saturday Review of Literature*, February 9, 1936, p. 5.

Seaver, R. W. Review of *The White Horses of Vienna and Other Stories*, in *Boston Transcript*, February 15, 1936, p. 3 [or 5].

Spanier, Sandra Whipple. *Kay Boyle, Artist and Activist*, Carbondale, IL: Southern Illinois University Press, 1986.

Walton, Edith. Review of *The White Horses of Vienna and Other Stories*, in *New York Times*, February 9, 1936, p. 7.

West, Ray B., Jr. *The Short Story in America*, Chicago: Henry Regnery Company, 1952.

Further Reading

Bell, Elizabeth S. *Kay Boyle: A Study of the Short Fiction*, Boston: Twayne Publishers, 1992.
   A study of Boyle's short stories. She also includes interviews with the author and critical commentary on her work.

Hamann, Brigitte. *Hitler's Vienna: A Dictator's Apprentice*, New York: Oxford University Press, 1999.
   This well-researched book explores Hitler's years in Vienna and their affect on his future development.

McAlmon, Robert. *Being Geniuses Together*, Garden City, NY: Doubleday & Company, 1968.
   McAlmon recalls the expatriate scene in Europe during the 1920s. The book includes supplementary chapters by Boyle.

Pelzer, Peter G. J. *The Rise of Political Anti-Semitism in Germany and Austria*, Cambridge: Harvard University Press, 1998.
   This revision of a classic text explores the roots of anti-Semitism in Austria and Germany and their effects on the political situation that evolved in Europe.

Spanier, Sandra Whipple. *Kay Boyle, Artist and Activist,*
Carbondale, IL: Southern Illinois University Press, 1986.
    Spanier presents in-depth analysis of Boyle's writ-
    ings. The study draws on unpublished documents as
    well as author interviews and correspondence.

Why I Live at the P.O.

Eudora Welty
1941

Eudora Welty's "Why I Live at the P.O." was inspired by a lady ironing in the back room of a small rural post office who Welty glimpsed while working as publicity photographer in the mid-1930s. Wetly had just started to write, and the story, which appeared in *Atlantic* magazine in 1941, was among the first she published. It was also included in her first collection of short stories, *A Curtain of Green,* which appeared that same year. Though Welty writes in many different styles and moods, "Why I Live at the P.O." is representative of her masterful evocation of vital, idiosyncratic southern speech. Both dark and hilarious, "Why I Live at the P.O." is one of Welty's most beloved stories and one of her own favorites. Throughout her long career she has frequently chosen it when invited to read from her work.

"Why I Live at the P.O." takes the form of a dramatic monologue. Sister, the first-person narrator, tells her side of the family spat that has led her to leave the family home where she had lived into adulthood and move into the local post office. She appeals to the reader to take her side as she indignantly recounts her younger sister's unjust maneuvers in turning the rest of the family against her, but her self-pity and exaggeration render her position unintentionally humorous. Though the story is comic, its underlying themes are complex, concerning the tensions between family affiliation and independence, the relative nature of truth, and the insularity and uniqueness of life in a small southern community.

Author Biography

Welty was born on April 13, 1909, in Jackson, Mississippi. Her father, an insurance executive, and her mother, a teacher, offered a stable and loving family for Welty and her two younger brothers. Her parents encouraged Welty intellectually and artistically, but were also very protective. In her autobiography *One Writer's Beginnings* she lovingly memorializes the ''sensory education'' in listening and observation offered by her parents and names their way of life as an important influence on her art.

Welty attended public high school in Jackson. She began college at Mississippi State College for Women in Columbus and transferred to the University of Wisconsin to finish her bachelor's degree. Welty majored in English Literature in college, but never formally studied writing or moved in literary circles. She is considered a self-taught writer, preferring the education provided by reading voraciously and listening carefully to the natural storytellers around her. In 1930, planning to equip herself to make money, Welty went on to study advertising at Columbia University's School of Business in New York City. Her graduation at the height of the Depression in 1931 and her father's death that same year led her to return to Jackson and move back into the family home. In Jackson, Welty took jobs at several newspapers and a radio station before accepting a job as a photographer with the Works Progress Administration (WPA). From 1933 to 1936 she traveled throughout Mississippi taking publicity photographs of WPA projects in the state, observing and listening to her fellow Missispians.

In 1936 Welty's first short story appeared in a small magazine called *Manuscript*. Over the next several years she published six more stories, including ''Why I Live at the P.O.,'' culminating in her first collection, *A Curtain of Green,* in 1941. The collection was well received, and from this point forward Welty committed herself to writing full time. She has continued to publish novels, short stories, and nonfiction ever since and has received most of the major American writing awards and honors, including a Guggenheim Fellowship, a Pulitzer Prize, an O. Henry Prize, the Presidential Medal of Freedom, and the Modern Language Association Commonwealth Award.

Though she has taken temporary teaching appointments in other states, Welty has remained a resident of Jackson, Mississippi. She enjoys socializing, reading, and gardening, and has described her life as sheltered and uneventful. Never married, Welty continues to live in the home in Jackson where she grew up.

Plot Summary

The events of ''Why I Live at the P.O.'' are set in motion when Stella-Rondo, the narrator's sister, returns to the family home in China Grove, Mississippi. The narrator, known as Sister, claims that up to this point she has gotten along well with her mother, uncle and grandfather. Sister has a competitive and contentious relationship with Stella-Rondo, and her return sets off a chain of petty family arguments that serve to explain why Sister has moved out and now lives at the local post office.

It is the Fourth of July. Stella Rondo has left her husband, Mr. Whitaker, a man Sister had once dated, and brings home a daughter, a two-year-old child named Shirley T. The family did not know of Shirley T.'s existence and her age suggests that she was conceived before the marriage took place. Stella-Rondo explains that Shirley T. is adopted, which everyone accepts except for Sister. Sister claims that the child looks like Papa-Daddy, their maternal grandfather, with his beard cut off. At lunch that day Stella-Ronda tells Papa-Daddy that Sister thinks he should cut off his beard. This is something he would never do, so Papa-Daddy gets angry with Sister and implies that she is ungrateful to him for using his influence in the community to get her a job at the post office. The sisters squabble about what Sister had really said and their mother takes Stella-Rondo's side. The conversation ends when Shirley T. throws up.

After dinner Papa-Daddy goes out to his hammock to sleep and Uncle Rondo—Sister and Stella-Rondo's uncle—who is drunk, appears in the hall wearing a kimono that had been a gift to Stella-Rondo from Mr. Whitaker. He goes downstairs to talk to Papa-Daddy who, according to Sister, tries to turn Uncle Rondo against her, but he is too drunk to listen. Stella-Rondo notices Uncle Rondo in her kimono and is upset. Still angry, Sister responds by insulting the kimono. Stella-Rondo snipes back at her, implying that Sister is jealous. Stella-Rondo adds that Uncle Rondo looks like a fool wearing the kimono and Sister defends him, telling Stella-Rondo that she is not in a position to criticize since she has just returned home separated and with a child no one knew about. Stella-Rondo is angry with sister for referring to Shirley T, which she had asked her not to.

Sister then goes to the kitchen to make green-tomato pickle and has a conversation with Mama about Stella-Rondo's situation. Sister says that if she were in Stella-Rondo's position, Mama would not have been as accepting, and reiterates her belief that Shirley T. is not adopted. Mama denies her favoritism and says that Sister is wrong not to believe Stella-Rondo's word. Sister refers to a cousin who "went to her grave denying the facts of life" with whom Mama has feuded and Mama slaps her in response. Then it occurs to Sister that Shirley T. has not said a word, so she tells Mama that she thinks the child has a mental disability and cannot talk. Mama calls to Stella-Rondo and asks if Shirley T. can talk. Stella-Rondo is offended by Sister's theory and makes Shirley T. sing and dance. Mama is tells Sister to apologize and, when she refuses, walks away furious.

At this point, everyone in the household has been "turned against" Sister except for Uncle Rondo, whom Sister considers an ally in the family. But at supper Stella-Rondo wins Uncle Rondo's favor by serving him and, when Sister asks him if it's wise to eat ketchup while wearing the kimono, Stella Rondo tells him that earlier Sister had sneered at him for wearing it. He tears off the kimono in anger and does not listen when Sister tells him she thinks he looked all right. Being drunk, he does not do anything to retaliate that night, but the next morning he sets of a string of firecrackers in Sister's bedroom. Sister decides that since Stella-Rondo has now turned the whole family against her, she will leave home and move into the post office.

Sister goes about the house collecting items that she feels are rightfully hers. Her mother argues with her about some of the items, calling her ungrateful, and says she'll never come to the post office again. Stella-Rondo concurs, and Sister once again refers to Stella-Rondo's failure to explain the existence of her child. Mama tells Sister to sit down and play cards with them, but Sister says that it is too late to stop her from leaving, and if they want to see her they'll need to come to the post office. Papa-Daddy says he will never come, and Uncle Rondo adds that she should stop reading his postcards. Sister points out that Stella-Rondo will have no way to get in touch with Mr. Whitaker if they refuse to use the mail and goes on to speculate that it is Mr.

Eudora Welty

Whitaker who has left Stella-Rondo, causing her to leave the room in tears. Sister again refuses to Mama's command to apologize and marches off with her possessions.

The story ends with Sister explaining that she has been living at the post office for five days and has not seen anyone in her family during that time. She has set up house and claims to like it there, despite the fact that there is little mail because her family is boycotting the post office and some of the people of the town have taken their side in the dispute. Sister proclaims, "I want the world to know I'm happy," and asserts that if Stella-Rondo decided to explain what happened with Mr. Whitaker, she would "simply put my fingers in both ears and refuse to listen."

Characters

Mama

Sister and Stella-Rondo's mother, Mama, is asked to mediate between her two daughters but, according to Sister, always ends up taking Stella-Rondo's side. In particular, she chooses not to question Stella-Rondo when she says that Shirley T.

Media Adaptations

- Eudora Welty reads "Why I Live at the P.O." on a 1998 Caedmon audio cassette entitled "Eudora Welty Reads."

---

is adopted. This bothers Sister, who sees it as evidence of her mother's favoritism toward Stella-Rondo and a willful denial of unpleasant or difficult facts.

Papa-Daddy

Papa-Daddy is Sister and Stella-Rondo's maternal grandfather and the patriarch of the household. By the standards of the rural community where he lives, he a rich man and he has gotten Sister her job as local postmistress, using sway that he aggrandizes as "my influence with the government." Papa-Daddy becomes the first family member who Stella-Rondo succeeds in turning against Sister when he accepts Stella-Rondo's story that Sister thinks he should cut off his very long beard, which is to him a profound insult.

Shirley T.

Shirley T., Stella-Rondo's blond-haired two-year-old daughter, is the major source of contention between Stella-Rondo and Sister. Shirley T., named for child star Shirley Temple, is too old to have been conceived during Stella-Rondo's marriage to Mr. Whitaker. Stella-Rondo maintains that she is adopted and the rest of the family goes along with this explanation, but Sister thinks she looks like a cross between Papa-Daddy and Mr. Whitaker, and keeps asserting that that the child is Stella-Rondo's. This carries the implication that Shirley T. was conceived out of wedlock, a fact that is particularly crucial to Sister, since she was dating Mr. Whitaker before Stella-Rondo won him "unfairly."

Sister

Sister, the narrator and protagonist of the story, is a young woman who lives with her family and works as a postmistress in a small Southern town. She nicknamed for her relation to her younger sister, Stella-Rondo, and defines herself through competition and comparison with her. She claims that Stella-Rondo has always been spoiled and even seems to blame her for having the same birthday, suggesting that Stella-Rondo's very existence takes something away from her. The competition and resentment that clearly has existed since childhood was exacerbated when, according to Sister, Stella-Rondo stole the affection of Mr. Whitaker, a traveling photographer who Sister had been dating, and married him herself. As the story opens, Stella-Rondo has separated from Mr. Whitaker and returned home with a two-year-old daughter she claims is adopted. Sister is convinced that the child is Stella-Rondo's and, by implication, that she got pregnant out of wedlock—a fact that the rest of the family has no interest in acknowledging. It is due the denial of this fact and the way that Stella-Rondo's additional lies turn the family against her that Sister leaves home and moves to the post office. Sister may be correct in her assessment of Stella-Rondo's situation, but her own exaggerated sense of self-pity and persecution render her less than creditable.

Stella-Rondo

Stella-Rondo is Sister's younger sister and the object of her resentment. She returns unannounced to her family home with a two-year-old daughter because her marriage has not worked out. She says nothing about what has gone wrong in her marriage and claims that her daughter, Shirley T., is adopted. The rest of the family is satisfied with this, but Sister feels that Stella-Rondo owes her an explanation and takes her deceptions as a personal affront. Stella-Rondo knows that Sister is jealous of her for winning Mr. Whitaker and for leaving China Grove and she uses this to get back at her for confronting her about Shirley T's parentage. She tells lies that alienate the rest of the family from Sister and displaces her in the family home. According to Sister, Stella-Rondo "always had anything in the world she's wanted and then she'd throw it away." But by the end of the story Sister has theorized that it was her husband, Mr. Whitaker, who had ended the marriage.

Uncle Rondo

Uncle Rondo is Mama's only brother and the sisters' uncle. He is the pharmacist in China Grove and is drunk for most of the story on what Sister coyly calls a "bottle of that prescription." He is the last member of the family to turn against Sister and she remembers his allegiance to her in the past. But when Stella-Rondo tells him that Sister said he did not look good in her kimono, he is enraged at her, though it was in fact Stella-Rondo who had earlier made this claim. He gets revenge on Sister by lighting firecrackers in her room, which precipitates Sister leaving home.

Joe Whitaker
See Mr. Whitaker

Mr. Whitaker

Mr. Whitaker is a traveling photographer and, according to Sister, "the only man ever dropped down in China Grove." He never appears in the story, but is significant as the central source of tension between the two sisters. Sister had dated Mr. Whitaker first, but Stella-Rondo broke them up and married him herself. Sister says that Stella-Rondo won him unfairly by telling the lie that she is bigger on one side than the other. This interpretation seems inadequate and the existence of Shirley T. suggests that his decision might have had more to do with the fact that Stella-Rondo had premarital sex with him and became pregnant.

Themes

Individual and Family Identity

Welty's use of names suggests the degree to which the members of the family in "Why I Live at the P.O." define themselves in relation to one another. Mama and Papa-Daddy are given no proper names. Stella-Rondo is named after her uncle, and Sister has only a nickname, one that suggests that her entire identity is tied up in her relationship with Stella-Rondo. On the one hand, Sister is completely alienated from her family and their way of dealing with the "facts of life," but, on the other, her entire way of understanding herself and her world is based on her position in the family. When Sister decides she must save her pride and move away from the home after Stella-Rondo has turned everyone against her, she has no recourse but to go to the post office where her grandfather has gotten

her a job and where her family provides most of the business. "There are always people who will quit buying stamps just to get on the right side of Papa-Daddy," she explains with feigned indifference at the story's close. Her self-exile at the post office has accomplished nothing but to draw the rest of the community—most of whom are relatives anyway—into "taking sides" in the family feud. Thus her bid for freedom and individuation from her family merely serves to underscore Sister's entrenchment in their insular world.

Truth and Falsehood

In "Why I Live at the P.O." the question of what is true and what is a lie divides Sister's family. Sister firmly believes that she knows the truth about Stella-Rondo's treachery in stealing Mr. Whitaker and her deception regarding Shirley T.'s parentage. Furthermore, she takes Stella-Rondo's sketchy version as a personal attack on her. While Sister "draws her own conclusions" about Stella-Rondo's recent history, the rest of the family is more than willing to go along with her face-saving fiction about Shirley T's adoption. Mama says she "prefers to take her children's word for anything when it's humanly possible," a position that Sister insinuates is "denying the facts of life." Papa-Daddy and Uncle Rondo believe Stella-Rondo's reports of Sister's insults toward them, which Sister's narration presents as bald-faced lies.

While Sister sees herself as the champion of truth, the extreme self-centeredness and self-pity of her narration creates the impression that her own version of reality is just as skewed and self-protective as that of Stella-Rondo. Sister feels aggrieved because those around her refuse to see the truth about Stella-Rondo's short marriage, but there is much that she herself cannot see. Sister is portrayed as a character who cannot see outside of herself and is thus incapable of insight into the ambiguities of human relations and the complexities and gradations of truth that result.

Communication

The hilarity of "Why I Live at the P.O." results, in part, from the havoc Stella-Rondo's return wreaks on her family's ability to communicate. Sister feels that she deserves an explanation of what happened in Stella-Rondo's marriage to Mr. Whitaker

Topics for Further Study

- Several early reviewers complain that Welty's stories all concern people who are ''abnormal.'' Katherine Anne Porter goes so far as to describe Sister as ''a terrifying case of dementia praecox,'' or schizophrenia. Welty has responded that the characters are regular people who are accustomed to speaking in an exaggerated way. Do you think that Sister is mentally ill? To what degree are the family conflicts Welty portrays abnormal?

- Robert Penn Warren describes the central theme running through Welty's writing as the conflict between love and separateness. This is a conflict that clearly applies to Sister. In your opinion, what does Sister need more—her family's love or independence from them?

- A sibling rivalry between Sister and Stella-Rondo shapes the conflict in the story. Read some psychological theories about the sources of sibling rivalry or use your own experiences with the phenomenon. How does the concept of sibling rivalry to help you understand the dynamics between the sisters and the rest of the family members?

- Welty is famous for capturing the patterns and expressions of Southern speech. Read a favorite passage from ''Why I Live at the P.O.'' aloud. What particular words, phrases, or word patterns make the sound of Welty's writing distinctive? How does this distinctive Southern voice affect your enjoyment of the story and your understanding of the characters?

- Welty has stated that a definite sense of place in a work of fiction enhances the universality of its themes. Describe the sense of China Grove, Mississippi that Welty creates in ''Why I Live at the P.O.'' Does this, in your opinion, add or detract from the story's universality?

---

and an admission that Shirley T. was conceived out of wedlock, but Stella-Rondo's return to family life depends upon the other family members' cheerful denial of the obvious. Stella-Rondo seeks to simply cut off communication about the touchy subjects. ''Sister, I don't need to tell you that you got a lot of nerve and always have and I'll thank you to make no future reference to my adopted child whatsoever.'' But when Sister goes on to do just that again and again, Stella-Rondo responds by bending the accusations Sister has made against her into comments that create tension between Sister and the rest of the family. The denials and further accusations create a farcical effect. For example, after Sister says that Shirley T. looks just like Papa-Daddy with his beard cut off, Stella- Rondo tells Papa-Daddy that Sister thinks he should shave, something she knows will seriously offend him. Sister denies this account, but Papa-Daddy not only believes it, but extrapolates further falsehoods. ''I says, 'Papa-Daddy, you know I wouldn't anymore want you to cut off your beard than the man in the moon. It was the furthest thing from my mind! Stella-Rondo sat there and made that up while she was eating breast of chicken.' But he says, 'So the postmistress fails to understand why I don't cut off my beard. Which job I got you through my influence with the government. Bird's nest-is that what you call it?''' The dispute is never resolved.

Through the setting of the post office Welty offers further development of the theme of communication and its failure. The post office is the family's source of contact with the outside world. After Sister leaves home, the feud continues with the family's refusal to send or receive mail. Their inability to communicate with each other is a result of their insularity and also leads to their further isolation. The family is cut off from communicating beyond their immediate environs by post. And Sister, who serves as a hub of communication in her capacity as postmistress, becomes even more cloistered than she had been at home.

Style

Setting

Sister narrates the story of her estrangement from her family from her new 'home' at the China Grove post office, the second smallest post office in the state of Mississippi and the point of connection between the provincial community and a distant outside world. The events that make up the main part of the plot all take place in the family home where Sister has lived all her life with her mother, uncle, and grandfather. Her sister, Stella-Rondo, has gotten away from the insular world China Grove by marrying and going to Illinois. But Sister's only point of reference and only source of identity come from her wacky, strong-willed relatives and the small rural community where their ways are taken for granted. The family is prominent in the town and relatively wealthy. They have black servants to whom they unselfconsciously refer as ''niggers,'' a practice that was not uncommon in the 1930s and 1940s. However, the story does not reflect the racial tensions that were taking place in the South, nor does it reflect broader social and cultural changes connected to rapid urbanization, modernization, the Depression, and the onset of World War II. Instead, the tensions between family members over beards and kimonos take on gigantic proportions within the insular setting of the family home.

Point of View

In a story that is so deeply preoccupied with ''taking sides,'' the issue of point of view is paramount. Stella-Rondo and Sister's different versions of the truth and the responses that each version elicits from the family generate the plot of ''Why I Live at the P.O.'' Though Sister narrates the story in the first person and thus has every opportunity to make a persuasive case for herself, Welty leads readers to question her accuracy. Welty lets Sister's voice and her perspective dominate the story, giving her plenty of rope with which to hang herself. In places, Sister's version of events simply seems implausible—as in her explanation of why she and Mr. Whitaker broke up. In others, her sense of victimization is so out of proportion as to seem comic—as when she complains of the terrible plight of having to ''stretch two chickens over five people'' instead of four. Despite her claims of championing the truth, Sister is rendered an unreliable narrator. She seeks to convince her audience that she is unambiguously in the right in her dispute with her family and that she has made a successful break from them by moving to the post office, but her account creates the opposite impression.

The Southern Idiom

Idiom is the specialized vocabulary, grammar, and word order of a language or regional dialect. Welty is famous for her skill in catching the rhythms and inflections of spoken language—particularly, the unique idiom of the American South. As reading the plot summary will reveal, the events of ''Why I Live at the P.O.'' lose both their humor and their poignancy without the vital tone created by Sister's emphatic voice and colloquial language. Welty's use of the speech patterns and figures of speech endemic to rural Mississippi gives ''Why I Live at the P.O.'' its most striking stylistic feature. Sister's first-person exposition, as well as the quoted speech, is replete with sentence fragments, exclamation points, and emphases that capture the sound of talk. Papa-Daddy ''l-a-y-s down his knife and fork!'' Stella-Rondo ''raises the window and says *'Oh!'* You would've thought she was mortally wounded.'' Colorful colloquialisms like ''dizzy as a witch,'' ''kiss my foot,'' and ''Miss Priss'' root ''Why I Live at the P.O.'' in a local way of talking that reflects the particularity and insularity of life in China Grove. The family is bound to the place and their mode of expression reflects this. The emphasis and diction also indicate Sister's hyperbolic sensibility. She perceives small gestures as major events and takes everything personally, which is reflected in the language that she uses to describe them. ''She's always had anything in the world she wanted and then she'd throw it away. Papa-Daddy gave her this gorgeous Add-a-Pearl necklace when she was eight years old and she threw it away playing baseball when she was nine, with only two pearls.''

Historical Context

Modern America and the Provincial South

Over first few decades of the twentieth century, the lifestyles of citizens across the United States became more homogeneous, and a sense of a unified national identity and culture began to solidify. This was the result of a complicated combination of factors, including urbanization, increased centralization of the government, the growing international

Compare
&
Contrast

- **1930s:** The number of U.S. post offices is down from its peak of almost 77,000 at the turn of the century, but free collection and delivery are not available in all areas and many people must go to their local post offices to send and receive mail.

  1990s: The vast majority of Americans receive their mail at home, delivered daily by mail carriers. For various reasons, a small fraction continue pick up their own mail at post office boxes and windows.

- **1930s:** In the late 1930s the United States begins to recover from the economic devastation of the Great Depression, but President Roosevelt estimates that one-third of the nation lives in poverty. For the most part, the other two-thirds have not experienced dramatic change in fortune. In particular, small town life remains largely undisturbed by economic crisis.

  1990s: The national economy is robust. The rural population is at its lowest level in national history, while technology has allowed agricultural production to grow to its highest level. Mass culture, information technology, and transportation have eroded the distinct culture of small town America.

- **1930s:** For the first time in decades, there is a reverse in the rural-urban migration pattern, with slightly more people leaving cities and returning to their towns of origin than vice versa.

  1990s: Fewer and fewer people live in rural communities and small towns, but a trend of "neo-traditionalism" or "new urbanism" attempts to recreate the intimacy of a small town community in a urban or suburban settings. Strategies include centralized businesses, common public places, and pedestrian scale. For example, a "neo-traditional" community would have a local post office within walking distance for most residents.

- **1930s:** The popularity of radio surges. The same schedule of music, drama, and news shows is available to a national audience, contributing to a more unified and homogeneous American culture than ever before.

  1990s: Radio is still a significant medium for music, with national franchises running the majority of local stations. The dominance of television has led to the end of radio dramas and has severely curtailed the importance of radio news.

---

economic and military power of the United States, and the rise of mass culture mediums such as film and radio. In significant ways, however, the South was set apart from this trend. More than any other region, the South retained a separate culture from the rest of the country. In the Civil War the South had lost the right to secede from the Union, but this defeat served in some ways to strengthen regional identity. In particular, in contrast to the mainstream American ethos of progress and change, the South remained rooted in history and in sometimes romanticized visions of the agrarian past. This was reflected in the conservatism and traditionalism of the region in comparison to the rest of the country. One of the most important aspects of southern identity

was the small town and rural lifestyle, with close-knit family and community at its center.

Welty attended graduate school in New York City. A few years later she returned home and took a job that required her to travel throughout rural Mississippi. Thus, shortly before she wrote "Why I Live at the P.O.," Welty observed two extreme examples of American culture. New York was the center of everything new in art, style, custom, and business. It was fast—paced and dynamic but also alienating and isolating. Upon returning to Mississippi and spending time in its most isolated rural communities, Welty was able to see more clearly the uniqueness of the traditional southern society, with its emphasis on family and community. "Why

I Live at the P.O.'' reflects the insularity of small-town southern life. Sister is largely oblivious to the world outside of her family and community. However, some of her tension with Stella-Rondo is based on Stella-Rondo's wider experiences in the North and her greater sophistication. The presence of popular culture and name-brand consumer items in the family home also suggests the influence of modern national culture on traditional southern society.

Women in the South

The conservatism of southern culture was reflected in the status of women and gender relations. While during the ''roaring twenties'' premarital sex had become much more widely accepted among sophisticated urbanites, in the 1930s and 40s it still remained strictly taboo in the rural South. This explains the family's complicity in the face of Stella-Rondo's unconvincing account of Shirley T.'s origins. In small communities women typically lived at home until marriage and their choices for mates were few. Sister's description of Mr. Whitaker as ''the only man ever dropped down in China Grove'' reflects the narrow field of romantic options. Middle-class social standards determined that an acceptable choice was not only a man of the right age and class, but preferably a local resident as well. Marriage to someone outside of the community was frowned upon and women seldom had the opportunity to meet men provided by leaving home for school or work. Unmarried women, known by the derogatory term of spinster, had to depend on their families to support them.

Southern women were more likely than other American women to work outside of the home, attributable to a higher rate of poverty in the South than any other region. However, most of these women worked in traditionally female roles such as domestic help, nurses, and teachers. The percentage of women working in traditionally male professions was lower than the national average. Sister's position at the tiny post office is largely honorary and would not have given her either the status or the financial power to make a greater bid for independence from her family.

Critical Overview

When it appeared in 1941, Welty's first book, *A Curtain of Green,* was met with mostly good re-views. However, reviewers who made up the northern literary establishment tended to find Welty's characters abnormal, a quality they chauvinistically associated with the South. ''Like many Southern writers, she has a strong taste for melodrama and is preoccupied with the demented, the deformed, the queer, the highly spiced,'' reads a *Time* review. A mixed review in *Books* includes a similar comment: ''As a whole, *A Curtain of Green* shows too great a preoccupation with the abnormal and grotesque. Some day some one might explore this tendency of Southern writers.'' However, the collection also won some very positive reviews. Interestingly, those critics who liked the book tended to focus on an opposite characteristic—Welty's beautiful and subtle portrayal of the normal. For example, the *New York Times*'s Miriam Hauser states that ''few contemporary books have ever impressed me quite as deeply as this book . . .To explain just why . . .appears as difficult as to define why an ordinary face, encountered by chance on the street, might suddenly reveal miraculous beauty, through a smile perhaps, or an unexpected expression of beauty.'' The reviewer for the *New Yorker* also points out Welty's extraordinary rendering of the ordinary. ''Miss Welty's stories are deceptively simple. They are concerned with ordinary people, but what happens to them and the manner of the telling are far from ordinary.'' In her introduction to the collection Katherine Anne Porter seems to ascribe to the former view when she describes Sister of ''Why I Live at the P.O.'' as ''a terrifying case of dementia praecox,'' the Latin term for schizophrenia. But she also states that ''there are almost perfect stories'' in the collection and praises Welty's ''blistering humor and her just cruelty.''

Though Welty went on to become a beloved and respected writer, contradictory perceptions of her work have persisted. She is sometimes grouped with writers of the ''Southern grotesque'' school who portray the dark underbelly of the gracious Southern lifestyle. And sometimes she is characterized as a ''Southern regionalist,'' a warm and funny writer who affectionately portrays the foibles of her own tribe. In *Eudora Welty: A Study of the Short Fiction*, Carol Anne Johnston suggests that both views undervalue Welty's artistry. Johnston claims that only way to account for such a discrepancy in interpretations is to recognize that Welty's genius lies in the merging and balancing of opposites. In her opinion, the first critic to do this was novelist Robert Penn Warren. His influential 1944 essay

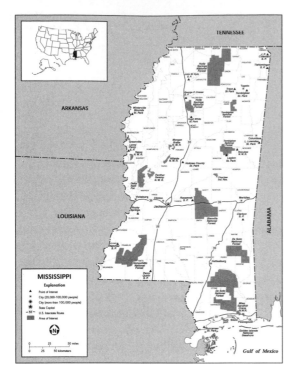

Map of Mississippi.

"Love and Separateness in Eudora Welty" explores the tension between intimacy and independence running through her first two collections of short stories. Focusing on the paradoxes of Welty's theme, he shows how, again and again, her characters love deeply and then are isolated.

Critical responses to Welty's fiction are almost always preoccupied, in one way or another, with its Southernness. But in her own critical writing Welty has made it clear that, while she is inspired by her cultural surroundings, she also sees herself as part of a broad, international literary tradition. In her book of literary criticism, *The Eye of the Story,* she discusses authors ranging from Chekov to Austen, drawing parallels between their aesthetics and her own. Welty's reputation has been overshadowed by that of her contemporary and fellow Mississippian, William Faulkner, one of the great American modernists. Though Faulkner also roots his writing deeply in his native state, his work has not been reduced as "regionalism." A number of scholars have compared the two writers' treatments of Southern themes. Some conclude that Welty has been labeled quaint because of her focus on female characters and "feminine" themes of love and family, while Faulkner's more "masculine" themes of history and legacy are seen as universal.

In general, Welty's most interested and insightful commentators have been other writers, and she has not been studied extensively by scholars. However, this is beginning to change. In recent years, literary critics have begun to apply a range of contemporary theories to her works. Regardless of scholarly trends, Welty's fiction has won her a loyal following and "Why I Live at the P.O." remains a perennial favorite among students and readers.

Criticism

Sarah Madsen Hardy

Madsen Hardy has a doctorate in English literature and is a freelance writer and editor. In the following essay, she discusses the implications of the first-person narrator's unbalanced perspective in "Why I Live at the P.O."

"Why I Live at the P.O." takes the form of a dramatic monologue, with Sister's emphatic first-person account of her sister's return home and her own eventual self-exile at the post office given in a direct appeal to the reader. Sister argues her position on the family argument forcefully, presenting overwhelming evidence of Stella-Rondo's craftiness and her own terrible persecution. Furthermore, she presents her case with the fierce conviction that she is in the right, and with no indication that the matter is anything but of the gravest order. By giving Sister's voice complete free reign, Welty would seem to give Sister every possible advantage in winning the reader to her side. There is no place in the story where Mama, Papa-Daddy, Uncle Rondo, or especially Stella-Rondo get to present the facts of the feud from their perspectives. The only information available is that provided by Sister. However, this does not mean that the reader is likely to be convinced by Sister's version of events. I would hazard to guess that most readers respond to Sister's list of grievances with some skepticism and that very few indeed fail to see the humor in the situation that she herself takes so seriously. "I was trying to write about the way people who live away off from nowhere have to amuse themselves by dramatizing every situation that comes along by exaggerating it," Welty explains in a *Conversations with Eudora Welty.* In this essay I will look at Welty's use of Sister's own dominating voice to reveal the weaknesses in her understanding of the family fight and family dynamics, focusing on Welty's playful references to physical and ethical disproportion.

What Do I Read Next?

- *The Wide Net and Other Stories* (1943), her highly acclaimed second collection of short stories, portrays a series of southern characters in Welty's inimitable voice.

- *One Writer's Beginnings* (1984), a brief autobiography by Welty, focuses on her relationship to literature and the influences that shaped her vision as an artist.

- *The Collected Stories of Katherine Anne Porter* (1965) represents the finest work by another southerner and modern master of the short story form.

- *The Collected Stories of William Faulkner* (1999) includes 42 short stories by the most famous modernist from Mississippi.

- *Everything that Rises Must Converge* (1965) presents the final collection of short stories by Flannery O'Connor, whose portraits of the underside of southern life are extreme and grotesque.

- *Member of the Wedding* (1946), a short novel by Carson McCullers, is the story of a Georgia 12-year-old's search for a sense of family belonging.

- *Shiloh and Other Stories* (1982), a collection of short stories by Bobbie Anne Mason, reflects the tensions of family life and relationships in the contemporary South.

Sister doesn't ask readers for sympathy so much as she asserts her right to it. The story is one long, self-righteous justification of why Sister left home and moved to the post office, a situation that benefits her not at all except in her right to claim the moral high ground. According to Sister, the entire community is now divided into "sides"—those who see the justice of Sister's position and those who "will quit buying stamps just to get on the right side of Papa-Daddy." The irony of Sister's vehement appeal to the reader to take her side relates to her inability to see it as just that—a self-interested and subjective perspective. Sister speaks as if people who want to stay on the "right side" of Papa-Daddy are self-serving and biased, while those who agree with her are simply correct. In Sister's view, there is only one way to see the truth—her own way. But true justice is predicated on balance and perspective—the ability to measure and evaluate evidence from more than one side, as represented in the icon of the scales of justice. Sister employs illogical logic, evoking the abstract principles of fairness in a manner that shamelessly and transparently skews the scales of justice in favor of her own point of view.

The central issue in the conflict between Sister and Stella-Rondo is the affection of Mr. Whitaker.

In the opening paragraph of the story, Sister asserts her initial claim to Mr. Whitaker and offers a somewhat perplexing explanation of how Stella-Rondo broke them up. "Told him I was one-sided. Bigger on one side than the other, which is a deliberate, calculated falsehood: I'm the same." Throughout the story, Sister represents Stella-Rondo as amazingly successful at turning those closest to Sister against her by telling bald-faced lies about her. But, in this first example of Stella-Rondo's deceit that Sister cites, the reader is in no position to judge the facts of the matter. In *Eudora Welty: A Study of the Short Fiction* critic Carol Ann Johnston explains that Stella-Rondo's accusation that Sister is "one-sided" and "bigger on one side than the other," refers to the folk wisdom that every woman has one breast that is slightly larger than the other. "Sister's reaction to this accusation is very telling," Johnston writes, "She takes it personally, denying it vehemently, when she might just as well have said, 'Well, so is Stella-Rondo and so is every woman.' But, as we see over and over in the story, Sister takes every comment and accusation as an intensely personal attack." While Stella-Rondo's accusation may or may not be true in regard to the issue of the symmetry of Sister's breasts, by introducing the sisters' conflict with this description,

---

" Part of Sister's frustration with Stella-Rondo is that she works within a different value system, refusing to acknowledge the rules of fair competition by which Sister wishes to play, and using a range of tactics to reframe, deny, and invert Sister's claims of truth."

Welty makes reference to the flagrant bias that circumscribes Sister's perspective and renders her ''one-sided'' as a narrator. To build on Johnston's point, Sister's might just as well have admitted that everyone is ''one-sided'' in their view of personal events that involve them. If she had, her perspective on events would be much more convincing and much less funny. In the points of view as well as breasts, no one is perfectly balanced. In her attempt to convince her audience of Stella-Rondo's misdeed, Sister reveals herself as incapable of comprehending—let alone admitting—that she is not fair and objective in her overblown account of the family argument.

Sister holds Stella-Rondo responsible for taking what she sees as rightfully hers, starting with being born on her first birthday. As Sister goes on to characterize Stella-Rondo as someone who ''always had anything in the world she wanted and then she'd throw it away,'' readers can affirm that Sister is unable to see any situation related to Stella-Rondo in an even-handed way. Sister recounts Stella-Rondo's profligacy with a ''gorgeous Add-a-Pearl necklace,'' clearly categorizing this item, coveted from childhood, along with Mr. Whitaker. Sister is so self-centered that she presents the fact that Stella-Rondo once lost a necklace as if it were a personal affront to her, deliberate and calculated. Among the things that Stella-Rondo takes from Sister is the good opinion of the other family members. Sister understands the family as being composed of two ''sides''—hers and Stella-Rondo's—that are perpetually uneven. The favor of loved ones—like the

charm bracelet that Stella-Rondo tries to steal, and the radio that Sister triumphantly receives from Uncle Rondo after he takes it back from Stella-Rondo—volleys from to one sister or the other, but can never be shared by them both.

Sister's tension with the rest of the family is triggered by her indignation at Stella-Rondo's deception regarding Shirley T. Again, she reacts as if the principle of honesty was at stake, rather than the very personal questions regarding two sisters' relationships with the same man. As if the competition between the two sisters was not enough to render family dynamics topsy-turvy, the arbiters of the sisters' struggle are themselves portrayed as out of kilter in both their capacity for judgement and their physical appearance. Papa-Daddy is self-centered and self-important, a quality that is embodied in the excessively long beard to which he is excessively attached. Mama is an unreliable judge for the opposite reason; she seems to lack her own perspective, and is thus too easily won over by Stella-Rondo's. When Sister appeals to her to face up to the ''facts of life'' about Shirley T.'s parentage, she adopts Stella-Rondo's attitude of blithe denial, saying ''*I* prefer to take my children's word for anything when it's humanly possible.'' Mama ''weighs two hundred pounds and has real tiny feet,'' a physical description that is also suggestive of being precariously off-balance. And Uncle Rondo, running around the house drunk in a negligee, is ''a good case of a one-track mind.'' He is the last family member to be ''turned against'' Sister, but only because he has been too dizzy to follow the argument.

Sister is so focused on Stella-Rondo's persecution of her and her family's ''unfair'' taking of sides that she does not bother to address the question that remains as to why Mr. Whitaker would leave Sister based merely on the unevenness of her breasts. She sees herself as a champion of truth and uses abstract justification for why Stella-Rondo ought to reveal to the family just what happened between her and Mr. Whitaker, but she doesn't admit that Stella-Rondo's accusation comments in an obscure way on her sexuality, an intensely personal issue that is at the repressed center of their conflict. Sister was the first one to meet the travelling photographer and she dated him before he became involved with Stella-Rondo and chose her instead. It is easy enough to see why Sister would resent Stella-Rondo for this reason, and to wonder about what defect on her own part led to his choice. Instead of admitting her vulnerability or hurt feelings, Sister positions herself as the victim of injustice. With the childish view that good and bad life events ought to be doled out equally, she cries "no fair!" As the elder sister, convention dictates that she ought to be considered first for marriage. But, as the existence of Shirley T. proves, Stella-Rondo and Mr. Whitaker's courtship did not follow rules of propriety and convention. Part of Sister's frustration with Stella-Rondo is that she works within a different value system, refusing to acknowledge the rules of fair competition by which Sister wishes to play, and using a range of tactics to reframe, deny, and invert Sister's claims of truth.

In the powerful voice that makes "Why I Live at the P.O." such a stylistic tour de force, Sister describes as "lies" statements that may have gradations of meaning, double meanings, or subtexts, and misses out on a good deal of the truth herself in the process. Sister's voice and perspective crowd out everything else. It is as if she must keep talking because if she doesn't, somebody else will. And in Sister's world, this is a grave matter, because saying things seems to have the power to make them so. "If Stella-Rondo should come to me this minute, on bended knees, and *attempt* to explain the incidents of her life with Mr. Whitaker—that is, to offer that truth in defense of which Sister has given up everything—"I'd simply put my fingers in both ears and refuse to listen," reads the story's last line. Sister narrates the story from this posture, with her ears blocked to other perspectives. But at the end of her diatribe against Stella-Ronda's lies, Sister concludes with lie of her own.

Source: Sarah Madsen Hardy, "The One-Sided Narrator in *'Why I Live at the P.O.'*" for *Short Stories for Students*, The Gale Group, 2000.

Diana R. Pingatore

In this essay, Pingatore traces the publication history of Why I Live at the P.O., *through Welty's inspirations and influences, to offer an interpretive critical analysis.*

Publication History

The *Atlantic Monthly* published this story in April 1941 on pages 443–50. "Why I Live at the P.O." was the second story of Welty's to appear in the *Atlantic Monthly*; it followed the February appearance of "A Worn Path" and preceded the publication of "Powerhouse" in June 1941. According to Kreyling (1991), the acceptance of these three stories by the *Atlantic Monthly* signaled the clear arrival of Welty on the national literary scene. This advance in Welty's literary stature also ful-

filled a major aspiration for her literary agent, Diarmuid Russell, who predicted such national acclaim would insure for Welty the publication of a book, and so it did. The story was included in Welty's first collection of short stories, *A Curtain of Green*, published in November of 1941 by Doubleday, Doran. The first British edition of *A Curtain of Green* appeared in July 1943, published by the Bodley Head.

Although it was to become one of Welty's most popular stories, "Why I Live at the P.O." suffered an inauspicious beginning. Its history of rejection began in October 1938, when Whit Burnett, editor of *Story*, offered consoling words to buffer his rejection of yet another of Welty's early submissions. She had submitted "Keela, the Outcast Indian Maiden" and "Petrified Man" earlier in the year, but Burnett could not secure editorial consensus about any of the three, and so rejected each of them in turn. Nonetheless, he encouraged Welty, noting in a letter housed at the Mississippi Department of Archives and History that "Why I Live at the P.O." "'is the closest yet'" (Marrs 1988).

Kreyling reports that Welty sent "Why I Live at the P.O." to Russell in the summer of 1940, after its rejection by both *Southern Review* and *Harper's Magazine*. Polk (1994), however, points out that the manuscript submitted to *Southern Review* in April 1939 was titled "Sister" and that Welty denied in a 1989 interview that this story was a earlier working of "Why I Live at the P.O." Upon receipt of the manuscript, the Russell & Volkening agency submitted the story to some six magazines, including the *New Yorker*, *Collier's*, *Harper's Bazaar*, *Good Housekeeping*, *Mademoiselle*, and *Harper's*, before its acceptance at the *Atlantic Monthly*. Referring to a 1941 letter from Welty to Russell, Kreyling remarks that the sale of "Why I Live at the P.O." to the *Atlantic Monthly* probably "saved it altogether" as it seems Welty was considering giving up on it. A copy of the *Atlantic Monthly* in which the story appears is housed at the MDAH, complete with Welty's signature on its cover (Marrs 1988).

The MDAH also holds an undated typescript copy of this story, which Marrs notes differs considerably from the published versions and from the other two typescripts held at the MDAH. These changes are not elaborated on by Marrs, nor are they addressed by McDonald (1983) or Lewis (1988), who examine the changes in the story only between its appearance in the *Atlantic Monthly* and in *A Curtain of Green* a few months later. Both report

> "As with a number of her early works, the deceptively simple surface permits, or even invites, fairly straightforward observations of the kind encouraged by early reactions to the story and even by Welty herself. But another line of interpretation, of a somewhat more complex nature, might also be investigated."

only slight variations, most of which are limited to alterations in punctuation. Lewis identifies three variants that either expand the discussion of Papa-Daddy's beard and Uncle Rondo's dizziness, for instance, or provoke speculation, such as the change from "Negroes" in the *Atlantic* version to "niggers" in *A Curtain of Green.* The undated typescript also contains a note to John Robinson, Welty's friend and fellow writer, directing him: "'My new theme read it & throw it away'" (qtd. in Marrs).

This favorite of Welty's stories was often selected for inclusion in reissuings of her work. "Why I Live at the P.O." was included in the Modern Library's 1954 *Selected Stories of Eudora Welty,* the 1965 selection of *Thirteen Stories* by Ruth M. Vande Kieft, and its reissuing as *Moon Lake and Other Stories* by the Franklin Library in 1980, the same year that Harcourt Brace published *The Collected Stories of Eudora Welty,* in which the story also appears. The story was also reprinted in *The House of Fiction,* edited by Caroline Gordon and Allen Tate and published by Scribner's in 1950, as well as in *Readings for a Liberal Education,* edited by Louis G. Locke and colleagues and published in 1957 by Rinehart. The story has appeared in numerous literary anthologies as well. For example, Mordecai Richler's edition of *The Best of Modern Humor,* published by Knopf in 1958; *A Collection of Classic Southern Humor: Fiction and Occasional Fact, By Some of the South's Best Storytellers,*

edited by George William Koon and published in 1984 by Peachtree; *Look Who's Talking: An Anthology of Voices in the Modern American Short Story,* edited by Bruce Weber and published by Washington Square Press in 1986; and *The Norton Book of American Short Stories,* edited by Peter S. Prescott and published by Norton in 1988.

Welty recorded her reading of the story for Caedmon Records in 1952, a recording that was reissued as an audiocassette in 1986. At least two dramatic adaptations of the story have been undertaken: one by Gloria Baxter, which was produced at Memphis State University in 1981, and another in 1979 by the University of Illinois, which Marrs notes was combined with the granting of an honorary degree to Welty. Welty discusses that production in an interview with Joanna Maclay in 1980 (Prenshaw 1984). She notes her worry about how the story would translate to the stage and voices concerns that she felt about actually seeing, on stage, characters whom Welty had not "seen" herself, given that the original story comes only from Sister's representation of the rest of her family. Welty concurs with the interviewer that the production avoided the pitfalls she had feared.

Circumstances of Composition, Sources, and Influences

As with all of the stories that Welty composed before the beginning of her thirty-year association with Diarmuid Russell, little, if anything, is known about the circumstances of the composition of the story. However, by the time she submitted "Why I Live at the P.O." for publication, she had published some ten or eleven stories in small literary magazines, including the *Southern Review,* and had begun to establish a network of literary relationships with such influential people as Robert Penn Warren, Cleanth Brooks, Ford Madox Ford, and Katherine Anne Porter. Welty was beginning to make her way onto the national literary scene, and, despite early rejections, continued to write for the joy of writing.

The most direct source for "Why I Live at the P.O." was mentioned by Welty in an interview with two of her own students, Royals and Little, in 1978; the comment has been much repeated by Welty scholars and critics, despite Welty's own disclaimers as to the significance of this event in the germination of the story. The incident noted by Welty entails her catching sight from a train window of a woman ironing in the back of a post office. But when asked about the incident, Welty retorts that the sight of the woman in the post office is ''a good example'' of something ''that's a fact but nothing like the truth'' (Prenshaw). ''The sight of the lady ironing was the striking of the match that set it off, but I wouldn't have written a story just about seeing somebody with an ironing board in the post office.'' Stories, according to Welty, ''have long fuses that run a long way back,'' so that while a particular incident might ignite the spark, it does not provide the fuel for the story's insight.

Literary influence is not an issue much addressed in relation to this story, except in the most general of terms. Appel (1965), for instance, likens the quality of Welty's humor in ''Why I Live at the P.O.'' to that of Mark Twain and Ring Lardner. Calling it ''one of the finest pieces of American humor,'' Appel extols the virtues of the story, among which he includes the fact that its comic antics are tempered by a ''sympathy that is generous yet unsentimental.'' Most commentators simply note its adept use of figures commonplace in local color stories, a tradition in Southern literature. An example is Skaggs's (1972) brief consideration of Sister as an essentially harmless eccentric whose provincial ways of thinking and speaking permit the reader to feel a sense of superiority. Du Priest (1982) detects allusions to Homer's *Iliad* in ''Why I Live at the P.O.'' in terms of both its subject matter and its structure: ''The pattern is this: a history of war, a world at war, nations at war, a town divided, a family at battle, two sisters who've never gotten along, and finally one person not at peace with herself.''

Relationship to Other Welty Works

Both Drake (1960) and Buswell (1961) draw parallels between Sister as a first-person female narrator and Edna Earle, her counterpart in Welty's novella *The Ponder Heart*. Both females are loquacious, opinionated, assertive, and compelling narrators. Both Drake and Buswell identify the two women as representative of the ''old maid'' figure, who nonetheless commands, by her very presence, a certain authority and recognition in the community. Sister, like Edna Earle, assumes a traditionally male responsibility by securing work outside the home, yet remains within the conventions of the feminine by what Drake labels ''a vocation of service.'' While both chafe at the restrictions of that vocation from time to time, neither protagonist is ever entirely free to sever those family ties completely, as Sister seems to begin to discover at the end of her amusing narrative.

Romines (1989) cites ''Circe'' as the story most similar to ''Why I Live at the P.O.'' She does so based on her assessment of both stories as exemplars of ''how not to tell a story.'' In Romines's view, both Circe and her narrative counterpart, Sister, exempt themselves from the communal nature of storytelling that Welty depicts as essential in some of her other fiction, such as in her novel *Losing Battles*. Both of these female narrators appropriate their stories from the control of others, Odysseus and Stella-Rondo respectively, who, in each narrator's view, misconstrue the tale to the detriment of the narrator. Sister, like Circe, sets out to make right the misrepresentation of facts that serve to malign each woman in ways she finds intolerable.

These narrative preemptive strikes constitute acts of courage and authority, according to Romines. ''Sister refuses to subside as a helpless violated victim. Instead, she recasts herself as a hero. The source of this renewal is her essential self-possession.'' However, the autonomy Sister claims for herself as mistress of her own fate is juxtaposed against the isolation to which she has subjected herself in order to assert her hard-won independence. Ultimately, Romines observes, Sister, like Circe, is a failed narrator because each female, in her striving to resist another's definition of the self, has severed the very ties to community that are intrinsic to the act of storytelling.

Finally, a number of critics link ''Why I Live at the P.O.'' to ''Petrified Man'' as stories that demonstrate Welty's consummate skill in capturing the Southern idiom, particularly in female speech (Vande Kieft ([1962] 1987); Appel 1965; Skaggs 1972; Howard 1973; and Schmidt 1991). Towers cites ''Why I Live at the P.O.'' as a prime example of Welty's ''mastery of the demotic speech of the region'' and nominates the story as ''a small classic of the genre'' (1980).

Interpretation and Criticism

Much of the surprisingly limited scholarly attention accorded this most popular of Welty's stories focuses on certain questions readers repeatedly ask. ''Is Sister insane?'' ranks as an inquiry that surfaced early and has remained a lively source of discussion. Katherine Anne Porter, in her noted introduction to the 1941 edition of *A Curtain of Green*, initiated the debate by nonchalantly remarking that ''the heroine of 'Why I Live at the P.O.' is a terrifying case of dementia praecox.'' While some commentators, such as Drake (1960) and Herrscher

(1965), directly challenge Porter's assessment of Sister's sanity, others, like Ruth Vande Kieft, build their interpretations around the assumption that Sister acts "with the insane logic of the paranoid" (1962). It is not until 1982 that Vande Kieft retracts this early assumption, when she labels the diagnosis of "paranoic schizophrenia" as "the Ur-blooper of Welty criticism."

Presumably, it is Welty's own response to the question of Sister's sanity that helped to stem, if not stop, the growth of this issue as a dominant feature in the discussions of this story. In a 1965 interview with *Comment* magazine, Welty directly addressed the ineptness of Porter's diagnosis. "It never occurred to me while I was writing the story (and it still doesn't) that I was writing about someone in serious mental trouble" (qtd. in Prenshaw 1984). Instead, Welty suggests, Sister's predicament consists primarily of isolation and the need "to amuse" herself by "dramatizing every situation that comes along by exaggerating it—'telling it'." Welty's emphasis on the salient aspect that performance plays in this phenomenon is taken up by some critics, such as Eisenger (1979), who calls the story nothing less than "an ingenious accomplishment" of a "fiction absorbed with its own language."

Welty's own comments seem to confirm observations such as Eisenger's. Welty told Bill Ferris in a 1977 interview that "Why I Live at the P.O." "was an exercise in using the spoken word to tell a story." Again she mentions the geographical isolation of Southerners as a motivation that "encourages our sense of exaggeration and the comic" as well as expresses the true concern that such people feel for each other. Welty also calls the process by which the artist converts ordinary speech into artistic prose "a transformation, a magician act," thus calling attention to the aspect of performance involved in this story, an activity shared by Welty and her narrator.

Drake's 1960 designation of "Why I Live at the P.O." as a "cater-cornered epic" corresponds to Welty's description of her intention to depict what she heard and saw around her in the South. He proclaims that Sister's predisposition to exaggerate fits perfectly into the form of the "mock-epic because it is the absurd that has been exalted to the sublime." Unlike Vande Kieft and Appel, who find the story representative of one of Welty's darker comedies, Drake and Herrscher view the story as a triumph of both sanity and aesthetics. Herrscher, in fact, makes the argument that not only is Sister *not*

insane, but she emerges as the only sane person in "a childish, neurotic, and bizarre family." He maintains that, far from being paranoid or schizophrenic, or merely vulgar, Sister represents unerring good sense and admirable mastery over the reality in which she finds herself. He attributes her "competence" to her status as a firstborn child who has had to take on an early responsibility for the blundering family; she chooses to abdicate that serious undertaking only when she finds her "own sanity and stability" in some jeopardy.

May (1978) also challenges the reductive view of Sister as merely paranoid and proposes an alternative approach to the reading of the story, one that incorporates the reader's response to the story as a salient feature of the story's interpretation. The key, for May, lies in the dynamics of Sister's relationship to her family, and in particular, to Stella-Rondo. In this, May joins several critics (such as Vande Kieft 1962, 1987; Drake 1960, 1970; Tarbox 1972; Pickett 1973; Romines 1989; and Schmidt 1991) who find the sibling rivalry an important consideration in "Why I Live at the P.O."

Employing the phenomenological theories of R. D. Laing, May points out that Sister's narrative involves a splitting of her psyche into the subjective realm of desire and fear, which she claims for herself, and the objective depiction of those desires or fears, which Sister attributes to Stella-Rondo, who, according to May, acts "out Sister's subjective feelings." As examples of the "divided self" the story reveals, May offers the sisterly disputes over who said what about Papa-Daddy's beard or what Uncle Rondo looked like in his niece's kimono. Schmidt (1991) takes up a similar line of thought and describes this internal conflict in terms of Sister's "own self-revulsion," noting that while she clearly expresses a strong desire for autonomy and authority, Sister nonetheless has "internalized" her family's negative characterizations of her as the selfish and uncaring female. Thus Sister is inclined to judge herself deserving of the self-imposed isolation of living at the post office rather than being in her rightful place as the favored child of her family.

Tarbox (1972) mentions Sister as representative of the "loser" characters in Welty's fiction who are finally unsuccessful in their quest for maternal love. Tarbox views Sister's sensitivity to noise as a counterpart to her compulsion to talk; each represents an aspect of her sadomasochistic nature, which in turn reveals her untenable position as the sibling displaced in the family's affections. Drake, on the other hand, suggests that it is Stella-Rondo's "lack of penitence" that disturbs and finally alienates Sister from her prodigal sibling.

Welty's use of the war metaphor in "Why I Live at the P.O." interests Du Priest. While Schmidt comments on the "war of words" (1991) that constitutes Sister's narrative, and Romines notes that words are used as "a highly elaborated weapon" in the family arsenal (1989), Du Priest extends the discussion of war as a metaphor for the entire story, an idea alluded to previously by Drake, who identifies the dynamics of Southern family life as militaristic in nature: "Many Southerners, especially those from big families, are perfectly familiar with the guerrilla warfare which exists within that secular Communion of Saints which is the family" (1960). Du Priest embellishes Drake's comment by taking note of the July 4 date, which DuPriest claims celebrates a military conquest, and the use of images connected to ideas of the East versus the West such as the references to the kimono and the town's name, China Grove. Welty's purpose, according to Du Priest, is to examine "the etiology of war" and to locate it in the family (1982). Pride is the culprit, in this critic's view, the factor that contributes to familial disputes and that is transposed to the global arena ultimately.

The remaining commentary on this story revolves around an analysis of its formalistic features: the nature of its comedy and the ways in which Welty achieves her hilarious effects. Vande Kieft (1962) leads off the discussion by identifying this story as representative of comedies of rigidity; her identification is based on Henri Bergson's categories of the sources of laughter. The repetitive nature of human thought and action provokes a comic response to the perversity of the situations, as is the case in Sister's narrative. Vande Kieft determines that the story succeeds due to Welty's expert depiction of Sister's "inexorable logic," including its exposure of her metaphysical alienation, as well as to Welty's superb command of the "Southern idiom." Calling Sister's monologue "elliptical and baroque," Vande Kieft sets the tone and tenor for subsequent discussions of the rhetorical features of this masterful achievement. Appel (1965) echoes Vande Kieft's analysis but adds that the story also serves as "a farcical treatment of the often obsessive Southern concern with 'kin'."

Schmidt extends Vande Kieft's designation of the story as exemplary of the comedies of rigidity to

suggest that such stories are representative of the early Welty canon and that they offer a strong contrast to the later "comedies of rebirth." He finds "Why I Live at the P.O." indicative of the earlier group of stories but inclusive of features such as Sister's assertiveness that anticipate the latter category. He observes that "a majority of her [Welty's] early comic stories . . . satirize rigidities in behavior, especially in women, whereas later collections . . . shift the comic balance to include a much greater role for the satirization of men . . . and a corresponding rise in interest of comedies of rebirth—stories featuring motifs of escape and transformation."

Pickett (1973) and Howard (1973) both provide brief analyses of the rhetorical choices Welty makes in this story to achieve her comic effects. Howard cites Welty's use of the "hyperbolic cliche" and slang as crucial to the success of the story and Welty's unfavorable depiction of white lower-class women. Pickett identifies "irony, word manipulation, oblique details, fallacies in logic, and characterization" as the stylistic techniques that Welty employs in "Why I Live at the P.O.". Although Sister's ironic self-exposure as a petty and jealous sibling comprises a pivotal device to convey the humor in the story, Pickett also describes how word manipulation, such as Sister's description of her sister's kimono as a "terrible flesh-colored contraption," adds to the humorous exposure of Sister's own self-deceptions, as does her use of oblique detail, such as the inclusion of brand names. Through the skillful employment of such rhetorical devices, Pickett argues, Welty manipulates the colloquial style of the story so that it serves a thematic purpose by suggesting which values are enduring, for example, the sanctity of family life, and which are not.

Wages (1973) provides a brief commentary on the relationship between the use of the family name Rondo and the structure of the story, a feature that others make note of as well (Schmidt and May, for instance). He reminds readers that the *rondo* is a form of musical composition that restates the dominant theme recursively, interspersing minor themes between the major ones. "The circular motion of a static situation accounts for part of the humor of the story," in Wages's view, as does the ironic deployment of "familial sobriquets."

Graves (1977) raises an issue that is not considered by other critics: that of the identity of Shirley-T's father. Graves attempts to make a case for naming Uncle Rondo for the position. She points out that the child calls him ''Papa,'' and that Sister believes the child ''was the spit-image of Papa-Daddy if he'd cut off his beard,'' which, Graves argues, would make Papa-Daddy like his son, Uncle Rondo; if Uncle Rondo had fathered Stella-Rondo's child, it would, in Graves's view, account for the long rift between Stella-Rondo and her uncle, during which time she refuses to be called by his name. The implication in Graves's argument is that such incestuous occurrences are not unheard of in the time and place of Welty's story.

There is much to be said even yet about this very well-known and much admired story of Eudora Welty's. As with a number of her early works, the deceptively simple surface permits, or even invites, fairly straightforward observations of the kind encouraged by early reactions to the story and even by Welty herself. But another line of interpretation, of a somewhat more complex nature, might also be investigated. Critical theories that enable a more sophisticated assessment of the linguistic elements in the story and align those elements to theme and structure would be welcome. The narrative as an act of performance seems a particularly promising area inadequately investigated thus far. Another avenue of exploration entails a deeper and perhaps more audacious examination of the relationship between the author and her work. For instance, a number of the features that Schmidt points out as characteristic of Sister also apply in a ''cater-cornered'' fashion to Welty herself. From her literary autobiography, *One Writer's Beginnings*, we learn that the author, like her protagonist, was the favored child until the birth of her two younger brothers; like Sister, Welty assumed the traditionally male responsibility of contributing to the family finances after her father's death; thus she achieved a position of recognized authority in the outside world as well as within the family as is the case with Sister. Surely, as a young woman fresh out of graduate school and longing to become a writer, the young Welty must have entertained fleeting thoughts about striking out on her own, just as Sister did. Indeed, we know that from time to time Welty did extricate herself from her family situation long enough to spend extended periods of times in such places as San Francisco and Europe. Further exploration of the ways in which Welty envisioned these independent gestures and the possible ramifications of these may be induced, however, from a closer analysis of those early stories about independent, if conflicted, females. As Schmidt cautions, any resemblances need to be explored tentatively and carefully, not so much as clues to Welty's personal life but as clues to the process by which the author transforms those ordinary life experiences into art.

Source: Diana R. Pingatore, ''*A Curtain of Green and Other Stories*: 'Why I Live at the P.O.,''' in *A Reader's Guide to the Short Stories of Eudora Welty*, G. K. Hall & Co., 1996, pp. 69–79.

Charles E. May

In the following essay, May advocates a close, analytical reading of Why I Live at the P.O. *to extract a more insightful understanding of the complex comical and psychological dynamics that are involved in the story's composition.*

Often in literary studies a well-known artist will turn critic briefly and make an offhand comment about the work of a fellow writer that becomes solidified into dogma and thus creates a critical or interpretative dead end. Such seems to be the case with the one-liner that Katherine Anne Porter tossed off over thirty years ago about Eudora Welty's popular little family comedy, ''Why I Live at the P.O.'' Porter's classifying of the story as a ''terrifying case of dementia praecox'' seems so ''right'' that no one has ever bothered to examine or challenge her judgment. If the story is a case study, albeit an hilarious one, of paranoia in action, then little is left for the critic to do except nod his head with a knowing smile.

However, this alone does not account for the lack of discussion of one of the most anthologized stories of a writer whose other stories are discussed widely. Another reason for critical silence on the work is that it is comic. No interpretation can fully account for what makes it so funny, and no one wants the thankless task of explaining a joke. One could point out, as Ruth M. Vande Kieft has, that the narrator of the story nicely illustrates Bergson's notion that mechanical rigidity in human beings is laughable. There is certainly nothing flexible about Sister's persecution obsession. One could suggest, as Sean O'Faolain has, that the story, like most good humor, is a very mixed affair and thus hides a groan somewhere behind the joke. Again, it seems clear that if we laugh because the characters of the story seem so obsessed with trivia, we also despair to think that people *can* be so obsessed with trivia. After making these general comments, critics have found little else to say about the humor of the story except to admire Welty's ability to capture a particular humorous verbal idiom. Everyone agrees that the story is a *tour de force*.

An additional problem that faces Welty critics who would interpret "Why I Live at the P.O." is the fact that its tone and technique seem radically different from Welty's usual fictional milieu. Best known and most discussed for stories that take place in a "Season of Dreams" where reality is transformed into fantasy and fable, and, as R. P. Warren has noted in a famous essay, the logic of things is not the logic of ordinary daylight life, Welty, in this, one of her most widely-read stories, creates a season that is not one of dream at all; the reality of things seems to remain stubbornly, almost militantly, real. Warren has suggested that the dream-like effect of the typical Welty story seems to result from her ability to squeeze meaning from the most trivial details. However, here in a story that depends on the triviality of things, there is no dream-like effect; the trivial details are comically allowed to remain trivial. They are never transformed into hierophanic entities the way they are in such typical Welty fables as "First Love," "Livvie," "Death of a Traveling Salesman," or "A Worn Path." No one has dared to try to show how Sister's green-tomato pickle or Stella-Rondo's flesh-colored kimono are transformed from the profane into the sacred.

For these reasons the story seems almost impervious to critical analysis. Aside from Robert Drake's interesting but inconclusive analysis of the story as a "cater-cornered epic" several years ago in *The Mississippi Quarterly*, the only comments that have been made about the form of the story are the suggestions made by several readers that it is a monologue similar to Ring Lardner's "Haircut," for Sister reveals more about her moral status than she intends to or is aware of. Drake never makes clear just what the nature of the "cater-cornered epic" genre is. He suggests that it involves the exalting of the everyday and the familiar to the level of the heroic and epic; yet the result is not mock-heroic, but rather something harder to define than that. Somehow, the cater-cornered nature of the story is related to a multiple point of view in which sister seems inwardly aware of the absurdity of her position in the P.O., but must justify her position anyway. Because Drake does not make the connection between Sister's psyche and the story's structure clear, I am left unsure about how the work is epical, cater-cornered, butt-ended, parallel-parked, or otherwise geometrically arranged.

> **"However, the literary character that Sister resembles even more is Dostoevsky's Underground Man. As it is for Dostoevsky's nameless antihero, Sister's logic is not so much insane as it is the rational pushed to such an extreme that it becomes irrational and perverse."**

I have reviewed these desultory comments about Welty's little story at such length because they illustrate certain basic interpretative problems about the work. The problem of calling Sister a schizophrenic is the resulting temptation to leave the issue there and thus ignore both the structural implications the phenomenon has for the story and the phenomenological implications it has for the characters. The problem of making such general comments about the story's monologue genre, its insane logic, its geometrical design, or its trivia-saturated detail is that all these remarks seem to be critical dead ends. None lead to a unified interpretation of the story or an appreciation of the complexity of its human content and artistic structure. R. P. Warren says that Welty's typical fictional character is, in one way or another, isolated from the world. Around this character, Warren further suggests, Eudora Welty creates either the drama of the isolated person's attempt to escape into the real world, or the drama of the discovery, either by the isolated character or by the reader, of the nature of the particular predicament. Of these two types, "Why I Live at the P.O." seems clearly to belong to the latter. Moreover, it seems equally clear that since Sister is less interested in discovering than justifying her situation, the drama of the story resides in the reader's gradual discovery of just exactly why Sister does live at the P.O. Consequently, although the story, by its very nature, seems to resist interpretation, by its very nature also it requires interpretation. The drama of the story exists as the drama of the reader's analysis of sister's basic situation as she herself describes it.

To make this discovery, I suggest the reader play the role of phenomenologist rather than psychoanalyst. To say that Sister's motives, actions, and intentions are other than those she proclaims is to indulge in the obvious and get nowhere. To attempt to analyze Sister's phenomenological situation in relation to her family, particularly her relation to her sister, Stella-Rondo, is to participate in the drama of discovery that Welty's story demands. R. D. Laing rather than Freud seems to be the best guide here. If Sister is indeed a schizophrenic, whatever that means, her predicament should not be analyzed *in vacuo*, but within the family nexus itself. I don't pretend that the method developed by R. D. Laing and Aaron Esterson in *Sanity, Madness and the Family* for analyzing families of schizophrenics can be adopted whole cloth to apply to the situation of "Why I Live at the P.O." After all, we do only have Sister's word on evening that happens, and, as everyone agrees, she is not to be trusted. Moreover, we are dealing here with the static, closed form of the art work, not the open, dynamic situation of existential reality. Yet, to use Laing's Sartrean terminology, we cannot make "intelligible" what the basic situation of the story is until we very carefully retrace the steps from what is going on (the "process") to who is doing what (the "praxis"). If the action of the story, or Sister's recounting of it, is "cater-cornered," circular, "one-sided," or "cut on the bias," then we must determine the existential source of both Sister's logic and the story's geometry.

A close look at the events of Sister's momentous Fourth of July indicates that she is an example of what Laing has termed the "unembodied self." She does nothing directly, but rather observes and criticizes what the body experiences and does. More specifically, in this story, Sister is one who does things subjectively rather than objectively. Welty dramatizes Sister's divided self by splitting her quite nearly into a subjective side, Sister herself, and an objective side, Stella-Rondo, who is "exactly twelve months to the day younger." Stella-Rondo acts out everything that Sister subjectively thinks or feels. In this sense Sister is right when she insists throughout the story that she does nothing, that everything is Stella-Rondo's fault. Yet the reader is also right in suspecting that everything that happens is Sister's doing. It is Sister who first dates Mr. Whitaker, but it is Stella-Rondo who marries him and moves away from the family; both are

desires which Sister harbors but cannot act out. Stella-Rondo did not break up Sister and Mr. Whitaker by telling him that she was "one-sided," or as Sister says, "bigger on one side than the other." Rather, Stella-Rondo's action dramatizes that the one side which is sister is the subjective side that cannot act.

According to Sister, Stella-Rondo turns the other members against her one by one. However, what Stella-Rondo really does throughout the story is act out Sister's subjective feelings. First, Sister says that Shirley-T is the "spit-image of Papa-Daddy if he'd cut off his beard." A bit later at the table, Stella-Rondo turns Papa-Daddy against Sister by telling him, "Sister says she fails to understand why you don't cut off your beard." Although Sister's defense—"I did not say any such of a thing, the idea!"—is literally true; that is, she did not say these exact words, it is obvious that "the idea" was indeed hers. Next, when Uncle Rondo appears in Stella-Rondo's flesh-colored kimono, Sister says he looks like a "half-wit" in it. Later, Stella-Rondo echoes Sister by saying that Uncle Rondo "looks like a fool." At supper, Stella-Rondo thus articulates Sister's feelings when she tells Uncle Rondo that Sister said he looked like a fool in the pink kimono. Again, although Sister did not use these exact words, she thought what Stella-Rondo voices. When Sister asks the imaginary listener, "Do you remember who it was really said that?" the listener should remember all too well.

Sister communicates everything in this oblique, cater-cornered way; she does not express her feelings directly, but rather diagonally through Stella-Rondo. Consequently, she can cause a great many events to occur, yet disclaim responsibility for any of them. She can sit in the post office, proclaiming, "I didn't do anything," and thereby believe that she preserves her freedom, her individuality, her blamelessness, and her inviolate self. R. D. Laing's description of the schizoid individual indicates the nature and result of Sister's self justification: she tries to preserve the self by withdrawing into a central citadel and writing off everything else except the self. The tragic paradox of this situation, says Laing, is that the more the schizoid person tries thusly to defend the self, the more he or she destroys it. The real danger stems not from the "enemies" outside, but rather from the destructive defensive maneuvers inside.

Once we see that Stella-Rondo is the objective side of Sister's subjective self, the inevitability of

Sister's being driven out of the house precisely because she urges the exile of Stella-Rondo becomes clear. If Stella-Rondo is a female version of the prodigal son returned, then like the good and faithful son who stayed home, Sister resents the fact that Stella-Rondo has failed in the prodigality of the venture that Sister's subjective side has sent her out on. M. H. Abrams, in his study, *Natural Supernaturalism*, has reminded us that the prodigal son story is a figure for life as a circular rather than a linear journey. The leaving of home is a fall from unity into self-dividedness; the return is the circularity of the return to union. It is precisely this union of subjectivity and objectivity that Sister does not want.

Sister now desires to remain safe at home where she can manipulate the family from her position as dutiful daughter. However, given her subjective/objective split, the very existence of this desire means that Stella-Rondo will become the favorite while Sister becomes the exile. The psychological mechanism here is similar to that which Edgar Allan Poe describes as the "perverse"—that "radical, primitive, irreducible sentiment" often overlooked by moralists and psychologists alike.

Thus, in a very complex way the story illustrates the schizoid self-deception of the unembodied self. Moreover, it also dramatizes the results of a complete failure of communication when people not only refuse to listen to each other, but refuse to listen to themselves as well. The basic irony of the story is that although Sister spends the whole tale explaining why she lives at the P.O., she really does not know why. Although she talks, talks, talks, no one listens to what she says, not even herself. In fact, no one listens to anyone else in the story; the motif is constant throughout. When Sister denies that she said Papa-Daddy should shave off his beard, Stella-Rondo says, "Anybody in the world could have heard you, that had ears." And the more Sister protests, the less Papa-Daddy listens; "he acts like he just don't hear me," says Sister. "Papa-Daddy must of gone stone deaf." When Sister warns Uncle Rondo not to go near Papa-Daddy, he ignores her and goes on "zigzagging right on out to the hammock" anyway.

Sister, of course, is the character most guilty of not listening in the story, even though she is always accusing others of this. She tells Mama that if it had been her that had run away to Illinois and returned, Mama would not have been so overjoyed to see her. When Mama insists that she would have, Sister says, "she couldn't convince me though she talked till she was blue in the face." The last words of the story further emphasize Sister's refusal to listen, and sum up her situation: "And if Stella-Rondo should come to me this minute, on bended knees, and *attempt* to explain the incidents of her life with Mr. Whitaker, I'd simply put my fingers in both my ears and refuse to listen." The fact is, Sister has been telling the whole story with her fingers figuratively in both ears. She will not listen to Stella-Rondo because she will not listen to herself. Consequently, she will go to her grave denying the facts of life, as she claims Stella-Rondo will do. Our response to Sister as we read the story might best be expressed in the Southern colloquialism, "I just wish you could hear yourself talk." It is precisely the point of the story that Sister cannot.

A speech to a listener that the speaker cannot actually hear, a speech in which the speaker reveals herself unawares, is, of course, the kind of utterance that we often attribute to the dramatic monologue form. However, Welty's story poses an important difference. The monologue speakers in Robert Browning's poems, for example, have dramatized listeners to whom they speak, with definite strategies in mind. Andrea del Sarto, Fra Lippo Lippi, the infamous Duke, all either have certain aims in speaking as they do to their listeners, or else they speak as a way to discover just what their situation is. A closer analogue to "Why I Live at the P.O." is Browning's "Soliloquy of the Spanish Cloister." The poem is not a soliloquy in the sense that it is a set speech, a delivery of feelings or ideas previously arrived at by the speaker, but rather a soliloquy in the sense that it is spoken to no one. The particular ironic nature of the "Soliloquy of the Spanish Cloister" which makes it closer to "Why I Live at the P.O." than the work with which it is usually compared, Ring Lardner's "Haircut," is that the speaker in Browning's poem is "guilty" precisely of those sins which he attributes to Brother Lawrence. Consequently, he damns himself even as he believes he is damning Brother Lawrence. No one hears him, not even himself, but he is damned nevertheless. Similarly, Sister alienates herself from the family in the very act of trying to alienate Stella-Rondo.

However, the literary character that Sister resembles even more is Dostoevsky's Underground Man. As it is for Dostoevsky's nameless antihero, Sister's logic is not so much insane as it is the rational pushed to such an extreme that it becomes irrational and perverse. Sister's story, an apologia, but not an apology, is an argument that becomes nonsense. The whole story that Sister tells (not the story Welty creates) is nonsense, not because of the triviality of objects and concerns that the argument seems to be about, but rather because the subjective is completely cut off from objective reality. If the story is about schizophrenia, this is the nature of the pathology. Although, as is typical of her, Sister accuses the members of her family of "cutting off your nose to spite your face," this is exactly what she does to herself. By pulling herself into her underground P.O., by casting off everything except her own subjectivity, Sister, like Dostoevsky's underground man, becomes involved in a constant verbal defense of the autonomy of the self that only serves to further destroy the self, to eat it up with its own subjectivity.

At the end of the story when Sister's "revolution" against the family on the Fourth of July has divided up the whole town into two camps that correspond to her own divided self, she believes she has established a separate peace. "Peace, that's what I like. . . . I want the world to know I'm happy." But as long as everything in Sister's life is "cater-cornered," which is indeed the way she likes things, she will never have peace. Like the Ancient Mariner, she will grab every Wedding Guest who enters the P.O. and once again tell her oblique and slanted story, therefore never uniting her ghost-like subjective self with the objective world of others. The real drama of the story is the reader's discovery of the logical and phenomenological circle in which Sister is trapped.

Source: Charles E. May, "Why Sister Lives at the P.O.," in *The Critical Response to Eudora Welty's Fiction*, edited by Laurie Champion, Greenwood Press, 1994, pp. 43–49.

Axel Nissen

In the following essay, Axel Nissen discusses the effects of "perspectival principle" in Welty's story.

In her introduction to the first edition of *A Curtain of Green and Other Stories* (1941), Katherine Anne Porter describes the heroine of "Why I Live at the P.O." as "a terrifying case of dementia praecox," effectively labeling her as a mental basket case. Though Ruth Vande Kieft has described Porter's comment as "the Ur-blooper" of Welty criticism ("Question"), the idea has stuck and poor Sister has been on the psychiatrist's couch ever since. In his monograph published in 1965, Alfred Appel, Jr. more or less accepts Porter's diagnosis and writes:

"As the narrator continues her straightforward account, the reader becomes aware of penetrating inconsistencies." Marie-Antoinette Manz-Kunz also follows Porter's lead when she states that the "story is a sheer clinical study of the distortions of reality caused by mental disorder." Charles E. May, in an essay entitled "Why Sister Lives at the P.O.," analyzes the patient in the light of a much more sophisticated psychological theory than his predecessors, but his conclusion is much the same: "in a very complex way the story illustrates the schizoid self-deception of the unembodied self." A final judgment from Nell Ann Pickett will suffice to show that Sister has had a lot of "bad publicity" down through the years. Pickett writes: "Sister's step-by-step explanation of each incident leading up to her move to the post office convinces us not that her family has mistreated her but rather that Sister is deceiving herself."

What all these critics are doing is applying the *perspectival principle* to the story, which is a reader strategy for dealing with perceived inconsistencies, tensions and incongruities in a text. In the words of Tamar Yacobi, the perspectival principle "brings divergent as well as otherwise unrelated elements into pattern by attributing them, in whole or in part, to the peculiarities and circumstances of the observer through whom the world is taken to be refracted." Because Sister's world is a topsy-turvy one, critics conclude that there must be something wrong with her way of seeing it. They are implying that Sister is an *unreliable narrator*: "as everyone agrees, she is not to be trusted" (May).

If this assessment correctly reflects the author's intention, it would mean that the story is structured in such a way that the reader sooner or later will realize the narrator cannot be taken at her word and feel there is a secret communication between the reader and the implied author, behind Sister's back. If Sister is an unreliable narrator it means we should be able to apply certain criteria to her, *qua* narrator. Shlomith Rimmon-Kenan has outlined three main sources of unreliability as "the narrator's limited knowledge, his personal involvement, and his problematic value-scheme." To determine whether Sister is in fact an unreliable narrator we must consider these factors and answer the following questions: Do the facts and the outcome of the story contradict the narrator's view and, in effect, prove her wrong? Does her personal involvement prevent Sister from giving us a reliable account and is this shown by the way the characters' views consistently clash? Does Sister have a problematic value-scheme and does her language contain internal contradictions and double-edged images?

To take the facts first. Even among Sister's detractors there is an unstated assumption that Sister does not tell outright lies; there is no evidence that she actively distorts the facts nor biases her narrative of the events leading to her leaving home, so as to give us a false impression of the participants and actions. As we have seen, Appel describes it as a "straightforward account." Ergo: we can believe that people said what they really said and did what they really did. Without this basis in fact, in actual words and actions, the interpretation of the story would be an entirely equivocal activity and lost in endless speculations about what really happened.

From the story we can thus "read out" the following fictional facts and make the following inferences:

(1) Sister never tries to conceal the real reason for her resentment towards Stella-Rondo. Her dislike and jealousy of her sister is never just implied, it is stated outright from the beginning. Sister has a frank dislike of her younger sibling, who "always had anything in the world she wanted and then she'd throw it away."

(2) Sister makes herself useful while the rest of the family lounges about. There is evidence that Sister might quite possibly be the family dredge, something her status as an unmarried daughter still living at home also indicates (Drake; Herrscher).

(3) Sister has not in fact said any of the things Stella-Rondo quotes her as saying. She has not said that Papa-Daddy should cut off his beard, nor that Uncle Rondo looks ridiculous in Stella-Rondo's flesh-colored kimono. The alienation of Sister is thus based on the active involvement of Stella-Rondo in outright lying.

(4) Sister is in fact treated unpleasantly by all the members of her family. Papa-Daddy calls her a "hussy," Mama takes Stella-Rondo's side against her, criticizes her cooking and assaults her physically. Uncle Rondo upsets her with firecrackers, Shirley-T. sticks her tongue out at her, not to mention Stella-Rondo's machinations. We notice that Sister is not included in the family games. Despite her ill-treatment, she shows remarkable patience and forbearance. She never complains about the physical and verbal abuse she is subjected to, and only objects to the scheming Stella-Rondo is involved in because it is what most insults Sister's sense of justice. She emerges as something of a stoic in the midst of egoists.

(5) The members of Sister's family are all unbalanced to the extent that they are hypersensitive to certain stimuli. These we can observe from their reactions to Stella-Rondo's well-placed insinuations. Papa-Daddy rants on about his beard at the slightest suggestion that he should cut it off. Uncle Rondo is very touchy on the subject of his looks and throws what can only

> "Sister's narrative is an unwitting, _high burlesque_ of daily life in her family, where a quite trivial chain of events is narrated as if it were the second coming."

be described as a temper-tantrum at the suggestion (again from Stella-Rondo) that the pink kimono might not be the most becoming thing he might wear. Mama actually strikes Sister just for mentioning a member of the family, Cousin Annie Flo, who "went to her grave denying the facts of life." Not least of all, there is Stella-Rondo who shows much the same tendency as Annie Flo, resolutely denying the fact that Shirley-T. is her biological daughter and finally having a fit of hysterics. Sister might quite easily be seen as the most sane one of the bunch; she has a steady job, is responsible for the household diet and is the only one who seems, quite reasonably, to want a rational explanation for the appearance of Shirley-T. Sister also expresses gratitude towards Uncle Rondo, with whom she appears to have had a special rapport, and does not raise an eyebrow at his eccentricities.

Critics have been quick to condemn Sister's way of speaking as evidence of her vulgarity and distance from the implied author's norms. Zelma Turner Howard writes: "Sister's speech pattern lacks rhythm, cadence, aphorisms, and all the positive qualities of a natural idiom." Does Sister's language give her away and is it the verbal wasteland Howard suggests? If her speech is meant to lead us towards a negative appraisal of her character, we would expect it to be contrasted in important ways with speech patterns of the other characters (as is the case in the scene in the doctor's office in "A Worn Path"). Yet Sister's speech patterns do not differ markedly from those of the rest of her family.

When it comes to her style, be it a "natural idiom" or not, Sister has a remarkable store of vivid expressions, hyperboles and proverbs at her disposal, and in fact makes a very good storyteller. Just because her speech is not "poetic" in its imagery and rhythm is not reason enough to take it as evidence that she is a negatively judged character. Appel has noted that Sister has a fine ability to sum up her fellow human beings in a few short phrases, as this description shows: "You ought to see Mama, she weighs two hundred pounds and has real tiny feet.'' Sister is very much the equal of the others at verbal jousting and has a vein of irony, which clearly reveals her intelligence.

The implied author gives us one final and telling clue as to Sister's real situation in the household. This is what the members of her family call her. We never know her proper name, but to the rest of the family she is simply ''Sister,'' indicating very clearly how she is defined as secondary to Stella-Rondo and of inferior status.

Based on this evidence it is possible to come to a completely different conclusion regarding Sister's mental state than have the great majority of critics. Despite her idiosyncracies, Sister is a character to be believed and what she is offering us is not a grossly distorted presentation of reality due to mental illness, but rather evidence of an entirely sane though unhappy state.

It is relatively easy to poke fun at critics for, in a manner of speaking, taking the story and its narrator too seriously (or maybe it is a case of them not taking her seriously enough?). It is more difficult to explain why so many have read ''Why I Live at the P.O.'' as a textbook example of unreliable narration. It is possible that the publication of Wayne Booth's book *The Rhetoric of Fiction* in the early sixties, which discussed the question of reliability extensively after a long period of silence (Yacobi), also produced an oversensitivity to signs of unreliability, and then especially in stories of this frankly subjective type.

In ''Why I Live at the P.O.'' the point of view is dominated by Sister, the protagonist-narrator. The important difference between this narrative and traditional first-person narration (e.g. Welty's ''A Memory'') is that Sister's story is transmitted orally. Welty sets up a fictional storytelling situation, with Sister's narration in the form of one long continuous speech. The story is completely imitative of an oral narrative.

Keeping the story's unusual narrative structure in mind, I believe Sister's perceived unreliability is mainly the result of a disjunction between the style and content of her monologue. The style of narration is highly realistic, while the characters and events teeter on the edge of the blatantly absurd. To analyze this contrast we need to account for the means by which Welty creates the illusion of living speech in print, because it is this that creates a disjunction with the bizarre content of her story.

The verisimilitude of the story's narrative structure is hard to describe objectively unless we compare Sister's monologue to some model of real oral narratives. The noted American sociolinguist William Labov has provided us with such a model. He has described the constituent features of the fully developed *natural narrative* as follows (in roughly chronological order): abstract, orientation, complicating action, evaluation, resolution and coda. The *abstract* is a short summary (usually one or two sentences) of the story that narrators generally provide before recounting the story proper and which is meant to encapsulate the point of the story. The *orientation* serves to ''identify in some way the time, place, persons, and their activity or situation'' (Pratt) and usually occurs immediately before narrative proper begins. *Complicating action* and *resolution* are the core of the narrative. The former begins with the first narrative clause in the speech act, the latter usually ends with the last narrative clause. By *evaluation* Labov is referring to ''the means used by the narrator to indicate the point of the narrative, its *raison d'etre*, why it was told and what the narrator was getting at.'' The *coda*'s general function is to ''close off the sequence of complicating actions and indicate that none of the events that followed were important to the narrative.''

The deep structure of ''Why I Live at the P.O.'' follows this model to a remarkable degree. Abstract, orientation, complicating action, resolution and coda are all in place and in the right order. The first line of the story is the abstract: ''I was getting along fine with Mama, Papa-Daddy and Uncle Rondo until my sister Stella-Rondo just separated from her husband and came back home again.'' Here Sister tells us in a nutshell what the story is going to be about, and also gives us a clue as to what motivates the telling of it. The orientation to the listener follows directly, with the presentation of the antagonist Stella-Rondo and the events leading up to the beginning of the narrative situation. The complicating action and the narrative proper begins with the line ''Mama said she like to made her drop dead for a second'' and continues on through a number of scenes, where the resolution begins with the line, ''And I'll tell you it didn't take me any longer than a minute to make up my mind what to do.'' The coda is separated from the rest of the story by a blank line and quite properly closes off the story by bringing us back to the storytelling situation and the present.

The realism of the story's deep structure is also seen in its surface structure, as Welty recreates the idiolect of a small-town, upper middle-class spinster. Welty has Sister use a wide range of expressions and figures, such as *colloquialisms* and *slang* (e.g. "as sure as shooting," "piecing on the ham," "no more manners than the man in the moon," a conniption fit" and "kiss my foot"); *cliches* ("thank her lucky stars," "I shudder to think," "till she was blue in the face"); *euphemisms* ([Shirley-T.] "lost the Milky Way") and *understatement* and *hyperbole* ("I made no bones about letting the family catch on to what I was up to," "before you could say 'Jack Robinson,'" "tickled her nearly to death"). Both part of Sister's verbal rhetoric and the monologue's verisimilar effect is her use of the *historic present* particularly in the speech tags. The use of italics to indicate emphasis and simple connectives rather than complex adverbs as transitions (mostly "so," but also "but" and "then") also contribute to making "Why I Live at the P.O." a uniquely convincing representation of an oral narrative.

This is an unbelievable story with a believable discourse, bizarre content in a highly realistic form. Thus the perceived contradictions in the story are not caused by willful deception nor by a warped mind, but rather by a willingness to feel things strongly and to see the dramatic in everyday conflicts, which every member of the family shares. This is *not* a sinister story in the manner of Ring Lardner ("Haircut" [1926]) or Ambrose Bierce ("Oil of Dog" [1909–12]). Rather, the effect of "Why I Live at the P.O." is highly comic.

In the beginning of his essay, May discusses why there have been so few critical analyses of this story (relative to its popularity and acclaim) and concludes that it is at least partly due to the difficulty of explaining its highly comic effect: "No interpretation can fully account for what makes it so funny, and no one wants the thankless task of explaining a joke." He mentions Vande Kieft's attempt at an explanation, which includes a reference to Bergson's theory that anything that suggests rigidity in a human being is laughable and thus ascribes the humorous effect to Sister's (perceived) *idee fixe* (*Eudora Welty*). Appel relies on another theoretician of the comic and writes that the story's "grim humor" is due to its being told gravely, as a humorous story should be, according to Twain's "How to Tell a Story."

There is nothing particularly grim about the humor in "Why I Live at the P.O." and its comic effect needs to be tied to the story's burlesque character. Sister's narrative is an unwitting, *high burlesque* of daily life in her family, where a quite trivial chain of events is narrated as if it were the second coming. Robert Drake touches on the same idea when he writes: "The whole point of Miss Welty's delicious ... story is its exalting of the everyday and familiar to the level of the heroic and epic." When I choose to call the story high burlesque it is because, in the manner characteristic of this literary mode, Sister's rhetoric is used to raise the everyday to the plane of high drama and seriousness in a way analogous to the classic example, Pope's "Rape of the Lock," though with one important exception: Sister's style is not formal or pompous but rather exalts through her direct involvement, her acting it out before us in a highly convincing way. The coda clearly solidifies the total comic impression: "And that's the last I've laid eyes on any of my family or my family laid eyes on me for five solid days and nights." The short time that has actually passed since the events took place puts the whole "drama" of Sister's exodus in an even more comic perspective, and makes us wonder how long it will be before she is back home again in the bosom of her eccentric family.

In seeking a more unified and complex understanding of "Why I Live at the P.O.," in all its facets—comic and tragic, melodramatic and farcical—we have focused on the relation of the story to the person telling it and asked what motivates Sister's long speech, what it tells us about her and why Welty has chosen this particular point of view. As we have seen, the answers to these questions may be quite different from the critic's regular analysis. They look at the story clinically, as a psychological study in some form of mental illness, or consider that its chief aim is not to narrate, but rather to indict and indirectly, hold up to ridicule. This line of interpretation makes unreliability the entire rationale of the story, and thus fails to look beyond this perceived technique to the actual fictional situation. To these readers, the medium ultimately seems more important than the message and they run the risk of fitting Edna Earl Ponder's description of the worst kind of listener (as so often, the heroine of *The Ponder Heart* is here talking about her uncle, Daniel): "I used to dread he might get hold of one of these occasional travelers that wouldn't come in unless they had to— the kind that would break in on a story with a set of questions, and wind it up with a list of what Uncle Daniel's faults were. . . ." Attaching psychological labels to the narrator, or to the other characters for that matter, prevents us from enjoying the humor of the story in its full breadth. The only dignosis we are able or need to pose is that Sister is a lonely woman. As the story so vividly shows, living in a family is no guarantee against loneliness and Sister's monologue is fundamentally a symptom of her lonesome state. The form of the story is, as often in Welty's fiction, the surest indicator of the basic motif.

Source: Axel Nissen, "Occasional Travelers in China Grove: Welty's 'Why I Live at the P.O.' Reconsidered," in *The Southern Quarterly*, Vol. 32, No. 1, Fall, 1993, pp. 72–79.

Peter Schmidt

In the following essay, Peter Schmidt employs character analyses for detailed insight into Welty's story.

One way to think of the Rondo family in "Why I Live at the P.O." is as an exceptionally noisy family of paper cutouts. Certainly the characters are as delightfully two-dimensional, and as farcically posed, as the cutouts described in "*Women!!*" but the story is also a comedy about fashion, gender differences, and power.

"Why I Live at the P.O." is set in China Grove, Mississippi, and features Sister as the narrator, Stella-Rondo (her younger sister), Papa-Daddy (Sister's grandfather), Mama (Sister's mother), Uncle Rondo, Stella-Rondo's two-year-old daughter Shirley-T., and (briefly) a dying woman named Old Jep Patterson. In the beginning of Sister's monologue, most readers tend to share Sister's view of the absurdity of her family members. Sister's main tactic is to show how false their language is. Stella-Rondo, Shirley-T., Mama, Papa-Daddy, and Uncle Rondo all speak an inflated language filled with euphemisms and the brand names of fashionable commercial products. When Stella-Rondo displays the clothes she has brought home, for example, she shows her sister something she has never seen before—a kimono that "happens to be part of my trousseau, and Mr. Whitaker took several dozen photographs of me in it." By replacing her sister's ignorance with exotic and fashionable words such as "kimono" and "trousseau," Stella-Rondo reminds Sister that although she may be older and have a job at the P.O., it is her younger sister Stella-Rondo who married the man they both dated and who escaped to live in the wide world. Thus she plays the sophisticated, well-traveled belle, full of polite condescension and a histrionic sense of martyrdom. In retelling her versions of these events, however, it is Sister and not Stella-Rondo who has the last word: the kimono becomes "a terrible-looking flesh-colored contraption I wouldn't be found dead in." Sister uses a similar tactic when relaying Papa-Daddy's speech to us. "This is the beard I started growing on the Coast when I was fifteen years old," Papa-Daddy boasts, but Sister deflates this boast with the comment, "he would have gone on till nightfall if Shirley-T. hadn't lost the Milky Way she ate in Cairo." All these examples are insults made after the fact, private acts of revenge taken during the retelling of the events to make up for her not being able to have her say earlier. Many of the most delightfully vulgar commercial references in the story, such as Shirley-T.'s Milky Way and the Add-a-Pearl necklace, furthermore, were not in Welty's early draft of the story; neither was fancy vocabulary like "disport" and "trousseau" (originally, merely "eat" and "underwear"). In revising, Welty carefully highlighted the story's comic contrasts of diction.

In Sister's war of words with her family, she continually seeks to draw our attention to the fact that their versions of the events are supposedly much less reasonable. Instead of admitting that her marriage to Mr. Whitaker has failed and that she has had to return to her family home with her two-year-old child, for instance, Stella-Rondo steadfastly maintains that the girl is adopted. Stella-Rondo's "proof" consists of nothing more than repeating her assertions more and more loudly—something that seems to work especially well in the Rondo family. Our sympathy for the narrator increases even further when Stella-Rondo lies about what her sister said about her grandfather's beard to turn her grandfather against her: "'Papa-Daddy,' she says. . . . 'Papa-Daddy, Sister says she fails to understand why you don't cut off your beard.'" The narrator's anger at her sister's airs becomes understandable after a few such scenes, and we begin to relish the ways in which Sister gives others their comeuppance, both in her original retorts and again, even more successfully, in her later storytelling. The victories she gains through storytelling are especially sweet because at last she seems to have an audience who sides with her, not with her sister. As she says triumphantly to her imagined listeners at one point, when she relates how her sister accuses her of calling Uncle Rondo a fool in his kimono: "Do you remember who it was really said that?." Welty's witty last name for this family denotes a musical form that has a refrain occurring at least three times between contrasting couplets. In the Rondo family, however, repetition and contrast produces only discord and disorder.

As "Why I Live at the P.O." progresses, the reader cannot but begin to notice that the narrator has many of the same family traits that she so despises in others. This is especially true of the way she talks and the way in which she deals with inconsistencies in her account of the events. Sister's vanity infects her language as thoroughly as that of the other characters infects theirs. At the beginning of the story we may not notice it as readily because Sister has so carefully placed the other characters and their foolish actions at the center of our attention. But as her story approaches the tale of her climactic break with her family, her own pretensions become more prominent. When she describes her Uncle Rondo's throwing firecrackers into her room at 6:30 A.M., for instance, her language is as comically inflated as anything that Stella-Rondo or Papa-Daddy has ever said.

> [A]t 6:30 A.M. the next morning, he threw a whole five-cent package of some unsold one-inch firecrackers from the store as hard as he could into my bedroom and they every one went off. Not one bad one in the string. Anybody else, there'd be one that wouldn't go off.
>
> Well, I'm just terribly susceptible to noise of any kind, the doctor has always told me I was the most sensitive person he had ever seen in his whole life, and I was simply prostrated. I couldn't eat! People tell me they heard it as far as the cemetery, and old Aunt Jep Patterson, that had been holding her own so good, thought it was Judgment Day and she was going to meet her whole family. It's usually so quiet here.

As this superbly comic passage develops, Sister's language becomes less controlled and ironic. Self-praise and self-martyrdom converge, and by the end she imagines that the entire town heard the indignities perpetrated against her, and the perfectly timed concluding phrase, "It's usually so quiet here," adds a new twist to the humor. The sentence is comic because its speaker does not realize that we have to take it as an absurdity; we have heard nothing but noise since the story began. This comment also has a sinister edge to it, for the longing for separation and silence that it reveals foreshadows the dark edge to the ending of the story, when "quiet" at great cost is finally achieved.

Once we begin to doubt the narrator's reliability, evidence to increase our doubt begins cropping up everywhere when the story is reread. The tale's wonderful opening paragraph is a case in point. "I was getting along fine with Mama, Papa-Daddy and Uncle Rondo until my sister Stella-Rondo just separated from her husband and came back home again. Mr. Whitaker! Of course I went with Mr. Whitaker

> ❝ These other secrets include her desire to be the authority figure in her family and to play the traditional role of the fashionable, worldly wife, but her secrets also include her own self-revulsion--her lingering belief that her family's view of her as a monster may be right."

first, when he first appeared here in China Grove, taking 'Pose Yourself' photos, and Stella-Rondo broke us up. Told him I was one-sided. Bigger on one side than the other, which is a deliberate, calculated falsehood: I'm the same. Stella-Rondo is exactly twelve months to the day younger than I am and for that reason she's spoiled."

As this passage reveals, the causes for Sister's anger lie much deeper than any resentment she has for specific things that Stella-Rondo has done to her, such as taking Mr. Whitaker from her and marrying him. The paragraph begins and ends with references to Stella-Rondo's being the younger sister whose birth caused her parents to spoil her and slight her older sister. In returning home with her child, Stella-Rondo clearly disrupts the privileged status of the parent's favorite child that Sister has managed to regain during her sister's absence. Because the two sisters share the same birthday, moreover, their rivalry is all the more galling to the older one; Stella-Rondo seems to have come on the scene exactly a year after Sister's birth to usurp her identity along with her birthday. Welty enforces this point by having Stella-Rondo's name mentioned repeatedly throughout the story, whereas the narrator, when she is addressed at all, is called merely "Sister," as if she has no identity except in (subordinate) relation to her favored younger sibling.

The status that Sister briefly had in the family with Stella-Rondo gone was much more various than the role of only child. Because of her job as the postmistress at the post office of China Grove, she is also able to hold the honored (and traditionally male) status as the family's principal breadwinner. (The fact that Papa-Daddy is rich and Uncle Rondo a pharmacist is, to Sister's mind, irrelevant; of the immediate family, she is the only member with a salaried position of authority in the outside world.) Indeed, Sister may even be said *to have become the family's father*: no husband for Mama is mentioned in the story, a telling omission; there is only Uncle Rondo and Papa-Daddy, Mama's father. With Stella-Rondo gone, Sister thus seems (at least in her own imagination) to gain the two most prominent positions of authority possible within a family—that of the head male breadwinner and that of the favorite child. Upon Stella-Rondo's return, however, she is immediately relegated to the role of female servant. Welty emphasizes the trauma of this demotion early in the story by having Sister indignantly portray herself "over the hot stove, trying to stretch two chickens over five people and a completely unexpected child into the bargain, without one moment's notice." As the story continues, the baby Shirley-T. takes over the role of the favored child, Stella-Rondo and Mama play the only available authoritative female roles, and both Papa-Daddy and Uncle Rondo reassert their place as male authority figures.

Originally, Welty's story used the name Adam rather than Rondo, implying that issues of gender, priority, and power are indeed central to Welty's conception of the root cause of the family's feuding. By fleeing to the P.O., Sister tries to gain a new family and new authority. The citizens of China Grove who must use the P.O. every day will see her, listen to her story of her family's cruelty, and commiserate. Raiding her home of all the possessions that will make her feel at home in the back room of the P.O.—including a cot, an oscillating fan, a charm bracelet, a fern, a ukelele, a sewing machine motor, a thermometer, a calendar, and many jars of preserves, fruits, and vegetables—Sister reconstructs an orderly and quiet Eden-like world in the back of the P.O., a public rebuke to her family. Welty's revisions to the list of possessions Sister carries away with her well shows her genius as a writer of comedy: by changing "sewing-machine" to "sewing-machine motor," for example, she makes Sister's actions even more comically futile, and by changing "bottle-opener" to "the Hawaiian ukelele" she stresses Sister's need to feel in touch with a world of broader horizons she feels has been unfairly denied her. Sister's paradise regained at the P.O. becomes an Eden as it might be imagined in a Woolworth's advertisement.

In the last three paragraphs of the story Sister's picture of self-reliance darkens considerably, though, as the language Sister uses becomes less pastoral and the social dimensions of her domain suddenly shrink. For in cutting herself off from her family, she is more or less cutting herself off from any larger "world." Despite vague references to other "people" and "folks" in China Grove, the only other resident of China Grove who is named in the story, significantly, is the dying old Aunt Jep Patterson, her family's last surviving member.

> Of course, there's not much mail. My family are naturally the main people in China Grove, and if they prefer to vanish from the face of the earth, for all the mail they get or the mail they write, why, I'm not going to open my mouth. Some of the folks here in town are taking up for me and some turned against me. I know which is which. There are always people who will quit buying stamps just to get on the right side of Papa-Daddy.
>
> But here I am, and here I'll stay. I want the world to know I'm happy.
>
> And if Stella-Rondo should come to me this minute, on bended knees, and *attempt* to explain the incidents of her life with Mr. Whitaker, I'd simply put my fingers in both my ears and refuse to listen.

The "world" and the authority that Sister will have at her P.O. thus seem largely self-created, a poor substitute for the position she had in her family before Stella-Rondo's return.

The most sinister aspect of the story's last paragraphs is not the sudden shrinking of Sister's world but the gruesome combination of a need to speak and a determination to be silent. Sister's flight and silence, like so many other elements in the story, are reminiscent of a child's temper tantrum caused by jealousy towards a sibling who seems to be favored by her parents. In a fit of pique Sister resolves never to speak to her family again, but like a child sulking in her bedroom she comically cannot but help break her resolve sooner or later—her family surrounds her. Sister's story is wholly constructed of desperate refutations and retellings of Stella-Rondo's stories, but the only audience that we are shown Sister convincing is one that she herself has imagined.

Thus we may revise one of the summarizing sentences at the end of "Why I Live at the P.O." to say "I want *myself* to know I'm happy." Despite the many legitimate reasons Sister has for feeling that she has been unfairly treated by her family, her story proves she knows that her own vanity, jealousy, and insecurity are at least partly to blame for her having to live in a post office's back room. The secret target of Sister's refutations is not only Stella-Rondo but herself, and her narrative at its deepest level is tragicomically inspired by her own guilt as well as Stella-Rondo's. Like Stella-Rondo's hilarious description of her as being "bigger on one side than on the other," Sister's narrative is both monomaniacal and lopsided. What she intends to assert as the story develops becomes increasingly unbalanced with the weight of other secrets that she does not know are there: as Welty said of her in *One Writer's Beginnings,* "how much more gets told besides!" These other secrets include her desire to be the authority figure in her family and to play the traditional role of the fashionable, worldly wife, but her secrets also include her own self-revulsion—her lingering belief that her family's view of her as a monster may be right. She has internalized all of her family's words against her and seems condemned to try forever to talk them down. The slapstick comedy that makes much of the story so hilarious changes somewhat near the end, as unsuspected pain and self-torment sound through the pratfalls, darkening the cartoon-bright narrative surface of the story like a bruise. . . .

Source: Peter Schmidt, "Rigidity and Rebirth: Eudora Welty and Women's Comedy," in *The Heart of the Story: Eudora Welty's Short Fiction*, University Press of Mississippi, 1991, pp. 109–203.

Ann Romines

In the following essay, Ann Romines explores Eudora Welty's rare, yet "memorable" use of first person narration in "Why I Live at the P.O."

Eudora Welty's fiction overflows with gifted, loquacious storytellers; it resounds with their voices. So, for me at least, it is surprising to realize how few of the stories are actually told in the first person. Welty is much more likely to depict storytelling as a kinetic exchange, an unpredictable process of reply, response, and mutual invention. *Losing Battles*, with its "fray" of voices, is the epitome of this process.

In that novel, one of the Beechams' main strengths (however terrifying) is their capacity to draw everyone and everything into a communal, continual story which becomes their own, as when they invent a paternity for Gloria which makes her one of the family. Such storytelling is a constant interchange, a game which everyone can—and

> **Obviously, Sister has found no real independence. Instead, she has denied some of her own deepest impulses. One of those impulses is her sense of the centrality of family to human life, to which her language often attests."**

must—play. A great moment of *Losing Battles*, weighted with danger and possibility, occurs when Lady May Renfro, the baby whose genealogy has been "decided" by the previous day's round of storytelling, finds her own voice, and thus begins her own life as a storyteller. Opening her eyes, "She put her voice into the fray, and spoke to it the first sentence of her life: 'What you huntin', man?'" Her sentence is a question, which demands a response: a story.

But occasionally, Welty has created a character who spurns such a communal storytelling. In such cases, we readers are unforgettably bombarded with direct address. This occurs most memorably in two great, singular stories: "Why I Live at the P.O." and "Circe."

The narrator protagonists of these stories, Sister and Circe, frame their tales as definitive assertions of their own commanding visions; they brook no interruptions and no replies. Both women tell stories because they have been confronted with a version of experience they refuse to accept. For both are pitted against rivals who insist on being protagonists. These rivals, Stella-Rondo and Odysseus, aggressively advance their own tales and their own heroism. Circe and Sister can combat them only be reinventing their worlds. And they do so by preempting the story's voice for their exclusive use. In each case, that voice belongs to a single woman, uncomfortable with the place she finds herself assigned in others' narratives. Circe, the nonhuman sorceress, and Sister, the incapacitated woman, deny humanity by refusing the communion of storytelling. But they also act to preserve themselves, by grappling with conventional female plots which would constrict them. Their failures as story-tellers, and as heroines, are among Welty's most stunning successes.

Sister's very title, "Why I Live at the P.O., is an act of appropriation; it asserts that *she* is the center of attention and that the reason for her domicile is of pressing interest to us. But then in her first sentence we learn that she has seized the power of narration because someone else snatched the role of protagonist: her prodigal sister, Stella-Rondo, who makes a spectacular reappearance at the family home on Independence Day—with a surprise two-year-old in tow. Against such peremptory claims for attention, Sister fights for control, by means of her narrative. Virtually the only information she imparts about her sister's absent husband, for example, is that *she* "went with" him first. The very scene of Stella-Rondo's return, dramatic as it must have been, is omitted. Instead, in Sister's first dramatized scene she places herself at the absolute center of the household, "over the hot stove," trying gamely to perform feats of domestic magic and to "stretch two chickens over five people and a completely unexpected child."

For Sister, her family is the world, and the optimal position for herself, as her tale begins, is the traditional domestic locus of power: feeding the family. Her family's importance is so self-evident to her that she does not think to tell us what their surname might be. Almost all Sister's relatives—Mama, Papa-Daddy, Uncle Rondo, and Sister herself—are referred to only by names which designate family relationships. The exception, of course, is Stella-Rondo. She is named for a star and a man (her mother's brother), and by stealing Mr. Whitaker from her sister, she managed to accomplish what Sister has not—to project herself outside the family house and the state of Mississippi. When Stella-Rondo acquired a daughter, she determinedly named her in the language of a larger world, outside the self-referential family vocabulary. Her child is Shirley-T., for Shirley Temple.

Newly equipped with daughter, Stella-Rondo is formidable competition for her sibling. According to Sister, she can lie effectively at the drop of a hat, discrediting Sister in the most humiliating ways. She arrives back home equipped with the paraphernalia of sexual experience, notably a seductive trousseau and a child. But Stella-Rondo denies that she is the child's biological parent. To admit that she bore Shirley-T. would be to acknowledge that she was subject to the uncertainties and indignities of conception and pregnancy, and that admission might also subject her (and her child) to the stigma of an out-of-wedlock pregnancy. She prefers to present herself as an adoptive parent, who exercised the powers of choice. If she is lying about Shirley-T.'s parentage, as seems likely, Stella-Rondo denies her own involvement in one of the most common female stories. By asserting that Shirley-T. is adopted, Stella-Rondo places herself in a position of clear-cut power which biological motherhood cannot afford: without the encumbrances of sexual passion and pregnancy, she chose her time and her child, as surely as she chose Shirley-T.'s defiant name.

When Stella-Rondo eloped with Mr. Whitaker, it must have seemed to Sister, and to all of China Grove, Mississippi, that she was this family's shooting star, its wanderer, its questing protagonist. But now she appears a fixed star, instead—returned to her place in the family constellation. Presumably, Mama once made the same return with her two daughters. For Mama too lives in *her* parental house, and there is no mention of the man who fathered Stella-Rondo and Sister. Stella-Rondo's return brings on a set of reversals, repetitions, and complications so disturbing for Sister that she must grapple for retrospective control of the situation by means of her plotted monologue.

Sister comprehends that plot is power; it is for her, as in Peter Brooks's definition, "the logic and dynamic of narrative, and narrative itself is a form of understanding and explanation." Thinking back over the events of the last few days, Sister gropes for an explanatory arrangement of those events, a plot which will reinforce her version of the self she wishes she were. She once had a secure place and was "getting along fine," as she asserts in her first sentence. She was well entrenched as postmistress and as dutifully domestic daughter. But when Stella-Rondo came back, Sister found herself a defending protagonist, locked in combat with her antagonist.

The plot-battle which ensues is conducted almost entirely through language. Sister's monologue itself is a highly elaborated weapon. According to her, Stella-Rondo puts up an unfair fight, for her weapons are lies. She tells her uncle and grandfather that Sister made mocking or critical remarks about them. But by Sister's account, it was Stella-Rondo herself who said the words she attributes to Sister—for example, Stella-Rondo actually said that Uncle Rondo "looked like a fool" as he swayed across the lawn in a peach silk kimono. Sister is especially infuriated by this treachery; she admonishes her audience, to make sure we don't miss Stella-Rondo's duplicity, asking, "Do you remember who it was really said that?"

In Sister's story, she presents herself as the speaker of a solicitous language, that of the loving housekeeper who makes heroic domestic efforts to take care of everything and everyone, sweetly warning her drunk uncle against dripping ketchup on her sister's silk lingerie. By her inspired lies, Stella-Rondo robs Sister of her own (hypocritical) caretaking language—and thus of the secure position she thought she had. Stella-Rondo's lies are the instrument by which she reshapes Sister's story. And the lies also isolate Sister, as a single woman, by destroying her alliances with male power. Just as she once stole Mr. Whitaker, by lying to him that Sister "was one-sided," she now steals the allegiance of Papa-Daddy and Uncle Rondo.

Under the pressure of Stella-Rondo's attack, Sister tries to win points with a display of domestic faculty. But her efforts are souring by the minute, turning as tart as the green-tomato pickles she stirs up on the Fourth of July—"Somebody had to do it," she claims. A less essential food than green tomato pickle can scarcely be imagined, and Sister's effort to consolidate her powers at the stove cuts no ice with Mama, who "trots in. Lifts up the lid and says, 'H'm! not very good for your Uncle Rondo in his precarious condition, I must say. Or poor little adopted Shirley-T. Shame on you!'"

Sister's response is "That made me tired." And well she might be. It is Independence Day, but she is at the stove, expected to suit her cooking to whatever kinfolk might turn up, in whatever condition. She ends her account of her kitchen efforts with an admission of defeat—no longer claiming authority but, instead, asking for pity: "I stood there helpless over the hot stove." She has become that most threadbare of domestic clichés—a mocked, overburdened, hearth-bound Cinderella, ripe for a godmother.

Sister makes one major effort to fight Stella-Rondo by her own methods. She attempts to discredit her sister's trump card—Shirley-T. Realizing the child has not spoken since her arrival, she deliciously imagines "something perfectly horrible" and asks, "'Can that child talk?'" The most fitting debility Sister can imagine for her new niece is to rob her of the defending, denying, shaping powers of speech. But Shirley-T. wins the engage-ment by yelling in a deafening "Yankee voice," "'OE'm Pop-OE the Sailor-r-r Ma-a-n!' and then somebody jumps up and down in the upstairs hall. In another second the house would of fallen down."

Shirley-T. has asserted her otherness from Sister and her invulnerability in every possible way: she is adopted, and not blood kin; she has all her faculties; she is a Yankee, not a Mississippian, and she is strong enough to bring the house down—or so it seems to Sister. And the child identifies not with a woman, but with a strong man, Popeye the Sailor, another figure from the mass culture which gave Shirley-T. her name. It is a complete rout for Sister—and from a two-year-old!

The last straw comes when Sister loses her last ally, Uncle Rondo, to Stella-Rondo's "lies." Angrily, Uncle Rondo throws a lit string of firecrackers into Sister's bedroom. Stella-Rondo's lies have already destroyed Sister's credibility with her family; the language by which she maintained her sense of her own dignity and power under their roof is no longer effective there. The firecrackers are not only phallic—aggressively male—and antidomestic; they are also pure, explosive, inhuman sound, absolutely outside Sister's control. And she prides herself on her sensitivity to noise.

Sister's response to the firecrackers is the turning point in her plot. This is the moment when she sees herself as most helpless; she says, "there I was with the whole entire house . . . turned against me." She describes herself in terms which emphasize her youthful *female* vulnerability: she is a "young girl" along in her bedroom, traumatized by an explosive invasion. But Sister refuses to subside as a helplessly violated victim. Instead, she recasts herself as a hero. The source of this renewal is her essential self-possession: "If I have anything at all I have pride."

Sister's story is fueled by that pride. Her family is no longer a haven or a receptive audience. So she changes her locale—she moves into "the next-to-smallest P.O. in Mississippi," where (thanks to Papa-Daddy) she holds the position of postmistress. By deciding to move and then by incorporating that decision into a story, Sister rescues herself; she becomes her own fairy godmother.

Once she has decided to move, Sister describes herself in newly decisive language. She "marches" through the house, "snatching" her possessions. Stella-Rondo is now routed, reduced to tears at the thought that a family boycott of the P.O. will cut her off from her husband. Mama exclaims helplessly,

'''Oh, I declare . . . to think that a family of mine should quarrel on the Fourth of July, or the day after, over Stella-Rondo leaving old Mr. Whitaker and having the sweetest little adopted child! It looks like we'd all be glad!''' Mama extols the sentimental ideal of the family. She believes in holidays and games (her solution to family discord is '''Why don't you all just sit down and play Casino?'''). If villains exist, they are outside the family, as is ''old Mr. Whitaker.'' Although she may assume the postures of power under her father's roof, shaking her finger at Sister over the stove, she is incapacitated for movement and action in a larger world, for she ''trots'' about with only tiny feet to support her 200 pounds. Mama's daughters have little choice but to conclude that staying home could mean for them what it did for her—triviality and ineffectuality.

Gathering up her movable possessions, Sister says to Mama with new independence, '''You 'tend to your house, and I'll 'tend to mine.''' The new force of her language contrasts with Mama's. She says, leaving, '''*He* left *her*—you mark my words. . . . That's Mr. Whitaker. After all, I knew him first. I said from the beginning he'd up and leave her. I foretold every single thing that's happened.''' Thus Sister pronounces herself a spiteful oracle and demonstrates that she has exchanged places with her sister. Now Stella-Rondo is the displaced victim; now Sister is the adventuring protagonist, setting out to occupy a new world.

In her new world, the P.O., Sister has a title which is not familial, as an agent of the U.S. Mail. As postmistress she should, ideally, facilitate China Grove's exchange with the distant outside world. Thus she is also allied with the U.S. male, for in this story the world of distances is associated with men. For example, Uncle Rondo ''was in France,'' and it was he who financed Sister's one major journey, to Mammoth Cave. When a woman travels, it is with the aid or provocation of a man. When Mama, impressed by Sister's new oracular authority, questions her about where Mr. Whitaker has gone, Sister replies, '''probably to the North Pole, if he knows what's good for him.'''

Sister's own short journey to the P.O. has led, she claims, to a happy ending: ''Oh, I like it here. It's ideal. . . . I want the world to know I'm happy.'' But the ideal world she asserts she has created in her five days of domestic life at the P.O. is as far from the hectic bustle of her roomy home as the North Pole—and as chilly. The last thing Sister collected from her home was the kitchen clock. She has appropriated and brought with her domestic time, as an immigrant woman might carry household rituals into a new country. But Sister has simply created a miniaturized version of the family house, crammed with the hideous appurtenances of domesticity, arranged to her own perverse taste, ''everything cater-cornered, the way I like it.''

Whatever the faults of Sister's family house, it was at least a model of domestic process. Nothing was stale or static there; everything was in a constant state of change and renewal. Allegiances shifted, and shifted again; a wanderer reentered as prodigal. Sister's ideal world at the P.O. is created by rearranging an especially motley selection of domestic props. But her arrangement is fixed. And thus process is thwarted.

The process of the U.S. Mail is thwarted too, for Sister's family, by her account ''the main people of China Grove,'' refuse to patronize the P.O.; and many townspeople, taking sides in the dispute, have ''quit buying stamps just to get on the right side of Papa-Daddy.'' Sister and the P.O. are a bottleneck; the exchange of communication, of storytelling, and of domestic life at its best, has become impossible. Sister has ''won''—by the last page, she has shaped and narrated her own self-centered tale, and she has denied Stella-Rondo's rival version. Sister concludes triumphantly, with a declaration of independence: ''And if Stella-Rondo should come to me this minute, on bended knees, and *attempt* to explain the incidents of her life with Mr. Whitaker, I'd simply put my fingers in both my ears and refuse to listen.''

Obviously, Sister has found no real independence. Instead, she has denied some of her own deepest impulses. One of those impulses is her sense of the centrality of family to human life, to which her language often attests. (She refers to Judgment Day itself as an occasion for meeting one's ''whole family''.) Another of Sister's deepest impulses is to hear. Insatiably curious, she habitually eavesdrops around her family home. But now she boasts of stopping her ears against her sister's voice, shutting out the one story she most wants to hear. Finally, Sister has incapacitated herself as storyteller. For her true subject was the conjunction of her sister's life and her own, the pattern of rivalry, speech and silencing, setting forth and return which they mutually wove. Just as Stella-Rondo earlier destroyed the authority of Sister's voice, Sister now refuses Stella-Rondo a hearing. And she is her own victim: fingers in ears, she is rendered deaf.

Sister's story is a triumph of rearrangement. But in that very triumph, she has ignored what Eudora Welty calls "a storyteller's truth: the thing to wait on, to reach there in time for, is the moment in which people reveal themselves. You have to be ready, in yourself; you have to know the moment when you see it" (*Eye*). The story Eudora Welty wrote is very different from the one Sister tells, for it captures/invents Sister in her very moment of self-revelation, which is the telling of this story. But recognizing revelation is beyond Sister's powers. She is not "ready, in herself" for that discovery. . . .

Source: Ann Romines, "How Not to Tell a Story: Eudora Welty's First-Person Tales," in *Eudora Welty: Eye of the Storyteller*, Kent State University Press, 1989, pp. 94–104.

Sources

Hauser, Marianne. *New York Times*, November 16, 1941, p. 6.

Johnston, Carol Ann. *Eudora Welty: A Study of the Short Fiction*, New York: Twayne Publishers, 1997.

Porter, Katherine Anne. Introduction to *A Curtain of Green and Other Stories* by Eudora Welty, New York: Harcourt, Brace, 1941.

Prenshaw, Peggy Whitman, ed. *Conversations with Eudora Welty*, Jackson: University of Mississippi Press, 1984.

Review of *A Curtain of Green*, in *Books*, November 16, 1941, p. 10.

Review of *A Curtain of Green*, in *New Yorker*, Vol. 17, November 15, 1941.

Review of *A Curtain of Green*, in *Time*, November 24, 1941, p. 110.

Further Reading

Bloom, Harold, ed. *Eudora Welty*, New York: Chelsea House, 1986.
> A collection of critical essays on Welty's fiction by the most well known Welty scholars of the past several decades.

Johnston, Carol Ann. *Eudora Welty: A Study of the Short Fiction*, New York: Twayne Publishers, 1997.
> A clear and comprehensive introduction to Welty's writing, this volume includes an analytical essay, excerpts from Welty's own writings on fiction, and selected reviews and articles reflecting how Welty's writing has been interpreted from the 1940s through the present.

Waldron, Ann. *Eudora: A Writer's Life*, New York: Doubleday, 1998.
> This first biography of Welty to be written offers a great deal of factual information about the life and achievements of the very private writer.

Welty, Eudora. *The Eye of the Story: Selected Essays and Reviews*, New York: Random House, 1979.
> This highly readable collection of Welty's non-fiction writing offers her perspectives on other authors of her generation, earlier authors who influenced her, and the craft of fiction.

Wolfe, Margaret Ripley. *Daughters of Canaan: A Saga of Southern Women*, Lexington: University of Kentucky Press, 1995.

Glossary of Literary Terms

A

Aestheticism: A literary and artistic movement of the nineteenth century. Followers of the movement believed that art should not be mixed with social, political, or moral teaching. The statement ''art for art's sake'' is a good summary of aestheticism. The movement had its roots in France, but it gained widespread importance in England in the last half of the nineteenth century, where it helped change the Victorian practice of including moral lessons in literature. Edgar Allan Poe is one of the best-known American ''aesthetes.''

Allegory: A narrative technique in which characters representing things or abstract ideas are used to convey a message or teach a lesson. Allegory is typically used to teach moral, ethical, or religious lessons but is sometimes used for satiric or political purposes. Many fairy tales are allegories.

Allusion: A reference to a familiar literary or historical person or event, used to make an idea more easily understood. Joyce Carol Oates's story ''Where Are You Going, Where Have You Been?'' exhibits several allusions to popular music.

Analogy: A comparison of two things made to explain something unfamiliar through its similarities to something familiar, or to prove one point based on the acceptance of another. Similes and metaphors are types of analogies.

Antagonist: The major character in a narrative or drama who works against the hero or protagonist. The Misfit in Flannery O'Connor's story ''A Good Man Is Hard to Find'' serves as the antagonist for the Grandmother.

Anthology: A collection of similar works of literature, art, or music. Zora Neale Hurston's ''The Eatonville Anthology'' is a collection of stories that take place in the same town.

Anthropomorphism: The presentation of animals or objects in human shape or with human characteristics. The term is derived from the Greek word for ''human form.'' The fur necklet in Katherine Mansfield's story ''Miss Brill'' has anthropomorphic characteristics.

Anti-hero: A central character in a work of literature who lacks traditional heroic qualities such as courage, physical prowess, and fortitude. Anti-heroes typically distrust conventional values and are unable to commit themselves to any ideals. They generally feel helpless in a world over which they have no control. Anti-heroes usually accept, and often celebrate, their positions as social outcasts. A well-known anti-hero is Walter Mitty in James Thurber's story ''The Secret Life of Walter Mitty.''

Archetype: The word archetype is commonly used to describe an original pattern or model from which all other things of the same kind are made. Archetypes are the literary images that grow out of the ''collective unconscious,'' a theory proposed by psychologist Carl Jung. They appear in literature as incidents and plots that repeat basic patterns of life. They may also appear as stereotyped characters. The ''schlemiel'' of Yiddish literature is an archetype.

Autobiography: A narrative in which an individual tells his or her life story. Examples include Benjamin Franklin's *Autobiography* and Amy Hempel's story ''In the Cemetery Where Al Jolson Is Buried,'' which has autobiographical characteristics even though it is a work of fiction.

Avant-garde: A literary term that describes new writing that rejects traditional approaches to literature in favor of innovations in style or content. Twentieth-century examples of the literary *avant-garde* include the modernists and the minimalists.

B

Belles-lettres: A French term meaning ''fine letters'' or ''beautiful writing.'' It is often used as a synonym for literature, typically referring to imaginative and artistic rather than scientific or expository writing. Current usage sometimes restricts the meaning to light or humorous writing and appreciative essays about literature. Lewis Carroll's *Alice in Wonderland* epitomizes the realm of belles-lettres.

Bildungsroman: A German word meaning ''novel of development.'' The *bildungsroman* is a study of the maturation of a youthful character, typically brought about through a series of social or sexual encounters that lead to self-awareness. J. D. Salinger's *Catcher in the Rye* is a *bildungsroman*, and Doris Lessing's story ''Through the Tunnel'' exhibits characteristics of a *bildungsroman* as well.

Black Aesthetic Movement: A period of artistic and literary development among African Americans in the 1960s and early 1970s. This was the first major African-American artistic movement since the Harlem Renaissance and was closely paralleled by the civil rights and black power movements. The black aesthetic writers attempted to produce works of art that would be meaningful to the black masses. Key figures in black aesthetics included one of its founders, poet and playwright Amiri Baraka, formerly known as LeRoi Jones; poet and essayist Haki R. Madhubuti, formerly Don L. Lee; poet and playwright Sonia Sanchez; and dramatist Ed Bullins. Works representative of the Black Aesthetic Movement include Amiri Baraka's play *Dutchman,* a 1964 Obie award-winner.

Black Humor: Writing that places grotesque elements side by side with humorous ones in an attempt to shock the reader, forcing him or her to laugh at the horrifying reality of a disordered world. ''Lamb to the Slaughter,'' by Roald Dahl, in which a placid housewife murders her husband and serves the murder weapon to the investigating policemen, is an example of black humor.

C

Catharsis: The release or purging of unwanted emotions—specifically fear and pity—brought about by exposure to art. The term was first used by the Greek philosopher Aristotle in his *Poetics* to refer to the desired effect of tragedy on spectators.

Character: Broadly speaking, a person in a literary work. The actions of characters are what constitute the plot of a story, novel, or poem. There are numerous types of characters, ranging from simple, stereotypical figures to intricate, multifaceted ones. ''Characterization'' is the process by which an author creates vivid, believable characters in a work of art. This may be done in a variety of ways, including (1) direct description of the character by the narrator; (2) the direct presentation of the speech, thoughts, or actions of the character; and (3) the responses of other characters to the character. The term ''character'' also refers to a form originated by the ancient Greek writer Theophrastus that later became popular in the seventeenth and eighteenth centuries. It is a short essay or sketch of a person who prominently displays a specific attribute or quality, such as miserliness or ambition. ''Miss Brill,'' a story by Katherine Mansfield, is an example of a character sketch.

Classical: In its strictest definition in literary criticism, classicism refers to works of ancient Greek or Roman literature. The term may also be used to describe a literary work of recognized importance (a ''classic'') from any time period or literature that exhibits the traits of classicism. Examples of later works and authors now described as classical include French literature of the seventeenth century, Western novels of the nineteenth century, and American fiction of the mid-nineteenth century such as that written by James Fenimore Cooper and Mark Twain.

Climax: The turning point in a narrative, the moment when the conflict is at its most intense. Typically, the structure of stories, novels, and plays is one of rising action, in which tension builds to the climax, followed by falling action, in which tension lessens as the story moves to its conclusion.

Comedy: One of two major types of drama, the other being tragedy. Its aim is to amuse, and it typically ends happily. Comedy assumes many forms, such as farce and burlesque, and uses a variety of techniques, from parody to satire. In a restricted sense the term comedy refers only to dramatic presentations, but in general usage it is commonly applied to nondramatic works as well.

Comic Relief: The use of humor to lighten the mood of a serious or tragic story, especially in plays. The technique is very common in Elizabethan works, and can be an integral part of the plot or simply a brief event designed to break the tension of the scene.

Conflict: The conflict in a work of fiction is the issue to be resolved in the story. It usually occurs between two characters, the protagonist and the antagonist, or between the protagonist and society or the protagonist and himself or herself. The conflict in Washington Irving's story "The Devil and Tom Walker" is that the Devil wants Tom Walker's soul but Tom does not want to go to hell.

Criticism: The systematic study and evaluation of literary works, usually based on a specific method or set of principles. An important part of literary studies since ancient times, the practice of criticism has given rise to numerous theories, methods, and "schools," sometimes producing conflicting, even contradictory, interpretations of literature in general as well as of individual works. Even such basic issues as what constitutes a poem or a novel have been the subject of much criticism over the centuries. Seminal texts of literary criticism include Plato's *Republic,* Aristotle's *Poetics,* Sir Philip Sidney's *The Defence of Poesie,* and John Dryden's *Of Dramatic Poesie.* Contemporary schools of criticism include deconstruction, feminist, psychoanalytic, poststructuralist, new historicist, postcolonialist, and reader-response.

D

Deconstruction: A method of literary criticism characterized by multiple conflicting interpretations of a given work. Deconstructionists consider the impact of the language of a work and suggest that the true meaning of the work is not necessarily the meaning that the author intended.

Deduction: The process of reaching a conclusion through reasoning from general premises to a specific premise. Arthur Conan Doyle's character Sherlock Holmes often used deductive reasoning to solve mysteries.

Denotation: The definition of a word, apart from the impressions or feelings it creates in the reader. The word "apartheid" denotes a political and economic policy of segregation by race, but its connotations—oppression, slavery, inequality—are numerous.

Denouement: A French word meaning "the unknotting." In literature, it denotes the resolution of conflict in fiction or drama. The *denouement* follows the climax and provides an outcome to the primary plot situation as well as an explanation of secondary plot complications. A well-known example of *denouement* is the last scene of the play *As You Like It* by William Shakespeare, in which couples are married, an evildoer repents, the identities of two disguised characters are revealed, and a ruler is restored to power. Also known as "falling action."

Detective Story: A narrative about the solution of a mystery or the identification of a criminal. The conventions of the detective story include the detective's scrupulous use of logic in solving the mystery; incompetent or ineffectual police; a suspect who appears guilty at first but is later proved innocent; and the detective's friend or confidant—often the narrator—whose slowness in interpreting clues emphasizes by contrast the detective's brilliance. Edgar Allan Poe's "Murders in the Rue Morgue" is commonly regarded as the earliest example of this type of story. Other practitioners are Arthur Conan Doyle, Dashiell Hammett, and Agatha Christie.

Dialogue: Dialogue is conversation between people in a literary work. In its most restricted sense, it refers specifically to the speech of characters in a drama. As a specific literary genre, a "dialogue" is a composition in which characters debate an issue or idea.

Didactic: A term used to describe works of literature that aim to teach a moral, religious, political, or practical lesson. Although didactic elements are often found in artistically pleasing works, the term "didactic" usually refers to literature in which the message is more important than the form. The term may also be used to criticize a work that the critic finds "overly didactic," that is, heavy-handed in its delivery of a lesson. An example of didactic literature is John Bunyan's *Pilgrim's Progress.*

Dramatic Irony: Occurs when the reader of a work of literature knows something that a character in the work itself does not know. The irony is in the contrast between the intended meaning of the statements or actions of a character and the additional information understood by the audience.

Dystopia: An imaginary place in a work of fiction where the characters lead dehumanized, fearful lives. **George Orwell's** *Nineteen Eighty-four,* and Margaret Atwood's *Handmaid's Tale* portray versions of dystopia.

E

Edwardian: Describes cultural conventions identified with the period of the reign of Edward VII of England (1901-1910). Writers of the Edwardian Age typically displayed a strong reaction against the propriety and conservatism of the Victorian Age. Their work often exhibits distrust of authority in religion, politics, and art and expresses strong doubts about the soundness of conventional values. Writers of this era include E. M. Forster, H. G. Wells, and Joseph Conrad.

Empathy: A sense of shared experience, including emotional and physical feelings, with someone or something other than oneself. Empathy is often used to describe the response of a reader to a literary character.

Epilogue: A concluding statement or section of a literary work. In dramas, particularly those of the seventeenth and eighteenth centuries, the epilogue is a closing speech, often in verse, delivered by an actor at the end of a play and spoken directly to the audience.

Epiphany: A sudden revelation of truth inspired by a seemingly trivial incident. The term was widely used by James Joyce in his critical writings, and the stories in Joyce's *Dubliners* are commonly called ''epiphanies.''

Epistolary Novel: A novel in the form of letters. The form was particularly popular in the eighteenth century. The form can also be applied to short stories, as in Edwidge Danticat's ''Children of the Sea.''

Epithet: A word or phrase, often disparaging or abusive, that expresses a character trait of someone or something. ''The Napoleon of crime'' is an epithet applied to Professor Moriarty, arch-rival of Sherlock Holmes in Arthur Conan Doyle's series of detective stories.

Existentialism: A predominantly twentieth-century philosophy concerned with the nature and perception of human existence. There are two major strains of existentialist thought: atheistic and Christian. Followers of atheistic existentialism believe that the individual is alone in a godless universe and that the basic human condition is one of suffering and loneliness. Nevertheless, because there are no fixed values, individuals can create their own characters—indeed, they can shape themselves—through the exercise of free will. The atheistic strain culminates in and is popularly associated with the works of Jean-Paul Sartre. The Christian existentialists, on the other hand, believe that only in God may people find freedom from life's anguish. The two strains hold certain beliefs in common: that existence cannot be fully understood or described through empirical effort; that anguish is a universal element of life; that individuals must bear responsibility for their actions; and that there is no common standard of behavior or perception for religious and ethical matters. Existentialist thought figures prominently in the works of such authors as Franz Kafka, Fyodor Dostoyevsky, and Albert Camus.

Expatriatism: The practice of leaving one's country to live for an extended period in another country. Literary expatriates include Irish author James Joyce who moved to Italy and France, American writers James Baldwin, Ernest Hemingway, Gertrude Stein, and F. Scott Fitzgerald who lived and wrote in Paris, and Polish novelist Joseph Conrad in England.

Exposition: Writing intended to explain the nature of an idea, thing, or theme. Expository writing is often combined with description, narration, or argument.

Expressionism: An indistinct literary term, originally used to describe an early twentieth-century school of German painting. The term applies to almost any mode of unconventional, highly subjective writing that distorts reality in some way. Advocates of Expressionism include Federico Garcia Lorca, Eugene O'Neill, Franz Kafka, and James Joyce.

F

Fable: A prose or verse narrative intended to convey a moral. Animals or inanimate objects with human characteristics often serve as characters in fables. A famous fable is Aesop's "The Tortoise and the Hare."

Fantasy: A literary form related to mythology and folklore. Fantasy literature is typically set in non-existent realms and features supernatural beings. Notable examples of literature with elements of fantasy are Gabriel Garcia Marquez's story "The Handsomest Drowned Man in the World" and Ursula K. LeGuin's "The Ones Who Walk Away from Omelas."

Farce: A type of comedy characterized by broad humor, outlandish incidents, and often vulgar subject matter. Much of the comedy in film and television could more accurately be described as farce.

Fiction: Any story that is the product of imagination rather than a documentation of fact. Characters and events in such narratives may be based in real life but their ultimate form and configuration is a creation of the author.

Figurative Language: A technique in which an author uses figures of speech such as hyperbole, irony, metaphor, or simile for a particular effect. Figurative language is the opposite of literal language, in which every word is truthful, accurate, and free of exaggeration or embellishment.

Flashback: A device used in literature to present action that occurred before the beginning of the story. Flashbacks are often introduced as the dreams or recollections of one or more characters.

Foil: A character in a work of literature whose physical or psychological qualities contrast strongly with, and therefore highlight, the corresponding qualities of another character. In his Sherlock Holmes stories, Arthur Conan Doyle portrayed Dr. Watson as a man of normal habits and intelligence, making him a foil for the eccentric and unusually perceptive Sherlock Holmes.

Folklore: Traditions and myths preserved in a culture or group of people. Typically, these are passed on by word of mouth in various forms—such as legends, songs, and proverbs—or preserved in customs and ceremonies. Washington Irving, in "The Devil and Tom Walker" and many of his other stories, incorporates many elements of the folklore of New England and Germany.

Folktale: A story originating in oral tradition. Folktales fall into a variety of categories, including legends, ghost stories, fairy tales, fables, and anecdotes based on historical figures and events.

Foreshadowing: A device used in literature to create expectation or to set up an explanation of later developments. Edgar Allan Poe uses foreshadowing to create suspense in "The Fall of the House of Usher" when the narrator comments on the crumbling state of disrepair in which he finds the house.

G

Genre: A category of literary work. Genre may refer to both the content of a given work—tragedy, comedy, horror, science fiction—and to its form, such as poetry, novel, or drama.

Gilded Age: A period in American history during the 1870s and after characterized by political corruption and materialism. A number of important novels of social and political criticism were written during this time. Henry James and Kate Chopin are two writers who were prominent during the Gilded Age.

Gothicism: In literature, works characterized by a taste for medieval or morbid characters and situations. A gothic novel prominently features elements of horror, the supernatural, gloom, and violence: clanking chains, terror, ghosts, medieval castles, and unexplained phenomena. The term "gothic novel" is also applied to novels that lack elements of the traditional Gothic setting but that create a similar atmosphere of terror or dread. The term can also be applied to stories, plays, and poems. Mary Shelley's *Frankenstein* and Joyce Carol Oates's *Bellefleur* are both gothic novels.

Grotesque: In literature, a work that is characterized by exaggeration, deformity, freakishness, and disorder. The grotesque often includes an element of comic absurdity. Examples of the grotesque can be found in the works of Edgar Allan Poe, Flannery O'Connor, Joseph Heller, and Shirley Jackson.

H

Harlem Renaissance: The Harlem Renaissance of the 1920s is generally considered the first significant movement of black writers and artists in the United States. During this period, new and established black writers, many of whom lived in the region of New York City known as Harlem, published more fiction and poetry than ever before, the first influential black literary journals were established, and black authors and artists received their first widespread recognition and serious critical appraisal. Among the major writers associated with this period are Countee Cullen, Langston Hughes, Arna Bontemps, and Zora Neale Hurston.

Hero/Heroine: The principal sympathetic character in a literary work. Heroes and heroines typically exhibit admirable traits: idealism, courage, and integrity, for example. Famous heroes and heroines of literature include Charles Dickens's Oliver Twist, Margaret Mitchell's Scarlett O'Hara, and the anonymous narrator in Ralph Ellison's *Invisible Man*.

Hyperbole: Deliberate exaggeration used to achieve an effect. In William Shakespeare's *Macbeth*, Lady Macbeth hyperbolizes when she says, ''All the perfumes of Arabia could not sweeten this little hand.''

I

Image: A concrete representation of an object or sensory experience. Typically, such a representation helps evoke the feelings associated with the object or experience itself. Images are either ''literal'' or ''figurative.'' Literal images are especially concrete and involve little or no extension of the obvious meaning of the words used to express them. Figurative images do not follow the literal meaning of the words exactly. Images in literature are usually visual, but the term ''image'' can also refer to the representation of any sensory experience.

Imagery: The array of images in a literary work. Also used to convey the author's overall use of figurative language in a work.

In medias res: A Latin term meaning ''in the middle of things.'' It refers to the technique of beginning a story at its midpoint and then using various flashback devices to reveal previous action. This technique originated in such epics as Virgil's *Aeneid*.

Interior Monologue: A narrative technique in which characters' thoughts are revealed in a way that appears to be uncontrolled by the author. The interior monologue typically aims to reveal the inner self of a character. It portrays emotional experiences as they occur at both a conscious and unconscious level. One of the best-known interior monologues in English is the Molly Bloom section at the close of James Joyce's *Ulysses*. Katherine Anne Porter's ''The Jilting of Granny Weatherall'' is also told in the form of an interior monologue.

Irony: In literary criticism, the effect of language in which the intended meaning is the opposite of what is stated. The title of Jonathan Swift's ''A Modest Proposal'' is ironic because what Swift proposes in this essay is cannibalism—hardly ''modest.''

J

Jargon: Language that is used or understood only by a select group of people. Jargon may refer to terminology used in a certain profession, such as computer jargon, or it may refer to any nonsensical language that is not understood by most people. Anthony Burgess's *A Clockwork Orange* and James Thurber's ''The Secret Life of Walter Mitty'' both use jargon.

K

Knickerbocker Group: An indistinct group of New York writers of the first half of the nineteenth century. Members of the group were linked only by location and a common theme: New York life. Two famous members of the Knickerbocker Group were Washington Irving and William Cullen Bryant. The group's name derives from Irving's *Knickerbocker's History of New York*.

L

Literal Language: An author uses literal language when he or she writes without exaggerating or embellishing the subject matter and without any tools of figurative language. To say ''He ran very quickly down the street'' is to use literal language, whereas to say ''He ran like a hare down the street'' would be using figurative language.

Literature: Literature is broadly defined as any written or spoken material, but the term most often refers to creative works. Literature includes poetry, drama, fiction, and many kinds of nonfiction writing, as well as oral, dramatic, and broadcast compositions not necessarily preserved in a written format, such as films and television programs.

Lost Generation: A term first used by Gertrude Stein to describe the post-World War I generation of American writers: men and women haunted by a sense of betrayal and emptiness brought about by the destructiveness of the war. The term is commonly applied to Hart Crane, Ernest Hemingway, F. Scott Fitzgerald, and others.

M

Magic Realism: A form of literature that incorporates fantasy elements or supernatural occurrences into the narrative and accepts them as truth. Gabriel Garcia Marquez and Laura Esquivel are two writers known for their works of magic realism.

Metaphor: A figure of speech that expresses an idea through the image of another object. Metaphors suggest the essence of the first object by identifying it with certain qualities of the second object. An example is "But soft, what light through yonder window breaks?/ It is the east, and Juliet is the sun" in William Shakespeare's *Romeo and Juliet*. Here, Juliet, the first object, is identified with qualities of the second object, the sun.

Minimalism: A literary style characterized by spare, simple prose with few elaborations. In minimalism, the main theme of the work is often never discussed directly. Amy Hempel and Ernest Hemingway are two writers known for their works of minimalism.

Modernism: Modern literary practices. Also, the principles of a literary school that lasted from roughly the beginning of the twentieth century until the end of World War II. Modernism is defined by its rejection of the literary conventions of the nineteenth century and by its opposition to conventional morality, taste, traditions, and economic values. Many writers are associated with the concepts of modernism, including Albert Camus, D. H. Lawrence, Ernest Hemingway, William Faulkner, Eugene O'Neill, and James Joyce.

Monologue: A composition, written or oral, by a single individual. More specifically, a speech given by a single individual in a drama or other public entertainment. It has no set length, although it is usually several or more lines long. "I Stand Here Ironing" by Tillie Olsen is an example of a story written in the form of a monologue.

Mood: The prevailing emotions of a work or of the author in his or her creation of the work. The mood of a work is not always what might be expected based on its subject matter.

Motif: A theme, character type, image, metaphor, or other verbal element that recurs throughout a single work of literature or occurs in a number of different works over a period of time. For example, the color white in Herman Melville's *Moby Dick* is a "specific" *motif,* while the trials of star-crossed lovers is a "conventional" *motif* from the literature of all periods.

N

Narration: The telling of a series of events, real or invented. A narration may be either a simple narrative, in which the events are recounted chronologically, or a narrative with a plot, in which the account is given in a style reflecting the author's artistic concept of the story. Narration is sometimes used as a synonym for "storyline."

Narrative: A verse or prose accounting of an event or sequence of events, real or invented. The term is also used as an adjective in the sense "method of narration." For example, in literary criticism, the expression "narrative technique" usually refers to the way the author structures and presents his or her story. Different narrative forms include diaries, travelogues, novels, ballads, epics, short stories, and other fictional forms.

Narrator: The teller of a story. The narrator may be the author or a character in the story through whom the author speaks. Huckleberry Finn is the narrator of Mark Twain's *The Adventures of Huckleberry Finn.*

Novella: An Italian term meaning "story." This term has been especially used to describe fourteenth-century Italian tales, but it also refers to modern short novels. Modern novellas include Leo Tolstoy's *The Death of Ivan Ilich,* Fyodor Dostoyevsky's *Notes from the Underground,* and Joseph Conrad's *Heart of Darkness.*

O

Oedipus Complex: A son's romantic obsession with his mother. The phrase is derived from the story of the ancient Theban hero Oedipus, who unknowingly killed his father and married his mother, and was popularized by Sigmund Freud's theory of psychoanalysis. Literary occurrences of the Oedipus complex include Sophocles' *Oedipus Rex* and D. H. Lawrence's "The Rocking-Horse Winner."

Onomatopoeia: The use of words whose sounds express or suggest their meaning. In its simplest sense, onomatopoeia may be represented by words that mimic the sounds they denote such as "hiss" or "meow." At a more subtle level, the pattern and rhythm of sounds and rhymes of a line or poem may be onomatopoeic.

Oral Tradition: A process by which songs, ballads, folklore, and other material are transmitted by word of mouth. The tradition of oral transmission predates the written record systems of literate society.

Oral transmission preserves material sometimes over generations, although often with variations. Memory plays a large part in the recitation and preservation of orally transmitted material. Native American myths and legends, and African folktales told by plantation slaves are examples of orally transmitted literature.

P

Parable: A story intended to teach a moral lesson or answer an ethical question. Examples of parables are the stories told by Jesus Christ in the New Testament, notably ''The Prodigal Son,'' but parables also are used in Sufism, rabbinic literature, Hasidism, and Zen Buddhism. Isaac Bashevis Singer's story ''Gimpel the Fool'' exhibits characteristics of a parable.

Paradox: A statement that appears illogical or contradictory at first, but may actually point to an underlying truth. A literary example of a paradox is George Orwell's statement ''All animals are equal, but some animals are more equal than others'' in *Animal Farm.*

Parody: In literature, this term refers to an imitation of a serious literary work or the signature style of a particular author in a ridiculous manner. A typical parody adopts the style of the original and applies it to an inappropriate subject for humorous effect. Parody is a form of satire and could be considered the literary equivalent of a caricature or cartoon. Henry Fielding's *Shamela* is a parody of Samuel Richardson's *Pamela.*

Persona: A Latin term meaning ''mask.'' Personae are the characters in a fictional work of literature. The persona generally functions as a mask through which the author tells a story in a voice other than his or her own. A persona is usually either a character in a story who acts as a narrator or an ''implied author,'' a voice created by the author to act as the narrator for himself or herself. The persona in Charlotte Perkins Gilman's story ''The Yellow Wallpaper'' is the unnamed young mother experiencing a mental breakdown.

Personification: A figure of speech that gives human qualities to abstract ideas, animals, and inanimate objects. To say that ''the sun is smiling'' is to personify the sun.

Plot: The pattern of events in a narrative or drama. In its simplest sense, the plot guides the author in composing the work and helps the reader follow the work. Typically, plots exhibit causality and unity and have a beginning, a middle, and an end. Sometimes, however, a plot may consist of a series of disconnected events, in which case it is known as an ''episodic plot.''

Poetic Justice: An outcome in a literary work, not necessarily a poem, in which the good are rewarded and the evil are punished, especially in ways that particularly fit their virtues or crimes. For example, a murderer may himself be murdered, or a thief will find himself penniless.

Poetic License: Distortions of fact and literary convention made by a writer—not always a poet—for the sake of the effect gained. Poetic license is closely related to the concept of ''artistic freedom.'' An author exercises poetic license by saying that a pile of money ''reaches as high as a mountain'' when the pile is actually only a foot or two high.

Point of View: The narrative perspective from which a literary work is presented to the reader. There are four traditional points of view. The ''third person omniscient'' gives the reader a ''godlike'' perspective, unrestricted by time or place, from which to see actions and look into the minds of characters. This allows the author to comment openly on characters and events in the work. The ''third person'' point of view presents the events of the story from outside of any single character's perception, much like the omniscient point of view, but the reader must understand the action as it takes place and without any special insight into characters' minds or motivations. The ''first person'' or ''personal'' point of view relates events as they are perceived by a single character. The main character ''tells'' the story and may offer opinions about the action and characters which differ from those of the author. Much less common than omniscient, third person, and first person is the ''second person'' point of view, wherein the author tells the story as if it is happening to the reader. James Thurber employs the omniscient point of view in his short story ''The Secret Life of Walter Mitty.'' Ernest Hemingway's ''A Clean, Well-Lighted Place'' is a short story told from the third person point of view. Mark Twain's novel *Huckleberry Finn* is presented from the first person viewpoint. Jay McInerney's *Bright Lights, Big City* is an example of a novel which uses the second person point of view.

Pornography: Writing intended to provoke feelings of lust in the reader. Such works are often condemned by critics and teachers, but those which can be shown to have literary value are viewed less harshly. Literary works that have been described as pornographic include D. H. Lawrence's *Lady Chatterley's Lover* and James Joyce's *Ulysses.*

Post-Aesthetic Movement: An artistic response made by African Americans to the black aesthetic movement of the 1960s and early 1970s. Writers since that time have adopted a somewhat different tone in their work, with less emphasis placed on the disparity between black and white in the United States. In the words of post-aesthetic authors such as Toni Morrison, John Edgar Wideman, and Kristin Hunter, African Americans are portrayed as looking inward for answers to their own questions, rather than always looking to the outside world. Two well-known examples of works produced as part of the post-aesthetic movement are the Pulitzer Prize-winning novels *The Color Purple* by Alice Walker and *Beloved* by Toni Morrison.

Postmodernism: Writing from the 1960s forward characterized by experimentation and application of modernist elements, which include existentialism and alienation. Postmodernists have gone a step further in the rejection of tradition begun with the modernists by also rejecting traditional forms, preferring the anti-novel over the novel and the anti-hero over the hero. Postmodern writers include Thomas Pynchon, Margaret Drabble, and Gabriel Garcia Marquez.

Prologue: An introductory section of a literary work. It often contains information establishing the situation of the characters or presents information about the setting, time period, or action. In drama, the prologue is spoken by a chorus or by one of the principal characters.

Prose: A literary medium that attempts to mirror the language of everyday speech. It is distinguished from poetry by its use of unmetered, unrhymed language consisting of logically related sentences. Prose is usually grouped into paragraphs that form a cohesive whole such as an essay or a novel. The term is sometimes used to mean an author's general writing.

Protagonist: The central character of a story who serves as a focus for its themes and incidents and as the principal rationale for its development. The protagonist is sometimes referred to in discussions of modern literature as the hero or anti-hero. Well-known protagonists are Hamlet in William Shakespeare's *Hamlet* and Jay Gatsby in F. Scott Fitzgerald's *The Great Gatsby.*

R

Realism: A nineteenth-century European literary movement that sought to portray familiar characters, situations, and settings in a realistic manner. This was done primarily by using an objective narrative point of view and through the buildup of accurate detail. The standard for success of any realistic work depends on how faithfully it transfers common experience into fictional forms. The realistic method may be altered or extended, as in stream of consciousness writing, to record highly subjective experience. Contemporary authors who often write in a realistic way include Nadine Gordimer and Grace Paley.

Resolution: The portion of a story following the climax, in which the conflict is resolved. The resolution of Jane Austen's *Northanger Abbey* is neatly summed up in the following sentence: "Henry and Catherine were married, the bells rang and every body smiled."

Rising Action: The part of a drama where the plot becomes increasingly complicated. Rising action leads up to the climax, or turning point, of a drama. The final "chase scene" of an action film is generally the rising action which culminates in the film's climax.

Roman a clef: A French phrase meaning "novel with a key." It refers to a narrative in which real persons are portrayed under fictitious names. Jack Kerouac, for example, portrayed various his friends under fictitious names in the novel *On the Road.* D. H. Lawrence based "The Rocking-Horse Winner" on a family he knew.

Romanticism: This term has two widely accepted meanings. In historical criticism, it refers to a European intellectual and artistic movement of the late eighteenth and early nineteenth centuries that sought greater freedom of personal expression than that allowed by the strict rules of literary form and logic of the eighteenth-century neoclassicists. The Romantics preferred emotional and imaginative expression to rational analysis. They considered the individual to be at the center of all experience and so placed him or her at the center of their art. The Romantics believed that the creative imagination reveals nobler truths—unique feelings and attitudes—than those that could be discovered by logic or by scientific examination. "Romanticism" is also used as a general term to refer to a type of sensibility found in all periods of literary history and usually considered to be in opposition to the principles of classicism. In this sense, Romanticism signifies any work or philosophy in which the exotic or dreamlike figure strongly, or that is devoted to individualistic expression, self-analysis, or a pursuit of a higher realm of knowledge than can be discovered by human reason. Prominent Romantics include Jean-Jacques Rousseau, William Wordsworth, John Keats, Lord Byron, and Johann Wolfgang von Goethe.

S

Satire: A work that uses ridicule, humor, and wit to criticize and provoke change in human nature and institutions. Voltaire's novella *Candide* and Jonathan Swift's essay ''A Modest Proposal'' are both satires. Flannery O'Connor's portrayal of the family in ''A Good Man Is Hard to Find'' is a satire of a modern, Southern, American family.

Science Fiction: A type of narrative based upon real or imagined scientific theories and technology. Science fiction is often peopled with alien creatures and set on other planets or in different dimensions. Popular writers of science fiction are Isaac Asimov, Karel Capek, Ray Bradbury, and Ursula K. Le Guin.

Setting: The time, place, and culture in which the action of a narrative takes place. The elements of setting may include geographic location, characters's physical and mental environments, prevailing cultural attitudes, or the historical time in which the action takes place.

Short Story: A fictional prose narrative shorter and more focused than a novella. The short story usually deals with a single episode and often a single character. The ''tone,'' the author's attitude toward his or her subject and audience, is uniform throughout. The short story frequently also lacks *denouement*, ending instead at its climax.

Signifying Monkey: A popular trickster figure in black folklore, with hundreds of tales about this character documented since the 19th century. Henry Louis Gates Jr. examines the history of the signifying monkey in *The Signifying Monkey: Towards a Theory of Afro-American Literary Criticism,* published in 1988.

Simile: A comparison, usually using ''like'' or ''as,''of two essentially dissimilar things, as in ''coffee as cold as ice'' or ''He sounded like a broken record.'' The title of Ernest Hemingway's ''Hills Like White Elephants'' contains a simile.

Social Realism: The Socialist Realism school of literary theory was proposed by Maxim Gorky and

established as a dogma by the first Soviet Congress of Writers. It demanded adherence to a communist worldview in works of literature. Its doctrines required an objective viewpoint comprehensible to the working classes and themes of social struggle featuring strong proletarian heroes. Gabriel Garcia Marquez's stories exhibit some characteristics of Socialist Realism.

Stereotype: A stereotype was originally the name for a duplication made during the printing process; this led to its modern definition as a person or thing that is (or is assumed to be) the same as all others of its type. Common stereotypical characters include the absent-minded professor, the nagging wife, the troublemaking teenager, and the kindhearted grandmother.

Stream of Consciousness: A narrative technique for rendering the inward experience of a character. This technique is designed to give the impression of an ever-changing series of thoughts, emotions, images, and memories in the spontaneous and seemingly illogical order that they occur in life. The textbook example of stream of consciousness is the last section of James Joyce's *Ulysses.*

Structure: The form taken by a piece of literature. The structure may be made obvious for ease of understanding, as in nonfiction works, or may obscured for artistic purposes, as in some poetry or seemingly ''unstructured'' prose.

Style: A writer's distinctive manner of arranging words to suit his or her ideas and purpose in writing. The unique imprint of the author's personality upon his or her writing, style is the product of an author's way of arranging ideas and his or her use of diction, different sentence structures, rhythm, figures of speech, rhetorical principles, and other elements of composition.

Suspense: A literary device in which the author maintains the audience's attention through the build-up of events, the outcome of which will soon be revealed. Suspense in William Shakespeare's *Hamlet* is sustained throughout by the question of whether or not the Prince will achieve what he has been instructed to do and of what he intends to do.

Symbol: Something that suggests or stands for something else without losing its original identity. In literature, symbols combine their literal meaning with the suggestion of an abstract concept. Literary symbols are of two types: those that carry complex associations of meaning no matter what their contexts, and those that derive their suggestive meaning from their functions in specific literary works. Examples of symbols are sunshine suggesting happiness, rain suggesting sorrow, and storm clouds suggesting despair.

T

Tale: A story told by a narrator with a simple plot and little character development. Tales are usually relatively short and often carry a simple message. Examples of tales can be found in the works of Saki, Anton Chekhov, Guy de Maupassant, and O. Henry.

Tall Tale: A humorous tale told in a straightforward, credible tone but relating absolutely impossible events or feats of the characters. Such tales were commonly told of frontier adventures during the settlement of the west in the United States. Literary use of tall tales can be found in Washington Irving's *History of New York,* Mark Twain's *Life on the Mississippi,* and in the German R. F. Raspe's *Baron Munchausen's Narratives of His Marvellous Travels and Campaigns in Russia.*

Theme: The main point of a work of literature. The term is used interchangeably with thesis. Many works have multiple themes. One of the themes of Nathaniel Hawthorne's ''Young Goodman Brown'' is loss of faith.

Tone: The author's attitude toward his or her audience may be deduced from the tone of the work. A formal tone may create distance or convey politeness, while an informal tone may encourage a friendly, intimate, or intrusive feeling in the reader. The author's attitude toward his or her subject matter may also be deduced from the tone of the words he or she uses in discussing it. The tone of John F. Kennedy's speech which included the appeal to ''ask not what your country can do for you'' was intended to instill feelings of camaraderie and national pride in listeners.

Tragedy: A drama in prose or poetry about a noble, courageous hero of excellent character who, because of some tragic character flaw, brings ruin upon him- or herself. Tragedy treats its subjects in a dignified and serious manner, using poetic language to help evoke pity and fear and bring about catharsis, a purging of these emotions. The tragic form was practiced extensively by the ancient Greeks. The classical form of tragedy was revived in the sixteenth century; it flourished especially on the Elizabethan stage. In modern times, dramatists have attempted to adapt the form to the needs of modern society by drawing their heroes from the ranks of ordinary men and women and defining the nobility of these heroes in terms of spirit rather than exalted social standing. Some contemporary works that are thought of as tragedies include *The Great Gatsby* by F. Scott Fitzgerald, and *The Sound and the Fury* by William Faulkner.

Tragic Flaw: In a tragedy, the quality within the hero or heroine which leads to his or her downfall. Examples of the tragic flaw include Othello's jealousy and Hamlet's indecisiveness, although most great tragedies defy such simple interpretation.

U

Utopia: A fictional perfect place, such as ''paradise'' or ''heaven.'' An early literary utopia was described in Plato's *Republic,* and in modern literature, Ursula K. Le Guin depicts a utopia in ''The Ones Who Walk Away from Omelas.''

V

Victorian: Refers broadly to the reign of Queen Victoria of England (1837-1901) and to anything with qualities typical of that era. For example, the qualities of smug narrow-mindedness, bourgeois materialism, faith in social progress, and priggish morality are often considered Victorian. In literature, the Victorian Period was the great age of the English novel, and the latter part of the era saw the rise of movements such as decadence and symbolism.

Cumulative Author/Title Index

Nationality/Ethnicity Index

Subject/Theme Index